THE
YEARBOOK OF ENGLISH STUDIES
VOLUME 23
1993

VOL. 23

1993

THE YEARBOOK

OF

ENGLISH STUDIES

*Early Shakespeare
Special Number*

Editor
ANDREW GURR

Assistant Editor
PHILLIPA HARDMAN

Reviews Editor
LIONEL KELLY

Modern Humanities Research Association

The Yearbook of English Studies

is published by

THE MODERN HUMANITIES RESEARCH ASSOCIATION

and may be ordered from

The Honorary Treasurer, MHRA

King's College, Strand, London WC2R 2LS, England

ISSN 0306-2473

ISBN 0 947623 50 7

Printed in Great Britain by

W. S. MANEY AND SON LTD   LEEDS LS9 7DL   ENGLAND

Contents

REVIEWS

EDITORIAL NOTE

The special number for 1994 will be concerned with Ethnicity and Representation in American Literature. For 1995 the special subject will be non-standard Englishes and the new media. The number for 1996 will be "Strategies of Reading: Dickens and After" relating readerly approaches to formal length, novel, serial form or short story. Articles for the 1995 and 1996 issues and books for review submitted to *YES* and *MLR* should be sent to the Editor, Department of English, University of Reading, P.O. Box 218, Reading, Berks. RG6 2AA, U.K.

ANDREW GURR
PHILLIPA HARDMAN

Shakespeare and Marlowe: Censorship and Construction

RICHARD DUTTON

University of Lancaster

With neither of them that take offence was I acquainted, and with one of them I care not if I never be: the other, whom at the time I did not so much spare, as since I wish I had [. . .] because myself I have seen his demeanour no less civil than he excellent in the quality he possesses. Besides, divers of worship have reported, his uprightness of dealing, which argues his honesty, and his facetious grace in writing, that approves his art. (Henry Chettle, 'To the Gentleman Readers', prefacing *Kind-Heart's Dream*.)

I know that nothing can be so innocently writ, or carried, but may be obnoxious to construction. (Ben Jonson, Dedicatory Epistle to *Volpone*).[1]

While Shakespeare, as a personality, remains enigmatically elusive, the opposite might be said to be true of his exact contemporary, Marlowe. So much so, that there are few authors with whom it is necessary to discriminate so vigilantly between the man and his writings as it is with Christopher Marlowe. For the temptation to read one 'Marlowe' in the light of the other remains as strong today as it apparently was for his contemporaries. The 'over-reaching' protagonists of the plays mirror the man of aggressively heterodox views who came under Privy Council scrutiny, while some ideas voiced in the plays are very close to opinions that Marlowe himself was supposed to hold and which were recorded as incriminating. Richard Baines's deposition 'containing the opinion of one Christopher Marly concerning his damnable judgement of religion and scorn of God's word' records Marlowe as claiming 'that the first beginning of religion was only to keep men in awe', which is not far removed from Machiavel's 'I count religion but a childish toy, | And hold there is no sin but ignorance' in *The Jew of Malta* (Prologue, ll. 14–15). Baines's claim that Marlowe also held 'that all they that love not [. . .] boys were fools' finds apparent corroboration in the

This essay is a revised and expanded version of the one that was joint winner of the 1990 Hoffman Prize for Distinguished Publication on Christopher Marlowe. It draws in parts on the author's *Mastering the Revels: the Regulation and Censorship of English Renaissance Drama* (London: Macmillan; Iowa: University of Iowa Press, 1991.) The author is grateful for the publishers' permission to reproduce that material here.
[1] The passage from *Kind-Heart's Dream* is quoted from S. Schoenbaum, *William Shakespeare: A Compact Documentary Life*, rev. ed. (Oxford and New York: Oxford University Press, 1987), p. 154. That from the Dedication to *Volpone* is from *Ben Jonson: Five Plays*, edited by G. A. Wilkes (Oxford and New York: Oxford University Press, 1988), p. 224.

provocative opening of *Dido Queen of Carthage*, where 'is discovered *Jupiter* dandling *Ganymede* upon his knee'.[2]

The manner and timing of Marlowe's death only compounded the pressure to identify the man with his literary creations, as we see in the sonnet appended to Gabriel Harvey's 'Newe Letter of Notable Contents' (September 1593), where the death of 'Tamberlaine' is listed as one of the notable events of the 'wonderful yeare', 1593, and a gloss declares how death, 'smiling at his Tamberlaine contempt [. . .] sternly struck home the peremptory stroke'. Puritan divines similarly seized upon the 'poetic' justice of the ungodly end in the Deptford tavern, as 'apt' in its way as the deaths of Edward II or the Jew of Malta; Thomas Beard's pointedly titled *Theatre of God's Judgements* declared Marlowe to be an actor in the sight of God 'not inferior to any [. . .] in Atheisme and impietie', insisting that he died with an oath on his lips.[3] More on the level of tabloid journalism Francis Meres supposed that Marlowe had paid the penalty, Faustus-like, for his unnatural presumption in sexual matters (and a parallel carelessness in social ones): 'As the poet Lycophron was shot to death by a certain rival of his, so Christopher Marlowe was stabd to death by a bawdy serving-man, a rival of his in his lewde love.'[4] Even now, though stripped (we hope) of Harvey's, Beard's, and Mere's triumphalism (and even though we know that Meres was wrong about the 'bawdy serving-man'), such configurations still powerfully grip the imagination.

Yet these are not the only 'readings' of the-man-in-the-works, the-works-in-the-man that Marlowe's own contemporaries sanctioned. The testimony of those who conveyed some of his works into print offers a very different construction. Richard Jones, the printer of *Tamburlaine* (1590) informed his 'Gentlemen Readers, and others that take pleasure in reading Histories' that 'I have purposely omitted and left out some fond and frivolous gestures, digressing and, in my poor opinion, far unmeet for the matter, which I thought might seem far more tedious unto the wise than any way else to be regarded. Though haply they have been of some vain-conceited fondlings greatly gaped at, what times they were showed upon the stage in their graced deformities, nevertheless now, to be mixtured in print with such matter of worth, it would prove a great disgrace to so honourable and stately a history' (*Christopher Marlowe*, p. 5). Jones does not actually deny that this comic material was written by Marlowe himself, but implies that it was unworthy of 'the author', whose 'eloquence' he leaves to speak for itself. In dedicating *Hero and Leander* (1598), Edward Blount more circumspectly reminds Sir Thomas Walsingham of 'entertaining the parts of reckoning and worth

---

[2] References to Marlowe's works and to the Baines deposition (Appendix, pp. 511–14) are normally to the Everyman *Christopher Marlowe: Complete Plays and Poems*, ed. by E. D. Pendry and J. C. Maxwell (London: Dent, 1976). The exception is to comparisons of the 1604 texts of *Dr Faustus*, where I refer to W. W. Greg's parallel-text edition: see note 51.

[3] Thomas Beard, *The Theatre of God's Judgements* (1597), p. 149.

[4] *Palladis Tamia* (1598), fol. 286.

which you found in [the unhappily deceased author], with good countenance and liberal affection' and suggests that Marlowe would have looked for a similar reception for 'this unfinished tragedy' as he himself had received (*Christopher Marlowe*, p. 400). Both of these construct an essential Marlowe, a gentleman scholar (implicitly the author of what Jonson was to dub the 'mighty line'), which is to be distinguished from his unfortunate associations with the popular theatre, from other unnamed qualities (doubtless those stressed by Harvey, Beard, and Meres), and from an incompleteness which is common both to the life and some of the works.

Both of these 'constructions' underpin distinct schools of thought in the modern appreciation of Marlowe, including one which takes its cue from Jones and sees him as a great poet but as rather less of a dramatist, and that which in effect endorses Harvey and Beard in seeing him as the 'demon' of Elizabethan culture, though it sometimes celebrates rather than castigates him for it. A. P. Rossiter was representative of the former in claiming that 'Marlowe, except in *Edward II* is a dramatist only in his dramatic poetry — in 'great vistas of *mind* rather than of the slip-knot of fate or events pulling tight on human lives'.[5] This view — based on a very partial sense of what constitutes drama — is less prevalent than it was, though Roma Gill's recent attempt to deny Marlowe's hand in even those comic scenes of *Dr Faustus* that were printed in the 1604 'A' text (she ascribes them to Thomas Nashe and the clown John Adams) still derives ultimately from an unwillingness to associate the author of 'the mighty line' with the supposed banalities of the popular theatre.[6] Stephen Greenblatt typifies the latter school of thought in finding in Marlowe's work 'a subversive identification with the alien', of a kind that 'flaunts society's cherished orthodoxies, embraces what the culture finds loathsome or frightening'.[7] By the same token, these potentially antithetical 'constructions' — Marlowe the scholar poet, and Marlowe the demon — predictably underpinned the debate about the theology and dramaturgy of *Dr Faustus*, which was for so long polarized between those who saw it was orthodoxly Christian and its ending poetically 'closed', and those who saw it as an embodiment of Renaissance humanist aspiration and the ending provocatively indeterminate.[8]

It is pointless now to enquire whether either of these early 'readings' of Marlowe was inherently more objective or truthful; we cannot escape the fact that the record is ambivalent, self-contradictory. But we must be alert to the fact that each item of the testimony is as much a product of Elizabethan

[5] A. P. Rossiter, *English Drama from Early Times to the Elizabethans* (London: Hutchinson, 1950; repr. 1969), p. 174.
[6] *The Complete Works of Christopher Marlowe*, ed. by Roma Gill, II: *Dr Faustus* (Oxford, 1990), Introduction, pp. xv–xxi.
[7] Stephen Greenblatt, *Renaissance Self-Fashioning* (Chicago: Chicago University Press, 1980), pp. 203, 220.
[8] See Max Bluestone, '*Libido Speculandi*: Doctrine and Dramaturgy in Contemporary Interpretations of *Dr Faustus*', in *Reinterpretations of Elizabethan Drama*, ed. by N. Rabkin (New York: Columbia University Press, 1969).

culture as was Marlowe himself, and susceptible to deconstruction on those grounds. Baines was a paid informer, and whether or not he was under orders to paint Marlowe in the worst light possible, it seems highly likely that his testimony would be coloured by his apprehension of what his paymasters wanted to hear. Harvey is characterized by the *Dictionary of National Biography* as 'a man of arrogant and censorious spirit, far too conscious of his own considerable abilities, while but little disposed to recognise the merits and claims of others'.[9] Gloating on the death of Marlowe is in part the sour grapes of one Cambridge man who felt thwarted in his own academic career but resentful of anything resembling success on the part of fellow scholars who had deserted their colleges for the flesh-pots of London. Richard Jones was no paragon, either. The Stationers' Company twice fined him for disorderly printing and once (1583) commited him to prison for printing without a licence; in 1592 Nicholas Breton complained that Jones had printed his *Bower of Delighte* 'altogether without my consent and knowledge, and many thinges of other mens mingled with a few of mine'. Jones's usual fare, moreover, was ballads, chap-books, and popular romances, so the attempt in the preface to *Tamburlaine* to ingratiate himself with 'Gentleman Readers' and to imply a shared disdain for 'fond and frivolous gestures' hardly rings entirely true. Edward Blount, by contrast, was altogether more respectable, the publisher of John Florio's Italian-English Dictionary and later of his translations of Montaigne; he is best remembered as one of the consortium that published the Shakespeare first folio which, like his own translation from the Italian of Lorenzo Ducci's *Ars Aulica; or The Courtier's Arte* (1607), was jointly dedicated to the Herbert Earls of Pembroke and Montgomery.[10]

Respectability, however, is no guarantee of objectivity. Blount's dedicatee, Sir Thomas Walsingham, had certainly known Marlowe, and the two of them may well have been at his funeral: 'We think not ourselves discharged of the duty we owe to our friend when we have brought the breathless body to the earth', (*Christopher Marlowe*, p. 400). Indeed, when the Privy Council issued a warrant for Marlowe's arrest, on 18 May 1593, they ordered a messenger of the Queen's chamber 'to repair to the house of Mr Thomas Walsingham in Kent, or to any other place where he shall understand Christopher Marlowe to be remaining': the association between Marlowe and Walsingham was well known in a body of which the latter's cousin, Sir Francis Walsingham, had been a key member until his death three years before.[11] A. L. Rowse is one who has readily assumed that Marlowe and the younger Walsingham were jointly employed by Sir Francis

[9] *The Compact Edition of the Dictionary of National Biography*, 2 vols (Oxford: Clarendon Press, 1975), I, 908.
[10] *DNB*, I, 1098–99, 175, on Jones and Blount.
[11] *Acts of the Privy Council of England, 1542 etc.*, ed. by J. R. Dasent (London: H.M.S.O., 1890–), *1592–93*, p. 244.

on espionage missions in the 1580s.[12] Others have assumed much more: Ingram Frizer, the man who killed Marlowe on 30 May 1593, was the Walsinghams' business agent, and it is only too easy to speculate about the death being premeditated expediency rather than Frizer's self defence in a dispute over the reckoning at the Deptford tavern (the version of events accepted by the inquest jury, and which secured Frizer a prompt pardon).[13] As the Privy Council (and Baines) closely scrutinized Marlowe's affairs, was Walsingham afraid of what might emerge about his association with the poet?

Or, if not Walsingham himself, what of the other notables with whom Marlowe had been associated? Baines's deposition mentions 'one Heriots, being Sir W. Raleigh's man': a reference to the mathematician, Thomas Hariot, who was in Raleigh's service; it is apparent elsewhere that Marlowe was associated with the Raleigh circle, and according to one report 'Marlowe [. . .] hath read the atheist lecture to Sir Walter Raleigh and others' (*Christopher Marlowe*, pp. 513, 512). When Marlowe was detained in Flushing by Sir Robert Sidney on suspicion of coining (January 1592) he boasted himself that he was 'very well known both to the Earl of Northumberland and my Lord Strange'.[14] 'The Wizard Earl' and the enigmatic Ferdinando, Lord Strange are names as charismatic as Raleigh's to conjure with. Conjuring — or perhaps juggling — is, however, all we can finally do with these names and circumstances. There is no evidence that the death did not occur exactly as Frizer claimed it did, and the precise relationship of Marlowe to these men of power and influence simply cannot be determined. The one object-lesson which may be said to follow from this complex tissue of suggestive association and pure speculation, in the shadow-land of the court and its acolytes, is that Blount's dedication of *Hero and Leander* to Walsingham cannot be accepted as entirely 'innocent', in the sense that it cannot be divorced from the pressures of patronage, factional disputation, and political intrigue that were inescapable facts for the privileged classes of Elizabethan England, making their public faces matters of considerable value.[15] To this extent the dedication, like others of its type, was a calculated public act, and the view of Marlowe it propagates cannot but have been composed with the reciprocal interests of Walsingham and Blount himself in mind.

Everywhere to look, in short, we find that the views of Marlowe propagated by his contemporaries, and overlaid upon his writings, are radically unreliable, 'constructions' liable to deconstruction. Indeed, in so far as they continue (however subtly) to inform our current reading of Marlowe's

---

[12] *Chrisopher Marlowe: A Biography*, rev. edn (London and Basingstoke: Macmillan, 1981), pp. 29, 30.

[13] Rowse, pp. 197–200.

[14] See R. B. Wernham, 'Christopher Marlowe at Flushing in 1592', *English Historical Review*, 91 (1976), 344–45.

[15] I am thinking here of 'patronage' in the wide sense of a Renaissance 'psychological system', as suggested by Robert C. Evans in *Ben Jonson and the Poetics of Patronage* (Lewisburg, PA: Bucknell University Press, 1989), p. 29.

works, they require deconstruction. The same is true of more recent 'narratives' of Marlowe, including the 'conspiracy theory' of his death, which only became possible when Leslie Hotson uncovered the details of the inquest and so of the personnel involved. It was in fact Hotson himself who first saw such possibilities in what he had discovered and argued for them in *The Death of Christopher Marlowe* (London: Nonsuch Press, 1925). The 'conspiracy theory', however elaborated, triumphantly underscores the 'demonization' of Marlowe: it is the twentieth-century's answer to Thomas Beard, political skulduggery standing in for the hand of God.

Shakespeare, as I observed earlier, resolutely resists reduction to narratives of this type. While it is entirely possible to construct 'documentary lives', or to chronicle at least the last twenty years of his career, the personality behind the factual record remains shadowy and indistinct. Yet, if we examine the early commentary on Shakespeare in the same spirit as we have that on Marlowe, we can see that it contains equally potent, if less melodramatic constructions, and ones that have subtly rooted themselves in subsequent readings of his works. It has become something of a commonplace to observe that Shakespeare is remade by each new generation of actors, critics, and audiences in their own image, but it is often assumed, as in the most iconoclastic of recent arguments to this effect, Gary Taylor's *Reinventing Shakespeare* (London: Hogarth Press, 1990), that this is a process which only got under way when he was comfortably part of the nation's literary history. On the contrary, it began before a word of his was in public print.

The extract from Henry Chettle's *Kind-Heart's Dream* which stands at the head of this essay is a famous reaction to an even more famous comment: the earliest allusion to Shakespeare's activity as a dramatist, which occurs in Robert Greene's *Groatsworth of Wit, Bought with a Million of Repentance*, published posthumously in 1592: 'There is an upstart crow, beautified with our feathers, that with his *tiger's heart wrapped in a player's hide* supposes he is as well able to bombast out a blank verse as the best of you; and, being an absolute *Johannes Factotum*, is in his own conceit the only Shake-scene in a country'.[16] As I have observed elsewhere, nothing can be taken for granted about this passage: only the punning on 'Shake-scene' and the barbed misquotation of a line from a play whose authorship is not beyond dispute ('O tiger's heart wrapped in a woman's hide' (*3 Henry VI*, 1. 4. 138)) links it with Shakespeare, what it actually says about him is far from clear, and even the fact that Greene wrote it can be doubted — it certainly was at the time.[17] Nevertheless, whoever wrote it certainly chose to channel a general grudge against actors (the passage is preceded by embittered comments on 'those puppets [...] that spoke from our mouths, those antics garnished in our

---

[16] Quoted in Schoenbaum, *Shakespeare: A Compact Documentary Life*, p. 151.
[17] See Richard Dutton, *William Shakespeare: A Literary Life* (London: Macmillan, 1989), pp. 17–20.

colours'), into specific complaints against one of them who, '*wrapped in a player's hide*, supposes he is as well able to bombast out a blank verse as the best of you'. The 'you' seems to embrace all fellow authors, and the nub of the complaint appears to be that this 'only Shake-scene' has got above himself, pretending to the status of a dramatist which the author tacitly reserves to university-educated men like himself. Where Harvey scorned Marlowe for prostituting his scholarship to the theatre, 'Greene' snubbed 'Shake-scene' for presuming above his academic and social standing: the pecking-order was a complex one, and in flux, but all the more fiercely contested for that.

This is how Chettle came to be involved. With Greene dead, suspicions that he might not have written the pamphlet, and complaints about its contents, focused on the man who oversaw it for the press. The 'apology' in *Kind-Heart's Dream* addressed complaints from two aggrieved parties: 'with neither of them [. . .] was I acquainted, and with one of them I care not if I never be'. All the circumstantial evidence points to this having been Marlowe, whose learning Chettle properly respects while resenting what appear to have been threats against him ('him I would wish to use me no worse than I deserve') and alluding darkly to a passage in Greene's pamphlet which he had edited out for the press: 'Had it been true, yet to publish it, was intolerable'. A charge of atheism, or of homosexuality? While Chettle concurs with Robert Jones and Edward Blount in acknowledging Marlowe's scholarship, he anticipates more wholeheartedly the constructions of Thomas Beard and Richard Barnes which made him out to be mad, bad, and dangerous to know.

His response to the other complainant, who all the circumstantial evidence suggests must be Shakespeare, is very different: 'Myself have seen his demeanour no less civil than he is excellent in the quality he professes: besides, divers of worship have reported, his uprightness of dealing, which argues his honesty, and his facetious grace in writing, that approves his art.' In short, he was what we should call a gentleman: his behaviour demonstrates it, and reliable witnesses vouch for the fact. For the Elizabethans being a gentleman was not a matter of good manners but of precise social status. The 'divers of worship' who have spoken for Shakespeare's good standing are explicitly gentlemen (just as 'divers of honour' would explicitly have been noblemen).[18] Shakespeare was not yet of their number, though he was to join their ranks in 1596 when his father acquired the right to bear arms by virtue of having once been bailiff of Stratford. Chettle is acknowledging that he is all but a gentleman; and so rebutting Greene's slur against the 'player', which takes most of its force from the fact that actors who operated outside the official famework of licensing and patronage had the

---

[18] See William A. Ringler, Jr, 'Spenser, Shakespeare, Honor and Worship', *Renaissance News*, 14 (1961), 159–61.

legal standing of vagabonds, sturdy beggars, and masterless men.[19] So far from his being such, Chettle assures us, Shakespeare demonstrates his quality in his (reported) 'facetious grace in writing, that approves his art'.[20] A further edge to Greene's contempt for a man portrayed as 'bombast[ing] out a blank verse' is that what he wrote was clumsy, and at best functional, the work of an artisan, not a scholar or artist. 'Facetious [polished, urbane] grace', speaks to the social standing of the writing as much as to its quality; a gentleman writes not only well but with at least the appearance of cultured ease, as Sir Philip Sidney had with his 'idle work' the *Arcadia*, which he described as 'but a trifle, and that triflingly handled'.[21] In his manner, in his behaviour, and even in his writing, Chettle avers, Shakespeare is a gentleman in all but name. As Olivia says of Viola, 'Thy tongue, thy face, thy limbs, actions, and spirit | Do give thee five-fold blazon' (*Twelfth Night*, 1.5.282–83).

Kind-Heart's Dream did not itself contribute to the myth of an 'artless' Shakespeare since its reference to him was not appreciated until the myth itself, of 'Fancy's child | Warbl[ing] his native wood-notes wild' (Milton, 'L'Allegro'), was already well entrenched. But we do see in it the seeds from which that myth derived, and one intriguing feature of the circumstances in which Chettle's words came to be printed is that they leave room to suppose that it was Shakespeare himself — or, at least, the 'divers of worship' who vouched for him — who laid those seeds, insisting on his gentility (and all that implied about his writing) in the face of 'Greene's' calumnies. Schoenbaum sums up numerous contemporary testimonies to his good nature (several of which use the term 'gentle') with the slightly whimsical observation 'Shakespeare is enshrined in consciousness as Gentle Will Shakespeare. One cannot imagine a more fitting designation for the innate gentleman who was not gently born' (p. 255). This vacillates between Elizabethan and modern uses of the term, and may not entirely do justice to the importance Shakespeare himself attached to the formal status of a gentleman. It was almost certainly a flourishing William Shakespeare who acquired the family coat of arms on behalf of his then impoverished father. And the following year he acquired New Place, an eminently suitable property for a country gentleman, which is what he seems to have been intent on being when he severed his links with the theatre.

This, moreover, was the image his old friends and colleagues, Heminge and Condell, sought to preserve when they published his *Comedies, Histories and Tragedies* in 1623:

---

[19] See A. L. Beier, *Masterless Men: The Vagrancy Problem in England, 1560–1641* (London: Methuen, 1986).
[20] Early copies, such as those in the Bodleian and Folger libraries, read 'factious'. But the careful change to 'facetious', which required a substitution of 'that' for 'which' to make space, indicates that this is what Chettle intended. See Schoenbaum, *Shakespeare: A Compact Documentary Life*, p. 155 and note.
[21] Sir Philip Sidney, *The Countess of Pembroke's Arcadia*, ed. by Maurice Evans (Harmondsworth: Penguin, 1977), p. 57.

Who, as he was a happy imitator of nature, was a most *gentle* expresser of it. His mind and hand went together, and what he thought he uttered with that easiness that we have scarce received from him a blot in his papers. (my emphasis)[22]

It is generally assumed that Shakespeare did not publish his own plays (unlike *Venus and Adonis* and *The Rape of Lucrece*) because of his contractual arrangement with the Lord Chamberlains' | King's Men, and their wish to keep his work out of the hands of his rival companies. But it is also highly likely that he was sensitive to both the status (at least in the early years of his career) of 'play books' and also to the stigma of the paid artisan which attached to most writing for public print.[23] The decision by Heminge and Condell to publish the First Folio reflects in large part the very different status of both plays and print by the end of the Jacobean era, compared to that which had obtained for most of Elizabeth's reign. But they were determined to preserve through these changes Shakespeare's standing as a 'gentle' writer, a man who wrote with natural ease: in all essentials an amateur, however much he did it for the money. There is no wonder that this so grated with Ben Jonson, whose own example had done so much to bring about the changed perception of 'playbooks' to which Heminge and Condell were responding: 'I remember the players have often mentioned as an honour to Shakespeare, that in his writing, whatsoever he penned, he never blotted out line. My answer hath been, "Would he had blotted a thousand"; which they thought a malevolent speech.'[24] The actors were belatedly according Shakespeare what could now be seen as the accolade of public print, but pointedly dissociating him from what Jonson had insisted was its essential concomitant, the rigorous discipline of a professional man of letters.

The myth of the artless genius thus entered the public arena alongside the plays that were its living proof, many never printed before, and never before collected in a form which so powerfully registered their range and sustained invention. That myth has coloured their reception ever since, partly because, as Heminge and Condell foisted it on the world, it betrayed little (unlike *Kind-Heart's Dream*) of the social pressures which had made it such a *necessary* fiction during Shakespeare's own lifetime. The afterlife of this myth cannot be my concern here. But I wish to consider one effect of its persistence on modern readings of Shakespeare's works. Because, just as the Baines deposition and the 'great reckoning in a little room' have so coloured modern readings of Marlowe, the presumption of a 'gentle', artless Shakespeare contributed for many years to the idea that his writings, unlike those of so

---

[22] 'To The Great Variety of Readers' in *William Shakespeare: The Complete Works*, ed. by Stanley Wells and Gary Taylor and others (Oxford: Clarendon Press, 1986), p. xiv. All references to Shakespeare's works are to this edition.

[23] See J. W. Saunders, 'The Stigma of Print: a Note on the Social Bases of Tudor Poetry', *Essays in Criticism*, 1 (1951), 139–59.

[24] 'Timber, or Discoveries' in *Ben Jonson*, ed. by Ian Donaldson (Oxford: Oxford University Press, 1985), pp. 521–94, ll. 658–70. I have discussed Jonson's reaction to this, and other aspects of his criticism of Shakespeare, at greater length in *Ben Jonson: Authority and Criticism* (Harvester Wheatsheaf, forthcoming).

many contemporaries, were essentially apolitical. Or, to put it another way, that they mirrored so complacently the attitudes of Elizabethan England shared by all reasonable and educated men, that they were for practical purposes politically uncontentious, so centrist as to be invisible.

This view has, of course, been widely contested in recent years from a variety of new historicist, feminist, and poststructuralist perspectives. Most of these have, however, been more than usually open to the charge of addressing what Shakespeare represents to the late twentieth century, in ways that might arguably distort what he could have meant to his contemporaries. I wish to further this debate by examining our relative constructions of Shakespeare and Marlowe in relation to the one attentive contemporary reading we know that virtually all plays for the public theatre received after 1581, that of their censor and licenser, the Master of the Revels. What this amounted to, however, is at least as contentious as the texts themselves and, as we shall see, just as liable to (mis)appropriation in the service of modern readings it is sometimes invoked to subserve.

To begin with, the notion is abroad of a Marlowe whose plays have come down to us seriously distorted by the attentions of the censor. The most sustained attempt to discern the hand of censorship on Marlowe's work is William Empson's posthumous and unfinished *Faustus and the Censor*.[25] I should say firstly that I regard this book as a sorry monument to a great and enlivening critic, and think it was a mistake that it was published at all. But since it is in the public domain and carries something of Empson's unique authority, I must take issue with those parts of the book which depend on a wholly uncritical or uninformed view of the mechanics of Elizabethan stage censorship. To that extent it is not altogether untypical, though more bluntly stated than most works; so my consideration of what Empson has to say has general implications, and that is my justification for paying such attention to the book. Motivated at least in part by a desire to rebut readings of *Dr Faustus* as an orthodox Christian work, Empson tried to establish how a play as heterodox as he takes it to be (he suggests Marlowe intended to imply that Faustus found a way of avoiding Hell (p. 64)) could be both staged and printed. In the process, he invokes censorship as the sole explanation for the two separate states of the text of *Dr Faustus* which have come down to us.

He assumes that Edmund Tilney, the Master of the Revels, first gave a licence to the play, the full heretical implications of which were only apparent in performance; that it was withdrawn when these implications were realized (p. 52); and that Tilney then threw the play to the wolves, possibly as the price for keeping his job, which Empson, following Glynne Wickham, assumes was at risk with the establishment in 1589 of a joint commission, involving representatives of the Archbishop of Canterbury and

---

25 William Empson, *Faustus and the Censor: The English Faust-book and Marlowe's 'Dr Faustus'*, recovered and edited with an introduction and postscript by John Henry Jones (Oxford: Blackwell, 1987).

the Lord Mayor of London, and Tilney himself, to oversee the censorship of public plays (pp. 50–51).[26] However, having savagely marked the play for cuts, he was prepared to license a transcript of what could still be used (the 1604 or 'A' Text), so badly mangled it was only fit for use in the provinces (pp. 54–55), while Henslowe managed to negotiate for a restitution of some of the cut scenes (though why Tilney should ever have felt the need to cut some of the comic scenes he is latterly supposed to have restored is never explained) and so produced the 1616 or 'B' Text (pp. 55–56), the version he supposes the Lord Admiral's Men performed throughout the 1590s. There is no evidence for *any* of these assumptions. Moreover, there is no consideration of any of the other factors which so routinely produced corrupt and incoherent versions of Elizabethan plays: revisions (Henslowe certainly paid William Birde and Samuel Rowley for some in 1602);[27] adaptations for touring productions (*Dr Faustus* was performed by English actors on the continent as well as in the provinces — another possible derivation of the 1604/1616 differences); memorial reconstruction for illicit publication. Neither text is inherently any worse, say, than the 1600 quarto of *Henry V* or the 1603 quarto of *Hamlet* where censorship had never been suspected as a major cause of their inadequacies. The availability in 1616 of the Birde/Rowley additions is by far the most plausible explanation for the longer text, and it taxes the imagination to see how the new scenes might ever have been thought more theologically subversive than what was originally allowed into print.

This is no place to reconsider the relationship between the 'A' and 'B' texts of the play. I wish solely to address the picture of the role of the Master of the Revels which Empson (and his editor) interweave into their account to explain the various supposed stages of composition. In the first place there are any number of minor inaccuracies, which suggest that Empson had not examined the issue at all closely and was relying on a defective memory. For example, he assumes (p. 55) that Tilney would have had to write on every leaf of a text for his licence to be valid, but it is clear from manuscripts like *The Second Maiden's Tragedy* and Massinger's *Believe as You List* that a single signed licence at the end of the 'allowed' copy was all that was required. He declares that 'censors were not theatregoers' (p. 54): in fact Tilney's primary responsibility was one of 'perusing' plays in performance to check their suitability for presentation at court. Thomas Heywood speaks in his *Apology for Actors* of Tilney's own quarters in the old palace of St John's 'where our Court playes have beene in late daies yearely rehearsed, perfected, and

---

[26] The documents relating to the commission are printed in E. K. Chambers, *The Elizabethan Stage*, 4 vols (Oxford: Clarendon Press, 1923), IV, 306–07 (hereafter cited as *ES*). Empson is following Glynn Wickham, *Early English Stages 1300–1600*, 4 vols (London: Routledge, 1959–72), II, Part I, p. 88.
[27] See Neil Carson, *A Companion to Henslowe's Diary* (Cambridge: Cambridge University Press, 1988), p. 114.

corrected before they come to the publike view of the Prince and Nobility'.[28] Moreover, we know in the case of one of Tilney's successors, Sir Henry Herbert, that he had the right to use a box in each of the theatres under his jurisdiction, and this was presumably established in Tilney's time.[29] Empson also records Tilney a knighthood he never received (p. 50), a common error, and confuses Ben Jonson's (self-proclaimed) voluntary imprisonment over *Eastward Ho* with his compulsory imprisonment over the *Isle of Dogs* affair (p. 53).

These are, however, details and it is the broad, implicit picture that is really at issue: in this, Tilney is singled out as 'appointed by the Queen' (p. 50) and 'the Queen's censor' (p. 52), as though this conferred some special status on him; he is envisaged as (belatedly) engaging in minute theological enquiry into the implications of what happens to Faustus after his death; it is assumed that his licence would be required for the performance in the provinces of so contentious a play (p. 55, note 46); it becomes a critical part of the argument that Tilney's post as censor might be on the line as a result of the 1589 commission, so that he 'must have done something decisive to save himself, for example throwing Marlowe to the wolves' (p. 51). This blends together two not entirely compatible notions: one of a strict Crown censor, with nationally recognized authority; the other of an official whose laxness on matters of theology made him potentially subject to removal by an ever-scrupulous Archbishop of Canterbury. Both of these are fallacious, in ways that distort not only Tilney's actual role but also the kinds of constraints that playwrights like Marlowe and Shakespeare would in reality have faced in dealing with the Master of the Revels as a censor.

Tilney did not, strictly, censor plays for the public stage by virtue of his post in the Revels Office (in which he was confirmed in 1579), where he was responsible for providing theatrical entertainment at court. He did so, rather, on the strength of a royal patent of 24 December 1581 which, among other provisions, gave him power

to warne commaunde and appointe in all places within this our Realme of England [. . .] all and every plaier or plaiers with their playmakers, either belonging to any noble man or otherwise, bearinge the name or names of usinge the facultie of playmakers or plaiers of Comedies, Tragedies, Enterludes or whatever other showes soever, from tyme to tyme and at all tymes to appeare before him with such plaies, Tragedies, Comedies or showes as they shall have in readines or meane to sett forth, and them to recite before our said Servant [. . .] whom we ordeyne appointe and aucthorise by these presentes of all such showes, plaies, plaiers and playmakers, together with their playing places, to order and reforme, auctorise and put downe, as shalbe thought meete or unmeete unto himself. (*ES*, IV, 285–87)

---

[28] Thomas Heywood, *An Apology for Actors* (1612), quoted from extracts in *The Seventeenth Century Stage*, ed. by Gerald Eades Bentley (Chicago, IL: Chicago University Press, 1968), p. 14.
[29] See *The Dramatic Records of Sir Henry Herbert*, ed. by Joseph Quincey Adams (New Haven: Yale University Press, 1917), p. 67.

He was also given powers to punish anyone who resisted him in this.

This was the ultimate basis of Tilney's authority to licence acting companies and their theatres, to censor and licence plays, and to charge fees for doing it. It is often seen as creating a system of state regulation of the theatre and is so categorical as to suggest that modern attempts to discover daring or subversive elements in those plays must be wrong-headed, or require (as in Empson's case) special explanations. G. E. Bentley, for example, states:

The hypotheses so often and so solemnly advanced by many critics and readers of Tudor and Stuart plays about the dramatist's 'advice to the queen' or 'protests against the law' or 'assertions of his religious dissent' must be made either in ignorance of the powers of the Master of the Revels or in assumption of his incompetence or his venality.[30]

In this, Bentley gives definitive voice to an attitude to the government of the period that was widely prevalent for much of this century: that the regime was in principle ruthlessly authoritarian, if often in practice incompetent, and underpinned by graft and corruption. That being so, the drama of the day must have been anodynely non-controversial from the point of view of the authorities, except for the odd blunder or when 'dangerous matter' somehow found a surreptitious path to the stage.

This is very much the attitude reflected throughout *Faustus and the Censor*, and it is compounded by Glynne Wickham's argument (based on a long view of Reformation theatrical controversy and the gradual suppression of amateur religious drama in the provinces) that 'the relationship between Church, State and individual being [. . .] was the very subject matter which the whole machinery of censorship and control had been devised to police and suppress'.[31]

But there must be real doubts whether there was any deliberate intention behind Tilney's patent to set up the repressive system of censorship that Bentley assumes, or if the system actually instituted was as focused on 'the relationship between Church, State and individual being' as Wickham suggests. The provision that anyone involved in the theatre should be required to 'appear before' Tilney, and 'presente and recite' anything from their repertoire for him, relates to his primary responsibility which, as I have observed, was to provide suitable entertainment for the court. The Master's duties had long included 'perusing and reforming of plays sundry times as need required for her Majesties' liking' — the kind of work that Philostrate had tried in vain to do with Peter Quince's 'tedious brief scene of Pyramus | And his love Thisbe' (v, 1, 56–57) and sundry other dubious entertainments offered for Theseus and Hippolyta's wedding night.[32] Tilney's 1581 patent was primarily to further such activities: to provide suitable and economical

[30] G. E. Bentley, *The Profession of Dramatist in Shakespeare's Time, 1590–1642* (Princeton: Princeton University Press, 1971), p. 149.
[31] Wickham, *Early English Stages 1300–1600*, II, Part I, p. 94.
[32] Philostrate in the Quarto text; Egeus in the Folio.

entertainment for the Queen, he was given unequivocal, catch-all powers over whatever theatrical facilities the country had to offer, but especially in the burgeoning commercial theatres around London, which *could* provide high-quality entertainment relatively cheaply. With this support, he succeeded to the extent that the Revels Office performed its functions more economically in the 1580s than in any other decade of Elizabeth's reign.[33]

In practice (apart from the boy companies of the choir schools, who had been attached to the court since their inception) Tilney's attention was focused almost exclusively on the principal professional acting companies who, since 1576, had acquired semi-permanent London bases at the Theatre, the Curtain, and their successors: at any one time a small selection of these were recognized as the 'allowed' companies, who might be accorded a venue at court. Only gradually would Tilney and his successors attempt to translate their powers into authority over the commercial theatre throughout the kingdom, whether or not it had a bearing on what might be offered at court. This explains an otherwise perplexing letter from the Privy Council of April 1582, requesting the Lord Mayor of London 'to allow of certain companies of plaiers to exercise their playeng in London, partly to the ende that they might thereby attaine to the more dexteritie and perfection in that profession, the better to content her majestie', urging the appointement of 'some fitt personnes who maie consider and allow of suche playes onely as be fitt to yeld honest recreacion and no example of evell' (*ES*, IV, 287–88). That is, what the Privy Council here proposed seems to be covered by what Tilney had been authorized to do only four months before. Yet there is no mention of him in the letter. Whatever his patent might say, he was not in 1582 censoring plays performed within the city limits of London and the Lord Mayor's jurisdiction.

It was only six years since James Burbage had erected the Theatre, and theatrical activity was increasing rapidly as the swelling population of London provided regular audiences: a crucial factor in Tilney's calculations for court entertainment. But it was doing so in the face of fierce resistance from the city authorities who (both literally and metaphorically) equated the actors with the plague. The Theatre and the Curtain were both built just outside their jurisdiction, though close enough to be seen as a real nuisance. Tilney's relationship with the companies using these theatres was thus, to an extent, in defiance of the city authorities, who would have preferred to see the actors put out of business altogether. Once Tilney had 'perused' a play and given it his 'allowance' he had in effect ruled that it was fit to be performed at court. No one could challenge such a ruling, or the right of a properly-licensed company to perform elsewhere a play given such clearance. The relationship that grew up between the Master of the Revels and the

[33] See *Jacobean and Caroline Revels Accounts 1603–1642*, ed. by W. R. Streitberger, Malone Society Collections, XIII (Oxford: The Malone Society, 1986), Introduction, pp. x, xvi–xxi.

companies he licensed was thus a curiously symbiotic one. On a professional level he needed to foster them to help him provide entertainment for the court; on a private level, his position provided him with a steady income, over and above his court allowances. The actors probably regarded this arrangement as a reasonable price to pay to avoid harassment from less well-disposed authorities and to keep open the possibility of lucrative court commissions. It accorded them a far more secure status than they would otherwise have enjoyed.

All of this doubtless had consequences for the kind of censorship that Tilney actually enforced. He had not been installed as a repressive agent of the state ('the Queen's censor', to quote Empson), to police a narrowly-defined Tudor orthodoxy, as the church authorities who censored printed works may be said to have been. He was looking to promote what would be acceptable to the court itself, and the emphasis here was rather different. At the outset of her reign (16 May 1559) Elizabeth herself issued a procla-mation, instructing her officers throughout the country on what was to be permissible in plays performed under their jurisdiction: 'her majestie doth [. . .] charge every one of them, as they will aunswere: that they permyt none to be played wherein either matters of religion or of the governaunce of the estate of the common weale shalbe handled or treated, beyng no meete matters to be wrytten of treated upon, but by menne of aucthoritie, learning and wisedome, nor to be handled before any audience, but of grave and discreete persons' (*ES*, IV, 263–64). To the best of our knowledge, Tilney himself received no more specific guidance on his responsibilities than this; as an educated man of the court, and one of some literary accomplishment (his *The Flower of Friendship*, 1568, advising the Queen on the desirability of marriage, went through several editions and his later days were devoted to compiling an exhaustive Diplomatic Manual on Europe), he was expected to know where to draw the line.[34]

In this context, the explicit reservation that 'matters of religion or of the governaunce of the estate of the common weale' were not in all circum-stances proscribed subjects, but might be written on by fit authors for an audience 'of grave and discreet persons' is suggestive. It echoes earlier provisions that only such plays in the vernacular were to be subject to such restrictions, not those in Latin. Within such contexts as the Inns of Court and the court itself, the limits of toleration were much greater, which explains how a play like *Gorboduc*, which openly and forcefully deals with 'matters of [. . .] the governaunce of the estate of the common weale', could be staged in both settings, and before the Queen herself. The evidence suggests that, in mediating between the court and the public theatres, Tilney rather exported the court standard of what was permissible than imported

---

[34] See W. R. Streitberger, *Edmond Tyllney, Master of the Revels and Censor of Plays: A Descriptive Index of His Diplomatic Manual on Europe* (New York: AMS Press, 1986).

the restraints supposedly in force in the country at large. To take only the most obvious example: it is hardly possible that Tilney would have permitted the large number of English history plays that were actually staged during his term of office, and were so obviously susceptible to 'application' to current political circumstances, if he had been enforcing a narrow interpretation of the 1559 proclamation. This is not to say that Tilney was a lax or indulgent censor. In the only manuscript to have survived which shows his attentions, that of *Sir Thomas More*, his strict instructions to 'leave out the insurrection wholly' and other detailed points, show that he took his responsibilities seriously. At the same time, however, it says a lot that the dramatists who worked on that play expected him to 'allow' a piece on a man who had gone to the block for resisting the Queen's own father and was widely regarded as a Catholic martyr (though they are extremely discreet about the issues involved). There is no evidence that the subject matter in itself struck Tilney as inadmissible: a telling point in weighing how far he might police the political and religious content of what he licensed.

It does seem, however, that he could be sensitive to 'matters of religion', as may be seen in his reaction to the actors' involvement in the 'Martin Marprelate' controversy of 1588–90. On 6 November 1589 Sir John Harte, Lord Mayor of London, wrote to Lord Burghley: 'Where by a lettre of your Lps, directed to mr. Yonge it appered unto me, that it was your honours pleasure I sholde give order for the staie of all playes within the Cittie, in that mr. Tilney did utterly mislike the same.' The minute of a Privy Council letter of 12 November suggests that what had upset Tilney (and subsequently the Council) was the religious and political content of certain plays 'in that the players take upon themselves to handle in their plays certen matters of Divinytie and of State unfitt to be suffred' (*ES*, IV, 305, 306). Nothing specifically connects the Privy Council's activity here with 'Martin Marprelate', but his unlicensed pamphlets attacking the Church of England had scandalously called into question the Elizabethan settlement of church and state, and John Lyly had suggested in 'Pappe-with-an-Hatchet' (October 1589) that the actors were ready to join in the controversy: 'Will they not be discouraged for the common players? Would these comedies might be allowed to be plaid that are pend, and then I am sure he would be decyphered, and so perhaps discouraged'.[35] The likely inference is that it was Tilney who had refused to licence the plays that had been 'pend', that one or more of them had been staged in spite of this, and that both Tilney and the Privy Council had taken a dim view of the fact. The striking feature of this, if it was the case, is Lyly's implication that the plays which had not been 'allowed' were *anti*-Martinist, that they might be beneficial in unmasking him or at least discourage him from publishing more pamphlets. If so, Tilney

---

[35] Quoted from *The Complete Works of John Lyly*, ed. by R. W. Bond, 3 vols (Oxford: Clarendon Press, 1902), III, 408.

was motivated not by a desire to suppress disloyal sentiments, but presumably by a determination to keep so controversial a subject off the public stages altogether. Again, he was not acting as 'the Queen's censor', but with a broad concern for public order (which may well also have underlain his concern about the anti-alien 'insurrection' in *Sir Thomas More*, since there was a number of such incidents in London in the early 1590s) and latterly out of outrage that his own authority had been flouted.

This whole business probably led to the setting up of the Commission of Censorship that so exercised Wickham and Empson, since it was on 12 November 1589 that letters went out to the Archbishop of Canterbury, the Lord Mayor of London, and Tilney himself, requiring the latter to join with persons ('to be men of learning and judgement') appointed by the two former in such a commission, with explicit powers to censor the plays of 'the several companies of players' (presumably that means all the acting companies) and to ensure that only works passed by the three of them should be performed, on pain both of punishment and of disqualification from ever performing for a living again (*ES*, IV, 306–07). What Wickham and Empson fail sufficiently to acknowledge is that these letters are the first and last we ever hear of this commission, which may never in fact have come into being at all. Certainly there is no mention of it in Philip Henslowe's *Diary*, which begins to record his theatrical affairs from February 1592; the Master of the Revels is the only regulatory official mentioned there. We can only speculate as to why the commission was not established on a permanent basis, but one likely factor must be that it would have done nothing to address the real concerns of the London authorities: they were far less interested in regulating what was performed than in banning performances altogether. It is noticeable in Harte's letter of 6 November that he had very probably exceeded his authority in suspending all playing within the city at this juncture. The Privy Council had actually written to Richard Young, Justice of the Peace for Middlesex and so with jurisdiction over the Theatre and the Curtain, in one of which the unlicensed performances presumably took place. The Lord Mayor judged that, in the charged atmosphere caused by the 'Marprelate' pamphlets, it would not be too openly an act of defiance to close the theatres under his control. Normally the Privy Council would have protected the right of the actors to perform there, as Lord Chamberlain Hunsdon did when his newly-formed company wanted to use the Cross Keys Inn in October 1594.[36]

For the London authorities to have collaborated in the commission would have been for them to connive in the institutionalization of the actors, when what they really wanted was their eradication. This is apparent from a letter of 25 February 1592, which the then Lord Mayor wrote to the Archbishop of

---

[36] See Schoenbaum, *Shakespeare: A Compact Documentary Life*, p. 182. The Privy Council protection of the actors' use of inn-yard theatres within the city's jurisdiction only lasted, at latest, until 1596, by when it was forbidden (*ES*, IV, 360).

Canterbury, asking him 'to voutchsafe us your good favour and help for the reforming and banishing of so great evill [i.e. the actors and all the ills attendant upon them] out of the Citie'. In this letter Tilney, far from being seen as an ally, is specifically singled out as an impediment: 'Hee being authorized to refourme exercise or suppresse all manner of players, playes and playeng houses whatsoever, did first licence the said playeng houses within this Citie for hir Majesties sayed service, *which before that time lay open to all the statutes for the punishing of these and such lyke disorders*' (my emphasis, *ES*, IV, 307–08). Since the pretext for Tilney's authority was that 'the Q. Majestie is and must be served at certen times by this sort of people' who need to practise their skills, he suggests that this 'may easily bee don by the private exercise of hir Majesties own players in convenient place'. Whitgift raised a practical issue, to which the Lord Mayor referred in his own next letter (6 March): 'As touching the consideracion to bee made to Mr Tilney [...] for the better effecting and continuance of this restraint of the sayed playes in and about this Citie, wee have appointed certain of our Bretheren the Aldermen to confer with him forthwith' (*ES*, IV, 308). They approached the Guild of Merchant Taylors (and very probably the other Livery Companies too), inviting them 'to yield to the payment of one annuity to one Mr Tilney, master of the revels of the Queen's house, in whose hands the redress of this inconveniency doth rest, *and that those plays might be abandoned out of this city*' (my emphasis, *ES*, IV, 309). This states as bluntly as anything that their ultimate aim was not control, but eradication. This initiative came to nothing, however. Later that year the plague intervened, and the theatres were closed anyway, remaining so until the autumn of 1594; just before this closure Greene died, and during it Marlowe was killed.

What does all this tell us about the censorship to which Marlowe's plays were subjected? In the first place it makes a nonsense of the supposition that the Commission of Censorship left Tilney in fear of losing his role as censor, and so willing to contemplate 'throwing Marlowe to the wolves' (*Faustus and the Censor*, p. 51). When the chips were down, the only way to remove the obstruction that he represented was to buy him off, and for one reason or another plans to do this did not come to fruition. For another, it makes higly questionable Tilney's role in a 'whole machinery of censorship and control [that] had been devised' to suppress theatrical discussions of 'the relationship between Church, State and individual being', at least in the sense that Empson construes Wickham's formulation. The 'Martin Marprelate' affair does demonstrate that Tilney would use his authority to prevent the theatrical discussion of religious matters that had a specific bearing on the political constitution of the country, but in doing so he apparently silenced orthodox rather than heretical voices. And this falls a long way short of demonstrating that he would have had any serious theological interest in a play like *Dr Faustus*, where the religious issues are broadly apolitical. In as much as the play is partisan at all, it is conventionally Protestant in its sympathies, with elements of anti-Papal farce; if some might argue that in both these regards it is essentially disrespectful of the institutions of all organized religion, one would have to say that this is a level of sophistication that does not seem to have troubled Tilney about, say, Shakespeare's *King John*, or his successor, Sir George Buc, about the depiction of the church in Webster's tragedies, which some would regard as anti-clerical as much as anti-Catholic. The very failure of the 1589 Commission, and the subsequent negotiations over Tilney's position, demonstrate that he was never a party to the church's censorship role: the city authorities looked to Whitgift not as Tilney's superior, who might bring him into line, but as an ally with whom they hoped to make common cause against a man whose court authority made him an impediment to aims they both held dear.

On all these counts, Empson's argument about Tilney's role in the evolution of the text of *Dr Faustus* simply will not hold water. At this point, however, I wish to reiterate that the force of my case is not only directed at a book which is manifestly unsatisfactory in any number of other particulars. It also calls into question the version of censorship advanced, for example, in Jonathan Dollimore's influential *Radical Tragedy: Religion, Ideology and Power in the Drama of Shakespeare and His Contemporaries* (Brighton: Harvester, 1984), which is to an extent representative of other new historicist and cultural materialist works of the last decade. He assembles his case in a rather unsystematic manner: 'That the theatres [. . .] were a potentially subversive context is evidenced by the fact of their censorship. [. . .] The authorities feared the theatre' (pp. 22–23). Oddly, his main evidence for this last assertion derives from the puritans, Philip Stubbes and William Prynne, who were hardly orthodox establishment figures. He goes on to cite the very passage from Wickham about 'the relationship between Church, State and individual human being' which Empson deployed so centrally, adding that 'the suppression was ideologically in the sense that it went far beyond simply forbidding the performance of controversial material; it was also designed to predetermine the nature of all drama' (p. 23). This is followed by the observation that 'in order to get beyond the the hostility of the City government, playhouses were built in the suburbs, areas which, interestingly enough, were noted for discontent, rioting and opposition to authority generally', which makes it sound as if this was a consequence of the 'actively ideological' policy of 'suppression', rather than a matter of shrewd business sense and collusion with the court authorities on the part of Burbage and subsequent entrepreneurs.

Dollimore then belatedly picks up Wickham's theme, maintaining that 'the authorities expressed particular anxiety when stage plays became an alternative to the church. There was here a double threat: not only were people abandoning what was then thought to be the principal institution of social discipline and control, they were frequenting instead an alternative which contradicted and challenged much of what it stood for' (p. 24). This is questionable on a number of counts. Firstly, people were not presented with a choice between the church and the theatre, 'abandoning' one for the other: plays were not allowed to be performed while church services were being held, and at least a minimum attendance at the latter was required by law. Moreover, what are we to make of this 'actively ideological' censorship, 'designed to predetermine the nature of all drama', if it allowed through plays 'which contradicted and challenged much of what [the church] stood for'? Dollimore concludes his case:

Lastly, we should remember that the dramatists were actually imprisoned and otherwise harassed by the State for staging plays thought to be seditious. [. . .] There is also evidence to the effect that the dramatists fell foul of the law outside as well as inside the theatre: sedition, atheism, homosexuality and espionage are among the charges made against them. (pp. 24–25)

This is provocatively phrased: 'the dramatists' implies that they were all alike and all suffered equally at the hands of a repressive state. While it is true that many of them were called to account by the authorities, quite a few of them appear not to have been troubled at all; Shakespeare and Heywood spring to mind. Moreover, in the closing sentence, there is a very clear inference to be drawn (but no evidence advanced) that the way 'the dramatists fell foul of the law outside [. . .] the theatre' is somehow connected with their activities within it: that they were marked men because they wrote plays.

This brings us squarely back to Marlowe. To the best of my knowledge, he is the only dramatist of the period to have been accused of as many as three out of four of the 'crimes' cited: atheism, homosexuality, and espionage. (In the latter case it appears that Marlowe's activities in Rheims were at the behest of the English authorities rather than aimed against them, but this was not generally understood).[37] The question remains, however, whether the kind of evidence assembled by the likes of Baines (which, we should remember, was never examined in any court of law) has any connexion at all with Marlowe's activities as a playwright. Dollimore constructs a picture of Elizabethan and Jacobean playwrights as uniformly alienated and marginalized figures, constantly subject to repressive censorship and legal harassment, bravely finding ways of voicing subversive opinions in the face of the state's thought-police apparatus. Later in the book, *Dr Faustus* is examined as a text important for the way it shows Faustus 'transgressing and demystifying the limiting structure of his world without there ever existing the possibility of his escaping it' (p. 119), its religious framework readily translatable into the malcontent socio-political terms of Jacobean drama. In this, of course, he flatly contradicts Empson, whose fundamental thesis was that Marlowe's Faustus *did* find a way of escaping God's judgement and hell. And censorship is only an issue to him in as much as it supposedly limited

[37] Rowse, *Christopher Marlowe*, pp. 27–30.

Marlowe's subversion to 'demystifying' the issues rather than (by implication) openly speaking his mind. Nevertheless, in their different ways,
Empson and Dollimore both propound variants on the construction of
Marlowe as the 'demonized' rebel, whose plays give voice (albeit muted by
censorship) to the heterodox opinions he held in his own life.

But it will be apparent that my account of the evolution of the role of the
Master of the Revels as censor of plays challenges Dollimore's suggestion
that he formed part of an ideologically coherent establishment, at odds with
the fact of theatre itself, as much as it does the conspiratorial improbabilities
of Empson's theory. He only existed at all because the court — the dominant
centre of power, but not the only one — found the actors useful to them, not
only as entertainers but as contributors to the conspicuous self-display
which was an important adjunct of power in the Renaissance. As John Cocke
sarcastically put it in his 'character' of 'A Common Player' (1615): 'players
may not be called rogues: *For they bee chiefe ornaments of his Majesties Revells*'
(cited in *ES*, IV, 255–57). Within limits the Master of the Revels offered them
protection rather than repression, and T. H. Howard-Hill has aptly
observed that 'his relationship with the players although ultimately authoritarian was more collegial than adversarial'.[38]

Tilney was thus never 'the Queen's censor' in quite the sense that Empson
implied. Like any court official, he owed his post, and the additional powers
of his 1581 patent, to royal favour. But that royal favour was engineered by
Tilney's cousin and patron, Lord Charles Howard (subsequently Lord
Howard of Effingham, Lord Admiral and Earl of Nottingham).[39] The
patronage system, with its reciprocal benefits and obligations, was designed
to bind the privileged classes to the existing power structure; but in as much
as it was inherently competitive (individuals vying with each other for
specific posts, their more elevated patrons competing with each other for the
royal ear) and since, moreover, the ties between patrons and their clients
were more characteristic of an extended family (which was not necessarily
uniform even in religious adherence), than of what we should describe as a
political party, the resulting 'establishment' was anything but ideologically
coherent.

In such a context, a 'state' view on many of the central religious and
political issues of the day was a meaningless concept, and Tilney, as a
product and beneficiary of this factional court, never sought to enforce one as
such. Rather, his censorship aimed to keep commentary within the limits
tacitly accepted at court itself; it insisted on a suitable fictional veiling of
topical issues, so as not to cause specific offence either to identifiable
individuals of note or to friendly foreign powers; it required pre-eminently

[38] T. H. Howard-Hill, 'Buc and the Censorship of *Sir John Van Olden Barnavelt* in 1619', *Review of English Studies*, n.s. 39 (1988), 39–63, p. 43.
[39] W. R. Streitberger, 'On Edmond Tyllney's Biography', *Review of English Studies*, n.s. 29 (1978), 11–35, p. 20.

that his own authority to draw the line be respected: the margin of what was permissible was that much greater, as long as all involved subscribed to the system of authority itself. In all of this there is no evidence that a Master of the Revels ever objected to what any playwright *thought*, much less that any was ever punished for his doctrines alone. Tilney could accept, apparently with equanimity, the vigorous puritanism of a Robert Wilson and the tacit sympathy for a Catholic martyr shown by the authors of *Sir Thomas More*; he could 'allow' Shakespeare's travesty of the Lollard 'martyr' Sir John Old-castle in *I Henry IV* (even if a latter-day holder of the Cobham title subsequently insisted that the name be changed) just as he could 'allow' the much more complimentary *Sir John Oldcastle* plays performed by the rival Lord Admiral's Men. And — the point of all this — there is no evidence whatever that he objected in any shape or form to what Marlowe wrote for the stage.

I say this despite Janet Clare's attempt to suggest otherwise in *'Art made tongue-tied by authority': Elizabethan and Jacobean Dramatic Censorship* (Manchester: Manchester University Press, 1990). This is a far more balanced and empirically-driven account of the subject than that deriving from Glynne Wickham and deployed to such different effects by Empson and Dollimore, but its view of the Master of the Revels is still that he was 'the agent of that most arbitrary and punitive instrument of state control' (i.e. censorship, p. 215). That being so, she is inclined to detect his hand in matters which are often explicable on other grounds. This is so, again, in relation to *Dr Faustus*, where she argues that 'the status of the so-called "A" version as a performance-based text, combined with the political referentiality of one of the passages absent in "A" and present in the "B" version, suggests interference by Tilney' (p. 27). The passage she singles out 'is the early part of the scene in Rome depicting the humiliation of Saxon Bruno' (p. 28). Her grounds for focusing on this particular scene, among so many others also missing from the earlier printed text, are that stylistically and in subject-matter it has echoes of other work by Marlowe, that its depiction of the excommunication by a Pope of a German Emperor would be too strong meat in the early 1590s, given Pius V's excommunication of Elizabeth in 1570, but might be less contentious later; and that the name Bruno, not in the historical sources, might have been 'intended [as] an allusion which would have appealed to the more initiated in his audience' to Giordano Bruno, the unorthodox Dominican philosopher and heretic magician imprisoned by the Holy Office in May 1592.

This is in fact a tottering edifice of suppositions to get around the fact that by far the likeliest explanation for the existence of this scene (as others) in the 'B' text but not in the 'A' is that of the 'adicyones in doctor fostes' for which Philip Henslowe paid William Birde and Samuel Rowley in November 1602.[40] If it indeed echoes Marlovian themes and style (notoriously difficult to quantify) this is hardly surprising since these men were writing for the company that had

[40] See note 28, above.

all his major works in their repertoire, and they were specifically adding to one of his best known works: an element of pastiche or imitation was only too likely; if indeed papal excommunication was a less touchy issue later rather than sooner (a debatable contention given the height of anti-Catholic feeling that remained at least till the time of the Gunpowder Plot) it is all the more likely that the scene was written later, rather than censored from an early version and revived later; if there *is* an allusion to Giordano Bruno, it is more likely to have resonated after his execution at the stake in 1600 (the death to which 'Saxon Bruno' is condemned in the text (B–1616, III.1.993–94)) rather than mere imprisonment in 1592. Saxon Bruno's escape from that fate, apparently engineered by Mephostophilis, would thus add topical defiance to Faustus's mockery of the Pope, though the fact that Giordano Bruno had *not* so escaped would also ironically foreshadow the fate of the magician Faustus. In short, the case for seeing the scene as a late addition is at least as compelling as that for seeing something of Marlowe's own hand in it, while the case for supposing Tilney's involvement here as an agent of that 'most arbitrary and punitive instrument of state control' is itself arbitrary and tendentious.

'Gentle Will' Shakespeare of course, has rarely been suspected of troubling the Master of the Revels. Virginia C. Gildersleeve, in what remained until recently the standard work on the question of government regulation of Renaissance drama, spoke for many when she described him as 'obviously in sympathy with the government and the customs prevailing in his time' and central to her perception that 'the Elizabethan drama was, indeed, essentially non-controversial. It was chiefly romantic concerned not with how things ought to be, but with how they might appear most splendid, most thrilling, most effective [. . .] it dealt rather with analysis of human character, of the foibles of human nature, than with political and social problems'.[41] This is a curiously blinkered statement at the end of an account of how dramatists as varied as Jonson and Chapman, Marston and Daniel, Middleton and Massinger are all known to have incurred the wrath of the authorities for their plays.

In the case of Shakespeare, who is not known to have troubled the authorities in anything more subversive than a failure to pay a small sum in property taxes, her case is at least superficially compelling.[42] But close textual scrutiny, especially of discrepancies between quarto and folio versions of his plays, does reveal a number of instances where censorship may best account for certain omissions and clumsinesses. Many of these relate to the period between the *Isle of Dogs* controversy (when a number of Pembroke's Men, including the part-maker of the play, Ben Jonson, were jailed for staging an offensive play in 1597) and the Essex rebellion (1601),

[41] Virginia Crocheron Gildersleeve, *Government Regulation of the Elizabethan Drama* (New York: Columbia University Press, 1908), p. 135.
[42] See Schoenbaum, *Shakespeare: A Compact Documentary Life*, p. 211.

which in many ways was the culmination of the political in-fighting that underlay the tensions arising from the succession question. The 1600 quarto text of *2 Henry IV* is a case in point. Compared with the 1623 folio text of the play it lacks all but one reference to Richard II (the *locus classicus* of an English King deposed by rebellion) and the arguments of the rebels within the play itself are significantly curtailed.[43] It is quite probable, however, that if these variations of the text *are* the result of censorship, they derive from the actions of those who licensed the play for printing, rather than from the Master of the Revels. Janet Clare doubts this, on the grounds that it was entered in the Stationers' Company, without surveillance by one of the ecclesiastical 'correctors' (p. 70). But this is simply to underplay the extent to which the Stationers' Company itself was implicated in the whole process of control. The preservation of their cartel was always a strong argument for not allowing anything to be published that might cause offence. In some ways it was a more effective mechanism of control than relying on the ecclesiastical 'correctors', whose judgement and attention to duty were not above reproach, as was to be demonstrated in the case of Dr John Hayward's *The First Part of the Life and Reign of Henry IV*.

The beauty of the argument that any censorship affecting Shakespeare plays was for the press rather than for the theatre, from the point of view of those who prefer to see him as an uncontentious and apolitical author, is that it allows for the possibility that what he wrote was uncontroversial when he wrote it (and so in intention), and only became suspect in the light of unforeseen developments. This is one way of approaching the most notorious single instance of suspected censorship in relation to a Shakespeare play, that of the abdication scene in *Richard II* (IV.1.145–308). This is a familiar theme, which I do not intend to rehearse in detail here. Essentially, the first three editions of the play (1597/8) did not contain the scene, which first saw print in 1608. In as much as there is a consensus on the matter, it is probably that the scene was cut for the press in 1597, deposition or abdication being seen (again by the Wardens of the Stationers' Company, rather than by an ecclesiastical censor) as too touchy an issue at a time when tensions over the succession were intensifying. Such fears could only have been confirmed as Hayward's *The First Part of the Life and Reign of Henry IV* (1599), which dealt with much of the same history as the Shakespearean play, caused a scandal; and then what was very probably Shakespeare's own play was performed on the eve of the Essex rebellion. But such considerations no longer pertained by 1608.

It is a comfortable doctrine, acknowledging on the one hand that the play clearly became dangerous but absolving Shakespeare himself of anything like subversive intention. Fortuitiously, we do not even know if he was

---

[43] See Janet Clare, '*Art made tongue-tied by authority*', pp. 68–70, for the argument that virtually all such discrepancies are ascribable to censorship of one sort or another.

personally involved in that performance on the eve of the Essex rebellion. We know he continued to act as late as 1603 (*Sejanus*) but not, apparently in all of the Lord Chamberlain's Men's productions (*Every Man Out of His Humour*, 1599), and though the authorities looked into that questionable performance they spoke to another of the company's principals, Augustine Phillips, rather than to its 'ordinary poet', Shakespeare. Anyone looking to absolve Shakespeare even more conclusively of complicity with 'dangerous matter' in respect of *Richard II* might revive the suggestion (first made by David Bergeron) that the abdication scene was never, in fact, cut from the play: that it was, rather, an addition (following a theatrical revival) to the 1608 Quarto, the title page of which proclaims: 'With new additions of the Parliament Scene, and the deposition of King Richard, as it hath been lately acted by the King's Majesty's Servants at the Globe.' The line which follows the 'cut' passage, the Abbot of Westminster's 'A woeful pageant have we here beheld' (IV.1.309), might refer equally to the arrest of the Bishop of Carlisle on a charge of treason (which preceded it in the 1597/8 Quartos) or to the abdication of the king, as in the later version. It is custom, rather than inherent sense, which predisposes most readers to adopt the later reading as always intended, and the recently-growing conviction (largely stemming from studies of the text of *King Lear*) that Shakespeare did sometimes purposefully revise his plays adds weight to the possibility that this is what may have happened here.[44] It has, after all, long been recognized that the 'missing' scene contains nothing particularly inflammatory. It concentrated on Richard's self-dramatization rather than the constitutional implications of the events, and it is difficult to enter the mind of a censor who would cut the abdication (rather than deposition) of a king but leave intact the depiction of his brutal murder.[45]

The fact is that we are unlikely ever to know the truth of *Richard II* and its 'censorship'. It will remain for ever a tangle of charged possibilities which we shall construe (or not) according to our dispositions. I wish merely to point out here how the balance of scholarship has, consciously or otherwise, almost always bent to avoid implicating Shakespeare in anything intentionally subversive, indeed in any personal confrontation with a censor. There is, in fact, no overpowering reason in this case to suppose that the scene was not simply cut by Tilney when the play first went to him. Had the play been by Marlowe I would hazard a guess that that would have been most scholars' first instinct. Therein lies the power of the 'constructions' I have been tracing.

Against that power it is sometimes necessary to state the obvious even more forcefully than usual. In the case of Marlowe we know, with quite

---

[44] See David Bergeron, 'The Deposition Scene in *Richard II*', *Renaissance Papers 1974* (1975), 31–37; also Leeds Barroll, 'A New History for Shakespeare and His Time', *Shakespeare Quarterly*, 30 (1988), 441–64.
[45] See *Richard II: the Variorum Edition*, ed. by Matthew W. Black (Philadelphia, PA: Lippincott, 1955), pp. 369–77.

exceptional specificity, that virtually all his plays were performed, and remained long in the repertoire, because they were either written for, or subsequently acquired by, companies with whom Henslowe was involved; the only exception is *Dido Queen of Carthage*, and even for that the title page of the 1594 Quarto assures us that it was 'Played by the Children of her Majesties Chappell': as much evidence of actual performance as we have for most plays of the period. As they have survived in print, although the texts of *Dr Faustus* and *The Massacre at Paris* are manifestly unsatisfactory, there is nothing whatever to associate the mangling of their limbs with censorship. Whatever we make of the debate over *Richard II*, the gruesome and demeaning death of Marlowe's Edward II had unequivocally been 'allowed' on the stage by Tilney and published in 1594: hardly evidence that the sacredness of kingship was to be respected at all times, as some who argue for the repressive nature of the censorship would have us suppose. Moreover, Edward Alleyn built much of a prosperous career on playing major Marlovian roles — certainly Tamburlaine and the Jew of Malta, probably Faustus — and this does not appear to have impeded his progress to a pious and respectable old age, Master of the Royal Game of Bulls, Bears, and Dog Mastiffs and founder of the College of God's Gift at Dulwich.

In short, the notion that Marlowe's plays were themselves dangerous properties, either mangled themselves by a censor or barely the survivors of his ideologically rigorous attentions, is a myth, one vicariously fuelled by the image of Marlowe himself as an Icarus-style over-reacher, and everything which that image in turn implies about the era in which he lived. If we pause to separate the man from the works, we can see that timing itself may well be responsible for the lasting force of the vivid configuration of Marlowe as the rebellious 'outsider'. Yes, the Privy Council had issued a warrant for his arrest on 18 May 1593. But two days later 'Christopher Marlowe of London, gentleman, being sent for by warrant from their lordships, hath entered his appearance for his indemnity therein; and is commanded to give his daily attendance on their lordships until he shall be licensed to the contrary'.[46] Unlike Marlowe's former room-mate, Thomas Kyd, who had been precipitately imprisoned for his supposed involvement in the touchy subject of anti-immigrant propaganda, Marlowe himself was formally recognized in his status as a gentleman and allowed to remain at liberty. Kyd's papers had been searched, and among them were found 'vile heretical conceits denying the deity of Jesus Christ our Saviour', apparently fragments of a Socinian treatise, which Kyd (under torture, and doubtless in fear of his own life) claimed had belonged to Marlowe and been accidentally shuffled with his own papers when they lodged together. He does not seem to have claimed that Marlowe wrote the treatise, but the latter's association with it appears to have precipitated the order for his arrest. It is entirely possible, however,

---

[46] Rowse, *Christopher Marlowe*, p. 192.

that Marlowe himself was only marginal to the Privy Council's anxiety: that they were most concerned about the anti-immigrant propaganda, an inflammatory issue with immediate public order implications, which seems to have been Edmund Tilney's first concern over *Sir Thomas More*. They may well have been particularly anxious to identify influential men (Northumberland, Raleigh, Walsingham?) shielding anyone writing such material. Their interest in Marlowe may not have extended beyond the help he could give them in furthering such enquiries. But the sudden and violent death ten days later, while the warrant was still in force, left the matter unresolved, and has left imaginations to dwell on it ever since.

No one can pretend that Marlowe was an easy man to live with. Even allowing for prejudice, hearsay, and sensationalism, there is evidence enough that he had a quick temper, was involved in the hot-blooded death of one man (William Bradley) and suspect activities like 'coining', had some dubious associates, held opinions that at least some people would find offensive, and was not averse to voicing them provocatively. But this is some way short of the marginalized rebel which he is so often held to be — and not only by a Jonathan Dollimore, who might well accept the description of marginalized rebel for himself. E. M. W. Tillyard, the very antithesis of such rebellion, allowed Marlowe two grudging entries in his *Elizabethan World Picture* and then only to emphasize how 'exceptional' is a passage on the warring of the elements in *Tamburlaine* from which he quotes.[47] Figures like Sir John Davies and even 'one of the more pedestrian poets, Davies of Hereford' (p. 31) are accorded far more centrality and representative status. By concentrating on the lack of censorship, so far as we can determine, on the fact that his works were allowed on to the stage and into print, with minimal apparent interference, I wish to query just how marginal as a writer (and possibly even as a person) Marlowe actually was, just how ostracized in fact by his own contemporaries, just how intellectually eccentric: to ask whether it is not more reasonable to consider him, even if somewhat unorthodox, as well within the spectrum of opinion that authority 'allowed'.

Although I reach these conclusions by a very different route I find myself largely concurring with the views of Simon Shepherd in *Marlowe and the Politics of Elizabethan Theatre* (Brighton: Harvester, 1986), where he questions over-easy assumptions about the 'demonized' or heretical Marlowe, emphasizing the centrality — one might almost say normality — of the dramatist's concerns as an educated Elizabethan, though one sceptical of the age's pieties, especially as represented on the stage: 'The Marlowe texts could be said to take a number of ideological truths of the Elizabethan theatre and reveal them to be discourses, and to show those discourses spoken within power relations' (p. 210).

[47] (London: Chatto, 1943; repr. New York: Random House, [n.d.]), p. 64.

For the record, it should be acknowledged that Marlowe did not entirely escape the attentions of the Master of the Revels after his death. The hand of the censor is clearly evident in one particular: the 'B' text of *Dr Faustus* has been revised to bring it into conformity with the 1606 Act 'to Restrain Abuses of Players', which made it law that 'if at any tyme or tymes [. . .] any person or persons do or shall in any Stage play [. . .] jestingly or profanely speake or use the holy Name of God or of Christ Jesus, or of the Holy Ghoste or of the Trinitie, which are not to be spoken but with feare and reverence, shall forfeite for everie such Offence by him or them committed Tenne Pounde'.[48] This is just about the clearest directive that Tilney and his successors were ever issued with, and all the evidence is that they were punctilious about enforcing it. So the 1616 text of *Dr Faustus* loses the riveting: 'See see where Christs blood streames in the firmament, | One drop would save my soule, halfe a drop, ah my Christ' (A, 1463–64) for a barely intelligible 'One drop of bloud will save me; oh my Christ', while 'And see where God stretcheth out his arme, | And bends his irefull browes' (A, 1468–69) becomes more blandly 'And see a threatning Arme, an angry Brow'. There are some cuts and many other minor amendments, which are also probably ascribable to this, such as: (A, 298) 'Is stoutly to abjure the Trinitie' [B: abjure all godlinesse]; (A, 519) 'If unto God [B: unto heaven,] hee'le throwe thee downe'; (A, 1505) 'My God, my God [B: O mercy heaven], looke not so fierce on mee'.[49] Thinking once more of Empson, it is difficult to conceive of Tilney or his successor, Buc, simultaneously tidying up such theological minutiae and relaxing their standards on what they saw as out-and-out heresy. The posthumous amendment of oaths remains the only proven intervention of the censors in relation to Marlowe's works, a trivial detail in the face of the provocation which he is conventionally held to have represented.

Janet Clare sees more in this than I do: 'The extent and nature of the censorship of the "B" text — beyond simple expurgation of oaths — suggest that [. . .] it was [. . .] censored in accordance with recent legislation and what seems to be a more pronounced anti-Catholic attitude toward doctrinal issues and sacred reference on stage' (p. 106). While it is true that the more oblique references to 'Christ' and to 'God', especially in Faustus's last soliloquy, blunt the impact of a play depicting a man at odds with his putative maker, some of the changes may well be down to Rowley and Birde at the time of their 'adyciones' and there is no compelling reason to construe any of them as more than a pragmatic accommodation with the express will of Parliament (which was after all, a more representative body than the crown, the court, or the Revels Office). In this respect it met, it would seem, with exactly the same treatment as the plays of Shakespeare.

---

[48] Quoted in Gill, *Dr Faustus*, p. xvii.
[49] A fuller account than this may be found in *Marlowe's 'Dr. Faustus' 1604–1616*, ed. by W. W. Greg (Oxford: Clarendon Press, 1950), pp. 85–87.

To take only one example: *Othello* was produced at court in 1604/5, before the Act to Restrain Abuses. A version of the text from that period got into print as late as 1622. This may have been because the Act did not specifically apply to printed texts, as distinct from what was spoken on stage, or because there was some confusion at the time about the authority to license play-texts for the press. Tilney's successor as Master of the Revels, Sir George Buc, had acquired that authority even before Tilney's death, but lost control over the process in his later years, when he was under tremendous pressure and went mad; it took his successors, Sir John Astley and Sir Henry Herbert, some little time fully to re-assert their authority in this sphere. Nevertheless, the text of *Othello* in the 1623 Folio shows all the attentions of a Master of the Revels to a text needing to be brought into conformity with the Act to Restrain Abuses. Possibly Heminge and Condell were being particularly scrupulous in connexion with a volume dedicated to the Lord Chamberlain (and his brother), the superior at court of the Master of the Revels. More likely they were following, at least in this respect, the King's Men's current 'allowed copy' of the play. We know that *Othello* was in their repertoire as late as 1613, when it was again presented at court. By then Buc would have insisted that it conform with the Act to Restrain Abuses.

In this respect, then, as in so many others, the plays of Marlowe and Shakespeare received identical treatment from their licensers and censors. The 'readings' of Tilney and Buc that implicitly underlay their 'allowance' of Marlowe's plays in a variety of contexts are not as forceful as those of Harvey and Beard, nor necessarily as respectful as those of Jones and Blount, but in some respects they might lay claim to be more representative than any of them. It is the normality of the treatment Marlowe received as a writer that stands out, ironically casting shadows over the long-perceived normality of attention accorded to Shakespeare. The testimony of the censors, approached as far as possible without prior constructions, calls into question the traditional construction of the ideological relationship between those exact contemporaries from Canterbury and Stratford, the one a perfect heretic, the other a perfect conformist.

The Sacralizing Sign: Religion and Magic in Bale, Greene, and the Early Shakespeare

KURT TETZELI VON ROSADOR

University of Münster

[To] signify the godhead, one Persian speaks of a bird that somehow is all birds; Alanus de Insulis, of a sphere whose center is everywhere and circumference is nowhere; Ezekiel, of a fourfaced angel who at one and the same time moves east and west, north and south. [...] Perhaps the gods might grant me a similar metaphor, but then this account would become contaminated by literature, by fiction. Really, what I want to do is impossible, for any listing of an endless series is doomed to be infinitesimal. (Jorge Luis Borges, 'The Aleph')

One God, one king, one faith, one profession is fit for one monarchie, and common wealth. (Edwin Sandys, *The Sermons*)

I

All culture (culture defined with Clifford Geertz as 'webs of significance [man] himself has spun')[1] is the site of the battle of signs which is the Reformation.[2] The discourse of the sacred constitutes and circumscribes the main arena in which this battle is fought.[3] The priest's altar, the preacher's pulpit, the monarch's throne, the printer's workshop, the scholar's study, the scientist's laboratory, the magician's circle, the dramatist's and player's stage are among the more important *loci* in this arena. The Word is pitted against words, and words are set against visual, tangible signs. The status, authority, significance, and (pragmatic, political) use of the Word,[4] of words, of signs, sacred or otherwise, of Scripture and scriptures, are being questioned and are hence in play. The Puritan's trust in the full presence of the Word collides with the Catholic's reliance on the sacramental character of the visible Church and its ceremonies. Royal power is both realized and

---

[1] *The Interpretation of Cultures* (New York: Basic Books, 1973), p. 5.
[2] See Robert Weimann's revision of traditional Marxist positions in *Shakespeare und die Macht der Mimesis* (Berlin and Weimar: Aufbau-Verlag, 1988), pp. 36, 54–89, which approaches such a view and would probably have been less hedging had it been published after the winter of state-socialism's discontent, 1989.
[3] See Stephen Greenblatt, 'Shakespeare and the Exorcists', in *Shakespearean Negotiations: The Circulation of Social Energy in Renaissance England* (Oxford: Clarendon Press, 1988), pp. 94–128.
[4] The fairly vigorous conflict of the spoken vs the written word during the sixteenth and seventeenth centuries can be ignored in this context. But see the stimulating and detailed accounts by Terence Cave, *The Cornucopian Text: The Problems of Writing in the French Renaissance* (Oxford: Clarendon Press, 1979), and Martin Elsky, *Authorizing Words: Speech, Writing, and Print in the English Renaissance* (Ithaca, NY and London: Cornell University Press, 1989).

subverted by its representation. And the drama's form, force, and development is to no small extent dependent on the answer to the question whether it should be seen or heard.[5] These are certainly not conflicts easily defined or readily resolved into binary oppositions. Nor can they be rigidly contained within the separate disciplines of theology, politics, or aesthetics. There are no fixed boundaries. Thus, to sketch roughly but one segment of the cultural field, the power of the monarch is inextricably entwined with that of the ecclesiastical hierarchy — 'No bishop, no King' in James's succinct phrase at the Hampton Court conference of 1604. It is mediated, established, and subverted, by the theatricality of its representation, be it in Elizabethan pageantry or the Stuart masque.[6] And it must defend and preserve the charismatic basis of its authority by delimiting, containing, or annihilating rival charismas, such as magic's.[7] It is impossible, even if it were desirable, to map definitely and comprehensively the complex dynamics of these interrelated processes, the movements of boundaries, the invasion and appropriation of territories. What can be essayed, is to revise some of the traces of this discursive field.

II

The long drawn-out conflict of religion and magic as it becomes visible in the sixteenth century belongs to this field. It is a conflict the medieval Church had tried to marginalize, if not to smother totally, by practically appropriating magical procedures for its own kind of ecclesiastical magic, by blurring the distinctions between prayer and charm, between holy and magical objects and rites. The use of holy water to make the crops grow, the ringing of consecrated bells to dispel thunderstorms and such like actions turn the Church into 'a repository of supernatural power which could be dispensed to the faithful to help them in their daily problems'.[8] Of course, such appropriation of magical techniques and modes of thought acknowledges the power of magic over the popular mind and brings into the open the rivalry which existed between the cunning folk, the wise men and women, on the one hand

---

[5] For a brief, but highly suggestive discussion of the aesthetic side of the problem see Andrew Gurr, *Playgoing in Shakespeare's London* (Cambridge: Cambridge University Press, 1987), pp. 85–97.

[6] See Stephen Orgel's excellent account *The Illusion of Power: Political Theater in the English Renaissance* (Berkeley: University of California Press, 1975). See also the more controversial study of Jonathan Goldberg, *James I and the Politics of Literature: Jonson, Shakespeare, Donne, and Their Contemporaries* (Baltimore, MD: Johns Hopkins University Press, 1983). For two recent, opposing points of view see David Scott Kastan, 'Proud Majesty Made a Subject: Shakespeare and the Spectacle of Rule', *Shakespeare Quarterly*, 37 (1986), 459–75, and Paul Yachnin, 'The Powerless Theatre', *English Literary Renaissance*, 21 (1991), 49–74.

[7] I have argued this in "The Power of Magic: from 'Endimion' to 'The Tempest' ", *Shakespeare Survey*, 43 (1991), 1–13.

[8] Keith Thomas, *Religion and the Decline of Magic: Studies in Popular Beliefs in Sixteenth and Seventeenth Century England* (London: Weidenfeld and Nicholson, 1971), p. 32. The passage is much indebted to Thomas's brilliant and detailed study.

and the (local) clergy on the other.[9] This is a rivalry which increased in hostility with the Reformation and the Protestant tendency to deny all reality and efficacy to magic, exiling it into a realm of shadows and diabolically induced illusions.[10] The rivalry is expressly stated by the country character in George Giffard's, the Puritan minister's, *A Dialogue concerning Witches and Witchcraftes*. When told that some of her acts intended to prevent misfortune must have been 'taught by the devill', she takes the pragmatic popular stand:

Is that witchcraft? Some scripture man hath tolde you so. Did the devill teach it? Nay the good woman at R. H. taught it my husband: she doeth more good in one yeare than all these scripture men will doe so long as they live.[11]

The Scripture, the Word, which, internalized and preached, is the main concern of the Protestant reformed clergy, is contrasted with the pragmatics of alleviating petty everyday misfortune, achieved by the help of charms written on slips of paper, amulets, shears, crystal stones, and similar objects used and distributed by the cunning men and women. Verbal and tangible signs are the respective weapons in this battle for the bodies and souls of the English populace.

The battle-lines, however, are by no means clearly drawn; they become blurred when the forces of Catholicism are mustered. For the Catholic Church miracles have not ceased, as the Elizabethan literature of demonology repeatedly insists, nor would a Catholic agree with Richard Hooker, the Anglican theologian, who talks of '[God's] surceasing to speake to the world since the publishing of the Gospell of Jesus Christ'.[12] (Note Hooker's transliteration of Christ's life, the Incarnation and Passion, into published speech!) For the Catholic, transcendence manifests itself ever and again in the Church Visible, its saints and sacraments, its rites and exorcisms. This is the stuff antipapistical polemics thrive on, by pointing out the identity of magical and Catholic thought and ritual. Hence, according to William Perkins, 'if a man will but take a view of all poperie, he shall easily see, that the most part is meere Magique',[13] with transubstantiation as the most prominent instance. But it is also 'that *pompous and carnall decking of the house of God*, rather to please the eie, then affect the heart, rather as a Pallace for the god of this world to revel in, and prey upon new-fangled and silly soules, then a place of *spirituall worship*'[14] which is violently objected to. In other words: it

[9] Thomas, p. 263, and passim. See also Alan Macfarlane's painstaking survey of witchcraft in Essex, *Witchcraft in Tudor and Stuart England: A Regional and Comparative Study* (London: Routledge, 1970), p. 121 and passim.

[10] 'An illusion is a worke of Satan, whereby he deludeth or deceiveth man. And it is two-fold; either of the outward senses, or of the minde.' (William Perkins, *A Discourse of the Damned Art of Witchcraft* (Cambridge, 1608), p. 22).

[11] (London, 1593), sig. M3ᵛ.

[12] *Of the Lawes of Ecclesiastical Politie*, The Folger Library Edition of The Works of Richard Hooker, ed. by W. Speed Hill, 2 vols (Cambridge, MA: Harvard University Press, 1977), I, 127.

[13] *The Works* (Cambridge, 1603), p. 36.

[14] Thomas Cooper, *The Mystery of Witchcraft* (London, 1617), p. 98.

is the visual signs' appeal to the eye which is attacked because it obscures or annihilates the Word speaking to the ear, heart, and spirit. In its reliance on the sensual, tangible sign Roman Catholicism is, in the Protestant view, indistinguishable from magic.

This, however, constitutes but another segment of the battlefield. In a different sociological and philosophical area, that held by Neo-Platonism,[15] the rivalry between religion and magic is no less explosive. However cautiously phrased, this rivalry becomes apparent in Agrippa's or Ficino's claims:

Wise men conceive it no way irrationall that it should be possible for us to ascend [...] through each World, to the same very originall World it self, the Maker of all things, and first Cause, from whence all things are, and proceed.[16]

The entire striving of our soul is that it become God. Such striving is no less natural to men than the effort to flight is to birds. For it is always in men everywhere. Likewise it is not a contingent quality of some men but follows the nature itself of the species. [...] Therefore the human effort to become God can some day be fulfilled. For who but God, Himself, whom we seek, would have inserted this into our souls?[17]

It is in vain that both Agrippa and Ficino intend such claims to belong exclusively to the spiritual world, that their aspiration to godhead is based on self-purgation and spiritual discipline, that this is meant to describe an inward process leading to a mystical experience of atoneness. The literal sense and the vocabulary of ascension and strife or of military conquest, as in the following statement by Ficino, formulates another kind of desire:

But in what pertains to the desire for victory, the immense magnificence of our soul may manifestly be seen from this, that he will not be satisfied with the empire of this world, if, having conquered this one, he learns that there remains another world which he has not yet subjugated. [...] Thus man wishes no superior and no equal and will not permit anything to be left out and excluded from this rule. This status belongs to God alone. Therefore he seeks a divine condition. (II, 491)

This is not the language of an interiorized spiritual experience; this is the language of power politics, of a Machiavellian *libido dominandi*. And it is a dominion not over the self, spiritualized into godlike self-sufficiency, but over the material, natural, social world:

The human mind vindicates to itself a right to divinity not only forming and shaping matter through the methods of arts, as we have said, but also in transmuting the species of things by command, which work is indeed called a miracle. [...] Here we

---

[15] Basic information as well as stimulating speculation on the subject of Neoplatonism and hermetic magic may be found in D. P. Walker, *Spiritual and Demonic Magic from Ficino to Campanella* (London: Warburg Institute, 1958); Michael J. B. Allen, *The Platonism of Marsilio Ficino* (Berkeley: University of California Press, 1984); Stephen A. McKnight, *Sacralizing the Secular: The Renaissance Origins of Modernity* (Baton Rouge, LA: Louisiana State University Press, 1989); John S. Mebane, *Renaissance Magic and the Return of the Golden Age: The Occult Tradition and Marlowe, Jonson, and Shakespeare* (Lincoln, NE: University of Nebraska Press, 1989), Chapters 1-4.
[16] Henry Cornelius Agrippa, *Three Books of Occult Philosophy* (London, 1651), p. 2.
[17] Marsilio Ficino *Theologia Platonica de immortalitate animorum*; quoted in, and translated by Charles Trinkaus, *In Our Image and Likeness: Humanity and Divinity in Italian Humanist Thought*, 2 vols (Chicago: University of Chicago Press, 1970), II, 487.

marvel that the souls of men dedicated to God rule the elements, call upon the winds, force the clouds to rain, chase away fogs, cure the diseases of human bodies and the rest. (II, 486)

This is no whit different from what a Medea claims or what a Prospero abjures. And it is achieved by means of natural, sympathetic magic, by (to use Faustus's refraction) the 'Metaphisickes of Magicians', by 'Lines, circles, sceanes, letters and characters'.[18] Small wonder that the Catholic Church feels threatened, warily watches Florentine practitioners, persecutes a della Porta, and burns a Giordano Bruno, when it finds its own domain invaded and its own system of holy signs used without permission. But what is the proper religious use of lines, circles, scenes, letters, and characters? Are any signs at all proper either for the (re)presentation of the holy or for religious use, if cunning folk and Neoplatonic magicians employ the verbal signs of charms and spells, if Catholic ritual, based on the visual, the tangible sign, is seen to be nothing but another version of magic?

Moreover: if the meaning, use, and power of religious signs have become a matter of controversy, what happens to the theatrical representation of these signs? Is there such a thing as a Protestant dramaturgy, being based upon and presenting the Word?[19] How far does the drama, the stage, given that their natures are necessarily subdued by, and suffused with, what they work in, namely verbal and visual signs, reflect and intervene in this controversy? By selecting and reading three plays, one written for the purpose of Protestant propaganda, the other two both for popular entertainment, but of different generic orientation, some traces within a highly intricate, even labyrinthine cultural field may become visible.

III

John Bale's *Thre Lawes, of Nature, Moses, and Christ, Corrupted by the Sodomytes, Pharysees and Papystes*, written in the middle of the 1530s and at least twice revised to keep up with the rapid and radical politico-religious changes of the sixteenth century, can be read as an early dramatic answer to such questions from a Protestant point of view. It is rigidly constructed. Each of its three middle acts presents one of the titular laws and its corruption by Infidelitas and his respective hench(wo)men. These processes are contained within Deus Pater's transcendental realm and government, as staged in

---

[18] *Marlowe's 'Doctor Faustus' 1604–1616: Parallel Texts*, ed. by W. W. Greg (Oxford: Clarendon Press, 1950), A 79, 81.
[19] Some aspects of this paper are thus related to recent attempts to describe a specifically Protestant poetics, based on the Bible and a definite set of ideologicl tenets and rhetorical strategies; see Barbara K. Lewalski's pioneering study *Protestant Poetics and the Seventeenth-Century Religious Lyric* (Princeton, NJ: Princeton University Press, 1979). Also John N. King, *English Reformation Literature: The Tudor Origins of the Protestant Tradition* (Princeton, NJ: Princeton University Press, 1982) and Ritchie D. Kendall, *The Drama of Dissent: The Radical Poetics of Nonconformity, 1380–1590* (Chapel Hill and London: University of North Carolina Press, 1986).

Acts I and V.[20] Such a framing sets up two opposed worlds, that of the temporal and that of the transcendental, and poses the question how the one is to be mediated through the other. The second act, presenting Naturae Lex and its disfigurement by Infidelitas, Idololatria, and Sodomismus, can be taken paradigmatically. It foregrounds the conflict of religion and magic, never totally absent in the rest of the play, most vigorously and extensively.

Like each of the three middle acts, Act II opens with the self-introduction and self-explanation of the Law governing it. Naturae Lex presents itself exclusively verbally with statuary dignity as a 'knowledge [. . .] whom God in Man doth hyde' (l. 165).[21] The interiorized existence of this law and its reliance on words are starkly contrasted with the presentation of Infidelitas, who enters singing his pedlar's chant of 'Brom, brom' (l. 176) and offering quite different wares:

> I wolde have brought ye the paxe,
> Or els an ymage of waxe
>   If I had knowne ye heare.
> I wyll my selfe so handle
> That ye shall have a candle
>   Whan I come hyther agayne. (l. 184)

Naturae Lex's words are opposed to Infidelitas's material objects. But it is not only the materiality of the objects which is emphasized. The deliberate choice of specific objects, 'the paxe', 'an ymage of waxe', 'a candle', makes clear that they are also used as signs — signs of the holy, as understood in Catholicism and magic.

It is Idololatria, 'decked lyke an olde wytche' (p. 121), who embodies this identification of Catholicism and magic most clearly in Bale's play. This is an identification regularly employed throughout the sixteenth century for purposes of antipapistical satire. Underlying the satire, however, the battle of signs, which is a battle over the policing of the sacred and thus a battle for power, becomes visible. Idololatria's powers, as pictured in her programmatic speeches, range from the working of 'wyles in battle' (l. 446) to curing the headache (ll. 537–38), from the minutiae of daily life to the fate of states. Her means are coercively deployed, visual, tangible signs. Hence Idololatria is furnished with 'holye oyle and watter' (l. 442), with 'bedes' (l. 502), with 'a God [. . .] of a chyppe' (l. 668) and 'a purse of rellyckes, | Ragges, rotten bones, and styckes, | A taper with other tryckes' (ll. 679–81), while each of the Laws is equipped with but one visible object, the stony tables of Moses or a book: the word made visible as scripture.

Thus a very clear-cut opposition between Catholicism, magic, and visual signs and Protestantism, religion, and the word is firmly established. This

[20] For a discussion of the act structure see Klaus Sperk, *Mittelalterliche Tradition und reformatorische Polemik in den Spielen John Bales* (Heidelberg: Carl Winter, 1973), pp. 75–78.
[21] All quotations from the play are taken from *The Complete Plays of John Bale*, ed. by Peter Happé, 2 vols (Cambridge: Brewer, 1986).

opposition is extended, in the course of the play, by that between spiritual
inwardness and ritual ceremony as the third Law, Evangelium, puts it:

> My church is secrete   and evermore wyll be,
> Adorynge the Father   in sprete and in veryte.
> By the worde of God   thys church is ruled onlye,
> And doth not consyst   in outwarde ceremonye.   (l. 1351)

Hence the attack of the Vices is in no small degree directed against the status
and authority of the word or even the Word, when Infidelitas makes use of
the 'Tetragrammaton' for conjuring purposes (l. 392). The word/Word is
further corrupted by the Vices' incessant swearing, their parody of prayer
(ll. 699–703) and of the creed (ll. 1163–76). In Ambitio's words:

> The keye of knowledge   I wyll also take awaye
> By wrastynge the text   to the scriptures sore decaye.   (l. 1101)

To counter this attack the forces of good have dramatically very little else at
their command but to insist on the purity and power of the word/Word itself.
While they are thus necessarily restricted to eloquence as their only action,
the Vices truly come into their own by presenting a world of sensuality, of
corporeality, including breaking wind (l. 194), making love (ll. 475–86), and
feasting and drinking (ll. 1767–68).

Consequently, new forces begin to rank themselves on either side of the
front: rhetoric, spirituality, and inwardness oppose action, corporeality, and
ceremony. The latter, being quite obviously basic components of all dramatic representation, have (not unexpectedly) provoked numerous Protestant
accusations of theatricality against Catholic magic or magical Catholicism,
the Mass and transubstantiation being favourite points of attack. This is one
of many sixteenth-century polemics, possibly Bale's:

> To the good playne people ye turne your backes
> And playe manye a pratye jugling caste/
> Brandon the juglare had never goodlyer knackes
> Than ye have at your masse/bothe fyrste and laste.[22]

The accusation rings through the sixteenth century, culminating in Samuel
Harsnett's works who not only in his *Egregious Popish Impostures* but also in *A
Discovery of the fraudulent practices of John Darrel* uses the extended conceit of
'the Pope his play house' and the Catholic religion as 'a pageant of
Puppites'.[23] It is, however, not unanswerable. The tables can fairly easily be
turned. For the word/Word staged is also the word/Word represented and
handed over to any play-acting Tom, Dick, and Harry as an

---

[22] For a perceptive comment on the relationship between ritual, juggling, and the stage see Thora
Balslev Blatt, *The Plays of John Bale: A Study of Ideas, Technique and Style* (Copenhagen: G.E.C. GAD, 1968),
pp. 132–35 (p. 132).
[23] (London, 1599), sig. A3.

infamouse companie of common minstrelles and entrelude plaiers, who be all brothers of youre fraternitie, membres of youre corporation, and in so good credite emongest yow, that they have their charge of dispensing the worde as well as yow.[24]

Intending to stage the Word, Bale has impaled himself on the horns of a dilemma. His somewhat simplistic Protestant dramaturgy demands clear-cut binary oppositions, pitting Protestant religion against Catholic magic,[25] inwardness against ceremony, the Word against the visual, tangible sign, presence against representation. But he evokes the (Vices') world of ceremony, visible signs, and corporeality almost exclusively through words, yet still has to embody the Word in a dramatis persona — enter Deus Pater: 'I am Deus Pater, a substaunce invysyble' (1. 36). Whatever the outward appearance of Deus Pater may have been, by merely entering the platform even absolute Presence, 'substaunce invysyble', partakes of the theatricality of all dramatic performance. With the play's first paradoxical line Bale has unwittingly deconstructed all the binary oppositions he will be setting up in the course of the play and has entered the realm of representation, in which his signs, verbal or visual, both signify and construct, both present and stage the holy.

IV

If Bale's *Thre Lawes* with its straightforward dualizing strategies fails to achieve its intention, no other drama can escape the play of representation. Certainly none written around 1590, the decade which saw not only the flourishing of an increasingly complex drama but also the precarious religious settlement commonly known as the Anglican compromise. That Greene's *Friar Bacon and Friar Bungay*, regarded until quite recently as little else but a jolly medley of motives and genres, can be read as a reflection of, and intervention in, this issue may come as somewhat of a surprise.[26] But sixteenth-century magic is so deeply implicated in the many-sided contest of *res* and *verba*, of verbal and visual signs, of scripture and ceremony (as the many modern allegories of reading its dramatization as that of artistic endeavour prove)[27] that this conflict cannot, whenever magic is put on the stage, be totally obscured or excluded, even though it can be moved to the periphery of the plays.

---

[24] Thomas Dorman, *A Proufe of Certeyne Articles* (Antwerp, 1564), p. 123.
[25] So far my reading tallies with that of Ritchie D. Kendall's in his brilliant study *The Drama of Dissent*, pp. 101–11. But even though Kendall has much to say on Bale's 'deepest anxieties about the potentially satanic nature of play' (p. 109) and, earlier on, about the slippery nature of language, he underestimates both the subversive power of theatrical representation as such and the problematics of staging the holy.
[26] The turning-point in the history of the play's reputation may be located in Norman Sanders's paper, 'The Comedy of Greene and Shakespeare', *Stratford-upon-Avon Studies*, 3 (1961), 35–53.
[27] For a recent presentation of such a view see Andrew V. Ettin, "Magic into Art: The Magician's Renunciation of Magic in English Renaissance Drama" *Texas Studies in Literature and Language*, 19 (1977), 268–93.

As almost invariably in the late Elizabethan and Jacobean plays from *Doctor Faustus* to *The Tempest*, in *Friar Bacon and Friar Bungay* magic's power seems to be wholly based on words in the form of scripture, on magical books. 'Attulisti nos libros meos de necromantia?' (II. 3), is Bacon's opening question.[28] He 'can by Books | Make storming Boreas thunder from his cave | And dim fair Luna to a dark eclipse' (II. 46–48), and 'the devils pleads homage to his words' (VI. 4). We even hear a charm pronounced — 'Per omnes deos infernales, Belcephon' (II. 116) — and witness the power of the words when a devil obeys them.[29] Hence, in *Friar Bacon and Friar Bungay*, magical words replace the Word as the origin of power. For in exact accordance with Greene's near-obliteration of Bacon's religious profession, his status as a Catholic churchman, still quite prominent in the source, in the play Holy Scripture is reduced to the 'portace' (VI. 136), the breviary Friar Bungay intends to employ for the marriage of Margaret and Lacy. Otherwise it is conspicuous only for its absence.

If the Word is absent in Greene's *Friar Bacon and Friar Bungay* and magical words are accorded considerable power, the status of words, their legitimacy and proper use, cannot go unquestioned. That it is the Fool who introduces the subject of books and book-learning into the play (I. 45–48), as he does that of magic, functions in itself as an implied criticism. This implicit problematization is continued with Latinity being presented as an essential quality of books (II. 3–5), evoking the controversy over both the proper language for the sacred, be it the Scripture or the liturgy, and the right to read and interpret it. And the power of books, the legitimacy of book-learning are wittily parodied, when Bacon magically produces the 'book' his rival, Burden, 'keeps at Henley for himself':

Masters, stand still; fear not. I'll show you but his book.
    Here he conjures.
Per omnes deos infernales, Belcephon.
    Enter a woman with a shoulder of mutton on a spit, and a devil.

(II. 115–16 S.D.)

Here the word is indeed turned into flesh, into mine hostess of Henley, and a pretty piece of flesh she is, her nature being sufficiently indicated by the mutton she carries. The legitimacy and power of books and words are devastatingly criticized by their gross results, staged as a parody of transubstantiation. And (Catholic) religion, seemingly marginalized, enters the play as a cultural context and parodic target.

If the authority of words is thus subverted — and Bacon undercuts it further by refusing, in most unscholarly fashion, to dispute (IX. 128–29, 150–51) — the magical sign, visual or tangible, does not fare much better in

---

[28] All quotations are taken from Daniel Seltzer's edition in The Regents Renaissance Drama Series (Lincoln, NE: University of Nebraska Press, 1963).
[29] A second charm, however, is less successful. But it is the German Vandermast's (IX. 138–40) and thus inferior to Bacon's English power.

Friar Bacon and Friar Bungay. Its status is presented and tested through the results its two most spectacular instances produce, the glass prospective and the brazen head. As a means of magical representation, the glass prospective demonstrates the illusory nature not only of all magical shows and ceremonies, making the Prince of Wales 'think the shadows substances' (VI. 130), but also, by analogy, of all theatrical representation, briefly opening up vistas of infinite regress. That such a show, such an illusion can produce 'tragedy' (XIII. 36) and death is not a contradiction, but an affirmation of the illegitimacy of magic's signs. In Greene's play the glass, the tangible sign, is nothing but a vehicle. It is blind man who acts. And man is blinded by his passions, be they those of ambition or love. This is also the story which the fashioning and destruction of the brazen head tells — with a slight twist. For the destruction of the brazen head is not man's work (as it was Bacon who shattered the glass): '*a hand appears that breaketh down the* Head *with a hammer*' (XI. 74 S.D.); but whose hand? This is a question never answered. Bacon seems to ascribe the deed to the envy of the fiends (XI. 106–10). Emblematic tradition, however, images God as a triangle or a hand.[30] For a brief moment, a transcendental power becomes visible, suggesting a religious context wherein the play is contained.

But both the brevity of this appearance and its ambiguous, indefinite nature counteract any certainty of clearly lodging the play within a given religious cosmology, Catholic or Anglican. Nowhere else does the play even hint at such a possibility. On the contrary: the questioning of the status of both the word and the tangible sign is accompanied by a somewhat implicit, but nevertheless continuous satiric undercutting of all religious authority. For the magical 'wresting of the holy name of God' (XIII. 92) to which Bacon like Bale's Vice confesses is not the only way religious texts are abused. When Miles pointedly misquotes a psalm (II. 4–5) or parodies a liturgical formula ('et nunc et semper. Amen' (II. 172)), when Friar Bungay, stricken by his more powerful *confrère*, can produce nothing but 'Hud, hud' out of the breviary (VI. 151 S.D.), the poking of fun affects the status of religious authority. The question raised by the gross parody of transubstantiating the word into the hostess of Henley must now be placed within the wider context: that magic and Catholicism claim to produce, by words and ceremony, 'substances'. If any doubt were left about the comic subversion of religion in Greene's *Friar Bacon and Friar Bungay*, Scene XIV dispels it. In this scene Margaret, thinking herself deserted by her lover, the Earl of Lincoln, intends to enter a convent. The scene is introduced with an obscenity, 'holy mutton' (XIV. 44), Margaret is confronted most bluntly with the choice of 'God or Lord Lacy' (XIV. 83), and her mundane choice is commented on with

---

[30] Examples can be found in abundance in *Emblemata: Handbuch zur Sinnbildkunst des XVI und XVII Jahrhunderts*, ed. by Arthur Henkel and Albrecht Schöne (Stuttgart: Metzler, 1967).

an obscene pun about the nature of women, 'be they never so near God, yet they love to die in a man's arms' (XIV. 103–04).

Both the word and the visual, tangible sign are thus tested and found wanting. The status and power of magic and religion, as they both rely on the word and the visual sign, are subverted by parody or the results they produce. Who or what is it, then, that licenses, polices, legitimizes the use of signs in Greene's play? The last scene seems to stage an unambiguous answer. Its contents and functions have been carefully prepared. For Greene strategically intersperses between all scenes in which magic and religion are represented scenes of court ritual (IV, IX, XII). And he opens the last scene of the play with the ceremonial representation of royal power:

Enter the Emperor *with a pointless sword; next, the* King *of* Castile, *carrying a sword with a point;* Lacy, *carrying the globe;* Ed[ward]; Warr[en], *carrying a rod of gold with a dove on it;* Ermsby, *with a crown and scepter.* (XVI. S.D.)

The pomp and circumstance of such an entry with the regalia of royal authority in full display seem to vindicate the power of the visual sign, if and as wielded by the monarch. Royal power is triumphantly staged. Within such a frame magical religion/religious magic can find its legitimate, if subordinate place: Bacon and the word find their integral place in the world of the play through the prophecy — a verbal activity — of the future monarchical glory of 'Diana's rose' (XVI. 62). Both the verbal and the visual sign, both magic and religion are thus handed over and subjected to political, royal power. And royal power, staged as a dumb discourse, need not rely on words: it is seen but not heard, it just *is*. Elizabeth, Defender of the Faith and Head of the Church, ought to have been delighted.

And yet: if all (religious and magical) representation in Greene's play because of its essence and/or its theatricality contains the seeds of (self-)-subversion, how can royal representation escape being tinged and invaded? Certainly, the question is never raised explicitly in *Friar Bacon and Friar Bungay* (as it will be in *The Tempest*). But analogy does its subversive work. Is that the reason why the representation of royal power is not given the final say or rather sight, why nine out of sixteen scenes of the play,[31] including the last, end with an invitation to eat and drink? Why the play abounds with references to the rich materiality of English life?[32] For whatever the status, the authority, the power of the word or the visual sign, of magic, of religion or of the monarchy, man (and woman) must eat and will drink. And it needs no Bakhtin to tell us what such a joyous celebration of the material and the instincts entails.

---

[31] As noticed by J. A. Lavin in the introduction to his edition of the play in The New Mermaids (London: Benn, 1969), p. xxxi.
[32] A somewhat speculatively orthodox reading of these matters is Cecile Williamson Cary, 'The Iconography of Food and the Motif of World Order in *Friar Bacon and Friar Bungay*', *Comparative Drama*, 13 (1979–80), 150–63.

V

Greene's *Friar Bacon and Friar Bungay* thus puts, as it were, the impact, the urgency of the Reformation battle of signs to the test of daily experience by placing magic's and religion's claims alongside the immediacy of basic human needs. There are, no doubt, glimpses of these needs (and of plebeian life) again and again to be caught in Shakespeare's tripartite *Henry VI*, most extensively in Part 2, most substantially in Cade's vision of a once and future English land of Cockaigne (IV.2.65–70), most movingly in the exit-line of Simpcox's wife after the exposure of her husband's fraud: 'Alas, sir, we did it for pure need' (II.1.154).[33] And there is also a glimpse of the radical nature of the cultural conflict thus implied when Cade accuses the Lord Say not only of having 'most traitorously corrupted the youth of the realm in erecting a grammar school' but also of having men about him 'that usually talk of a noun and a verb, and such abominable words as no Christian ear can endure to hear' (IV.7.32–41). Important as this incipient conflict of classes and cultures is both dramatically and historically, it is but a part of Shakespeare's exploration of the 'nature, origins, and transfer of power' in the *Henry VI* plays.[34] This is an exploration which is not limited to such problems- as a history or chronicle play cannot avoid dramatizing because of its subject matter, such as those of historical causation, the nature and legitimation of power, the ethos of politics.[35] It is an exploration which, since there is magic in the plays' web, necessarily has to come to theatrical terms with the Reformation discourses in which magic is embedded, such as the rivalry of religion and magic becoming visible in a battle of signs.

The extent to which the *Henry VI* plays are immersed in, and suffused by, religious issues has only recently become visible. In a brilliant analysis Leah Marcus has elucidated the topicality of the trilogy, especially 'the subversive potential of Joan, a defective analogue of the queen, to suggest flaws in the royal composite itself'.[36] And she has demonstrated how religious ritual and witchcraft, female power and royal ceremony are closely linked and contribute to the topicality of the plays. This is, according to Marcus, a topicality in which the audiences' fantasies, anxieties, aggressions about Elizabeth, her status and her politics, are acted out; while being necessarily confined to indirection, implication, latency in the staging. Nor could wider or more

---

[33] All quotations are taken from *The Riverside Shakespeare*, ed. by G. Blakemore Evans (Boston: Houghton Mifflin, 1974).
[34] The phrase is Michael Hattaway's in the introduction to his edition of *1 Henry VI* in the New Cambridge Shakespeare (Cambridge: Cambridge University Press, 1990), p. 17.
[35] These issues have (under new historicist auspices) been excitingly revised and brilliantly extended to include, among others, matters of historical construction, theatrical representation, and the role of women, by Phyllis Rackin, *Stages of History: Shakespeare's English Chronicles* (London: Routledge, 1990).
[36] *Puzzling Shakespeare: Local Reading and Its Discontents* (Berkeley, Los Angeles, and London: University of California Press, 1988), p. 100. See Chapter 2; also the brief reference to the place of religion in the trilogy in Susan Bassnett, 'Sexuality and Power in the Three Parts of *Henry VI*', *Shakespeare Jahrbuch*, 124 (1988), 183–91, p. 187.

basic religious controversies be treated differently, in the face of a royal proclamation against any plays treating matters of religion and of the ever-present threat of a deliberately erratic censorship.

The opening scene of the trilogy introduces the matter, sets the tone, and clarifies the method of presentation. The sudden death of the nostalgically idealized Henry V makes the nobles not only lament it ceremoniously but also inquire into its causes:

> EXETER   What? Shall we curse the planets of mishap
> That plotted thus our glory's overthrow?
> Or shall we think the subtile-witted French
> Conjurers and sorcerers, that, afraid of him,
> By magic verses have contriv'd his end?
> WINCHESTER He was a king blest of the King of kings.
> Unto the French the dreadful Judgment Day
> So dreadful will not be as was his sight.
> The battles of the Lord of hosts he fought;
> The Church's prayers made him so prosperous.
> GLOUCESTER The Church? where is it? Had not churchmen pray'd,
> His thread of life had not so soon decay'd.   (I. I. 23)

A whole bundle of controversial historical, political, and religious issues are encoded in this exchange. The question of historical causation is raised by Exeter's contrasting first and efficient causes, the working of fate, and magical manipulation.[37] He simultaneously and involuntarily questions the legitimacy of Henry's and Lancastrian rule in considering that magic may have touched the life of the king, which orthodox demonological theory deemed to be immune against any such attacks, provided the monarch held his or her office legitimately.[38] Against the efficacy of magical charms Winchester sets the church's right and benevolent use of words: 'The Church's prayers made him so prosperous.' Spoken over the king's corpse Winchester's claim acquires a deeply ironical meaning which Gloucester does not hesitate to explicate: 'Had not churchmen pray'd, | His thread of life had not so soon decay'd.'

Thus the question of the power and proper use of words is explicitly, if briefly, brought to the fore only to be turned aside by the squabbling of Winchester and Gloucester about their respective political ambitions. Still, Gloucester's equation of magical charms and Catholic prayers voices a deep anxiety about the malevolent power of words, which surfaces again and again in the plays. Words are believed to have the power if not to kill (Exeter's question and Gloucester's accusation remain unanswered) then to hurt as the Lieutenant warns the Duke of Suffolk: 'First let my words stab him, as he hath me' (IV. I. 66). Or they are the means of deception, especially

---

[37] For a stimulating discussion see Rackin, Chapter 2. The Augustinian influence has been somewhat one-sidedly stressed by John Cox, *Shakespeare and the Dramaturgy of Power* (Princeton, NJ: Princeton University Press, 1989).
[38] For a fuller discussion of this problem see my 'The Power of Magic', pp. 2–5.

when used by Joan la Pucelle, the Countess of Auvergne, and Margaret. Joan may serve as an exemplar when 'by fair persuasions, mix'd with sug'red words' (III.3.18) she entices the Duke of Burgundy to desert his English allies, an effect the Duke himself ascribes to witchcraft (III.3.58).

The linkage of the malevolent potential of words, of witchcraft, of (French) female power, and the Catholic religion is surely a highly dangerous, a potentially subversive one in a play where all the actors, the English included, are 'professors of one faith' (V.1.14). For, if words are malevolent how can a religion which puts its faith solely and exclusively into the Word escape being implicated and corrupted (just as the verbal art of the dramatist might under such auspices need some justification)? Strategies have to be evolved to minimize and contain these implications. Shakespeare's two main strategies to do so are both deployed in the opening scene. The first is an attempt to export the problem, as it were. Both Gloucester's antagonism against Winchester, the Romish priest, and his equation of magical charms with Catholic prayers turn him into a proto-Protestant. His exposure of Simpcox affirms the Protestant axiom that miracles have ceased since Christ's passion and that hence no divine intervention in terrestrial affairs is to be expected till the Last Judgement. Right from the beginning this Protestant Englishness is contrasted with French magical Catholicism. The 'magical verses' ascribed to the French by Exeter are embodied in Joan la Pucelle in the second scene of *1 Henry VI*. Joan presents herself as empowered by the Virgin Mary, indeed as a *figura* of the Virgin:

> Heaven and our Lady gracious hath it pleas'd
> To shine on my contemptible estate.
> Lo, whilest I waited on my tender lambs,
> And to sun's parching heat display'd my cheeks,
> God's Mother deigned to appear to me,
> And in a vision full of majesty
> Will'd me to leave my base vocation
> And free my country from calamity.
> Her aid she promis'd, and assur'd success;
> In complete glory she reveal'd herself;
> And whereas I was black and swart before,
> With those clear rays which she infus'd on me
> That beauty am I blest with which you may see.
> (I.2.74)

Consequently, Joan can and will claim, and is accorded, charismatic power, transcendentally legitimized, as a new Virgin and a saint throughout the play. This, her figural status, is right from the beginning undercut by the double entendres of the French courtiers and her inscription as a witch by the English. It is finally exploded by her trafficking with devils (V.3) and the blasphemous re-enactment of an immaculate conception:

YORK   Now heaven forfend, the holy maid with child?
WARWICK   The greatest miracle that e'er ye wrought!
(V.4.65)

The tradition of female, French, magical, Catholic malevolence which includes the malevolent abuse of words is royally carried on by Margaret who ravishes the King in the beginning of Part 2 even more by 'her grace in speech' (1.1.32) than by her beauty and who lives on 'to fill the world with words' (v.5.44) at the end of Part 3, finally to prophesy and curse in *Richard III*.

If antagonistic, alien forces can thus be saddled with the abuse of words no inopportune questions need to be asked about the proper use. Shakespeare attempts to ensure that such questions will not be asked by the second strategy: one of abstention. Nowhere in the plays is the true nature, the essence of the Word or of words directly or explicitly discussed and therefore questioned. Furthermore, questions about the true essence of the Word or of words are suppressed, if not totally excluded, since the plays present no competing system of signs of any significance, thus marginalizing the contrast of, and conflict between, the verbal and the visual, tangible sign. However the conjuration scenes in Parts 1 and 2 may actually have been staged, the explicit and implicit stage-directions demand little else than some kind of talisman for Joan (v.3.2) and a magical circle plus a charm for Bullingbrook (1.4.22, S.D.). Fitting as it might have been, there is little magical ceremony in the *Henry VI* plays — fitting, since it might have easily been blamed on the French and/or Catholicism. Although, as Phyllis Rackin puts it, it may be that 'Talbot, the English champion, and Joan, his French antagonist, speak alternative languages', her claim that 'the play defines their conflict as a contest between English *words* and French *things*' (pp. 150–51) is in need of substantiation. There are very few *things* in the plays altogether and most of them are indeed 'dumb significants' (11.4.26) like the roses plucked by the opposing factions in the Temple garden: they have to be inscribed, have to be given meaning, which the parties involved punningly, vociferously, and controversially do straightaway.[39] But the signifying practice is verbal.

However, there are two visual, tangible signs, strikingly effective in the trilogy, one the object of all strife and coming gradually into theatrical prominence, namely 'the golden circuit' (*2 Henry VI*, 111.1.352), the other, the ever-present means to gain it: the sword. The latter truly dominates the *Henry VI* plays and circumscribes their world of power politics in which the central question is the one of appropriate means. Hence it is a world blind to all questions of first causes, focusing exclusively on efficient ones. It is therefore in their political use and function that words are analysed (and that their true nature can go unquestioned). This analysis insistently pits the use and power of words against those of the sword. As in all other matters of authority and power, the dead Henry is the ideal whose 'deeds exceed all

[39] See John W. Blanpied, '"Art and Baleful Sorcery": The Counter-consciousness of *Henry VI, Part I*' *Studies in English Literature*, 15 (1975), 213–27, pp. 219–22.

speech' (I. I. I5), if in nothing else, in that all the nobles try to emulate him, from Gloucester who 'will not answer [Winchester] with words, but blows' (I. 3. 69) to Richard who states baldly:

> Sword, hold thy temper; heart, be wrathful still:
> Priests pray for enemies, but princes kill.
>
> (*2 Henry VI*, V. 2. 70)

Jack Cade cannot profit from 'this word "sallet"' (*2 Henry VI*, IV. 10. 10) after all, but is killed by Iden whose sword therefore is sacralized: 'Sword, I will hallow thee for this thy deed' (V. 10.67). And Joan's threat is the greater since she wields the sword, attempting to occupy a male preserve. Although she claims transcendental legitimation and holy status verbally, she validates her claim in combat with the Dauphin, with her 'keen-edg'd sword' (I. 2.98). Under the reign of the sword the power of words is drastically diminished. It becomes the domain of witches and women, preferably French, of Joan, the Countess of Auvergne, the Duchess of Gloucester, Margaret. Thus the latent anxiety about the malevolent potential of words finds a local habitation which can be policed and checked by traditional patriarchal structures.

One question, however, the fundamental question of the Reformation and of Protestant drama remains, being always implied but never articulated. It is the question of the status, the nature of the *logos*, the Word, if it cannot enter the world and stage but through the *logoi*, the words, thus necessarily partaking in the play of representation (Bale) or being put to the radical test of basic human needs (Greene) or the sword (Shakespeare).

Devils and Power in Marlowe and Shakespeare

JOHN D. COX

Hope College

Between the two of them, Marlowe and Shakespeare put actual devils on stage in only three plays: *Dr Faustus*, *1 Henry VI*, and *2 Henry VI*, respectively. At first glance this seems an unremarkable coincidence, particularly since the *Henry VI* plays are early minor plays by Shakespeare, while *Dr Faustus* is Marlowe's supreme dramatic achievement. Moreover, Shakespeare's devils are marginal, showing up briefly in only one scene in each play, without fireworks, gymnastic slapstick, obscenities, or temptingly equivocal arguments — indeed in *1 Henry VI* without any words at all — whereas in *Dr Faustus* Mephastophilis is present almost from first to last, and his subtlety has provoked endless comment. Yet the limited staging of devils by both young playwrights makes better grounds for comparing them than may appear at first. For one thing, both shared a keen interest in the Vice, a close stage relative of devils: Vice adaptations appear in three of the six plays Marlowe wrote besides *Dr Faustus*, and Shakespeare created central or important roles based more or less closely on the Vice in plays as diverse as *Titus Andronicus*, *Richard III*, *Much Ado*, *1 Henry IV* and *2 Henry IV*, *Othello*, and *Cymbeline*. Beyond this, and more importantly, differences in the way the two young playwrights stage actual devils is a revealing index to other differences between them, especially differences in their response to political power. For while Marlowe seems to challenge and defy received traditions that gave rise to stage devils in the first place, Shakespeare explores the world those traditions imply in a critical and thoughtful but fundamentally affirmative manner.[1]

Defiance and subversion have long been suspected in *Dr Faustus*, yet no one has been able to establish conclusively that the play is heterodox, while the defenders of its essential orthodoxy have stoutly resisted imputations to

---

[1] Marlowe and Shakespeare have frequently been compared, though no one, to my knowledge, has compared *Dr Faustus* and *1 Henry VI*. See F. P. Wilson, *Marlowe and the Early Shakespeare* (Oxford: Clarendon Press, 1953); Nicholas Brooke, 'Marlowe as Provocative Agent in Shakespeare's Early Plays', *Shakespeare Survey*, 14 (1961), 34–44; Irving Ribner, 'Marlowe and Shakespeare', *Shakespeare Quarterly*, 15 (1964), 41–53; Harold F. Brooks, 'Marlowe and Early Shakespeare' in *Christopher Marlowe*, ed. by Brian Morris (London: Benn, 1968), pp. 67–94; Marjorie Garber, 'Marlovian Vision/Shakespearean Revision', *Research Opportunities in Renaissance Drama*, 22 (1979), 3–9; Carol Leventen Duane, 'Marlowe's Mixed Messages: A Model for Shakespeare?', *Medieval and Renaissance Drama in England*, 3 (1986), 51–67; Kenneth Muir, 'Marlowe and Shakespeare' in '*A Poet and a filthy Play-maker': New Essays on Christopher Marlowe*, ed. by Kenneth Friedenreich, Roma Gill, and Constance Kuriyama (New York: AMS Press, 1988), pp. 1–12.

the contrary.[2] An issue of such complexity cannot be settled in an essay that is only partly about *Dr Faustus*, but it is important to acknowledge at the outset that an open declaration of dissent was impossible for Marlowe, or any other contemporary playwright who valued his freedom to write or even to live, while the appearance of conformity does not necessarily point to the reality. Marlowe's handling of devils may thus parallel his handling of other dramaturgical features that he inherited from medieval religious drama, such as the structure of homiletic plays, for example. David Bevington has demonstrated Marlowe's familiarity with traditional morality play form in five of his seven plays — in both parts of *Tamburlaine*, *The Jew of Malta*, *Edward II*, and *Dr Faustus*.[3] Yet in every case, Bevington points out, the result is ambiguous: Marlowe's apparent aim to enhance his individualized heroes is compromised by the implicit moral causality of his inherited structure. What Bevington poses conservatively as an aesthetic dilemma for Marlowe may be viewed more radically as a deliberate strategic choice. The possibility of choice is strongly suggested by the contrasting example of Shakespeare, for in his case the argument from the limitations of professional troupe structure does not work. From the very beginning, Shakespeare experimented with a wide variety of dramatic forms, perhaps in some cases while writing for the same acting company as Marlowe.[4] The young Shakespeare's most important rival can be seen as deliberately choosing to challenge homiletic assumptions if we grant that Marlowe's aim was subversive, that modifying homiletic form was a ready means to that end, and that Marlowe did what he wanted to do: create an ambiguous structure.[5] The dramaturgical appearance of conformity may in fact have been a stalking horse for defiance.

[2] For representative contributions to the argument that *Dr Faustus* is heterodox, see Paul H. Kocher, *Christopher Marlowe* (Chapel Hill; University of North Carolina Press, 1946), pp. 104–19; Robert Ornstein, 'Marlowe and God: The Tragic Theology of *Dr Faustus*', *PLMA*, 83 (1968), 1378–85; Wilbur Sanders, *The Dramatist and the Received Idea* (Cambridge: Cambridge University Press, 1968), pp. 205–42; Edward A. Snow, 'Marlowe's *Doctor Faustus* and the Ends of Desire' in *Two Renaissance Mythmakers* (Baltimore: Johns Hopkins University Press, 1977), pp. 70–110. For the contrary view, see Leo Kirschbaum, 'Marlowe's *Faustus*: A Reconsideration', *RES*, 19 (1943), 225–41, and 'Religious Values in *Dr. Faustus*' in *The Plays of Christopher Marlowe* (Cleveland, Ohio: Meridian Books, 1962), pp. 101–13; W. W. Greg, 'The Damnation of Faustus', *MLR*, 41 (1946), 97–107; Helen M. Gardner, 'Milton's Satan and the Theme of Damnation in Elizabethan Tragedy', *English Studies*, n.s. 1 (1948), 46–66; Douglas Cole, *Suffering and Evil in the Plays of Christopher Marlowe* (Princeton: Princeton University Press, 1962), pp. 191–243.

[3] David M. Bevington, *From 'Mankind' To Marlowe* (Cambridge MA: Harvard University Press, 1962), pp. 199–262.

[4] Henslowe records income throughout 1592 and 1593 for 'harey the vj', which may be one or more of Shakespeare's plays. *Henslowe's Diary*, ed. by R. A. Foakes and R. T. Rickert (Cambridge: Cambridge University Press, 1961), pp. 16–20. The *Diary* also records income for 'the Jewe of malta' throughout the same period and into 1594. Income for 'titus' and 'titus & ondronicus' is recorded for 1593 and 1594.

[5] Marlowe's ambiguity has been recognized by many critics besides Bevington and has been construed in various ways. The favoured explanation is that Marlowe himself was ambivalent, psychologically predisposed to indeterminacy. The most influential argument of this kind is Harry Levin's *The Overreacher* (London: Faber and Faber, 1954), though it had appeared much earlier in Una Ellis-Fermor's *Christopher Marlowe* (London: Methuen, 1927). For other defenders of the 'subjective' view of Marlowe's ambiguity, see Max Bluestone, '*Libido Speculandi*: Doctrine and Dramaturgy in Contemporary Interpretations of Marlowe's *Doctor Faustus*' in *Reinterpretations of Elizabethan Drama*, ed. by Norman Rabkin (New York and

By the same token the apparent orthodoxy of the devils in *Dr Faustus* need not be proof that the play is orthodox nor disproof that it is subversive. Indeed, if Marlowe aimed to challenge the values that gave rise to stage devils in the first place, it would be in his interest to present his devils as compellingly as possible, and the perennial popularity of the play before the closing of the theatres suggests that he was successful. To dismiss his devils as mere psychological projections or theatrical spectacle is to underestimate the extent to which they conform to orthodox expectation and are all the more effective for doing so. Is it surprising that Mephastophilis gives Faustus orthodox answers about devils and hell? Not at all, says Robert West, who knows more than any other of the play's modern critics about the complexity of Renaissance demon lore: 'The fact is that treatises of witchcraft do insist that in order to maximize their sins the devil reveals himself and his aims to his victims before he signs them'.[6]

How, then, can we identify the subversive ambiguity in Marlowe's devils? Let us begin with a specific instance of Mephastophilis's cunning orthodoxy: his explanation of how angels became demons. (This is a particularly important instance, since it effectively explains the originating docrine behind a long tradition of both devils and vices on the English stage.) 'Tell me', demands Faustus of Mephastophilis in the scene of their first meeting,

What is that Lucifer thy Lord?
MEPHASTOPHILIS   Arch-regent and commander of all spirits.
FAUSTUS   Was not that Lucifer an angel once?
MEPHASTOPHILIS   Yes Faustus, and most dearly lov'd of God.
FAUSTUS   How comes it then that he is prince of devils?
MEPHASTOPHILIS   O by aspiring pride and insolence,
For which God threw him from the face of heaven.[7]

What Mephastophilis accurately recounts here is the patristic doctrine of *libido dominandi*, the lust for domination, key point in one of the first and most

London: Columbia University Press, 1969), pp. 33–88; Constance B. Kuriyama, *Hammer or Anvil* (Rutgers University Press, 1980), pp. 95–135; Jonathan Dollimore, *Radical Tragedy* (Brighton: Harvester, 1984), pp. 109–19. Others eschew the readings of the plays through the poet, preferring a deliberate and calculated ambiguity. For examples of this view, see Judith Weil, *Christopher Marlowe: Merlin's Prophet* (Cambridge: Cambridge University Press, 1977), pp. 50–81; Joel Altman, *The Tudor Play of Mind* (Berkeley and Los Angeles: University of California Press, 1978), pp. 321–88; T. McAlindon, 'The Ironic Vision: Diction and Theme in Marlowe's *Doctor Faustus*', *RES*, 32 (1981), 9–41; Lawrence Danson, 'Christopher Marlowe: The Questioner', *ELR*, 12 (1982), 3–29; Leventen, 'Marlowe's Mixed Messages', who usefully reviews various approaches and advocates for Marlowe the kind of indeterminacy that Norman Rabkin finds in Shakespeare, in *Shakespeare and the Problem of Meaning* (Chicago and London: University of Chicago Press, 1981). An extensive reading of indeterminacy in *Dr Faustus* is Johannes H. Birringer, *Marlowe's 'Dr Faustus' and 'Tamburlaine': Theological and Theatrical Perspectives* (Frankfurt a.M.: Lang, 1984), but Maurice Charney's review of Birringer's book points out that it borrows extensively without acknowledgment from a 1979 University of California dissertation by Thomas Cartelli. Charney's review is in *Renaissance Quarterly*, 38 (1985), 165–66.
[6] Robert H. West, 'The Impatient Magic of *Dr Faustus*', *ELR*, 4 (1974), 222. My understanding of Mephastophilis is much indebted to West, though he and I interpret the effect of a lying devil differently.
[7] Quotations from *Dr Faustus* are from the edition by Roma Gill, *Complete Works*, II (Oxford: Clarendon Press, 1990), with spelling modernized in keeping with quotations from Shakespeare. Gill uses the A Text as her copy text, following recent arguments that it has more authority than the 1616 B Text. I confine my remarks about the play entirely to the A Text, and I follow Gill in the spelling of Mephastophilis's name, since it is the preferred form in the A Text.

influential of Christian theodicies, Augustine's explanation for the fall of Lucifer in Books 11 and 12 of *The City of God*.[8] Marlowe may well have encountered the idea in Augustine himself, but he could have found it in innumerable other places as well (there is a hint of it in his source, the English Faustbook), and it was a very old idea on the English stage before Marlowe, since it had appeared in all the extant dramatic versions of the angels' fall from grace. Though Marlowe is very unlikely to have seen any of these plays himself, it is important to bear in mind that the last of them had been staged in the early 1580s, during the years he was studying at Cambridge. Many people in Marlowe's earliest audiences could have imagined easily what Mephastophilis describes because they had seen it literally performed on stage within ten years of the time Marlowe's play first alluded to it on the public stage.

Mephastophilis's description of archetypal *libido dominandi* is noteworthy not only because of its stage history but because of its centrality in *Dr Faustus*. From an orthodox point of view, Faustus perpetuates the medieval stage tradition by repeating Lucifer's sin in his own turn. 'Pride and insolence' (a strangely orthodox phrase for the devil to use) led to Lucifer's overthrow, and pride is the key concept in Faustus's story: initially he wishes to go beyond the bounds of received knowledge because it is 'too servile and illiberal for me' (1. 36), and he believes the conjuring of devils will afford him 'a world of profit and delight, | Of power, of honor, of omnipotence' in which 'All things that move between the quiet poles | Shall be at my command' (1. 53–57). Pride is the first in the pageant of the Seven Deadly Sins, answering the Evil Angel's temptation to Faustus: 'Be thou on earth as Jove is in the sky, | Lord and commander of these elements' (1. 76–77). No less than Tamburlaine before him, Faustus is a Marlovian hero who rises from an inauspicious background ('Now is he born, his parents base of stock' (Prol. l. 11)), and eventually comes to believe that he can have the means to 'reign sole king' over everyone he encounters (1. 94).

The play's demonology is thus defensibly orthodox. That it is also ambiguous and subversive, however, can be seen in two ways. First, in other descriptions of Lucifer's fall and in parallel descriptions of Faustus's fall. According to Mephastophilis, the aspiring pride and insolence of Lucifer are answered by God's throwing him from the face of heaven, and this description is closely anticipated by the opening Chorus's description of what happened to Faustus as well:

> Till swoll'n with cunning of a self-conceit,
> His waxen wings did mount above his reach,
> And melting heavens conspir'd his overthrow.   (Prol. l. 20)

---

[8] In Appendix D, 'Libido', of *The Overreacher*, Harry Levin briefly outlines the history of *libido dominandi*. Despite allusions to Augustine's *Confessions*, however, Levin misses Augustine's contribution (which is undoubtedly the most influential in Western intellectual history) and attributes the phrase to Pascal (p. 202), who almost certainly learned it from *The City of God*.

What both descriptions emphasize is the power and malignity of the limiting heavens: 'God threw him' and 'heavens conspir'd his overthrow'. Roma Gill points out that the Prologue's phrase appears in *1 Tamburlaine*, where the conqueror imagines divine support against the 'frame of Heaven' if it should 'conspire my overthrow' (*Dr Faustus*, p. 52, n. 22). Moreover, this emphasis on a powerful God reappears in the closing Chorus, which refers again to 'the hellish fall' of Faustus:

> Whose fiendful fortune may exhort the wise
> Only to wonder at unlawful things
> Whose deepness doth entice such forward wits,
> To practise more than heav'nly power permits.   (Epil. l. 5)

Here too the sole characteristic of heaven is power. From the beginning, damnation had been understood as a logical necessity of divine love, yet love is nowhere a characteristic of God in *Dr Faustus*, merely punitive power.[9] It is not enough in this case to reply that Faustus only *perceives* God as merely powerful because Faustus is unwilling to repent, for both the opening and closing choruses use the same terms. In Marlowe's rendering of the story, what Lucifer and Faustus both lose is merely a power struggle, not a cosmic struggle of wilful and derivative evil against creative and loving goodness.

Marlowe alludes once more to Lucifer's fall in *Dr Faustus*, and when he does so he introduces still another characteristic ambiguity: the play of homoerotic wit. When Mephastophilis describes the women he can supply to Faustus, he promises:

> She whom thine eye shall like, thy heart shall have,
> Be she as chaste as was Penelope,
> As wise as Saba, or as beautiful
> As was bright Lucifer before his fall.   (v. 158)

The switch from female chastity and wisdom to male beauty is easy to miss as the exotic catalogue unfolds, yet it has the same witty quality that appears in a similar catalogue in *Hero and Leander*:

> There might you see the gods in sundry shapes,
> Committing heady riots, incest, rapes:
> For know, that underneath this radiant flow'r
> Was Danae's statue in a brazen tow'r,
> Jove slyly stealing from his sister's bed,
> To dally with Idalian Ganimed.   (i. 143)

Indeed, we do not have to go as far afield as *Hero and Leander* to find parallel instances of such wit, for it is apparent elsewhere in *Dr Faustus*, particularly in the intense eroticism of the scene with Helen, whom Faustus apostrophizes with another switch of gender like that in Mephastophilis's allusion to Lucifer's fall:

---

[9] Paul Kocher makes the same point about *Tamburlaine* as well (*Christopher Marlowe*, p. 71), and later compares 'Jove' of the earlier play to the God of *Faustus* (p. 118).

> O thou art fairer than the evening air,
> Clad in the beauty of a thousand stars,
> Brighter art thou than flaming Jupiter,
> When he appear'd to hapless Semele,
> More lovely than the monarch of the sky
> In wanton Arethusae's azur'd arms,
> And none but thou shalt be my paramour.   (XII. 94)

An orthodox defence of *Dr Faustus* might well explain such descriptions as the depraved imaginings of a devil and a reprobate: in the words of the Old Man

> most vile and loathsome filthiness,
> The stench whereof corrupts the inward soul
> With such flagitious crimes of heinous sins,
> As no commiseration may expel,   (XII. 32)

but this explanation does not adequately account for the rhetorical power of such passages or for their similarity to the undisguised homoeroticism of *Hero and Leander*. A more satisfactory explanation is that Marlowe deliberately subverted the orthodox seriousness of *Dr Faustus* with occasional flashes of irreverent wit.[10] To suggest that the beauty of the unfallen Lucifer was powerfully erotic is to read his fall very differently from the way it had been read by Augustine or by the orthodox tradition indebted to Augustine.[11]

The second way in whch Marlowe creates a subversive ambiguity in the devils of *Dr Faustus* is more pervasive and more substantive: by exploiting their traditional reputation for lying and equivocation in the context of Faustus's struggle to enhance his power. For if Faustus seems to be 'overthrown' on one hand by an absent, punitive, malignant, and merely powerful God, he is destroyed on the other by the lying promises and empty threats of the demons. Faustus's bid for power is thus hopeless from the outset, and his condition has been aptly described in Constance Kuriyama's cunning neologism, 'omnimpotence' (*Hammer or Anvil*, pp. 95–135). Such a condition can again be defended from an orthodox point of view: God seems absent and punitive to Faustus because of Faustus's own pride and despair, and the demonic sifting of the conjuror is not only painful but successful

---

[10] Edward Snow, '*Doctor Faustus* and the Ends of Desire', p. 72, also sees Faustus's repeated midnight invocation, 'Come Mephastophilis' (v. 26–29) as erotic. Constance Kuriyama was the first to remark on the change of gender in Faustus's hyperbolic descriptions (*Hammer or Anvil*, pp. 119 and 123), and her explanation is neither that the wit is mimetic nor intentionally heterodox, but that it is a subsconscious expression of Marlowe's own sexually ambivalent imagination. For an argument heavily dependent on Kuriyama's subjective approach but designed to show that Faustus is struggling toward heterosexuality, see Kay Stockholder, '"Within the massy entrailes of the earth": Faustus's Relation to Women', in '*Poet and filthy Play-maker*', pp. 203–19.

[11] In an important essay, C. L. Barber argues that *Dr Faustus* depends for its effect on a lively sense of blasphemy, '"The form of Faustus' fortunes, good or bad"', *TDR*, 8 (1964), 92–119. Barber cites Mephastophilis's lines about the beauty of Lucifer as an example of language which condemns its users 'by the logic of a situation larger than they are' (p. 99). He is referring to Lucifer's pre-fallen happiness, however, not to the gender switch, which in context also depends on blasphemy for its effect.

because God has given him up to his own devices, by which he can do nothing apart from God. The humble faith of the Old Man is the play's orthodox proof of Faustus's infidelity and despair, for the Old Man urges a course of repentance and faith, by which he himself eventually 'triumphs' over hell and the devil (xii. 106).

That the play indeed admits an orthodox reading of demonic equivocation should be no surprise, because (to reiterate) no play could have survived at the time *Dr Faustus* was written and staged if it had not been capable of sustaining an orthodox reading and sustaining it fairly convincingly. As in the case of homiletic structure, however, *Dr Faustus* subverts the orthodoxy of its lying devils, and it does so by making them the only effective influence on Faustus and by presenting his dilemma as no more than a struggle for power. Even the Old Man is identified rhetorically with this struggle. His final speech in the play is a cry of victory with more than a hint of gloating in it:

> My faith, vile hell, shall triumph over thee.
> Ambitious fiends, see how the heavens smiles
> At your repulse, and laughs your state to scorn.   (xii. 106)

The defiant certitude of this declaration is rhetorically related to the idealized defiance of tortured and dying martyrs in Foxe's *Book of Martyrs*, including their echo of the Bible. (The old Man alludes to Psalms 2.1.). In the immediate context of *Dr Faustus* the Old Man's declaration in fact culminates a sequence of similar claims, all made by Faustus himself, which originate with a mockery of Catholic ritual in bitterly sarcastic terms reminiscent of virulent anti-Catholic propaganda:

> How? bell, book, and candle, candle, book, and bell,
> Forward and backward, to curse Faustus to hell.
> Anon you shall hear a hog grunt, a calf bleat, and an ass bray,
> Because it is St. Peter's holy day.   (vii. 84)

Protestants were accustomed to believing that the Roman Catholic Church was an instrument of Satan, but *Dr Faustus* is a rare (if not unique) Elizabethan instance of the devil intervening explicitly on the Protestant side. Faustus appropriates a power superior to the Pope's to make the Pope look like a gull and an asshead, just as the Old Man will appropriate a power apparently superior to the devil's to smile at hell's repulse and laugh its state to scorn. In between those two victories are four more, all won by Faustus, in league with Mephastophilis: a vindication of learning against courtly arrogance (ix), a similar vindication against clownish aspiration (x), a demonstration of intellectual prowess before a duke (xi), and a demonstration of similar prowess before fellow academics (xii). All of Faustus's victories are presented in deeply sympathetic terms, beginning with his victory over the Pope: he is courted by the most powerful ruler in Europe and demonstrates his invulnerability to courtly detraction; he vanquishes lower-class demands for justice with scornful ease; he handily wins the unfeigned admiration of the powerful and learned. In short, his career embodies a fantasy of upwardly mobile Protestant power in the late sixteenth century.

Viewed in the context of the sequential victories that make up the second half of the play, the Old Man's ultimate victory has less to do with a triumph of faith over despair (or of cosmic goodness over evil) than it does with making sure one joins the winning side from the outset — provided, that is, that one can know what the winning side is going to be. And this is where the equivocation of Marlowe's fiends is crucial. Faustus's wish to enhance his power leads him naturally to reject traditional affirmations of human limitation, because to acknowledge those limitations would be to give up before one begins. Having recognized the cosmic determinism of traditional theology, Faustus scorns the theological truisms he hears from Mephastophilis:

> What, is great Mephastophilis so passionate,
> For being deprived of the joys of heav'n?
> Learn thou of Faustus manly fortitude,
> And scorn those joys thou never shalt possess. (III. 83)

If one's dominion that exceeds in magic is to stretch as far as does the mind of man, it will have to stretch farther than traditional hopes and fears about the human condition, even when those are voiced in apparent sincerity by the devil himself. In retrospect and from an orthodox perspective, of course, Faustus's refusal to listen to what Mephastophilis tells him is fatal and ironic. In context, however, it is an affirmation of the manly fortitude that set him on his course in the first place. Given the triumph he enjoys as a consequence of his choice, he appears to have made the right choice, despite occasional doubts, because he is clearly on the winning side: successful, admired, powerful, Protestant, and fully aware of his deserving superiority.

Yet the devils who seem to offer Faustus a means to escape traditional limitations are the means of his undoing in the end, the duplicitous source of him 'omnipotence'. This is not to say that their equivocation can be taken to affirm a true and loving God. Rather, the demons play a role in *Dr Faustus* that is analogous to the role of Barabas in *The Jew of Malta* or of Mortimer in *Edward II*, who are characters based on the Vice, a close stage analogue to devils. These human characters' parallel with the devils in *Dr Faustus* is in their essential hypocrisy and their illimitable thirst for power, their *libido dominandi*. The defeat of Faustus in the cosmic power struggle offers no proof of a good and loving God, any more than Barabas's defeat in the human power struggle is proof of justice in human affairs. For all we know of the God in *Dr Faustus*, he is no better than Ferneze: what both have indubitably in common is that they win in the end, and in a struggle for mere power only winning counts. The difference in *Dr Faustus* is that the Barabas-like characters (i.e., the devils) are not defeated either, or at least not in the short term. Despite allusions to their one-time defeat by God, they triumph maliciously over the only character who is defeated in the short term — a mortal loser in the stakes for cosmic omnipotence.

In *Dr Faustus* Marlowe thus reinterprets the popular dramatic tradition in innovative Renaissance terms: the ancient Christian doctrine of *libido dominandi* gets a sharp new secular edge in a context where dissimulation was advocated as the essential means to acquire and maintain power. *Allegoria*, says Puttenham, is 'the Courtly figure', because we use it 'when we speake one thing and thinke another, and that our wordes and our meanings meet not':

> no man can pleasantly utter and perswade without it, but in effect is sure never or very seldome to thrive and prosper in the world, that cannot put it in ure, in somuch as not only every common Courtier, but also the gravest Counsellour, yea and the most noble and wisest Prince of them all are many times enforced to use it, by example (say they) of the great Emperour who had it usually in his mouth to say *Qui nescit dissimulare nescit regnare*. Of this figure therefore which for his duplicitie we call the figure of *false semblant or dissimulation* we will speake first as of the chief ringleader and captaine of all other figures, either in the Poetical or oratorie science.[12]

Marlowe was the first English dramatist to allude to Machivaelli, but as N. W. Bawcutt points out, the essential characteristics of Marlowe's 'Machevil' in *The Jew of Malta* had long been associated with the word 'policy' in the popular dramatic tradition, and the masters of 'policy' were the Vices, sometimes actually called 'Policy'.[13] In recapturing the lust for power as the source of native dramatic diablerie, Marlowe simultaneously updated it to reflect contemporary courtly reality. In doing so, he did not need to turn to an authority as foreign and exotic as Machiavelli. Puttenham's *Arte*, published in 1589, offered an extensive English vocabulary for many of the same courtly insights that Machiavelli was condemned for. As Machevil incisively observes, 'To some perhaps my name is odious, | But such as love me guard me from their tongues' (*Jew of Malta*, Prol. l. 5).

The focus of demonic dissimulation in *Dr Faustus* is the bargain itself, as it is in Barnabe Barnes's *The Devil's Charter*, an early Jacobean spin-off of Marlow's play. While Barnes's devils trick their human victim by means of a verbal quibble like those in *Macbeth* (another early Jacobean play inspired by Marlowe, where the telling combination of equivocation, the lust for power, and the demonic supernatural again appears), Marlowe explores more forthrightly the inherent instability of a bargain supposedly in good faith with a power-seeking master of deceit. That the pact is really a means to make Faustus *submit* (rather than giving him a means to dominate, as he hopes to do) is apparent from the moment Mephastophilis explains

---

[12] George Puttenham, *The Arte of English Poesie*, ed. by Gladys Willcock and Alice Walker (Cambridge: Cambridge University Press, 1936), p. 186. On the social and political commitments of the courtesy tradition (of which Puttenham's work is a Tudor culmination), see Frank Whigham, *Ambition and Privilege: The Social Tropes of Elizabethan Courtesy Theory* (Berkeley and Los Angeles: University of California Press, 1984).

[13] N. W. Bawcutt, '"Policy", Machiavellianism, and the Earlier Tudor Drama', *ELR*, 1 (1971), 195–209).

blasphemy as a sign of potential interest in submission to demons (III. 46–54). Yet even this claim needs to be regarded as a demonic feint in Mephastophilis's incessant battle to control Faustus ('O what will I not do to obtain his soul?' (v. 73)), because Mephastophilis always seeks to dominate Faustus rhetorically and always succeeds. Like Tamburlaine, he is a master of 'working words', by which he overpowers his victim, rather than by violence; like Theridamas, Mephastophilis serves a power-seeker whose sole aim is to 'enlarge his kingdom' (v. 40). To take an example we noticed earlier, Mephastophilis's phrase to describe the motive for Lucifer's rebellion is 'aspiring pride and insolence', which precisely captures God's view of the matter (III. 67). Since Mephastophilis presumably does not hope to convert Faustus to God's view, however, he must be using orthodox diction to tempt Faustus to persevere in 'manly fortitude', because that kind of perseverance is really a submission to the devil. The rhetorical effect on the audience is precisely what it is on Faustus: to make them feel the force of orthodox limitation.

The bargain itself is another demonic feint, as the Good Angel and the Old Man (who, for the purpose of this argument, we will assume are not liars) make clear in their assurances of divine mercy long after Faustus has signed. For if the bargain were indeed what Mephastophilis claims it is, he would not pursue his victim after the signing but would expend his energy elsewhere, confident that he could abandon Faustus to his own waywardness. Mephastophilis 'serves' Faustus not in good faith in response to a bargain but because he is vigilant to 'obtain his soul', that is, to dominate him by pretending to serve him. This is why Mephastophilis's threats are empty but effective: the devil cannot literally harm Faustus, any more than he can harm the Old Man, because Faustus still has the option to 'repent', that is, to go over to God's side. At the same time, as long as Faustus still thinks he has something to gain from Mephastophilis, he does not want to abandon the opportunity to gain it. Lies and truth thus become so intermingled that they are difficult, if not impossible, to distinguish:

FAUSTUS	Come. I think hell's a fable.
MEPHASTOPHILIS	Aye, think so still, till experience change thy mind.
FAUSTUS	Why? thinkest thou then that Faustus shall be damn'd?
MEPHASTOPHILIS	Aye, of necessity, for there's the scrowl, Wherein thou hast given thy soul to Lucifer. (v. 130)

Mephastophilis appears to take one step backward in affirming the real existence of hell in order to take two steps forward in lying about the efficacy of the bargain in Faustus's domination. But if the reality (as Marlowe presents it) is that Lucifer and God are locked in a power struggle, then the truth of what opposes the devil is not guaranteed either, any more than Ferneze's truth is guaranteed simply because he is a Christian. If the aim of both sides is to gain Faustus's soul, what will they not do to obtain it? In *Dr Faustus* Marlowe reproduces the effect of multiple liars that he had created in

The Jew of Malta, but the effect apears on a cosmic scale, and the stakes are correspondingly higher.[14] The rhetoric of the prologue and Epilogue to *Dr Faustus* renders both Lucifer and God's spokesmen equally untrustworthy as reliable guides to human action. Harry Levin is surely right that Marlowe was drawn to hyperbole, or what Puttenham calls the 'over reacher' and the 'loud liar', but hyperbole is a species of 'allegoria' for Puttenham, and Mephastophilis follows Puttenham's advice precisely in using dissimulation as the chief ringleader and captain of all other figures in rhetorical science.

In short, Faustus begins to lose the moment he seeks to win, and the sequence of apparent Renaissance/Reformation triumphs that define the second half of the play reveals a pattern that signals his decline, even as he seems to be rising. His triumph over the Pope is profoundly ambiguous, for he succeeds only by the means that Protestants invariably attribute to the Pope himself: by demonic power. Where secular courts are concerned, far from reigning 'sole king', as he had hoped to do (I. 94), Faustus is no more than an eminent visitor, first at the emperor's palace and then at the duke's. In neither case is he a part of the permanent power structure, and the movement from emperor to duke suggests a pattern of steady decrease in Faustus's spheres of influence, a pattern confirmed by the intervening triviality of a triumph over uppity clowns. The learning that wearied Faustus at the beginning is all he has left in the end, despite his conjuring to exceed it, for his ability to produce grapes out of season derives from common knowledge about the earth's hemispheres that was familiar to the ancient Greeks. (The passage is in fact closely paraphrased from the English Faustbook.) Finally in the academic sphere, Faustus may be impressive to his colleagues in his ability to conjure up an image of Helen of Troy, but Marlowe was much too familiar with academic self-importance to confuse it with real power, and he therefore puts it last in the sequence of ambiguous triumphs. While the raising of Helen is a genuine rhetorical climax, in context it signals a severe delimiting of Faustus's initial aspirations: for Faustus, 'working words' effect no deeds but produce only a demonic illusion, the ultimate image of his ironic enslavement to what he vainly thinks he dominates.

Marlowe's return to his dramaturgical roots in *Dr Faustus* thus has the effect of subverting what originated and sustained them. Though Marlowe revitalizes Augustine's doctrine of *libido dominandi* and insightfully explores

---

[14] See Coburn Freer's useful essay, 'Lies and Lying in *The Jew of Malta*' in '*Poet and filthy Play-maker*', pp. 143–65, especially the following: 'When a majority of characters in a play lie to each other and themselves, their verbal behavior will not only shape the action but will also give that action a multitude of meanings, some of them inevitably contradictory' (p. 145).

its implications as the originating idea behind a long tradition of stage devils, he clearly does not take the doctrine in the same sense that Augustine himself did. If he had, he would not have included a moment of homoerotic wit in describing Lucifer's fall, nor would he have presented the dilemmas of Faustus and Lucifer as no more than parallel losses in a cosmic power struggle, nor would he have made demonic equivocation a means of substantive ambiguity in the play itself. Faustus emerges as a double loser, since the devils were defeated by God and somehow serve God's purpose, and Faustus is defeated by the devils and serves their purpose. God and the devils become effectively indistinguishable as the guarantors of Faustus's humiliation and destruction. Augustine's attempt to offer an imaginatively persuasive account of divine justice and love as the underpinning of human hope becomes in *Dr Faustus* a grimly sardonic picture of cosmic injustice and malice as the underpinning of human aspiration and despair.

Turning from *Dr Faustus* to Shakespeare's brief staging of devils in *1 Henry VI* and *2 Henry VI* admittedly seems a move from high seriousness to farce, but a consideration of Shakespeare's devils in their context makes a fruitful comparison with Marlowe, whether or not Shakespeare knew *Faustus* at the time he wrote the *Henry VI* plays. Shakespeare understands the devil's relation to power no less clearly then Marlowe, and he assumes, as Marlowe does, that devils are closely identified with the human lust for power, but Shakespeare reduces the focus of his plays to human action per se, and he puts devils onstage very briefly only to emphasize human depravity in the quest for power, not (as in *Dr Faustus*) to emphasize the cosmic gulling of human fools. To be sure, the character who consorts with 'fiends' (as the Folio stage direction identifies them) in *1 Henry VI* is also gulled by them, but the point of her duping is not that such things are the making of human tragedy; rather, her defeat is a small eddy in the maelstrom of human politics, the source of whose chaotic energy is a purely secular struggle for power. In *2 Henry VI*, the women who consults a 'spirit' is gulled not by it but by those who arrange the conjuring, because they also arrange for her to be caught redhanded in the act of resorting to black magic, thus offering an opening to powerful nobles who wish to destroy her husband.

The character who consorts with fiends in *1 Henry VI* is Joan la Pucelle, in many respects a parody of Marlovian overreachers and of Tamburlaine in particular. Like him, she is born of socially ignoble parents (in fact, like Tamburlaine's parents, Joan's are shepherds), and her sudden astounding rise to power and pre-eminence is achieved not only by her unaccountable military success but by her irresistible rhetorical ability. As Tamburlaine persuades Theridamas to desert Mycetes and join him, so Joan persuades Burgundy to desert the English, in a thirty-line speech of moving patriotism (III. 3. 41–77) whose force he keenly feels (though earlier he had dismissed her as the dauphin's 'trull' (II. 2. 28)): 'she hath bewitched me with her words' (III. 3. 58), and again:

> I am vanquished: these haughty words of hers
> Have battered me like roaring cannon-shot
> And made me almost yield upon my knees.   (III.3.78)[15]

Joan's cynical response ('Done like a Frenchman: turn and turn again' (III. 3. 85)), parallels Tamburlaine's aside to Techelles, after his intensely moving speech to Zenocrate: 'Techelles, women must be flattered' (*1 Tamburlaine*, I. 2. 303).

But Tamburlaine is not the only Marlovian overreacher who has a parallel in Joan. She is like Faustus as well, in that she achieves her astonishing worldly success through the agency of hell, though she dissimulates the source of her strength, piously attributing it to heaven.[16]

> Dauphin, I am by birth a shepherd's daughter,
> My wit untrained in any kind of art.
> Heaven and our Lady gracious hath it pleased
> To shine on my contemptible estate.
> Lo, whilst I waited on my tender lambs
> And to sun's parching heat displayed my cheeks,
> God's Mother deignèd to appear to me
> And, in a vision full of majesty
> Willed me to leave my base vocation
> And free my country from calamity.   (*1 Henry VI*, I. 2. 72)

Shakespeare's anti-Catholicism is closer to Elizabethan expectation than Marlowe's: Joan's hypocrisy and hellish inspiration as a Catholic saint are characteristic of Protestant propaganda, and Shakespeare in fact took most of his portrait of Joan from the English chroniclers, Hall and Holinshed, who write with a strong anti-French and anachronistically Protestant bias.[17] Whether or not Shakespeare was writing with a knowledge of *Dr Faustus*, he created a character in Joan whose sexual avidity parallels Faustus's concupiscence, though hints of this trait in Joan are offered by Hall. By the end of *1 Henry VI* Joan appears to have seduced two French noblemen besides the dauphin (V. 4. 72–78), but he is her first and easiest conquest (I. 2. 65–150). In contrast to the gullible dauphin, the heroic English warrior, Talbot, stoutly resists Joan, because he immediately recognizes her demonic motivation:

---

[15] *1 Henry VI*, quoted from *The Complete Works of Shakespeare*, ed. by David Bevington (New York: HarperCollins, 1992). *2 Henry VI* is quoted from the same edition.

[16] Joan's character has provoked more comment from modern critics than any other aspect of *1 Henry VI*, and my assumption that she is duplicitous, while it is the majority view, is by no means universal. As recently as 1951, F. S. Boas was so impressed by the contradictions in Joan's character that he made them the basis for an arguement that *1 Henry VI* is the product of multiple authorship, 'Joan of Arc in Shakespeare, Schiller, and Shaw,' *Shakespeare Quarterly*, 2 (1951), 39.

[17] *Narrative and Dramatic Sources of Shakespeare*, ed. by Geoffrey Bullough, 8 vols (London: Routledge; New York: Columbia University Press, 1966), III, 56–58; 75–76. Richard F. Hardin thoroughly surveys all the chronicle sources about Joan and judiciously assesses the way Shakespeare presents her in the light of his sources in 'Chronicles and Mythmaking in Shakespeare's Joan of Arc', *Shakespeare Survey*, 42 (1990), 25–35.

Here she comes — I'll have a bout with thee;
Devil or devil's dam, I'll conjure thee:
Blood will I draw on thee — thou art a witch —
And straightway give thy soul to him thou serv'st.   (I. 5. 4)

Even Talbot is daunted by Joan as long as her derivative power is ascendant, but he never ceases to believe that she is a pious fraud: 'Heavens, can you suffer hell so to prevail?' ((I. 5. 9; cf II. 1. 25–27; III. 2. 38–40, 52, 64, 122).

Joan and Talbot would appear to be two sides of a warrior portrait in *1 Henry VI* that effectively corrects the portrait in *Tamburlaine*.[18] Talbot's success derives from his feudal piety: kneeling before King Henry with 'submissive loyalty of heart' (III. 4. 10), Talbot frankly 'ascribes the glory of his conquest got | First to my God, and next unto your grace' (III. 4. 11–12). He makes no claims to self-derived virtue, as Tamburlaine does, and his double allusion to Icarus, a favourite Marlovian image, is not the boast of an overweening aspirer but the courageous determination of a father to fight beside his son to his last breath against overwhelming odds:[19]

Then follow thou thy desp'rate sire of Crete,
Thou Icarus; thy life to me is sweet.
If thou wilt fight, fight by thy father's side,
And, commendable proved, let's die in pride.   (IV. 6. 54)

As it turns out, young John Talbot is killed first, and his father again compares him to Icarus for his courage:

Dizzy-eyed fury and great rage of heart
Suddenly made him from my side to start
Into the clust'ring battle of the French;
And in that sea of blood my boy did drench
His over-mounting spirit; and there died
My Icarus, my blossom, in his pride.   (IV. 7. 11)

What makes Talbot heroic are two qualities: first, the ambition proper to a soldier ('the big wars that make ambition virtue', as Othello says), in contrast to the cowardice of the French, and second, the 'submissive loyalty of heart' that directs his energy into channels of service to God, king, and national interest. These qualities contrast not only with Tamburlaine but with Joan, who effectively acquires the negative qualities of Tamburlaine with little or none of his ambiguity, and who thus becomes a demonic parody

[18] David Riggs also sees Joan and Talbot 'as two sides of a complex statement about aristocratic values' in response to Tamburlaine, but his interest is in classical rhetorical theory, not in the two playwrights' medieval dramatic heritage, *Shakespeare's Heroical Histories* (Cambridge, MA : Harvard University Press, 1971), pp. 100–13 (p. 101). Where Riggs understands Shakespeare to be reformulating Marlowe's heroic values, I see him deliberately eradicating the characteristic ambiguities of power in *Tamburlaine* and instead emphasizing an astute secular assessment of power, since neither Joan nor Talbot ultimately makes any difference to the outcome of events.

[19] Coppélia Khan understands Talbot to be interpreting his son's death as punishment for his pride, *Man's Estate: Masculine Identity in Shakespeare* (Berkeley and Los Angeles: University of California Press, 1981), pp. 53–54, but this reckons without the wide number of meanings that 'pride' had for Shakespeare. The *OED* cites this passage from *1 Henry VI* under 'pride' sb.[1] II.9.a, 'The best, highest, most excellent or flourishing state or condition; the prime; the flower'.

of Talbot.[20] Following Hall, Shakespeare emphasizes the impropriety of a female warrior: Joan's promise to 'exceed my sex' (I. 2. 90) is not merely descriptive but an implicit self-condemnation for exceeding presumably natural limitations.[21] Her meteoric social rise is not, as she claims, the work of heaven, but of hell, ultimately producing the wilful self-deception that goes with deception by fiends (as in *Faustus* and *Macbeth*) and leads her to reject her peasant father:

> Decrepit miser, base ignoble wretch!
> I am descended of a gentler blood:
> Thou art no father nor no friend of mine.   (V. 4. 7)

She is a liar (denying not only her parenthood but her league with hell (V. 4. 42)), a hypocrite, a sexual and social overreacher, and a dupe of the spirits to whom she resorts for temporary dominance. At the height of her success, after the destruction of Talbot, her fiendish assistants abandon her. Appearing in response to her conjuration, they mutely refuse to serve her further and eventually depart (V. 3. 1–29). 'My ancient incantations are too weak', laments Joan, 'And hell too strong for me to buckle with' (V. 3. 27–28). Faustus makes the same discovery, also to his loss.

While Shakespeare thus offers a portrait of demonic involvement with human beings that is much closer to orthodox expectation than Marlowe's,

---

[20] On Joan as an 'antitype', 'grotesque inversion', and 'parody' of Talbot, see Edward I. Berry, *Patterns of Decay: Shakespeare's Early Histories* (Charlottesville: University Press of Virginia, 1975), pp. 1–28.

[21] Shakespeare's characterization of Joan manifestly caricatures and demeans female assertiveness, and it has elicited a great deal of thoughtful comment. David Bevington first pointed out her deviation from expectations of female submissiveness and compared her thematically to the Countess of Auvergne and Margaret of Anjou, 'The Domineering Female in *1 Henry VI*' *Shakespeare Studies*, 2 (1966), 51–58, but Leslie Fiedler offered perhaps the first feminist reading of Joan as a projection of Shakespeare's own troubled sexuality, a common male malady of the late sixteenth century, *The Stranger in Shakespeare* (London: Croom Helm, 1973), pp. 56–63 and 77–81. Coppélia Kahn (above, n. 19) made a similar argument to Fiedler's but saw Shakespeare as criticizing the patriarchal values that produced the kind of bifurcated gender identity represented by Joan and Talbot. Writing at the same time as Kahn, Marilyn French came to very similar conclusions, though she saw Shakespeare sharing the male prejudice that produced Joan, and she followed Riggs in understanding the divided kingdom as 'a struggle to define legitimacy', *Shakespeare's Division of Experience* (New York: Simon and Schuster, 1981), pp. 43–75 (p. 45). (Compare Riggs, *Shakespeare's Heroical Histories*, p. 104.) Linda Bamber, *Comic Women, Tragic Men: A Study of Gender and Genre* (Stanford: Stanford University Press, 1982), contrasts Joan the warrior in *1 Henry VI* with Isabel the overseer of a garden in *Richard II* and suggests a gradual change in Shakespeare's view of women in history (pp. 135–38). In contrast, Marilyn French had noted that neither Joan nor any other woman in *1 Henry VI* actually achieves anything militarily: they work by trickery and subterfuge, not by physical prowess and courage, and they come up empty-handed (*Shakespeare's Division of Experience*, p. 47). In fairness, it should be noted that the prowess and heroism of Talbot also achieve nothing, a point that is generally not noted by those who focus their comments on Joan. Writing without recognition of other feminist critics, Phyllis Rackin sees Shakespeare's females (particularly Joan of Arc) as subversive in male-dominated history, 'Anti-Historians: Women's Roles in Shakespeare's Histories', *Theatre Journal*, 37 (1985), 329–44. The most thoroughgoing revisionist view of Joan is Gabrielle Bernhard Jackson's 'Topical Ideology: Witches, Amazons, and Shakespeare's Joan of Arc', *ELR*, 18 (1988), 40–65. Jackson reads Joan as an elaborate topical allusion to Elizabeth I, not only in the epithets used to describe her but in her military cross-dressing (after the manner of Elizabeth at Tilbury), and her sardonic retort to Talbot ('Belike your lordship takes us then for fools,| To try if that our own be ours or no' (III. 2. 62–63)), for Talbot, in Jackson's view, is Essex. Jackson rejects attempts to understand Joan as a consistent character, preferring the older view of radical inconsistency in her portrait that led Boas to doubt whether *1 Henry VI* is by one author (above, n. 16). Also topical but less tendentious where Joan is concerned is Leah Marcus's *Puzzling Shakespeare: Local Reading and Its Discontents* (Berkeley and Los Angeles: University of California Press, 1988), pp. 67–83.

1 Henry VI is more than a patriotic potboiler, for at the same time that he eradicates Marlowe's particular ambiguities, Shakespeare introduces new complexities of his own about the human struggle for power: complexities that Marlowe never hints at. Joan and Talbot are undoubtedly the most heroic characters in *1 Henry VI*, but they ultimately make no difference to the outcome of events. Talbot's defeat is brought about not by Joan's demonic power but by the factionalism of the English court, which prevents effective relief from reaching Talbot in time, and the French eventually triumph because of English division, not because of Joan. The real cause of Talbot's destruction is the erupting quarrel between York and Lancaster, prompting each to blame the other for England's defeat, as the choric Sir William Lucy recognizes: 'Whiles they each other cross, | Lives, honors, lauds, and all, hurry to loss' (IV. 3. 52–53). England's war with France at first appears to have a kind of providential clarity about it: the properly humble Talbot is ranged against overweening Joan, submission to heaven against submission to hell, cosmic order against disorder. But the clarity of this struggle is of no assistance in determining how to judge the play's principal action which involves endless infighting at the English court. Lacking effective central power, England is adrift in a chaos of competing political interests: Winchester v. Gloucester (I. 3), Somerset v. Suffolk (II. 4), York v. the King himself (II. 5), Suffolk v. Gloucester (v. 3 and v. 5), and, potentially, Suffolk and Margaret v. the King (v. 5).

Shakespeare thus puts his only staged devils on the margins of *1 Henry VI* for strategic reasons: unlike Marlowe in *Dr Faustus*, Shakespeare does not focus on the cosmic frame of human action but on human action itself. Both playwrights acknowledge *libido dominandi* as the motive for demonic activity (hence Joan's overweening character), but whereas Marlowe recalls the ancient doctrine in order to subvert it, Shakespeare takes it for granted and de-emphasizes it in favour of the struggle for power among human beings themselves, quite apart from overt demonic motivation.[22] The cosmic implications of this secular struggle are difficult, if not impossible, to determine. We cannot even be certain that Joan's fiends abandon her because Providence has overruled their power. To what purpose? York captures and destroys Joan, to be sure, but in the same scene that York finally achieves what Talbot could not, Suffolk and Margaret of Anjou seduce each other, with consequences that clearly portend disaster for England: the loss of Maine and Anjou without a blow being struck and the elevation of an overbearing French woman to the English throne. Joan's captor, York, is a principal contributor to English political chaos, even though he is the immediate instrument of the French witch's undoing. Demons seem to

---

[22] Edward Berry, *Patterns of Decay*, p. 15, comments incisively on the 'narrowly political and ethical' concerns of *1 Henry VI*, implied in the ultimate irrelevance of Joan and Talbot. I would only add that a similar narrowness of concern is characteristic of all Shakespeare's histories, in contrast to the tragedies.

contribute little to the distress of human political life, in comparison to what human beings contribute on their own. *1 Henry VI* does not deny the lust for power as the root of evil, but it certainly seems to question whether demonic motivation can always be clearly assigned to particular human actions and especially to the most destructive of them.

The marginal fiends of *1 Henry VI* are complemented by a single marginal 'spirit' in *2 Henry VI*, whose name, 'Asnath', is presumably an anagram of 'Sathan'.[23] This spirit appears in a context that again recalls the Luciferian archetype: Asnath is evoked by Bolingbroke, a conjurer, and Margery Jourdain, a witch, at the behest of Eleanor Cobham, who hopes to enlist supernatural aid in gaining the throne for her husband, Humphrey Duke of Gloucester, uncle to King Henry. Eleanor's overweening ambition is repeatedly emphasized in a way that makes her Joan la Pucelle's thematic successor and, like Joan, a spiritual and rhetorical successor to Tamburlaine. She demands of Gloucester

> Why are thine eyes fixed to the sullen earth,
> Gazing on that which seems to dim thy sight?
> What seest thou there? King Henry's diadem,
> Enchased with all the honors of the world?
> If so, gaze on, and grovel on thy face,
> Until thy head be circled with the same.
> Put forth thy hand; reach for the glorious gold.
> What, is't too short? I'll lengthen it with mine;
> We'll both together lift our heads to heaven
> And nevermore abase our sight so low
> As to vouchsafe one glance unto the ground. (1.2.5)

Like Lucifer, Eleanor longs for power and a throne that are not rightly hers, and her determination to have them is her undoing, as it was Lucifer's before her.

Shakespeare complicates this picture, however, in ways that make Eleanor more sympathetic than Joan and that make Asnath even less important than Joan's fiends. Indeed, Asnath is Shakespeare's invention; in Hall's account, no one conjures, but Margery Jourdain makes a wax image of the king for Eleanor, 'whiche by their sorcery, a litle and litle consumed, entendyng therby in conclusion to waist, and destroy the kynges person, and so to bryng hym death'.[24] Nothing in the conjuring scene in *2 Henry VI* involves a threat to the king, as the wax image does in Hall's history. Asnath utters a series of ambiguous prophecies, including one about the king that might be construed as favouring Gloucester, at least in the mind of one (like

---

[23] I am grateful to Randall Martin for reminding me of Asnath, whom I had overlooked in an earlier version of this essay, presented in a seminar session at the 1992 meeting of the Shakespeare Association of America.

[24] Edward Hall, *The Union of the Two Noble and Illustre Famelies of Lancastre and Yorke* (1548), in Bullough, *Narrative and Dramatic Sources*, III, 102.

Eleanor) who desperately wants him to succeed, but this prophecy works in the same way as the prophecies of the equivocating fiends in *Macbeth*:

> The duke yet lives that Henry shall depose,
> But him outlive, and die a violent death. (1.4.31)

The most serious threat in the conjuring scene is not Eleanor or even Asnath but Hume, a priest whose aid Eleanor seeks in securing the services of Bolingbroke and Jourdain. Departing from Hall, Shakespeare makes Hume a double agent: having been hired by Eleanor, he also hires himself as an informer to Winchester and Suffolk who wish to destroy Gloucester (1.2.87–107). This is an unpleasant bit of business, and it succeeds in ruining the good duke, but it has nothing to do with demonic power. For its motivation is ordinary courtly dissimulation and treachery, and in fact the conjuring incident, which *does* involve demonic power, is bracketed on one side by Hume's plotting and on the other by York's surprise interruption of the conjuring. As in *1 Henry VI*, the real evil in the political life of England is not demonic (Eleanor comes across as pathetic rather than wicked) but human.

More influential than demons in the *Henry VI* plays would appear to be human derivatives of the devil's close stage relation, the Vice. The chaos of civil strife eventually yields to a single potent character who is brilliantly modelled on the Vice, Richard, Duke of Gloucester, afterwards King Richard III. But Richard has antecedents in the earlier plays, principally William de la Pole, the Earl of Suffolk, in *1* and *2 Henry VI*, and Richard Plantagenet, afterwards the Duke of York, the father of Richard III, in *2* and *3 Henry VI*. Suffolk is introduced as a young nobleman studying at the Inns of Court, who takes an ominously self-centred view of his profession:

> Faith, I have been a truant in the law
> And never yet could frame my will to it,
> And therefore frame the law unto my will.   (II. 4. 7–9)

Suffolk is a major contributor to the outbreak of hostility that will issue in the wars of the roses, and he seduces Margaret of Anjou at the play's end. As Bernard Spivack points out, Suffolk's self-serving rationalization in this scene ('She's beautiful, and therefore to be wooed; | She is a woman, therefore to be won' (v. 3. 78–79)) echoes similar statements by Aaron the Moor in *Titus Andronicus* and by Richard of Gloucester in *Richard III*, both immediately derived from the Vice.[25] In *2 Henry VI* Suffolk will be the principal agent behind the destruction of Humphrey, Duke of Gloucester, the only remaining bulwark preventing complete political chaos, as all things meet in mere oppugnancy. Suffolk has little of the theatrical brilliance that characterizes Richard III, but he anticipates Richard, and also looks

---

[25] Bernard Spivack, *Shakespeare and the Allegory of Evil* (New York: Columbia University Press, 1958), pp. 386–87.

back to the Vice, in his inexplicable viciousness and his determination to sow dissent and mistrust.

One might well conclude that the difference between the devils in *Dr Faustus* and the *Henry VI* plays is the difference between tragedy and history. Marlowe seems predisposed to tragedy: even Tamburlaine discovers the limitations of mortality, despite the inability of mere fellow mortals to impede his bloody progress, and *The Jew of Malta*, while it is certainly the funniest of Marlowe's plays, offers only sardonic irony and wit and could hardly be thought of as comedy, by any definition. The fullest development of Marlowe's tragic vision is *Dr Faustus*, where irony again prevails, but not so strongly that Faustus is denied a genuine measure of tragic grandeur in his decline. Mephastophilis is a liar, as I have argued, and his lies are the play's principal source of ambiguity, but he gloats very little over his victim (much less than Iago gloats over Othello, for instance), and his lies are therefore harder to detect and their effect on Faustus is less demeaning than would be the case if Marlowe's devil were as openly theatrical as the morality play Vice. In short, what makes Mephastophilis so credible is his opacity, a quality that perhaps inclined Harry Levin to state (erroneously) that Mephastophilis does not tempt Faustus (*The Overreacher*, p. 138). The credibility of opaque power-seekers is a quality Shakespeare also discovered in his second tetralogy, where Henry IV and his son are displayed in an utterly naturalistic and politically compelling portrait of single-minded determination to seize or maintain effective power. Their motivation is ancient, if not timeless, and their dramatic heritage may well be demonic, but their opacity heightens the effectiveness of their dissimulation and makes it hard for us to know precisely what is truth and what is not. That epistemological dilemma is Faustus's dilemma as well, but in his case, as in Hamlet's and Macbeth's, the stage is universal and the stakes are cosmic. In the Lancastrian history plays, what is at issue is mere power between mortals, and what we cannot know is what any human being could not know in contemplating the competition for power at court, where those who did not know how to dissimulate did not know how to reign.

Stagecraft and Imagery in Shakespeare's
Henry VI

ALAN C. DESSEN

University of North Carolina

When dealing with Shakespeare's *Henry VI* on the page or on the stage, a critic, an editor, or a director immediately confronts the question of the integrity of the three plays as they have survived in the two quartos (among the earliest of Shakespeare's works to appear in print) and the First Folio (where Part One first appears). Since the eighteenth century, scholars and theatrical professionals have shown little confidence in or enthusiasm for these histories as intact entities, worthy of analysis as discrete units, but rather have either lumped them together as one item that can be dealt with summarily or raided them so as to appropriate detachable elements that suit the interpreter's agendas. For example, directors often graft Richard of Gloucester's speeches from Part Three on to *Richard III* (the Olivier movie is the best known but by no means the only instance); several recent scholars have written tellingly about Joan de Pucelle;[1] and other distinctive parts have been singled out for attention or analysis, with one line ('The first thing we do, let's kill all the lawyers', *2 Henry VI*, IV. 2. 70)[2] achieving a cult status. Admittedly, starting in the 1960s and 1970s a few academic critics have argued forcefully on behalf of thematic or imagist integrity;[3] at least two directors (Terry Hands, Jane Howell) have treated the scripts with respect. But for the most part both scholars and theatrical professionals (weaned on standards and assumptions derived from subsequent plays in the canon) have only intermittent interest in this trilogy other than as context for *Richard III*.

The reasons for such neglect or atomization are no secret. For the academic critic, the interpretative tools that for generations have worked well for later Shakespeare plays, whether for analysis of 'character', imagery,

[1] See Leah Marcus, *Puzzling Shakespeare* (Berkeley and Los Angeles: University of California Press, 1988), pp. 51–96; Gabriele Bernhard Jackson, 'Topical Ideology: Witches, Amazons, and Shakespeare's Joan of Arc', *English Literary Renaissance*, 18 (1988), 40–65; Nancy A. Gutierrez, 'Gender and Value in *1 Henry VI*: The Role of Joan de Pucelle', *Theatre Journal*, 42 (1990), 183–93. For a recent provocative interpretation of one episode in *2 Henry VI*, see Craig A. Bernthal, 'Treason in the Family: The Trial of Thumpe v. Horner', *Shakespeare Quarterly*, 42 (1991), 44–54.

[2] Citations from Shakespeare are from *The Complete Pelican Shakespeare*, general ed. Alfred Harbage (Baltimore: Penguin, 1969).

[3] See in particular J. P. Brockbank, 'The Frame of Disorder: *Henry VI*', in *Early Shakespeare*, ed. by J. R. Brown and Bernard Harris, Stratford-upon-Avon Studies 3 (1961), 72–99; David Riggs, *Shakespeare's Heroical Histories: 'Henry VI' and its Literary Tradition* (Cambridge, MA: Harvard University Press, 1971); and Edward Berry, *Patterns of Decay: Shakespeare's Early Histories* (Charlottesville: University Press of Virginia, 1975).

or structure, do not provide satisfying results when applied to *Henry VI*. As to the latter, the Elizabethan fondness for episodic structure or multiple unity here collides with a post-Elizabethan prizing of concentration and subordination of elements (as seen also in comparable discomfort among critics with the rebel scenes in *2 Henry IV* or the Aumerle rebellion in *Richard II*). Despite a long series of apologias (starting in the early 1950s with H. T. Price),[4] interpreters have therefore sensed formlessness rather than coherence in this trilogy (a problem only 'solved' with the emergence of Richard of Gloucester as a focal figure).

Such an introduction, as a reader of scholarly essays will recognize, is a prelude to The Answer, a formulation that will set the record straight now and forever so that The Problem will no longer bother future readers. Sadly (for I would be delighted to set things aright), such is not the case, for I lack the insights that would enable me to descend from Mount Sinai to deliver the reader of these plays to the promised land. Rather, I offer a paradox linked to a closed loop, a version of the infamous hermeneutic circle. Thus, perhaps more than with any other group of Shakespeare plays, the key to each of the three parts of *Henry VI* as a discrete unit, a play with its own distinctive shape and rationale (regardless of the interpretation eventually to be drawn from that shape and rationale), lies in the play as an onstage event, the play as seen-heard rather than the play-as-read (and few will quarrel with the limitations of this trilogy as plays-to-be-read). Such a claim, in turn, usually leads to a paeon on behalf of performance-oriented interpretation. That approach, however (although now much in fashion), is keyed to often unexamined assumptions drawn from twentieth-century theatre, whereas the rationale behind Elizabethan staging (especially in the early 1590s when that rationale was still taking shape) can be different, in ways both subtle and obvious, from what we take for granted today. In my terms, Shakespeare, his fellow players, and his playgoers shared a theatrical vocabulary accessible, even obvious, then but easily blurred or eclipsed today.

Paradoxically, one consequence of this situation is that the staging of these three plays in our theatres rather than helping to bridge this gap in our understanding can instead widen it (so as to become part of the problem rather than part of the solution). When treating these plays as playscripts to be enacted by modern actors before today's audiences, theatrical professionals inevitably make many adjustments that in turn eliminate or blur elements important for the original strategy. My point is not to fault actors and directors (who to survive must take into account the theatrical vocabulary they share with their paying customers and whose negative attitude towards these plays has been heavily conditioned by critics, scholars, and

---

[4] Hereward T. Price, 'Construction in Shakespeare', *University of Michigan Contributions in Modern Philology*, 17 (1951), 1–42 (pp. 24–37).

editors) but rather to lament that what can be a valuable tool for investigating other scripts (seeing the play-on-the-page come to life on the stage) is often denied the would-be interpreter of *Henry VI*.

Two recent and highly visible productions can serve as instructive paradigms. Both Michael Bogdanov (English Shakespeare Company 1987–88) and Adrian Noble (Royal Shakespeare Company 1988–89) elected to present the first tetralogy to their audiences by condensing four plays into three, with *Richard III* standing alone and the three parts of *Henry VI* compressed into two plays (the ESC's plays were entitled *The House of Lancaster* and *The House of York*, the RSC's *Henry VI* and *The Rise of Edward IV*). The choices necessitated when setting up such compressed versions of event-filled history plays can then be instructive (e.g., what is deemed essential versus what is treated as disposable), especially in the context of the commercial and artistic success of the RSC's 1977–78 Terry Hands *Henry VI* trilogy (played 'warts and all' with few cuts) and the significant achievement of Jane Howell's first tetralogy for the BBC's 'The Shakespeare Plays' (one of the strongest items in that series). The plays *are* do-able, as demonstrated by Hands (along with Alan Howard, Helen Mirren, Emrys James, Peter McEnery, Julian Glover, and others),[5] Howell, and Pat Patton (whose Part Three in 1977 was one of the strongest shows I have seen in fifteen years of playgoing at the Oregon Shakespeare Festival).

As experienced directors, both Bogdanov and Noble were much concerned with the commercial as well as the artistic advantages of presenting three rather than four plays, so the choice to streamline the received script came easily. Some of Noble's rationale is set forth in the preface to the printed edition of his script where he describes himself as continuing a process started by Shakespeare. For example, Shakespeare saw 'the dramatic advantages of shape and focus achieved by running several events into one', a process, Noble observes, 'which we have taken further'. In his conclusion, moreover, he notes: 'We all had to learn to value narrative over "character moments" and to value storytelling over psychology.'[6] Clearly, a different rationale is at work behind these plays, one that demands some adjustments from both the modern theatrical professional and the playgoer. Moreover, any compression of three event-filled plays into two is going to necessitate major omissions and adjustments ('running several events into one').

Both adaptations of the *Henry VI* material, in turn, followed the same general pattern. The material from Part One was allotted roughly ninety minutes so as to be completed by the first interval; the second half of the first

---

[5] For accounts of this production see Homer D. Swander, 'The Rediscovery of *Henry VI*', *Shakespeare Quarterly*, 29 (1978), 146–63; David Daniell, 'Opening up the text: Shakespeare's *Henry VI* plays in performance', *Themes in Drama*, 1 (1979), 247–77; G. K. Hunter, 'The Royal Shakespeare Company Plays *Henry VI*', *Renaissance Drama*, 9 (1978), 91–108.
[6] *The Plantagenets* (London and Boston: Faber, 1989), pp. vii, xiv.

play then contained the first three acts of Part Two; the last two acts of Part Two and the first two acts of Part Three (with much restitching of elements) occupied the pre-interval section of play number two; the remaining three acts of Part Three then finished the job.

Given such a master plan, certain problems emerge, problems that, in turn, can provide some insights into distinctive features of the three plays. First, the structural integrity of Shakespeare's Part Two was undermined. For example, the prophecies of Act I Scene 4 were not fulfilled. Both directors cut the references to Walter-water; indeed, Noble cut the entire scene (IV. 1), so that even though Suffolk's head did appear in Margaret's hands, the playgoer has no clue as to how he died (the plot summary in the programme informed the reader that Suffolk 'is murdered aboard ship as he leaves England'). Somerset, moreover, died in the next play (with no reference to castles or ale-house signs). The kind of implicit structure provided by the working out of prophecies or riddles (best seen in *Macbeth*) was therefore gone.

The same was true for the genesis of the Cade rebellion. Noble provided a powerful image to open *Edward IV*, with the Cade supporters rising from grated traps and filling the stage, but this subterranean emergence meant something very different at the outset of a new play as opposed to being experienced in Act IV Scene 2 of a continuum. Similarly, Bogdanov began his second play with a train station scene to show York's return from Ireland (V. 1), then switched to a Cade meeting hall rally (IV. 2). Gone therefore from both productions was any link between this new force unleashed upon England and the deaths of Gloucester, the Cardinal, and Suffolk or the earlier machinations of York; gone as well was any analogy to *Julius Caesar* where again a major political murder at the centre of the play comparable to the assassination of Gloucester opens the way to violence and war. To look closely at such compressions is therefore to bring into focus Shakespeare's sense of structure or cause and effect.

Both the RSC and ESC versions economized upon battle scenes in the second play so as to combine the first battle of St Albans (that ends Shakespeare's Part Two) with the battles that begin Part Three (and this alteration necessitated a host of other significant changes).[7] The most telling consequence of this compression was that a high percentage of the violence in Shakespeare's Parts Two and Three was now concentrated in the

---

[7] For example, owing to the transposition of elements young Clifford presented his angry speeches from the beginning of Part Three (e.g., I. 1. 159–60) *before* the death of his father at the end of Part Two, the event that occasioned his pronouncement that 'my heart is turned to stone' (v. 2. 50). Some of the elements from Part Two, v. 1 were retained, but moving and reshaping them eliminated the climactic position of the first confrontation between the parties of York and Lancaster (and one potentially telling element, the choice by Salisbury not to kneel to Henry VI, was gone). To the degree that the sequence of elements is an integral part of theatrical 'meaning' and effect, the treatment of the end of Part Two and the beginning of Part Three by both Bogdanov and Noble was a translation rather than an interpretation.

ninety-minute segment that begins the second play, for this stretch contained all the violence of Part Two (e.g., the Cade scenes, done by Noble with
many onstage decapitations and a host of severed heads on poles, York
versus Clifford, Richard versus Somerset) and then most of the violence in
Part Three (the battles of Acts I and II, the murders of Rutland and York, the
death of young Clifford). At the interval of Noble's production, one observer
(who did not know Shakespeare's script) asked me: 'What are we watching
— a Renaissance *Full Metal Jacket?*' Controlled use of onstage violence in the
original scripts has (in this segment) yielded to theatrical overkill.

Of the many changes and elisions I shall consider several small choices
that had a disproportionately large impact. Thus, Bogdanov pared down
considerably the 'common man' scenes from the first two acts of Part Two
(although, unlike Noble, he did retain the Simpcox episode), so that Peter
and his master Horner disappeared from view. No charge of treason was
therefore brought against York by means of Horner's reported comments, so
that, in turn, no particular reason remained for choosing Somerset over York
as Regent of France (Gloucester recommends to the king that Somerset get
the regency 'because in York this breeds suspicion' (1.3.203–04)).
Bogdanov's King Henry, moreover, not Gloucester, provided 'this doom'
(l.202). Although on the surface only an innocuous series of cuts and
changes, such giving of the decision to Henry had a significant effect upon
the portrayal of three major figures. First, Henry appears much more
decisive as a politician than is the case anywhere else, a shift that sets up a
very different progression to his one strong moment when, after recovering
from his swoon at the news of Gloucester's death, he banishes Suffolk in
Act III Scene 2. Secondly, Gloucester loses one of his two highly visible
judgements (the other coming with Simpcox) and hence some of his special
stature, a diminution that contributed to one of the weak spots in this
production. Thirdly, an insight into the danger posed by York is eliminated,
as was also true in some other cuts made by Bogdanov (most notably the
elimination of York's speech that ends Act I Scene 1 and the paring down of
Gloucester's final speech in Act III Scene 1, including his reference to 'dogged
York, that reaches at the moon, | Whose overweening arm I have plucked
back' (ll. 158–59)). Having Henry deliver the 'doom' therefore has a
significant impact upon three of the key figures in this play and upon the
dynamics of Part Two as a whole.

Comparable small but telling changes can be noted in Noble's production.
In both Shakespeare's Part Three (IV.8.38–50) and Noble's adaptation,
Henry VI has a speech in which he naïvely concludes that, because he has
been mild and merciful, the people will support him rather than Edward in
the coming conflict. In Noble's version, Henry exits after this speech (so
some playgoers were surprised to see him turn up in prison a few scenes
later); in Shakespeare's scene, however, he is immediately confronted and
arrested by the Yorkists (whom the people *have* supported) so that the speech

serves as the first half of a one-two punch, with the second element, the deflation, gone from Noble's version. Similarly, in Shakespeare's Part Three, a Henry VI anxious to relinquish kingly power gives over his political authority to both Warwick and Clarence (IV. 6), but in Noble's version only Warwick is so designated. Shortly thereafter (v. 1) Clarence arrives at Coventry (where his brothers are besieging Warwick) and decides to change sides, forsaking Warwick in favour of the Yorkist cause. Does it not make a difference to our understanding why Clarence makes this switch whether he is or is not a sharer in kingly power? At the least, a figure who has left his brothers in order to gain half a kingdom (however provisionally) is not faced with the same choice as a figure who has played second fiddle to an older brother and now is to be second again to Warwick (as in Noble's stripped down version).

Such choices and resulting problems are (perhaps) inevitable given the squeezing of three plays into two, but that three-into-two choice is itself a product of a series of assumptions (both aesthetic and commercial) about the dramaturgy and coherence of these early Shakespeare plays. What if, in contrast, these histories do have a distinctive theatrical shape or logic (as suggested above in my account of the prophecies and the role of Gloucester's assassination in Part Two), albeit one not as accessible today as that found in later comparable plays?

To pursue such a defence of the integrity of these plays I will focus upon a few distinctive and revealing configurations. My emphasis will be upon scenes and images that, although easily blurred for a reader today, would be hard for a playgoer in the 1590s to miss; that depend more upon visual-theatrical than upon poetic-verbal effects (or are underdeveloped in poetic-verbal terms); and that were omitted or blurred significantly in the RSC and ESC productions (and, in a few instances, were realized meaningfully in other productions).

Let me start with one of the least discussed moments in the most maligned of the three plays, *1 Henry VI*. At the nadir of her fortunes, just before her capture by York, Joan de Pucelle appeals for help to a group of onstage '*Fiends*' (v. 3. 7. s. d.), but in response these fiends, according to the Folio stage directions, '*walk, and speak not*', '*hang their heads*', '*shake their heads*', and finally '*depart*' (s.ds at ll. 12, 17, 19, 23). This exchange has not fared well on the page or on the stage, for to deal with this script is inevitably to run foul of this scene and this appeal-rejection that in several ways tests the reflexes of today's interpreters. The Folio's call for fiends and for specific reactions is unusually clear (and presumably would have posed few problems in the 1590s for playgoers attuned to *Doctor Faustus*), but Elizabethan onstage presentation of the supernatural repeatedly strains 'our' paradigms of credibility (and canons of taste), with this moment a particular challenge.

Directors have therefore tinkered with the Folio signals. In Howell's rendition for television, Joan speaks her lines while staring at the camera so that no supernatural entities are in sight to walk, refuse to speak, hang their heads, and eventually depart. In Noble's rendition, various onstage corpses from the previous battle rose as if animated to provide an onstage audience but without the reactions to Joan's pleas specified in the Folio. In the Hands production, amid the onstage cannons that dominated the battlefield set, Joan offered herself to the fiends who appeared suddenly 'looking like gas-masked soldiers from the French trenches of the First World War'.[8] Bogdanov cut the fiends and altered the text, so that, alone on stage and looking at the audience, his Joan directed her appeal not to any diabolic entities but rather to the Virgin Mary, a change that eliminated any infernal climax for this sequence.[9] In contrast, in his 1975 Oregon Shakespeare Festival production, Will Huddleston introduced his fiends earlier (thinly disguised as Joan's followers, later her torturers) and then did stage the rejection; at the close of the play, moreover, the fiends make a final appearance above (with midnight tolling in the background) to snarl at the playgoers.

Even to a casual reader the interaction between Joan and the fiends leaps off the page in vivid (and, to many, offensive) fashion: a good example of what I term theatrical *italics*. To explore the potential in this moment, consider Joan and her devils not as a one-shot effect but as the climactic example of a larger progression of images and moments that starts in Act II. From her first appearance Joan has claimed supernatural powers (see 1.2.72–92), a claim tested in the first meeting between Joan and Talbot that results in a stand-off; still, Joan scorns his strength (1.5.15) and leads her troops to victory at Orleans. Moments later, Talbot, aided by Bedford and Burgundy, scales the walls and regains the town, so that a united English force wins back what had just been lost. The three leaders working together therefore accomplish what Talbot, facing Joan alone, could not.

Shakespeare then provides a gloss on both this victory and the larger problem of unity-disunity by means of Talbot's interview with the Countess of Auvergne. Her trap for Talbot fails, as he points out, because she has only caught 'Talbot's shadow', not his substance. The set of terms is repeated throughout the remainder of the scene (e.g., 'No, no, I am but shadow of myself. | You are deceived, my substance is not here') and is explained by the appearance of his soldiers, at which point he observes:

[8] Daniell, 'Opening up the text', p. 257.

[9] Bogdanov did some radical surgery here by transposing the beginning of Act V Scene 3 to Act V Scene 4 so that one sustained sequence involving Joan followed the Suffolk-Margaret part of Act V Scene 3. The juxtaposition of the two French women remained, but the value of that link was changed (e.g., Joan's capture by York was not immediately followed by Suffolk's capture of Margaret). Bogdanov also cut Joan's shepherd father. His Joan, moreover, had her own distinctive music, but without the Folio fiends as a final comment this production offered no clear signal as to whether that music (and the auspices for her final moments) was holy or witchly. Here, as elsewhere, Bogdanov provided an engaging story, but the original punchline as set up in the Folio had been drastically changed.

> Are you now persuaded
> That Talbot is but a shadow of himself?
> These are his substance, sinews, arms, and strength,
> With which he yoketh your rebellious necks.   (II. 3. 45)

The individual standing alone, no matter how heroic (one thinks of Corio-lanus), is but a shadow without the substance of his supporters, his army, his country.[10]

This play, however (as two generations of critics have reminded us), is about division, not unity, a division that has already been displayed in the split between Winchester and Gloucester and that widens in the Temple Garden scene (immediately following Talbot's lecture to the countess), with its symbolic plucking of red and white roses. The figures who had joined Talbot in the victory at Orleans, moreover, soon disappear (Bedford dies, Burgundy changes sides). Factionalism thrives, to the extent that the division between York and Somerset (unhistorically) undoes Talbot himself who, in the terms of Act II Scene 3, is denied his substance and must face death (along with his son) as a shadow of his heroic self. Sir William Lucy's listing of Talbot's titles (IV. 7. 60–71) can then be mocked by Joan as 'a silly stately style indeed', for 'him that thou magnifi'st with all these titles, | Stinking and flyblown lies here at our feet' (ll. 72, 75–76).

Joan's scene with her devils follows less than a hundred lines after her exchange with Lucy. With the French forces fleeing the conquering York, all Joan can do is call upon her 'speedy helpers' or 'familiar spirits' to help with their 'accustomed diligence', but neither the offer of her blood, with which she has fed them in the past, a member lopped off, her body, or even her soul will gain the needed support. She therefore concludes:

> My ancient incantations are too weak,
> And hell too strong for me to buckle with.
> Now, France, thy glory droopeth to the dust.   (V. 3. 1)

No one makes grandiose claims for the imagery of this sprawling play. But a verbal patterning involving shadow and substance is clearly set forth in Act II and echoed thereafter (see Alencon's speech, v. 4. 133–37); moreover, Talbot eventually falls (and France ultimately is lost to England) because of divisions whereby 'substance' is denied and the hero must stand alone as shadow of himself. In her scene with the fiends, Joan too is deserted, denied by those who formerly supported her. Like Talbot, her heroic status cannot exist alone, so she becomes a mere shepherd's daughter, not the figure who raised the siege at Orleans and was a match for Talbot in battle. The denial by the fiends is here equivalent to the squabble between York and Somerset that undoes Talbot, a link that can be reinforced through the staging. For

---

[10] For treatments of Act II Scene 3, see especially Daniel C. Gerould, 'Principles of Dramatic Structure in *Henry VI*', *Educational Theatre Journal*, 20 (1968), 376–88 (pp. 379–80); Berry, *Patterns of Decay*, pp. 1–28; James A. Riddell, 'Talbot and the Countess of Auvergne', *Shakespeare Quarterly*, 28 (1977), 51–57; Alexander Leggatt, *Shakespeare's Political Drama* (London and New York: Routledge, 1988), pp. 1–8.

example, what if the fiends' scripted reactions to Joan's offer echo similar walking apart, hanging and shaking of heads, and departures by York and Somerset in Act iv Scene 3 and Act iv Scene 4 in response to Lucy's pleas on behalf of Talbot? If so, the playgoer would see two or three parallel failures by first Lucy and then Joan, rejections that visibly set up the deaths of the two previously unbeatable or 'heroic' figures. Just as Lucy fails to get the necessary support, a failure that means Talbot must give way to the new factions, so Joan fails to get the support that she too desperately needs and must give way to the third Frenchwoman, Margaret (who appears immediately upon Joan's exit with York). However interpreted in theological or political terms, these highly visible fiends can function as part of an ongoing pattern of images or configurations linked to the central themes of the play.

Of the three plays, Part One has been the most disparaged, but in both the Bogdanov and Noble three-into-two adjustments Part Two suffered the greatest damage because its elements were split into two separate plays. As noted earlier, such a split calls attention to the different kinds of through-lines or pay-offs set up in earlier scenes and realized later (as is most obvious with the prophecies). Other cuts and changes made by the two directors call attention to comparable links and images. For example, Noble manufactured a fresh image in Act iv Scene 2, for his Cade not only knighted himself (ll. 107–08) but also knighted Dick the Butcher, underscoring even further the indictment of titles and hierarchy. As part of his streamlining of Act v of Part Two, however, Noble cut Henry VI's knighting of Alexander Iden (v. 1. 78); in the first play he had also cut Henry's grant of a dukedom to a kneeling Suffolk as a reward for bringing Margaret as bride (Part Two, 1. 1. 61–63). Shakespeare's own sequence of giving new titles to kneeling figures was therefore gone, with two instances of number two in the series but no number one and no number three.

All three plays but particularly Part Two gain much of their distinctive shape from such visible repetitions, but with many of these elements eliminated, transposed, or located in two different plays (and hence two different evenings) much of that rationale was gone. For example, Gloucester tells his wife that 'I must offend before I be attainted', for his foes, no matter how powerful, 'could not procure me any scathe | So long as I am loyal, true, and crimeless' (ii. 4. 59, 62–63). Two acts later, Lord Say tells the king and Buckingham: 'The trust I have is in mine innocence, | And therefore am I bold and resolute' (iv. 4. 59–60). At their next appearances, however, both figures are accused and swiftly convicted by their enemies and are murdered shortly thereafter (with Gloucester's body and Say's head subsequently brought onstage). If such elements, however, are pared down or cut completely and placed in two separate plays, no such analogy or structural link is available (whatever interpretative spin one chooses to place upon it).

Part Three suffered the least from adaptation and compression, for several clearly linked moments were retained and were in the same play. Thus, in

Shakespeare's Act I the Lancastrians led by young Clifford kill a Yorkist child (Rutland) and the symbol of the Yorkist cause (Richard); in Act V, the Lancastrians do the same: the three brothers kill Prince Edward, and in the following scene Richard of Gloucester murders Henry VI in the Tower. In Patton's Oregon production a highly visible detail added to this patterning, for Margaret's taunting of York with the napkin bearing Rutland's blood left blood on Richard's face. Such a bloody face was then seen again on the father contemplating the son he has killed (II. 5) and most tellingly on Margaret herself after she had kissed her murdered son Edward (V. 5).

The streamlining occasioned by making three plays into two, however, did take its toll. Indeed, what may seem to the adapter redundancies and hence cuttable episodes looked at another way can add up to a distinctive feature of this play. For example, in his speech to his captors in Act III Scene 1 (pared down in both versions) Henry VI first raises questions about oaths and obedience but then laments the frailty of human nature:

> Look, as I blow this feather from my face
> And as the air blows it to me again,
> Obeying with my wind when I do blow
> And yielding to another when it blows,
> Commanded always by the greater gust —
> Such is the lightness of you common men.
> But do not break your oaths   (III. 1. 84)

Many disparate episodes in the next two acts provide demonstrations of this thesis: that, regardless of their pretensions about oaths and principles, feather-like men and women are 'commanded always by the greater gust'. In the next scene (III. 2) that greater gust is King Edward's lust for the beautiful widow that takes precedence over political allegiances, most notably his bond with Warwick; that turnabout is quickly paralleled in Warwick's rapid switch in reaction to this disgrace in which he tells his hated enemy Queen Margaret 'let former grudges pass, | And henceforth I am thy true servitor' and she responds: 'Warwick, these words have turned my hate to love, | And I forgive and quite forget old faults' (III. 3. 195–201). The most obvious example comes when Clarence, who marches in ready to fight against his own brothers on behalf of Warwick, with little ado throws his red rose at his former ally and rejoins the Yorkists (eliciting Richard's delicious line: 'Welcome, good Clarence. This is brotherlike' (V. 1. 105)).

Easily lost in this sequence of events, however, is Act IV Scene 7, a scene omitted from the two streamlined versions (and also from Patton's Oregon production) but one of the gems of Howell's rendition. Here Edward gains access to the city of York by vowing that he has come as duke, not as a would-be king ('I challenge nothing but my dukedom, | As being well content with that alone' (ll. 23–24)), but the arrival and threatened departure of Sir John Montgomery ('Then fare you well, for I will hence again. | I came to serve a king and not a duke' (ll. 48–49)) puts Edward on the spot (in a manner that closely parallels the dilemma faced by Edward's father in Act I Scene 2: whether to keep his bargain with Henry VI or seek the crown now). In the spirit of 'like father, like son' Edward quickly caves in to the urgings of Richard and Hastings, so that, in Howell's rendition, with drums sounding in the background, the Mayor (rather than a soldier) shakily reads the proclamation of Edward's kingship and Montgomery, visibly itching for action, stands by impatiently, snatches away the paper, and offers his open challenge to single combat. The rapidity of Edward's switch in his professed intentions yields both dark comedy and a telling insight into the value of oaths and protestations in this political jungle.

In the spirit of Henry's speech on 'the greater gust', the sequence of turnabouts by key figures such as Edward, Warwick, and Clarence heightens the uncertainties and lack of any firm principles or beliefs in this Darwinian society and, if played in full, helps to explain the rise of Gloucester and the genesis of Richard III and *Richard III* (the first, longest, and most famous of Gloucester's speeches is positioned just after Edward's decision to marry his widow in Act III Scene 2). The streamlined versions tell the same story (often with considerable panache), but the repeated betrayals or apostasies (like the recapitulation in Act V of the brutal killings of Act I) are the bones and sinews from which this play takes its distinctive shape. To cut the Countess of Auvergne, Peter-Horner, and Sir John Montgomery is to economize on time and personnel so as to enhance the narrative pace, but the price-tag involves the elimination of paradigms that, if attended to, can call attention to central themes and images. Whether with shadow-substance in Part One, the many analogous situations in Part Two, or the action following Henry's feather speech in Part Three, the repetitions, even apparent redundancies (according to today's sensibilities), *are* the essence of the plays.[11]

In calling attention to such losses, my goal is to bring into focus a broader and deeper interpretative problem. The stage directions for the fiends' reactions to Joan's pleas are unusually explicit, but the absence of any comparable signals for the reactions of York and Somerset to Lucy's pleas for help makes any claims about linkage between the two moments conjectural. Such lack of specific signals, however, is the norm in the extant playscripts, for in most cases clear indications of stage business or properties have not

---

[11] As shrewd, experienced directors, both Bogdanov and Noble were well aware of the opportunities for strong visual links between episodes. For example, Noble had Margery Jourdain's death at the stake (in his first play) repeat the fate of Joan (events divided between Shakespeare's Parts One and Two); also in his first play, the first meeting of Margaret and Suffolk (just before the interval) was echoed in the plays final moments when Margaret cradled Suffolk's severed head. Twice, moreover, Noble found strong images (albeit in two different plays) to convey the price-tag for the power associated with the throne. First, the dead Mortimer (at the end of Shakespeare's Part One, II. 5) descended in his cage-prison, an object then replaced with Henry VI's golden throne (a disturbing and effective juxtaposition). Then, at the end of the second play the body of the murdered Henry VI descended in a similar fashion, to be replaced by a throne inhabited by Edward. In both instances, the image of a body under the throne was strong and meaningful.

survived. Such gaps in our knowledge of what may have been obvious in the 1590s are compounded by the changes in theatrical vocabulary between then and now, for inevitably our inferences about how an Elizabethan company would have staged X are heavily conditioned by how *we* would stage X.

As a particularly useful example, consider the moment in Part Three when Edward IV, having been surprised and captured by Warwick and Clarence, is carried onstage '*in his gown, sitting in a chair*' (IV. 3. 27. s. d.). In the Howell television rendition, Edward is bound to his chair so that the image for the spectator is that of a prisoner (comparable to Gloucester in the blinding scene of *King Lear*). Howell's choice makes immediate sense to a viewer today, but it may also blur a distinctive effect keyed to the original stage conventions.

For what we today do not recognize is that, in the age of Shakespeare, bringing a figure onstage in a chair was the primary way of signalling '*enter sick*' or '*as if sick*'. To cite only a few of the many examples, in *Westward Ho* Mistress Tenterhook, pretending to be sick, calls for 'a chaire, a chaire'; a companion says 'shees sicke and taken with an Agony'. In *Othello*, after 'finding' the wounded Cassio, Iago cries 'O for a chair | To bear him easily hence' (v. 1. 82–83) and mentions the chair twice more (ll. 96, 98); when the chair arrives, he adds: 'Some good man bear him carefully from hence. | I'll fetch the general's surgeon' (ll. 99–100) and 'O, bear him out o'th' air' (l. 104); the 1622 Quarto (but not the Folio) then directs Cassio in the next scene to be brought in '*in a Chaire*' (N1ʳ). Elsewhere in Shakespeare's plays, chairs are specified for sick and dying figures in *1 Henry VI* (II. 5. 0. s. d., III. 2. 40. s. d.), *2 Henry VI* (II. 1. 66. s. d.), and *King Lear* (IV. 7. 20. s. d., TLN 2771). Examples are also plentiful in the plays of Fletcher and Brome and can be found as well in Peele, Chapman, Dekker, Heywood, Marston, Massinger, Markham, Haughton, and Ford and in many anonymous plays.[12]

---

[12] Thomas Dekker, *Westward Ho*, v. 1. 196–201 in *The Dramatic Works*, ed. by Fredson Bowers, 4 vols (Cambridge: Cambridge University Press, 1953–61), II, 379 (for another example from the Dekker canon, see I, 374). For examples roughly contemporary with *Henry VI*, see George Peele, *The Battle of Alcazar*, ed. by W. E. Greg, Malone Society (Oxford, 1906), l. 1302; Peele, *Edward I*, ed. by W. W. Greg, Malone Society (Oxford, 1911), ll. 48–49 and *Locrine*, ed. by Ronald B. McKerrow, Malone Society (Oxford, 1908), l. 33. For a further sampling of the evidence, see *The Works of Francis Beaumont and John Fletcher*, ed. by Arnold Glover and A. R. Waller, 10 vols (Cambridge: Cambridge University Press, 1905–12), I, 374, 378; IV, 76; VI, 254; IX, 375; Richard Brome, *The Dramatic Works*, 3 vols (London: Pearson, 1873), I, 218, 257; II, 127 (*The Queen and Concubine*); III, 180, 263, 546; George Chapman, *The Gentleman Usher*, ed. by John Hazel Smith (Lincoln, NE: University of Nebraska Press, 1970), IV. 3. 0. s. d., v. 4. 39. s. d,; Thomas Heywood, *The Dramatic Works*, 6 vols (London: Pearson, 1874), I, 155; Philip Massinger, *The Plays and Poems*, ed. by Philip Edwards and Colin Gibson, 5 vols (Oxford: Oxford University Press, 1976), III, 461; Gervaise Markham and William Sampson, *Herod and Antipater* (1622), H3ʳ, 12ᵛ; William Haughton, *Englishmen for My Money*, ed. by W. W. Greg, Malone Society (Oxford, 1913), l. 2434; *A Yorkshire Tragedy*, ed. by Sylvia D. Feldman, Malone Society (Oxford, 1973), l. 720. Sick-chairs are also to be found in plays as diverse as Marston's *Sophonisba*, Middleton's *Hengist King of Kent*, Jonson's *The Magnetic Lady*, Ford's *The Broken Heart*, May's *The Old Couple*, Drue's *The Duchess of Suffolk*, *A Warning For Fair Women*, *The Second Maiden's Tragedy*, *The Soddered Citizen*, and *The Telltale*.

To return to the scene in Part Three, when Edward is carried onstage '*in his gown, sitting in a chair*', the initial signal for the original spectator would have been that this figure is entering '*sick*' or '*as sick*'. In this instance, however, the signals would be misleading, for Edward is embarrassed and vulnerable but not sick. But keep in mind that this play starts and ends with throne scenes, with that royal seat a symbol of the disorder in a kingdom in which three different figures are seen sitting upon the English throne. Indeed, in the opening scene the titular king, Henry VI, comes onstage to discover Richard of York seated upon his throne, an initial usurpation that typifies what is to follow. The presence of a king (or pseudo-king) brought onstage in what appears initially to be a sick-chair is therefore more than a momentary trick played upon the spectator. Rather, that initial confusion of throne-chair and sick-chair calls attention to an important set of associations that links disease to kings and power-brokers, associations reinforced by the unkinging, rekinging, and unkinging of Henry VI in the last three acts. Memories of both the opening confusion about the throne and the momentary sick-chair image of Act IV Scene 3 should then inform the final moments, where the surface order assumed by Edward ('Now am I seated as my soul delights, | Having my country's peace and brothers' loves' (v. 7. 35–36)) is undercut by a continuing sense of the kingdom's diseases, as typified in Richard's asides (e.g., 'I'll blast his harvest' (l. 21)). The momentary effect with Edward in his chair therefore reinforces a potentially meaningful iterative pattern that links disease imagery to the throne and to the larger political concerns of the play.

Nor is this sick chair-royal chair image limited to Part Three. Squabbles in the presence of Henry and his throne are a major symptom of what is wrong in Part One, so that in Howell's production Exeter delivers his choric speech on 'this base and envious discord' (and recalls the prophecy 'that Henry born at Monmouth should win all | And Henry born at Windsor should lose all') while pointing to the empty throne (III. 1. 186–200). The scenes that precede and follow this chaotic activity around the boy-king seated on his throne are instructive. First, Shakespeare presents the plucking of red and white roses by Suffolk and York in the Temple Garden scene (II. 4), a symbolic beginning to the divisions to come. Moments later, Mortimer, who is '*brought in a chair*' by his jailers (II. 5. 0. s. d.), provides a long disquisition to Richard about the Yorkist claim to the throne. This claim, passed from this dying figure to the up-and-coming Richard, is linked visually to a figure in a sick-chair. Mortimer's ominous laying on of hands (see lines 37–38) is immediately followed by our first view of the young Henry VI, presumably on his throne, who is unable to control the squabble between Gloucester and Winchester or the fight, offstage and then onstage, between their serving-men. The one action this vulnerable king does take, however, is to restore Richard to his dukedom, so that the figure bequeathed a claim to the throne in the previous scene by a figure in a sick-chair is now given status and power by a demonstrably weak occupant of the royal seat. This sequence is then extended in the next scene where, during the loss and recapture of Rouen, the dying Bedford is '*brought in sick in a chair*' (III. 2. 40. s. d.) to witness Falstaff's cowardice and then the English victory. At the climax of this action, '*Bedford dies and is carried in by two in his chair*' (l. 114. s. d.).

Throughout the play, Henry's 'throne scenes' act out his inability to control internal divisions and, hence, England's diseases, but his first appearance in Act III Scene 1, sandwiched between scenes displaying figures dying in their sick-chairs, neatly sums up the problems linked both to the Yorkists' claim to the throne (symbolized by Mortimer) and the dying off of that loyal older generation devoted to the good of the country rather than factional interests (symbolized by Bedford). As with Joan's fiends and Talbot's shadow versus substance, much of the theatrical coherence of this episodic play arises from such linked images and configurations. If the final scene also has an onstage throne (as in Part Three), Suffolk's convincing the king to take Margaret as his bride (made ominous by Suffolk's closing reference to Paris and the implicit analogy between Margaret-Helen and England-Troy) enacts a climactic link between the royal chair and potential diseases to come. Again, even in this early play, a set of associations made accessible by conventional theatrical practice (*enter sick*) can be used to italicize important meanings and effects.

In Part Two, such chair-throne patterning is present but less emphatic, for Shakespeare uses violent deaths and the Cade rebellion to highlight the kingdom's diseases. The dead or dying Gloucester and Winchester are displayed onstage but (apparently) in sick-beds rather than sick-chairs. The impostor Simpcox, however, enters '*between two in a chair*' (II. 1. 66. s. d.) in front of a weak king who, early in the same scene, is unable to control the quarrel between Gloucester and Winchester. Humphrey's uncovering of Simpcox's fraud acts out his important role in keeping some semblance of order in England, but, owing to Elinor's disgrace and his own naïvete, Humphrey's position is soon undermined. Simpcox in his chair therefore prepares us for a hapless Henry on his throne who is unable to protect Humphrey or Lord Say (the latter linked to the palsy and 'full of sickness and diseases' (IV. 7. 81, 85)); this king is therefore vulnerable to an obvious fraud (Cade) in Act IV and defenceless against a formidable opponent (York) in Act V (so, as a result, Henry finds York seated on his throne in the first scene of Part Three). When the inevitable confrontation does come, York's critique pinpoints the vulnerability of Henry as possessor of the royal seat, for he begins 'No! thou art not king', then cites the attributes of kingship ('That head of thine doth not become a crown; | Thy hand is made to grasp a palmer's staff | And not to grace an awful princely sceptre'), and concludes: 'Give place. By heaven, thou shalt rule no more | O'er him whom heaven created for thy ruler' (V. 1. 93, 96–98, 104–05). As in the other two plays, such powerful accusations are enhanced by a subliminal memory of the purportedly lame Simpcox exposed as a fraud and forced to 'give place' from *his* chair (and leap over a stool) by the beadle. The whole may be greater than the sum of its parts, but first an interpreter must have all the parts and some sense of how they might work.

The productions cited in this essay provided a great deal of narrative excitement so as to engage and entertain playgoers (and television viewers) unfamiliar with the scripts. The many cuts and transpositions (along with the telescoping of disparate figures into one to economize on personnel) could be seen as the price-tag for mounting *Henry VI* at all (although the 1977–78 Hands trilogy provides testimony that three-into-two is not the only available route). In singling out some representative choices, my purpose therefore has not been to mount an indictment of the director-as-vandal. Rather, I have sought to bring into focus both the assets and liabilities of such modern onstage interpretations as a tool for understanding the original dramaturgy, theatrical vocabulary, and potential meanings. For the theatrical historicist, the changes made by Bogdanov and Noble can be especially revealing when the original onstage logic (whether linked to analogical thinking, distinctive images, or signifiers in a lost vocabulary) is no longer seen or appreciated, so that directoral adjustments serve as signposts that point to differing notions of how a play works or how that play is (or should be) put together. Such signposts can be particularly revealing in productions of *Henry VI* where the overall shape (or sense of organization) may be more in tune with Spenser's *The Faerie Queene* or Sidney's *Arcadia* than with *Henry V* or *Hamlet*.

The changes made by Bogdanov and Noble can therefore serve as a useful window into an Elizabethan theatrical logic (linked to a 1590s sense of analogy, imagery, and onstage story-telling) that is difficult (at times impossible) to recapture today. Some directoral decisions or adjustments can produce considerable theatrical excitement (and in this area I have not done justice to any of the productions). Other changes, however, fail to achieve the intended goal (a graceful elision of three long, ungainly plays) but rather constitute radical surgery or, for a different metaphor, provide not an adaptation but a translation into a new and different theatrical language. Both Talbot's lecture on shadow versus substance and Henry VI's lament about the feather commanded by the greater gust should serve as chastening thoughts for interpreters of this trilogy on the stage or on the page.

Sexual Perversity in *Venus and Adonis*

JONATHAN BATE

University of Liverpool

Late in 1589, Thomas Lodge published his poem *Scillaes Metamorphosis: Enterlaced with the unfortunate love of Glaucus*. In so doing, he established a new poetic genre, the witty love-poem dressed in the manner of Ovid. Following in Lodge's wake, Marlowe wrote *Hero and Leander* and Shakespeare *Venus and Adonis* — to judge by frequency of allusions to the former and reprintings of the latter, two of the most popular poems of the age.

An earlier tradition, extending back through the middle ages, had moralized Ovid's tales: in the prose dedication to the first edition of his translation, Arthur Golding wrote that the myths of the *Metamorphoses* were 'outwardly moste pleasant tales and delectable histories', but that they were 'fraughted inwardlye with most piththie instructions and wholsome examples'.[1] With not inconsiderable ingenuity, Golding peeled off the narrative skin and found hidden 'inner' moral meanings in the text; he thus contrived to make Ovid sound at least a little like the other major author whom he translated into English: John Calvin. Lodge's poem, by contrast, sets out to enjoy Ovid's poetry of passion, as the Roman poet did himself. Lessons may be learnt from this world of desire and metamorphosis, but they are lessons about the games and the anguish of love. The examples are *not* wholesome, the instruction is not moralistic. Lodge and his successors show how love is; they don't moralize about how behaviour should be. Golding's argument is that if you give in to passion, you will suffer, whereas the argument of late Elizabethan Ovidianism often seems to be that however you behave, whether you rein in your passion or not, love will make you suffer. Hero and Leander embrace love and end up dead. Adonis rejects love and ends up dead. In Lodge's poem, first Glaucus woos a reluctant Scilla, then Cupid fires an arrow that stops up his wound and cures him of his love; but Cupid also fires at Scilla, so she is in turn afflicted and tries to seduce a now reluctant Glaucus. Cupid, the blind, diminutive, and illegitimate child of Venus, is in every respect a contrary little bastard.

But these poems cannot be described as tragedies of love. This is partly because, as in Ovid, metamorphosis lets the characters off the hook: they are arrested in the moment of intense emotion and released into a vital, vibrant, colourful world of anthropomorphic nature. And it is also, pre-eminently, because the poet is ultimately more interested in the beginnings than the

---

[1] *The Fyrst Fower Bookes of P Ovidius Nasos Worke, intitled Metamorphosis, translated oute of Latin into Englishe meter by Arthur Golding Gent.* (London, 1565), dedication to Leicester, dated December 1564.

ends of love. The primary focus is upon the psychological causes of love —
what is it that the lover desires? — and the linguistic arts with which the
love-object is pursued. Lodge in *Scillaes Metamorphosis*, Marlowe in *Hero and
Leander*, and Shakespeare in *Venus and Adonis*, devote most of their attention to
the arguments of the characters, in particular to the topos of the persuasion
to love. The pleasure for the Elizabethan reader resides in the cunning
rhetoric; Shakespeare was above all known as a sweet, witty, mellifluous,
honey-tongued writer.

The skill of the writers of erotic narrative poetry manifested itself in their
way of combining two Ovids: the witty preceptor of love, the poet of arguing
one's way into bed, as in the *Amores* and the *Ars Amatoria*, is brought together
with the weaver of 'interlaced' mythological tales of metamorphosis. Thus
Leander makes use of an argument from the *Amores* about how a woman's
sexual treasure (her virginity) should, like all wealth, be used instead of
hoarded.[2] In the terms of William Keach, the best modern reader of the
genre, Ovid's irony is combined with his pathos — his witty detachment and
his emotional intensity are fused.[3] Love is acknowledged to be confusing and
painful, but desire is also revealed to be comic and undignified. The world of
these quintessentially Elizabethan poems is not so far from that of David
Mamet's play, *Sexual Perversity in Chicago*: the language may be smooth
where Mamet's is rough in the extreme, but in each world the characters
wisecrack and bully their way in love because they are ultimately extremely
uncomfortable in it. They try to be cool in their dealings with the opposite
sex, but in fact they are constantly hot under the collar. Mamet's word
'perversity' is apt in suggesting the contrariness of desire, whilst also
summoning up yet staving off the idea of 'perversion'.

It is easy to share the cultivated Elizabethan reader's delight in the
conceits of the genre. The resourceful Venus has many a memorable
example:

> I'll be a park, and thou shalt be my deer.
> Feed where thou wilt, on mountains or in dale;
> Graze on my lips, and if those hills be dry,
> Stray lower, where the pleasant fountains lie.[4]

Shakespeare's handling of his source in the writing of *Venus and Adonis* is
characteristic. Ovid tells the story in less than a hundred lines, Shakespeare
in more than a thousand: the classical text provides a narrative famework
into which the Elizabethan writer inserts elaborate arguments, thus demonstrating his own rhetorical skills. Because the persuasions given to the

---

[2] *Hero and Leander*, 1.231–40 is a translation and expansion of *Amores*, 1.8.51–53 (also trans. by Marlowe
in his *Ovid's Elegies*).
[3] *Elizabethan Erotic Narratives: Irony and Pathos in the Ovidian Poetry of Shakespeare, Marlowe, and Their
Contemporaries* (New Brunswick, NJ: Rutgers University Press, 1977).
[4] *Venus and Adonis*, ll. 231–34. The poem is quoted from *The Complete Works*, ed. by Stanley Wells and
Gary Taylor (Oxford: Clarendon Press, 1986).

characters are the major interpolations into the source, critical readings tend to concentrate on them.[5] But it will be the contention of this essay that within Shakespeare's poem there are signals that we must consider the Ovidian source-text to be much broader than the seventy or so lines of direct material. Golding's outward/inward distinction works differently in Shakespeare's reading of Ovid: whilst the moral translator claimed to find meaning 'inwardlye' but in fact imposed it from outside the text, the creative imitator interprets his source narrative partly by means of other narratives that lie both outside and inside, around and within it. Surrounding the text is a distinctly unwholesome context.

When Shakespeare read Book x of the *Metamorphoses*, the first thing he was told about Adonis was that he was the 'misbegotten chyld' of the union between Myrrha and her father, Cinyras.[6] At the same time, he would have learned that the lovely boy was born not from his mother's womb, but by the splitting open through Lucina's agency of the tree into which his mother had been metamorphosed.[7] Incest and a kind of posthumous caesarean section — a bizarre birth like that of Marvell's 'Unfortunate Lover' — initiate the reader into a world of 'unnatural' swervings of gender and generation.

Ovid's story of Venus and Adonis is narrated by Orpheus as part of his long lament to the trees and wild animals after his loss of Eurydice. The Orphic section of the *Metamorphoses* begins with a series of tales of homosexual love. Orpheus says that after losing his Eurydice he shunned all love of woman and turned to boys instead:

> And *Orphye* [. . .] did utterly eschew
> The womankynd. [. . .]
> He also taught the *Thracian* folke a stewes of Males too make
> And of the flowring pryme of boayes the pleasure for too take.
>
> (x. 87–92)

Orpheus is the patron saint of homosexuality, or, more precisely, of pederasty. Among the trees to which he sings is the cypress, etiologized as the metamorphosed form of a boy loved by Apollo, Cyparissus, who erroneously killed a tame stag whom he loved and consequently resolved to die himself, asking as a last boon that he should be allowed to mourn for ever. He is thus 'sad cypress' — there is a resonance forward in Shakespeare's career, to the figuration of love's sorrows in *Twelfth Night*, where, as with Ovid's Orphic narration, the context is homoerotic, Orsino's desire for Cesario echoing Apollo's for Cyparissus. More locally, there is a prefiguration of and

[5] See, for example, the strong rhetorically-orientated reading of the poem by Heather Dubrow in her *Captive Victors: Shakespeare's Narrative Poems and Sonnets* (Ithaca, NY: Cornell University Press, 1987).
[6] *The XV Bookes of P. Ovidius Naso, entytuled Metamorphosis, translated oute of Latin into English meeter, by Arthur Golding Gentleman* (London, 1567), quoted from *Shakespeare's Ovid: being Arthur Golding's Translation of the Metamorphoses*, ed. by W. H. D. Rouse (London: Centaur Press, 1961), x. 577.
[7] Should we think forward to Ariel's re-birth from a tree through Prospero's agency in *The Tempest* and thence to the other strange re-births of that play, such as Prospero's extraordinary image of his own labour on the sea-voyage?

variation on Adonis: both boys are loved by gods, while one slays and the other is slain by accident.

Cyparissus homoeroticizes the audience of Orpheus. The singer himself then picks up the motif: he tells of Ganymede, loved by Jove (and impersonated, we may add, by the gender-bending Rosalind in *As You Like It*), then of Hyacinth, loved by Apollo. The latter is a second prefiguration of Adonis, in that he loves hunting. He is inadvertently killed by Apollo's discus while sporting with him; the flower that grows from his blood has Apollo's lament ('AI AI') inscribed upon it — as with Venus and Adonis, the story ends with the creation from the beloved boy's blood of a plant that is also a signifier of grief. George Sandys's commentary speaks of 'an afflicted ingemination, charactred in the leaves', a phrase nicely catching the two key elements which the story shares with that of Adonis: floral inscription and repetition (the story is retold with each year's new growth).[8] Having argued that homoerotic desire is licensed by the fact that the gods practised it, Orpheus then turns to some examples of real perversion: the Propoetides, the first prostitutes; Pygmalion, who makes love to his statue; and Myrrha, who falls in love with her father.

Elizabethan and Jacobean interest in perverse sexuality found a strong focus in Book x of the *Metamorphoses*, as may be seen from Marston's *Metamorphosis of Pigmalions Image* (1598) and William Barksted's *Myrrha, the Mother of Adonis; or Lustes Prodegies* (1607). The final act of *The Winter's Tale* is exceptional in its way of reworking the Pygmalion story without any implication of perversity or, in Paulina's term, unlawfulness. The traditional moralization of Book x is summarized by Golding in the epistle prefixed to his 1567 translation:

> The tenth booke cheefly dooth containe one kynd of argument,
> Reproving most prodigious lusts of such as have bene bent
> Too incest most unnaturall.
>
> (Epistle, l. 213)

But the intentions of Ovid's Orpheus are not quite this simple: he sings with a lighter touch ('leviore lyra')[9] of the delights as well as the dire consequences of sexuality. And insofar as Orpheus's songs are an apology for homoeroticism, the moralizing Golding is forced to read the text against the grain.

Even in the case of incest, Ovid is more interested in exploring the lover's mental state than condemning her. Myrrha may resort to a bestial comparison ('animals commit incest, so why shouldn't humans?'), but she is revealed to be a tortured victim of desire, as she lies restlessly at night:

---

[8] Sandy's *Ovids Metamorphosis Englished, Mythologiz'd, and Represented in Figures* (Oxford, 1632), p. 359.
[9] *Metamorphoses*, x. 152. Latin quotations are from the Loeb edn. (London: Heinemann, 1916, repr. 1976).

Shee wisshes and shee wotes not what too doo, nor how too gin.
And like as when a mightye tree with axes heawed rownd,
Now reedye with a strype or twaine to lye uppon the grownd,
Uncerteine is which way to fall and tottreth every way:
Even so her mynd with dowtfull wound enffeebled then did stray
Now heere now there uncerteinely, and tooke of both encreace.

(x. 419)

This kind of representation of the mind under the stress of conflicting emotions is Ovid's prime gift to the Elizabethan narrative poets. Like their master, Marlowe and Shakespeare as poets are psychopathologists rather than moralists.

As so often in the *Metamorphoses*, a festival in honour of a god provides the occasion for resolution of the Myrrha story; rather as the 'holiday' moment in Shakespearean comedy precipitates transformative action, the festival's interruption of the quotidian provides the impulse which causes the tottering tree to fall. With characteristic Ovidian irony, the festival in question is that of Ceres, goddess of fertility — in these circumstances, foison is the last thing Myrrha needs. Sandys's commentary reminds the Renaissance reader of the distance between Myrrha and Ceres, to whose worship 'none were admitted that were either uncleane, or whose consciences accused them of any secret crime' (p. 363). Cinyras's wife goes off to celebrate this distinctively female festival, leaving him alone in his bed for nine nights; a nurse offers to provide him with comfort in the form of a girl who loves him. She gives a false name, but says that the 'pretye lasse' is Myrrha's age; she escorts her to the bedroom in the dark and father makes love to daughter, ignorant of her identity. Ovid observes the behaviour of the lovers with his usual perspicuity and irony: 'by chaunce as in respect of yeeres | He daughter did hir call, and shee him father' (x. 536–37). The encounter ends with his 'cursed seede in [her] wicked womb' (l. 538). Adonis is the fruit of that seed.

The Venus and Adonis story must be seen in the broader context of this series of narratives concerning destructive passion, female desire — Book x teems with aggressive female wooers — and homoerotic charm. Venus the lover is also Venus the mother: 'hot, faint, and weary with her hard embracing [. . .] like the froward infant stilled with dandling, | He now obeys' (ll. 559–63); 'Like a milch doe whose dwelling dugs do ache, | Hasting to feed her fawn hid in some brake' (ll. 875–76). Such juxtapositions of sexuality and parenting suggest that Adonis is forced to re-enact, with gender and generational roles reversed, his mother's incestuous affair.

The contextual pressure of Myrrha is signalled by Shakespeare's two explicit allusions to Adonis's mother. As part of her argument that the lovely boy should accept love, Venus says:

Art thou obdurate, flinty, hard as steel?
Nay, more than flint, for stone at rain relenteth.
Art thou a woman's son, and canst not feel
What 'tis to love, how want of love tormenteth?

> O, had thy mother borne so hard a mind,
> She had not brought forth thee, but died unkind.
>
> (l. 199)

She suggests that he somehow owes it to his mother's experience of love to love himself. In the light of Book x, it is a richly ironic suggestion: Myrrha found that love 'tormented' as much as — more than — 'want of love' did. The 'mind' that she bore was hardly exemplary; the child 'brought forth' by her, the fruit of incest, would have been better unborn. She would have 'died unkind' if she hadn't loved a man and thus borne a child, says Venus — but it would have been better if she had died untouched by her own kind, her kin. In the incestuous bed she was a little more than kin and more than kind. As for Venus's phrase 'died unkind', ironically it was only in death that Myrrha achieved a kind of kindness or softness. She is metamorphosed into the 'weeping' myrrh tree, oozing drops that signify her repentance.

Later, Venus addresses the sun: 'There lives a son [i.e. Adonis] that sucked an earthly mother | May lend thee light, as thou dost lend to other' (ll. 863–64). The sun/son pun invokes Adonis's mother for a second time. Again the irony rebounds on Venus: Myrrha never did suckle Adonis, since he was born from the tree after her death. Instead, Venus herself eventually becomes a surrogate mother, suckling Adonis — she ends the poem with his flower in her breast, imaged as the 'cradle' in which she 'rock[s]' him (ll. 1185–86). Adonis's life begins with a father and daughter in bed together, and ends with sexual desire for him being sublimated into an image of a mother by the bed of her baby son. For Ovid, Venus's love for Adonis is the direct consequence of Myrrha's illicit desire: 'Dame *Venus* fell in love with him: wherby | He did revenge the outrage of his mothers villanye' (x.604–05). Venus is held responsible for Myrrha's love, since she is the goddess of love, even in its illicit forms, and she is punished by being smitten with unrequited love herself.

The Myrrha story, then, provides an ironizing, darkening pre-text for the tale of Venus and Adonis, which points to the perverse origins of desire. A second parallel narrative occupies a position as what might be called an *in-text*. When Ovid's Venus advises Adonis not to hunt the boar, she tells a story to support her case. Embedded within Orpheus's tale of Venus and Adonis is Venus's tale of Atalanta, a girl who has been told by an oracle that if she takes a husband she will die. Being a fast runner, she repels her suitors by saying that they must race her: if they win she will be the prize, if they lose they will die. The youthful Hippomenes initially scorns men who are willing to risk their lives in a race for a girl, but when Atalanta strips off to run, he is won over by her beauty, 'the which was like too myne, | Or rather (if that thou wert made a woman) like too thyne' (x.674–75) explains Venus, taking the opportunity to dwell on Adonis's female charm, which is further echoed in Hippomenes's 'maydens countenance' (l. 742). Atalanta promptly falls in love herself: suddenly she is uncertain whether she wants to win or lose this race. Golding's translation is flat-footed at this point; a modern version catches more concisely Ovid's exquisite account of Atalanta's attempt to rationalize her faltering:

> It's not his beauty
> That touches me (though that could touch me too);
> But he is still a boy; it's not himself
> That moves me but his tender years, his youth.
> Think of his courage, unafraid of death.[10]

The parenthesis is a wonderfully revealing moment. His beauty has of course touched her. As with Myrrha, the mind is pulled in conflicting directions, love induces weakness, and then a disastrous mistake is made: the oracle is disregarded.

Hippomenes, being in love, invokes the assistance of the love-god Venus. She assists him by throwing three golden apples at strategic moments during the race, causing Atalanta to go off course and pick them up. Hippomenes thus wins both the race and her. Venus points the moral:

> Thinkst thou I was not woorthy thanks, *Adonis*, thinkest thow
> I earned not that he too mee should frankincense allow?
> But he forgetfull, neyther thanks nor frankincense did give.
> By meanes wherof too sooden wrath he justly did me drive.

(x. 798)

She accordingly turns against the young lovers, determining to have her revenge and make an example of them. She inflames them with sexual desire while they are in the temple of Cybele; they defile it by making love there, and Cybele transforms them into lions.

Ostensibly, Venus tells Adonis this story in order to persuade him not to go hunting dangerous beasts like lions and boars. But it's not really a tale warning against wild animals; it is Venus saying 'don't rile me', 'do as I say, I'm a powerful woman'. The key moment is the one where she addresses Adonis directly, demanding that he assent to her claim that she deserved a thank-offering and was justified in taking revenge when not given one. She tells the story to demonstrate her power. But the song is still that of Orpheus — it is a narrative within a narrative, creating the kind of multiple perspective allowed for by the Shakespearean play within a play. For Orpheus, the story is another warning against love: Atalanta submitted to desire and no good came of it. So Venus is saying to Adonis 'do not resist love', while simultaneously Orpheus is saying to his audience 'resist love'. The Orphic context undercuts Venus's rhetoric. The story is being *used* by both characters; narratives about love, Ovid seems to be saying, are never disinterested. The narrator always has ulterior motives, is always driven by his or her own desires.

---

[10] *Metamorphoses*, x. 614–16, trans. by A. D. Melville, Worlds Classics (Oxford: Oxford University Press, 1987).

I have described the embedded Atalanta narrative at some length because of a striking fact about the structure of Ovid's Venus and Adonis. Forty lines are devoted to Venus falling in love with Adonis, then one hundred and forty-seven lines to Venus telling her admonitory tale, and finally thirty-two to Venus's departure and Adonis's being gored by the boar and metamorphosed. The discourse of Venus thus occupies twice as much space as the story's action. The narrative of Atalanta fulfils the role in Ovid that Venus's rhetorical persuasions to love do in Shakespeare. Shakespeare's Venusian discourse — the traditional *carpe diem* arguments of the male lover put into the mouth of the aggressive female wooer — is engendered by Adonis's active resistance to love, a resistance which is the major alteration to the source (Ovid's Adonis likes hunting, but does not object to love on principle as Shakespeare's does). Like all good imitators, Shakespeare enters into the same arena as his model, but does his own turn there. His version is very much his own, as Ovid's is his (the *Metamorphoses* do not lean particularly on the older versions of the Venus and Adonis story, such as that of Theocritus). In Ovid, Atalanta goes against the advice of the oracle in falling for Hippomenes; in Shakespeare, Adonis goes against the advice of Venus in hunting the boar. Atalanta's death results from the way that she does not resist love, Adonis's from the way that he does resist it. Put the two stories together and one reaches the irresistible conclusion that whichever way you turn love will destroy you. It is essentially something out of your control, a force that drives you rather than vice versa.

In both Ovid and Shakespeare the story ends with the death of Adonis, described as a pattern which will be repeated perpetually. This sense of inevitable future repetition is what gives the story its mythic, archetypal quality. In Ovid, Venus creates a flower (the anemone) from Adonis's blood as a 'resemblance' (l. 848) of her suffering. The passing of the seasons will be a figuration of love's sorrows; the flower symbolizes the transience of beauty. *Venus and Adonis* moves towards an etiology of love's anguish: 'Since thou art dead, lo, here I prophesy | Sorrow on love hereafter shall attend' (ll. 1135–36). Ovid closes Book x with an image of the flower blasted by the wind and shed all too soon; so too, according to Shakespeare's Venus, love will 'bud, and be blasted, in a breathing-while' (l. 1142). Adonis's flower is the purple of the blood from which it springs, the colour a reminder of the violence and death that will attend on love. Venus then plucks it: 'She crops the stalk, and in the breach appears | Green-dropping sap, which she compares to tears' (ll. 1175–76). This comparison between liquid drops falling from vegetable matter and tears reintroduces Myrrha, whose guilt and sorrow are symbolized by the gum that drops from the Arabian tree into which she is metamorphosed. '"Poor Flower," quoth [Venus], "this was thy father's guise — | Sweet issue of a more sweet-smelling sire"' (ll. 1177–78). It is a brilliant variation: where Ovid begins his tale with Adonis as a son issuing from a tree, Shakespeare ends his with a flower issuing from Adonis, who thus becomes a father. Shakespeare's Venus acts out an extraordinary family romance. By imaging her lover as a father, she makes herself into the mother and the flower into the fruit of their union. But the logic of the imagery dictates that the flower is her sexual partner as well as her child, for it clearly substitutes for Adonis himself — she comforts herself with the thought that it is a love-token, which she can continually kiss. The fusion of lover and mother in the context of vegetative imagery makes Venus into Myrrha once again. It is as if, having slept with her father, the girl is now sleeping with her son.

In the next and last stanza, Venus flies off to Paphos, the site of her principal temple on Cyprus. The naming of the place takes the mythologically literate reader back to Orpheus's narrative in Book x, for Cyprus is the location of the stories of the Propoetides, Pygmalion, and Myrrha, the figures associated with Venus and with the rapacious female sexuality that Orpheus uses to justify his misogyny. Ovid explicitly states that the name Paphos derives from the child of the union between Pygmalion and his statue; Paphos in turn produces Cinyras, who, thanks to the incestuous union with Myrrha, is both father and grandfather of Adonis. Golding and Sandys took Paphos to be a boy ('a Sun that Paphus hyght', Golding, x. 323), presumably because they read 'quo' as ablative masculine in Ovid's line 'Illa Paphon genuit; de quo tenet insula nomen' (x. 297: 'she [the statue] bore Paphos, from whom the island takes its name'), but the next line makes the child feminine: 'Editus hac ille est' ('he [Cinyras] was borne by *her*'). Ovid *could* be deliberately confusing the gender — that would be in accordance with the sexual ambiguity of Book x — but it is more likely that 'quo' is a manuscript error for 'qua' and a girl is intended. The Renaissance, however, stuck to the masculinized name Paphus: Marston ends his *Metamorphosis of Pigmalions Image* with the lines: 'Paphus was got: of whom in after age | Cyprus was Paphos call'd, and evermore | Those Ilandars do Venus name adore.'[11] Whatever the gender, the identification of Venus with Paphos further embroils her in the incest plot.

If we are alert to the signals in *Venus and Adonis* that activate the other parts of Book x of the *Metamorphoses*, it becomes much clearer that this is a poem about transgressive sexuality. And since it is supposed to be an etiology of sexual love — the goddess of love's own experience of desire sets the tone for everybody else's — there is a strong implication that sexual love is always at some level transgressive. The broader Ovidian context reveals two persistent characteristics of sexual desire: it is bound up first with the polymorphous perversity of family romance and second with a dissolution of the conventional barriers of gender, for in these stories women take the active role usually given to men and young men always look like girls. The first

---

[11] Stanza 39, in *Elizabethan Minor Epics*, ed. by Elizabeth Story Donno (NY: Columbia University Press, 1963).

characteristic is an essentially destructive one, associated above all with the Myrrha pre-text. The second, which is partly a function of Orpheus's conversion to homosexuality, is also potentially destructive, as may be seen from the fate of the singer at the beginning of Book XI. Orpheus's narratives may charm rocks and trees and birds, but they cut no ice with a horde of Thracian women who descend on him in bacchic fury and tear him to pieces in punishment for his attitude to their sex.

The girlish-boy motif also takes the reader to other parts of the *Metamorphoses*. Adonis is one of Ovid's many beautiful young men on the threshold of sexual maturity; like the sixteen-year-old Narcissus, 'he seemde to stand beetwene the state of man and Lad' (III. 438). Venus herself makes the link, first in her persuasion to love — 'Is thine own heart to thine own face affected? [...] Narcissus so himself himself forsook, | And died to kiss his shadow in the brook' (ll. 157–62) — and again in her final lament to the flower, 'To grow unto himself was his desire' (l. 1180). Coppélia Kahn sees this association as the key to the poem: 'In Adonis, Shakespeare depicts not only a narcissistic character for whom eros is a threat to the self, but also a boy who regards women as a threat to his masculinity. But the real threat is internal, and comes from this very urge to defend against eros.'[12] Narcissism, then, is another aspect of destructive sexuality in *Venus and Adonis*. What is it that the lover desires? If not her parent, like Myrrha, then himself, like Narcissus — it is not a happy prognosis.

But Echo never gets near Narcissus; the physical interplay between a desiring female and a resistant male, the poem's body-contact, derives from neither the tale of Adonis nor that of Narcissus but another Ovidian narrative, that of Salmacis and Hermaphroditus.[13] Golding moralized the fate of Hermaphroditus as a warning against effeminacy (Epistle, l. 116), but Shakespeare, I would suggest, read it very differently. If the perverse, quasi-incestuous aspects of *Venus and Adonis* are derived primarily from Book x of the *Metamorphoses* and the self-consuming absorption of Adonis from Narcissus, the poem's playfulness and delicate eroticism, its enjoyment of sexuality and the dissolution of gender barriers, owe much to the Hermaphroditus tale in Book IV.

The nymph Salmacis's wooing of the coy youth Hermaphroditus is a bravura performance, in which the norms of seduction poetry are systematically reversed. It is the boy who blushes and looks more sexually desirable as a result, the boy who has a perfectly-formed body resembling a work of art (swimming in the translucent water, he looks like an ivory figure encased in glass), the girl who hides in a bush and watches the object of desire undress

[12] *Man's Estate: Masculine Identity in Shakespeare* (Berkeley and Los Angeles: California University Press, 1981), p. 33.
[13] This story has long been recognized as a supplementary source for *Venus and Adonis*: see, for example, Geoffrey Bullough, *Narrative and Dramatic Sources of Shakespeare*, vol. 1 (London: Routledge, 1957, repr. 1966), pp. 161–63.

to bathe. Both Ovid and the Elizabethans usually give the male reader the pleasure of a prurient gaze on the gradual stripping of Diana, Arethusa, and the rest; but here the tease is for the benefit of the reader (male or female) who likes fresh-limbed boys:

> and by and by amid
> The flattring waves he dippes his feete, no more but first the sole
> And to the ancles afterward both feete he plungeth whole.
> And for to make the matter short, he tooke so great delight
> In coolenes of the pleasant spring, that streight he stripped quight
> His garments from his tender skin.
>
> (IV. 421)

And in the scene of aquatic love-making, it is the male breast that is reached for: 'And willde he nillde he with hir handes she toucht his naked brest' (l. 446), the female who presses down 'with all hir weight' (l. 458). Salmacis ultimately achieves total intercourse with her object of desire (notice how the force which effects the union is 'hir hugging and hir grasping'):

> The bodies of them twaine
> Were mixt and joyned both in one. To both them did remaine
> One countnance. Like as if a man should in one barke beholde
> Two twigges both growing into one and still togither holde:
> Even so when through hir hugging and hir grasping of the tother
> The members of them mingled were and fastned both togither,
> They were not any lenger two: but (as it were) a toy
> Of double shape: Ye could not say it was a perfect boy,
> Nor perfect wench: it seemed both and none of both to beene.
>
> (IV. 462)

At one level the story is meant as an etiology of the Hermaphrodite. Hermaphroditus gets the last word — just as he, not Salmacis, keeps his name — and the final image is of enfeeblement, of the waters in which the union took place having the power to convert a man into a half-man ('semivir', IV. 386). This is the basis of Golding's moralization in terms of effeminacy. The description of interpenetration, however, with its wonder-filled sense of total coition, suggests not halving of strength but doubling of perfection. As so frequently in Ovid, the moment of wild passion paradoxically seems to outlast the subsequent stasis. This, we feel, is an image of how sex should be.

So it was that the Renaissance did not always read the hermaphrodite as a transgressive abomination. An alternative interpretation made it into an image of the complete union and interpenetration that Donne strives for in 'The Extasie': 'the *form* of the hermaphrodite was uniquely that of perfect love because it alone imaged that mystical union wherein the two sexes became one self-sufficient sex that contains both'.[14] The paradox of the

---

[14] A. R. Cirillo, 'The Fair Hermaphrodite: Love-Union in the Poetry of Donne and Spenser', *SEL*, 9 (1969), 81–95 (p. 94). Cirillo here cites Benedetto Varchi, *Lezzioni* (Venice, 1561). For a more complex and less affirmative reading of the hermaphrodite in *The Faerie Queene*, see Lauren Silberman, 'The Hermaphrodite and the Metamorphosis of Spenserian Allegory', *ELR*, 17 (1987), 207–23.

hermaphrodite is even more condensed than Stephen Greenblatt supposes: in his essay 'Fiction and Friction', he argues that the discourses of hermaphroditism and 'normal sexuality' are 'the same discourse, for the knowledge that enables one to understand the monstrous conjunction in one individual of the male and female sexes is the identical knowledge that enables one to understand the normal experience of sexual pleasure';[15] Greenblatt's sense of 'identical' depends on the Foucauldian notion of discourses containing their own opposites, whereas in the positive Renaissance reading of Ovid the figure of the hermaphrodite is more directly, indeed is precisely, an image of the normal experience of sexual pleasure. Spenser used the figure thus when describing the passionate union of Amoret and Scudamour in the 1590 ending of *The Faerie Queene*:

> No word they spake, nor earthly thing they felt,
> But like two senceles stocks in long embracement dwelt.
> Had ye them seene, ye would have surely thought,
> That they had beene that faire *Hermaphrodite*.[16]

It is, I think, highly significant that the story which provides the ideal image of union between a man and a woman is one in which the initial desire for that union stems from the woman. Women in both Ovidian and Elizabethan poetry usually have to be seduced and hence to some degree coerced — the dividing-line between the verbal coercion of rhetoric and the physical one of rape is thin, as Shakespeare shows in *The Rape of Lucrece* and the Countess of Salisbury scenes in *Edward III*. Salmacis and Hermaphroditus is a rare example of a union that is not tainted by the exercising of male power.

'How does all this relate to *Venus and Adonis*?', it will be asked. Surely the point there is that coitus is not achieved. Granted, Shakespeare derives the style of Adonis's behaviour from Hermaphroditus and the 'woman on top' position from Salmacis, but there the resemblance ends. The nymph's love for her boy is never aggressive to the point of grotesquerie, as the goddess's is in, for example, the stanza concerning her kisses:

> Even as an empty eagle, sharp by fast,
> Tires with her beak on feathers, flesh, and bone,
> Shaking her wings, devouring all in haste
> Till either gorge be stuffed or prey be gone,
>> Even so she kissed his brow, his cheek, his chin,
>> And where she ends doth anew begin.

(l. 55)

But perhaps the difference is the point. The resemblance of Adonis to Hermaphroditus is denoted by his beauty, his blushing, and his petulance. The reader who recognizes those marks will perceive Adonis's *potential* to participate in an ideal Salmacian/Hermaphroditic union. But such a union

---

[15] *Shakespearean Negotiations* (Oxford: Clarendon Press, 1988), p. 77.
[16] *The Faerie Queene*, III, 12, stanzas 45–46, in the 1590 edn, quoted from the edn by A. C. Hamilton (London: Longmans, 1977). The 'two stocks' recall Ovid's image of the two twigs growing into one.

never takes place — coitus only occurs in the form of perverted, parodic variations, as Adonis is nuzzled by the boar[17] and Venus cradles the flower — because the partners are not equals. An oppressive power-relation has to exist: after all, this is a goddess dealing with a mortal. Shakespeare has some fun inverting the traditional power structure — Venus's problem is that she can't actually rape Adonis, as Jove rapes Danaë, Neptune Theophane, and Apollo Isse — but in the end the poem shows that a sexual relationship based on coercion is doomed. The inequality is highlighted by the difference in age of the two characters; one function of the allusions to Adonis's mother is to suggest that the sexual dealings of partners of greatly unequal age are bound at some level to replicate the archetypal relationship based on an unequal power-structure, incest between a parent and a child.

Venus and Adonis is a disturbing poem in that perversity takes the place of the unfulfilled Salmacian/Hermaphroditic potential. But stylistically it is a poem that bubbles along in the manner more of the story it is not telling than of the one that it is. Of the later poems in the genre, the one that is closest to it is not Barksted's prurient *Myrrha, the Mother of Adonis; or Lustes Prodegies*, but Beaumont's glittering *Salmacis and Hermaphroditus*, a narrative full of youthful energy and unabashed sexuality, of 'lovers sweet delight'.[18] Salmacis and Hermaphroditus achieve oneness because they are of the same age and the same kind (a naiad and a boy who has been nursed by naiads), as well as because the girl has attributes that are traditionally seen as male and the boy ones that are traditionally female. Their union is an enduring reminder of the creative potential of sexuality. By incorporating the tone of their tale, its lightness of touch and its delight in the charm of androgyny, Shakespeare makes his poem into a celebration of sexuality even as it is a disturbing exposure of the dark underside of desire.

---

[17] The image of the boar kissing Adonis (l. 1114) is traditional to the story (it is to be found in Theocritus, a Latin epigram by Minturno, and elsewhere — see Douglas Bush, *Mythology and the Renaissance Tradition* (New York: Norton, 1963), p. 140n.), but in Shakespeare it adds to the flavour of perverse, violent sexuality. Ovid's Calydonian boar also lies behind some of the details of the Shakespearean hunt.

[18] *Salmacis and Hermaphroditus* (1602, attributed to Beaumont in edn. of 1640), line 254, quoted from *Elizabethan Minor Epics*.

'Silence, like a Lucrece knife': Shakespeare and the Meanings of Rape

CAROLYN D. WILLIAMS

University of Reading

Brief allusions to rape occur throughout Shakespeare's work, combining maximum effect with minimum critical perturbation. Issues often appear reassuringly simple: Macbeth's vision of 'wither'd murder' (II. 1. 52) stealing with 'Tarquin's ravishing strides' (l. 55) depicts rape as an act of unmitigated evil, inflicting irreversible damage on helpless innocence; *The Tempest* offers no reason for the audience to wish Caliban's attempt on Miranda had succeeded. Complexities are also part of the act; when Henry V threatens the maidens of Harfleur with 'hot and forcing violation' (III. 3. 21), his speech may sound like fair warning from a just prince or a reminder of the moral degradation war can inflict on victors; either way, Shakespeare is in charge. Titania's hint to Bottom that the flowers are 'lamenting some enforced chastity' (*A Midsummer Night's Dream*, III. 1. 209) strikes a subtler chord. Sexual aggressors posing as defenceless targets cut a comic figure, yet Titania retains a half-contemptuous, half-sympathetic awareness that in some quarters, rape is a serious matter. These are still Shakespeare's ironies. He even copes elegantly with non-events, making it clear that Helen's 'fair rape' (*Troilus and Cressida*, II. 2. 148) is only seduction.

Shakespeare's detailed treatments of rape are less satisfactory. Responses to *The Rape of Lucrece* and *Titus Andronicus* suggest he has failed to take intellectual and artistic control. Titus's daughter Lavinia is raped by Demetrius and Chiron, who cut off her hands and tongue, then subject her to a barrage of sick humour. Titus avenges this and other atrocities by killing the rapists and serving their flesh to their mother, Tamora, and stepfather, the Emperor Saturninus, in a pie. During the table-talk, Titus elicits from Saturninus the opinion that a father is justified in killing his ravished daughter. Titus thereupon kills Lavinia; the play moves swiftly to its close with the deaths of Tamora, Titus, and Saturninus, and the election of Lucius Andronicus as Emperor of Rome. Lavinia's prolonged sufferings and perfunctory death make an uncomfortable spectacle. Rather than contemplating Lavinia herself, critics and directors prefer to make her a symbol of 'the destruction of the Roman political order'.[1] With *Lucrece*, Shakespeare's own vision seems to falter; it gives Ian Donaldson 'a sense — so rare in

---

[1] William Shakespeare, *Titus Andronicus*, ed. by E. M. Waith (Oxford: Oxford University Press, 1984), p. 36.

Shakespeare's work as to be doubly remarkable — that the central moral complexities of the story are in some ways curiously evaded, while the simpler outlying issues are decoratively elaborated'.[2] Certain key questions are traditionally raised by Lucrece's dilemma, concerning the nature of her consent and the ethical implications of her suicide. Shakespeare seems unwilling to concentrate on providing answers. C. Knox Pooler charitably detects 'a determination to leave nothing of the truth untold'.[3] Yet apparently peripheral matters may be central to Shakespeare's perception of his subject. Better understanding of *Lucrece* and *Titus Andronicus* can be achieved with clearer recognition of the 'truth' Shakespeare tries to tell.

The cases of Lavinia and Lucrece will be examined in the light of Renaissance ideas about rape. Evidence is drawn from poetry, drama, religious and legal writings; legal practice; and modern theories on rape which make explicit assumptions that Shakespeare and his contemporaries apparently take for granted. All this material, particularly the last, must be used with extreme caution; as Roy Porter observes, rape 'is a subject fiendishly difficult to research and interpret'.[4] Two related concepts emerge from this examination: rape as a process that suppresses or invalidates female utterance; and the violated, silenced female body as a middle term in a transaction between men. No definitive solution to all the problems raised by *Lucrece* and *Titus Andronicus* can be expected; by present-day standards, some aspects of Shakespeare's thinking are irredeemably confused. But at least the origins of that confusion can be understood.

I   *Her chaste and honest hart*

The early modern rape victim faces, in their acutest form, the contradictions in the position of all women in her society. She is a man's possession, yet a responsible human agent. Her chief duty is to subordinate her will to her master's. Lavinia is exemplary, unprotestingly obedient when her father arranges for her to marry Saturninus, despite her prior betrothal to Bassianus. Lucrece calls neither body nor soul her own: 'both were kept for heaven and Collatine' (l. 1166). Rape is consequently a crime against property and an offence against the person.

The former view typifies the values of a 'shame' culture, the latter those of a 'guilt' culture. 'Shame' and 'guilt' are diametrically opposed in the importance they attribute to the victim's statements. By the 'shame' code, her refusal of consent, whether indicated by protests and struggles during the rape, or story afterwards, is irrelevant; her physical condition determines her status. She is a contaminant to her entire family; if she cannot be married

---

[2] *The Rapes of Lucretia: A Myth and its Transformations* (Oxford: Oxford University Press, 1982), p. 40.
[3] William Shakespeare, *Poems*, ed. by C. Knox Pooler (London: Methuen, 1911), p. xlvii.
[4] Roy Porter, 'Rape — Does it Have a Historical Meaning?' in *Rape: An Historical and Cultural Enquiry*, ed. by Sylvana Tomaselli and Roy Porter (Oxford: Blackwell, 1989), pp. 216–36 (p. 216).

to her ravisher, she must be segregated from former contacts. In ancient Rome, such pollution — whether incurred by rape or adultery — could be removed only by death. Any public announcement of her plight increases her humiliation; her acknowledged violation may also cast doubt on her veracity.[5] Rape either gags her or robs her words of significance. 'Guilt' standards, however, focus attention on the victim's mind. Her utterance is crucially important. Lack of consent defines the rape; the law on consenting under-age girls is the exception that proves the rule, for consent is not theirs to give. Her ability to tell her story afterwards vindicates her honour. But if she *does* consent, the pangs of tormented conscience exacerbate her open shame.

In his analysis of *Lucrece*, Donaldson associates 'shame' and 'guilt' with Roman and Christian standards respectively, complaining of Shakespeare's 'wavering between different criteria for judgement' (p. 44). Norman Bryson finds this enriching rather than obfuscating:

In Renaissance terms, Lucretia is a *topos* interesting because it brings together pagan and Christian frameworks, and the issue is whether or not she is to be admired, or whether a Christian or pagan view should be taken of her case. Shakespeare consciously alternates these frameworks.[6]

While this is true to a great extent, much of the contradictoriness in Shakespeare's treatment of Lucrece, and Lavinia too, can be accounted for by the incompatibilities — all the more damaging when not explicitly acknowledged — of 'shame' and 'guilt' values operating simultaneously in early modern Britain; this double standard can also be seen at work in earlier texts which profoundly influenced Shakespeare's culture.

Deuteronomy 22 juxtaposes 'guilt' with 'shame' by first correlating the victim's innocence with her inaudibility, then indicating drastic impairment of her eligibility and cash value. Furthermore, comparison of an innocent victim to a murdered man indicates the finality with which she is cut off from normal life within her community. Even more ambiguity appears in the 1597 Geneva Bible, where two marginal notes (italicized and bracketed in the following quotation) increase the tension between 'shame' and 'guilt':

23   If a maid be betrothed unto an husband, and a man find her in the towne and lie with her,
24   Then shall ye bring them both out unto the gates of the same citie, and shall stone them with stones to death: the mayde because she cried not, *being* in the citie, and the man, because hee hath humbled (*Or, defiled*) his neighbours wife: so thou shalt put away evil from among you.
25   But if a man find a betrothed maid in the field, and force her, and lie with her, then the man that lay with her, shall die alone:

[5] Donaldson, p. 24. Anna Clark, *Women's Silence, Men's Violence: Sexual Assault in England 1770–1845* (London: Pandora, 1987), p. 47.
[6] Norman Bryson, 'Two Narratives of Rape in the Visual Arts: Lucretia and the Sabine Women', in *Rape: An Historical and Cultural Enquiry*, pp. 152–73 (p. 171).

26   And unto the maid thou shalt doe nothing, because there is in the mayde no cause of death: (*Or, no sinne worthie death*) for as when a man riseth against his neighbour and woundeth him to death, so is this matter.

27   For he found her in the fields: the betrothed maid cried, and there was no man to succour her.

28   If a man find a maid that is not betrothed, and take her, and lie with her, and they be found,

29   Then the man that lay with her, shall give unto the maides father fiftie *shekels* of silver: and she shall be his wife, because he hath humbled her: hee cannot put her away all his life.

In the first instance, changing 'humbled' to '*defiled*' would move towards 'shame', by substituting physical effect for emotional response; in the second, '*sinne worthie death*' would stress 'guilt' values by emphasizing the victim's moral purity.

The two classical sources which Shakespeare used for *Lucrece* are Ovid's *Fasti*, ii. 721–852 and Livy's *Ab Urbe Condita*, i.lvii–lx. Both counterpoint 'guilt' and 'shame' by stating Lucretia's essential innocence, while presenting her suicide as none the less admirable. Her husband Collatinus and father Lucretius exonerate her completely, and Lucretia herself distinguishes between spiritual guilt and physical pollution, yet she cannot demonstrate this split to her own satisfaction without cutting her soul free from her tainted body. William Painter translates as follows in *The Pallace of Pleasure* (1566): 'But it is my body only that is violated, my minde God knoweth is guiltles, whereof my death shalbe witnesse.'[7] Political considerations predetermine Lucretia's death: her martyrdom legitimizes the expulsion of the Tarquins and the foundation of the Roman Republic. If her predicament is considered realistically, however, one suspects that the sorrow of Collatinus and Lucretius might be tempered by relief that she has done the decent thing.

Lucretia's case is complicated by the fact that she yielded Tarquin a measure of consent: technically, she is an adultress. According to Livy, Tarquin said 'that he would kill her, and when she was slain, he woulde also kill his slave, and place him by her, that it might be reported howe she was slaine, being taken in adulterie'. Depiction of her response varies, but all agree he had his way. Livy suggests she incurred some guilt, but in overwhelmingly mitigating circumstances: 'She vanquished with his terrible and infamous threate, his fleshlye and licentious enterprice overcame the puritie of her chaste and honest hart, which done he departed.'[8] Ovid just says 'succubuit famae victa puella metu' ('the girl yielded, overcome by fear of scandal') (*Fasti*, ii. 810).[9] Shakespeare, possibly apprehensive that deliberate compliance, if depicted in his slow-motion technique, would appear

---

[7] *Narrative and Dramatic Sources of Shakespeare*, ed. by Geoffrey Bullough, 6 vols (London: Routledge, 1958–66), i, 198.

[8] Bullough, i, 198.

[9] Ovid, *Fasti*, ed. and trans. by J. G. Frazer, Loeb Classical Library (London: Heinemann, 1989).

indefensible, makes Lucrece resist to the last. She screams until Tarquin gags her with her nightgown: 'With her own white fleece her voice controll'd | Entombs her outcry in her lips' sweet fold' (ll. 678–79). Later, however, she expresses remorse for guilty complicity: 'I fear'd by Tarquin's falchion to be slain' (l. 1046). Shakespeare then offers a compromise solution: Tarquin's threat weakened her resistance by paralysing her with terror (ll. 1265–67). She finally presents this version of events to Collatine and Lucretius: 'Mine enemy was strong, my poor self weak, | And far the weaker with so strong a fear' (ll. 1646–47).

To Christian readers, the classical Lucretia must always be a woman who 'valued her Virtue more than her Life; but her Reputation more than her Virtue'.[10] In Roman terms, this ordering of priorities might itself be virtuous: Norman Bryson shows how her 'concern for reputation' is truly 'laudable'. (p. 165). If she resists, her inviolate but inarticulate corpse will become the subject of Tarquin's lies; if she survives to tell her story, she will save her entire family from dishonour. In the circumstances, preservation of chastity might seem self-indulgent. To the author of *Measure for Measure*, the preservation of female chastity ought to be a non-negotiable position. Nevertheless, Shakespeare stresses family concerns in Tarquin's threat:

> 'So thy surviving husband shall remain
> The scornful mark of every open eye;
> Thy kinsmen hang their heads at this disdain,
> Thy issue blurr'd with nameless bastardy.'
>
> (l. 519)

The Roman Lucrece sacrifices herself with a generosity forbidden to the Christian Isabella.

For Renaissance readers, the best-thumbed guide to ancient riots, incests, and rapes is Ovid's *Metamorphoses*. He repeatedly stresses the victims' innocence, presenting their subsequent torments in ways that invite the reader to consider them monstrously unfair. But his treatment of Calisto shows that innocence alone cannot prevent a victim from internalizing, as guilt, the shame she knows she will incur in the eyes of her community. Diana's fanatical devotee, her chastity is beyond question. No victim could plead more overwhelming force; her assailant is Jupiter, 'pater omnipotens' (ii. 401).[11] In the version by Arthur Golding,

> This wench against him strove as much as any woman could:
> I would that *Juno* had it seene: for then I know thou would
> Not take the deed so heynously: with all her might she strove:
> But what poore wenche, or who alive could vanquish mighty Jove?
>
> (l. 541)

[10] U.A., *The Gentleman's Magazine*, 6 (1736), 547.
[11] All quotations are from Ovid, *Metamorphoses*, ed. and trans. by F.J. Miller, 2 vols, Loeb Classical Library (London: Heinemann, 1971), I.

Afterwards Calisto suffers anxiety, depression, and guilt, with extreme reluctance to reveal her situation:

> She prankes not by hir mistresse side, she preases not to bee
> The foremost of the companie, as when she erst was free,
> She standeth müet.

$$(l. 557)^{12}$$

Her condition resembles modern rape trauma syndrome, which can be exacerbated by fear of an unsympathetic hearing.[13] Ovid, however, does not apportion her distress between reaction to her violation, and fear of its consequences. To the pregnant Calisto, the distinction is meaningless. Ovid's language seems to endorse her guilt: 'Oh Lord how hard a matter ist for guiltie hearts to shift, | And kepe their countnance?' (ll. 555–56). Ovid uses the same word for guilt, *crimen* (l. 447), when describing the revelation of her pregnancy (l. 462): Golding translates: 'Then with hir naked body straight hir crime was brought to light' (l. 574). Ovid may be using ironic point-of-view presentation, showing how Calisto appears to others, even herself. (The Latin does not even state definitely that the *crimen* is hers!) Yet it is significant that he does not cast the slightest doubt on her virtue until after she has lost her virginity.

Silenced by her own shame, then others' hostility, Calisto is alienated from the articulate community. Diana banishes her: 'Fie beast (quoth *Cynthia*) get thee hence thou shalt not here defile | This sacred spring' (ll. 576–77). Juno's 'punishment' (l. 579) turns her into a bear: in her indiscriminate yet unrelenting cruelty, Juno, patron goddess of marriage, appears to embody the inflexible social processes that stigmatize every rape victim under the 'shame' dispensation. Calisto's very identity is now obscured. Eventually, her son tries to kill her. Jupiter averts matricide by turning her into a constellation, but Juno bars her from descending to Ocean: 'Ne let that strumpet vyle | By bathing of hir filthie limmes your waters pure defile' (ll. 662–63). Unable to assert her innocence, Calisto is visibly, and indelibly, polluted.

Among other speechless victims is Io, whom Jupiter turns into a cow in a vain attempt to protect her from Juno. She is so demoralized by this shattering experience that, after restoration to human shape, she fears to speak in case she starts to moo (1. 745–46). Philomela, the direct source for Shakespeare's Lavinia, has her tongue cut out by her ravisher, her brother-in-law Tereus. She weaves an account of her misfortunes into a cloth which she sends to her sister, Procne. Procne pities Philomela and vows revenge on her husband. While Procne is debating whether to kill Itys, her son by Tereus, Philomela's silence makes up her mind (vi. 633). The sisters serve up

---

[12] All quotations are from Ovid, *Metamorphoses*, trans. by Arthur Golding (London: Seres, 1567), reprinted (London: Centaur, 1961).

[13] J. Temkin, 'Women, Rape and Law Reform' in *Rape: An Historical and Cultural Enquiry*, pp. 16–40 (pp. 16–20).

Itys's flesh to the unwitting father. While fleeing Tereus's nauseated wrath, Philomela turns into that most vocal of birds, the nightingale. She owes her comparative success in seeking justice to the fact that someone was prepared to believe her story.

Probably less frequently consulted than Ovid, but more fundamentally constitutive of Renaissance society, is *De Civitate Dei* by St Augustine (350–430). He reinforces Deuteronomy's insistence on the innocence of non-consenting victims, asserting their right to live against the popular Roman concept of suicide as a vindication of honour. For Augustine, suicide is a form of murder (I. xxi). If Lucretia killed herself to declare her innocence, the medium compromises the message. Her suicide can be read as an admission of guilt or commission of sin: 'Si adulterata, cur laudata? si pudica, cur occisa?' ('If she was an adultress, why was she praised? if chaste, why was she killed?') (I. xix). Yet Augustine admits the possibility that a ravished woman, however unwilling, may feel unbearable shame if there is any chance that she might be thought to have consented — especially if, as Augustine thinks probable, she experienced physical pleasure. In that case her suicide should not be judged too harshly (I. xvii). Shakespeare's Lucrece, debating whether to live or die, begins with an idea not mentioned by Augustine: suicide would be pointless ·because, since she consented to rape, it is not her body but her soul that is polluted (ll. 1056–57). Then she fears suicide would incur 'with my body my poor soul's pollution' (l. 1157), implying that rape has left her soul untouched. Finally she fears spiritual pollution is only a matter of time:

> 'Ay me! the bark peeled from the lofty pine,
> His leaves will wither and his sap decay;
> So must my soul, her bark being peel'd away.'

(l. 1167)

Shakespeare fails to pronounce judgement on any of these positions; Donaldson finds *Lucrece* 'raises more questions than it manages to answer' (p. 49). An explanation of Shakespeare's failure lies in Augustine's echoing silence: although he defends those ravished nuns who bravely decide to live, he offers no full rehabilitation to other women who have suffered this experience. Ultimately, he cannot advise such women to regard violation as fundamentally irrelevant to their spiritual essence. He endeavours to reinforce their wavering faith by arguing that God ordained this humiliation as a means of checking or preventing excessive pride in their chastity. He takes it for granted that rape has changed their status (I. xxviii). Like the ancient Jews, Greeks, and Romans, and early modern Christians, Augustine lives in a society that cares less about women's minds than their bodies.

II   *This hainous offence*

The late sixteenth century is a watershed in rape law. From Anglo-Saxon times, rape was defined as the abduction of a woman against the will of her male guardian. Consent was often irrelevant; violation was a side-issue: the crime was essentially theft, either by direct removal of goods, or by marrying an heiress to gain control of her fortune. But as Nazife Bashar points out, 'statutes of 1555 and 1597 treated abduction separately from rape, and had the indirect effect of establishing rape and abduction as separate offences'.[14] In *The Institutes of the Laws of England* (1628), Edward Coke lists two related crimes: 'Rape', followed by 'Felony for carrying away a woman against her will'.[15] Coke takes both crimes seriously; among a hundred felonies, listed in order of gravity (IV. B2^r), they come eleventh and twelfth, incurring the death penalty without benefit of clergy. Rape is 'this hainous offence', traditionally held in 'detestation'. It consists of 'carnall knowledge and abuse of any woman above the age of ten years against her will, or of a woman child under the age of ten years with her will, or against her will'. Definition of 'carnall knowledge' is clinically precise: 'If there be no penetration, that is, *res in re*, it is no rape' (IV.60). 'Carrying away a woman' lays more stress on a woman as property, or a means of transfering property from one man to another. For abduction to be felonious, the woman must be propertied, 'taken away against her will', and not be 'ward or bondwoman to the person that taketh her [...] only as his ward or bondwoman'. She must also be forcibly married or 'defiled (that is, carnally known)'. Although lack of consent appears to place decisive emphasis on the woman's will, Coke refers to a milder but none the less 'good and profitable statute' against taking away girls under sixteen, with or without consent (IV,62). Abduction has a spectacularly wide range of victims, occurring 'to the greatest displeasure of God, and contrary to the King's Laws, and disparagement [unequal marriage] of the said women, and utter heavinesse, and discomfort of their friends, and to the evill ensample of all other' (IV,61).

Lavinia's career illustrates the relationship between rape as abduction and rape as violation. Her first 'rape' occurs on stage, in public, as she is carried off to be married to Bassianus, who claims her as 'my true betrothed love' (*Titus Andronicus*, I.1.406). Bassianus is aided by her brothers and wise uncle Marcus. She returns a few minutes later, a virgin bride. The whole episode might pass off as a romantic frolic of eminent respectability, were it not that the transaction occurs against the will of the men with strongest rights to ownership: Titus and Saturninus. Titus, feeling 'dishonour'd' (l. 345) by the abduction, kills his son Mutius in an effort to prevent it. Saturninus regards Lavinia as degraded, 'that changing piece' (l. 309). Yet she has remained silent and passive. Marcus reduces her to a chattle: '*Suum cuique* [to each his own thing] is our Roman justice' (l. 280). Lucius, while conceding that his sister is alive, makes this state conditional on her marriage to Bassianus; he will return her to Saturninus 'dead, if you will; but

[14] 'Rape in England between 1550 and 1700', in *The Sexual Dynamics of History: Men's Power, Women's Resistance*, ed. by The London Feminist Group (London: Pluto, 1983), pp. 28–42 (p. 41).
[15] *Institutes of the Laws of England*, 4 vols (New York and London: Garland, 1979), IV, A3^r.

not to be his wife' (l. 207). The bitterness engendered by this first rape facilitates the second. It is a very different experience for Lavinia, but its consequences are similar in nature, if larger in scale. It costs the lives of Bassianus, two more brothers, and Lavinia herself; Titus performs the deed Lucius had only threatened: once again, he kills his own child to avert dishonour. A better example of the 'utter heavinesse, and discomfort' arising from abduction would be hard to find.

In practice, it is very hard for early modern victims to prove rape has actually taken place. Since the victim is the chief, perhaps the only witness, her evidence is of paramount importance. According to T. E.'s *The Lawes Resolutions of Womens Rights*, the victim ought 'to go straight way and with Hue and Cry complaine to the good men of the next towne, shewing her wrong, her garments torne and any effusion of blood', then report her case to other authorities, including 'the chief constable and Justices before whome she was againe to reintreat her Appeale'.[16] He fails to warn her that, even if she commands the financial and psychological resources to achieve this harrowing task, the chances of bringing a case to trial are slim: according to Nazife Bashar, 'the proportion of rape cases rejected "ignoramus" in the seventeenth century was usually more than twice as high as for cases involving other crimes' (p. 34). Conviction rates are also disproportionately low: 'Male judges and juries were loath to punish in any way other males for any sexual offence against females' (p. 40). This may be partly due to the misogyny inherent in many aspects of contemporary society. A possible contributory factor is class difference: judges and juries may disapprove of the legal innovation which gives women without property an opportunity to put rapists in fear of their lives. Prosecutions are most likely to succeed when the victim can be considered as property herself. In the home counties between 1558 and 1599,

The only convictions that were imposed were on men accused of raping young girls. [. . .] Rape of a virgin, a young woman, was regarded as the theft of her virginity, the property of her father to be used in procuring an advantageous marriage (p. 42).

Not even virginity guaranteed success. Apart from the inertia or hostility of the legal system, a victim faced her assailant's efforts to silence or discredit her testimony. These problems appear clearly in the case of Margery Evans, an 'illiterate fourteen-year-old servingmaid'. In 1631 she claimed, credibly, to have been forcibly deflowered by the influential Philbert Burghill. Undeterred by his death threats, she 'raised Hue & Cry', only to be imprisoned without charge when she caught up with him. Two women who examined her 'secrett partes' and 'verely judged that she was ravished', later unaccountably changed their testimony. Although a special Commission of the Peace found Burghill 'guiltie of Rape', the grand jury at the assizes refused to

---

[16] T. E. [Thomas Edgar?], *The Lawes Resolutions of Womens Rights* (London: John Grove, 1632), p. 392.

send him for trial.[17] After exceptionally intense political activity, a trial did take place: despite a hostile summing-up, Burghill was acquitted. Margery Evans's aunt, who had borne the prosecution expenses and was deeply in debt, could not obtain reimbursement. Burghill threatened both women with trial in the Star Chamber. All in all, he took much trouble to make Margery wish her 'partes' had remained 'secrett'. Many women found the pressures for silence overwhelming.[18]

In theory, only fear of the law stopped Burghill emulating Tereus. Coke's chapter on abduction is followed by 'Felonie for cutting out of Tongues, and putting out of Eyes, &c'. 'Misdoers' used to perform these outrages 'when one had been beaten, wounded, maimed, or robbed, etc. to the end that the party grieved might not be able to accuse them'. Before they were declared a felony, such acts were 'daily done' (iv, 63). To an Elizabethan audience, Lavinia's mutilation has a hideous common-sense logic. To a twentieth-century spectator, the main practical objection to this precaution, like Tarquin's blackmail attempt, is pointlessness: when redress is unobtainable, rendering the victim silent and helpless is superfluous. But hindsight must be avoided when plotting the doomed trajectories of Lavinia and Lucrece against Elizabethan parameters. Our present knowledge suggests that if Tarquin, Demetrius, and Chiron had been tried for rape in Shakespere's England, they would have been acquitted. Yet this information is unavailable to Shakespeare, whose treatment of the ravishers makes such an outcome appear improbable and undesirable. It would be more helpful to study the range of attitudes to rape in the community at large. We can then see how Shakespeare reflects beliefs which make it hard for fictional victims to survive, or real victims to get a fair hearing.

III   *Lust in action*

Students of rape today recognize three distinct views of rape, regarded as a transaction between rapist and victim. Firstly, rape is a source of female pleasure: the 'deadly' male myth that 'ALL WOMEN WANT TO BE RAPED'.[19] The resulting 'no-means-yes' syndrome reduces the victim's protests to nonsense. Secondly, rape may be a response to the frustration experienced in sexually repressive communities.[20] Though unsupported by correlation between repression and rape statistics,[21] it appeals to those who see rape as a 'normal' act, unacceptable only because of its inappropriate context. Emphasis on male desire makes the woman's reaction irrelevant.

[17] Leah S. Marcus, 'The Milieu of Milton's *Comus*: Judicial Reform at Ludlow and the Problem of Sexual Assault', *Criticism*, 25 (1983), 293–327 (pp. 293, 297, 301, 298).
[18] Bashar, p. 37.
[19] Susan Brownmiller, *Against Our Will: Men, Women and Rape* (London: Secker and Warburg, 1975), p. 311.
[20] Edward Shorter, 'On Writing the History of Rape', *Signs*, 3 (1977), 371–82.
[21] Porter, pp. 220–21.

Thirdly, female suffering could be the object of the exercise: rape 'is a violent act aimed at humiliating women'.[22] The first two concepts appear frequently in Renaissance literature; the third is seldom spelled out, but Shakespeare and his contemporaries seem aware of its implications.

The proof text on female insatiability is Ovid's *Ars Amatoria*, a cynically sophisticated guide to fornication. The poet — or his rakish persona — tells the man about town that if he resists the temptation to ravish a woman, she will only pretend to be pleased; attack would meet token resistance (I.673–78).[23] As that devout Ovidian Christopher Marlowe observes in *Hero and Leander*, 'In such wars women use but half their strength' (II.296).[24] In *The Faithful Shepherdess* by John Fletcher, the lustful Cloe takes rape to its logical vanishing-point: 'It is impossible to Ravish mee, | I am soe willing' (III.1.212–13).[25] Yet she is distinguished from other women, such as the chaste Clorin and Amoret. Dramatists utilize differing female responses to suit their purpose. In *The Alchemist* Ben Jonson achieves a satirically amoral comic resolution by making Dame Pliant take offence at Surly's noble refusal to exploit her sexuality. In *Volpone*, he maximizes indignation at a man who prostitutes his wife by making Celia a chaste woman who begs her assailant to kill her instead. When Buckingham advises Gloucester to 'play the maid's part, still answer nay, and take it' (*Richard III*, III.7.50), Shakespeare is displaying the plotters' hypocrisy, not making an authoritative pronounce-ment on female desire. Still, the remark's proverbial nature indicates that it might be uphill work for a rape victim to have her plight taken seriously.

It is often hard to tell when a rape is depicted as a simple failure to control natural desire, and when the introduction of force perverts the whole process. The differentiation between heterosexual rape and 'Buggery, or Sodomy', which precedes rape in Coke's order of gravity and is considered 'against the ordinance of the Creator, and order of nature' (IV, 58), tacitly supports the notion that rapes performed by men on women are 'normal'. Courtship may degenerate into rape when a woman's coldness is resented. In *The Two Gentlemen of Verona* Proteus, after asking Silvia for 'one calm look' (V.4.42), exacts a severe penalty for refusal: 'I'll woo you like a soldier, at arms' end, | And love you 'gainst the nature of love, — force ye' (ll.57–58). Marlowe's Leander is ultimately indifferent to Hero's expressed wishes: 'Love is not full of pity (as men say) | But deaf and cruel where he means to prey.' (*Hero and Leander*, II.287–88). One problem (in art as in life) is the event's differing significance for rapist and victim. In *Valentinian*, Fletcher depicts rape as a tragic breakdown in communication; after seeking Lucina's

---

[22] Clark, p. 39.
[23] Ovid, *Art of Love and Other Poems*, ed. and trans. by J. H. Mozley, Loeb Classical Library (London: Heinemann, 1962).
[24] Christopher Marlowe, *Complete Poems and Translations*, ed. by Stephen Orgel (Harmondsworth: Penguin, 1971), p. 39.
[25] *The Dramatic Works in the Beaumont and Fletcher Canon*, ed. by Fredson Bowers and others, 7 vols (Cambridge: Cambridge University Press, 1966–89), III, 538.

love by every means he and his pandars can think of, the Emperor rapes her. Afterwards, he vows 'Ile ever love, and honour you' (III. 1. 59). She scornfully retorts, 'can there be a love in violence? (l. 61). He continues to believe she will come to 'love her wrongs, | And doate upon her rape' (IV. 1. 7–8), until she dies of 'greife, and disgrace' (l. 5).[26] Fletcher also provides an unambiguous embodiment of rape as different in kind from other sexual acts in the Sullen Shepherd. He is a violent misogynistic loner, who 'lusts after every severall beauty, | But never yet was known to love or like' (*The Faithful Shepherdess*, (I. 2. 200–01). He is incapable of establishing harmonious relations with any sentient being; even his 'nye starved flockes | Are alwaies scabby, and infect all sheepe | That feede withall' (ll. 204–06).[27] In the end, he is banished: no decent community can tolerate him.

Demetrius, Chiron, and Tarquin pass with deplorable rapidity through all three interpretations of rape. The brothers begin as chivalrous lovers, seeking 'to serve, and to deserve my mistress' grace' (*Titus Andronicus*, II. 1. 34). Reification and fragmentation set in, as Demetrius's romantic aspirations precipitate into adulterous lust: 'Easy it is | Of a cut loaf to steal a shive' (ll. 86–87). Aaron knows she is too chaste to comply willingly, so hatches a plot for them to 'strike her home by force, if not by words' (l. 118). For Demetrius, Lavinia has become depersonalized, 'the stream | To cool this heat' (ll. 133–34). In the final phase he sees Lavinia as a person once more, so that he can rationalize rape as vengeance:

> This minion stood upon her chastity,
> Upon her nuptial vow, her loyalty,
> And with that painted hope she braves your mightiness:
> And shall she carry this unto her grave?
>
> (II. 3. 124)

The brothers' jokes show how deeply they despise her for the degradation they inflict:

> CHIRON   An 'twere my case, I should go hang myself.
> DEMETRIUS If thou hadst hands to help thee knit the cord.
>
> (II. 4. 9)

Tarquin's first recorded words in Lucrece's bedroom depict a parallel transition from pleading lover to impersonal conqueror to avenger, punishing her provocative beauty:

> The colour in thy face, —
> That even for anger makes the lily pale,
> And the red rose blush at her own disgrace, —
> Shall plead for me and tell my loving tale;
> Under that colour am I come to scale
>   Thy never-conquer'd fort: the fault is thine,
>   For those thine eyes betray thee unto mine.
>
> (l. 477)

[26] Beaumont and Fletcher, IV, 316, 335.
[27] Beaumont and Fletcher, IV, 510.

Afterwards, 'This hot desire converts to cold disdain' (l. 691). Tarquin typifies the effects of 'lust in action': 'no sooner had, | Past reason hated' (*Sonnet* CXXIX, 2, 6–7). Shakespeare, like Marlowe and Fletcher, understands that if rape is an act of love, 'love' needs drastic redefinition.

IV *Womanhood denies my tongue to tell*

Although Renaissance writers maintain that rape is not only possible but, in certain circumstances, extremely cruel and destructive, their testimony offers little help to a victim trying to prove in open court that those circumstances prevailed in her case. Worse still, they offer few precedents for her to appear in court at all. Fictitious victims find it extremely difficult to tell their story in approved legal style, since this itself would injure their modesty. Literary conventions spare them this cumbersome ordeal: their rape is authenticated by death. Death, usually by suicide but occasionally, as with Lucina, from natural causes, serves artistic purposes by heightening pathos and removing loose ends. It also produces practical benefits desirable in real life: it prevents moral deterioration, preserves family honour, terminates pregnancy, and frees for remarriage a husband otherwise trapped with a wife whom he can neither divorce nor take to his bed without shame. Writers do not recommend suicide unequivocally: 'Elizabethans believed that a woman ought to preserve her chastity to the point of death, but they were uncertain about the relative values of lust and suicide as deadly sins.' Titus's initiative was an even less acceptable solution because murder was considered worse than suicide.[28] Nevertheless, the theme of the dead rape victim is repeated with subtly prescriptive force.

This appears as early as Livy, whose Lucretia kills herself both to assert her spiritual chastity, and to avoid setting a precedent for survival that could be abused by lying adultresses; Shakespeare renders this more generally: 'No dame, hereafter living | By my excuse shall claim excuse's giving' (ll. 1714–15). This line of reasoning, if followed to its logical conclusion, would lead a sad procession of aspiring Lucretias to an early grave. Michael Drayton in *The Barons Warres* shows suicide as the last resort of a ravished virgin. His setting is the anarchy of medieval civil war, but many women in his own lifetime faced similar problems:

> None would be found to whom she could complain;
> And crying out against th' adult'rer's force,
> Her plaints untimely did return in vain; ...
> She, spoil'd of fame, was prodigall of breath,
> And made her life clear by her resolute death.
>
> (IV. 370–76)[29]

---

[28] Nancy Cotton Pearse, *John Fletcher's Chastity Plays: Mirrors of Modesty* (Lewisburg, PA: Bucknell University Press, 1973), pp. 94, 97.
[29] Michael Drayton, *The Barons' Wars*, in *Works of the English Poets*, ed. by A. Chalmers, 21 vols (London: J. Johnson, 1810), IV, 44.

In *The Revenger's Tragedy*, sometimes ascribed to Cyril Tourneur but probably by Thomas Middleton, suicide after rape brings not only vindication
but glory to Lord Antonio's wife: 'Sh'as made her name an empress by that
act' (I.4.50).[30]

The necessity of speedy death is emphasized by the unseemly conduct of
victims who persist in living. Bianca, in Middleton's *Women Beware Women*, is
a carefully designed case study of moral degeneration. At first she resists the
Duke of Florence vigorously, but soon after the rape falls in love with him
and becomes his mistress, then (after her husband's murder) his bride. She
attempts to murder the Duke's virtuous brother, and when the Duke dies
instead, finally commits suicide, not to make a statement of her worth or
expiate dishonour, but because she simply cannot bear to go on living. Less
amenable to schematization is the story of Boadicea the British queen who,
when she was beaten and her daughters raped by occupying Roman forces,
started a war. Their eventual suicide was provoked by defeat. In *Bonduca*
Fletcher shows considerable embarrassment. He depicts the daughters
alternately as comical vixens and tragic heronies. They inspire admiration
by their deaths, but appear despicable when they try to speak and act for
themselves in ways that do not involve self-destruction. He makes them
infuriate their chivalrous uncle Caratach by their breach of military convention when they use feminine wiles to take Roman prisoners:

> 2. DAUGHTER   We will have vengeance for our rapes.
> CARATACH   By —
> You should have kept your legs close then.   (III.5.70–71)[31]

John Milton adds no such episode to his *History of Britain*; he finds the
accounts of previous historians too imaginatively indecorous as they stand.
He is particularly incensed by Boadicea's address to her troops:

A deal of other fondness they put into her mouth, not worth recital; how she was
lash'd, how her Daughters were handl'd, things worthier silence, retirment, and a
Vail, then for a Woeman to repeat, as don to hir own person, or to hear repeated
before an host of men.[32]

If Leah Marcus's interpretation of *Comus* is correct, Milton combines deep
respect for the innocence of rape victims with awareness of the difficulties
they face in obtaining justice (pp. 316–22). Yet his ideal of feminine delicacy
makes their task no easier. The more modest the victim (and, therefore, the
more potentially credible), the harder she should find it to state her case.
And, as Middleton and Fletcher show, the fact that she is still alive renders
her suspect.

Renaissance presentation of rape victims follows classical tradition in
making the victim's body, living or dead, communicate with an eloquence

---

[30] Cyril Tourneur, *Plays*, ed. by George Parfitt (Cambridge: Cambridge University Press, 1978), p. 26.
[31] Beaumont and Fletcher, IV, 202.
[32] John Milton, *Complete Works*, ed. by Frank Allen Patterson and others, 20 vols (New York: Columbia University Press, 1931–40), X, 68.

and credibility beyond the range of words. Livy's Lucretia tells her story in businesslike fashion (Livy never misses a chance to compose a stirring speech), but still feels the need to punctuate it with a dagger. Ovid's Lucretia is more reticent; the verse mimes her hesitation:

> Quodque potest narrat: restabant ultima: flevit:
> Et matronales erubuere genae.
>
> (*Fasti*, II.827)

(She told them what she could: the final horrors remained unspoken: she wept: and a blush stained her matron's cheeks.)

In *Valentinian* Lucina, afte several long speeches expressing her determination to denounce her ravisher, cannot find words to tell her husband what happened. Luckily, Maximus needs no telling: 'Already in thy teares, I have read thy wrongs' (III.1.157).[33] Shakespeare's Lavinia is so modest that, even while imploring to be spared from rape, she cannot command the language to explain exactly what she wants.

> 'Tis present death I beg: and one thing more
> That womanhood denies my tongue to tell.
>
> (*Titus Andronicus*, II.3.173)

Afterwards, Lavinia's mutilations are enough to make Marcus and Titus fear she has been raped (II.4.26–27; IV.1.49). When she scrapes three words in the sand, '*Stuprum* [rape], *Chiron, Demetrius*' (IV.1.78), she is believed without question and avenged without mercy.

Lavinia's plea for death is her only expressed wish not to outlive violation. Titus's action can be viewed as a substitute for the suicide she cannot manage alone, providing the audience forgets about it before Marcus and Lucius offer to kill themselves by jumping off a nearby monument — a feat requiring no manual dexterity. The dialogue before her death makes Titus, rather than Lavinia, chief actor and sufferer. Saturninus says Virginius was right to kill his allegedly ravished daughter Virginia,

> Because the girl should not survive her shame,
> And by her presence still renew his sorrows.
>
> (v.2.41)

'Because' here means 'in order that': 'should' consequently expresses the father's purpose, not the daughter's moral responsibility. Titus kills Lavinia to end his own suffering:

> Die, die, Lavinia, and thy shame with thee;
> And with thy shame thy father's sorrow die!
>
> (l.46)

Livy's Virginius kills his daughter to prevent her rape; lack of prior consultation is forced upon him by the need to improvise (III.xlviii.5). But in *Apius and Virginia* by R. B., there is a long conversation in which Virginia

---

[33] Beaumont and Fletcher, IV, 319.

exhorts Virginius to save her chastity by beheading her (ll. 920–70).[34] Lavinia shows similar initiative in *The History of Titus Andronicus* (c. 1750): 'At his daughter's request he killed her.'[35] Whether a woman's death prevents or follows rape, most early modern authors like to make it an authentic part of *her* story. Is Shakespeare being careless, over-economical, uncompromisingly classical — or simply more realistic in his depiction of a man's emotional response?

The dishonour inflicted on a man by the sexual pollution of a woman in his domain makes it difficult and painful to break the news to him. In any patriarchal society, 'men's bonds with women are meant to be in a subordinate, complementary, and instrumental relation to bonds with other men'.[36] Rape, seduction, and other irregular triangulations fasten interloper, woman, and rightful owner in an agonizing stranglehold that can be released only by the death of the first two, perhaps all three. A man is less intimately connected with his other possessions than with his womenfolk, especially those parts of them which are dedicated to carrying on a legitimate line of succession. Man and wife, particularly, are one flesh. When Petruchio pronounces Kate 'my horse, my ox, my ass, my anything' (*The Taming of the Shrew*, III. 2. 235), he might as well leave out 'any': marriage endows him with a vagina. The law of *suum* (rather than *suam*) *cuique* defines Lavinia as Bassianus's thing, not his woman. In *The Winter's Tale* Leontes describes adultery in language which reduces a woman to an extension of her vagina, then attaches the entire structure to her husband:

> she has been sluic'd in his absence,
> And his pond fish'd by his next neighbour, by
> Sir Smile, his neighbour: nay, there's comfort in't,
> Whiles other men have gates, and those gates open'd,
> As mine, against their will.
>
> (I. 2. 194)

Cuckolding is a sexual act performed by one man upon another, though few injured husbands go so far towards eliminating the middle term as Maximus:

> Would he had ravish'd me, I would have payd him,
> I would have taught him such a trick, his Eunuches
> Nor all his black-eyd boyes dreamt of yet.
>
> (*Valentinian*. III. 3. 118)[37]

The cuckold's dishonour is an 'unfelt sore' (*Lucrece*, l. 828) until he is enlightened. It is the same with male relatives. Pity, as well as shame, may be

---

[34] R. B., *Apius and Virginia, 1575* (Chiswick: The Malone Society, 1911), D3ʳ⁻ᵛ.
[35] *Titus Andronicus*, ed. by E. M. Waith, p. 204.
[36] Eve Kossofsky Sedgwick, *Between Men: English Literature and Male Homosocial Desire* (New York: Columbia University Press, 1985), p. 51.
[37] Beaumont and Fletcher, IV, 333.

indicated when Lavinia 'flies away' from Marcus, and tries to 'draw back' when he leads her to her father (*Titus Andronicus*, II. 4. 11, 56).

Yet this stern necessity must be met. It is especially urgent for a wife, who must avoid intercourse with her husband. This act consummates his shame. The horror and disgust aroused by the prospect can be gathered from Othello's hysteria (IV. 1) and Diomedes's contempt for Menelaus (*Troilus and Cressida*, IV. 1. 61–62). A sign that a powerful, if unarticulated, convention operates is the frequency of plot manipulations preserving husbands from a fate worse than death, as in *The Changeling* by Thomas Middleton and William Rowley, where Alsemero is saved by a bed-trick contrived to save his bride's reputation. With a sense of inescapable yet unbearable duty Lucrece, facing husband, father, and 'consorted lords' (l. 1609), 'modestly prepares to let them know | Her honour is ta'en prisoner by the foe' (ll. 1607–08).

How can a modest woman speak the unspeakable? *Lucrece* explores the heroine's disastrous relationship with language. The poem is organized by the things people say, or might say, about Lucrece, and the things Tarquin tries to stop her saying. It starts when Collatine's boasting arouses Tarquin's lust, and 'closes as it opened, as men rhetorically compete with each other over Lucrece's body',[38] Reading *Lucrece* for the story, or even a conclusive argument, is a frustrating experience. C. S. Lewis dismisses as 'three stanzas of digression' the passage where the narrator rebukes Collatine for foolishly blazoning Lucrece's charms. Lewis also finds Lucrece 'too rhetorical in her agonies', numbering among the poem's imperfections her preoccupation with 'the style of her letter to her husband'; judging Lucrece as an attempt at realistic character drawing by Elizabethan standards, he concedes 'perhaps it is not impossible that a woman of the nineties, brought up by a humanist tutor, might, even at such a moment, have remembered the claims of *eloquentia*'.[39] Shakespeare's Lucrece, however, is probably best understood as his representation of the archetypal rape victim, struggling to state her case in a way that will get her the fair hearing she desperately needs, but fears she will never obtain. She settles on a noncommittal communication; she cannot trust words, written or spoken, to do her justice:

> She dares not thereof make discovery;
> Lest he should hold it her own gross abuse,
> Ere she with blood had stain'd her stain'd excuse.

> Besides, the life and feeling of her passion
> She hoards, to spend when he is by to hear her;
> When sighs, and groans, and tears may grace the fashion
> Of her disgrace.

(l. 1314)

[38] Nancy J. Vickers, '"This heraldry in Lucrece' face"', in *The Female Body in Western Culture*, ed. by S. R. Suleiman (Cambridge, MA: Harvard University Press, 1986), pp. 209–22, p. 218.
[39] C. S. Lewis, *English Literature in the Sixteenth Century Excluding Drama* (Oxford: Clarendon, 1954), pp. 500, 501.

Ian Donaldson notes that, unlike Lavinia, 'Lucrece talks of her griefs, but her talk seems to get her nowhere' (p. 42). According to Richard Lanham, *Lucrece* is 'about the rhetoric of display, about the motives of eloquence'.[40] Yet *Lucrece*, like *Titus Andronicus* and many other texts dealing with rape, is also about inducements to concealment and silence, and the subtler pressures that make women's words ineffectual or meaningless if unsupported by self-destructive action.

---

[40] Richard Lanham, *The Motives of Eloquence: Literary Rhetoric in the Renaissance* (New Haven, CT and London: Yale University Press, 1976), p.82.

Willobie his Avisa and *The Passionate Pilgrim*: Precedence, Parody, and Development

JOHN ROE

University of York

Commentators have long been foxed and fascinated by the peculiar relationship between Canto XLVII of *Willobie his Avisa* and poem XVIII ('When as thine eye hath chose the dame') of *The Passionate Pilgrim*. Not only that, but a tantalizing relationship with Shakespeare has been forged for each. The speaker of the Willobie poem is given the initials W. S., while *The Passionate Pilgrim* is a more or less pseudo-Shakespearian miscellany, authenticated in parts by some genuine pieces. That Shakespeare might have been the author of either of the poems is too improbable to warrant serious conjecture. However, I hope to show that the one poem develops in response to, and indeed somewhat parodies, the other; and in discussing the relationship between them it is relevant to assess the role of Shakespeare's *name*, if not his personal intervention, in the proceedings.

Willobie his Avisa was published in 1594 shortly after Shakespeare's poem *The Rape of Lucrece* to which it carries a fulsome compliment.[1] The resemblance between Canto XLVII of *Willobie* and 'When as thine eye hath chose the dame' is well known and has in turn given rise to speculation on how or whether they may be connected. William Jaggard published *The Passionate Pilgrim* (a miscellany of twenty sonnets and lyrics) under Shakespeare's name, though as far as can be known without authority. Canto XLVII of *Willobie* bears the initials W. S. W. S. figures in a dialogue with H. W. in this part of the poem and offers the latter advice on how to conduct matters with the virtuous and intractable heroine, Avisa. The canto then is spoken by W. S. Since this figure has never emerged from behind his initials, there is no saying who he might have been. Many have casually supposed that he is indeed Shakespeare, a tradition of identification which A. B. Grosart unquestioningly followed in his 1880 edition of *Willobie his Avisa* when he wrote, 'I am inclined to conjecture that Shakespeare may have sent his friend H. W. this identical poem'.[2] H. W. is of course the Henry Willobie who

---

[1] See the verses 'In praise of Willobie', etc., immediately preceding the main poem and which contain lines such as, 'Yet Tarquyne', etc. in *Willobie his Avisa*, ed. by G. B. Harrison (London: Bodley Head, 1926; repr. Edinburgh: Edinburgh University Press, 1966), pp. 19–20.
[2] See *Willobie his Avisa*, ed. by A. B. Grosart (Manchester: for subscribers, 1880), p. xii.

provides the Willobie of the title and whose full name recurs at several points. But who that Willobie may have been is equally open to conjecture.[3]

Before proceeding further along this line, it is worth pausing over the makeup of *Willobie* itself. The poem consists in the main of seventy-four cantos which take the form of arguments between the chaste and virtuous Avisa, a woman of modest social status (the wife of an innkeeper, in fact) and various disreputable suitors who ply her with courtship both before and after her marriage. The husband never appears except in allusion. Her would-be seducers include 'Ruffians, Roysters, young Gentlemen, and lustie Captaines', including a 'Cavaleiro' (Harrison, p. 56). This accent on the misdoings of lesser nobility emphasizes the poem's championship of the class to which Avisa belongs: merchants of good yeoman stock who, like similar figures in the novels of Deloney, represent English values at their best. Avisa is assailed in turn by various unsavoury Continentals, a Frenchman, a German, and a 'Hispano-Italiensis', Petrarchist figure called Henrico Willobego, who is of course none other than Henry Willobie himself, courting the lady in an absurd and affectedly poetic posture.[4] The author appears to have had in mind a version of the Lucrece story set in a familiar English social context in which chastity manages to prevail over sexual adventuring. The fact that her wooers tend to be richer and of a nobler, or at least more elevated class, than Avisa provides an instructive analogy with the Roman tale in which the son of a king undertakes to abuse one of his father's subjects. A patriotic note is further struck in that those of Avisa's wooers who ply their suit at any length in the poem are from beyond the British Isles and represent the hostility and distrust their countries inspire at an economic and political level.[5]

The stanza pattern differs from the rhyme royal of *The Rape of Lucrece*, being in sixains or six-line octosyllabics. This reduces the capacity for

---

[3] See the *DNB* entry by Sir Sidney Lee who plausibly identifies a Henry Willoughby who matriculated at Oxford in 1591, aged sixteen. Whether this historical person is in fact the author of the poem to which he contributes his name is uncertain since no evidence of his being an author survives. The title-page of course bears no name of author. Another figure who plays a prominent role in the presentation of the poem is Hadrian Dorrell who announces himself as Willobie's friend. Grosart indeed thinks that Dorrell is the real author, hiding his artistry behind his description of his friend's vicissitudes (p. xii). But since the historical Dorrell is even more obscure than Willoughby this speculation is practically worthless.

[4] It is hard to share Harrison's conviction (p. 213) that Henrico Willobego cannot be Willobie on the grounds that H. W., his suit having failed, is as Willobie puts it, 'striken so dead, that hee hath not yet any farder assaid, nor I thinke ever will, and where [whether] he be alive or dead I know not, and therefore I leave him'. It is a conventional Petrarchan touch for the lover to describe himself as more dead than alive and so beside himself as truly not to know his own condition. Evidently, 'Willobego' is the identity Willobie assumes during his preposterous and misguided Italianate courtship of Avisa — an identity he discards in reverting to his simpler, English character at the end when he accepts the wisdom of Avisa's chastening reproof.

[5] The poem may be a source for the comedy *Englishmen for my money*, written by William Haughton for Henslowe at the Rose in 1599. In this salutary comedy, an English-domiciled Portuguese merchant's three daughters prefer plain English husbands to the Continental matches at which their father aims. The outwitted Dutch, Italian, and French suitors all speak a 'funny' prose macaronics. In other respects, the play demonstrates as much the determination, not to say wilfulness, of women (its sub-title is 'A Woman will have her Will') as their simple-hearted virtue, and the equation of marital chastity and old-fashioned patriotism is much less evident than in *Willobie his Avisa*.

rhetoric and reflectiveness of the usual heroic pentameter line and issues in
straightforward, vigorous metrical statements, of which the poem's opening
stanza is as good an example as any:

> Let martiall men, of Mars his praise,
> Sound warlike trumpe: let lust-led youth,
> Of wicked love, write wanton layes;
> Let sheepeheards sing, their sheepecoates ruth:
> The wiser sort, confesse it plaine,
> That these have spent good time in vaine.
>
> (Harrison, p. 21)

In its forthright way, the poem stands then as an emulation of *The Rape of
Lucrece*, though set in a plainer English key which partially repudiates the
other poem's grander stylistic excesses, while serving as a reminder that if
good sense prevails then the tragic denouement invariably associated with
the urges of an irresistible passion need not follow.

Despite the play on names, it offers no invitation to seek further in the way
of identification; but the allegorical yearnings of scholars have taken no heed
of that. Harrison himself was quite convinced that the poem was written in
support of Sir Walter Ralegh, then under investigation on charges of atheism
in the neighbourhood of Cerne Abbas, which the geographical details of the
poem more or less reveal to be its supposed setting. To support Ralegh
means to attack Ralegh's enemy Southampton and with him the patron-
pleasing Shakespeare; all this despite the compliment to Shakespeare's
genius in the preliminary verses already referred to. According to Harrison's
conjecture H. W. ceases to be Willobie and reveals himself instead as Henry
Wriothesley (the Earl of Southampton) and W. S. is naturally Shakespeare
(Harrison, p. 214). These speculations of Harrison's which undermine the
credibility of his otherwise fine edition have never taken hold and need not be
dismantled now.

A further attempt at allegorical interpretation was made by B. N. De Luna
in a more recent edition of the poem; she argued that Avisa, despite her
clearly humble social standing which serves the poem with a necessary
moral point, is no less a person than the Queen herself. The poem provides
no internal evidence for such a reading: on the contrary everything supports
the view that Avisa is the wife of an innkeeper, albeit a superior example of
the breed. But De Luna, having fixed on Elizabeth, has no difficulty in
revealing the appropriate identities of the suitors, identifying them as Philip
of Spain, the Duke of Alençon, Essex, and so on. The book's Latin description of Avisa (added in the edition of 1596) as 'conjunx cauponis, filia
pandochei' which translates straightforwardly as 'the wife of an innkeeper,
the daughter of an inn-keeper' De Luna allegorically reconstrues as 'the wife
of a shop-keeper [England], the daughter of a harlot [Anne Boleyn]'.[6] The

---

[6] The odd-looking 'pandochei' is the Greek for innkeeper and is introduced simply to balance and vary
the Latin version, 'cauponis'.

tissue of suppositions forming the main fabric of this argument was effectively dealt with by Douglas Hamer in a review which seems to me to be quite final.[7]

The composition of *The Passionate Pilgrim*, on the other hand, may shed some light on the connexion between W. S. and Canto XLVII. When Jaggard put the miscellany together as Shakespeare's he was presumably anxious that it should appear genuine, or at least deceive its readers into believing in Shakespeare's authorship. Since he had little of Shakespeare's own work (five poems out of the twenty) this was far from easy. Jaggard's ploy seems to have been to include poems not by Shakespeare but on a theme popularly associated with him: hence the inclusion of several sonnets on the love of Venus for Adonis (Shakespeare's erotic narrative currently seeing its fifth printing in six years). There is no evidence that Shakespeare wrote any of these sonnets, and indeed the author of one of them (and perhaps others?) was subsequently identified as Bartholomew Griffin. But the connexion was made. Jaggard, looking for other 'Shakespearean' specimens may have lighted on Canto XLVII of *Willobie*, which with its initials looked Shakespearean enough. In addition, the canto appears preceded by a prose description of the conversation between W. S. and H. W. which provides enough information for anybody determined to make the identification with Shakespeare:

H. W. being sodenly infected with the contagion of a fantasticall fit [. . .] pyneth a while in secret grief, at length [. . .] bewrayeth the secresy of his disease unto his familiar frend W. S. who not long before had tryed the curtesy of the like passion, and was now newly recovered of the like infection; yet finding his frend let bloud in the same vaine, he took pleasure for a tyme to see him bleed, and in steed of stopping the issue, he inlargeth the wound, with the sharpe rasor of a willing conceit, perswading him that he thought it a matter very easy to be compassed, and no doubt with payne, diligence and some cost in time to be obtayned. Thus this miserable comforter comforting his frend with an impossibilitie, eyther for that he now would secretly laugh at his frends folly, that had given occasion not long before unto others to laugh at his owne, or because he would see whether an other could play his part better then himselfe, and in vewing a far off the course of this loving Comedy, he determined to see whether it would sort to a happier end for this new actor, then it did for the old player.

(Harrison, pp. 115–16)

References to 'Comedy' and to W. S. as an 'old player' might, given Shakespeare's reputation as a dramatist and actor, forge a connexion between him and H. W.'s dubious counsellor. In fact, the representation of love as a comedy or theatrical spectacle is as common to sonnet sequences as to the stage, witness Thomas Nashe's introduction to the unofficial publication of *Astrophel and Stella* of 1591:

let not your surfeted sight, new come fro such puppet play, think scorne to turn aside into this Theater of pleasure, for here you shal find a paper stage streud with pearle,

[7] See *RES*, 22 (1971), 335–40.

an artificial heav'n to overshadow the fair frame, & christal wals to encounter your
curious eyes, whiles the tragicommedy of love is performed by starlight.[8]

But it would be enough for such as Jaggard, keen to give his miscellany as
Shakespearean a character as possible to seize on the evidence and include in
it a poem remarkably like if not derived from *Willobie* Canto XLVII. There lies
the question. Was the connexion already in the minds of readers, as seems
quite possible? Did Jaggard insist on it by including 'When as thine eye'?
Furthermore, did he perhaps commission an approximate imitation of
Canto XLVII, close enough to identify its source and yet distinct enough not to
risk seeming a mere copy? The question is further complicated by the
existence in manuscript of two other versions of 'When as thine eye'. Do they
precede the poem printed in *The Passionate Pilgrim* or do they derive from it?
The answers to all such questions can probably never be run to earth, but
something may be gained by closely comparing the canto from *Willobie* with
'When as thine eye'.
    I give both poems in sequence:

W.S

Well, say no more: I know thy grief,
And face from whence these flames aryse,
It is not hard to fynd reliefe,
If thou wilt follow good advyse:
    She is no Saynt, She is no Nonne,   5
    I thinke in tyme she may be wonne.

arsveteratoria At first repulse you must not faint,
Nor flye the field though she deny
You twise or thrise, yet manly bent,
Againe you must, and still reply: 10
    When tyme permits you not to talke,
    Then let your pen and fingers walke.

Apply her still with dyvers thinges,
Munera (For giftes the wysest will deceave)
(crede mihi) Sometymes with gold, sometymes with ringes,   15
placant No tyme nor fit occasion leave,
hominesq: Though coy at first she seems and wielde,[9]
Deosq:.   These toyes in tyme will make her yielde.

Looke what she likes; that you must love,
And what she hates, you must detest,   20
Where[10] good or bad, you must approve,
The wordes and workes that please her best:
    If she be godly, you must sweare,
    That to offend you stand in feare.

[8] *The Works of Thomas Nashe*, ed. by R. B. McKerrow, 2nd edn, rev. by F. P. Wilson, 5 vols (Oxford: Oxford University Press, 1958), III, 329.
[9] wielde] wild.
[10] Where] Whether.

Wicked
wiles to
deceave
witles
women

You must commend her loving face,   25
For women joy in beauties praise,
You must admire her sober grace,
Her wisdome and her vertuous wayes,
   Say, 'twas her wit and modest shoe,[11]
   That made you like and love her so.   30

You must be secret, constant, free,
Your silent sighes and trickling teares,
Let her in secret often see,
Then wring her hand, as one that feares
   To speake, then wish she were your wife,   35
   And last desire her save your life.

When she doth laugh, you must be glad,
And watch occasions, tyme and place,
When she doth frowne, you must be sad,
Let sighes and sobbes request her grace: 40
   Sweare that your love is truly ment,
   So she in tyme must needes relent.

   (*Willobie his Avisa*, Canto XLVII; Harrison, pp. 121–23)

When as thine eye hath chose the Dame,
And stalde the deare that thou shouldst strike,
Let reason rule things worthy blame,
As wel as fancy (partyall might).
   Take counsell of some wiser head,   5
   Neither too young, nor yet vnwed,

And when thou comest thy tale to tell,
Smooth not thy toung with filed talke,
Least she some subtil practise smell,
A Cripple soon can finde a halt,   10
   But plainly say thou lovst her well,
   And set her person forth to sale.

And to her wil frame al thy waies,
Spare not to spend, and chiefly there,
Where thy desart may merit praise   15
By ringing in thy Ladies eare,
   The strongest castle, tower and towne,
   The golden bullet beats it downe.

Serve alwaies with assured trust,
And in thy sute be humble true,   20
Unlesse thy Lady prove unjust,
Prease never thou to chuse anew:
   When time shal serve, be thou not slacke,
   To profer though she put thee backe.

[11] shoe] show.

What though her frowning browes be bent,   25
Her cloudy lookes wil calme yer[12] night,
And then too late she wil repent,
That thus dissembled her delight.
    And twice desire yer it be day,
    That which with scorne she put away.   30

What though she strive to try her strength,
And ban and braule, and say thee nay:
Her feeble force wil yeeld at length,
When craft hath taught her thus to say:
    Had women been so strong as men,   35
    In faith you had not had it then.

The wiles and guiles that women worke,
Dissembled with an outward shew:
The trickes and toyes that in them lurke,
The Cocke that treades them shall not know: 40
    Have you not heard it sayd full oft,
    A woman's nay doth stand for nought.

Thinke Women still to strive with men,
To sinne and never for to saint,
There is no heaven (be holy then)   45
When time with age shall them attaint,
    Were kisses all the joys in bed,
    One Woman would an other wed.

But soft enough, too much I feare,
Lest that my mistresse heare my song,   50
She will not stick to rounde me on th'are,[13]
To teach my toung to be so long:
    Yet wil she blush, here it be sayd,
    To heare her secrets so bewraide.[14]

Although it is hardly necessary to demonstrate the already well-known resemblances between the two poems, it is worth noting some common features. They are both advice-to-lovers poems. In each case a speaker of some assurance in matters of the heart encourages an ingénu to adopt various tactics which are bound eventually to succeed. Both speakers advise the novice to woo the lady with gifts and praise. Both tacticians advocate using the Petrarchan posture as a stratagem, i.e., asserting one's loyalty and trust, not as an example of selfless devotion, but in the expectation that unlike the typical Petrarchan lady whose constancy to the vow of chastity never wavers, the woman in question will sooner or later submit. The siege of love need not be endless; on the contrary a thorough preparation of the

---

[12] yer] ere.
[13] are] ear.
[14] I have used the version of the poem printed in *William Shakespeare: The Complete Works, Original-Spelling Edition*, ed. by Stanley Wells and Gary Taylor (Oxford: Oxford University Press, 1986), pp. 885–86, which is based on the first octavo of 1599, though re-punctuated. A check with the facsimile reproduction by Joseph Quincy Adams (New York: Scribners, 1939) shows that the Oxford text is accurate in all particulars, except for the printing of 'the' for 'thee' in line 32.

ground will force an inevitable capitulation. As we know from events in *Willobie his Avisa*, these confident assurances of W. S. do H. W. no good at all; Avisa is more than equal to his arguments in love and the final lesson is that of moral resolution which she teaches him. The situation envisaged by the speaker in 'When as thine eye' is altogether different. The assumption that perseverance will succeed is never challenged in that poem, which, unlike the *Willobie* canto, does not appear to belong to a larger narrative framework. Furthermore, reinforcement of the speaker's views comes from his confident, and confidential, revelations about his own mistress, who is about to chastise him for giving away secrets concerning the true nature of women. Whereas chastity prevails over seduction in the larger perspective of *Willobie his Avisa*, 'When as thine eye' seems to laugh it mercilessly out of court. This difference raises the question whether the poem which found its way into *The Passionate Pilgrim*, assisted as already argued by the spurious if plausible evidence provided by the initials W. S., does not offer itself as a parody of the assumptions underlying the *Willobie* canto. H. W.'s suit is doomed to failure as W. S. secretly seems to know (judging by the prose passage about the 'old player'),[15] Avisa's chastity emerging ultimately as triumphant. But whereas W. S. proceeds cautiously, outlining prospective satisfaction in terms of a decorous and rewarded transition from suffering to solace, the speaker of 'When as thine eye' positively riots in his anticipation of the protesting lady's backsliding. Here is the concluding stanza of Canto XLVII of *Willobie*:

> When she doth laugh you must be glad,
> And watch occasion, tyme and place,
> When she doth frowne, you must be sad,
> Let sighes and sobbes request her grace:
> > Sweare that your love is truly ment,
> > So she in tyme must needes relent.
>
> (l. 37)

The comparable moment is reached in the fifth and pivotal stanza (there are nine in all) of 'When as thine eye':

> What though her frowning browes be bent,
> Her cloudy lookes wil calme yer night,
> And then too late she will repent,
> That thus dissembled her delight.
> > And twice desire yer it be day,
> > That which with scorne she put away.
>
> (l. 25)

While W. S. offers H. W. the prospect of her relenting 'in tyme' (a discreet, even euphemistic way of putting things), 'When as thine eye' increases the erotic tempo considerably with its confident prediction that once night has spread its all-concealing cloak we shall witness a remarkable turnabout on the lady's part, modesty and chaste denial transforming themselves into

---

[15] See above, p. 114.

unappeasable appetite. Not only will she submit but she will insist on a
repetition ('*twice* desire') of 'that which with scorn she put away'.

With the establishment of this point a more thoroughgoing ribaldry than
anything offered by the comparatively circumspect tone of the *Willobie* canto
begins to dominate:

> Thinke Women still to strive with men,
> To sinne and never for to saint,
> There is no heaven (be holy then)
> When time with age shall them attaint,
>   Were kisses all the ioyes in bed,
>   One Woman would an other wed.[16]
>
> (l. 43)

Lines and phrases resemble the opening stanza of Canto XLVII: 'There is no
heaven' (i.e., 'there is nothing heavenly about them, women') accords with
'she is no Saynt', etc., while 'saint' occurs in both stanzas to a similar
sceptical purpose. But Canto XLVII fails or refuses to contemplate further
erotic possibilities: 'I thinke in tyme she may be wonne', the concluding line
of stanza 1, is merely echoed by the poem's last line, 'so she in tyme must
needes relent'; whereas 'When as thine eye' moves swiftly into the bedroom,
depicting love as a wrestling match and revealing feminine restraint to be
nothing more than instinctual cunning. 'At first Repulse', which in *Willobie*
means 'rebuff' becomes a literal and physical contest in the stanza which in
the other poem begins, 'What though she strive to try her strength' (l. 31),
and so on.

I should like to suggest that the tone of the two poems, assuming that they
are connected and not just accidentally similar, helps decide which is the
original and which the imitation or parody. Canto XLVII looks like a poem
uneasily trying to have it both ways: W. S. advocates a posture of Petrarchan
or troubadour service which will earn the lover eventual gratification in a
manner which Petrarchanism normally denies. As long as he goes through
the forms of devoted love, says the right things and plies her with enough
gifts, everything should work to his advantage. The spuriousness of this
position is doubtless intended by the poem since one sure way of vindicating
Avisa's chastity is to expose the insincerity of such lovers as H. W. as well as
the speciousness of such advisers as W. S. However, 'When as thine eye'
neatly steps in to short-circuit such contrived demonstrations of female
worthiness by announcing frankly that women are exactly as W. S. describes
them, if not a good deal more so. I believe that the latter poem gains much of
its momentum and exuberance by a carefree demolition of the positions held
tenuously in balance in Canto XLVII. 'When as thine eye' is subsequent

---

[16] This stanza is in an unsatisfactory state in the octavo version. Wells-Taylor's chosen emendation 'be
holy then', based on the mansucripts, is the one I prefer; though the sense would be even clearer without
the brackets, e.g.: 'There is no heaven: be holy then, When time', etc. I give the o1 and manuscript
versions below.

because it is a parody of the other poem, written in cheerful reaction to its doubly preposterous premises: 'doubly' both in that the stratagem advocated by W. S. puts H. W. in the ridiculous position of the yearning Petrarchanist milksop, not unlike that of the hopelessly deluded Roderigo in *Othello*, and in that the ploy is unnecessary anyway, such chastity as Avisa's being a mere Petrarchan invention.[17]

For all its debunking of *Willobie his Avisa*,[18] 'When as thine eye' is in fact more complimentary to women than the poem it parodies. A more equal relationship, one that is perfectly honest in its own terms, is envisaged:

> Serve always with assured trust,
> And in thy sute be humble true,
> Unlesse thy Lady prove unjust,
> Prease never thou to chuse anew.
>
> (l. 19)

This evokes the other side of troubadour love in which a lover who has gained acceptance now acknowledges his own obligations to serve faithfully. The distinction lies between the commitment of faith rewarded (troubadourism à la Arnaut Daniel) and the blind service of a love without reward (troubadourism as modified by Petrarchanism). In contrast to this W. S.'s advice is simply to apply the Petrarchan line in the hope that something materially satisfying might come of it.

The point at which the two poems most echo one another is in their respective third stanzas in which they each speak of the effectiveness of 'gold':

> Apply her still with dyvers thinges,
> For giftes the wysest will deceave)
> Sometymes with gold, sometymes with ringes,
> No tyme nor fit occasion leave,
>   Though coy at first she seeme and wielde,
>   These toyes in tyme will make her yielde.
>
> (Canto XLVII, l. 13)

---

[17] I apply the terms 'Petrarchan' and 'Petrarchanist' in preference to 'Petrarchist', which denotes a stylistically more mannered poetry evolving out of the Petrarchan movement. While such developments were already taking place on the Continent, English poetry does not properly embrace them until the seventeenth century, and then largely in the defiant practice of Cavalier lyrists. 'Petrarchanism' seems apter to describe the comparatively unsophisticated manner of *Willobie*, which concerns itself more with the misapplication of traditional Petrarchan ethics than with subtleties of style.

[18] She is not really *his* Avisa since of course he never possesses her; she is rather, punningly, his 'adviser', an ideal or honest broker as opposed to the dealer in false wisdom represented by W. S. In addition, her name puns in different ways: she signs herself in conclusion 'Alway the Same' (Harrison, p. 170), suggesting that the Latin Avisa is a contraction or portmanteau for the English motto. Hadrian Dorrell in the 'Epistle to the Reader' (Harrison, p. 67) further comes up with the formula:

A.   V.   I.   S.   A.
Amans.   Vxor.   Inuiolata.   Semper.   Amanda.

Finally Harrison himself offers the view that the name puns on 'Avis' (bird), and indeed finds one or two women so called in the Cerne Abbas register, without significantly advancing his allegorical claims (Harrison, pp. 197–98).

And to her wil frame al thy waies,
Spare not to spend, and chiefly there,
Where thy desart may merit praise
By ringing in thy Ladies eare,
   The strongest castle, tower and towne,
   The golden bullet beats it downe.

('When as thine eye', l. 13)

W. S. urges H. W. to ply the lady with gifts, discreetly of course, which 'in tyme will make her yield'. Underscoring such advice is the reminder that she should be allowed to accept such 'toyes' in seeming modesty and at a 'fit occasion', otherwise she will appear merely brazen and not 'coy'. The 'gold' and 'ringes' are clearly gifts of money and jewellery. Comparing the two stanzas we can see how the one adopts and stylistically modifies the terms of the other, and, interestingly, the *Willobie* stanza enables us to resolve an awkward reading in 'When as thine eye', over which the manuscripts are at variance. Let us take the comparison between the stanzas first.

The author of 'When as thine eye' adopts the image of gold and rings and alters it subtly: the physical object 'ringes' modulates into the 'ringing' of 'praise', while 'gold' changes into the image of 'golden bullet' which might be interpreted as smooth-tongued oratory. Might be, but not necessarily; since the phrase 'Spare not to spend' reminds us of the strong likelihood of hard cash bolstering the fulsome compliments. What 'When as thine eye' seems to do is to take over a straightforward and poetically unambitious idea from *Willobie*, that of buying favours, and give it a more subtle ambivalence: gifts of cash and trinkets make a lover's praise more attractive. The connexion between money and oratory is so much the more artfully rendered. Developments such as this from the one poem to the other convince me that 'When as thine eye' was written in reaction to Canto XLVII.

The stanza from 'When as thine eye' is, as noted above, subject to slightly conflicting interpretations depending on what importance we allow the manuscripts. The couplet ending the stanza prior to this one, 'But plainly saye thou loust her well, | And set her person forth to sale' (ll. 11–12) reads markedly differently in both manuscripts. For the sake of clarity I will give the relevant two stanzas in each version, the printed *Passionate Pilgrim* text and the composite manuscript reading:

And when thou comst thy tale to tell,
Smooth not thy toung with filed talke,
Least she some subtil practise smell,
A Cripple soone can find a halt,
   But plainly saye thou lovst her well,
   And set her person forth to sale.

And to hir wil frame all thy waies,
Spare not to spend, and chiefly there,
Where thy desart may merit praise

By ringing in thy Ladies eare,
  The strongest castle, tower and towne,
  The golden bullet beats it downe.

(l. 7)

And when thou comest thy tale to tell
whet not thy tongue with filed talke
least she some subtle practice smell
a cripple soone can spie a halt
but plainely saye thou lovest her well:
and set thy body forth to sell.

Unto her will frame all thy waies
spare not to spend and chiefely there
where thy expence may sound thy praise
and still be ringinge in her eare
the strongest towres fort or towne,
the goulden bullet beateth downe.

(l. 7)[19]

The only serious difference between the manuscripts is that for 'body' (l. 12) MS 1.112 reads 'person', as in the printed text. But note that both manuscripts use the possessive adjective 'thy' for this object as opposed to the printed text's 'her'. A recommendation of the lady's person (the printed version) is set against promotion of one's own (person or body). The manuscript readings are closer to the terms of the *Willobie* poem, though that canto lacks an equivalent line for 'And set her/thy person forth'. It is logical that if the lover is equipping himself mainly with an argument based on cash (as he clearly is in the *Willobie* canto), then it is his own saleability that needs underlining. In so far as they do this, the manuscripts follow *Willobie*. But the *Passionate Pilgrim* text makes the important switch of person from him to her: it is the lady's person who should be 'set forth to sale' (i.e., she is to be convinced of her value in the eyes of her lover). A further instructive difference is that the manuscripts read 'expence' (MS 1.112 'expences') in l. 15 whereas the printed text has 'desart'. The choice of 'expence' accords with the cash angle and makes it clear that the 'sound' of praise is equivalent to the noise made by coins jingling — a crude enough point but consistent, I feel, with the *Willobie* canto's simple advice. By contrast, the printed version's reading 'desart' sets up a nice equivocation between her praise and his, what is owed to her and what to him, which accords well with the poem's greater subtlety as well as its impression of a more reciprocal relationship between lover and lady. Whereas Canto XLVII goes about its wooing in a slyly craven fashion, 'When as thine eye' proposes a much more equal exchange between the wooer and his mistress. While the pretence of chastity is

---

[19] *William Shakespeare: A Textual Companion*, ed. by Stanley Wells and Gary Taylor (Oxford: Oxford University Press, 1987), p. 456. Wells and Taylor print Folger MS 2071.7 (now reclassified as MS V.a.339) with slight emendations from Folger MS 1.112 (now MS V.a.89). The Folger cross-reference system allows the manuscript to be consulted using either reference.

boisterously exposed as a sham, and the erotic instinct degraded to the level of farmyard 'treading' (see l. 40), the loss of dignity is more than compensated for by the intimacy that follows the shedding of illusions. If Canto XLVII speaks of resolution under fire in a conventional image of the lover braving the lady's disdain ('At first repulse you must not faint', etc.), 'When as thine eye' recommends no less loyal a service — but to the lady herself rather than to the god of love:

> Serve alwaies with assured trust,
> And in thy suit be humble true,
> Unlesse thy Lady prove unjust,
> Prease never thou to chuse anew:
>   When time shal serve, be thou not slacke,
>   To profer, though she put thee backe.
>
> (l. 19)

These lines combine the notion of service in the field (the same military-erotic idea as that controlling the *Willobie* line quoted above) as well as faithfulness in requited love. Of the two kinds of service, sexual fidelity is likely to be more impressive to her than mere persistence. W. S.'s advice is full of rather unpleasant manoeuvres designed to deceive her into giving in. Only dissemble: 'If she be godly, you must sweare, | That to offend you stand in feare' (ll. 23–24). Avisa herself calls that sort of bluff, but being chaste, she can only refute it in conventional virtue's cheerfully hortatory, narrow, and uncomplicated terms:

> If honest love could breed content,
> And frame a liking to your will,
> I would not sticke to give consent,
> To like you so, and love you still,
>   But while lust leades your love awrie,
>   Assure your selfe, I will denie.
>
> (Canto LXIV, Harrison, p. 150)

Through *not* complimenting the lady on her virtue, 'When as thine eye' gives her marks for perceptiveness: none of these dissembler's tactics will work for the reason that she is too adept at guile herself to be taken in for a moment: 'A Cripple soone can finde a halt.'[20] This is a backhanded compliment but it helps ensure the poem's more realistic parameters. It also leads the lover to adopt the morally more acceptable posture of speaking plainly and without duplicity. For all its simplicity of expression, H. W.'s poem betrays his moral footwork quite painfully — an effect undoubtedly to be attributed to the author's intention but not something that makes for stylistic interest. In 'When as thine eye' the notion of wooing strategies breaking down before a superior instinctual guile while the direct approach is rewarded has, by

---

[20] i.e., something out of joint; 'halt' means a limping motion.

contrast, much to commend it despite the fact that the coarseness of its expression has proved too much for some readers.[21]

I have argued in the foregoing analysis that 'When as thine eye' succeeds *Willobie his Avisa* Canto XLVII chronologically, just as the printings of the two texts follow each other at an interval of five years. I have tried to show that the later poem was written in direct response to the former and that it parodies its terms of 'advice' as well as mocking its unreal assumptions about female chastity which are upheld generally in the poem by the figure of Avisa. Although the parody has little patience for the ideal, it is a more intelligent and morally more attractive poem, and indeed more sympathetic in tone, despite some scurrilous counter-assertions concerning the sexual character of women. It stands in relation to *Willobie*'s championship of ideal virtue rather as Shakespeare's Sonnet 130 does to the Petrarchist tradition. However, this is not to claim it as Shakespeare's. As argued above (pp. 115–17), all that connects it for certain with Shakespeare is Jaggard's decision to include it in a group of poems he brought out under Shakespeare's name, and that decision in turn was doubtless influenced by contemporary speculation that W. S. might indeed be Shakespeare. It is more likely that Jaggard took advantage of the association, already forming in contemporaries' minds, than that he planted the idea himself.[22] The third stanza, in particular, of 'When as thine eye' appears to be a modification of and ultimately a riposte to the woefully bland arguments of the *Willobie* canto.

In 1599 *Willobie his Avisa* was 'called in' by order of the Archbishop,[23] but unlike some other satirical, and in certain cases, pornographic works, it appears not to have been suppressed. Both Harrison (p. 186) and De Luna (p. 2) believe that political intrigue underlay the decision, but their assumptions are undermined by the plausibility we allow their theories (see above pp. 113–14). There is possibly more substance in C. F. Tucker Brooke's view that the action resulted from the publication in 1596 of *Penelope's Complaint* by Peter Colse, which attacks *Willobie his Avisa*.[24] The Bishops were nervous of literary quarrels, as witness their calling in of the respective publications of Harvey and Nashe. But it may have been the subject and tone of *Willobie his Avisa* that came up for inspection, rather than deeper, and frankly improbable, allegorical considerations. The tone is innocuous enough,

[21] For example, the Arden editor F. T. Prince dismisses it as 'ugly and stupid' (*William Shakespeare: The Poems* (London: Methuen, 1960), p. xxiii).
[22] The existence of more than one manuscript version of 'When as thine eye' argues that matters were beyond Jaggard's contriving. Although *The Passionate Pilgrim* seems to have been put together to meet 'Shakespearean' expectations, especially in its inclusion of the Venus and Adonis sonnets, it does not bear the mark of a very careful fabrication. Several of its poems are obviously filler pieces, patently without resemblance to anything of Shakespeare's style or themes, while certain items even then could be attributed to other authors.
[23] Harrison, p. 185.
[24] See 'Willobie's Avisa' in C. F. Tucker Brooke, *Essays on Shakespeare and other Elizabethans* (New Haven, CT: Yale University Press, 1948), pp. 173–77.

though some stanzas might have given pause to anybody bent on a vigorous clean-up of literary expression:

> Art thou preciser than a Queene:
> Queene Joane of Naples did not feare,
> To quite mens love, with love againe:
> And *Messalina*, 'tis no newes,
> Was dayly seene to haunt the stewes.
>
> (Harrison, p. 36)

But it is just as likely, indeed more so, that what prompted the action was the currency given to the poem, as a result of the parody of Canto XLVII circulating in ever more scurrilous manuscript versions and finally achieving print in *The Passionate Pilgrim*.

The Name of the Rose in *Romeo and Juliet*

CATHERINE BELSEY

University of Wales College of Cardiff

I

Is the human body inside or outside culture? Is it an organism, subject only to nature and independent of history? Or alternatively is it an effect of the signifier, no more than an ensemble of the meanings ascribed to it in different cultures, and thus historically discontinuous? Or, a third possibility, is this question itself reductive, a product of our wish to assign unambiguous causes and straightforward explanations?

When it comes to sexual desire, our culture is dominated by two distinct and largely contradictory models, both metaphysical in their assumption that we can identify what is fundamental in human nature. One metaphysic proposes that sex is a matter of the body, originating in the flesh and motivated by it, however people might deceive themselves with fantasies about romance. The other holds that love is a marriage of true minds, and that sex is (or ought to be) the bodily expression of this ideal relationship. Both models take for granted a dualist account of what it is to be a person, a mind on the one hand, and a body on the other, one of them privileged, the two either in harmony or in conflict. This dualism is associated with the Enlightenment and the moment of its crystallization is the Cartesian *cogito*.[1]

But in practice desire deconstructs the opposition between mind and body. Evidently it exists at the level of the signifier, as it imagines, fantasizes, idealizes. Desire generates songs and poetry and stories. Talking about it is pleasurable. At the same time, however, desire palpably inhabits the flesh, and seeks satisfaction there. Desire undoes the dualism common sense seems so often to take for granted.

The human body, we might want to argue in the light of our postmodernity, is subject to the imperatives of nature, but at the same time it does not exist outside culture. It owes to the differentiating symbol its existence as a single unit, with edges, limits. Psychoanalysis adds the presence of the symptom, evident on the body, the mark not of organic disease but of disorder at the level of the signifier, and psychoanalysis identifies the 'talking

I am grateful to Alan Dessen and Cynthia Dessen for their incisive comments on an earlier version of this essay.

[1] The dualism of the Enlightenment differs from Plato's and Augustine's. Both Platonic and medieval souls are immortal and their affiliations are divine. But the Cartesian mind is predominantly secular and human. Nor is its relation to the body always one of superiority. Enlightenment science, paradoxically, had the eventual effect of reversing Descartes's hierarchy.

cure' as the disorder's remedy.[2] Desire, it urges, is an effect of difference, in excess of the reproductive drive. Furthermore, it knows itself as desire to the degree that it reads both the signifying practices of the body and the cultural forms in which desire *makes sense*. It is not possible to isolate the human body as natural organism, even methodologically: such a body would precisely not be human.

Romeo and Juliet is a play about desire. It is also a text poised on the brink of the Enlightenment, and it can be read, I want to suggest, as engaging with some of these issues, putting forward for examination in the process paradoxes that, for all the historical difference, a postmodern moment can find sympathetic. The bodies of the lovers are inscribed and, crucially, tragically, named. Their own account of love, while it displays a longing to escape the constraints of the symbolic order, reveals in practice precisely the degree to which it is culture that enables love to make sense. In *Romeo and Juliet* desire imagines a metaphysical body that cannot be realized.

II

Though there can be no doubt that Renaissance culture was profoundly and distinctively patriarchal, one sphere in which Shakespeare's women are perfectly equal to men is their capacity for experiencing sexual desire. Venus, Cleopatra, Portia in *The Merchant of Venice*,[3] and, of course, Juliet, are presented as sharing with their near-contemporaries, Alice Arden, the Duchess of Malfi, Beatrice-Joanna and Ford's Annabella, for example, an intensity of passion which is not evidently exceeded by that attributed to the men they love. These women are shown as subjects and agents of their own desire, able to speak of it and to act on the basis of it.

Meanwhile, Thomas Laqueur's *Making Sex* assembles persuasive documentation from the Greeks to the Renaissance of similar asumptions among European analysts of physiology and anatomy. Laqueur finds in this distinct sphere of knowledge, which is also, of course, a distinct discursive genre, what he calls the 'one-sex' model of the human body. The one-sex understanding of the body prevailed, he argues, until modern science redefined women and men as *opposite* and antithetical sexes. In the one-sex body the sexual organs are understood to be similarly distributed among men and women, though externally visible in men and internal in women. Thus the vagina commonly corresponds to the penis, the uterus to the scrotum, and so

<hr/>

[2] Charles Shepherdson, 'Biology and History: Some Psychoanalytic Aspects of the Writing of Luce Irigaray', *Textual Practice*, 6 (1992), 47–86. I owe to the clarity of that essay the theoretical framework of my argument here.
[3] *The Merchant of Venice*, III. 2. 108–14. Shakespeare references are to *The Riverside Shakespeare*, ed. by G. Blakemore Evans and others (Boston: Houghton Mifflin, 1974).

on. Laqueur is clear about the implications of this account for the understanding of erotic impulses themselves: both sexes were capable of intense
sexual pleasure; both sexes experienced desire. Indeed, it was widely held
that female pleasure was necessary to conception, and this was consequently seen as an important project of male sexual activity. Desire was
not in any sense a masculine prerogative. On the contrary,

The process of generation might differ in its nuances as the vital heats, the seeds,
and the physical qualities of the substances being ejaculated differed between the
sexes — but libido, as we might call it, had no sex.[4]

Some Renaissance physicians would have gone even further. Jacques Ferrand, for example, whose second treatise on lovesickness was published in
Paris in 1623, argues that, being less rational than men, women are
correspondingly more subject to violent erotic desires, and less able to
resist their own impulses. A woman, according to Ferrand, 'is in her Loves
more Passionate, and more furious in her follies, then a man is'.[5]

Laqueur does not, of course, imply that the one-sex body was the
product of a less patriarchal culture. On the contrary, the male body
represented the ideal of perfection; the female body, meanwhile, differed
from it because women possessed less of the vital heat which pushed the
sexual organs outwards. But the difference was one of degree, Laqueur
insists, not kind. Women, less perfect than men, were in consequence less
entitled to power and prestige. But they were not men's opposite, passive
and passionless where men were active and desiring. That antithesis
belongs to a later epoch.

Renaissance medical knowledge is neither a source of the plays nor a
guarantee of their meanings. It is too easily supposed that we can read off
the true meaning of fictional texts from the other knowledges of the period,
as if the culture somehow shared a single, homogeneous account of the
world, and was in that respect simpler, less diverse than our own.[6] We

---

[4] Thomas Laqueur, *Making Sex: The Body and Gender from the Greeks to Freud* (Cambridge, MA: Harvard
University Press, 1990), p. 43.

[5] Jacques Ferrand, *Erotomania*, trans. by Edmund Chilmead (Oxford, 1640), p. 214. Female desire was
widely taken for granted in the Middle Ages, and natural philosophy commonly presented women as
more libidinous than men (Mary Frances Wack, *Lovesickness in the Middle Ages: The 'Viaticum' and its
Commentaries* (Philadelphia: University of Pennsylvania Press, 1990), pp. 110–25.

[6] The New Historicism sets out to break with this version of the Elizabethan world picture by insisting
on the single anecdote which is not offered as 'representative'. But though it produces acute insights, the
New Historicist juxtaposition of fiction with quite different knowledges, as if it could be taken for granted
that they illuminate each other, risks repeating Tillyard's unifying and simplifying gesture. In 'Fiction
and Friction', for example, after a number of disclaimers Stephen Greenblatt goes on to identify
Renaissance England as 'a culture that knows, as a widely accepted physical truth, that women have
occulted, inward penises' (*Shakespearean Negotiations: The Circulation of Social Energy in Renaissance England*
(Oxford: Clarendon Press, 1988), pp. 66–93, p. 87). He then uses this medical knowledge to explain the
transvestite theatre, female cross-dressing in Shakespeare's comedies, and homoerotic desire in the
period. All this is suggestive, inventive, and challenging, but it fails to take account of the counter-
knowledge, evident in the bawdy jokes of the theatrical tradition itself, that women lacked what men

should not now expect popular romance to depict the world in the same way as psychoanalysis, and even current pornography frequently takes precious little account of elementary anatomy. I invoke Laqueur's extremely valuable work here simply as additional evidence that it was possible in the sixteenth and seventeenth centuries to imagine female desire, and even to take it seriously.

But there are also significant generic differences between Renaissance anatomy and Renaissance fiction. In the medical treatises libido had no necessary moral implications: this was a knowledge which set out to record the world it found in the authorities and in experience. The drama, however, makes no attempt at value-free analysis. It cannot avoid showing the implications of the passions it depicts, and consequently it tends, whether incidentally or as its main project, to offer an assessment and evaluation of female desire. But the judgements it makes are by no means univocal or monolithic. As my examples suggest, desire may lead women into bad ways (*Arden of Faversham, The Changeling*); it may be radically misdirected (*'Tis Pity She's a Whore*), or innocent in itself but unfortunate in its consequences (*The Duchess of Malfi*); its moral status may be profoundly ambiguous (*Antony and Cleopatra*); it may be seen as lyrical but at the same time absurd (*Venus and Adonis*). But alternatively, desire reciprocated may be the foundation of conjugal marriage and (we are invited to assume) the nuclear family, as it is in Shakespeare's comedies. It was the Enlightenment, according to Laqueur, which insisted on the two-sex model of male and female bodies, the woman's lacking what defined the man's. And it was also the Enlightenment which tended to polarize male erotic activity and female passivity. Not until the nineteenth century was it established as a fact of nature that good women had no sexual feelings at all. The oppositional stereotypes of sexless virgin and voracious whore are not helpful in making sense of the work of Shakespeare and his contemporaries.

III

There was of course a convention, not that women should feel nothing, but that they should appear aloof in order to intensify male desire. This is the convention that Juliet unwittingly breaks when she declares her love at her window, only to be overhead by Romeo. It is quite late in their discussion, however, that she alludes, perhaps rather perfunctorily, to the proprieties of female behaviour: 'Fain would I dwell on form, fain, fain deny | What I have

---

possessed. Greenblatt himself cites Viola's 'a little thing would make me tell them how much I lack of a man' (*Twelfth Night*, III.4.302–03). Gratiano's 'would he were gelt that had it' is comic if Nerissa is understood to be 'gelded' (*The Merchant of Venice*, v. 1. 144). See also: '"That's a fair thought to lie between a maid's legs." "What is?" "Nothing."' (*Hamlet*, III.2.118–21), and David Wilbern, 'Shakespeare's Nothing', in *Representing Shakespeare: New Psychoanalytic Essays*, ed. by Murray Schwarz and Coppélia Kahn (Baltimore: Johns Hopkins University Press, 1980), pp. 244–63.

spoke, but farewell compliment!' (*Romeo and Juliet*, II. 2. 88–89). The moment
for observing the conventions has clearly passed, and propriety itself soon
becomes matter for a teasing romantic overture on her part:'If thou thinkest
I am too quickly won, | I'll frown and be perverse, and say thee nay, | So thou
wilt woo, but else not for the world' (II. 2. 95–97).

At the heart of the play it is Juliet who speaks most elequently and
urgently to define, perhaps on behalf of both lovers, the desire experienced in
the secret life of the body:

> Gallop apace, you fiery-footed steeds,
> Towards Phoebus' lodging; such a waggoner
> As Phaeton would whip you to the west,
> And bring in cloudy night immediately.
>
> (III. 2. 1)

The opening imperative, in conjunction with the image of the pounding,
burning hooves, suggests the speeding pulses and the impatient ardour of
desire, as well as its barely controlled power, and the allusion to Phaeton
which follows evokes the boy's failure to manage Apollo's unruly horses, and
so implies a surrender of what remains of restraint. Juliet's speech is entirely
explicit in its invocation of love performed, acted, possessed and enjoyed.
Their wedding night will be 'a winning match | Play'd' between a symmetri-
cally and reciprocally desiring couple 'for a pair of stainless maidenhoods'
(ll. 12–13). This necessarily clandestine love — perhaps the more thrilling
because it is clandestine, because the fear of discovery intensifies the danger
and the excitement[7] — is to be enacted in secret, in total darkness, and in
silence:

> Spread thy close curtain, love-performing night,
> That [th'] runaways's eyes may wink, and Romeo
> Leap to these arms untalk'd of and unseen!
> Lovers can see to do their amorous rites
> By their own beauties.
>
> (l. 5)

The (bed-)curtain of the dark is to exclude all outsiders, and the runaway
god of love himself will close his eyes,[8] so that no one sees their union, not
even the lovers. If 'see' is a metaphor (l. 8), they are to be guided in the
performance of their amorous rites by the beauty of each other's bodies.
Love, the conceit implies, has no need of light, since its mode of 'seeing' is
tactile, sensational. And the syntax here might lead us to suppose that if the
lovers are 'unseen' by themselves as well as other people, so too, perhaps, the
act is 'untalk'd of' by the lovers, since speech is also superfluous. Indeed,

---

[7] Julia Kristeva, *Tales of Love*, trans. by Leon S. Roudiez (New York: Columbia University Press, 1987),
p. 211.
[8] Gary M. McCown, '"Runnawayes Eyes" and Juliet's Epithalamium', *Shakespeare Quarterly*, 27 (1976),
150–70, pp. 156–65.

night is invited to obscure even the signifying practices of the virgin body: 'Hood my unmann'd blood, bating [fluttering] in my cheeks, | With thy black mantle' (ll. 14–15). It is as if Juliet imagines the presence of the desiring bodies as pure sensation, sightless, speechless organisms in conjunction, flesh on flesh, independent of the signifier. A rose by any other name, she had earlier supposed, would smell as sweet (ii. 2. 43–44): the same gases, emanating from the same petals, striking the same nostrils, its physical being separable from the word that names it. The name, the signifier, and the symbolic order in its entirety are to be relegated to a secondary position, the place of the merely expressive and instrumental.

But these isolated, unnamed bodies (and roses) are only imaginary. The human body is already inscribed: it has no existence as pure organism, independent of the symbolic order in which desire makes sense In the sixteenth-century text Juliet's imagined act of love is paradoxically defined in a densely metaphoric and tightly structured instance of signifying practice. The speech depends on invocations repeated with a difference ('Come civil night [. . .] Come night, come Romeo [. . .] Come gentle night, (ll. 10, 17, 20)), framing an elaborate conceit in which the love-performing darkness both is and is not synonymous with Romeo himself, the lover who is ultimately to be perpetuated in little stars (l. 22). The text specifies a wish in a tissue of formally ordered allusions, comparisons and puns, which constitute a poem, the zenith of signification, self-conscious, artful, witty. In order to bring before us its imagined bodies, the play here invokes a long poetic and rhetorical tradition, and in the process the lyricism which conjures up the act of love necessarily supplants it too. Moreover, this is a set piece, an epithalamion, though it is spoken, ironically, not by the assembled wedding guests, but by the bride herself, and in solitude.[9] What is enacted within it is desire imagining its fulfilment, and not the event itself, nor even any possible event. Love is inevitably performed within culture, within, indeed, a specific culture: bodies do not exist outside the cultural moment which defines them, and experience cannot be identified beyond the meanings a cultural tradition makes intelligible. What we call a rose might take any other name, but if it were nameless, outside difference, who is to say that its smell would be 'sweet'? Here too a whole cultural tradition underlies the recognition (re-cognition) of this sweetness — and its association with love.

Romeo and Juliet is about desire. It is also one of Shakespeare's most evidently formal, conventional texts. As Rosalie Colie points out, the play draws on the traditions of Roman comedy, with its young woman and two suitors, one of them approved by her father. The garrulous nurse belongs to the same genre. Meanwhile, the Prologues to Acts i and ii are sonnets, and the lovers converse in Petrarchan imagery. Mercutio, on the other hand, is an Ovidian figure. When the lovers are together they perform in joint

[9] McCown, '"Runnawayes Eyes"', p. 165.

and reciprocal set pieces: first a sonnet (1.5.93–106) and then an *aubade* (III.5.1–36). But there is no necessary contradiction, Colie proposes, between convention and desire: on the contrary, the effect in the text is precisely to naturalize the familiar forms. 'One of the most pleasurable, for me, of Shakespeare's many talents, is his "unmetaphoring" of literary devices, his sinking of the conventions back into what, he somehow persuades us, is "reality"'. The Petrarchan convention of love at first sight, she goes on to argue, 'is here made to seem entirely natural [...] its conventionality forgotten as it is unmetaphored by action.'[10]

In this respect, Colie might have added, Shakespeare's text is no more than a superlative instance of culture in general, which works precisely by unmetaphoring the device and naturalizing inherited forms. There is no unmediated experience located entirely outside the existing semiotic repertoire, though there are, as the play demonstrates, unexpected deviations, juxtapositions, turns, and resistances. In the play Ovid disrupts Petrarch; comic form leads to tragic denouement; choric narrative appropriates the lyric voice of the sonnet. Culture imagines the symbol as truth, and 'proves' its case by novelty, demonstrating that it is constantly possible to formulate something new, surprising or unexpected.

In a brilliant discussion of the formality of *Romeo and Juliet* Gayle Whittier argues that the play shows how the inherited word declines 'from lyric freedom to tragic fact.'[11] She points out that the poetic mode in which Romeo falls in love precedes him, and that he longs to be the author of the lover he becomes. But in Whittier's account the narrative mode of drama displaces the abstract and timeless paradoxes of Petrarchan poetry. It endows the word with flesh, and in the process necessarily subjects it to time and death. Poetry, Whittier argues, is transcendent: love is referential. The bodies of the lovers exist in time, and confront death: the poetry which precedes them also survives them.

The argument is extremely convincing, and it is eloquently presented. If in the end I put a slightly different case, the distinction between us is perhaps no more than a matter of emphasis. I want to stress the degree to which the letter invades the flesh, and the body necessarily inhabits the symbolic. This above all is the source of the tragedy of *Romeo and Juliet*. Petrarch, their names and the word of the Prince ('banished') are all decisive for the protagonists, but the symbolic order is not external to their identities: on the contrary, it is exactly the element in which they subsist. On the other hand, they exceed it too. The body which it defines is not contained by the symbol, and desire seeks to overflow the limits imposed by the differential signifier.

---

[10] Rosalie Colie, *Shakespeare's 'Living Art'* (Princeton, NJ: Princeton University Press, 1974), pp. 135–67, p. 145.
[11] Gayle Whittier, 'The Sonnet's Body and the Body Sonnetized in *Romeo and Juliet*', *Shakespeare Quarterly*, 40 (1989), 27–41, p. 27.

IV

In recognizing that the name of the rose is arbitrary, Juliet shows herself a Saussurean *avant la lettre*, but in drawing the inference that Romeo can arbitrarily cease to be a Montague, she simply affirms what her own desire dictates.

> O Romeo, Romeo, wherefore art thou Romeo?
> Deny thy father and refuse thy name;
> Or, if thou wilt not, be but sworn my love,
> And I'll no longer be a Capulet [. . .]
> 'Tis but thy name that is my enemy;
> Thou art thyself, though not a Montague.
> What's Montague? It is nor hand nor foot,
> Nor arm nor face, [nor any other part]
> Belonging to a man. O, be some other name!
> What's in a name? That which we call a rose
> By any other word would smell as sweet;
> So Romeo would, were he not Romeo call'd,
> Retain that dear perfection which he owes
> Without that title. Romeo, doff thy name,
> And for thy name, which is no part of thee,
> Take all myself.
>
> (II. 2. 33–49)

Identity, the speech acknowledges, exists in the symbolic as the Name of the Father. Juliet imagines a succession of (im)possibilities: that Romeo should repudiate his father's name, or she hers; that he should be named differently; and finally that he should simply remove his name, as if it were extrinsic, separable from identity. In place of Romeo's name Juliet offers her 'self', implying that beyond their names, as beyond the name of the rose, the lovers could exist as unnamed selves. This move to transcend the signifier, however, the play at once makes clear, is precisely a contradiction. In offering to take what she urges *literally*, Romeo can only propose punningly to assume another *name*, to adopt a different location in the symbolic:

> I'll take thee at thy word
> Call me but love, and I'll be new baptiz'd;
> Henceforth I never will be Romeo.
>
> (l. 49)

But the signifier, however arbitrary, is not at the disposal of the subject. Romeo's name precedes him, makes him a subject, locates him in the community of Verona. It is not optional. Later Romeo will offer to excise his murderous name, but he cannot do so without killing himself:

> O, tell me, friar, tell me,
> In what vile part of this anatomy
> Doth my name lodge? Tell me, that I may sack
> The hateful mansion.
>
> (III. 3. 105)

Unlike hand or foot, Romeo's name is not something that he can lose and retain his identity, continuing to be the specific, differentiated Romeo that Juliet loves.

Lovers are prone to perceive the imaginary essence of the object of desire, to identify a 'self', a presence which subsists beyond the symbolic order, the 'dear perfection' of the loved one independent of the public and external name. This is the evidence of their idealizing passion. A lover who might be expected to know better, the author of Jacques Derrida's sequence of postcards, also affirms something of this kind:

> you will never be your name, you never have been, even when, and especially when you have answered to it. The name is made to do without the life of the bearer, and is therefore always somewhat the name of someone dead. One could not live, be there, except by protesting against one's name, by protesting one's non-identity with one's proper name.[12]

Here too, the letter kills, we are invited to suppose, but desire gives life. The name is a trapping, inessential, inherited or given, a reminder that the individual's autonomy is always imaginary, the effect of a place allotted by others, by the family, by a whole culture.

But Derrida's amorous-philosophical text is not naïve (of course!). The name is dead because it is ancestral; it is dead because in differentiating the person that it names, it constitutes a reminder of all the other possible objects of desire, and the arbitrariness that singles out *this* one; and it is dead finally because it stands in for the person it names, and thus supplants the being who elicits so much intensity, intervening between the lover and the loved one. But there is no suggestion that it is possible to do more than protest against the imposed identity, to insist on non-identity with *that*, to refuse the imposition. Though it imagines it in an oxymoron ('I am calling you [...] beyond your name, beyond all names',[13] the text does not in the end suppose that the person could exist independently, a free-floating essence beyond nomenclature, which is to say beyond difference.

Nor, indeed, is Shakespeare's text naïve. The name of Montague, imposed, ancestral, *is* Juliet's enemy, the text as a whole makes clear. If Romeo's non-identity with his name legitimates their love, the repudiated name returns, nevertheless, to ensure their tragedy. Even though his name is no part of the man Juliet loves, the play at once draws attention to the impossibility of discarding the name which differentiates him. Hearing in the darkness a voice reply to her musings, the shocked Juliet demands, 'What man art thou?' (l. 52), and how else can Romeo indicate who he is but by reference to a name which precisely cannot be specified without identifying an opponent of all Capulets:

---

[12] Jacques Derrida, *The Post Card: From Socrates to Freud and Beyond*, trans. by Alan Bass (Chicago: University of Chicago Press, 1987), p. 39.
[13] Derrida, *The Post Card*, p. 130. Compare: 'But it is you I still love, the living one. Beyond everything, beyond your name, your name beyond your name' (p. 144).

> By a name
> I know not how to tell thee who I am.
> My name, dear saint, is hateful to myself,
> Because it is an enemy to thee.
>
> (II. 2. 53)

In the event, Juliet recognizes his voice, a property of the lover like hand or foot, or any other part, and promptly puts her recognition to the test — by naming him:

> My ears have not yet drunk a hundred words
> Of thy tongue's uttering, yet I know the sound.
> Art thou not Romeo, and a Montague
>
> (l. 58)

The question of names recurs at intervals throughout Derrida's 'Envois' to *The Post Card*. The text is at least in part an engagement with Oxford philosophy and its distinction between 'use' and 'mention' ('Fido is my dog'; '"Fido" is a possible name for a dog'). But this issue is part of a larger debate in Western philosophy concerning the question whether proper names have meaning. The answer to this question has implications for our understanding of the relationship between language and the world,[14] and this in turn is the problem Derrida has addressed throughout his work. Proper names imply that words may be no more than substitutes for things, labels for the objects they refer to, without meaning in themselves. What, after all, does 'Smith' mean? If names have no meaning, however, but only reference, what are we to say when the name is Medusa, and the referent does not exist? And is 'Homer' meaningless? Or does 'Homer' precisely *mean* the anonymous author(s) of the *Iliad* and the *Odyssey*, who must have existed, but probably not as Homer? If so, is meaning independent of what goes on in the world, a matter of shared, inherited knowledge, which may be false? Who does Homer's name belong to? To an individual? Or to a culture? What *gives* it its meaning?[15]

The 'Envois' to *The Post Card* consists of a series of love letters to an unnamed person, addressed poste restante 'because of all the families' (p. 45). The epistolary form throws into relief the problems of 'communication', and the story of a passionate clandestine love makes evident how much is at stake in the process of writing. The secret love letter is a paradigm case of the urgency and the impossibility of meaning as immediate, transparent, individual, exclusive *presence*. All language is subject to what Derrida calls 'the Postal Principle as differantial relay' (p. 54). The message is always differed and deferred (differantiated), since the intervals and the distance, the delays and relays, separate the people it was designed to unite. Much of Derrida's love story concerns a critical, definitive, 'true' letter which fails to

---

[14] See J. R. Searle, 'Proper Names and Descriptions', *The Encyclopaedia of Philosophy*, ed. by Paul Edwards, 8 vols (London: Collier Macmillan, 1967), VI, 487–91.
[15] I am grateful to Andrew Belsey for a discussion of the problem of proper names.

arrive. Instead it is eventually returned unopened, and remains for ever unread by the addressee, unopened by the sender, though it goes on to haunt the relationship, since its existence cannot be forgotten. This 'dead letter' is at once outside the living love affair and formative for it. In response to Lacan's account of *The Purloined Letter*, Derrida's text insists that the letter never arrives at its destination.

At the same time, *The Post Card* proposes, the letter can never ensure its own secrecy. However cryptic it is, however coded, designed exclusively for the recipient, if the message is intelligible, it is always able to be intercepted, read, misread, reproduced. Since it is necessarily legible for another, who does the letter belong to? To the sender, the addressee, or an apparently irrelevant unspecified third party, representative of the symbolic order in all its (dead) otherness? Their secret love does not belong exclusively to Romeo and Juliet. To the degree that it inhabits the symbolic, to the extent that it is relayed in messages and letters, even when the messages in question are those of the signifying body itself, love is tragically not theirs to control.

Derrida's text refuses to name its object of desire, the secret addressee of the love letters, though it plays with a succession of possible names (Esther, Judith, Bettina (pp. 71–73, 231)). It names others, however, who feature in the itinerary of the lover (Neil Hertz, Hillis, Paul, Jonathan, and Cynthia, and a woman who seems tantalizingly, comically, to be called Metaphysics (p. 197)). It thus keeps the reader guessing, about the identity of the beloved, and about whether the named and apparently non-fictional figures can be ruled out (p. 223). It names the writer, but only (punningly?) as acquiescent, as *j'accepte* ('this will be my signature henceforth [. . .] it is my name, that *j'accepte*' (p. 26)), leaving in doubt whether the whole story is fictional, or in some disguised and elusive way referential, 'true', and problematizing in the process those terms themselves. But though it withholds the name of the loved one, it substitutes a pronoun, 'you': a shifter, certainly, but no less differential for that. The amorous project is to locate the living object of desire beyond the inherited, dead signifier, to invest it with a transcendent existence outside mortality. At the same time, of course, *The Post Card* recognizes this impulse as imaginary, 'metaphysical', and perhaps in the process offers another clue — or possibly a red herring — which might lead us to identify the object itself:

You have always been 'my' metaphysics, the metaphysics of my life, the 'verso' of everything I write (my desire, speech, presence, proximity, law, my heart and soul, everything that I love and that you know before me).   (p. 197)

The beloved is not named, but is not nameless either, for the lover or the world:

I have not named you while showing you to others, I have never shown you to others with the name they know you by and that I consider only the homonym of the one that I give you, no, I have called you, yourself.   (p. 219)

'Yourself' is not an unmediated self. It is not a name, but at the same time it is not independent of the signifier. And as a shifter, it patently does not belong to the unnamed object of desire.

Romeo and Juliet are not reducible to their proper names, but they are not beyond them either, though in their idealizing, transfiguring imagery they repeatedly locate each other outside mortality, in the heavens, among the inauspicious stars, not at their mercy (II. 2. 2; 15–22; III. 2. 22–25). And their names are not their property: they do not belong to them in the same way as hand or foot, or any other part. As subjects, the lovers aspire both to love and to immortality only by virtue of the differentiating, inherited signifier, which subjects them, in the event, to death itself.

V

What is at issue in the *aubade* is the name of the lark.

> Wilt thou be gone? it is not yet near day.
> It was the nightingale, and not the lark,
> That pierc'd the fearful hollow of thine ear.

(III. 5. 1)

The referential truth is available here, but it is not what matters. The debate is about the significance of the birdsong that the lovers hear, its meaning: not ornithology, but the time of day. The same bird known by any other name would make the same sound, but it would be of no interest unless a culture had already invested the song with the meaning of dawn. It is the lark: Romeo proves it on the evidence of other signifiers:

> Look, love, what envious streaks
> Do lace the severing clouds in yonder east.
> Night's candles are burnt out

(l. 7)

The lark is already inscribed as 'the herald of the morn' (l. 6), and while the time of day is also referential, a matter of fact, it too is in question here in its meaning, as the signifier of the moment when Romeo's banishment takes effect, separating, because of their names, the desiring bodies of the lovers. The world of nature, of birdsong and morning, is already invaded by culture, even though it also exceeds it, and the knowledge that it purveys is necessarily at the level of signification.

Juliet's epithalamion is uttered, ironically, in the direct shadow of the Prince's sentence, immediately after it is pronounced (III. 1. 186–97), but thanks to the Postal Principle she does not yet know it. When the message that Romeo is banished is finally delivered by the Nurse, her account initially obscures the truth, and Juliet believes that Romeo is dead (III. 2. 36–70). Juliet's premature lament for Romeo here finds a parallel in the family's lamentations for her apparent death (IV. 5). Both are displaced, inappropriate, and yet not wholly irrelevant, since they anticipate the events of the play, as if the signifier lived a life of its own, partly but not entirely independent of the referent. Meanwhile, Friar Lawrence's letter fails to reach its destination and Romeo, in possession of another narrative, the public account relayed by Balthasar, tragically returns to act on Juliet's supposed death.

The Prince speaks the sentence of banishment, but it is to be carried out on Romeo's body, causing either his absence or his death. Romeo's absence is a kind of death for Juliet too, she affirms:

> Some word there was, worser than Tybalt's death,
> That murder'd me; I would forget it fain,
> But O, it presses to my memory
> Like damned guilty deeds to sinners' minds:
> 'Tybalt is dead, and Romeo banished.'
>
> (III. 2. 108)

The insistent signifier is determining for the bodies of the lovers, and yet at the same time it is not definitive, in the sense that its implications are not contained by its meaning. '"Romeo is banished": to speak that word, | Is father, mother, Tybalt, Romeo, Juliet, | All slain, all dead.' (ll. 122–24). The signifier, which differentiates, specifies limits and imposes boundaries, also evokes an unspeakable residue, boundless and unlimited: 'There is no end, no limit, measure, bound, | In that word's death, no words can that woe sound' (ll. 125–26). The woe exceeds the word because no word can make it present. Supplanted by the signifier, it exists as an absence hollowed out within the utterance — just as it does within the corresponding signifying practice of the body, the weeping which is to follow (ll. 130–31).

In the same way, the signifier cannot exhaust desire, since desire inhabits the residue that exceeds what can be said. Challenged to 'unfold' in speech the happiness of her marriage, Juliet replies:

> Conceit, more rich in matter than in words,
> Brags of his substance, not of ornament;
> They are but beggars that can count their worth,
> But my true love is grown to such excess
> I cannot sum up sum of half my wealth.
>
> (II. 6. 30)

Love, Juliet claims, like the unnamed rose or the untalked of act, is more substantial than mere words. For this reason, she continues, its substance cannot be counted, cannot be summed up in words. And she makes the affirmation in an ornamental metaphor, an analogy between love and wealth familiar to us from the *Sonnets* and from Theseus's opening speech in *A Midsummer Night's Dream*. The comparison, which brings the intensity of the love before us, simultaneously has the effect of supplanting it, replacing it by the signifier, so that the speech demonstrates precisely the impossibility it affirms of putting love into words. This excess of love over the signifier is what invests desire with metaphysics, and at the same time, if Derrida is to be believed, the metaphysical with desire. As speaking subjects, we long for the unattainable verso of signifying practice — proximity, certainty, presence, the thing itself. Lovers long to make present the unspeakable residue which constitutes desire.

VI

Shakespeare's play ends with death, the golden statues — and names again. At the beginning of the final scene Paris decorously strews Juliet's tomb with flowers and sweet water, in a gesture appropriate to a man who would have been her bridegroom. He is interrupted by her actual bridegroom, whose intentions, in contrast, are excessive, in every sense of the word: 'savage-wild, | More fierce and more inexorable far | Than empty tigers or the roaring sea' (v. 3. 37–39). Alan Dessen makes the point that modern productions commonly include a structure which represents the tomb. This, he argues persuasively, is not necessarily how the scene would have been staged in the 1590s. On the contrary, the tomb might well have been no more than a stage door or a trap door in the stage, and Juliet's body might have been thrust out on a bier at the point when the scene shifts to the inside of the tomb. Including the tomb, as they do, Dessen says, modern productions often leave out Romeo's mattock and crowbar. In consequence, they fail to do full justice to the emblematic contrast the scene sets up between Romeo and Paris, the one sprinkling scented water on the grave, and the other violating the tomb with an iron bar, forcing open what he himself calls this 'womb of death' (l. 45).[16] When Romeo, who is beside himself with passion, offers to *strew* the churchyard with the interloper's limbs, the contrast is surely complete.

Explaining his purpose, Romeo 'lies' to Balthasar:

> Why I descend into this bed of death
> Is partly to behold my lady's face,
> But chiefly to take thence from her dead finger
> A precious ring . . .

(l. 28)

The lie is also intelligible as a coded truth, a cryptic declaration of a real purpose, not intended to be legible to Balthasar, of re-enacting his clandestine marriage by a second exchange of rings. In the grotesque parody of the wedding night that follows, Romeo seeks a repetition in the tomb of the original darkness, silence and secrecy invoked so eloquently in Juliet's epithalamion, though once again these amorous rites are to be lit by beauty,

---

[16] Alan C. Dessen, 'Much Virtue in "As"' in *Shakespeare and the Sense of Performance: Essays in the Tradition of Performance Criticism in Honor of Bernard Beckerman*, ed. by Marvin and Ruth Thompson (Newark, NJ: University of Delaware Press, 1989), pp. 132–38.

as Juliet, who once taught the torches to burn bright (1.5.44), now 'makes |
This vault a feasting presence full of light' (v.3.85–86).

This time, too, the body signifies. There is blood in Juliet's face once more,
to the point where Romeo seems almost to read the message it puts out:

> O my love, my wife,
> Death, that hath suck'd the honey of thy breath,
> Hath had no power yet upon thy beauty:
> Thou art not conquer'd, beauty's ensign yet
> Is crimson in thy lips and in thy cheeks,
> And death's pale flag is not advanced there.
>
> (l. 91)

But because his understanding at this moment is constructed in accordance
with another narrative, he cannot read the story of Juliet's living body.
Again he turns to her, this time with a question: 'Ah, dear Juliet, | Why art
thou yet so fair?' (ll. 101–02). The audience could have told him the answer
(and perhaps did in early productions?). But Romeo, in the light of what he
thinks he knows, produces another hypothesis:

> Shall I believe
> That unsubstantial Death is amorous,
> And that the lean abhorred monster keeps
> Thee here in dark to be his paramour?
>
> (l. 102)

(It is tempting, especially in the context of Georges Bataille's current
popularity, to find an erotics of death in this conceit, but it is worth bearing
in mind that from the point of view of the audience, the account is ironic,
since it represents precisely the wrong answer.)[17] The re-enacting of the
wedding night remains in consequence imaginary.They die, as Juliet performed their epithalamion, separately. 'These lovers of the night remain', as
Kristeva puts it, 'solitary beings.'[18]

Their grave is not, however, a private place. On the contrary, it is the
family vault of the Capulets, a memorial, precisely, to the name, which is all
that remains of their ancestors, but which lives on to shadow the present so
tragically. Moreover, no sooner has he established the close-curtained
secrecy of this second wedding night, than Romeo interrupts his address to
Juliet to recognize the dead body of Tybalt in its bloody sheet (l. 97). Once
again Tybalt, who insisted on the importance of Romeo's name and the
'stock and honor' of his own kin (1.5.54, 58, 61), and who for that reason
fatally sustained the feud, intervenes between the lovers, as an emblematic
third party, representative of the inherited symbolic order in all its dead —
and deadly — otherness. Finally, the whole community crowds in, the

---

[17] See Georges Bataille, *Erotism: Death and Sensuality*, trans. by Mary Dalwood (San Francisco: City
Lights Books, 1986); and *The Tears of Eros*, trans. by Peter Connor (San Francisco: City Lights Books,
1989).
[18] Kristeva, *Tales of Love*, p. 216.

community which is ultimately responsible for the arbitrary and pointless ancestral quarrel, and which is powerless to reverse the effects of a violence carried on in the names of Montague and Capulet, and enacted on the bodies of the new generation.

VII

Romeo and Juliet are immortalized as signifiers. The promised golden statues are, of course, a metamorphosis, effigies of their bodies, beautiful, precious, and lifeless. Metamorphosis enacts something of the project of desire, arresting, and stabilizing the object, fixing it as possession — and supplanting it in the process. Like metaphor, metamorphosis offers an image in place of the thing itself, but the image is precisely *not the same*. Venus is able to hold the flower that Adonis becomes, but the flower is no longer Adonis. The reconciling golden statues appear too late to interrupt the fatal invasion of the signifier into the living organism. Verona will recognize the effigies of Romeo and Juliet, but the effigies will signify concord, not desire.

And yet finally, as is to be expected of signifiers, the lovers are incorporated into a love story, foretold by the Prince, dramatized by Shakespeare. The play closes, appropriately, with their names, which are not synonymous with the lovers themselves, but which are not independent of them either. The play, and the legend of love that the play has become, have been astonishingly popular from the Restoration period on. The text has been performed, adapted, cut, reinterpreted, rewritten as a musical, filmed,[19] and now produced as a movie starring cats. Even in death, therefore, the record of the lovers' desiring, inscribed bodies is preserved in the archive, filed, appropriately enough, under their names:

> For never was a story of more woe
> Than this of Juliet and her Romeo.
>
> (v. 3. 309)

Evidently it was possible, before the dualism of the Enlightenment separated us all neatly into minds and bodies, to identify another relationship between the organism and the culture in which it becomes a human being. *Romeo and Juliet* dramatizes the sexual desire which is produced at the level of the signifier and inscribes the body of the lover. The play also acknowledges the slippage between the signifier and the world it defines and differentiates. But above all, it puts on display the hopeless longing to escape the confines of the signifier, to encounter directly, im-mediately, the rose that exists beyond its name. And to this extent *Romeo and Juliet* suggests the degree to which the named, differentiated lover is always only a stand-in for

---

[19] See Jill L. Levenson, *Romeo and Juliet*, Shakespere in Performance (Manchester: Manchester University Press, 1987).

something which cannot be embraced, a reminder, as Plato proposes, of 'an ideal that is out of sight, but present in the memory.[20]

Does the continued popularity of the play, even in a predominantly Enlightenment culture, perhaps suggest a dissatisfaction with the neat Cartesian categories by which we have so diligently struggled to live?

---

[20] Kristeva, *Tales of Love*, p. 269.

Framing the Taming: Metatheatrical Awareness of Female Impersonation in *The Taming of the Shrew*

MICHAEL SHAPIRO

University of Illinois at Urbana-Champaign

Kate's speech of submission at the end of *The Taming of the Shrew* raises problems for producers and critics who want to dissociate Shakespeare from normative Elizabethan views about the subordination of married women to their husbands. Some modern directors have devised stage business for subverting Kate's declaration of submissiveness, occasionally using it to grant her subtle or not-so-subtle powers of manipulation and control. Although much of the critical debate over the play has centred on whether the ending subverts or reinforces patriarchal attitudes, Linda Woodbridge concludes a brief survey of feminist efforts to recuperate the play and its ending with the sceptical observation that 'I see little evidence that he was ahead of his time in his attitudes toward women'.[1] Other critics whose work is no less historically based than Woodbridge's find reason to argue that the play is more problematic than conventional. As Michael Hattaway asserts, 'there can be *no* authoritative reading.'[2]

Some directors and critics have tried to solve the problem by enclosing the submission of Kate in some kind of frame, thereby hoping to find an ironic perspective which undercuts the wife-taming, or at least qualifies it. In the Folio text, the Induction provides such a perspective, but unfortunately it disappears after the first act. Some directors, following Pope, adopt the ending from *The Taming of A Shrew*, the so-called 'bad' quarto published in 1594. Stanley Wells and Gary Taylor have recently buttressed the authority of this ending by suggesting that it may reflect 'Shakespeare's final text [. . .] more fully than the Folio does' or else may be a 'paraphrase or imitation' of an earlier Shakespearian text behind the Folio version.[3]

[1] Linda Woodbridge, *Women and the English Renaissance: Literature and the Nature of Womankind, 1540–1620* (Urbana: University of Illinois Press, 1984), pp. 221–22, n. 22.

[2] Michael Hattaway, 'Drama and society', in *The Cambridge Companion to English Renaissance Drama*, ed. by A. R. Braunmuller and Michael Hattaway (Cambridge: Cambridge University Press, 1990), p. 111. On the complexity of tone at the end, see also *The Taming of the Shrew*, ed. by H. J. Oliver (Oxford: Oxford University Press, 1982), pp. 40–43 and 56–57. The debate between 'revisionist' and 'anti-revisionist' critics is concisely summarized by John C. Bean, 'Comic Structure and the Humanizing of Kate in *The Taming of the Shrew*', in *The Woman's Part: Feminist Criticism of Shakespeare*, ed. by Carolyn Ruth Swift Lenz and others (Urbana: University of Illinois Press, 1980), pp. 65–66 and 75–76.

[3] Stanley Wells and Gary Taylor, 'No Shrew, A Shrew and The Shrew: Internal Revision in *The Taming of the Shrew*', in *Shakespeare: Text, Language, Criticism: Essays in Honour of Marvin Spevack*, ed. by Bernhard Fabian and Kurt Tetzeli von Rosador (Hildesheim: Olms-Weidmann, 1987), pp. 367–69.

New historicist criticism provides another kind of frame, the social context. Karen Newman cites an actual case of a skimmington, a traditional practice in which villagers directed mockery and 'rough music' at couples suspected of deviance from accepted patriarchal norms of family organization. On such occasions, young men impersonated wives believed guilty of adultery, scolding, and disobeying or beating their husbands, thereby presenting caricatured antitypes of the ideal obedient wife. Perhaps London theatre-goers recalled such ritualized female impersonations of unruly women when attending plays in which young male actors represented similar types of women. Newman suggests that idealized female stereotypes, such as the submissive Kate, might have been deconstructed by audiences' awareness of crossgender casting.[4] But as her reading of the play relies on framing-by-contextualization, she does not pursue the idea.

I propose to argue that the text itself, as originally performed by an all-male cast, generated deconstructive power of its own by creating a metatheatrical frame. Beginning with the Induction, the play flaunted its theatricality, principally by underscoring the use of male actors in female roles, and Shakespeare sustained that effect even after the Induction framework itself disappeared from view. As the female roles taken by these male performers were either idealized married gentlewomen or their unruly antitypes, they appeared not only as theatrical constructions but also as female stereotypes as outlined in conduct books and marriage manuals. Before exploring the play's exposure of its female characters as being both theatrically and culturally constructed, we need to consider the practice and probable effects of crossgender casting more broadly and in some detail.

I

Although casting of male actors in female roles was the accepted practice on the English stage, there is no way to prove if or when or to what extent spectators were aware of the performers representing female characters. Such awareness of the crossgender casting would have come not from the actors' deficiency, for the evidence indicates that the young male actors who specialized in female roles were quite capable of representing women, or of rendering the theatrical codes used to represent women. Although Colley Cibber was later to disparage the 'Boys, or young Men of the most effeminate Aspect' who played female parts as 'ungain Hoydens', most pre-Restoration accounts suggest that these 'boy-actresses', as Granville-Barker termed them, were highly skilled. There was ample time and opportunity to develop whatever talent they had, for they were apprenticed from the age of ten or

---

[4] Karen Newman, 'Renaissance Family Politics and Shakespeare's *The Taming of the Shrew*', *ELR*, 16 (1986), 100. The essay has been reprinted in Newman's book, *Fashioning Femininity and English Renaissance Drama* (Chicago: University of Chicago Press, 1991), pp. 33–50.

slightly older for seven or more years to individual members of adult companies, who were responsible for their training and maintenance.[5] Because puberty came several years later than it does now, they could play women well into adolescence, but probably with a seemingly precocious intellectual and emotional maturity proportionate with their chronological ages.[6] Extant casting lists for seven plays acted by the King's Men between 1611 and 1632 indicate that young performers like Richard Robinson, Robert Pallant, and Richard Sharpe changed from female to male roles at about the time their apprenticeships ended. Ezekiel Fenn was evidently nineteen when he played his first adult male role.[7]

It is not exactly clear just when female roles became the exclusive speciality of apprentices and younger actors. Doubling schemes printed on title pages indicate such specialization when all female roles are assigned to one or two actors.[8] Further evidence of such specialization is suggested by a short exchange in *Sir Thomas More* between the title character and the leader of an itinerant troupe consisting of 'ffoure men and a boy':

MOORE   But one boy? then I see, ther's but fewe women in the play.
PLAYER   Three my Lord: dame Science, Lady vanitie, and wisedome she her selfe.
MOORE   And one boy play them all? bir Lady, hees loden.[9]

More assumes correctly that all three female roles will be played by the same boy, whose doubling in these parts adds theatrical point to Witt's mistaking of Lady Vanity for Lady Wisedome.

By the 1590s, when the more successful troupes found more permanent venues in London, apprenticeships for younger actors might have become

---

[5] Cibber, *An Apology for the Life of Mr. Colley Cibber*, 2 vols (London: Nimmo, 1889), I, 90. Harley Granville-Barker, *Prefaces to Shakespeare*, 2 vols (London: Batsford, 1958), I, 14. Richard Flecknoe, 'A Character of a Proud Woman', *Aenigmatical Characters* (London, 1658), sig. B', denigrates the skill of female impersonation at the Red Bull playhouse, when he compares his haughty lady, who 'looks high and speaks in a majestic tone', to 'one that plaide the *Queens* part at the Bull'. On theatrical apprentices, see G. E. Bentley, *The Profession of Player in Shakespeare's Time 1590–1642* (Princeton: Princeton University Press, 1984), pp. 113–46. Bentley challenges the evidence for the theory that adult male actors played some female roles; see also Richard David, 'Shakespeare and the Players', in *Studies in Shakespeare: British Academy Lectures*, ed. by Peter Alexander (London: Oxford University Press, 1964), pp. 42–45; and J. B. Streett, 'The Durability of Boy Actors', *N&Q*, 218 (1973), 461–65.

[6] Richard Rastall, 'Female Roles in All-Male Casts', *Medieval English Theatre*, 7 (1985), 25–50.

[7] T. J. King, 'The Versatility of Shakespeare's Actors', in *Shakespeare and Dramatic Tradition: Essays in Honor of S. F. Johnson*, ed. by W. R. Elton and William B. Long (Newark: University of Delaware Press, 1989), pp. 144–50. See also T. J. King, 'The King's Men on Stage: Actors and Their Parts, 1611–32', in *Elizabethan Theatre*, 9 (1981), Papers from Ninth International Conference on Elizabethan Theatre, Waterloo, 1981, ed. by G. R. Hibbard, pp. 32–37. On Ezekiel Fenn, see G. E. Bentley, *The Jacobean and Caroline Stage*, 7 vols (Oxford: Clarendon Press, 1941–68), II, 433–34; Bentley reprints Henry Glapthorne's poem, 'For *Ezekial Fen* at his first Acting a Mans Part', from his 1639 Quarto, *Poems*.

[8] David Bevington, *From 'Mankind' to Marlowe* (Cambridge: Harvard University Press, 1964), p. 79, cautiously observes a gradual but uneven tendency for younger actors to specialize in female roles. On pp. 265–73, Bevington transcribes the doubling schemes on the title pages of plays 'offered for acting'. Specialization in female roles appears to be indicated by the doubling scheme in the manuscript of Merbury's *The Marriage of Wit and Wisdom* (1579), and on the title pages of the printed texts of Pikerying's *Horestes* (1567), *Trial of Treasure* (1567), Preston's *Cambyses* (1569–84), Wapull's *Tide Tarrieth No Man* (1576), Garter's *Virtuous and Godly Susanna* (1578), *Mucedorus* (1598), and *The Fair Maid of the Exchange* (1607).

[9] *The Book of Sir Thomas More*, ed. by W. W. Greg, Malone Society Reprints, 24 (Oxford, 1911), ll. 932–37.

readily available, more stable, and perhaps more attractive, with a concomitant rise in the quality of female impersonation. There seems no reason to doubt that boys or youths who assumed female roles for Shakespeare's troupe created compelling illusions of femininity. According to one spectator, Henry Jackson, who saw *Othello* at Oxford in 1610, 'Desdemona [and not the boy playing the role] moved the spectators with *her* expression' [my emphasis]. Other witnesses reflect spectators' ability to maintain a sense of the male actor playing the female role without any loss of aesthetic pleasure. Lady Mary Wroth uses the female impersonator, or 'play-boy', as a metaphor for technical virtuosity.[10] Defending the practice of female impersonation against puritan charges that it violated biblical injunctions against transvestism and so blurred gender boundaries, Thomas Heywood claimed that spectators recognized male actors and understood they were watching a temporary theatrical illusion:

To see our youths attired in the habit of women, who knowes not what their intents be? who cannot distinguish them by their names, assuredly, knowing they are but to represent such a lady, at such a time apoynted?[11]

Although Heywood assumes a high level of metatheatrical awareness of female impersonators, a dual consciousness of male actor and female character might also have been activated by moments of self-referentiality. The best known, of course, is Cleopatra's fear that a young male actor will 'boy' her greatness, but one should also consider references to such strong gender markers as primary or secondary sex characteristics, as when Cleopatra describes herself as suckling an asp. Crossgender disguise is another such gender marker, for as the female character assumed a fictive male identity, the male performer resumed his authentic male identity. But it also seems likely that female characters played by male actors were readily 'deconstructed' when seen next to other female characters portrayed in contrasting styles or representing other stereotypes. The dissonance produced by such contrasts alerted the audience to a fact, which, as Samuel Johnson says, spectators 'always know': that it was watching theatrical constructions of femininity created by male actors. Such awareness of theatrical artifice would inevitably lead to an awareness that these male

[10] Michael Shapiro, 'Lady Mary Wroth Describes a Boy Actress', *Medieval and Renaissance Drama in England*, 4 (1987), 187–94. Jackson is quoted on pp. 189–90.
[11] *An Apology for Actors* (London, 1612), C3ᵛ. Peter Holland, 'The Resources of Characterization in *Othello*', *ShS*, 41 (1989), 128, suggests 'divisions between [. . .] [boys] who play women's parts and those who do not', which seems plausible from the chapter on apprenticeship in G. E. Bentley, *The Profession of Player*, pp. 113–46, but I know of no detailed study of the problem. If Holland is right, then some boy actresses, e.g. Dick Robinson and Nicholas Burt, may have been all the more easily recognized, as Heywood claims.

performers were offering versions of femininity, versions which might reflect, refract, or refute images of women most readily available to the culture.[12]

Another way pointing up the phenomenon of female impersonation was for a male character deliberately to burlesque or caricature a female character, as in *Jack Juggler* (c. 1555), where Jenkin Careaway describes a fellow servant by the name of Alison Trip-and-go:

> She simperith, she prankith and getteth without faille
> As a pecocke that hath spred and sheweth hir gaye taylle
> S[h]e mynceth, she bridelethe, she swimmith to and fro
> S[h]e tredith not one here a wrye, she tryppeth like a do
> A brod in the stret going or cumming homward
> She quaverith and warbelith like one in a galiard
> Everie joint in her bodie and everie part
> Oh it is a joylie wenche to myns and devyd a fart.[13]

T. W. Craik comments on the contrasting styles:

As Alison makes an appearance in the play, there must have been visible points of difference between the acting of the boy playing her and that of the boy playing Jenkin and (in that character) burlesquing her. The former would mimic a woman's walk with little or no extravagance; the latter would lard his mimicry with every imaginable affectation.[14]

The situation is even richer than Craik suggests. Alison makes one very brief appearance and has a single speech (ll. 749–58), which is shorter than Jenkin's description/parody of her. Jenkin's burlesque of Alison is in fact preceded by a similar description/parody of Dame Coy, the other female character in the play. Although the title-page lists Dame Coy as a gentle-woman, Jenkin describes her as 'a verie cursed shrew [...] | And a verye divell' (ll. 211–12), who spares neither servants nor her husband corporal punishment and the rough side of her tongue.

What was the precise effect of Jenkin's burlesques? Did they make the female characters, when they appeared, seem more or less natural? Was Jenkin mocking women or was he rather mocking men's stereotyped ideas about women? Or both? On the one hand, the actors playing Alison and Dame Coy clearly offered a more 'natural' version of femininity than Jenkin did in his burlesques. On the other hand, his more obviously constructed travesties drove home the fact that both performances were theatrical constructions, especially when the audience was reminded of what it 'always knew', that both Dame Coy and Alison were played by male actors. As women, they corresponded to the familiar social constructs of the young flirt

---

[12] Samuel Johnson, 'Preface [to Shakespeare], 1765', in *Johnson on Shakespeare*, ed. by A. Sherbo, *Works*, 19 vols (New Haven: Yale University Press, 1958), VII, 77; and S. L. Bethell, *Shakespeare and the Popular Dramatic Tradition* (Durham, NC: Duke University Press, 1944), p. 26 and passim; and 'Shakespeare's Actors', *RES*, n.s. 1 (1950), 203. Bethell's position has been restated by P. H. Parry, 'The Boyhood of Shakespeare's Heroines', *ShS*, 42 (1989), 99–109.
[13] *Jack Juggler*, ed. by Eunice Lilian Smart, Malone Society Reprints, 75 (1933), ll. 229–36. I quote throughout from this text.
[14] T. W. Craik, *The Tudor Interlude* (Leicester: Leicester University Press, 1958), p. 45.

and the old shrew, but as female impersonations they seemed to correspond to two opposing theatrical constructions: one illusionistic and the other self-consciously parodic.[15]

Jenkin's burlesques of female characters anticipate the moments in later plays by Shakespeare and others when male characters impersonate women within the world of the play. One such moment occurs in *The Merry Wives of Windsor* when Falstaff appears disguised as the Witch of Brentford alongside Mistress Ford and Mistress Page. The effect produced depended on a clear contrast between Falstaff's farcical, awkward, deliberately unconvincing (to the audience) representation of a grotesque female figure and the apprentices' more realistic potrayal of female characters, as was their speciality. In other words, the play contrasts an adult male actor playing a man pretending to be a 'woman' with young male actors playing female characters.[16]

Usually the contrast between 'women' and female characters is more subtle. In the 'boy bride' plays listed by Victor Freeburg, young male characters are disguised as young 'women' in order to deceive other male characters, as in *The Merry Wives* where Slender and Caius each finds his intended bride to be 'a great lubberly boy'.[17] Such plays presented two levels of female impersonation: actors playing female characters (women), and actors playing boys playing 'women'. Unless a surprise effect was intended, as in *Epicoene*, one assumes a stylistic differentiation between the two levels — companies presented 'real' women more realistically than 'boy brides', or else relied on the audience's knowledge of context to create a sense of the difference. Whereas Chapman, Jonson, and Marston usually make the 'boy bride' part of a con game or practical joke, Shakespeare often heightens the metatheatricality of such moments, as in *A Midsummer Night's Dream*, where an amateur actor, Francis Flute the bellows-mender, is cast as Thisbe in the first mechanicals' scene, and is shown briefly rehearsing the role before finally performing it in the last act.

The casting scene of *A Midsummer Night's Dream* is in general a mine of reflexive effects, but in particular it uses Flute to promote metatheatrical awareness of female impersonation. Flute hopes to play a 'wand'ring knight'

---

[15] According to Susan Savitsky, *Red Pumps, Size 13: Drag Styles at the Pyramid Club* (unpublished master's thesis, New York University, 1987), the New York transvestite theatre uses the terms 'comic drag' and 'glamour drag', respectively, to refer to caricatured and naturalistic female characters played by men. Savitsky's work is cited in June Schlueter's unpublished paper for the seminar on female impersonation at the World Shakespeare Congress, 1991. I am also indebted to the other participants in the seminar, particularly to Henk Gras, Peter Hyland, Yoseharu Ozaki, Francis Barasch, and Bruce Smith.
[16] Crossgender disguise films like *Some Like it Hot* and *Tootsie* create similar effects, as women playing women in a relatively natural style are in constant relationship with men playing women in a much broader manner. English Pantomime regularly contrasts the Panto Dame, played farcically by an adult, male actor (often a comedian of large girth) with other female roles, not to mention the male lead, or principal boy, who is always played by an actress. See the interesting observations by the comedian Roy Hudd on the two chief contrasting styles of female impersonation included in an edition of *The Birth of Merlin* (Shaftesbury: Element Books, 1989), pp. 58–59.
[17] Victor O. Freeburg, *Disguise Plots in Elizabethan Drama* (New York: Columbia University Press, 1915), pp. 101–20. *The Merry Wives of Windsor*, in *Riverside Shakespeare*, ed. by G. B. Evans (Boston, MA: Houghton Mifflin, 1974), v. 5. 184. Unless otherwise noted, subsequent references to Shakespeare are to this edition.

(1.2.45), the romantic male lead of the play, and is thus unhappy at being assigned a female role: 'Nay, faith; let me not play a woman; I have a beard coming' (1.2.47–48). Although the mechanicals are referred to as men, the name Flute suggests a high voice, while both the touchy masculine pride and the allusions to the incipient beard suggest a boy of roughly the same age as those performing the four female roles in Shakespeare's play. As fifth female impersonator, Flute may not have been as good at it as the other four boys. More likely he was even better, possibly an experienced young actor now old enough to abandon female roles, perhaps like Dick Robinson in Jonson's *The Devil is an Ass*. Some Elizabethan spectators would have recognized Flute/Thisbe as a distorted reflection of what was happening within the larger play, where boy actors pretended to be Hippolyta, Hermia, Helena, and Titania.[18]

A similar situation occurs in *Hamlet*, where the female impersonator, like Flute, is first singled out for special attention and then seen performing in an inserted playlet before 'real' women. In his greeting to the players, Hamlet warmly welcomes them all (the stage direction in the second Quarto mentions '*The Players*', while the Folio specifies '*four or five Players*', although only three actors are required to play the scenes we see of 'The Murder of Gonzago'.) In greeting the Players, Hamlet takes particular notice of two — a man with a beard and a female impersonator — and notes their gender-marking attributes:

You are welcome, masters, welcome all. I am glad to see thee well. Welcome, good friends. O, old friend! why, thy face is valenc'd since I saw thee last; com'st thou to beard me in Denmark? What, my young lady and mistress! by' lady, your ladyship is nearer to heaven than when I saw you last, by the altitude of a chopine. Pray God your voice, like a piece of uncurrent gold, be not crack'd within the ring. Masters, you are all welcome. (II.2.421–29)

The adult male actor has grown a beard since Hamlet last saw him, while the boy has grown taller, by an amount Hamlet compares to an 'additional base [attached] to a lady's shoe to increase height'.[19] Like Flute, whose name may refer to a voice undergoing adolescent change, the boy's voice too may be 'crack'd within the ring', a phrase suggesting both the defectiveness of a

---

[18] William Ringler, 'The Number of Actors in Shakespeare's Early Plays', in *The Seventeenth-Century Stage*, ed. by Gerald Bentley (Chicago: University of Chicago Press, 1968), pp. 110–34, suggests that four adult actors doubled as Titania's attendants and as Flute and three other mechanicals. But this suggestion seems unlikely given the brevity of fairies' lines and Bottom's condescending attitudes toward them. Richard Fotheringham, 'The Doubling of Roles on the Jacobean Stage', *ThR*, 10 (1985), 21, also observes that III.1 and IV.1, the two scenes in which Titania's fairies appear, 'are both effectively directed by the major actors; the first by Titania [. . .] and the second by Bottom'. For fuller discussion of reflexive effects involving female impersonation in *A Midsummer Night's Dream*, see my essay in *Elizabethan Theatre XIII* (forthcoming). On Robinson, see Anne Barton, *Ben Jonson, Dramatist* (Cambridge: Cambridge University Press, 1984), p. 228.

[19] *Hamlet*, ed. by Philip Edwards (Cambridge: Cambridge University Press, 1985), II.2.389n. In Kosintsev's film, the boy dons a blond wig with one long thick braid, which replicates Ophelia's hair style and which Hamlet catches himself caressing.

damaged coin and the loss of (female) virginity, a playful confusion of real and feigned gender identities.

As in *A Midsummer Night's Dream*, where 'Pyramus and Thisbe' is performed before three ladies of the court, 'The Murder of Gonzago' is played to an audience which includes Gertrude and Ophelia. It is played twice, once as a dumb-show and once with dialogue. The dumb-show is obviously stylized and the spoken version, like the inserted playlet in *A Midsummer Night's Dream*, is stylized in terms of diction and metre and therefore asks to be presented in a different style as well in order to differentiate this fictive world from the world inhabited by the onstage spectators. Watching and listening to the Player Queen through Hamlet's eyes and ears, the playhouse audience sees the boy they had met previously now playing a noble lady devoted to her husband but wooed and finally won by his murderer. Played in a more formal style, she had seemed an icon of female constancy and so contrasted with the more naturalistically enacted roles of Gertrude and Ophelia, both of whose loyalties Hamlet has come to doubt, but in the end proved as weak and inconstant as they now seem to him, verifying his belief that 'frailty thy name is woman', in art no less than in life.

II

In *The Taming of the Shrew*, the two scenes of the Induction provide several opportunities for reflexive contrasts in levels and styles of female impersonation. The first Induction scene opens with the Hostess claiming that Sly owes her money 'for the glasses you have burst' (i. 7–8) and threatening to 'fetch the thirdborough' (i. 12), or constable. The Hostess is probably ejecting Sly from her premises by force, for in the following scene one of the Lord's servants tells him that in his recent state of 'distraction' he would speak 'idle words' such as claiming 'ye were beaten out of door' and would then 'rail upon the hostess of the house' (ii. 85–86). In short, the opening lines of the Folio text present a dominating, aggressively violent lower-class woman, played as always by a boy.

Moreover, the presence of the young male actor was not merely a latent metatheatrical fact, but became explicit when Sly's defiant response to the Hostess's threat to call the police includes the line, 'I'll not budge an inch, *boy*' (i. 14; my emphasis). Like most other editors, Ann Thompson glosses the word as 'a contemptuous form of address to a servant or inferior'. But the next sentence undermines this suggestion: 'This is the only example in Shakespeare of it being applied to a woman, so perhaps it is another drunken error.'[20] But surely not Shakespeare's. Assuming the word is not an error by

---

[20] *The Taming of the Shrew*, ed. by Ann Thompson (Cambridge: Cambridge University Press, 1984), p. 47n.

a scribe or compositor, Sly hurls 'boy' at the Hostess in order to insult her. In performance, this word may have indicated Sly's drunkenness, confusion, or anger, or simply been given to him to use as a meaningless intensifier, but it may also, like Cleopatra's 'boy my greatness', have reminded some if not all spectators of what they 'always knew' — that the female character was in fact played by a boy. This exposure of artifice in the play's opening lines reveals the Hostess to be a theatrical construct, just as the scuffle with Sly labels the character as a stereotypical social construct — the familiar scold of Tudor misogynist lore, literature, and legal records.

An even more explicit allusion to the theatrical representation of women by male performers occurs a few lines later, shortly after the players arrive. A stage direction, '*Enter* PLAYERS' (i. 78), preceding the Lord's invitation to 'bid them come near', indicates that at least two of them appear onstage, and indeed two of them have speeches. The Lord recalls having seen the company before and recognizes the First Player, 'Since once he play'd a farmer's eldest son' (i. 84). Addressing the actor directly, he remembers the play: ''Twas where you woo'd the gentlewoman so well' (i. 85), thereby accentuating the general practice of crossgender casting if not the presence of the same female impersonator who had played the role of the gentlewoman. As soon as the Players leave, the Lord orders a servant to recruit 'Barthol'mew my page, | And see him dress'd in all suits like a lady' (i. 105–06).

The exchange between Lord and Players is handled differently in the Quarto, where a stage direction clears up some of the uncertainties of the Folio: '*Enter two of the players with packs at their backs, and a boy.*'[21] They are clearly just in off the road, not yet in costume. The Lord does not recognize any of the Players nor does he refer to any previous roles. He asks the 'play-boy', to use Lady Mary Wroth's term, rather than his own servant to take the part of Sly's wife:

> And sirha go you make you ready straight,
> And dresse yourselfe like some lovelie ladie,
> And when I call see that you come to me,
> For I will say to him thou art his wife,
> Dallie with him and hug him in thine armes,
> And if he desire to goe to bed with thee,
> Then faine some scuse and say thou wilt anon.
> Be gone I say, and see thou doost it well.
>
> (i. 71)

The boy departs, promising to 'dandell him well enough | And make him thinke I love him mightilie'' (i. 79–80). As promised, the female impersonator

---

[21] *The Taming of a Shrew*, i. 57, in *Narrative and Dramatic Sources of Shakespeare*, ed. by Geoffrey Bullough, 8 vols (London: Routledge, 1957–75), I, 70. Subsequent citations refer to this text. The relationship of *A Shrew* and *The Shrew*, or Quarto and Folio as I shall for greater convenience refer to them, is still unclear. Some scholars believe the Quarto came first, others that it was derived from the Folio text, a third group that both derive from a lost version. The arguments are reviewed by Ann Thompson, pp. 164–74; and H. J. Oliver, pp. 22–34.

returns as Sly's 'wife', thereby reminding the audience that all female characters were played by male actors.[22]

In the Folio, the Lord's instructions are far more detailed. On one level, they need to be spelled out because the performer he recruits to play Sly's wife is a household servant and not the experienced professional female impersonator of the Quarto. The Folio Lord is also a connoisseur of acting, and although he may have forgotten the name of the actor who played the farmer's eldest son, he is 'sure that part | Was aptly fitted and naturally perform'd' (i. 86–87). Instead of simply ordering the boy to 'do [. . .] it well', the Folio Lord specifies the features involved in this construction of femininity, as well as suggesting some of the tactics to be employed to create the kind of naturalistic illusion he admired in the play he saw, and seems to relish in paintings as well.

Whereas the Quarto Lord simply envisions a 'lovelie ladie', the Folio Lord's instructions sketch a model of upperclass femininity, but its constructedness is readily apparent. As a model presented by an aristocratic male character for his youthful male servant to adopt in representing a 'woman', it not only alludes reflexively to the standard theatrical practice of crossgender casting but also conforms to the well-defined social role of a married gentlewoman:

> Tell him from me, as he will win my love,
> He bears himself with honorable action,
> Such as he hath observ'd in noble ladies
> Unto their lords, by them accomplished;
> Such duty to the drunkard let him do,
> With soft low tongue and lowly courtesy,
> And say, "What is't your honor will command,
> Wherein your lady, and your humble wife,
> May show her duty and make known her love?"
>
> (i. 109)

The Lord's idealized image of a married gentlewoman is derived from English and continental conduct books of the period, although Shakespeare emphasizes external features which can be readily represented both by the boy actor and the page. Conduct books regularly enjoin wives to silence, reverence, and obedience, and the ideal wife as constructed by the Lord is soft-spoken, deferential, and not only obedient to her husband's will but tenderly solicitous of his well-being.[23] Whereas the Quarto Lord advises the

---

[22] Scott McMillin, 'Casting for Pembroke's Men: The *Henry VI* Quartos and *The Taming of A Shrew*', *SQ*, 23 (1972), 152n, suggests that 'the boy actor of the visiting players (Induction) doubled as one of Alfonso's daughters in the rest of the play'. McMillin argues that Pembroke's Men regularly employed four female impersonators.

[23] Several secondary works survey the manuals and treatises on the duties and responsibilities of married women: see Ruth Kelso, *Doctrine for the Lady of the Renaissance* (Urbana: University of Illinois Press, 1956), pp. 78–135; Joan Larsen Klein, 'Women and Marriage in Renaissance England: Male Perspectives', in *The Elizabethan Woman*, *Topic*, 36 (Washington, PA: Washington and Jefferson College, 1982), pp. 20–37; Suzanne W. Hull, *Chaste, Silent and Obedient* (San Marino: Huntington Library, 1982), pp. 47–56; Ian Maclean, *The Renaissance Notion of Woman* (Cambridge: Cambridge University Press, 1980), pp. 51–59.

boy player to establish his role as wife chiefly if not solely through strong sexual advances to Sly, the Folio Lord urges his page to enact the role of noble lady by expressing concern for his welfare and thereby classifying potentially erotic gestures as wifely solicitude and celebration of his recovery:

> And then with kind embracements, tempting kisses,
> And with declining head into his bosom,
> Bid him shed tears, as being overjoyed
> To see her noble lord restor'd to health.

(i. 118)

The dallying and dandling of the Quarto 'wife' is discouraged by some conduct books on the grounds that married women should remain modest in connubial sexual behaviour, while even those tracts (mainly Puritan) which encourage sexual relations within marriage counsel moderation. While William Perkins in *Christian Economy* (1609) looks with favour on the 'due benevolence' of the marriage bed, he warns that 'even in wedlock excess in lusts is no better than plain adultery before God'.[24]

In the Folio, Shakespeare points up the artifice involved in the construction of a married gentlewoman by having the Lord instruct his page how to make himself cry real tears by means of a theatrical trick, women evidently having the ability to induce tears at will, if not by nature then by subtler artifices of their own:

> And if the boy have not a woman's gift
> To rain a shower of commanded tears,
> An onion will do well for such a shift,
> Which in a napkin (being close convey'd)
> Shall in despite enforce a watery eye.

(i. 124)

The Lord sends one of his servants off, perhaps remaining alone on stage and so giving additional emphasis to his final eight lines, which might be considered a soliloquy directed at the playhouse audience.

He begins this segment of the speech by reasserting his confidence in Barthol'mew's ability to imitate a real lady:

> I know the boy will well usurp the grace,
> Voice, gait, and action of a gentlewoman.

(i. 131)

In specifying such features as deportment, vocal quality, movement, and gesture, the Lord is again outlining a social construction of a married

---

[24] William Perkins, *Christian Economy* (1609). Chapter 10, 'Of the Communion of Married Folks, and of Due Benevolence'. Quoted in *Daughters, Wives, and Widows: Writings by Men about Women and Marriage in England, 1500–1640*, ed. by Joan Larsen Klein (Urbana: University of Illinois Press, 1992), p. 170. I am grateful to Professor Klein for allowing me to examine parts of the book in typescript and for commenting on a draft of this essay. Perkins's warning is amplified by R[obert] C[leaver], *Godly Forme of Householde Government* (1598): 'So that marriage is not a mad and dissolute estate, neither are husbandes to turne their wives into whores, or wives their husbands into whoremasters, by immoderate, intemperate, or excessive lust' (1600 edn, sig. K7ᵛ). See also sig. M4ᵛ and Kelso, p. 100.

gentlewoman such as the conduct books of the period describe. Wives should maintain a discreet but not total silence. Richard Braithwaite's advice in *The English Gentlewoman* (1631) is typical: 'Bashfull silence is an ornament to their Sexe. [. . .] It suites not with *her* honour, for a *young woman* to be prolocutor. But especially, when either men are in presence, or ancient Matrons, to whom shee owes a civill reverence, it will become her to tip her tongue with silence.'[25]

Whereas most conduct books concentrate on inward or moral aspects of married life, Braithwaite devotes some attention to such external considerations as carriage, for, as he puts it, 'It is no hard thing to gather the *disposition* of our *heart*, by the *dimension* of our *gate*'. He thus recommends that 'your *Carriage* [. . .] should neither be too precise, nor too loose', and later describes inappropriate kinds of 'gates' in scornful detail: 'What a circular gesture wee shall observe some use in their pace, as if they were troubled with the *vertigo*! Others make a tinkling with their feet, and make discovery of their light thoughts, by their wanton *gate*. Others with a jetting and strutting *pace*, publish their hauty and selfe-conceited minde.' Model women of 'preceding times' 'had not the art of imitating such huffing and mounting *gates*, as our light-spirited Dames now use'.[26]

'Grace' is a more elusive terms than 'voice', 'gait', and 'action', but can be glossed by the conduct books as modesty of demeanour, which Ruth Kelso defines as 'a kind of timidity, that is, a shrinking from drawing attention to oneself, a desire to be inconspicuous, a fear of adverse comment, or to give it positive force and a more praiseworthy connotation, moderation' (p. 105). He wants his page to represent this version of an idealized married gentlewoman with what he considers verisimilitude ('aptly fitted and naturally performed') rather than exaggerated theatricality. His own presence will prevent excessive mirth from deflecting the page's performance towards broad caricature.

In the second Induction scene a Lady enters, whom the audience has been prepared to recognize as Barthol'mew 'dressed in all suits like a lady'. However accurate his imitation of a great lady, spectators would have known that this 'boy bride', like female characters, was being played by a boy or young man. Although there may have been moments when the Page revealed himself non-verbally to the Lord or to other servants and hence to the audience without Sly's noticing it, the text stipulates no such 'breaking' of character, which suggests that the boy remained in his female role throughout the scene, solicitous about Sly's welfare and treating him with appropriate, perhaps ironically exaggerated, deference and humility: 'My husband and my lord, my lord and husband, | I am your wife in all obedience' (ii.105–07). In declaring her obedience to her husband's

[25] Richard Braithwaite, *The English Gentlewoman* (1631), p. 89 (sig. N). Compare Kelso, p. 101.
[26] Braithwaite, pp. 42, 82–83 (sig. G^v, M^v–M2). Compare Kelso, p. 106.

authority, Sly's 'lady' echoes the central duty of a wife according to manuals of the period. 'An Homily of the State of Matrimony' (1563), quoting 1 Peter 3.1, defines that duty quite simply: *'Ye wives, be ye in subjection to obey your own husband.'*[27] Carrying out his master's instructions, Barthol'mew thus provided a doubly theatrical construction of the social construction of a married gentlewoman, the role Kate will adopt by the end of the play.

A crisis in this doubly constructed performance occurs when Sly commands his wife to 'undress you, and come now to bed' (ii.117). Up to that point, the text gives him little opportunity to kiss and embrace Sly. The tinker's sexual appetite has already been whetted, by descriptions first of erotic mythological pictures and then of his wife, 'a lady far more beautiful | Than any woman in this waning age [. . .] the fairest creature in the world', even now her 'lovely face' although marred by tears, 'inferior to none' (ii.62–67). His wife enters, full of tender solicitude and obedience, as the Lord has directed Barthol'mew. Once Sly accepts her as his 'wife' and is reminded how to address her, his sexual interest is renewed when she laments that she has been 'abandoned from your bed', a lament possibly reinforced by kisses and embraces albeit in the manner of 'noble ladies' rather than the more forward manner of the Quarto 'wife'.

In Shakespeare's day, the enactment of some sexual intimacy in the world of the play and the possibility of still more to come may have raised some mild anxieties about the prospect of homoerotic contact between two male characters and two male actors. If so, then the audience was probably relieved when the page extricated himself from the problem of inventing the excuse, 'in character', that Sly's doctors have ordered 'her' temporarily to 'absent me from your bed', lest sexual activity cause a recurrence of 'your former malady'. But the page concludes with a possible sexual innuendo — 'I hope this reason stands for my excuse' (ii.122–24) — which Sly seizes upon to acknowledge the difficulty of sexual abstinence once he has been aroused: 'Ay, it stands so that I may hardly tarry so long. But I would be loath to fall into my dreams again. I will therefore tarry in despite of the flesh and the blood' (ii.125–28).

The Quarto abbreviates and modifies the equivalent passage. It omits the pictures, shortens the description of the wife, leaves out the farcical by-play of Sly's not recognizing her as his wife and not knowing what to call her, and

[27] 'An Homily of the State of Matrimony', *The Second Tome of Homilies* (1563), quoted in *Daughters, Wives, and Widows*, p. 17. The importance of the duty of obedience is stated with equal bluntness in one of the most often reprinted marriage manuals of the period, Juan Luis Vives, *A Very Fruitful and Pleasant Book Called the Instruction of a Christian Woman* (1523), trans. by Richard Hyrde (1529), *The Second Book of the Instruction of a Christian Woman*: 'Neither I wolde that she should love her husband as one loveth his friend or his brother, that is to say, I will that she shall give him great worship, reverence, great obedience, and service also; which thing not only the example of the old world teacheth us, but also all laws, both spiritual and temporal, and Nature herself cryeth and commandeth that the woman shall be subject and obedient to the man. And in all kinds of beasts the females obey the males, and waiten upon them, and fawn upon them, and suffer themself to be corrected of them. Which thing Nature sheweth must be and is convenient to be done.' (Quoted in *Daughters, Wives, and Widows*, p. 114). See also Kelso, p. 94.

allows her only a single speech, less noteworthy for its tenderness and deference than for its frank erotic appeal:

> Oh that my lovelie Lord would once vouchsafe
> To looke on me, and leave these frantike fits,
> Or were I now but halfe so eloquent,
> To paint in words what ile performe in deeds,
> I know your honour then would pittie me.
>
> (ii. 38)

The anticipated 'dandling' may have come toward the end or after this speech, the tone of which suggests not the decorous sexual behaviour of the conduct books but coarse sexual farce such as occurs in Italian popular comedy.[28] More of a seductress than is Barthol'mew's noble lady, the Quarto 'prettie wench' (ii. 37), as Sly first called her, comes on so strongly that Sly seems to recoil, postponing sexual intimacy by enacting his ale-house version of courtly largesse:

> Harke you mistresse, wil you eat a peece of bread,
> Come sit downe on my knee, *Sim* drinke to hir *Sim*,
> For she and I will go to bed anon.
>
> (ii. 43)

His drinking buddy 'Sim', i.e., the Lord, announces the readiness of the Players, perhaps, to extricate the boy from an awkward situation. The Quarto 'play-boy' had failed to heed the Lord's advice to devise an excuse, unlike Barthol'mew, and now seizes the opportunity to 'go bid them begin their plaie' (ii. 54). Sly orders his 'wife' to 'come againe' (ii. 55), but there is no indication that 'she' returns, although the boy may have reappeared in a female role in the play the company is offering for Sly's entertainment.

In the Folio, by contrast, Barthol'mew/Lady evidently remains at Sly's side after the messenger enters to announce the Players and they watch the first part of the play together. Where they watch from is not certain. They, and possibly some servants, may be 'aloft', as the initial stage direction of the second Induction scene stipulates, or if they are on the main playing level, as the Quarto suggests, perhaps they withdraw to one side or the rear of the main playing area.[29] In either case, Barthol'mew/Lady, this acknowledged female impersonator, known to the audience and all characters but Sly, remains visible to the audience at least through their one and only subsequent bit of dialogue at the end of Act 1 Scene 1.

Sly and his 'wife' are onstage and visible when Baptista and his two daughters enter at 1. 1. 47. The implied contrast between Barthol'mew/Lady on the one hand and Kate and Bianca on the other raised the same questions as did the contrast between Flute and the other female characters in *A*

---

[28] At various times, *commedia dell'arte* troupes contrasted romantic heroines played by women with low-comic servants played by men, as Frances Barasch demonstrates in an unpublished paper for the World Shakespeare Congress, 1991.

[29] See Ann Thompson, pp. 181–85.

Midsummer Night's Dream. A male character in the world of the play pretending to be a woman was exactly what several female impersonators were doing in the world of the playhouse. The deconstructive effect was even stronger in *The Taming of the Shrew* because Kate and Bianca may have already been seen as, or were understood to be, members of the troupe of players whom the Lord welcomed, onstage, in Induction 1, whereas Hypolita, Hermia, Helena, and Titania appeared only as women with no explicit allusion to male actors playing the roles in the world of the play.

As characters in a play performed before Sly and his 'wife', Kate and Bianca, like Thisbe, might have been played in a style that contrasted with Barthol'mew's Lady. They, after all, are supposedly being played by professional female impersonators, not by reluctant amateurs like Flute or eager but inexperienced amateurs like the Lord's page. In *Hamlet*, the inserted playlet of 'The Murder of Gonzago' is written in rhymed couplets and archaic diction, enforcing a stylistic differentiation between the onstage players and the onstage spectators. The Player Queen, who was seen as a boy in Act II Scene 2, contrasts with Gertrude and Ophelia, who were played by professional female impersonators in the world of the playhouse. If *Hamlet* is a guide, then Kate and Bianca, as characters in a play-within-a-play would have been played, at least initially, in a more stylized, artificial and theatrically self-conscious mode than the Lady. That possibility may seem unlikely to us, given our knowledge of the centrality of Kate and Bianca, but spectators seeing the play for the first time would not yet possess that knowledge.

Lucentio's opening speech of Act I Scene 1 suggests such stylization. It is a stiff, formulaic piece of exposition ostensibly informing his servant, who surely already knows, that they are now in Padua, that it is a famous university town, and that he has come there to study.[30] Petruchio's opening speech of Act II Scene 2 is a condensed version of the same formula. The entrance of the Minola family, along with Gremio and Hortensio, is presented as a kind of inserted playlet, 'some show to welcome us to town' (I.1.47), as Tranio puts it. He and Lucentio, who are themselves characters within a play performed before the mock-Lord and his Lady of the Induction, '*stand by*' like spectators to watch the scene.[31] To the naïve spectator, Baptista and his daughters are stock *commedia* figures, deriving from material domesticated decades before Gascoigne, to whose work, *The Supposes* (1566, published 1579), adapted from Ariosto's *I Suppositi* (1509), Shakespeare's play twice alludes. Nested within two other concentric planes of reality, the world of the playhouse and the world of the Induction, Kate and Bianca might well have been played at the outset in a style consistent with the conventionality

[30] H. J. Oliver, p. 60.
[31] G. K. Hunter, *John Lyly: The Humanist as Courtier* (London: Routledge and Kegan Paul, 1962), pp. 309–10; and Leo Salingar, *Shakespeare and the Traditions of Comedy* (Cambridge: Cambridge University Press, 1974), pp. 271–72. For another example of 'standing by', see I.2.142.

of the Italianate material. If so the male actor would have been required to offer a more self-consciously artificial representation of femininity than Barthol'mew's had provided in impersonating a married English gentle-woman along the naturalistic lines suggested by his Lord.

This initial pattern of stylistic differentiation, however, begins to change in the Folio version at some point after Sly and his 'wife' disappear following the end of Act I Scene 1. The change accelerates as Shakespeare adds disguises and intertwines or crosses different strands of the plot, and as Petruchio's wooing of Kate moves away from Italianate neo-classical comedy and evolves into a more vigorous and original adaptation of native oral tales of 'wife-taming'.[32] The Quarto, by contrast, sustains the Induction frame throughout and indeed ends the play with Sly's reflections on the 'dream' he has just had. But if the curtailment of the frame in the Folio text is deliberate and not the result, say, of faulty printer's copy, then the intended effect may well have been an intricate kind of eversion, whereby the play literally turns itself inside out, as the inner play comes gradually to eclipse the Induction framework, as figure and ground, frame and vision, switch places.[33]

The disappearance of the Induction characters may have stylistically enhanced this process of eversion, for once Sly's 'Lady', initially played by the Page in a relatively naturalistic mode disappeared from view, that style became available, so to speak, for the young male actor playing Kate, as did the image of the married gentlewoman, an explicitly theatrical recon-struction of the idealized wife of conduct books and marriage manuals.

Even before Kate's complex transformation into this idealized wife, Shakespeare found other ways to remind the audience of a slight variation on this doubly constructed image of a married young gentlewoman. The first wooing strategy he devises for Petruchio is to sketch this idealized lady in language. Although Petruchio has been told and clearly believes that Kate is 'an irksome, brawling scold' (I. 2. 187), he tells Baptista that he has heard of 'her beauty and her wit, | Her affability and bashful modesty, | Her wondrous qualities and mild behavior' (II. 1. 48–50) and tries to impose this image on Kate by a kind of verbal magic. First he tests this strategy in soliloquy, using stock similes for female attractiveness:

> Say that she rail, why then I'll tell her plain
> She sings as sweetly as a nightingale;
> Say that she frown, I'll say she looks as clear
> As morning roses newly wash'd with dew.
>
> (II. 1. 170)

[32] Jan Brunvand, 'The Folktale Origin of *The Taming of the Shrew*', *SQ*, 17 (1966), 345–59. Brunvand's doctoral dissertation (Indiana University, 1961), from which this article is derived, has been reprinted under the title *'The Taming of the Shrew': A Comparative Study* (New York: Garland, 1991).

[33] Barbara Freedman, *Staging the Gaze: Postmodernism, Psychoanalysis, and Shakespearean Comedy* (Ithaca, NY: Cornell University Press, 1991), p. 126. See also Figure 10, M. C. Escher's *The Print Gallery* (1956), p. 125, and Freedman's commentary on framed material enclosing its frames.

Abandoning the similes, he determines to create the model wife he seeks by simply superimposing his own version of reality on Kate's actual behaviour, substituting more direct language for the stock images:

> Say she be mute, and will not speak a word,
> Then I'll commend her volubility,
> And say she uttereth piercing eloquence.
>
> (II. 1. 174)

After an initial wit-combat with Kate, he tries out his plan:

> I find you passing gentle:
> 'Twas told me you were rough and coy and sullen,
> And now I find report a very liar;
> For thou art pleasant, gamesome, passing courteous,
> But slow in speech, yet sweet as spring-time flowers.
> Thou canst not frown, thou canst not look askaunce,
> Nor bite the lip, as angry wenches will,
> Nor hast thou pleasure to be cross in talk;
> But thou with mildness entertain'st thy wooers,
> With gentle conference, soft, and affable.
>
> (II. 1. 243)

One sign of the strain involved in this verbal magic is the simile of the hazel-twig, which leads him to describe her complexion as 'as brown in hue | As hazel-nuts' (II. 1. 254–55), which in fact may not be such a compliment, as fashionable Englishwomen covered their faces to preserve an aristocratic pallor. But Petruchio recovers adroitly, if somewhat menacingly, in finding her 'sweeter than the kernels', suggesting that her hard exterior can be cracked to expose the tender meat within.

The implied threat of violence is partly carried out once the play moves to Petruchio's house. Whereas many wife-taming tales involve direct physical assault of various kinds against the shrew, others displace the violence by having the husband kill or maim an animal by way of warning his wife.[34] Petruchio's cuffing or kicking of his household servants in Act IV Scene 1 (added by eighteenth-century editors) is the theatricalized comedic form of such aggression. But he quickly moves to another phase, borrowed not from oral tales but from techniques used in taming falcons and other hunting birds, the withholding of food and sleep. What links both phases, intimidation by violence and subjugation by deprivation, is the exaggerated solicitude Petruchio claims to be showing toward Kate and the exquisite politeness of his manners. At the verbal level, he is treating her as if she were an ideal gentlewoman, while at the physical level he is trying to terrify her with displays of violence and break her spirit by weakening her body.

Petruchio's tactics up to this point are unsuccessful, as they must be if the play is not to end prematurely. His next phase seems to involve a return to his initial gambit, superimposing the image of gentlewoman upon his

---

[34] See Brunvand for examples.

ungentle wife, only now done with clothing rather than with words. Although Petruchio several times disparages garments as inconsequential compared with the mind or soul, he tells Kate just after permitting her to eat and wishing 'Much good do it unto thy gentle heart!' (IV. 3. 51) that they will return to Padua dressed as befitting their rank —

> And revel it as bravely as the best,
> With silken coats and caps, and golden rings,
> With ruffs and cuffs, and fardingales, and things,
> With scarfs and fans, and double change of brav'ry,
> With amber bracelets, beads, and all this knav'ry.
>
> (IV. 3. 54)

As the use of loose syntax, bouncy rhythms and rhymed couplets implies, the offer is a ruse, for he will pretend to dislike the cap and the gown that the Haberdasher and Tailor have made for her on the grounds that they are excessively ornate. When Kate protests that 'gentlewomen wear such caps as these' he retorts that 'when you are gentle, you shall have one too | And not till then' (IV. 3. 70–72). As for the gown, in many productions Petruchio all but destroys it as he comments on its various features before ordering Grumio to take it 'up', i.e., away. From the sartorial details — a loose-bodied gown cut with perforations to reveal another layer of material, demi-cannon or trunk sleeves and a small compassed cape — it seems to be what the Tailor describes as made 'according to the fashion and the time' (IV. 3. 95).[35] The image of the gentlewoman is presented this time as clothing, possibly draped over a tailor's dummy, but again Petruchio dismisses garments as merely external, 'For 'tis the mind that makes the body rich' (IV. 3. 172), and he withholds them from Kate on the grounds that she cannot lay claim to attire appropriate to her social station until she is gentle in both senses of the word, that is, in behaviour as well as in rank.

In the scene on the way back to Padua, Kate appears to conform to Petruchio's desires, but it is not clear whether her obedience in the 'sun-moon' sparring, and in calling Vincentio a young woman represent an inner change on her part, a tactical submission, or a willingness to join her husband in madcap pranks intended to twit their stolidly bourgeois society. The idealized image of the gentlewoman appears again, not as clothing but rather as a purely verbal construction, as part of the joke on Vincentio. Petruchio conjures 'her' into existence by invoking 'her' social rank and standard physical attributes, this time with a Petrarchan coloration:

> Good morrow, *gentle* mistress, where away?
> Tell me, sweet Kate, and tell me truly too,
> Hast thou beheld a fresher *gentlewoman?*
> Such war of white and red within her cheeks!
> What stars do spangle heaven with such beauty
> As those two eyes become that heavenly face?

---

[35] See Walter Hodges's illustration of the gown and cap in the Cambridge edition, p. 33.

Fair lovely maid, once more good day to thee.
Sweet Kate, embrace her for her beauty's sake.

(IV. 5. 27; my emphases)

Perhaps determined not merely to obey her husband by following his lead in
teasing Vincentio, Kate outdoes him by accentuating the 'gentlewoman's'
sexual status as a pubescent girl and prospective wife:

Young budding virgin, fair, and fresh, and sweet,
Whither away, or where is thy abode?
Happy the parents of so fair a child!
Happier the man whom favorable stars
Allots thee for his lovely bedfellow!

(IV. 5. 37)

When Petruchio relabels Vincentio as 'a man' and then begins a new round
of teasing by adding increasingly derogatory adjectives ('old, wrinkled,
faded, withered'), Kate again trumps her husband's lead with overstated
and hence possibly ironic apologies:

Pardon, old father, my mistaking eyes,
That have been so bedazzled with the sun,
That everything I look on seemeth green;
Now I perceive thou art a reverent father.
Pardon, I pray thee, for my mad mistaking.

(IV. 5. 45)

The modest tone of a model gentlewoman is subtly mocked, not only by the
exaggerated deference toward Vincentio but by the allusion to Petruchio's
previous arbitrariness over the 'sun'.

The image of the young gentlewoman, which they had both created out of
words and images, much to Hortensio's alarm and Vincentio's consterna-
tion, they now dissolve. Whereas the image created by clothing was
destroyed by Petruchio's tyrannical edict and perhaps even by his violent
rending of the gown, the purely verbal image in this scene with Vincentio is
created at Petruchio's initiative in the spirit of play, play shared with his wife
at the expense of someone else.[36]

Although the text does not specify the motive for Kate's apparent change
in this scene or anywhere else, leaving the matter open for performance
choice and critical speculation, it does contrast her with several antitypes of
the ideal married gentlewomen. One such antitype is her own earlier
behaviour as a shrew. Another is her sister, who first appeared as a
stereotypically dutiful daughter, later became the object of Lucentio's

[36] Brunvand, p. 354, points out that the 'absurd statements' are found in many oral wife-taming tales.
For 'playful' readings of the play, see J. Dennis Huston, Shakespeare's Comedies of Play (New York:
Columbia University Press, 1981), p. 64; Marianne L. Novy, Love's Argument: Gender Relations in
Shakespeare (Chapel Hill: University of North Carolina Press, 1984), p. 61; Alexander Leggatt, Shake-
speare's Comedy of Love (London: Methuen, 1974), pp. 41–62. Camille Wells Slights, 'The Raw and the
Cooked in The Taming of the Shrew', JEGP, 88 (1989), 187–89, who finds that such 'playful' readings
overstress the separation of Petruchio and Kate from their community, argues that they, and Shakespeare, ultimately endorse its basic social values but assert active control over them.

romantic clichés, and finally emerges as a disobedient wife. The last antitype of upperclass femininity is yet another type of unruly woman, the Widow, that is, a woman who has lived independent of male authority and is therefore a threat or a source of anxiety, as reflected by some (male) authors of conduct books.[37]

In the Quarto, there is no Widow; instead Kate has a second sister who merely replicates Bianca. In the Folio version of the play, the introduction of Hortensio's 'wealthy widow', completes the triadic classification of women, in terms of their relationships to men, as maids, wives, and widows. In the Folio text, the introduction of this particular Widow adds a striking deviation from the ideal of the married gentlewoman to the ending of the play. We first hear of her in Act IV Scene 2, when Hortensio claims that he will marry her 'ere three days pass' (IV.2.38) and that she has loved him as long as he has been wooing Bianca. Tranio speaks of Hortensio's decision immediately after he leaves the stage almost as if this match will provide another 'show' to stand aside and watch: 'I'faith, he'll have a lusty widow now | That shall be woo'd and wedded in a day' (IV.2.50–51) and jokes with Bianca and Lucentio about whether Hortensio can apply to his bride the lessons he has learned at Petruchio's 'taming-school' (IV.2.54). Shakespeare makes Hortensio himself repeat this idea three scenes later, when, inspired by Petruchio's success, Hortensio closes the scene with a rhymed couplet:

> Have to my widow! and if she be froward,
> Then hast thou taught Hortensio to be untoward.
>
>   (IV.5.78)

But given the difference between Hortensio and Petruchio, the clear implication is that the Widow, now that she has a new husband whose authority she can defy, will become the type of unruly wife commonly labelled as a scold.

Just as the spectators first heard of Barthol'mew and the role he was to play before he entered as Sly's wife, so they hear of the Widow well before her first appearance onstage. Shakespeare implants the idea that she is both froward and lusty, conventional attributes of literary and theatrical widows, and that Hortensio, who is no Petruchio, will fail in his attempt to tame her. Not until the final scene does the audience actually get to see her, at which point she is Hortensio's wife. No sooner do Baptista's guests sit down at the banquet 'to chat as well as eat' (V.2.11), than Hortensio complains of his Widow, and Petruchio teases them both, her acerbic retorts lead to a flyting with Kate, and she inspires Bianca to ill-tempered bawdy repartee. From one point of view, the Widow underscores the play's orthodoxy: Kate's shrewishness has been displaced on to this late-arriving figure, a reminder of what Petruchio's wife had once been before becoming (or adopting the role of) a model married gentlewoman. From another point of view, however, the Widow is clearly an antitype of that model, and the two female characters

[37] See the section on widows in Kelso, pp. 121–32.

are obviously constructed at both theatrical and social levels. In contrast to Kate's enactment of a gentlewoman — polite, decorous, obedient to Petruchio — the Widow, joined by Bianca, scorns her husband's wishes and mocks Kate's demonstration of wifely obedience.

That demonstration is the play's final embodiment of the model of the married gentlewoman, a model earlier created by the Lord and his page, Barthol'mew, and now re-created by Petruchio and the boy actor playing Kate. Although a wager on the shrew's obedience is included in many of the oral tales cited by Brunvand, Shakespeare dilates and amplifies the motif. Kate comes at Petruchio's bidding, inquires 'What is your will, sir, that you send for me?' (v. 2. 100), and silently agrees to return to the parlour to 'fetch' the other wives. Although Petruchio has won the wager, he now proposes to win it

> better yet,
> And show more sign of her obedience,
> Her new built virtue and obedience.
>   (l. 116)

To test her, he orders her to throw her cap 'under-foot', perhaps the very cap he had earlier denied her, and then bids her chastise the other wives:

> Katherine, I charge thee tell these headstrong women
> What duty they do owe their lords and husbands.
>   (l. 130)

Petruchio's language not only invokes the duty of obedience as emphasized in homilies, the marriage service, and the conduct books, but also echoes Sly's 'wife' in her deferential declaration to her husband: 'My husband and my lord, my lord and husband, | I am your wife in all obedience' (ii. 105–07).

The climax of Kate's demonstration of obedience is the lecture to the other women, which ends with her own symbolic gesture of submission, placing her hands beneath Petruchio's feet, a gesture which can be staged as anything between humiliating self-abnegation and ironic verbal formula. Whether one takes Kate's lecture as genuine, feigned, or playful, it is the longest speech of the play and requires the performer to display a poise and self-confidence which can seem to belong to the character as well. Whatever intention that performer provides, the attitudes expressed in the speech are conventionally patriarchal. Although the speech makes no reference to God, the Bible, or the sacredness of holy matrimony, it asserts that women 'are bound to serve, love, and obey' (l. 164), and thus echoes the minister's question to the bride, found in the *Book of Common Prayer*, 'Wilt thou obey him, and serve him, love, honor, and keep him, in sickness and in health?'[38] Whereas the Quarto explicitly invokes the creation myth and the sin of Eve to justify the subordination of women, the Folio relies on the analogy of the

[38] 'The Form and Solemnization of Matrimony', from *The Book of Common Prayer* (1559), quoted in *Daughters, Wives, and Widows*, p. 6.

prince and the subject, and limited obedience to the 'husband's honest will' (v. 2. 158). Such limitation of a wife's obedience, perhaps more theoretical than actual, was based on the doctrine of Christian conscience and evidently originated with Erasmus in his *Institutio matrimonii christiani* (1526): 'If he orders you to do something that is contrary to faith or good manners, gently refuse to obey him; but if he persists in wishing to be obeyed, remember that it is better to obey God than men.'[39] In place of the Quarto's scripturally sanctioned denigration of woman, compressed into the familiar pun of 'woe of man' (xviii. 34), the Folio places conditions on wives' obdedience and bases it not on their inherent inferiority but on their sense of obligation and gratitude, and on their desire for domestic harmony, central tenets of many marriage manuals of the period.[40]

There are also possible ironies in the speech, as many directors and critics have noted: its praise of husbands who risk their lives to care for their wives points up the fact that most of the men in the play are landowning gentry or urban upper bourgeoisie, the declaration of women's weaker physical traits is made by a female impersonator, and the final gesture of submission, the hand beneath the foot, is absurdly hyperbolic. In original performance, given spectators' metatheatrical awareness of female impersonation, a straightforward delivery of the speech would have produced still deeper irony: Kate's transformation into the ideal of wifely obedience is labelled as the fulfilment of a male fantasy, constructed at many levels — by the male performer, by Kate, by Petruchio, by Barthol'mew, by the Lord, and hence by the patriarchal norms of both 'Padua' and early modern England.

This deconstruction of Kate as an icon of wifely obedience would have been enhanced by any doubling of male performers in the play's female roles. Some kind of doubling involving the Widow seems quite likely inasmuch as she does not appear until the play is more than half over, while boy actors appearing in the Induction had been available since the Induction framework disappeared, presumably by design, in the first act. If noticed, as I assume it would have been, such doubling would have emphasized the theatrical and social constructedness of the female roles by heightening the audience's metatheatrical awareness of crossgender casting and reminding them of the female roles these same performers had played in the Induction.

[39] Quoted and trans. by Constance Jordan, *Renaissance Feminism: Literary Texts and Political Models* (Ithaca, NY: Cornell University Press, 1990), p. 62, who comments as follows:

The parallel between the family and the state is a rediscovery of humanists, but Erasmus is the first of them to link a wife's obedience to the more general injunction against disobedience to governing authorities which applies to all Christians. Discussing instances in which a wife may disobey her husband, he follows a line of reasoning identical to that of Luther when he argues for the right of Christians to liberty of conscience.

Similar attitudes are expressed in other manuals. See Robert Cleaver's *A Godly Forme*: 'Yet must not this obedience so far extend, as that the husband should command any thing contrary to her honour, credit, and salvation, but as it is comely in the Lord' (sig. P2); compare sig. P5ᵛ–P6. For commentary, see Jordan, pp. 217–18.

[40] John C. Bean, pp. 67–71.

All of the doubling possibilities are rich in implications. (1) If the actor playing Barthol'mew/Lady doubled as the Widow, then that original model married gentlewoman now metatheatrically returned, but its constructed-ness was underscored by the fact that the same performer played both that model and its unruly antitype. This effect would have been heightened if the Hostess and Bianca were doubled by a third boy. (2) If the Hostess and the Widow were doubled, then the unruly antitype of the Induction returned greatly amplified by the repetition. But this male nightmare of rebellious womanhood was metatheatrically deconstructed into a male construct and hence weakened or contained, and also contrasted with its opposite male construct, Kate's embodiment of the role of idealized married gentlewoman. (3) The Widow was 'tripled' by the boy who played both the Hostess and Barthol'mew, which is possible as the former disappears early in the first scene of the Induction and the latter does not appear until well into the second scene. That possibility suggests that a skilled female impersonator, such as the boy who played the shrewish and the obedient Kate, could represent both idealized and unruly stereotypes, and had done so in the Induction.

However much such doubling scenes would have enhanced a metatheatrical frame, such an effect was based on the audience's awareness of male performers *per se*, whether or not they reappeared in successive roles. What is repeated at the end of the play is the reinstatement of the ideal married gentlewoman, the deliberate parallel between the reformed Kate, as played by a boy actor, and Sly's lady, as represented by Barthol'mew under his master's direction. Such a reprise of the Induction would have compensated for what many critics of the Folio version have lamented: its failure to complete the framework of the Induction by supplying a dramatic epilogue involving Sly.[41] The Quarto ending does indeed bring Sly back to conclude the frame and does so with acute irony, for he leaves the stage for his final exit as Petruchio's self-proclaimed disciple:

> I know now how to tame a shrew,
> I dreamt upon it all this night till now,
> And thou hast wakt me out of the best dreame
> That ever I had in my life, but Ile to my
> Wife presently and tame her too
> And if she anger me.
>
> (xix. 15)

Sly's swagger, followed by the Tapster's eagerness to accompany him home and 'heare the rest that thou has dreamt to night' (ll. 21–22), turns the drunken tinker into a theatrical spectacle to be witnessed offstage or at some future presentation. Sly's swagger also labels him as a hen-pecked husband in desperate need of a role-model like Petruchio, and makes a similar jibe at

[41] The debate on whether or not the dropping of the Sly framework is deliberate is concisely summarized by Ann Thompson, pp. 171–73.

male spectators who responded enthusiastically to this wishful fantasy of wife-taming.

The Folio ending is far more subtle. There is no explicit framing of the Petruchio-Kate plot to undercut it with irony. Instead, the text, as originally played with male actors in female roles, provides a metatheatrical frame, a perspective for reading Kate's evident submission as the final incarnation of an elaborately but transparently constructed ideal of upperclass femininity: that is to say, a doubly theatrical replication of a socially generated role. Instead of using Sly to subvert Petruchio as an icon of patriarchal authority, as the Quarto ending does, the Folio playfully contrasts opposing stereotypes of the gentlewoman and the scold and juxtaposes the ideal fantasy with the dreaded nightmare, exploiting the audience's realization that these familiar cultural constructs or roles were theatrical illusions created by male performers.

The Performance of Things in
The Taming of the Shrew

LENA COWEN ORLIN
The Folger Shakespeare Library, Washington, DC

From the opening complaint of the Hostess that Sly has 'burst' glasses for which he refuses to pay, *The Taming of the Shrew* is cluttered with references to and displays of objects, and especially household furnishings.[1] Add to these the text's preoccupations with apparel, with food, and with material wealth, again both described and exhibited, and we are confronted with a play unusually rich in 'things'.[2] Such things, especially those sufficiently common and flexible to be required with any confidence by an Elizabethan theatrical performance, would seem to have little mystery for us. According to Pierre Bourdieu, however, 'cultural consecration' confers not only upon the persons and situations it touches but also upon objects 'a sort of ontological promotion akin to a transubstantiation'.[3] For the sake of the argument of this essay, I intend to begin by treating the Elizabethan theatre as a discrete culture susceptible of ethno-historical investigation; to take as a case study in that theatrical culture *The Taming of the Shrew*; to investigate some ways in which *The Shrew* consecrates its objects; to proceed as if their 'transubstantiation' entails a form of personalization, an intuition of their motivation and agency; and to look then at the reflexive ontology that objectifies *The Shrew*'s persons.

To the extent that this essay offers a reading of *The Taming of the Shrew*, it engages the three most vexed issues of *Shrew* criticism: the relation of *The Shrew* to *The Taming of a Shrew*, the role of the induction, and the nature of Katherina's last speech. For the first, the exact textual and authorial relationship of *The Taming of the Shrew* and *The Taming of a Shrew*[4] is for me of less interest than is the interpretive significance afforded by their semiotic redundancy; *A Shrew* shares with *The Shrew* the three plots of the peasant

For direct and indirect encouragement in writing this paper, I would like to thank Andrew Gurr and Catherine Belsey. My greatest debt is to Leeds Barroll, who followed, challenged, redirected, and improved my argument through several versions of it.

[1] My text is The Riverside Shakespeare *The Taming of the Shrew*, ed. by G. Blakemore Evans (Boston: Houghton Mifflin, 1974).

[2] Camille Wells Slights also calls the world of the play 'a world of objects', although to the different end of characterizing it as 'almost too cluttered to move about in freely', with an 'oppressive atmosphere' (in 'The Raw and the Cooked in *The Taming of the Shrew*', *JEGP*, 88 (1989), 172).

[3] Pierre Bourdieu, *Distinction: A Social Critique of the Judgement of Taste*, trans. by Richard Nice (1979; Cambridge, MA: Harvard University Press, 1984), p. 6.

[4] For bibliography on the textual relationship between *The Shrew* and *A Shrew*, see The Riverside Shakespeare, p. 140.

tricked into believing he is a lord, the taming of a shrew, and the courtship of her sister(s), and all three plots rely upon things: the goods that convince the peasant of his transformation, the items that are withheld for the purpose of taming the shrew, and the wealth that confirms the successful betrothal. For the second, I take the two opening scenes of the play (to which Pope first gave the name 'induction'[5]) just as we have received them, that is, as substantive elements which, very much because they function outside the narrative of the play 'proper', require no narrative resolution but which must in consequence be expected to and which from the present theoretical perspective do prove themselves ideologically inextricable from the whole; in fact, they point the theme of 'things' and their cultural meaning. Finally, for the third (and this last is the issue with which I am most explicitly concerned), I examine the role of 'things' in the accommodation that Katherina reaches; it is an accommodation that, to be read ironically, must be read characterologically,[6] and it is largely in order to pose an alternative to characterologic criticism that I have turned to the performance of things in this text.

My working notion is that things have a cultural project; my methodological hypothesis is that an analysis of the uses, values, trajectories, and imperatives of things may reveal the nature of their project. Before I proceed in this fashion to analyse the things of *The Taming of the Shrew*, however, I must clarify some points of reference. In citing Pierre Bourdieu, I mean to emphasize that the cultural consecration in which I am interested is fundamentally anthropological rather than specifically theatrical; that is, I am not here concerned with the stage symbolism of dramatic properties that has been so persuasively decoded in a series of publications by Alan Dessen, Frances Teague, and others.[7] Rather, my approach is principally informed by the work of Arjun Appadurai, who proposes that things have 'a social life'; by Igor Kopytoff, who suggests that they have 'a cultural biography'; by Mary Douglas and Baron Isherwood, for whom goods constitute 'an information system'; and by Maurice Godelier, who would dissolve the

---

[5] As Ann Thompson notes in her edition for The New Cambridge Shakespeare of *The Taming of the Shrew* (Cambridge: Cambridge University Press, 1984), p. 46n; and as David Daniell emphasizes in 'The Good Marriage of Katherine and Petruchio', *Shakespeare Survey*, 37 (1984), p. 24.

[6] John Bean has influentially divided *The Shrew* criticism into the 'two camps' of 'revisionists', who read Kate's last speech ironically, and 'anti-revisionists', who read the play as a farce. (See 'Comic Structure and the Humanizing of Kate in *The Taming of the Shrew*', in *The Woman's Part: Feminist Criticism of Shakespeare*, ed. by Carolyn Ruth Swift Lenz, Gayle Greene, and Carol Thomas Neely (Urbana: University of Illinois Press, 1983), p. 65.)

[7] See for example Alan C. Dessen, 'Hamlet's Poisoned Sword: A Study in Dramatic Imagery', *Shakespeare Studies*, 5 (1969), 53–69; *Elizabethan Drama and the Viewer's Eye* (Chapel Hill: University of North Carolina Press, 1977); and *Elizabethan Stage Conventions and Modern Interpreters* (Cambridge: Cambridge University Press, 1984). Just as I completed this essay, Frances Teague's useful *Shakespeare's Speaking Properties* was published (Lewisburg: Bucknell University Press, 1991).

distinction between 'the material and the mental', as well as by that of Bourdieu.[8]

The writings of these sociologists and anthropologists offer an important complement to Marcel Mauss's *Essai sur le don*, a work that has become a common tool of literary and social historians, that has been understood to have inaugurated an economic anthropology, and that is occupied with (in the familiar terms of Mauss's translator) 'the forms and functions of exchange'.[9] Appadurai, for example, assumes his revisionist posture as follows:

Even if our own approach to things is conditioned necessarily by the view that things have no meanings apart from those that human transactions, attributions, and motivations endow them with, the anthropological problem is that this formal truth does not illuminate the concrete, historical circulation of things. For that we have to follow the things themselves. [...] This methodological fetishism, returning our attention to the things themselves, is in part a corrective to the tendency to excessively sociologize transactions in things, a tendency we owe to Mauss.

Or, as Appadurai also argues, 'even though from a *theoretical* point of view human actors encode things with significance, from a *methodological* point of view it is the things-in-motion that illuminate their human and social context'.[10]

While I am indebted to Appadurai for his authorization of a methodological fetishism that initiated this essay (and that debt will become fully apparent below), I differ from him and from most anthropologists to the extent that their primary concern continues to be with things when they are 'in motion', in circulation or exchange: that is, as active commodities. The distinction may become clearer if I refer to Kopytoff, who, as Appadurai summarizes it, argues that 'the commodity phase of the life history of an object does not exhaust its biography. [...] Objects may be moved both into and out of the commodity state'. Kopytoff would construct a biography by considering the derivation and genesis of a thing, the possibilities inherent in its status and defined by its culture, the degree to which the thing realizes these possibilities, its recognizable ages or periods, its uses as they change over time, and its fate when it reaches the end of its usefulness, as well as its history of exchange.[11] Without using the term 'biography', Patrick Geary also

[8] Arjun Appadurai, 'Introduction: Commodities and the Politics of Value', in *The Social Life of Things: Commodities in Cultural Perspective*, ed. by Arjun Appadurai (Cambridge: Cambridge University Press, 1986), pp. 3–63; Igor Kopytoff, 'The Cultural Biography of Things: Commoditization as Process', in *The Social Life of Things*, pp. 64–91; Mary Douglas and Baron Isherwood, *The World of Goods* (New York: Basic Books, 1979); Maurice Godelier, *The Mental and the Material: Thought Economy and Society*, trans. by Martin Thom (n.p.: Verso, 1986). For related perspectives on the embeddedness of cultural and material meanings, see also Jean Baudrillard, *Le Système des Objets* (Paris: Gallimard, 1968), and Marshall Sahlins, *Culture and Practical Reason* (Chicago: University of Chicago Press, 1976).

[9] Marcel Mauss, *The Gift: Forms and Functions of Exchange in Archaic Societies*, trans. by Ian Cunnison (1925; New York: W. W. Norton, 1967). Mary Douglas identifies *The Gift* as the 'brilliant start' of economic anthropology in 'The Exclusion of Economics' (1973), collected in *In the Active Voice* (London: Routledge, 1982), p. 174.

[10] Appadurai, p. 5.

[11] Appadurai, p. 17; Kopytoff, pp. 66–68.

suggests one when he outlines the three stages of creation, evaluation, and circulation for commodities.[12] Because *The Taming of the Shrew* presents us with things at varying points in their own biographies, however, I am interested in objects at whatever phase of their career they enter the text, not just at that stage that makes them eligible for exchange.

This means that I cannot entertain some other common anthropological distinctions, in particular those regarding the forms of circulation. Geary, for example, categorizes those forms as including sale, exchange, gift, and theft (and he further defines theft as variously larceny, plunder, extortion, ransom, and tribute); Appadurai recognizes the three forms of commodity exchange, direct exchange (that is, barter), and gift exchange.[13] But some awareness of these forms is useful to the extent that they are not unrelated to the definition of things, or, rather, to their familiar separation into the categories of commodities, gifts, and currency; or, as Bronislaw Malinowski influentially put it, into those of commodities and valuables;[14] or even, most common of all, to the subdivision of commodities into necessaries and luxuries.

Objects of all definitions enter *The Taming of the Shrew*. To resort to a sixteenth-century legal distinction rather than a twentieth-century anthropological one, they tend most often to be movables or chattels; they include in the first place an assortment of apparel, rich and also shabby, a cap, a gown, a cloak, a hat, boots; various foods and drinks; horns and trumpets; such hunting apparatus as dead rabbits or a bow;[15] a basin, ewer, cups, and trenchers; hand cloths; a rope or scarf; two notes, or one used twice; a lute, some books; a candle or lantern; stools or chairs; a sword; perhaps a thimble; coins or a purse — routine and readily accessible items all.[16] In cataloguing some activities of these things I include not only the properties directly called for and listed above but also those figured for us through narrative, for what the text imagines is at least as suggestive of cultural meaning as what it shows.[17]

Douglas and Isherwood, whose notion that goods are an information system I finally find most useful, also argue persuasively against 'the Cartesian dichotomy between physical and psychic experience': 'Goods that minister to physical needs — food or drink — are no less carriers of meaning than ballet or poetry. Let us', they exhort, 'put an end to the widespread and

[12] Patrick Geary, 'Sacred Commodities: The Circulation of Medieval Relics', in *The Social Life of Things*, p. 169.

[13] Geary, pp. 169, 172; Appadurai, p. 9.

[14] Bronislaw Malinowski, *Argonauts of the Western Pacific* (London: Routledge, 1922).

[15] I assume such properties to bear out the stage direction '*Enter a Lord from hunting*', following the argument on this matter of Dessen, *Elizabethan Stage Conventions*, pp. 32–33.

[16] I include items of costume when they function as properties, as do Petruchio's wedding apparel and Katherina's gown and cap. I completed this catalogue before the publication of Frances Teague's *Shakespeare's Speaking Properties*, but her finding list (p. 158) congrues more or less with mine, is more rigorous, and provides helpful citations.

[17] For example: the beds of Sly and of Katherina, the Lord's wanton pictures, Gremio's possessions, the book and glass of wine abused by Petruchio during his wedding ceremony, and so on.

misleading distinction between goods that sustain life and health and others that service the mind and heart — spiritual goods'.[18] Certainly, *The Shrew* invokes the function of goods to supply subsistence needs; it primarily does so through want, when at Petruchio's house Katherina is surrounded by water to quench her thirst, food to satisfy her hunger, and a (reported) bed to ease her rest, but is permitted to make use of none. A basin of water is let fall; meat, trenchers, and cups are refused; pillow, bolster, coverlet, and sheets are flung aside, until she complains that she is 'starv'd for meat, giddy for lack of sleep'. Meat is brought on stage for a second time only to maintain the edge of her hunger; Petruchio enlists Hortensio to 'eat it up all' to prolong her enforced fast (IV. 3. 9, 35 s.d.–50). Petruchio explains in soliloquy that deprivation is his 'politic' method to 'curb her mad and headstrong humor' (IV. 1. 209). The text is conscious, in other words, that even this elemental quality of things is susceptible of social and political definitions and uses.

Douglas and Isherwood further advise that 'if it is said that the essential function of language is its capacity for poetry, we shall assume that the essential function of consumption is its capacity to make sense. [...] Forget that commodities are good for eating, clothing, and shelter; forget their usefulness and try instead the idea that commodities are good for thinking'.[19] What sorts of sense do things make in *The Taming of the Shrew*? Because the sorts that I propose to discuss in this first part of my essay are but one means to, not the end of, my argument, to list them is to appear to give them a greater substantive weight than I intend; but because a list will help to organize that argument, it follows.

1. They construct an environment.
2. They fix identity.
3. They register distinction.
4. They create a system of value.
5. They provoke competition.
6. They arouse expectation.
7. They substantiate deceit.
8. They effect social bonds.
9. They offer compensation.
10. They resist certain control.
11. They perform transactions.

This list numbers eleven projects of things in order to emphasize how artificial it is, incomplete, redundant, idiosyncratic, and very much guided by my interest in Douglas and Isherwood's notion that things make 'visible and stable the categories of culture'.[20]

[18] Douglas and Isherwood, p. 72.
[19] Douglas and Isherwood, p. 62.
[20] Douglas and Isherwood, p. 59.

1. The environment that things construct in *The Taming of the Shrew*, for example, is a specifically human environment, as distinct from the natural world, furnished with what we none the less call 'creature' comforts that appeal to all the 'natural' human senses, but more susceptible than is the wild to social and political control and cultural definition. Petruchio on his arrival at his theatrically imagined house calls for men to remove his boots and bring him slippers (IV.1.144, 153), thus marking the transition from a harsh outer world to the humanly determined and humanely hospitable interior; marking, too, the irony of a subverted transition for Katherina. Sly, like Katherina, is surrounded with things that serve to dislocate him, and the objects of the Lord markedly transcend his subsistence needs: the tinker is offered not just sustenance, but a banquet, served with basin, ewer, and diaper; not just water, but 'rose-water', in a 'silver basin' and 'bestrewed with flowers', to 'cool', not merely wash, his hands; as well as rings, clothes that are 'sweet', and a suit that is 'costly' (Induction, 1.38–59).[21] Key to the illusion of completeness with which Sly is presented is the Lord's orchestration of objects to activate all the senses: wanton pictures hung for sight; sweet wood burned for smell; musical instruments played for sound; sack and conserves served for taste; clothing and diaper offered for touch. As Sly observes, 'I do not sleep: I see, I hear, I speak; | I smell sweet savors, and I feel soft things' (Induction, 2.70–71).

In the self-contained theatrical space identified as the Lord's 'fairest chamber' (Induction, 1.46) and then again in that presented as Petruchio's 'house', objects, in other words, expand in significance to create the illusion of a little world, and apparent fullness and wholeness effect their own magical insinuation. For Sly, multiple sensory experiences countervail the arguments of memory and logic; in fact, his 'sense of self', precisely because it is less tangible, is vulnerable to the alternative and persuasive testimony offered by the physical senses as they are stimulated by objects. For Katherina, removal from a familiar physical context and from a familial support system and transport to an isolated and fully realized 'house' under Petruchio's exclusive control enact the common sixteenth-century notion that the domestic establishment launched by marriage is itself a little world or 'petty commonwealth',[22] with her own subordinate role in Petruchio's household kingship adumbrated by his command of its accoutrements (as well as of its fellows).

2. As Sly's dissociation in particular demonstrates, things fix identity. In fact, as often as the pronoun 'my' is coupled with an object — my hounds, my

---

[21] Other creature comforts (not needs) include the candle or lantern called for when, in the explicit setting of 'this chamber', Petruchio gestures to 'this light whereby I see thy beauty' (II.1.259, 273). Several references are made to stools or chairs, as Sly directs his 'wife' to 'sit by my side' (Induction, 2.142–43); as Bianca commands her tutors, 'here sit we down' (III.1.21); and as at her wedding banquet Petruchio exclaims that there is 'nothing but sit and sit, and eat and eat!' (V.2.12).

[22] For just one example, see John Dod and Robert Cleaver: 'A Housholde is as it were a little commonwealth', in *A Godly forme of Household Government* (London: 1598; STC no. 5382), sig. B1ʳ.

house, my port, my chamber, my goods, my chattels, my household stuff, my field, my barn — self-definition is asserted through possession. As an external trigger of identification and of role, clothing substantiates Lucentio's scheme to switch places with Tranio; cues Biondello's characterization of the Merchant as 'formal in apparel [. . .] surely like a father' (IV. 2. 64–65); and permits the Merchant's transformation to Lucentio's surrogate father, according to a stage direction 'dress'd like Vincentio', 'booted and bareheaded' (IV. 4. s.d.). Even as Tranio takes the part of Lucentio and the Merchant assumes the paternal function of Vincentio, through costume, so, too, Bartholomew adopts the role of Sly's fictive wife. The Lord orders his page to be 'dress'd in all suits like a lady' (Induction, 1. 106), a ruse that is of course threatened with exposure when Sly orders the page to undress for bed. Sly, who is persuaded by the Lord's goods-rich practice to 'forget himself' (Induction, 1.41), in his further susceptibility to Bartholomew demonstrates to us the semiotic capacity of clothing as well as of household objects.

Things are gender signifiers (and thus identifiers) through circles of association as well: the objects to which Katherina has linguistic recourse are domestic ones, reflecting the gender-determined sphere of her knowledge. Thus, she threatens to beat Hortensio with 'a three-legg'd stool'; she analogizes blood to cosmetic 'paint' (1.1.64–65); she calls Petruchio a 'moveable' and 'join'd-stool' (II. 1. 197–98); and she ends Petruchio's quibble over whether light is shed by sun or moon by offering, if he would have it so, to 'call it a rush-candle' (IV. 5. 14). Similarly, when Baptista orders Katherina to 'go ply thy needle' (II. 1. 25), he refers to the most common of household objects to 'place' and contain her in the context of an occupation socially acceptable for women.

3. Things also register class distinctions. The Lord convinces Sly that *he* is a lord by suggesting that he will have not only music, but the music of Apollo and of 'twenty caged nightingales'; not only a couch, but one 'softer and sweeter than the lustful bed | On purpose trimm'd up for Semiramis'; not only horses, but horses with 'harness studded all with gold and pearl' (Induction, 2.35–42). Goods are presented as status signifiers throughout. When Lucentio remarks to Tranio, 'Nor can we be distinguish'd by our faces | For man or master' (1. 1. 200–01) and then exchanges hat and cloak with him, and when Vincentio fears the consequences as he discovers Tranio wearing clothes more appropriate to master than to man (V. 1. 65–68), all acknowledge that because class is external to person, clothing is its necessary marker. Similarly, Tranio transforms the Merchant into a Vincentio by arranging 'to clothe you as becomes' a man of such position (IV. 2. 121), and Katherina recognizes of another object of apparel that 'gentlewomen wear such caps as these' (IV. 3. 70). Objects are necessary, that is, to the construction and perpetuation of status systems. In this activity the customary opposition of necessaries and luxuries is elided, because, as Douglas and

Isherwood observe, luxury, too, 'serves a cultural function' that is essential to its culture.[23]

Much of the humour of Sly's transformation derives from his stubborn incapacity to appreciate the objects offered him. Most obviously, he prefers small ale to sack and conserves of beef to conserves of fruit (Induction, 2.1–8).[24] Status preferences are not natural, in other words; they are learned, and Sly's vocabulary in the complex language of things is at best rudimentary. Other readers of *The Shrew* have emphasized that the Lord's 'wanton pictures' are interpreted for Sly in erotic terms, and Bourdieu relevantly observes that 'the capacity to see (*voir*) is a function of the knowledge (*savoir*). [...] A work of art has meaning and interest only for someone who possesses the cultural competence, that is, the code, into which it is encoded'.[25] It must be remembered, however, that Sly's exposure is at yet one more cultural remove even from Bourdieu's schema, for in *The Shrew* the pictures seem only to be described, not displayed, and the unillustrated myths of Cytherea and Adonis, Io and Jove, and Daphne and Apollo are undoubtedly commodities to which Sly again has no informed access and for which the descriptions of the Lord's servants may well be inadequately explicit (Induction, 2.48–60). The Lord finds his pleasure, in the event, in the reassurance that Sly provides him of his own solid superiority of taste. As Bourdieu again remarks, such objects 'fulfil a social function of legitimating social differences'.[26]

4. Further, things construct a system of value. The registrar of difference to whom we are first introduced is the Lord; the possessions of the Lord that we first encounter are his hounds. There are four frames of reference for his relationship with them: the first, his directions that they be 'tender[ed] well', pays tribute to their value; the second, his description of Silver's action in the hunt, establishes that the value of these possessions inheres in their performance to his pleasure; the third, his declaration that he 'would not lose [one particular] dog for twenty pound', translates that value into the terms of commodity; and the fourth, his argument concerning their varying performances, with Silver contextualized among Merriman, Clowder, Belman, and Echo, establishes that value is qualified by comparison, is not absolute, is subjective, and solicits an investment of the owner in the form of his judgement of them (Induction, 1.16–29). Building upon the thought of Georg Simmel, Colin Renfrew relevantly observes that to 'speak of value as if

---

[23] Appadurai calls luxuries 'goods whose principal use is *rhetorical* and *social*, goods that are simply *incarnated signs*. The necessity to which *they* respond is fundamentally political' (p. 38).

[24] Slights in 'The Raw and the Cooked' points 'a contrast between the cultivated and the brutish', but our readings thereafter diverge. She sees as entirely more benign the Lord's 'gracious familiarity' with, 'effortless authority' over, and 'protective care' for his servants, as well as their 'respectful deference' towards him (p. 169).

[25] Bourdieu, p. 2; for earlier readings of the scene, see especially Marjorie B. Garber ('These Ovidian reminiscences are of course a form of sexual temptation') in *Dream in Shakespeare: From Metaphor to Metamorphosis* (New Haven: Yale University Press, 1974), pp. 31–32.

[26] Bourdieu, p. 7.

it were inherent within the object or commodity' is to 'create a metaphor, or
mask a reality'; instead, 'value is a property that is assigned to an object in a
manner that arises from the social context in question'.[27]

As Douglas and Isherwood analyse the values that motivate consumption,
they conclude that 'if we reject envy [...] we are left with a mild wonder
about the irrational human wish for fine carpets and new kitchens, much as
one might question why dogs should want jeweled collars as well as food and
exercise'.[28] But *The Shrew* indicates that envy undergirds possession (or
possessiveness) as well as consumption. The Lord's boast that he would not
take twenty pounds for Silver suggests that some value resides in the
covetousness of others, or, at least, in the owner's happy presumption of
others' covetousness of his things.

5. Thus, things provoke competition. The Lord's argument with his First
Huntsman over the relative merits of Silver and Belman implies that the
accumulation and valuation of possessions incite rivalry. And clearly the
contest for Bianca's hand, for example, is impelled in part by the desire of her
suitors to demonstrate their ability to compete; clearly, too, they locate their
'ability' in their possessions. As has been frequently remarked, Baptista sees
the competition in material rather than affective terms: he 'that can assure
my daughter's greatest dower | Shall have my Bianca's love'. His challenge
elicits, first, Gremio's sensuous catalogue of his house, plate, gold, basins,
ewers, hangings, coffers, chests, arras, apparel, tents, canopies, linen,
cushions, valens, pewter, brass, cattle, and oxen; next, Tranio's implication
that he can multiply all this by three or four and then compound it with an
annual rental income of two thousand ducats; third, Gremio's counter of an
argosy; again, Tranio's rebuttal that he will inherit three argosies and,
moreover, two galliasses and twelve galleys; and, finally, Tranio's pre-
emptive assurance that he can put up 'twice as much, what e'er thou off'rest
next' (II.1.342–80). It is this last stroke, signalling to us that Tranio's is an
exercise in rhetoric rather than of catalogue, that removes competition from
its illusion of 'objective' basis in reality and reminds of the subjective needs
that even 'luxury' objects serve.

6. So familiar are the rules of things that their very presence projects
certain performances; so faithfully are the rules observed that only failure
occasions notice. Katherina's physical torture is intensified because she is
given every objective evidence that her hunger will be appeased, as the
basin, meat, and dishes are served in. Occupying the 'bridal chamber', with
its pillow, bolster, coverlet, and sheets, she similarly can expect no 'sermon

[27] Colin Renfrew, 'Varna and the Emergence of Wealth in Prehistoric Europe', in *The Social Life of Things*,
p. 158. See also Georg Simmel, *The Philosophy of Money*, 2nd edn, trans. by Tom Bottomore and David
Frisby (1907; London: Routledge, 1978), Chapter 1. I find Renfrew's emphasis upon the formative
influence of social context upon value particularly useful.
[28] Douglas and Isherwood, p. 19.

of continency' nor all-night 'watches' (IV. I. 178–202).[29] When the informational codes are disrupted by the intervention of a conflicting agenda, such as Petruchio's, in other words, goods stop making sense.

When expectations of them hold, however, things can carry the force of tradition and can perform as what Douglas and Isherwood call 'ritual adjuncts'. At one quotidian extreme of social ritual is the household custom of hand-washing before dinner, pointed with the offer of a basin (Induction, I.55; Induction, 2.76–77; IV. I. 149 s.d.). At the other extreme is the life passage of marriage, marked with special apparel, household furnishings, ceremonial objects, and celebratory feasts: Baptista, for example, follows ritual form, directing Bianca to 'help to dress your sister's chamber up' for the wedding day (III. I.83), 'prepar[ing] great store of wedding cheer' (III. 2. 186). Douglas and Isherwood assert that the 'more effective rituals use material things, and the more costly the ritual trappings, the stronger we can assume the intention to fix the meanings to be'.[30]

In this context, it is not surprising that things also carry the burden of moral expectation. Bourdieu, for example, associates with 'working-class people' the notion that 'every image [should] explicitly perform a function, if only that of a sign, and their judgements make reference, often explicitly, to the norms of morality or agreeableness. Whether rejecting or praising, their appreciation always has an ethical basis'.[31] In just this manner, Sly holds that the Hostess's bed must be a 'cold' one in complement of her behaviour toward him (Induction, I. 10).

7. Their semiotic force is such that things can substantiate deceit. They organize fictions as large as that of the devised world, identity, and life history of Sly; as small as the feigned tears of Sly's pretended wife, for which, according to the Lord, only an onion in a napkin is necessary provocation (Induction, I. 124–28); and as incidental as the inn hostess's practice of serving inadequate measures of ale by concealing them in 'stone jugs and no seal'd quarts' (or so Sly would have it (Induction, 2.88)). Clothing, too, cloaks fraud. As apparel effects the disguise of Bartholomew, so also for Lucentio, presenting himself as a master of philosophy; for Tranio, playing the part of his master; for Hortensio, posing as a master of music; and for the Merchant, enlisted as a surrogate father to the substitute Lucentio. In one case, that of Sly, disguise is imposed upon an unknowing wearer, and the disguised is deceived by his own disguise.

---

[29] A similar understanding informs Vincentio's disappointment when he is denied entry at the place indicated by Petruchio's assurance that 'here's the door, this is Lucentio's house'. His dismay is compounded by the violation of his paternal entitlement and by the public disgrace of social incapacity that follows upon an invitation he had issued in sanguine expectation: 'You shall not choose but drink before you go. | I think I shall command your welcome here; | And by all likelihood some cheer is toward' (V. I. 8–13).
[30] Douglas and Isherwood, p. 65.
[31] Bourdieu, p. 5.

8. Social relationships are mediated by objects: by gifts and by the artefacts of hospitality. Douglas and Isherwood write that 'sharing goods and being made welcome to the hospitable table and to the marriage bed are the first, closest fields of inclusion', and both table and bed are of the essence in a plot that in its brief course accomplishes the integration of two strangers into a community and into a family.[32] Newly arrived in Padua, Lucentio understands that his first business must be to 'take a lodging fit to entertain | Such friends as time in Padua shall beget'; even when his plans are diverted, Tranio will maintain the expected presence: 'Keep house and ply his book, welcome his friends, | Visit his countrymen, and banquet them' (I. I. 44–45, 196–97). Lucentio's house eventually requites his investment, as it shelters the travelling Merchant who provides assurance for his marriage, hosts marital negotiations with Baptista, and then celebrates the transfer of Bianca from her father's care to her new husband's with continued celebration and desserts after the 'great good cheer' of Baptista's wedding feast. In welcoming guests to his banquet, Lucentio prescribes that their purpose is 'to chat as well as eat' (v. 2. 10–11); as Douglas and Isherwood again observe, 'eating is always social; even during eating, the meal is subject to community rule, to conversation'.[33]

9. For a series of characters in the play, things offer compensation. Bianca, directed in to the protective shelter of her father's house — 'mew'd up', as Gremio, among others, would have it (I. I. 87, 183) — announces her resort: 'My books and instruments shall be my company, | On them to look and practice by myself (I. I. 82–83). When Gremio's hopes are frustrated, he, too, finds material consolation: 'My cake is dough, but I'll in among the rest, | Out of hope of all but my share of the feast' (v. I. 140–41). When language is inadequate or requires added emphasis, moreover, things serve as an alternate or compensatory medium of expression. For Katherina, they expand limited resources in expressing emotion, frustration, and anger, as when she breaks the lute over Hortensio's head. For Petruchio, they can be more shocking than words, as when he causes the book containing the marriage service to fall and when he throws sops in the sexton's face. He understands the supra-linguistic utility of objects: one of the most immediate ways for him to demonstrate Katherina's docility to others is by commanding her publicly to remove her cap and trample on it.

If there seem limits, though, to what things can do for Gremio and Hortensio (for, for them, even Katherina's dowry is insufficient to counterpoise her 'loud alarums' (I. I. 124–33)), the theme none the less finds its climax in Petruchio's avowal that wealth will make acceptable even the foulness of Florentius's love, the age of Sibyl, and the shrewishness of

---

[32] Douglas and Isherwood, p. 88. The Lord's welcome to the players is a distantly related form of hospitality that finally has more in common with charity; it is incumbent upon him as a responsibility of privilege.
[33] Douglas and Isherwood, p. 73.

Xanthippe. He then, of course, conducts the process of behavioural conversion that simultaneously transforms material compensation into overplus.

10. For Douglas and Isherwood, the consumer cannot be content merely to get information from the system that goods constitute: 'There has to be a concern to control it. If he is not in any position of control, other people can tamper with the switchboard, he will miss his cues, and meaning will be swamped by noise. So his objective as a rational consumer also involves an effort to be near the center of transmission and an effort to seal off the boundaries of the system.'[34] Goods thus require management, as do the Lord's hounds and as do Vincentio's transactions in Padua, and they demand protection, which is the objective of the various dowry negotiations and the reported terms of inheritance.

The text, however, is rife with anxiety about the effectiveness of such measures of control. Vincentio is notably less concerned with the health of his son, when he sees Tranio dressed in Lucentio's clothes, than with his own goods: 'O, I am undone, I am undone! While I play the good husband at home, my son and my servant spend all at the university' (v. 1.68–70). And attempts to compel obligation through reward are, throughout, redundant and ineffectual. To the point, Hortensio enlists Gremio and Tranio to support Petruchio in his courtship of Katherina, but his investment does not yield the expected return of Bianca's hand; Gremio purchases Lucentio's agency, but Lucentio, too, serves his own ends rather than Gremio's.[35] Goods, in other words, can have an uncertain trajectory. And their independence can read as a form of treachery. As Simmel usefully remarks, 'we call those objects valuable that resist our desire to possess them'.[36]

11. Finally, to return to the functions of things with which my anthropological sources began, they of course perform transactions. Tranio, for example, knows to offer gifts (a lute and a packet of books) and knows also (as does Mauss) that Baptista's acceptance of them engenders his obligation to honour Tranio's accompanying request that he 'may have welcome 'mongst the rest that woo, | And free access and favor as the rest' (II. 1.96–97).[37] The negotiation for which this is a mere intimation of a theme is, of course, the marriage settlement. Petruchio lays on the table the fact that he is his father's only heir; Baptista responds that Katherina will inherit half of his lands and then raises the stakes by pledging immediate transfer of twenty thousand crowns; Petruchio seals the bargain with assurance of provision in the event of Katherina's widowhood (II. 1.116–27). In this negotiation and in the satisfaction of their owners' differing objectives and desires, the possessions of Baptista and Petruchio achieve their optimal

[34] Douglas and Isherwood, p. 95.
[35] See I. 2. 214–15, 271–72, 275.
[36] Simmel, p. 67.
[37] See on this subject Mauss, pp. 10–12.

destinies. For Godelier, notably, 'property only really exists when it is rendered effective in and through a process of concrete appropriation'.[38]

As I indicated before embarking on this catalogue of the projects of things, the eleven listed are not intended to exhaust the active and provocative roles of objects in the text of *The Taming of the Shrew*. Nor are the items on the list mutually exclusive. Some categories are internally contradictory for, in what is in fact a further tribute to their power, things can both arouse expectation and frustrate it, can both compel control and resist it, and so on. Further, it is not as if *The Shrew* does not acknowledge that things are susceptible of manipulation to individual (human) satisfaction: Petruchio, after all, is a master manipulator (and violator) of things, object-ive expectations, and cultural consecrations. These eleven are merely the performances that strike me as most useful for attacking the cultural project of things in *The Shrew* text.

This is a text, after all, populated with characters for whom displays of wealth have superseded even the illusion of chivalric exploit. To wit, Gremio vows that Bianca is 'beloved of me, and that my deeds shall prove', but Grumio provides the gloss for 'deeds', 'and that his bags shall prove'. In the same manner, Baptista declares that ''tis deeds must win the prize' of his daughter's hand but immediately continues that 'he of both | That can assure my daughter greatest dower | Shall have my Bianca's love' (I. 2. 176–77; II. 1. 341–43). *The Shrew* is also a text in which the male lead makes the infamous declaration that Katherina 'is my goods, my chattels; she is my house, | My household stuff, my field, my barn, | My horse, my ox, my ass, my any thing' (III. 2. 230–32), incorporating her into the comprehensive catalogue of domestic objects that constitute his little kingdom. As remarked by one of the play's more instructive readers, Coppélia Kahn, 'his role as property owner is the model for his role as husband; Kate, for him, is a thing'.[39]

There are in fact many such depersonalizations of the text's characters, not all of them anti-feminine, as the Lord puts Sly through psychically disorienting paces to his own amusement, as the Lord forgets the name but remembers the pleasing performance of a player, as Baptista makes Katherina what Ruth Nevo calls 'nothing but an obstacle or a means to her sister's advancement',[40] as Hortensio and Gremio resolve to 'get a husband' for Katherina (I. I. 120), as Tranio resolves to 'get a man' to serve as Vincentio (III. 2. 131), as Petruchio takes the tailor and Vincentio as instruments to his practice upon Katherina, as Lucentio 'slip[s Tranio] like his greyhound, | Which runs himself, and catches for his master' (v. 2. 52–53), and as persons are analogized to animals throughout.

[38] Godelier, p. 81.
[39] Coppélia Kahn, *Man's Estate: Masculine Identity in Shakespeare* (Berkeley: University of California Press, 1981), p. 110.
[40] Ruth Nevo, *Comic Transformations in Shakespeare* (London: Methuen, 1980), p. 41.

The obvious corollary to a methodology that personalizes objects is one that objectifies persons. To put it another way, just as the things that I have charted are the inventions and properties of a dramatic text, so, too, are its 'artificial persons' (a term I borrow from Leeds Barroll).[41] And in fact, in *The Taming of the Shrew* the performance of persons intersects with that of things with significant regularity and in markedly similar ways. If I observe, for example, that persons, too, substantiate deceit (number 7), I mean not that Lucentio conceives a scheme to gain a place in Baptista's household, but that Tranio is deployed to facilitate the scheme in much the same way that a thing might be used; not that Tranio bargains with Baptista on Lucentio's behalf, but that in inventing a Vincentio to 'assure' Baptista of the marital agreement he manipulates the person of a merchant much as he does 'inanimate' apparel.

Similarly, persons arouse expectation (number 6), whether of role, as that Baptista ironically assumes for the false Vincentio, 'that like a father you will deal with him' (IV.4.44); of status, as that Baptista assumes for Lucentio, because his father is 'A mighty man of Pisa' (II.1.104); or of 'nature', as that Petruchio enforces for Katherina, that 'thus the bowl should run, | And not unluckily against the bias' (IV.5.24–25). Persons, too, ground social ritual: 'the servingmen in their new fustian' are necessary to the initiation of a new household (IV.1.47); guests are essential to the observance of marriage; and the wedding celebration cannot advance without bride and groom — or, in their default, without the surrogates Baptista assigns.[42] As is true for things, the expectations of persons are never more noticeable than in their violation, a fact that Petruchio (rather more even than Katherina) demonstrates. Baptista, for example, calls Petruchio's barbarous appearance on his wedding day a 'shame to your estate' ((III.2.100) that is, to his status and descent and the expectations they generate), and Tranio (speaking on behalf of Lucentio) stigmatizes Petruchio's costume as 'unlike yourself' (III.2.104), or, at least, unlike the 'self' anticipated either from his position or from his previous behaviour.

In related fashion, persons require management (number 10), as do the Lord's servants and Grumio; they demand protection, as do Bianca (the 'treasure' stored in Baptista's 'keep' (I.2.118)) and Katherina (of whom Petruchio threatens, 'touch her whoever dare, | I'll bring mine action' (III.2.234)); and they none the less resist certain control, as demonstrated when the courtship of Bianca proceeds even despite her 'mewing up'. Social restraints of order and taste are inadequate to contain Petruchio, who argues that a cap that 'doth fit the time' is 'lewd and filthy' (IV.3.65–69); who

---

[41] J. Leeds Barroll, *Artificial Persons: The Formation of Character in the Tragedies of Shakespeare* (Columbia: University of South Carolina Press, 1974).

[42] 'Lucentio, you shall supply the bridegroom's place, | And let Bianca take her sister's room' (III.2.249–50). One definition of 'room', according to *OED*, is 'the particular place assigned or appropriated to a person'.

dismisses a gown that is again made 'according to the fashion and the time' as instead 'masquing stuff' (IV. 3. 87–95); who avers that 'honor peereth in the meanest habit' (IV. 3. 174); and who violates religious sacrament, civic ceremony, and nuptial tradition.[43]

Like things, the text further asserts, persons construct an environment (number 1): Hortensio believes that to be married to Katherina is 'to be married to hell' (I. I. 125); Petruchio by taming her is able to predict a petty commonwealth of 'peace [...] and love, and quiet life, | [Of] aweful rule, and right supremacy'; both thus pay tribute to her atmospheric capability (V. 2. 108–09).[44] Persons fix identity (number 2): as Kahn recognizes, 'it is Kate's submission to him that makes Petruchio a man'.[45] They also register distinction (number 3): Sly's pretend wife is 'the fairest creature in the world'; the list of thirteen names in Petruchio's household gives some notice of his status (Induction, 2.66; IV. I. 89–136). They create a system of value (number 4): the two sisters comprise a polar, relative, and reversible scale that begins with Bianca as her father's treasure and ends with Katherina figured as 'another' and rarer daughter, 'for she is chang'd, as she had never been' (V. 2. 115).[46] Persons provoke competition (number 5), as Bianca inspires the rivalry of Grumio, Hortensio, and Lucentio. They effect social bonds (number 8): Bianca serves the purpose for those who compete over her, as Tranio observes when he enters the contest, inviting Hortensio and Grumio to 'quaff carouses to our mistress' health, | And do as adversaries do in law, | Strive mightily, but eat and drink as friends' (I. 2. 275–77). They offer compensation (number 9), of the sort the widow affords Hortensio after he loses the marital stakes for Bianca. And finally, persons, like things, perform transactions (number 11): Cambio and Litio are given as 'gifts', in deference, to Baptista, and Katherina is 'bestowed' during a negotiation in which her father says he 'play[s] a merchant's part, | And venture[s] madly on a desperate mart'. The high bidder for Bianca, Tranio, professes a similar understanding of her value (significantly employing the impersonal pronoun): ''Twas a commodity lay fretting by you. | 'Twill bring you gain, or perish on the seas' (II. I. 326–29).[47]

For all that the Induction and taming plot are concerned with enforced metamorphosis, the way in which the text manipulates its persons very

---

[43] Appropriate to Petruchio's sense of licence (if not to his precise class) is Bourdieu's remark of 'all aristocracies' that 'the essence in which they see themselves refuses to be contained in any definition' (p. 24).

[44] In another parallel with things, the persons of the text furnish creature comforts: the 'low submissive reverence' of the Lord's servants (Induction, 1.53) are as requisite to Sly's transformative pleasure as are the silver basin and the costly apparel.

[45] Kahn, p. 117.

[46] Jean E. Howard observes that in the course of the play 'the audience reverses its initial assumptions about the relative value of the two women' ('The Difficulties of Closure: An Approach to the Problematic in Shakespearian Comedy', in *Comedy from Shakespeare to Sheridan: Essays in Honor of Eugene M. Waith*, ed. by A. R. Braunmuller and J. C. Bulman (Newark: University of Delaware Press, 1986), p. 115).

[47] Appadurai is one of many to observe that 'marriage transactions might constitute the context in which women are most intensely, and most appropriately, regarded as exchange values' (p. 15).

much as it does its things is in fact nowhere more clear than in the 'courtship' plot (and in the last-scene denouement that brings together the courtship and taming plots). To begin with, the text finds two sisters the optimal number to perform its initial function of semiotic distinction (three are muddily redundant, as is demonstrated in *A Shrew*, where the two younger sisters are for all practical purposes indistinguishable as scripted). Contrast between only two can be clearly drawn, with the opposing values of the sisters powerfully conveyed through the surplus of attention to Bianca and the failure of demand for Katherina. But the text also discovers in accomplishing its reversal of this opening assessment that triangulation finally becomes more useful to it than does dichotomy: Katherina's value is appreciably more rare and her triumph emphatically more dramatic if she is unique among several. And so, as contested courtship is succeeded by trial of obedience, the two sisters are succeeded by three wives. The 'wealthy widow', Hortensio's eventual wife, is introduced by reference as late as the second scene of the fourth act and finally appears for the first time only during the closing scene, *femina ex machina*.

Again, female characters are not the only such objects of the text's deployments. For romantic purposes, for example, two suitors are entirely sufficient to the courtship of Bianca; instead, there are three. When Lucentio joins Gremio and Hortensio among her suitors, the text in fact acknowledges its unconventional surplus: 'She may more suitors have, and me for one. | Fair Leda's daughter had a thousand wooers, | Then well one more may fair Bianca have' (I.2.241–43). In any case, because the contest is pursued on two fronts, the plot in fact requires two different rivals for Lucentio. Disguised as Cambio, he satisfies the conventions of folk romance by gaining Bianca's affections in direct competition with Hortensio. Through his surrogate, Tranio, he simultaneously pursues the more significant competition regarding wealth and dower, in indirect competition with Gremio. Once the betrothal is accomplished, however, the text is careless of the two who have served its plot functions. Hortensio takes offence at Bianca's preference for a 'stale' and voids the romantic contest voluntarily. And Gremio acknowledges his defeat and then fades away, in a fashion that has disturbed readers more preoccupied with individual 'character' than is the text itself.[48]

Now, it can fairly be objected that in my earlier analysis of *The Taming of the Shrew* I have over-personalized things and that the activities that I have ascribed to them are 'merely' the functions of their use and manipulation by 'humans'. But obviously I wish to argue in turn that others have over-personalized *The Shrew*'s characters, 'who' are functions of their use and manipulation by the text. My anthropological superstructure and methodological fetishism were adopted in large part to dissolve the standard

---

[48] See on this subject Kristian Smidt, *Unconformities in Shakespeare's Early Comedies* (New York: St Martin's Press, 1986), pp. 67–69; see also Thompson, in her New Cambridge edition, pp. 163–64 (including her quotation of Gary Taylor).

dichotomy between persons and properties in a text. Or, more precisely, to recognize a dissolution of the dichotomy that is accomplished by the text itself.

The relevant paradigm that Claude Levi-Strauss has established, to take my argument to its next step, is of three parts rather than two: that is, he characterizes the forms of exchange that constitute social life as not only the exchange of wives and the exchange of goods but also the exchange of words or meaning, in correspondence with the three branches of anthropology: kinship, economics, and mythology.[49] This paradigm finds a parallel in *The Taming of the Shrew*, which in fact projects a sympathy of behaviour in persons, things, and plays through its central, synthetic metaphor of 'household stuff'.

The term refers first and most obviously to things. Second, in Petruchio's declaration that 'she is my goods, my chattels; she is my house, | My household stuff', these things are identified with, as if indistinguishable in function from, a(n artificial) person (a semiotic integration adumbrated in his earlier vow to 'bring [her] from a wild Kate to a Kate | Conformable as other household Kates' (II.1.277–78)).[50] But there is, further, a third association. In the Induction, an artificial person who is incidentally and totemically identified as a tinker — that is, a repairer of household objects — and who is practised upon in a manner that objectifies him to the delight of his multiple audiences, including us as well as the Lord, is presented with a self-reflexive theatrical performance:

> MESSENGER Your honor's players, hearing your amendment,
> Are come to play a pleasant comedy ...
> SLY ... let them play it. Is not a comonty a
> Christmas gambold, or a tumbling-trick?
> PAGE No, my good lord, it is more pleasing stuff.
> SLY What, household stuff?
>
> (Induction, 2.129–40)

In Sly's apparent misunderstanding, the text unites itself, by its nature or genre, with its things and persons. Through the term 'household stuff', the performances of things, of persons, and of plays are suggestively analogized.

The analogy holds, for example, in the way that a play text creates a human environment (number 1 again), its little world of rooms and streets and families and citizens, and in the way that it substantiates deceit (number 7),

---

[49] Levi-Strauss develops the paradigm in various texts (and in various formulations), especially in *The Elementary Structures of Kinship*, rev. edn, trans. by James Harle Bell, John Richard von Sturmer, and Rodney Needham (1949; London: Eyre & Spottiswoode, 1969) and *The Savage Mind* (1962; Chicago: University of Chicago Press, 1966). The formulation I present is preferred by Mary Douglas in 'Goods as a System of Communication', in *In the Active Voice*, p. 24; compare Douglas and Isherwood, pp. 87–88. In private conversation, James Boon has pointed out that Levi-Strauss's *femme* has too often been translated, as by Douglas, as 'woman', when the more accurate translation is 'wife'.

[50] In private correspondence, Andrew Gurr emphasizes the richness of the construction 'household Kate', which refers to an edible cate as well as to property. On this subject see Mary Douglas, 'Food as a System of Communication', in *In the Active Voice*, pp. 82–124.

as its actors body forth its brief illusion of 'reality'. This text, moreover, flatters the discrimination of its audience as the Induction does that of the Lord (number 3), for we, too, feel superior to the Sly who prefers small ale to sack, who requires interpretation of the wanton pictures, and, especially (the cream of the jest), who does not appreciate the play performed for him, who does not know what a comedy is, who 'nods' during the first scene, who knows not that more is to follow the first scene, and who sighs, 'would 'twere done!' (I. I. 249–54).

Of more moment, the text manipulates the members of its audience by arousing their expectations (number 6): all Grumio's scene-setting talk at Petruchio's house — 'Where's the cook? Is supper ready, the house trimm'd, rushes strew'd, cobwebs swept' (IV. I. 45–47) — is spoken to our hearing, not to Katherina's, so that we are as much taken by surprise (for us, to the comic end of our amusement) as is she by the unreadiness that she discovers. The 'Induction', too, engenders anticipation, preoccupying scores of readers with the frustration of their aesthetic demand for the closure of what they (but not the text) have categorized as a framing device. So does the very genre of the text, provoking our apparently inexhaustible desire that the play be a romantic comedy. And the text resists certain control (number 10), as evidenced particularly by the many conflicting readings of the purpose of the 'Induction' and of the meaning of Katherina's closing speech.[51]

The Levi-Straussian paradigm, cited above, effects distinctions (whether he intended them or not): three forms of exchange, three branches of anthropology. In applying it to *The Taming of the Shrew*, however, I am less interested in the three than in the one, in the significance of a sense of commonality in the performances of persons, objects, and playtexts as 'household stuff'. One meaning of this synthesis would have to be that the text recognizes its own economic nature. This meaning resonates in its semiotic twin, *The Taming of a Shrew*, where the Lord asks the travelling players 'what store of plaies have you' (with the word *store* suggesting the stockpiling of goods for marketing), and the first player responds: 'Marrie my lord you maie have a Tragicall | Or a commoditie, or what you will.' The second player corrects his Dogberry with 'comedie', but the transactive signification lingers.[52] This collapse of playtext into 'household stuff' and 'commoditie' is of interest primarily as a substantiating variation on my central themes of the cultural power of things and of the textual erasure of difference between persons and things; that is, *The Taming of the Shrew* implicates itself in a material world view.

For a concluding perspective on these themes, one that is inflected by Levi-Strauss's notion that the three categories of exchange are fundamental

[51] For the most recent reviews of the criticism, see Thompson's introduction to the New Cambridge *Taming of the Shrew*.
[52] My text is Geoffrey Bullough, *Narrative and Dramatic Sources of Shakespeare*, 8 vols (London: Routledge, 1957–75), I: *Early Comedies, Poems, Romeo and Juliet* (1957), pp. 69–108 (pp. 70–71).

components of social life, I add to my list one last project of things in the material culture theatrically represented by *The Taming of the Shrew*:

12. They legitimate the social order.

The early modern social order was constituted in hierarchies; that which concerns me here is gender rather than class. The gender issue, as for so many others in *The Taming of the Shrew*, is mooted in the Induction, where the idea of a woman proves itself a universally signifying object as a place-marker against which a man can position himself in the hierarchy. Sly lacks the *savoir* to appreciate the objects with which he is surrounded until he is told 'thou hast a lady'; his abilities to see, hear, speak, smell, feel — and believe — are released by this discovery.[53] Certainly the information system conveys implications of status: Bartholomew is directed to bear himself 'as he hath observ'd in noble ladies' (Induction, 1.111), and the Lord is confident that his servant will 'usurp' the behaviours of a 'gentlewoman'; but Sly is persuaded that 'I am a lord indeed' even before he has seen the lady, before he has apprehended her gentility, and also before he has marked her beauty: the news of her existence alone converts to belief. One experience that is universal to early modern men of all stations is that of male authority over women; Sly's previous experience of marriage proves his touchstone in this uncertain new world and provides a model for expanded authority; merely at the report of a wife, Sly is empowered to issue his 'lordly' commands over two 'objects': 'bring our lady hither to our sight, | And once again a pot o' th' smallest ale' (Induction, 2.72–75).[54] Through Sly we get our first glimpse in *The Shrew* of a power relationship that constructs male authority as key to social order.

Katherina's last speech makes explicit the notion that for women 'thy husband is thy lord'; more, he is 'thy life, thy keeper, | Thy head, thy sovereign'. A healthy measure of the speech is occupied with the political role of the wife, who in this world view is compelled to offer 'such duty as the subject owes the prince' and who is stigmatized as a 'foul contending rebel | And graceless traitor' when 'not obedient to his honest will' (v.2.146–60). But of particular interest to this essay is the way in which the husband's political roles of lord, head, and sovereign are grounded economically, in his roles as life and keeper:[55]

---

[53] Karen Newman similarly points out that 'Sly is only convinced of his lordly identity when he is told of his "wife"' in 'Renaissance Family Politics and Shakespeare's *The Taming of the Shrew*', *English Literary Renaissance*, 16 (1986), p. 88.

[54] I am interested in the relationship of 'lady' to 'pot' as objects to be commanded. But just as women can be commodified through marriage, so men can be commodified through service, as the Lord's men are in this very command.

[55] My (economic) reading of the term 'keeper' (i.e., as relating to Katherina's 'keep') differs from that of Valerie Wayne, who writes that '"keeper" suggests that a husband is an agent for imprisoning his wife as one might cage an animal, which Petruchio has nearly done', 'Refashioning the Shrew', *Shakespeare Studies*, 17 (1985), p. 173. But she continues that '"life" implies that she is so totally dependent on him for support and nurturance, as Kate sometimes appears to be, that she must have a husband in order to survive'; in this, our interpretations are more in sympathy.

> one that cares for thee,
> And for thy maintenance; commits his body
> To painful labor, both by sea and land;
> To watch the night in storms, the day in cold,
> Whilst thou li'st warm at home, secure and safe.
>
> (v. 2. 147)

Other readers have pointed out how little this description of the husband's activities corresponds to the (dramatized) facts of Petruchio's behaviour.[56] But the paradigm voiced by Katherina articulates a logic that is independent of the characterologic. This logic organizes a necessary social myth in the culture of the early modern period of which *The Taming of the Shrew* is an artefact.

The material culture of the English Renaissance was, notably, an expansive one. Joan Thirsk, Chandra Mukerji, and Jean-Christophe Agnew are among those who have described the economy of the period in terms, first, of the proliferation of available commodities and, second, of the ongoing reclassification of objects, as once-rare luxuries became increasingly popular and widely available possessions. Mukerji emphasizes that the market economy was an international one, as imported silks, glass, spices, and carpets, for just a few examples, found their way into private homes that ranged some distance on the social scale. Thirsk writes of how noblemen, gentlemen, yeomen, and merchants shared 'an almost encyclopedic body of knowledge' about the best market sources for an ever-enlarging inventory of goods.[57] The explosion of objects and choices necessarily effected a material consciousness of the sort that is witnessed in Gremio's catalogue of luxurious household stuff in *The Taming of the Shrew*.

One phenomenon is progenitor to such economic manifestations as Gremio's cushions from Turkey, valances from Venice, and argosy anchored at Marseilles; Mukerji's avidly collected imports; Katherina's mythical husband labouring on sea and land: it is travel. The early modern market was implicated in the move away from a culture of relatively high self-sufficiency and self-containment to one of getting, trading — and travelling — to achieve the new standard of living. And that phenomenon is of some significance to the construction of the gender order. By the end of the sixteenth century, a common formulation of marital roles held that:

The dutie of the husband, is to get goods: and of the wife, to gather them togeither, and save them. The dutie of the husband is, to travell abroad to seeke living, and the wives dutie is to keepe the house. The dutie of the husband is, to get mony and provision: and

---

[56] Peter Saccio, for example, calls the passage 'rich in private irony', but his characterological concern is the 'private' rather than the 'irony', as he distinguishes the presumed response of Katherina and Petruchio from that of the other characters, 'Shrewd and Kindly Farce', *Shakespeare Survey*, 37 (1984), p. 39.
[57] Joan Thirsk, *Economic Policy and Projects* Oxford: Clarendon Press, 1978); Chandra Mukerji, *From Graven Images: Patterns of Modern Materialism* (New York: Columbia University Press, 1983); Jean-Christophe Agnew, *Worlds Apart: The Market and the Theater in Anglo-American Thought, 1550–1750* (Cambridge: Cambridge University Press, 1986). See especially Thirsk, p. 119.

of the wives, not vainely to spend it. The dutie of the husband is, to deale with many men: and of the wives, to talke with fewe. The dutie of the husband is, to be entermedling: and of the wife, to bee solitarie and withdrawne. The dutie of the man is, to bee skilfull in talke: and of the wife, to boast of silence. The dutie of the husband is, to be a giver: and of the wife, to bee a saver. The dutie of the man is, to apparrell himselfe as he may: and of the woman, as it becometh her. The dutie of the husband is, to bee Lord of all: and of the wife, to give account of all. The dutie of the husband is, to dispatch all things without doore: and of the wife, to oversee and give order for all things within the house. Now where the husband and wife performeth these duties in their house, wee may call it a Colledge of quietnesse: the house wherein these are neglected, wee may terme it a hell.[58]

Notice how all manner of political roles and gender assignments proceed from the notion that that responsibility to 'get goods' belongs to the husband and that the responsibility entails his travel. Notice, too, how many of these 'duties' resonate with the operative order of *The Taming of the Shrew*, beginning with Katherina's mythical husband whose duty is to get goods, ending with Hortensio's notion that marriage to the undutiful Katherina might be termed a hell and with Petruchio's confidence that her taming will afford him a college of quietness.

Notice, finally, in the passage I have quoted from Katherina's last speech, the way in which the fiction that Petruchio must risk his (physical) life to get goods sustains the reciprocal notion that his provision of goods merits in exchange her (political) life. Katherina's set-piece figures her 'maintentance' or 'keep' as his service to her, accepts that that service is one for which she is indebted beyond the possibility of requital, and finds obedience 'too little payment for so great a debt'. The fact that Katherina's obedience is thus offered consentually accords with a hegemonic strategy that Godelier has recognized: 'For there to be such shared conceptions' as social order requires, 'the exercise of power must appear as a *service* rendered by the dominant to the dominated that creates a *debt* of the latter to the former — which can only be discharged by the gift in return of their goods, their labour, their services or even their lives'. As Godelier continues, consent, which 'involves a certain co-operation in the reproduction of this domination', is more effective in perpetuating hierarchy than is violence, 'is the portion of power added by the dominated to that which the dominant directly exercise over them'.[59]

The final turn of *The Shrew*, then (to appropriate Joel Fineman's apt wordplay[60]), with respect, that is, to things, is that things purchase the consent that perpetuates the gendered social contract. They enable the prevailing power relationship between men and women by grounding it in contractual terms, by lending it a logic: specifically, by interposing the

[58] Dod and Cleaver, sigs. M4^v-M5^r.
[59] Godelier, pp. 12–14.
[60] Joel Fineman, 'The Turn of the Shrew', in *Shakespeare and the Question of Theory*, ed. by Patricia Parker and Geoffrey Hartman (New York: Methuen, 1985), pp. 138–59.

economic logic of exchange. The dramatic text's erasure of difference between persons and things and its exposure of interest in the performance of things predict this social contract and expose its conceptual underpinnings.

'Trouble being gone, comfort should remain': Tranquillity and Discomfort in *The Merchant of Venice*

CHRISTOPHER HARDMAN

University of Reading

The last scene of *The Merchant of Venice* apparently realizes the consummation of a traditional definition of comedy, 'the beginning is troubled, the end tranquil',[1] yet it is a tranquillity which has often given rise to profound unease. It does not seem to be a natural conclusion developing from the body of the play. Instead, it is achieved by a series of daring strokes from 'tarry a little' (IV.1.301), when Shylock's fortunes are reversed by Portia's skilful legal quibble, until the restoration of Antonio's ships announced in the letter Portia has 'chanced on' by a 'strange accident' (V.1.278–79).[2] Many readers have experienced a sense that this is not quite an ordinary comedy, and some have consequently sought to qualify the description by suggesting that it is a 'dark' or 'problematic' foreshadowing of what they consider later generic hybrids. Would an Elizabethan have agreed that there was something less comforting to be considered alongside the comic tranquillity, or are these modern readings more sensitive and perceptive to a lack of harmony at the centre of the play perhaps not fully appreciated by their forebears?

Certainly an appreciation of discords to be registered alongside the dominant harmony would not, I think, have upset the generic categorization very much for any Elizabethan at all concerned about genre. Early theorists did have a category in which *The Merchant of Venice* might fairly readily be accommodated. A reader of Evanthius's essay *De Fabula* would doubtless have recognized *The Merchant of Venice* as one of the comedies he describes as 'active' rather than 'tranquil', and perhaps it is one in which the greater 'turbulence' that this kind of comedy stirs up is certainly never forgotten and never entirely calmed. I shall argue that *The Merchant of Venice* was always an 'active' comedy. It was intended to be 'turbulent', and if comic harmony was achieved structurally that in no way put an end to the turbulence of the issues themselves. Indeed, the uneasiness they arouse is functional, important, and positively exploited.

---

[1] Evanthius, *De Fabula*, in *Medieval Literary Criticism*, ed. by O. B. Hardison, Jr and others (New York: Ungar, 1974), p. 45. The references to 'active' and 'quiet' comedies which follow in the next paragraph are from the same page.
[2] All references to *The Merchant of Venice* are to the Arden edition edited by John R. Brown (London: Methuen, 1959)

The treatment of Shylock and the presentation of Christian behaviour in the play is of course the most familiar cause of uneasiness today, and has consequently been exhaustively treated. My subject here is a different source of unease: the relationship between Antonio and Bassanio and the treatment of love and friendship in the play. It might be thought that any unease about this is a modern phenomenon not shared by the original audience, which would be dissipated if the tradition of male friendship and its relationship to renaissance views about heterosexual love were properly recognized. Alternatively, modern students of the play are often inclined to suggest that one should question the unfamiliar idealism found in the treatment of friendship and love: recent critical interest in sexual difference has adjusted the focus on these relationships and on what is sometimes seen to be the covert homosexuality of the relationship between Antonio and Bassanio, and from time to time this has been presented overtly on the stage.[3] A simplistic approach might assume that the play presents the triumph of heterosexual love over homosexual passion. It can be developed to denigrate Bassanio — his treatment of Antonio showing a rather callous disregard for his feelings and a willingness to exploit his fortune. The Bassanio in Bill Alexander's Royal Shakespeare Company production in 1987 was described as a 'bisexual opportunist' and, more extremely, as existing 'on the instincts of a successful rent boy'.[4] Antonio becomes 'one of those men whose melancholy fate it is to give all their love to one of their own sex, and see that love used rather than returned'.[5] Naturally, this tarnishes Bassanio's image as the ideal suitor, the right lover sought by Portia's father who is to be carefully identified by his posthumous tests. If he does well in Belmont, such a view of his behaviour in Venice would suggest a Bassanio more skilful, perhaps more devious, than his naïve and foolish opponents, but essentially no more admirable and certainly demonstrating no greater moral probity.

Commentators often ask, uneasily, about Portia's knowledge of and attitude towards the relationship between Antonio and Bassanio. Bassanio has been judged to be a profligate and described as a 'sponge' and a 'professional cadger'.[6] Starting from such a point of view it is easy to see how his pursuit of Portia can be tainted with the accusation of fortune hunting for a lady 'richly left' (I. I. 161).

While it is, of course, impossible to recover the reaction of Shakespeare's contemporaries to the play with complete accuracy, it is the argument of this essay that, however important an understanding of friendship tradition is it

---

[3] See, for example, the description of the production at the RSC, Stratford-upon-Avon in 1957 directed by Bill Alexander in J. C. Bulman, *The Merchant of Venice*, Shakespeare in Performance (Manchester: Manchester University Press: 1991), pp. 117–42. The question of the relationship between Antonio and Bassanio has most recently been discussed by Catherine Belsey in *Shakespeare Survey*, 44 (1992), pp. 41–53.

[4] Bulman, p. 126.

[5] N. Coghill, 'The Governing Idea: Essays in Stage-Interpretation of Shakespeare; 1. *The Merchant of Venice*', *Shakespeare Quarterly*, Austrian Shakespeare Society, 1 (1948), pp. 1–18 (p. 14).

[6] Coghill, p. 14.

cannot entirely explain away our unease; nor would such an understanding of friendship as they had have obliterated the unease of a contemporary audience. There can, I think, be little doubt that (although perhaps not always in exactly the same way) issues of sexual difference, the relationship between friendship and love, the nature of heterosexual love and same-sex relations which exercise modern students, were issues which already exercised Shakespeare's original audience and would have caused unease.

The attitudes and behaviour of Shakespeare's Antonio would in some respects have seemed rather distant from everyday experience to a contemporary audience in the 1590s: his opinion of usury, though not unfamiliar, would have appeared old-fashioned and perhaps idealistic, while his attitude to friendship would not have reflected behaviour with which they were directly familiar, but, like the bond he makes with Shylock, would have seemed to be very much the stuff of traditional stories.

When Antonio seeks a loan from Shylock he breaks a habit to assist his friend:

> Shylock, albeit I neither lend nor borrow
> By taking nor by giving of excess,
> Yet to supply the ripe wants of my friend,
> I'll break a custom.

(1.3.56)

His behaviour here, as elsewhere, is traditionalist. Throughout the century on the continent and in England the discussion about the morality of taking interest had been prosecuted with some fervour. In 1571 the Bill Against Usury of 5 & 6 Edward VI, c. 20 (1552), repealing Act 37 Henry VIII, c. 9 (1545) allowing ten per cent, had been set aside.[7] However, dramatists continued to characterize usurers in the traditional fashion as idle bloodsuckers, and some preachers maintained their attack on the practice for a long time. It has also been suggested that in the new world of emerging capitalism the high ideals of friendship were frequently ignored.[8] Protestant theologians who reinterpreted the Mosaic law's prohibition against usury in the light of modern social and economic conditions were certainly more practical than idealistic. Polonius's advice to Laertes, 'Neither a borrower nor a lender be' (*Hamlet*, 1.3.75), is more in tune with new attitudes than Antonio's willingness to lend freely to a friend and Bassanio's to borrow. Many contemporary theologians would not have endorsed the ideal of a man standing surety for his friend in real life, as men so often did in friendship literature, even to the point of death. Luther, for example, considered it presumptuous, for man, he said, was by nature deceitful and unreliable: one should trust in God alone. For such men the adage of Lyly's 'lewd usurer' Cassander, giving advice (like Polonius) to his son Callimachus: 'he that

---

[7] Benjamin N. Nelson, *The Idea of Usury From Tribal Brotherhood to Universal Otherhood* (Princeton: Princeton University Press, 1949), p. 83.
[8] Nelson, pp. 141–64.

payeth another man's debts seeketh his own decay', was to be taken seriously. It is hardly surprising to find exactly the same maxim forming part of the advice given in all seriousness by the politic Lord Burghley to his son Robert.[9] Antonio's friendship for Bassanio is, like his attitude to borrowing, traditional and idealistic, not expedient and self-interested — unless we read it as the behaviour of a desperate and depressed homosexual seeking at whatever cost to cling to any opportunity of maintaining his emotional grip on his lover. In friendship terms Antonio's behaviour looks back to a renaissance tradition of male friendship which was idealistic, literary, and frequently aristocratic, echoing the classical encomiums of Plato, Aristotle, Cicero, and Plutarch. The most important treatise, Cicero's *De Amicitia*, was repeatedly translated during the sixteenth century, and friendship ideas found a place in collections of adages and in influential books of aristocratic manners, and received numerous imaginative treatments. The importance which Shakespeare placed on an examination of friendship alongside love in the play is obvious since the addition of friendship material to Ser Giovanni's story of the Lady of Belmont is entirely Shakespeare's. In *Il Pecorone* Antonio's prototype Ansaldo is the godfather rather than the friend of Giannetto, clearly a younger man who treats him with filial respect.

Friendship was traditionally treated as an exclusively male relationship and invariably considered superior to love of women. According to Montaigne the former was 'a generall and universal heat, and equally tempered, a constant and settled heat, all pleasure and smoothness', while sexual passion, by contrast, was 'a rash and wavering fire, wavering and divers: the fire of an ague subject to fits and stints, and hath but a slender holdfast of us'.[10]

Friendship was very different from 'lustful love' characterized by a 'mad desire in following that which flies us', (I, 199) and is specifically differentiated from what Montaigne described as 'Greek licence', provoked by 'external beauty' and animated by a passion of 'immoderate heat' which allowed the offer of 'all insolent and passionate violences' to 'tender youths flower'. In this there was, he said, a 'necessarie [. . .] disparitie of ages and difference of office between lovers' which was inimical to the equality required in the 'perfect union' of true classical friendship. Montaigne is clearly following the ideas expressed by Cicero both in the *De Amicitia* and the *Tusculan Disputations*. Though Montaigne did, momentarily at least, contemplate more favourably than Cicero the prospect of a relationship between men and women in which 'not only the mindes [. . .] but also bodies [had] a share of the alliance', both considered 'the ordinary sufficiency of

---

[9] Nelson, p. 147, quotes J. Lyly, *Euphues and his England* in *Complete Works* ed. by R. W. Bond, 2 vols (Oxford: Oxford University Press, 1902), II, 16, and *A Multitude of Counsellors*, ed. by Joesephus N. Larned (Boston and New York: Houghton Mifflin, 1901), p. 242.
[10] *Essays of Montaigne done into English by John Florio*, Tudor Translations, 3 vols (London: David Nutt, 1892), I, 199. All references are to this edition.

women' not to have strong enough minds for such relationships (I, 200). In the *Tusculan Disputations* Cicero is particularly dismissive of homosexual relationships between men which he too thought of as Greek, having their origin in the stripping of bodies in the Greek gymnasia.[11] For Cicero all who 'are transported with delight at the enjoyment of sexual pleasure are degraded' (p. 407), amorous passion is trivial, and induces a madness which is the most violent of all the disturbances of the soul (p. 413).

The theory and conventions of male friendship are obviously unfamiliar to modern audiences and, as I have already indicated, there has been a natural tendency for the relationship between Bassanio and Antonio to be interpreted in terms of current attitudes to homosexuality. It would be easy to assume that this is a historically determined reading and that a renaissance audience would have given little or no attention to the question of same-sex relations but would have looked only to friendship tradition. Clearly theorists were, as has been seen, concerned to make a distinction between passionate sexual relations, whether heterosexual or homosexual, and friendship. However, the original audience was not composed of theorists, and these attitudes would have seemed somewhat idealistic, old-fashioned, and not an account of how current sexuality was or was perceived. There is reason to think that the anxiety often generated today by the relationship between Antonio and Bassanio was paralleled by comparable anxiety in the sixteenth century, and alongside it there were anxieties which we experience rather less acutely, concerning the irrationality of and threat from heterosexual love. Both these issues relate in the play to questions of maturity and immaturity — though this is probably a less obvious concern to a modern audience in the case of relations between those of the same sex.

It is possible to recover something of the real-life context in which Shakespeare's first audiences would have viewed the relationship between Antonio and Bassanio, and the question of whether it gave any suggestion of covert homosexuality, from current views about same-sex relationships. The setting of the play in Venice could arouse some speculation: Venice seems to have had a reputation for sodomy from the later middle ages, and had a penal code framed to attempt to keep it under control.[12] In England the accusation of homosexuality, together with accusations of sexual licence in general, was not uncommonly directed at courtiers, though it was not until the reign of James that there was more open scandal and even then the connexion between his behaviour towards his favourites and sodomy is not usually overt.[13] Actual

[11] Cicero, *Tusculan Disputations*, trans. by J. E. King, Loeb Classical Library (London: Heinemann; New York: G. P. Putnam's Sons, 1927), p. 409. All references are to this edition.
[12] See Michael Goodich, *The Unmentionable Vice: Homosexuality in the Later Medieval Period* (Dorset Press: [n.p.], 1979), p. 12 and notes.
[13] See Laurence Stone, *The Crisis of the Aristocracy 1556–1621* (Oxford: Clarendon Press, 1965), p. 666; Stephen Orgel, '"Nobody's Perfect": Or Why Did the English Stage Take Boys for Women?', *South Atlantic Quarterly*, 88 (1989), 7–29; Roger Lockyer, *Buckingham: The Life and Political Career of George Villiers, First Duke of Buckingham 1592–1628* (London: Longman, 1981), p. 102.

charges of sodomy seem rarely to have been made alone, but usually to have accompanied other damaging accusations such as atheism, sedition, or witchcraft, to make up a catalogue of depravity. It is a pattern reflected in Bolingbroke's charges against Richard II in Shakespeare's play (III. 1.8–15). Orgel suggests that those who, like Hobbinol in Spenser's *Shepheard's Calender*, sought the love of one of their own sex, and who as E. K.'s gloss puts it, preferred 'pederastice' to 'gynerastia' were not necessarily assumed, as E. K. makes clear, to be guilty of what was thought to be the foreign vice of sodomy, whatever the facts might seem to indicate.[14]

Despite the disapproval of same-sex relationships between men and boys expressed by Montaigne, and Cicero before him, on the grounds that it was certainly not friendship between equals (a necessary part of the classical tradition), such relationships seem frequently to have passed without any disapproving comment. Clerimont, for example, in Jonson's *Epicene* is described as melting away his time 'betweene his mistris abroad, and his engle at home' (I. 1. 23–24). Ingles, like catamites and Ganymedes, always seem to be boys. This of course was in the classical tradition: 'Reciprocal desire of partners belonging to the same age category is virtually unknown in Greek homosexuality.'[15] One has the impression that relations between youths or between men and boys were seen as very different from those between adults.

Accounts of *The Merchant of Venice* often seem to suggest that Antonio is older than Bassanio. Some are very ready to accept this because they see it as compatible with the presentation of a relationship between an older homosexual and a younger man, perhaps unsure of his sexuality and willing to exploit his emotional hold over his lover. It was not only in Bill Alexander's production that Antonio was seen as 'a solidly middle-aged homosexual'.[16] Perhaps partly because Bassanio himself speaks of his prodigal youth it is assumed that a sober merchant of substance must be mature in years. Of course there is no reason why Antonio should not be young and wealthy, any more than why age and mature judgement should necessarily go together, as Aragon's choice of casket demonstrates. Although in the source the merchant Ansaldo is older than Giannetto, his godson, in Shakespeare's adaptation of the story there is no real evidence for concluding that there is a significant disparity in age between the two friends: indeed, by emphasizing

---

[14] See Orgel, p. 23 on E. K.'s gloss to the January Eclogue. For contemporary legal evidence see David F. Greenbury, *The Construction of Homosexuality* (Chicago, 1988). Interestingly, one of the abhorrent practices with which Francis Meres associated sodomy was usury. See *Palladis Tamia* (London, 1598), p. 322. I owe this reference to G. W. Bredbeck, *Sodomy and Interpretation: Marlowe to Milton* (Ithaca, NY and London: Cornell University Press, 1991), p. 5.
[15] K. J. Dover, *Greek Homosexuality* (Cambridge: Cambridge University Press, 1978), p. 16.
[16] Bulman, p. 126.

their friendship it might be thought that he suggests the opposite. However, I do not think it is only a modern audience which is liable to assume that Antonio is older: it seems to me that the anxiety about the nature of the relationship which is raised here would also have been shared by a renaissance audience. While they would have recognized more readily than a modern audience the ever-present elements of friendship tradition, they would also have been aware of the disquieting possibility that Antonio's and Bassanio's was a relationship between a man and a youth which might dangerously continue into maturity, or which might be divided with unhappy consequences if Bassanio once grown to mature sexuality should reject Antonio. Shakespeare's careful avoidance of specificity about their relative ages allows both views to be entertained.

The concern in the play with the differentiation between the disorderly passions of immaturity and the rationality of maturity is perhaps paralleled by this distinction of behaviour acceptable in boys but not in men. The audience is uneasy about how far this is or will become an issue, and once raised, the question is always there for consideration, particularly because this play returns so frequently to the motif of the choice, the trial, the test of faith, always inviting the audience to judge the actions and motives of friends and lovers.

As the plays develops, conventional ideas about friendship become very prominent both in the relationship between Antonio and Bassanio and, even more interestingly, in the relationship between Bassanio and Portia. It becomes clear that the inherent conflicts in these relationships are quite as productive of unease as suspicions of homosexual passion.

The friendship between Antonio and Bassanio can be explained in ideal terms, even at those points where modern audiences are most inclined to be critical. The first exchange between the friends makes it clear that Bassanio has been living beyond his means and now has little left to pay for the journey to Belmont. However, because of their mutual love Bassanio knows that he has a 'warranty' to confide his hopes in his friend. He stresses equally his dual obligations of money and of love. Antonio's response:

> You know me well, and herein spend but time
> To wind about my love with circumstance.
>
> (I. I. 153)

is not necessarily a sad rebuke, but can be interpreted as an insistence on the generosity of friendship in which there is no need to explain or persuade. It is characterized by selfless generosity. Antonio has already repeated the Ciceronian precept that one should refuse nothing virtuous to a friend and offer one's possessions and even one's person to serve his advantage. He answers him that his 'purse', his 'person', and his 'extremest means [. . .] Lie all unlock'd to [his] occasions' provided that his purpose stands 'as you yourself still do, | Within the eye of honour' (I. I. 136–39). Here is a whole collection of ideas which can be paralleled in the *De Amicitia*. True friend-ship, Cicero repeatedly stressed, 'cannot exist except among good men',[17] for it is virtue that 'both creates the bond of friendship and preserves it' (p. 207). Good men are those 'who are free from all passion, caprice and insolence' (p. 129). Consequently there can be no question of their seeking anything dishonourable from a friend for 'they will not demand from each other anything unless it is honourable and just' (p. 191).[18]

The mutual exchange of confidences, too, is only to be expected between friends.[19] Indeed, Bassanio's failure to tell his friend of his 'secret pilgrim-age' until now is undoubtedly the cause of Antonio's great anxiety at the beginning of the play, for there should be no secrets between friends. Antonio's melancholy at the beginning of the play is frequently over-emphasized by critics who wish to present him as a rejected lover. It should be remembered that the play begins, as Shakespeare's plays often do, in mid-conversation, and that Antonio's first words are an entirely natural expression of irritation at the probing questions of Salerio and Solanio. Antonio can be understood to be showing the conventional concern of one friend for another when secrecy has replaced frankness. His anxiety is entirely explicable when his friend is committed to a course which so easily and so frequently led to unhappiness, to disappointment, to frustration, and to destructive passion; one which had traditionally proved inimical to friendship in literature. No wonder Antonio is suspicious of a lady Bassanio has determinedly made something of a mystery.

An Elizabethan who accepted the traditional view of women's sexuality as a dangerous threat to male reason might well have found Bassanio's apparent defection to 'gynerastia'[20] more threatening to desired tranquillity than any suggestion of male love whether in the friendship tradition or not. The comparison between friendship and heterosexual passion is presented (humorously at first) in *The Winter's Tale* as between an idyllic sinless youth before the advent of puberty and a sinful adulthood of sexual temptations and faults (see 1. 2. 66–86). Here jesting soon turns to deadly earnest, friends are divided by unfounded sexual jealousy and suspicion. Carefree youth has not here been replaced by responsible maturity. The ideal reciprocity of lovers and the happy stability of marriage, family, and the assurance of dynastic order it encapsulates do not last. In place of the pattern of growth from youth to maturity, from the less to the more responsible, from male friendship to an adult heterosexuality which does not exclude but comple-ments the values of male friendship, in *The Winter's Tale* the image is instead

---

[17] Cicero, *De Senectute, De Amicitia, De Divinatione*, trans. by W. A. Falconer, Loeb Classical Library (London: Heinemann; New York: G. P. Putnam's Sons, 1922), p. 127. See also p. 177. All references are to this edition.

[18] See also p. 155.

[19] *De Amicitia*, pp. 131–32: 'What is sweeter than to have someone with whom you may dare discuss anything as if you were communing with yourself'.

[20] See above p. 192.

of a move from an unfallen to a clearly fallen world. As with Bassanio's fellow choosers, here age clearly does not equal maturity.

If Bassanio's circumlocutions do indicate any signs of reluctance, it may be taken to be the reluctance of an honourable man to seek financial assistance from a friend he knows is ever generous. A reader of Montaigne would certainly not have considered Bassanio a sponge. Montaigne wrote:

each [friend] seeking more than any other thing, to do his [friend] good, he who yields both matter and occasion, is the man sheweth himselfe liberall, giving his friend that contentment, to effect towards him what he desireth most. (1, 205)

In other words, Bassanio shows himself 'liberall' by giving Antonio an opportunity to do what he desires most, give proof of his friendship. It is interesting to compare what Laelius had to say about his friendship with Scipio in *De Amicitia*:

It is far from being true that friendship is cultivated because of need; rather, is it cultivated by those who are most abundantly blessed with wealth and power and especially with virtue, which is man's best defence; by those least in need of another's help; and by those most generous and most given to acts of kindness. Indeed, I should be inclined to think that it is not well for friends never to need anything at all. Wherein, for example, would my zeal have displayed itself if Scipio had never been in need of my advice or assistance either at home or abroad? (p. 163)

Montaigne continued that friends 'can neither lend or give to each other' for 'all things are by effect common between them' (1, 205). Again, Laelius had mentioned his own sharing with Scipio:

there was one home for us both; we had the same fare and shared it in common, and we were together not only in our military campaigns, but also in our foreign tours and on our vacations in the country. (p. 211)

If one feels that there is some disproportion in the advantages gained from their friendship by Bassanio and Antonio, Cicero makes it abundantly clear that any expectation that 'our goodwill towards our friends should correspond in all respects to their goodwill towards us' (p. 167) is

surely [. . .] calling friendship to a very close and petty accounting [requiring] it to keep an exact balance of credits and debits. [. . .] True friendship is richer and more abundant than that and does not narrowly scan the reckoning lest it pay out more than it has received; and there need be no fear that some bit of kindness will be lost, that it will overflow the measure and spill upon the ground, or that more than is due will be poured into friendship's bin. (p. 169)

As soon as Antonio knows the truth he does not reveal any jealousy towards Portia but rather protests his willingness to assist Bassanio and furnish his needs:

> Then do but say to me what I should do
> That in your knowledge may by me be done,
> And I am prest unto it.
>
> (I. I. 158)

Lack of hesitation in serving a friend is only to be expected. Cicero wrote 'let zeal ever be present, but hesitation absent' (p. 157). Antonio's immediate generosity is natural, for one 'should render to each friend as much aid as [one] can and [. . .] as much as he whom you love and assist has the capacity to bear' (pp. 181–82). The lengths to which Antonio is prepared to go to raise money are also explained in *De Amicitia*: 'How many things we do for our friends that we never would do for ourselves!' One of the examples reminds us of the distasteful dealing with Shylock in which Antonio willingly engages: 'At one time we beg and entreat an unworthy man' and do 'things not quite creditable in our own affairs but exceedingly so in behalf of our friends' (p. 167).

Antonio's willingness to bind his body to Shylock in return for the loan is a variation on yet another familiar friendship convention. True friends were commonly prepared to die for each other if the need arose,[21] and while Antonio does not directly pledge his life (indeed it seems very unlikely that the bond will be forfeit), when it is required of him he does not regret his agreement and willingly accepts the consequence of his pledge. This is a novel version of an old idea, especially as the money his pledge provides is intended to finance an amorous expedition — something all too often fatal to the relationship between friends. Further, the redemption of Antonio depends not upon the return of his friend just in time (as in the archetypal story of Damon and Pythias) but on Portia. The interdependence of friendship and love in the plotting is obvious. It is the same quality of interdependence which is equally clear in the definition of love which the play provides.

The relationship between Bassanio and Portia is very different from Montaigne's 'rash and wavering fire'. Indeed, some care seems to be taken to ensure that Cicero's view of the degradation of passion is countered by a careful balance between mature rationality and erotic desire. This is achieved largely by the employment of the language of friendship when speaking of love. We first learn about Portia from Bassanio immediately before her appearance. As observed above, his description of her has sometimes been censured, especially by those who see him as a sponge, for what is taken to be too great an interest in her wealth. It is true that her riches are mentioned first, but the lines, couched in the romantic hyperboles of the lover, have a climactic organization:

> In Belmont is a lady richly left,
> And she is fair, and (fairer than that word),
> Of wondrous virtues.
>
> (1. 1. 161)

In the end, of course, her greatest riches do indeed prove to be her virtues. The speech continues by pointing out her worth by comparison with the virtuous Roman matron who provided Shakespeare with her name. She is

---

[21] The best known examples were of course found in the classical stories of Damon and Pithias and Orestes and Pylades. The former was dramatized by Richard Edwards in 1561.

'nothing undervalu'd | To Cato's daughter, Brutus's Portia' (i. i. 165–66). It is instructive to read what Plutarch writes about Brutus's Portia. She was 'excellentlie well seene in Philosophie, loving her husband well, and being of noble courage, as she was also wise'. In seeking to prove herself worthy of her husband's confidences she inflicted a wound on herself and then asked what troubled him:

I being, O Brutus, (sayed she) the daughter of Cato, was married unto thee, not to be thy beddefellowe and companion in bedde and at borde onelie, like a harlot: but to be partaker also with thee, of thy good and evill fortune. Nowe for thy selfe, I can finde no cause of faulte in thee touchinge our matche: but for my parte, howe may I showe my duetie towardes thee, and howe muche I woulde doe for thy sake, if I can not constantlie beare a secret mischaunce or griefe with thee, which requireth secrecy and fidelity? I confesse, that a woman's wit commonly is too weake to keepe a secret safely: but yet, Brutus, good education, and the companie of vertuous men, have some power to reforme the defect of nature.[22]

A renaissance man would have recognized that the relationship to which Portia aspires here is something other than the normal marital relationship — which the translation describes in words echoing those of the marriage service: 'bonere and buxome in bedde and at the borde'.[23] Portia disparagingly rejects this: she wishes rather to participate in his counsels and confidences just like a friend. These ideas are in Cicero's *De Amicitia*, but for him women cannot enjoy ideal friendship, seeking instead only to make alliances for 'defence and aid' because of their weakness and helplessness (pp. 131–32).[24] Brutus's Portia is presented as admitting that women's wit is usually too weak to keep a husband's confidence as a true friend should, but arguing that her background and upbringing have remedied this natural defect and seeking to prove it by her demonstration of courage and steadfastness. Brutus's praise of her admits as much to be true. They furnish an example of that 'more compleat and full' friendship between the sexes which Montaigne thought impossible (i, 200). The name chosen for Shakespeare's heroine indicates that like her namesake she will prove an exception to the rule.

What we have here is an example of the extension of the language and ideas of male friendship into the language of heterosexual relations which became prominent in seventeenth-century puritan encomiums of marriage. These built on Erasmus's *Encomium Matrimonii* translated in 1530 as *A Right Frutefull Epystle [. . .] in Laude and Prayse of Matrymony*,[25] a text which, preferring the married state to virginity and consequently on the index of

[22] *Plutarch's Lives of the Noble Grecians and Romans Englished by Sir Thomas North (1579)*, Tudor Translations, 6 vols (London: David Nutt, 1896), VI, 193–94.
[23] *Monumenta Ritualia Ecclesiae Anglicanae*, ed. by Revd William Maskell (London: Pickering, 1846), p. 46.
[24] See also p. 157.
[25] Erasmus of Rotterdam, *A Right Frutefull Epystle [. . .] in Laude and Prayse of Matrymony*, trans. by Richard Tavernour (London: R. Redman, 1530). See the discussion of the relationship between Puritan attitudes to marriage and the history of friendship in Edmund Leites, *The Puritan Conscience and Modern Sexuality* (New Haven: Yale University Press, 1986), pp. 75–104.

prohibited books at the Sorbonne from 1547, offered a very different view of women's capacities from that endorsed, perhaps a little regretfully, by Montaigne. If for Montaigne women were incapable of friendship because 'their mindes [are not] strong enough to endure the pulling of a Knot so hard, so fast and durable' (1, 200), he recognized the attraction of a relationship in which 'not only mindes had the entire jovissance, but also bodies, a share of the alliance' and which would thereby make friendship 'more compleat and full' (1, 200). However, all the 'ancient schooles rejected' such a possibility and Montaigne is perhaps inclined to take and proclaim his stand on their authority all the more emphatically because of the dangerous ideas of an Erasmus who can ask 'what thynge is sweeter, then with her to lyve, with whome ye may be most streyghtly copuled, nat onely in the benevolence of the mynd, but also in the conjunction of the body' and believe it possible.[26]

While the first and third scenes of the play in Venice occasion unease for a variety of reasons, the scenes in Belmont, despite the suspense aroused by the choosing and the increasing tension as scenes reporting Antonio's losses and declining fortunes are interleaved with them, operate upon a different level. This is the world of romance where questions of the definition of love are treated in an environment of courtly idealism. When we first see Portia her words remind us of Bassanio's admission to his friend that he has until now spent his money 'like a wilful youth'. Both of them seem to be at the threshold of maturity. At first Portia expresses irritation at the curbs placed on her youthful affections by her father's will, playing on the word 'will' to emphasize that she considers his interference just as wilful as her own headstrong passions. But control is incumbent on those who seek real maturity, rather than simply becoming adult, and it is only those who master their passions who can be truly virtuous: 'Passions [. . .] if they be moderated [are] very servicable to vertue: if they be abused, and overruled by sinne, [are] the nurcerie of vices and pathway to all wickednesse.'[27]

Portia's growing maturity is signalled by her agreement to the conditions of her father's will, and by her acceptance of Nerissa's conviction that the casket device, which is presented as having something of a miraculous air: the good inspiration of a virtuous and holy man, will indeed help her to a husband who truly loves her and whom she 'rightly' loves. So, too, in choosing correctly Bassanio reveals not the irrational passions of youth, but true maturity, unlike his opponents Morocco and Arragon. From the outset Bassanio had insisted that his companion Gratiano curb his wild manners lest they be misunderstood and spoil his chances (II. 2. 171–79). The scroll which explains Morocco's reward emphasizes that he is not old in judgement and as for Arragon, the fact that there are old men with silver hair who

---

[26] Erasmus, *A Right Frutefull Epystle*, C6r. See Leites *The Puritan Conscience*, p. 81.
[27] Thomas Wright, *The Passions of the Minde in generall*, 2nd edn (London, 1604), pp. 18–19.

despite their mature appearance remain immature in their judgement, is revealed to him when the silver casket he has chosen proves to cover a fool's head. Although Portia is overcome with love, it is the importance of moderation which is stressed when Bassanio makes the correct choice:

> O love be moderate, allay thy extasy,
> In measure rain thy joy, scant this excess!
> I fear too much thy blessing, make it less
> For fear I surfeit.
>
> (III. 2. 111)

As the suitors proceed to their choice, we know from her comments that Portia recognizes clearly their lack of reasonable control, their lack of maturity, and when she encourages Bassanio, she recognizes that his protestations of love reveal his true self. As he is not deceived by fancy, neither is she. The moderation of their affection contrasts markedly with the attitude taken by Cicero to the disturbing effect of erotic passion,[28] suggesting rather something more characteristic of friendship. As the play proceeds the terms of ideal male friendship are again recalled in the depiction of love between the sexes.

When the message comes from Antonio Portia at once asks, as her classical namesake had done in different circumstances, to be taken into Bassanio's confidence, insisting:

> I am half yourself,
> And I must freely have the half of anything
> That this same paper brings you.
>
> (III. 2. 247)

She is of course referring to the commonplace that the friend is a second self and seeks to share his friend's fortunes be they good or bad. The traditional obligation of the friend to return to redeem his surety which the audience knew would arise from preceding scenes and which contextualized Bassanio's amorous success, is at once recognized by Portia. However, the complex development of the surety motif makes the outcome problematic. In the archetypal story of Damon and Pythias the latter is under sentence of death and his return, apparently fatal for him, redeems his friend. Here Bassanio is not in danger, and given Jessica's account of her father's desire for Antonio's flesh rather than twenty times the sum he is owed, even with Portia's willingness to pay Shylock's price, there is no reason to suppose that his return will save Antonio. Portia's recognition of the importance of the bond is signalled by the way in which Bassanio is despatched before the consummation of their marriage. There is no suggestion here that she feels threatened by Antonio, a conviction strengthened by her response to Antonio's claims of love in the letter which she reads at the very end of the scene: 'O love! — Dispatch all business and be gone!' (III. 3. 320). The

---

[28] See above p. 193.

understanding of friendship revealed by her behaviour is praised by Lorenzo: 'You have a noble and a true conceit | Of god-like amity' (III.4.2–3), and developed in her response. She recognizes that

> in companions
> That do converse and waste the time together,
> Whose souls do bear an equal yoke of love,
> There must be needs a like proportion
> Of lineaments, of manners and of spirit;
> Which makes me think that this Antonio
> Being the bosom lover of my lord
> Must needs be like my lord.
>
> (III.4.11)

While the assumption that Antonio and Bassanio share 'like proportion of lineaments' is presumably figurative it is probably intended as a demonstration of Portia's familiarity with the friendship tradition, for friends are often described as looking alike. The celebrated friendship of Titus and Gisippus recounted in Elyot's *The Governour* describes the two as alike in 'stature, proporcion of body, favour, and colour of visage, countenance and speche', so that 'without moche difficultie it coulde not be discerned of their propre parentes, which was Titus from Gysippus, or Gysippus from Titus.'[29] Since Portia obviously assumes that she too is like her lord, in conventional friendship terms a second self, Antonio must be like her and hence 'the semblance of my soul' who must be rescued 'from out the state of hellish cruelty' (III.4.20–21).

When all else seems hopeless Antonio turns to his friendship for Bassanio, though he holds out no hope of its saving him. His unselfish

> Repent but that you shall lose your friend
> And he repents not that he pays your debt.
>
> (IV.1.274)

produces a most striking proof of Bassanio's friendship:

> Antonio, I am married to a wife
> Which is as dear to me as life itself
> But life itself, my wife, and all the world
> Are not with me esteem'd above thy life.
> I would lose all, ay sacrifice them all
> Here to this devil, to deliver you.
>
> (IV.2.278)

These words sometimes give rise to a hostile reaction and make the audience uneasy but it is a superficial response which concludes that they indicate that he values Portia less than Antonio.[30] The passage certainly recalls familiar friendship stories, such as the story of Orestes and Pylades and its numerous

[29] Sir Thomas Elyot, *The Boke named The Gouernour*, ed. by Henry H. S. Croft, 2 vols (London: Kegan Paul, 1883), II, 134.
[30] *The Riverside Shakespeare*, ed. by G. Blakemore Evans and others (Boston: Houghton Mifflin, 1974), p. 253. This and the following references are to Anne Barton's introduction to *The Merchant of Venice*.

imitations in which a friend is willing to offer his life in place of his friend's, or that of Titus and Gisippus, where one friend gives up his lady to another. Bassanio is certainly not willing to give up Portia, as in the stories, to another lover, but since he values her as he values his life and neither, nor indeed all the world, more than Antonio — note he does not say he values any of them less — he must perforce be prepared to give up any or all of them. This protestation, by its manipulation of familiar commonplaces, emphasizes once more the relationship between the values of love and friendship central to the play. Gratiano's attempt to equal Bassanio in his generosity is humorously inept (one may perhaps compare Gobbo's parody of Portia's moral dilemma in Act II, Scene 1):

> I have a wife who I protest I love, —
> I would she were in heaven, so she could
> Entreat some power to change this currish Jew.
>
> (IV. 1. 286)

However, it serves to underline the point because it is a crude sexist parody. Gratianio's words make us all the more aware of the careful equation between love, friendship, and all the world in Bassanio's speech. In the end it is from the interrelationship of friendship and love and not from Portia's wealth, so freely offered to pay the debt many times over, that Antonio's redemption comes.

In Shakespeare's source, *Il Pecorone*, three ships fail to return one after the other. The first two were lost by his godson, Giannetto, in successive attempts to win the Lady of Belmont, for the test which had to be passed to win her could be attempted many times and to fail meant forfeiture of the ship. Ansaldo's fortunes therefore depended on the return of one ship, not of many: the ship in which Giannetto sailed for his third try. Given Giannetto's two failures there was no reason for confidence, indeed disaster was likely; and the third ship, of course, did fail to return because of Giannetto's careless disregard for the passage of time in his joy at winning the Lady of Belmont. Shakespeare introduced a new test which could be attempted only once, separated the loss of ships from the expedition to Belmont, increased the number of ships involved to six (III. 2. 267) — and these merchant ships trading throughout the world — and made them fail to return all at the same time. Shakespeare's alterations to his sources thus greatly increase rather than diminish the improbability of Antonio's bankruptcy and the forfeiture of the bond. A loss of this magnitude is a stroke of incredible ill-fortune which only in fiction can be regarded without surprise and disbelief. Critics who compare the values of Belmont and Venice sometimes see in Shylock a reflection of Arragon's determination to get what he deserves; perhaps Antonio (though through necessity not choice) depends, like Morocco, on the transitory riches of the world.

Antonio's redemption, however, is no more found in gold than is the picture of the lady contained in the golden casket. The wealth of love is what saves him. Portia's skill and her desire to employ it to help him is the return on his investment. Only when he has been saved in this way, is his material wealth also restored. Portia gives no explanation of how she came upon the news of the return of three of his argosies: 'You shall not know by what strange accident | I chanced on this letter' (v. 1. 278–79), and the event itself is entirely implausible. It is an audacious and obvious piece of dramatist's manipulation, which emphasizes that the restoration of his wealth is a secondary and less important consideration: merely a token, as it were, of his real redemption by love.

The concluding episode of the rings turns our attention to personal sexual bonds. With the accompanying jokes and bawdy and the complicity with the audience these bonds are treated very differently from the bond made by Antonio at the beginning of the play. Here Bassanio learns that it is Portia who has saved Antonio, and the interdependent circularity of friendship and love is set out. Another commonplace of friendship literature is alluded to here: true friendship was traditionally presented as taking precedence over heterosexual love, frequently to the complete exclusion of the latter. Antonio was concerned at the outset that love would destroy friendship. Here it appears that the reverse is likely: the bond of friendship which after some agonizing persuaded Bassanio to part with the ring:

> My Lord Bassanio, let him have the ring,
> Let his deservings and my love withal
> Be valued 'gainst your wife's commandement.
>
> (IV. 2. 445)

now seems to threaten love. Bassanio can hardly be said to have preferred friendship to love by doing as he did. Under the circumstances it is not easy to accept that Bassanio is 'wrong' to give up the ring, as Ann Barton claims (p. 253). The events do, however, certainly recall more serious examples of the demands of friendship being considered superior to those of love. An Elizabethan audience, then, might have been uneasy about a rather different conjunction of relationships here from that which modern readers sometimes perceive: not a conflict between homosexual and heterosexual desires, but between the loyalty of friendship and the fidelity of married love. Of course the audience is not as uneasy here as it was about the consequences of Bassanio's secret pilgrimage at the beginning, for here it shares the secret and knows that the women are teasing. Portia ignores Bassanio's reasons for parting with the ring, suggesting he has been unfaithful, threatening to pay him in the same coin and then implying, if only for a moment, that he and Gratiano have already been cuckolded. Bewildered by all this Antonio, characteristically solemn, is moved to pledge on his soul that Bassanio will not again break his faith. That Antonio should do his best to preserve a bond of which he was apprehensive at the outset suggests that, just as Portia demonstrably recognizes the value of friendship and acts to save it, Antonio is now prepared to defend conjugal love. His words are an intentional reminder of that familiar convention of the friend doing all he can for his friend:

> I once did lend my body for his wealth,
> Which but for him that had your husband's ring
> Had quite miscarried. I dare be bound again,
> My soul upon the forfeit, that your lord
> Will never more break faith advisedly.

(v. 1. 249)

It repeats his willingness to stand surety for Bassanio and it parallels Bassanio's protestation in the trial scene. Ann Barton is right that the ring episode demonstrates that there can be a 'latent antagonism' between love and friendship. Surely, however, the effect is not a matter of relegating friendship to a 'subordinate place' while love 'holds the upper and controlling hand' as Ann Barton, who emphasizes the 'solitude' of Antonio at the end, supposes (p. 253). The dramatic events suggest that love and friendship need not conflict if there is a proper recognition of their values, the similarity of which the play demonstrates; and if they do conflict they may, with good sense, be reconciled without one ousting the other.

However, many students remain uneasy about the conclusion and some are less aware of the contrived harmony of a comic denouement than of discords subverting that harmony. Certainly the issues raised and apparently resolved in this dramatic structure continue to be troubling. No one can doubt that the way in which the concluding harmony is achieved is a matter of daringly obvious dramatic artifice. One does not need the crude directorial decision that Antonio should remain solitary on stage, alienated from the harmony and sinking again into melancholy, to ensure that we do not forget our unease about friendship and love, the relationship between them, and the nature of Antonio's friendship for Bassanio. Uneasiness and embarrassment will always exist alongside the structurally contrived harmony of comedy in *The Merchant Of Venice*. Any work dealing with topics which have a history of theoretical utopian idealism alongside numerous examples of failure to live up to the ideal will carry within it potential material for the subversion of the harmonies it contrives. Shakespeare reveals a constant interest in a sophisticated and complex working out of the comic progression from trouble to tranquillity, from unease to comfort: his plays rarely present a simple conclusion of unmixed harmony. Leonato's words: 'Trouble being gone, comfort should remain' (*Much Ado About Nothing*, 1. 1. 100), offer a brief definition of what Evanthius would have described as a straightforward 'tranquil' comic structure. Shakespeare's comic structures are more often 'active'.[31] In *The Merchant of Venice* Shakespeare ensures that the issues raised in the play remain in the minds of the audience as a trouble to the comfort of the conclusion.

---

[31] See above p. 189.

Textual Signs in *The Merry Wives of Windsor*

ARTHUR F. KINNEY

University of Massachusetts

Despite a current ripple of interest,[1] Shakespeare's *The Merry Wives of Windsor* has in general attracted regrettably scant attention from scholars and critics; most seem content with the unfounded legend that the play was written in a fortnight for a queen who asked to see Falstaff in love.[2] Andrew Gurr's recent demonstration of how much *The Merry Wives*, properly situated in theatrical history, can tell us about Shakespeare's company, particularly in relationship to Henslowe's company, is one way in which this play can be made especially revealing. I want to propose that further examination of the text (or texts) of the play itself and of the England it purports to portray will show us more about the ways Shakespeare reacted to the other plays of his time, and about his use of drama to provide social commentary on his contemporary England, even by means of a farce. Finally, I want to suggest (during this present period of re-examining the transmission of playtexts) that *The Merry Wives* provides vital ways of understanding textual variants besides the theories of 'foul papers' or 'memorial reconstruction' (now increasingly discredited) or their fashionable replacement, the newly ascribed master-narrative of a playwright maturing, changing his mind, and so revising his earlier work (as in the case of Quarto and Folio *King Lear*) to perfect his art.

I

I want to begin with what H. J. Oliver, the editor of the New Arden text of *The Merry Wives*, calls 'the inviting title-page'[3] of the 1602 Quarto:

A | Most pleasaunt and | excellent conceited Co- | medie, of Syr *Iohn Falstaffe*, and the | merrie Wiues of *Windsor*. | Entermixed with sundrie | variable and pleasing humors, of Syr *Hugh* | the Welch Knight, Iustice *Shallow*, and his | wise Cousin M. *Slender*. | With the swaggering vaine of Auncient | *Pistoll*, and Corporall *Nym*. | By *William Shakespeare*. | As it hath bene diuers times Acted by the right Honorable | my Lord Chamberlaines seruants. Both before her | Maiestie, and else-where. | [*ornament*] | LONDON | Printed by T. C. for Arthur Iohnson, and are to be sold at |

---

[1] See especially the following essays in *Shakespeare Quarterly*: Gerald D. Johnson, '*The Merry Wives of Windsor*, Q1: Provincial Touring and Adapted Texts', 38 (1987), 154–65; Andrew Gurr, 'Intertextuality at Windsor', 38 (1987), 189–200; Leah S. Marcus, 'Levelling Shakespeare: Local Customs and Local Texts', 42 (1991), 168–78. I have also benefited from comments by Andrew Gurr and Eugene Hill

[2] The best discussion of this is by G. R. Hibbard in his Introduction to the New Penguin edition of *The Merry Wives of Windsor* (Harmondsworth: Penguin, 1973), pp. 10–12.

[3] H. J. Oliver, Introduction the the New Arden edition of *The Merry Wives of Windsor* (London: Methuen, 1971), p. viii. My citations throughout are to this text.

his shop in Powles Church-yard, at the signe of the | Flower de Leuse and the Crowne. | 1602.

Of the play's main characters — Falstaff, Mistress and Master Ford, Mistress and Master Page, Anne Page, Fenton, Slender, and Dr Caius — only two are actually given by name, and only two more referred to generically. For the emphasis of the title-page is not on the traditional dramatic characters but rather on their 'sundrie variable and pleasing humors'. They make the play a 'humour play', as if it were Shakespeare's version of Ben Jonson, or to put it another way, Shakespeare's representation of Jonson's representation of men and women whose particular imbalances of the humours in their body chemistries turn them into exaggerated caricatures.[4] Thus many of Shakespeare's characters in *The Merry Wives* are identified from the outset as one-dimensional, and the play develops, as Jonson's humour plays do, by juxtaposition and situation rather than by the growth and transformation of character. Shakespeare's Hugh Evans is a muddler, who confuses scriptural learning and biblical training with linguistic habit and proverb and tangles Welsh pronunciation with native English words; Justice Shallow tries to relive his daring and lustful youth; Slender is impossibly shy and inept; and Pistol and Nym in their arrogant, assertive, and blunt selfishness are crude counterparts to the arrogant but lazier Falstaff. Above all, there is Master Brook, the prototypical cuckold. To the printer, then, selling Shakespeare's play by comparing it to Jonson's could have seemed inspired or inevitable; and it helps us to date the play after 1598 when just such a description would have carried most meaning and weight. But there is also a fundamental distinction that may suggest why Shakespeare's apparent imitation of Jonson was so short-lived: whereas Jonson's characters show their humours primarily in their behaviour, Shakespeare encapsulates them primarily in language. It is the odd accent of Sir Hugh Evans and his references that are at the heart of his characterization, just as it is the expressions of Falstaff, Pistol, and Nym, and the inappropriate claims of Shallow, the insufficient comments of Slender, and the anxious and elaborate scheme of Brook that create their characters, and the fun. This insistence on verbal humour might, then (by 1602), not so much anticipate or imitate Jonson whose own humours comedies began in 1598, as burlesque him and 'humours comedies' generally.

Such burlesque is obvious. But Shakespeare's representations here do not mock Jonson, or not only Jonson: they also mock characters in Shakespeare's earlier works, as if *The Merry Wives* were even more essentially an exercise in *self*-mockery, *self*-burlesque. The Falstaff of *1 Henry IV* who, during the Gadshill robbery, is a 'coward on instinct' because he recognizes in disguise

---

[4] Curiously, this matter is not discussed by Russ McDonald in *Shakespeare and Jonson/Jonson and Shakespeare* (Lincoln, NE: University of Nebraska Press, 1988) nor James Shapiro, *Rival Playwrights: Marlowe, Jonson, Shakespeare* (New York: Columbia University Press, 1991).

and in the dark the 'true prince', or the Falstaff who, clearly a coward on the battlefield at Shrewsbury, tells us that to feign death is but discretion, 'the better part of valor', is surely related to the Falstaff of *The Merry Wives* who can say to Pistol, 'Indeed, I am in the waist two yards about, but I am now about no waste: I am about thrift' (I. 3. 38–40) and who can say directly to the audience (since his only audience in the play, Bardolph, has just exited to get him some sack),

Have I lived to be carried in a basket, like a barrow of butcher's offal, and to be thrown in the Thames? Well, if I be served such another trick, I'll have my brains ta'en out and buttered, and give them to a dog for a New Year's gift. The rogues slighted me into the river with as little remorse as they would have drowned a blind bitch's puppies, fifteen i'th'litter; and you may know by my size that I have a kind of alacrity in sinking: if the bottom were as deep as hell, I should down. I had been drowned but that the shore was shelvy and shallow — a death that I abhor: for the water swells a man; and what a thing should I have been when I had been swelled! I should have been a mountain of mummy (III. 5. 4–17).

This speech combines the ready wit of the explanation about running away at Gadshill with a soliloquy at the battle of Shrewsbury, both of them intended to address audiences. They are reminiscent of the Falstaff in *1 Henry IV* as the behaviour and comments of Justice Shallow in *The Merry Wives* — 'I have seen the time, with my long sword I would have made you four tall fellows skip like rats' (II. 1. 216–18) — are of Shallow in *2 Henry IV* ('I may say to you, we knew where the bona [robas] were and had the best of them all at commandment' (III. 2. 22–24)). At the same time, these are remarkably discrepant representations, and it is this difference that now seems more important: ever defensive, this Falstaff is nevertheless victimized by two middle-class citizens' wives, not a prince nor any enemy batallion — and so badly fooled by them that they can easily play a trick on him three separate times in apparently a two-day period. Indeed, his buffoonery at preening ('Good body, I thank thee. Let them say 'tis grossly done; so it be fairly done, no matter' (II. 2. 136–38)), at attempting to rut ('Come, thou canst not hide it' (III. 3. 59–60)), or at being bayed (by children dressed as fairies (V. 5. 55–103)) all reduce him to the level of a simple animal. Justice Shallow is likewise not the crafty justice of the peace from Gloucestershire who in *2 Henry IV* can aid and abet Falstaff in a greedy scheme to con the government by recruiting undertrained and underpaid soldiers; rather he is, from the opening of the play, helpless before the pickpocket expertise of Pistol and Nym and inadequate before the self-confidence and spontaneity of Falstaff.

This is not at all unlikely, especially in an occasional work; Gurr and others have recently been tracing how drama which took scripts from the same authors and set them into action by the same companies in the same theatres before roughly the same audiences, week by week and year by year in repertoire, both copied and mocked dramatic conventions, sometimes in witty jockeying and jousting for effect, sometimes in serious competition for attention and for audiences.[5] Taking our cue from a suggestive 1602 title-page or discrepant characterization, we will find that *The Merry Wives of Windsor* is continually sending up the resources and traditions of late Tudor drama generally. Sir Hugh Evans confuses a lyric by Marlowe with a sacred psalm; Master Fenton attempts to court Mistress Anne by pretending to compose a sonnet of Sidney's already in print; Falstaff as Herne the Hunter parodies Ovid in his lengthy invocation to Jove. The pattern of traditional comedy, of courtship and marriage or quarrelling and reconciliation, is parodied here by the ineptitude of Falstaff's pursuit of Mistresses Page and Ford and Master Slender's pursuit of Mistress Anne as well as by the cross-dressing of two boys in the final midnight scene. A disguise such as Julia's in *Two Gentlemen of Verona*, necessary for her courtship, or those of the courtiers in *Love's Labours Lost*, is in *The Merry Wives* reduced to Falstaff dressed in women's clothing as the fat woman of Brainford, the aunt of Mistress Ford's maid, in his attempt to escape a scene of courtship. The motif of eavesdropping that crucially turns the plot of *Love's Labours Lost* is likewise reduced to Falstaff cowering behind the arras. Dr Caius's revenge parodies that of Proteus or Oberon; his attempt to duel with the frightened Sir Hugh is reminiscent of challenges in *Two Gentlemen*.

Such representation as re-presentation can be seen as self-satire: so many allusions energize what at first seems so slight. Falstaff recalls Don Armado; as a schoolteacher Sir Hugh is reminiscent of Holofernes; Mistresses Page and Ford generally re-enact the situation of Silvia, the attitude of the Princess of France and her attendants, and the desire for revenge of Katherina in *The Taming of the Shrew*. The greasy fatness to which Falstaff keeps alluding recalls the fat wench who pursues Dromio of Syracuse in *The Comedy of Errors*. Falstaff, like Bottom, calls himself an ass. Sir Hugh's Latin lessons with their *double entendres* are reminders of Lucentio teaching Latin to Bianca disguised as the tutor Cambio. The ring song of the fairies as punishment for Falstaff echoes the more innocent ring song of the fairies in *A Midsummer Night's Dream*. Motifs are also burlesqued. The generational conflict of *The Taming of the Shrew* and *The Merchant of Venice* (or, more darkly, *Titus Andronicus*, *Romeo and Juliet*, or *Henry IV*) here becomes the recurring disagreement of Mistress Anne and her parents and of uncle Shallow and his nephew Slender. The deliberate pretence of Portia and Jessica, Proteus, and Berowne is made ludicrous when Falstaff feigns lovesickness. Valentine's duping of Thurio, Berowne's testing of the King of Navarre, and Portia matching wits with Shylock are all potentially captured in the entrapments of Falstaff by Mistresses Page and Ford. The cuckoldry of Antipholus of Ephesus is reworked in the scenes of Master Ford as Brook and Falstaff as Herne the Hunter with the antlers set squarely on his head. Indeed, the

---

[5] The Folger Insitute seminar held throughout the spring of 1990; see also Andrew Gurr, *Playgoing in Shakespeare's London* (Cambridge: Cambridge University Press, 1987).

overall theme of the biter bit, which Shakespeare employs in *The Merchant of Venice* as well as in *Two Gentlemen of Verona* and *Love's Labours Lost*, is in *The Merry Wives* alone made double and more: in the merry wives on Falstaff, in Falstaff on Brook/Ford, and in Fenton on all of them. More serious ideas in the other comedies are also reduced here to comic treatment: the notion of love as commodity in *The Comedy of Errors* and *The Merchant of Venice* to Falstaff's attempt to make his fortune from Slender and from the merry wives; the traditional argument of man's superiority to woman proposed by Lucina, Petruchio, and Theseus to the superior wit of Mistresses Page and Ford; love's bewitchment of Lysander, Helena, and Bottom to the self-delusion of Falstaff; the exorcism of Dr Pinch to the Fairy Queen and her retinue trained by Sir Hugh; and, perhaps darkest of all, the desire for revenge in Oberon and Shylock is now made comic in the reports of Falstaff's deception by Pistol and Nym to Masters Ford and Page. Even Shakespeare's signature technique is carried in *The Merry Wives of Windsor* to the very height of burlesque. The play-within-a-play, found in *Love's Labours Lost* and *A Midsummer Night's Dream*, extended to most of *The Taming of the Shrew*, and transformed into a theme and variations in the casket scenes, the courtroom scene, and the ring trick in *The Merchant of Venice*, is not only repeated in nearly identical ways twice with the buckbasket but then at the climax and denouement of the play, is carried to a power of five, all nestled within one another: Fenton making off with Mistress Anne in his scheme within the play of Falstaff as Herne the Hunter within the world of Hugh's children within the direction of the Fairy Queen played by Mistress Quickly within the situation staged by the two merry wives and their husbands. This elaborately staged finale, in fact, boldly burlesques the fairy scene conclud-ing *A Midsummer Night's Dream* as Mistress Quickly openly reminds her audiences:

> About, about;
> Search Windsor Castle, elves, within and out:
> Strew good luck, ouphs, on every sacred room
> That it may stand till the perpetual doom
> In state as wholesome as in state 'tis fit,
> Worthy the owner, and the owner it;
> The several chairs of order look you scour
> With juice of balm and every precious flower;
> Each fair instalment, coat, and sev'ral crest,
> With loyal blazon, evermore be blest;
> And nightly, meadow-fairies, look you sing,
> Like to the Garter's compass, in a ring;
> Th'expressure that it bears, green let it be,
> More fertile-fresh than all the field to see.
>
> (v. 5. 56)

This self-advertisement, like the inexplicable transformation of Mistress Quickly herself in posture and speech from her earlier appearance in *1 Henry IV*, makes no sense in *The Merry Wives of Windsor* as Shakespeare's sole representation of his own sixteenth-century England, his one contemporary play, but it makes very good sense indeed as burlesquing the drama of his time, and of himself. Even the ugly idea of the scapegoat as comic — alongside the earlier treatment of Shylock — is here represented, re-presented, as wholly comic justice. Such a juxtaposition seems bizarre and ill-suited. Yet either by coincidence or remarkable instinct, the anonymous author and printer of *Shakespeare Boiled Down*, published in 1890 as an instructive guide to adults and children by the New Home Sewing Machine Company of Orange, Massachusetts and distributed throughout America, juxtaposes a summary of the plot of *The Merry Wives* with the scene in *The Merchant of Venice* where Shylock is mocked and driven through the city.

II

It is axiomatic that such textual signs of burlesque come as a tradition dies out, not as it begins or flourishes, despite the attempt of the bookseller and printer to seize on the popularity of humours plays in making up their advertisement for the title-page. Internal textual signs in *The Merry Wives* date the play precisely at the cusp of change from humours comedy, parodied and mocked as commonplace or even old-fashioned, to the brand-new citizen comedy which uses comic satire to address more deeply troubling social concerns, a more reliable if still inferential means of dating than Leslie Hotson's attempt in *Shakespeare versus Shallow* (London: None-such Press, 1931) to date the play by the Garter Feast at the induction of Sir George Carey, second Lord Hunsdon, in 1597 — an induction that took place in fact at Whitehall and not in Windsor at all. Scattered critics have noticed that *The Merry Wives* takes the force of its plot and characterization from the anticipation of this new concern with a more serious comedy of the city, 'of the Elizabethan bourgeoisie [...] in a bourgeois setting', as G. R. Hibbard has it (pp. 16, 26).[6] This is not surprising if we recognize, with

---

[6] The first recent scholar to make this suggestion is Alexander Leggatt in his *Citizen Comedy in the Age of Shakespeare* (Toronto: University of Toronto Press, 1973). T. W. Craik, in his Introduction to the new Oxford edition (Oxford: Oxford University Press, 1990) raises the relationship of this play to citizen comedy only to dismiss it (pp. 41–42). It may be more instructive, however, to listen to the older work of Trevor-Roper who 'has rightly stressed the political and social division between the court and country gentry, the latter being those living demurely on their estates cut off from the fountain of patronage and favour' (quoted by Peter Ramsey in *Tudor Economic Problems* (London: Victor Gallancz, 1963), p. 129): despite the eventual royal patronage of his company, Shakespeare was more familiar with the merchant life of Stratford than he ever was with royal court life at London, Whitehall, Windsor, and elsewhere. Apparently in agreement with Craik, Richard Horwich observes connexions between *The Merry Wives* and citizen comedy only to find *The Merry Wives* too early in composition and so he traces its roots not in contemporary comedy but in the earlier drama of Plautus and work of Boccaccio and Chaucer ('*The Merry Wives of Windsor* and the Conventions of Companionate Marriage', forthcoming in *Shakespeare Yearbook*; first delivered at a conference at Kalamazoo in May 1991, and called to my attention by Anne Lake Prescott. I am grateful to both Professors Horwich and Prescott for this reference).

Gurr, that citizens made up an important segment of Shakespeare's audiences.[7] The actual Garter Inn in Tudor Windsor is not so much a public house in Shakespeare's play as it is the centre of business and of business transactions. Alan Everitt has written that 'the Stuart inn was in many ways unlike its modern counterpart, which is rather the descendant of the humble tavern or alehouse'. Rather, it was 'primarily a hotel, sometimes with thirty or forty rooms, [which also] supplied the place of a warehouse, bank, exchange, auction-room, scrivener's office, and coach and waggon park. By the turn of the seventeenth century it was also sometimes a posting-house, a centre for local lectures and exhibitions, and an information bureau of the commercial and social facilities of the area'.[8] While the town of Windsor did not provide an especially notable commerce in Shakespeare's time, his play transforms it, making the Garter Inn and Master Ford's prosperous home (with its huge daily supply of dirty linens for the buckbasket) suggestive of the wealth of the citizen and merchant class, signalling the centrality there of commerce and commodity.

In an early essay in *Past and Present* on the social and economic history of Tudor and Stuart England, Lawrence Stone notes that great interest focused on the 'two main requirements for upward mobility — capital and patronage' which, in turn, 'both hinged on the family. At a time when the interest rate was 10 per cent and long-term credit hard to come by, the easiest road to riches was through inheritance or marriage; for example eight per cent of London Jacobean aldermen had, when apprentices, married their master's daughter, while several of the richest merchants of Elizabethan Exeter had got a start by capturing the fancy of a rich widow. Similarly family connections usually provided the initial leverage to get a man started on a career'.[9] Nor was Shakespeare unaware of such interests: although it would not affect his own marriage prospects, in 1596 he was applying for a coat of arms for his merchant father, elevating him too, in Stratford, to gentleman status, and making himself armigerous in the second generation, his son in the third. But while increasing attention turned to a market economy and material advancement, a related issue, that of poverty and vagabondage, also grew more dramatically apparent: the year commonly assigned to the composition of *The Merry Wives* and its initial performances (1597) came on the heels of a new, forceful, and detailed proclamation (38 Elizabeth I) which cited 'certain most notable and lewd practices put in use by divers dissolute and audacious persons to the great slander of her majesty's service, and abuse, charge, and hindrance of her majesty's loving subjects'.[10]

---

[7] *Playgoing*, p. 50; but see pp. 59–60.
[8] 'Social Mobility in England', *Past and Present*, 33 (April, 1966), 56–73 (pp. 69–70). See also Peter Clark, *The English Alehouse* (New York: Longman, 1983), pp. 7–8.
[9] 'Social Mobility in England, 1500–1700', *Past and Present*, 33 (April, 1966), 16–55 (p. 38).
[10] 'Ordering Punishment of Persons with Forged Credentials', issued from Greenwich, repr. in *Tudor Royal Proclamations*, ed. by Paul L. Hughes and James F. Larkin (New Haven: Yale University Press, 1969), III: *The Later Years*, p. 159.

In such a context, we are made aware of something else that causes this citizen comedy to be unlike much of the rest of Shakespeare: Windsor Castle, to which the characters in *The Merry Wives* frequently allude, which Doctor Caius serves, and which Mistress Quickly as the Fairy Queen wishes to scrub clean, at least in the chapel, is never visited in the play itself; whereas nobility are often portrayed in Shakespeare and their palaces and great houses used as settings for his dramas, here the inn and the merchant's house displace the more customary quarters of royalty and nobility. Put another way, the citizens and servants in *The Merry Wives* consistently point out how their own society is marginalized by those who pass through Windsor Great Park and beyond the castle walls, so that their society imitates, but then itself marginalizes the nobility. As a result, they turn their attention from rank to wealth. It is the lack of money that forces the Host of the Garter Inn to take Bardolph as a tapster in lieu of Falstaff's payment of his bill, just as it is Falstaff who, in effect, indentures him; and it is Falstaff's need for capital (not love) that causes him to pursue Mistress Page and Mistress Ford with identical proposals, in letters that cause Mistress Page to 'warrant he hath a thousand' of them, 'writ with blank space for different names — sure, more — and these are of the second edition' (II. 1. 71–73). Cash is also Master Ford's way to bribe Falstaff when, disguised as Brook, Ford asks that the knight test his wife's fidelity: 'Want no money, Sir John; you shall want none' (II. 2. 248). The look and feel of money dim Falstaff's sight: he does not see that the anxious Brook is the fearful Ford because he does not know nor care to know him despite his fortune: 'Hang him, poor cuckoldly knave, I know him not. Yet I wrong him to call him poor: they say the jealous wittolly knave hath masses of money, for the which his wife seems to me well-favoured. I will use her as the key of the cuckoldly rogue's coffer, and there's my harvest-home' (II. 2. 259–64). Later, when he has survived the buckbasket, he is still looking for financial support from his new employer: 'I marvel I hear not of Master Brook; he sent me word to stay within. I like his money well' (III. 5. 52–53).

What is true of Falstaff's commodification of Mistresses Page and Ford is also, at least initially, true of gentle Master Fenton who, in appealing to Mistress Anne, notes that her father has attempted to preclude their match because

> He doth object that I am too great of birth,
> And that my state being gall'd with my expense,
> I seek to heal it only by his wealth;
> Besides these, other bars he lays before me —
> My riots past, my wild societies —
> And tells me 'tis a thing impossible
> I should love thee but as a property.
>
>   (III. 4. 4)

When Mistress Anne at first agrees, 'Maybe he tells you true' (l. 11), he denies thinking of her as merely a commercial investment although the metaphors he employs belie him:

No, heaven so speed me in my time to come!
Albeit I will confess thy father's wealth
Was the first motive that I woo'd thee, Anne,
Yet, wooing thee, I found thee of more value
Than stamps in gold or sums in sealed bags;
And 'tis the very riches of thyself
That now I aim at.

(l. 12)

Yet Shakespeare's representation of the chief characters of *The Merry Wives of Windsor* is as properties, as objects of possession, and sites of investment and fortune. Master Page's choice for his daughter Anne, rather than Master Fenton, is the foolish Master Slender and Anne knows why: it is because this embodiment of 'ill-favour'd faults | Looks handsome in three hundred pounds a year!' (III. 4. 32–33). His uncle Shallow, however, looking to line his own pocket, has a counter-offer: 'He will make you a hundred and fifty pounds jointure' (III. 4. 48–49). Mistress Page, Anne's mother, compounds her interest in money with an interest in power in choosing the professional French Dr Caius:

I'll to the Doctor, he hath my good will,
And none but he to marry with Nan Page.
That Slender, though well landed, is an idiot;
And he my husband best of all affects.
The Doctor is well money'd, and his friends
Potent at court: he, none but he, shall have her,
Though twenty thousand worthier come to crave her.

(IV. 4. 83)

The last scene of *The Merry Wives* reveals and confirms this fundamental concern; in his summary speech, in which we may find embedded the play's moral, Master Ford remarks that 'In love the heavens themselves do guide the state; | Money buys lands, and wives are sold by fate' (V. 5. 229–30): it is the verb *sold*, not the agent *fate*, that discloses his (and the play's) basic sense of values. Even the sing-song couplet by Master Ford that concludes the play deals with a business arrangement that is fulfilled and so closed:

Sir John,
To Master Brook you shall hold your word,
For he to-night shall lie with Mistress Ford.

(V. 5. 240)

The commercial forces that characterized the town of Windsor (rather than the royal castle at Windsor) are Shakespeare's real focus here.

III

Such observations about the relationship between humours comedy and citizen comedy which drives *The Merry Wives of Windsor* are generally true of the Folio text of 1623 and surely true of the text with which we are most often familiar, the composite text that emends the Folio with the other extant text, the Quarto of 1602, half its length.[11] But as Leah Marcus has recently pointed out, the 'use of a conflated text, in which Folio readings are combined with occasional borrowings from the Quarto, is likely to blur analysis [...] because it intermingles patterns that are relatively distinct in either version when considered separately'.[12] And in fact, she notes, when we turn back to the Quarto, published slightly more than two decades earlier and so far nearer to the original composition, we find a different play: a recognition unseen by any of the play's modern editors. Marcus argues generally that, unlike the Folio version,

in the Quarto the relationship between Anne and Fenton is presented in a sentimental and romantic vein; theirs is a love match predating the play. We never find out how much Anne is 'worth' in money, and it is clear that Fenton, although initially attracted to her, as he admits, for her wealth, remains attached to her out of love. In the Folio the match is only being negotiated as the play itself unfolds. Anne is explicitly worth £700 plus the inheritance expected from her father. Fenton is distinctly more mercenary throughout, less convincingly in love with Anne than with her money. The Quarto's sentimental benevolence extends to other characters like Ford and even to Falstaff himself: in that text, once properly reformed, he is forgiven his debt of £20 to Ford; in the Folio he is expected to pay up. (p. 177)

Thus the Quarto of 1602 records a different character and set of characterizations than those more widely preserved in the Folio and in later editions.

But the dissimilarity between Quarto and Folio texts of *The Merry Wives* is readily apparent: the beginning of the play, Act I, Scene 1, is virtually rewritten in the Folio; long passages in Act I, Scene 4 are added in the Folio, while the Folio drops the Quarto text at signatures B3–B3^v in that scene; and the Folio adds a great deal to Act II, Scene 1, the Latin scene in Act IV, Scene 1, and Act V, Scenes 1–4, for instance, producing a text nearly twice as long

---

[11] The only texts with any independent authority are these. In addition, there are also extant Q2 (1619), a reprint of Q1; Q3 (1630), a reprint of F1; and F2 (1632), F3 (1664), and F4 (1685), each directly derived from its predecessor.

[12] 'Levelling Shakespeare', p. 177. Modern textual scholars are unanimous in preferring the Folio text to the Quarto. They agree with W. W. Greg who in 1910 advanced the theory that Q1 was an imperfect memorial reconstruction. The New Arden text, ed. H. J. Oliver (1971), is 'based uncompromisingly on the Folio' and 'admits very few readings from the Quarto', as Hibbard observes in the New Penguin text (p. 51); but he, A. T. Quiller-Couch and J. Dover Wilson in the Cambridge edition (1921), Fredson Bowers in the Pelican edition (1963), and William Green in the Signet edition (1965), all follow suit. The most insistent is T. W. Craik in the Oxford text (1990), who agrees with his predecessors in finding F1's text based on an authorial manuscript transcribed by Ralph Crane while dismissing Q1 as 'a corrupt text reconstructed from memory and, where memory failed, from invention' (p. 48). Craik lists substitutions and expurgations of F1 and Q1 and then discusses at some length the types of error in Q1: inconsistent action and dialogue, misplaced fragments of speeches, echoes of other plays not in Shakespeare's version, and loose paraphrases and invented substitutions (pp. 49–51). He summarizes, 'Though Q's text is very unlike F's there is little likelihood that it is based on a much revised version used in a public theatre as distinct from the original court version. Most of its shortening can be explained by the reporter's failure to remember the full text' (p. 51). William Bracy's alternative view in '*The Merry Wives of Windsor*': *The History and Transmission of Shakespeare's Text* (Columbia, MO: University of Missouri Press, 1952), that Q1 is a carefully abridged version of the original text, has not won universal support, although the interpretations which Marcus and I make below about the play may also stimulate further interest in Q1.

as the Quarto. But Marcus's painstaking collation of the two texts reveals other more subtle changes that display a singular consistency. 'We will quickly discover', she writes, 'that the pattern of difference is quite regular';

the names of surrounding towns are similar in both versions, but in nearly every place where the Folio specifies a Windsor locale, the Quarto substitutes a more generalized location that could easily be London rather than Windsor. Falstaff's great 'buck-basket' is carried 'among the Whitsters in *Dotchet* Mead' in the Folio (TLN 1363–64), merely 'to the Launderers' in the Quarto (p. 565 (in the Muir–Allen facsimile)). (The fat knight ends up in the same river in either case, since both London and Windsor are on the Thames.) In the Folio one set of characters runs madly 'through the Towne (of Windsor) to *Frogmore*' while others run 'about the fields with mee through *Frogmore*' (TLN 1134–35, 1144–45). In the Quarto they go 'through the fields to *Frogmore*' (p. 563) — a slight change, but one that makes the line more parallel to the London experience of going 'through the fields' to reach the open countryside. Characters in the Folio text habitually offer exclamations and comparisons anchored in their locale: 'as any is in *Windsor*' (TLN 866), 'neuer a woman in *Windsor*' (TLN 514–15), 'for ye welth of *Windsor castle*' (TLN 1543). This trick of language does not exist in the Quarto text.

In nearly every case where the Folio refers to some feature of rural life in Windsor, enlivened by the presence of the court, the Quarto creates a more identifiably urban equivalent, but without any mention of the court. The Folio has Simple hiding in a 'Closett' and Doctor Caius on his way to court (TLN 438–65); the Quarto has Simple hiding in a 'Counting–house' and does not specify the Doctor's destination (p. 557). Mistress Quickly's long description of the court's visit to Windsor in 2.2 of the Folio (TLN 829–46) does not exist in the Quarto. The Folio's 2.2 has Ford praising Falstaff's 'war-like, court-like' preparations; in the Quarto, Falstaff is simply 'A man of such parts that might win 20. such as she' (p. 561); and in several other places, similarly, references to court to 'Windsor-chimnies' and the castle, which must be kept clean since 'Our radiant Queene, hates Sluts, and Sluttery' (TLN 2525–28), the Quarto has Puck sending Peane to the 'countrie houses' and Pead dispatched to a more recognizably urban setting:

> go you & see where Brokers sleep,
> And Foxe-eyed Seriants with their mase,
> Go laide the Proctors in the street,
> And pinch the lowsie Seriants face. (p. 576)

And of course, the Folio's long, elaborate blessing of the castle itself and St. George's Chapel does not exist in the Quarto:

> Search Windsor Castle (Elues) within, and out.
> Strew good lucke (Ouphes) on euery sacred roome,
> That it may stand till the perpetuall doome,
> In state as wholsome, as in state 'tis fit,
> Worthy the Owner, and the Owner it.
> The seuerall Chaires of Order, looke you scowre
> With iuyce of Balme; and euery precious flowre,
> Each faire Instalment, Coate, and seu'rall Crest,
> With loyall Blazon, euermore be blest. (TLN 2538)

Even Falstaff's language is sometimes more rural in the Folio than in the Quarto. In the Folio he says, 'I will vse her [Mistress Ford] as the key of the Cuckoldy-rogues Coffer, & ther's my haruest-home' (TLN 1026–28). For 'haruest-home' the Quarto has 'randeuowes [rendezvous]' (p. 562). And finally, his punishment as 'Herne the Hunter' in the Folio is imagined as part of an elaborate myth surrounding a long-dead keeper of Windsor Forest who haunts a giant oak known by all as 'Hernes

Oake' — a mysterious and 'ancient' rural 'tale' that is apparently Shakespeare's invention (TLN 2150–60). In the Quarto, 'Horne the Hunter' is the subject of superstition but is not associated with an ancient keeper of Windsor Forest, a giant oak, or any topographical fable. He haunts 'field' and 'woods' more generally, and is, through his name and lack of other associations, more directly a figure of cuckoldry than the mighty Herne of the Folio. As Horne, Falstaff still calls himself the fattest stag 'In all *Windsor* forrest' (p. 575), but that is almost the Quarto text's only reference to Windsor aside from the title itself.[13] The Folio version of *Merry Wives* is a comedy of small town and rural life, steeped in rustic customs and topography but also imbued with the 'high' presence of the royal court; the Quarto version is 'lower', more urban, closer to the pattern of city or 'citizen' comedy. (pp. 173–75)

Such documentation does not necessarily suggest London, but it does suggest that the printer of the Quarto text attempted to remove the original location with its habitation and a name (despite the title and four scattered references which indicate a fossilized initial version) to a place *like* London with no habitation or name.

I think we can build on Marcus's observations by adding to them our own understanding that *The Merry Wives of Windsor* is at pains to override a humours comedy with the sense of commercialism and commodification of the later city satires. If we bear this in mind, and work our way once more through the Folio text (in only the ways and places in which it departs from the 1602 Quarto) we shall find a further patterning. Marcus is right in noting that in emphasizing *Windsor*, the Folio also emphasizes a sense of contemporary Tudor town life, as in the following passages which all allude to local customs and, on occasion, to Windsor Great Park itself:

MR. PAGE   Wife, bid these gentlemen welcome: come, we have a hot Venison pasty to dinner; Come gentlemen, I hope we shall drinke downe all unkindnesse. (TLN 180–82)

[MISTRESS] QUICKLY   Goe, and we'll have a posset for't soone at night, (in faith) at the latter end of a Sea-cole fire. (TLN 406–07)

CAIUS   I will cut his troat in de Parke, and I will teach a scurvy Jack-a-nape Priest to meddle or make: — you may be gon: it is not good you tarry here: (TLN 497–99)

MISTRESS FORD   I would have sworne his dispostion would have gone to the truth of his words: but they doe no more adhere and keep place together, then the hundred Psalms to the tune of Greensleeves: What tempest (I troa) threw this Whale, (with so many Tuns of oyle in his belly a' shoare at Windsor? How shall I be revenged on him? (TLN 605–10)

PISTOL   Take heed, have open eye, for theeves do foot by night. Take heed, ere summer comes, or Cuckoo-birds do sing. (TLN 663–64)

PAGE   I will not beeleve such a *Cataian*, though the Priest o' th' Towne commend him for a true man. (TLN 682)

MISTRESS PAGE   Good husband, let us every one go home,
And laugh this sport ore by a Country fire. (TLN 2724–25)

---

[13] Actually, there are two others: 'halfe *Windsor*' (p. 566) and 'all *Windsor*' (p. 576) which Marcus also adds in note 11, p. 175. Clearly Shakespeare had first set the play in Windsor although it seems later to have been given a more generalized setting.

Such country matters are interlarded with some twenty explicit references to Windsor, Windsor Great Park, Windsor Forest, Windsor Castle, and Windsor Bell, as well as three references to Datchet Mead and two more to Frogmore. The setting of the Folio is not only indisputable: it deliberately reverberates in the ear.

At the same time, tracing those passages in the Folio that do not appear in the 1602 Quarto, there are just as many which make this town focus almost entirely on pecuniary matters of marriage settlements that overlap, or become confused with commercial ones. Here is a sampling to indicate how the Folio changes tonally:

SLENDER   Did her Grand-sire leave her seaven hundred pound?
EVANS   I, and her father is make her a pritter penny.
SLENDER   I know the young Gentlewoman, she has good gifts.
EVANS   Seven hundred pounds, and possibilities, is goot gifts. (TLN 58–61)

SHALLOW   Will you, (upon good dowry) marry her? (TLN 219)

FENTON   [to Mistress Quickly] Hold, there's money for thee: Let me have thy voice in my behalfe: if thou seest her before me, commend me. (TLN 540)

FORD   I have long lov'd her, and I protest to you, bestowed much on her: followed her with a doating observance: Ingross'd opportunities to meete her: fee'd her every slight occasion that could but nigardly give mee sight of her: not only bought many presents to give her, but have given largely to many, to know what shee would have given. (TLN 945–61)

FORD   Beleeve it, for you know it: there is money, spend it, spend it, spend more; spend all I have, onely give me so much of your time in exchange of it, as to lay an amiable siege to the honesty of this *Fords* wife: if any man may, you may as soone as any. (TLN 989–94)

SIMPLE   Why, sir, they were nothing but about Mistris *Anne Page*, to know if it were my Masters fortune to have her, or no.
FALSTAFF   'Tis, 'tis his fortune.
SIMPLE   What, sir?
FALSTAFF   To have her or no: goe; say the woman told me so. (TLN 2263–69)

Both these strains of marriage and money are dominant, and there is no way that an audience would not connect them. In fact, on several occasions the characters do the job for us, Falstaff, Shallow, Master and Mistress Ford, the parents and suitors of Anne Page, and, as in this instance, the go-between in these business-like dealings, Mistress Quickly:

Marry — this is the short, and the long of it: you have brought her into such a Canaries, as 'tis wonderfull: the best Courtier of them all (when the Court lay at *Windsor*) could never have brought her to such a Canarie: yet there has beene Knights, and Lords, and Gentlemen, with their Coaches; I warrant you Coach after Coach, letter after letter, gift after gift, smelling so sweetly: all Muske, and so rushling, I warrant you, in silke and golde, and in such alligant termes, and in such wine and suger of the best, and the fairest, that would have wonne any womans heart: and I warrant you, they could never get an eye-winke of her: I had my selfe twentie Angels given me this morning, but I defie all Angels (in any sort, as they say) but in the way of honesty: and I warrant you, they could never get her so much as sippe on a cap with the prowdest of them all, and yet there has been Earles: nay (which is more) Pentioners, but I warrant you all is one with her. (TLN 829–46)

Clearly, the overriding point of the Folio *Merry Wives* seems to be that monetary thinking governs all transactions in Windsor: an idea that, given the fuzzy locale and the de-emphasis on commercialism, is never a theme in the Quarto text of 1602.

That two distinctive texts such as these may harbour significantly different meanings is suggested by Annabel Patterson; she finds in the case of *Henry V* that substantive variants carry not only literary but ideological signification, to be taken as textual signs and markers.

For the first Quarto version is not only shorter than the Folio but tonally different from it. Among the most striking absences in the Quarto are all five Choruses and the final Epilogue; hence, in the fifth Chorus, the non-appearance of the allusion to Essex's anticipated return from Ireland, which Gary Taylor has called 'the only explicit, extra-dramatic, incontestable reference to a contemporary *event* anywhere in the canon'; and with no epilogue, there is no final let-down, no admission that the legendary victory at Agincourt accomplished nothing, since in the following reign the regents for Henry VI 'lost France, and made his England bleed' (TLN 3379). [...] Also missing from the Quarto is Act 1, Scene 1, where the bishops cynically discuss how they are to motivate the war and distract the House of Commons from their plan to reclaim ecclesiastical property; the Hostess's claim in 2:1 that Falstaff is dying because 'The King has killed his heart'; almost all of the Harfleur episode, including the famous 'Once more unto the breach' speech by Henry, and most of his threats of violence upon the besieged citizens; much of the material in the scene before the battle of Agincourt, especially Henry's closing soliloquy on the hardships of kingship; several scenes in the French camp; all of Burgundy's speech on the damages suffered by France in the war; and much of the wooing scene between Kate and Henry. [...] There is nothing in the stage-historical records to refute the Quarto's claim that it represents the play as it was 'sundry times' acted by the Chamberlain's Company. We simply do not know, in fact, what the performative version of *Henry V* was like; the Quarto may very well be closer than the Folio to what the London audiences actually saw on the stage at the absolute turn of the century.[14]

But she is certain of the ideological difference: 'The Folio can possibly sustain the hypothesis of ideological confusion or deliberate ambiguity', seeming to side with the Queen and also with Essex, 'whereas the theses of [Lily B.] Campbell and [E. M. W.] Tillyard could be better supported by *The Cronicle History of Henry the fifth*, the first Quarto version, which has long been ruled out of interpretive account by Shakespearean bibliographers, and placed in the evaluative category of the 'Bad Quartos', that is to say, beyond interpretive reach' (pp. 72–73). The Quarto of *Henry V* for Patterson thus accommodated itself to political authority (and pointedly, at the time of Thomas Cockson's heroic engraving of Essex circulating on February 2, 1600, and Sir John Hayward's imprisonment for insurrection in July of that year), while the later version recorded in the Folio (but most useful as

[14] *Shakespeare and the Popular Voice* (Oxford: Blackwell, 1989), p. 73.

political commentary between 1599 and 1601) interrogated such authority. I think the same case can be made (but in reverse) for the Quarto and Folio texts of *The Merry Wives of Windsor*, for the Quarto, in de-emphasizing the use of Windsor that we find in the Folio and substituting no other particular locale, may signal the reason why the setting of Windsor, first established in play and title, temporarily disappears once we replace the Quarto text back in its original time and place.[15]

IV

To return to the question of place: no modern editor of *Merry Wives* has examined contemporary towns such as Windsor, or Windsor itself, at the time of the Quarto, although the Folio keeps suggesting that we should. And there is good enough reason: the condition of towns in England including Windsor in the late 1590s was appalling; Peter Clark has described it thus:

English towns in the 1590s suffered from three principal, if interacting pressures: harvest failure, plague and overseas war. Following the dearth of 1586 the subsequent harvest years were tolerably good and those of the early 1590s attained near-glut proportions. But after 1593 there was a succession of climactic and agricultural disasters. As one observer noted: 'every man complains against the dearth of this time.' In the West Midlands the Shrewsbury town chronicle recorded for 1594: 'this year and most of the summer and part of the harvest time continually for the most part was great wet. [...] that where rye was at 18d or 20d the bushel and wheat 8 groats, now it is risen to 3s 2d rye and 5s 4d wheat.' There was a similar grim complaint at Coventry: it began to rain in May and 'rained every day or night till 28th July and in September great rains again.' 1595 was worse. Philip Wyot wrote at Barnstaple, 'By reason of rain and foul weather wheat is 9s a bushel.' The next year Wyot wrote, 'all this May has not been a dry day and night' [...] 'small quantity of corn brought to market [so] townsmen cannot have corn for money'; 'there is but little comes to the market and such snatching and catching for that little and such a cry that the like was never heard.' At Shrewsbury after another winter of storms and rain, corn reached 18s the bushel in May 1597; further downpours in July pushed it even higher at Barnstaple to 20s. Only in 1598 did the sun appear and the harvest improve. Even so there were renewed shortages in 1600. Though the west may have suffered worst from the weather, the sharp rises in corn prices in towns across the kingdom suggest that all felt the harsh pressures of harvest failure.[16]

More recently, Steve Rappaport has confirmed this. 'Throughout the Tudor period it is likely that no years were leaner than 1596 through 1598', he writes, the years in which *The Merry Wives* may first have been set, but 'from 1591–3, on the eve of the first of four successive harvest failures, to the peak of the inflationary crisis in 1596–8 the price of flour more than doubled and food prices in general rose by nearly 50 per cent, creating conditions which

---

[15] *Hamlet* may be another example with its changes between Quarto and Folio texts.

[16] Peter Clark, 'A Crisis Contained? The Condition of English Towns in the 1590s', in *The European Crisis of the 1590s: Essays in Comparative History*, ed. by Peter Clark (London: Allen & Unwin, 1985), pp. 44–66 (p. 45).

led to food riots in Gloucestershire, Somerset, Oxfordshire, Kent, Essex, and elsewhere in England.' For comparison, 'when Henry VIII took the throne in 1509 a bushel of flour cost about sixteen pence and a rabbit roughly tuppence. Half a century later, at the accession of his daughter, Elizabeth, the same bushel of flour cost three shillings and the rabbit had more than doubled in price. And by the decade of Elizabeth's death, marking the end of the Tudors' reign, the sixteen pence which had bought a bushel of flour a century earlier was worth little more than a peck. Rabbits too had roughly quadrupled in price'. Moreover, Rappaport continues, 'real wages plunged by 20 per cent from an average index of 76 during 1590–3 to 61 in 1596–8, greater than the loss half a century earlier. Though prices fell sharply in the following years, real wages never recovered all of the ground lost during 1594–8: workers suffered a net loss in real wages of five per cent from 1590–3 to 1600–9'.[17] While he generally finds London suffering less due to the support of livery companies as well as wards and parishes (pp. 377, 384), explaining perhaps why *The Merry Wives* seems in the 1602 Quarto to be removed from town life, all of England suffered more than in anyone's living memory. Statistics recently compiled by R. G. Outhwaite bear this out. Average wheat prices in nearby London shot up from 36s. in 1594 to 40s. in 1595, 61s. in 1596, and dropped to 44s. in 1597; on the other side of Windsor, in Oxford, prices rose from 37s. in 1594 to 81s. in 1595, 59s. in 1596, and 69s. in 1597 at their highest points.[18] A second chart by Outhwaite shows that taking the average indexed prices of particular grains between 1450 and 1499 as 100, the average indexed price in England for wheat was 578 in 1594–95, 607 in 1595–96, and 811 in 1596–97; for barley, 520 in 1594–95, 740 for 1595–96, and 971 for 1596–97; for oats, 765 in 1594–95, 574 in 1595–96, and 1148 in 1596–97; and for rye, 801 in 1595–96, and 1227 in 1596–97 (the figure being unavailable for 1594–95 (Table 2.3, p. 29). 'Nothing will sooner lead men to sedition than dearth of victuals', remarked William Cecil, Principal Secretary to Elizabeth I, just a short time earlier, although Thomas Starkey had made a similar warning as early as 1529.[19] 'The working class', John Walter adds, 'spent fully 80 to 90 per cent of their incomes upon food and drink; in such a country the harvest was the fundamental fact of economic life' (p. 84).

There was a direct relationship between poor harvest, high prices, and the mortality rate (exclusive of the plague). 'To know how far people did fear illness and premature extinction is to know something of profound importance about any society', Peter Laslett writes. 'Such knowledge is as

[17] Steve Rappaport, *Worlds within Worlds: Structures of Life in Sixteenth-Century London* (Cambridge: Cambridge University Press, 1989), pp. 282, 379, 160, 158.
[18] R. G. Outhwaite, 'Dearth and the English Crown', in Clark, pp. 23–43 (Table 2. 2, p. 28).
[19] Quoted in John Walter, 'The Social Economy of Dearth in Early Modern England', in *Famine, Disease and the Social Order in Early Modern Society*, ed. by John Walter and Roger Schofield (Cambridge: Cambridge University Press, 1989), pp. 75–128 (p. 76). Thomas Starkey, *A Dialogue between Pole and Lupset*, fol. 107; ed. by T. F. Mayer for the Royal Historical Society (London, 1989), pp. 116–17.

significant to a society's ideological and political life as it is to its economics, although far and away its greatest significance is for the ordinary, everyday life of ordinary people',[20] such as the citizens of Shakespeare's Windsor. 'At the local level', John Walter and Roger Schofield add, 'crisis mortality [from disease and famine] was never absent' (p. 59). In the Cambridge sample taken by Outhwaite, the crude death rate in 1593–94 was 20.8; in 1594–95, 21.1; in 1595–96, 24.1; and in 1596–97, 33.2.[21] He notes in addition 'the sharp rise in the proportion of those parishes experiencing an increase of burials of 50 per cent or more: from 4 per cent in 1595–6 to 18 per cent and then 33 per cent in the two succeeding years' (p. 35).[22] According to Joyce Youings, 'a run of five disastrous harvests from 1594 to 1598, largely due to very heavy and unseasonable rainfall' with 'great floods' and 'many impassable roads' and 'contagious fogs' heightened the chance of plague too. 'Parish registers tell a dreadful tale in the middle and later 1590s, not only of death by starvation but, easily detectable from the seasonal pattern, of heavy plague mortality. Almost every town of any size suffered.'[23]

At the same time that England was experiencing deteriorating harvests and an increasing death rate, there was vastly increased fear of further invasion by Spain. In 1595 the Spanish made a raid on Cornwall, in October 1596 the Spanish launched a second Armada which (fortunately for the English) was savaged by gale winds four days out to sea, and in July 1596 Spanish arms firing on Calais were heard in Greenwich if not in Windsor itself. To build and maintain any kind of notable defence the Crown attempted various means to raise capital by 'coat and conduct money' and by 'ship money'. In addition, between 1585 and 1603 England spent £1,420,000 supporting the war in the Low Countries against Spain and an additional £424,000 in France and £575,000 for other naval expeditions so that the balance in the national exchequer dipped to unprecedentedly low reserves: from £101,940 in 1596 to £26,003 in 1597, £17,045 in 1598, and £9,206 in 1599. In consequence, food riots began in London in 1595, spreading in time to general rebellion. According to Peter Clark,

The trouble began during June in Southwark, crowded with the poor and unemployed. According to Stow, 'some apprentices and other young people [...] being pinched of their victuals [...] took from the market people' a quantity of butter which was being sold at excessive prices. About the same time a gang of apprentices mobbed a crowd of Southwark fishwives who had been trying to monopolise supplies. The Southwark rioters acted in a responsible, customary way, eschewing violence and offering money for the goods they took, but the situation was explosive. The Southwark disorders coincided with renewed agitation against aliens, the circulation of seditious libels, probably against city leaders, and the forcible rescue

[20] Peter Laslett, 'Andrew Appleby: A Personal Appreciation', in Walter and Schofield, p. xii.
[21] Table 2.4, p. 35.
[22] Detailed statisitics bearing out these observations are given in E. A. Wrigley and R. S. Schofield, *The Population History of England 1541–1871* (Cambridge, MA: Harvard University Press, 1981); see esp. Appendices, pp. 485–738.
[23] *Sixteenth-Century England* (London: Allen Lane, 1984), pp. 151–52.

of a prisoner by a throng of apprentices. The government determined on a tough response. The Southwark rioters were tried in Star Chamber and sentenced to be flogged and set in the pillory on 27 June. None the less, two days later a major riot broke out on Tower Hill when a large force of young people, led by a former soldier, assaulted ward officials. Thomas Earl, the minister of St. Mildred, Breadstreet, noted in his commonplace book 'a foolish commotion of youths,' but the details are unclear. The government was badly shaken by the incident. On 4 July a proclamation was issued excoriating 'sundry great disorders committed in and about the city of London by unlawful great assemblies of multitudes of a popular sort of base condition.' A provost-marshal was appointed to enforce martial law, and five of the Tower Hill rioters were charged with high treason and condemned to be hanged, drawn and quartered — virtually the only occasion in the century before 1640 when such a ferocious punishment was meted out to ordinary rioters. Vigorous police action and a concerted official drive to improve food supplies seem to have kept the cauldron from boiling over, but discontent continued to seethe. In October 1595 there was a minor disorder near Cheapside; in July 1596 the mayor reported the arrest of Thomas Deloney for publishing a ballad containing 'a complaint of the great want and scarcity of corn,' and in September another outbreak of seditious libelling took place. Finally in the summer of 1598 there was a recurrence of apprentice agitation, with calls for a meeting in Islington Fields to be 'revenged' upon the Lord Mayor. (pp. 53–54)

To the north-west, in Wendlebury, a small Oxfordshire parish, the vicar noted in 1598 'that in the years of our lord god 1597 and 1596 wheate was solde for xis, barley for 7s, and beanes for vi^s viii^d. This was a sorroful time for the poore of the land god grant that such a darth and famyne may never be sene agayn'.[24] Evidence for the plight of the poor is fragmentary: F. J. Levy thinks the disastrous news may be unmentioned because hardship produced a 'conspiracy of silence';[25] but in 1596 the village of Kirtlington, just north of Oxford, decided to begin ploughing marginal land while at Christ Church in the city an attempt was made to cut the students' bread allowance. The most dramatic consequence was the proposed Oxfordshire uprising at Enslow Hill organized by James Bradshaw and Bartholomew Steer which was thought to have some 400 active supporters; that it failed to materialize at the appointed time lay not so much in a change of heart among the poor, it has been contended, as in their utter hopelessness and despair.[26]

In such an environment, individual charity was frequently extended where possible. Walter cites a Norfolk cousin of Sir Robert Sidney who sold his corn in the market below the asking price in the 1590s and in addition claimed to relieve 400 poor men each week at his door. In 1596 Sir Thomas Egerton, of the Queen's Privy Council, distributed alms to 62 inhabitants of St Dunstan's parish, London, each week. 'In just under three months in the dearth of 1597', Walter adds, 'Lord Buckhurst spent one hundred and

---

[24] Quoted in John Walter, 'A "Rising of the People"? The Oxfordshire Rising of 1596', *Past and Present*, 107 (May 1985), 90–143 (p. 95).
[25] In conversation with F. J. Levy in August 1991, following his examination of unpublished correspondence in the 1590s in England generally.
[26] Walter gives the fullest account, 'A "Rising"', pp. 90–143.

fifty-four pounds on purchasing imported rye to give away to "the hungry villagers" in six Sussex villages. In what was presumably also a reference to the harvest failures of the 1590s, Sir George Shirley was said to merit "the glorious title of father and nourisher of the poor" for "relieving during the great dearth 500 a day at his gate"'.[27] The heightened, even desperate concern is also recorded on 2 November 1596 in a proclamation by the Queen entitled 'Enforcing Orders against Dearth; Ordering Hospitality Kept in Country, and Defences Maintained'.

The multitude of her poor people having no grain growing of their own to sustain great lack, [the Queen] caused special orders to be made and published to all parts of her realm in what sort the justices of peace in every quarter should stay all engrossers, forestallers, and regraters of corn, and to direct all owners and farmers having corn to furnish the markets ratably and weekly with such quantities as usually they had done before time or reasonably might and ought to do; by which orders many other things were prescribed to be observed for the staying of the dearth and relief of the people. Yet nevertheless, her majesty is informed that in some parts of her realm the dearth doth not diminish but rather increase for lack of due execution of the said orders, and specially by the covetousness of the owners forbearing to furnish the markets as reasonably they might do and by secretly selling out of their houses to a kind of people that commonly are called badgers, at prices unreasonable, who likewise do sell and regrate the same out of the markets at very high and excessive prices.[28]

John Walter and Keith Wrightson note that prosecutions in Essex rose markedly during this period of dearth: while the harvest years of 1592–94 show an annual average of 78.6 prosecutions for theft, the corresponding count for each year of 1595–97 was an average of 178.3.[29] Both vagrants and petty criminals began noticeably to increase in London and were first confronted in 1594 when on 15 January the court of aldermen began a Friday night search and sweep; on 7 March, they appointed a committee to devise new ways to rid the city of rogues and organized watches; they increased the committee on 6 June. In time special funds were put in place in London to collect voluntary donations from householders which were converted to loaves of bread to distribute to the poor; in Bristol, the corporation required that each burgess provide a meal a day for at least one poor person.

The necessity and force of royal action, including the 'Acte for the Maintenance of Husbandrie and Tillage' (39 Elizabeth) passed in 1597–98, can be measured even more accurately by the observations of Sir Robert Cecil in a manuscript dated by scholars November 1597, now at Hatfield House:

[27] Walter, 'Social Economy', pp. 107, 115, 108.
[28] *Tudor Royal Proclamations*, III, 170.
[29] 'Dearth and the Social Order in Early Modern England', *Past and Present*, 71 (May 1976), 22–42 (p. 24). All of these statistics and the interpretations of them are continually being reassessed by John Walter, Carole Shammas and others, and such terms as 'poverty line' are being redefined. For further views, see Walter and Schofield generally and the earlier *English Towns in Transition 1500–1700*, ed. by Peter Clark and Paul Slack (London: Oxford University Press, 1976), esp. Chapter 8.

General reasons of state for both bills, both that of building and that of tillage. The great decay of people. The ingrossing wealth into few hands. Setting people to work in husbandry, whereby idleness, drunkenness, and vice are avoided. Swarms of poor loose and wandering people bred by these decays, miserable to themselves, dangerous to the state. Subjecting the realm to the discretion of foreign states either to help us with corn in time of dearth or to hinder us by embargos on our cloths, if we stand too much upon that commodity. Danger of famine. Some remedy expected in the country. The policy of former laws for seventy years past has provided precedent though with some penalties unfit to be put in execution. The necessity either by a new law or by the ancient laws of the crown to punish misdemeanours against the Commonwealth. The exceptions of all late pardons of these offences showing how odious they have ever been deemed.[30]

Clearly, at the time of *The Merry Wives of Windsor* the nation at large suffered from a crisis in the economy and in law enforcement that must have been agonizing to behold, and just as clearly Shakespeare, who grounded his play in contemporary topographical and cultural references, omitted any related political and social factors. The play has no distinctly persistent setting in the Quarto text (despite four references in passing to Windsor) since all places suffered, and no authentic suffering would do in a play which pretended to be a farce: Marcus is right to say the play (at least the Quarto text of the play) is neither repeatedly pronouncing its location in Windsor (as is true of the Folio text) nor in London (which, if Rappaport is right, had some means of allaying some of the pain) but in Nowhere, rather like Thomas More's Utopia.

Yet a further point must be that Shakespeare expected his audiences to apply such a contemporary play to their own present-day suffering: the most fundamental significations in *The Merry Wives* are, first, in its astounding silences — there are no analogous characters to the Robert Cecils, Lord Buckhursts, or Sir George Shirleys in this play — and next, in this 'natural perspective that is and is not' in the shocked reactions that such silence — such a conspiracy with silence — leads his audiences then (and even now) to acknowledge.[31] For the play is less and more than the farce it seems. Just as *The Merry Wives* is not innocent of the rising concerns of a market economy and a capitalist mentality in its treatment of the commodification of persons and of the institution of marriage, as Marcus has hinted, so it is not innocent either of increasing vagabondage and crime outside the walls of great Windsor Castle where the majority of Shakespeare's audiences lived — and precisely where (though nowhere in particular) the Quarto text takes place.

If we return to the text of the modern version, this is still clear. The play (as we have come to know it in all available editions) actually opens with this

[30] *Tudor Economic Documents*, ed. by R. H. Tawney and Eileen Power, 3 vols (London: Longman, 1924, 1965), I, 89. Compare a petition from the inhabitants of Norfolk against the restraint of exportation of corn dated loosely in the 1590s (in Tawney and Power, I, 162–63), in *The Stiffkey Papers*, ed. by H. W. Saunders, Camden Society, 1915.
[31] F. J. Levy has examined several private letters of the 1590s which strangely do not mention the dearth and its consequences.

concern: Justice 'Robert Shallow, Esquire' will 'make a Star Chamber matter' (I. I. 1–4) of Falstaff's crimes which are to him in his deprived circumstances tantamount to treason: 'You have beaten my men, killed my deer, and broke open my lodge' (I. I. 103–04). There can be no worse crime against the state or the self than the theft or destruction of property. Slender confirms this. He accuses Falstaff's 'cony-catching rascals, Bardolph, Nym, and Pistol' (I. I. 116–17) of stealing from him not only cash but rare cash investments, 'seven groats in mill-sixpences, and two Edward shovel-boards that cost me two shilling and twopence apiece of Yead Miller' (I. I. 140–42) and then physically beating him too. But money is what life is about for all of them: just as Shallow and Slender find property loss the greatest offence in the realm, Falstaff finds poverty to be the greatest shame, and the best motive for what others conceive as crime. He confesses at the opening of *The Merry Wives* that 'I am almost out at heels' (I. 3. 29); 'There is no remedy: I must cony-catch; I must shift' (I. 3. 31–32). It is not ceremony, as in a Garter Feast or Induction for which Windsor was known, among other things, but poverty which is, from the outset, what this play is really about.

As the play progresses, Falstaff means to recover his reputation, his self-respect, his very identity by increasing his fortune in this commercial world of the play (and of Shakespeare's time); and he means to do so, after crassly indenturing Bardolph, by fleecing Mistress Ford. This is doubtless his motive, as it is surely his need, but this is not how he represents it here. Rather, he tells his comrades that 'I do mean to make love to Ford's wife. I spy entertainment in her: she discourses, she carves, she gives the leer of invitation; I can construe the action of her familiar style, and the hardest voice of her behaviour, to be Englished rightly, is, "I am Sir John Falstaff's"' (I. 3. 40–45). Thus, 'I have writ me here a letter to her; and here another to Page's wife, who even now gave me good eyes too, examined my parts with most judicious oeillades: sometimes the beam of her view gilded my foot, sometimes my portly belly' (I. 3. 54–58). It is not so much his motive that is difficult to ascertain, but its signification in this play, for his singular poverty points to a more general and less obscure concern.

What overshadows commodification of people in this play, then, and what belies its comic innocence is that Shakespeare relies on his audience's knowledge of the authentic Windsor, their authentic world — a real place characterized by starvation, theft, and death — as more importantly a play about the haves and the have-nots. *The Merry Wives of Windsor* is not about the nobility at court but about the ignobility of not being there, the ignobility, further, that materialism forces into being and the general awareness that causes men and women to define themselves as properties or as investors where every person as well as every event is a potential commercial enterprise. It follows then that Falstaff — not the clever, controlling Falstaff of the history plays but the same fat Jack who lives for food and drink, for plenty even in a land characterized by dearth — is so resonant a focus for Shakespeare's sole play of contemporary England: his corpulence is both a signifying cause and a haunting reminder of those that prey on others, and of those who feel it most when out at heels.

Food and drink, the abundance of capitalist pleasure and satisfaction, are never themselves marginalized in this play with Falstaff at its centre, just as food and drink are never out of Falstaff's mind or sight. Master Page, who constantly invites his friends (but never Falstaff) to fatten themselves at his table of plenty is only the inversion of the Host of the Garter Inn who would serve Falstaff only after he is paid. Beneath the comic surface of the plot of nesting confidence games by Falstaff and by the suitors and parents of Anne Page, then, is the more savage reality. But just as Americans flocked to movies of romance and the good life at the height of their Great Depression (and invented the musical comedy as a new genre during that cruel time of grief and want and rising mortality) so too Falstaff calls up their equivalent in Tudor England with his references to the romance and quick fortunes of New World explorations. Besides Mistress Ford, he also finds Mistress Page is 'a region in Guiana, all gold and bounty. I will be cheaters to them both', precisely because 'they shall be exchequers to me: they shall be my East and West Indies, and I will trade to them both' (I.3.65–68). His own newly indentured servant, young Robin, Bardolph's replacement, is his emissary to 'sail like my pinnace to these golden shores' (I.3.76). But what for him is romance born of necessity is for Mistresses Ford and Page, given their financial situation, merely a joke. These haves can find fun at the expense of the needs of the have-nots. Thus Mistress Page notes that 'unless he know some strain in me that I know not myself, he would never have boarded me in this fury'; and Mistress Ford, herself alive to commercial thought and privateering imagery, replies in kind: '"Boarding" call you it? I'll be sure to keep him above deck.' And Mistress Page: 'So will I: if he come under my hatches, I'll never to sea again' (II.1.84–90). To all of them, then, the voyage of life is a voyage of commerce, and this journey of exploitation and conquest centres only on El Dorado, the land of unlimited wealth that is the most delusory of make-believe. Comic division between those with money and those without is annealed in their narrow commercial interests in which money drives every thought and deed.

It drives every thought and deed because the dearth, the high mortality rate, and poverty were seen as among the Court's great failings; and these must always have outweighted, every moment of every day for most of those in Shakespeare's audiences, the potential lack of chivalry or courage which Windsor as the home of the Order of the Garter attempted to foster and protect. Marcus's observations about the auction for Anne Page as a central subject of the play comes together with Gurr's observation that Lord Hunsdon seems not to have helped his ailing players when they most needed his moral (and financial) support; eventually, they would themselves steal the timbers of the Theatre, Falstaff-like, to build the Globe.[32] *The Merry Wives of Windsor* is about both the Court that is and the Court they might wish to have, aiding and protecting England in tandem with Parliament. That presence and absence, like the real dearth and the play's sunny setting, always work in tandem, generating the play's fundamental purpose and meaning. Whether the play was produced at Whitehall in Westminster on 23 April 1597, at a great Garter Ceremony honouring Lord Hunsdon, the new Lord Chamberlain, where it might be diplomatic to play up the farce, or at Southwark in commercial rivalry with Henslowe's company, the tricks of Falstaff served a darker purpose, the language and action of *The Merry Wives* nevertheless confront fact and authenticity in an especially direct and especially harrowing way in the unlocated geography of the 1602 Quarto. Regardless of site or performance, this may well explain why a corpulent character such as the indolent, self-indulgent Falstaff, a most promising character for a humours play, is cast instead in a citizen comedy. At some date later than 1602 it became possible, and fun, to restore *The Merry Wives* to the town of Windsor where it had been meant to be set all along. For later, things were much better: 'In 1620', Mildred Campbell notes, 'a year of low prices, wheat sold at slightly more than 22s. the quarter'.[33] In Durham, she records, sheep prices had levelled out (pp. 202–03). In the Berkshire countryside around Windsor, Campbell notes that the farmer Robert Loder kept close accounts:

In spite of occasional inaccuracies in arithmetic and certain omissions, [he] leaves us what must be a reasonably accurate picture of his earnings, expenses, and annual profits for the period 1612–18. His annual earnings during these years ranged from £319 0s. 9¼d. to £435 3s. 0½d. His expenses, including such items as labor, seed corn, tithes, king's tax, poor rate, etc., were from £120 14s. 7d. to £160 12s. 10½d. per annum. This left annual profits ranging from £181 15s. 7¼d. to £292 10s. 2d., the latter for 1619 being the most profitable year of the eight. (p. 216)

Her point is not one of rising exploitative profits, but the restabilization of an improving economy following the five years of bad harvest and the dearth of the 1590s. The farce could return as farce. 'The numerous intrigues and deceptions practised by the characters upon each other', which is how T. W. Craik sees the entire play in any of its forms, would not be 'calculated to arouse complex or conflicting emotions in the audience' but instead would arouse 'good humour and mirth' which Craik sees as the only possible outcome for the play.[34]

---

[32] Gurr, 'Intertextuality', p. 191.
[33] *The English Yeoman Under Elizabeth and the Early Stuarts* (New Haven: Yale University Press, 1942), p. 186. Soon afterwards prices increased again.
[34] Introduction, p. 29. In *Population History*, Wrigley and Schofield not that 'in the sixteenth century the relation between the demand for industrial products or tertiary services and urban growth had been uncertain, for although London grew, other towns experienced mixed fortunes. Urban population overall may well have increased but it is also possible that the percentage of the population living in towns fell since national population as a whole grew so markedly' (p. 472).

V

The Merry Wives of Windsor and *Henry V* are not the only Shakespearean plays with two remarkably different texts in Quarto and in Folio. Building on a talk by Michael Warren and perhaps earlier work on the stability of Shakespeare's texts by E. A. J. Honigmann,[35] Steven Urkowitz proposed in 1980 that Quarto and Folio *King Lear* were sufficiently different to be seen as two different plays, one a thorough and later revision of the other by Shakespeare himself. Urkowitz comments that

By every standard, the theory of Shakespearean revision as the basis for variants in *King Lear* offers a more powerful, more complete, and more coherent explanation for the data than any other theory so far stated. Every process envisioned in this theory is well within the observed performance range of the agents known to have influenced the text. No compositor is held responsible for brilliant strokes of stagecraft, no copyist is needed to have a rich supply of Shakespearean synonyms at the tip of his tongue, no bookkeeper is required to have acted suddenly in an innovative manner never before observed in bookkeepers. Instead, all that is needed is Shakespeare, capable of preternatural brilliance, well within his observed capacity to strike us dumb with amazement.[36]

This most sweeping of reasons for radically different texts accommodates Patterson's understanding of the two different ideologies behind Quarto and Folio *Henry V* and my own proposal here about the effect of different economic climates on the setting and force of *Merry Wives*; it is one which has won general tentative agreement and has come, in fact, to inform the activities of the Oxford Shakespeare. Speaking of the texts of *King Lear*, Stanley Wells writes that 'the most obvious hypothesis would be that they represent a deliberate rewriting of the text printed in the Quarto' although 'whether the reviser was Shakespeare or someone else might be debated, but we should clearly be faced with two versions of the play, each consciously and distinctly fashioned, which it would be wrong to confuse'.[37]

No such judgement about the two texts of *The Merry Wives of Windsor* has been made by the most recent textual scholars. In a comprehensive study of both Quarto and Folio texts, William Bracy, in *'The Merry Wives of Windsor': The History and Transmission of Shakespeare's Text*, concludes that 'there can be

---

[35] Michael Warren, 'Quarto and Folio *King Lear* and the Interpretation of Albany and Edgar', delivered to the International Shakespeare Congress in Washington, D.C.; see also his essay on Kent in *The Division of the Kingdoms: Shakespeare's Two Versions of 'King Lear'*, ed. by Gary Taylor and Michael Warren (Oxford: Oxford University Press, 1983), pp. 59–73; E. A. J. Honigmann, *The Stability of Shakespeare's Text* (Lincoln, NE: University of Nebraska Press, 1965). Honigmann confronts what he sees as the deconstruction of Shakespeare's text by those who, like Alice Walker, would see variants that would confuse the common understanding of the transmission of texts. Honigmann's work is important as the first to witness to modern textual editing disrupting any traditional sense of the transmission of texts, but he mediates, finally, between the earlier work of Greg and Pollard and more modern editing.
[36] Steven Urkowitz, *Shakespeare's Revision of 'King Lear'* (Princeton, NJ: Princeton University Press, 1980), pp. 148–49.
[37] Stanley Wells, 'Introduction: The Once and Future *King Lear*' in Taylor and Warren, *The Division of the Kingdoms* pp. 10–11. See also George Walton Williams in his review of Urkowitz's book for *Shakespeare Survey*, 35 (Cambridge: Cambridge University Press, 1981), quoted by Wells, p. 17.

no doubt that the evidence of deliberate revision is conclusive',[38] but assigns the Folio to a transcript by Ralph Crane of Shakespeare's holograph and the Quarto to memorial reconstruction by the actor playing the Host of the Garter Inn, noting that this 'text offers unquestioned evidence of extensive adaptation and abridgment for special production purposes' for a provincial tour (p. 97), since the nearly simultaneous shutting of the London theatres by the Privy Council at the request of the Lord Mayor and Aldermen of London on 28 July 1597 made playing outside London necessary. Bracy cites as evidence for this tour an entry in the account of the proceedings of the Privy Council:

A letter to Robert Wrote, William Fleetwood, John Barne, Thomas Fowler and Richard Skevington, esquires, and the rest of the Justices of Middlesex nerest to London. Her Majestie being informed that there are verie great disorders committed in the common playhouses both by lewd matters that are handled on the stages and by resorte and confluence of bad people, hathe given direction that not onlie no plaies shalbe used within London or about the citty or in any publique place during this tyme of sommer, but that also those play houses that are erected and built only for suche purposes shalbe plucked down, namely the Curtayne and the Theatre nere to Shorditch or any other within that country. (pp. 124–25)

This would account for a vastly inferior Quarto text. Bracy adds that 'the presence in the Folio text of errors attributable to handwriting, the careless omission of a line in the first scene of Act III, and numerous other variants and inaccuracies leave no doubt of the role of manuscript transcription' by Ralph Crane that is likewise faulty (p. 136). But 'its eventual release to the printer may have occurred after a revival of the play had renewed popular interest in the *Merry Wives* and made the sale of a discarded manuscript of some profit to the players' (p. 134). In his narrative of the printing of both Quarto and Folio, Bracy drew on earlier work of A. W. Pollard and J. Dover Wilson.[39] In 1987 the New Variorum editor of *The Merry Wives*, Gerald D. Johnson, took Bracy to task for merely updating Pollard and Wilson on 'the provincial acting hypothesis' and for following W. J. Lawrence who 'in 1935 argued that these quartos were abridged to suit a reduced cast by eliminating characters and arranging for the doubling of roles'.[40] While Johnson agreed that the Quarto text was a work of memorial reconstruction by the actor playing the Host and while he agreed that Ralph Crane and not Shakespeare was responsible for the text used in the Folio, he took Bracy still further to task for his ideas about cuts and doubling, for his 'method is lacking in rigor and attention to detail' (p. 155). 'A more stringent analysis of the probable casting pattern in the Quarto', he argued, 'makes it unlikely that the quarto text was deliberately adapted for a reduced cast' (p. 155), and he appended a chart (p. 165) which shows the need for a troupe of

---

[38] University of Missouri Studies, 25:1 (Columbia, MO: University of Missouri Press, 1952), p. 94.
[39] A. W. Pollard and J. Dover Wilson, 'Surreptitious Shakespearean Texts', *TLS* 9 January 1919, p. 18.
[40] Gerald D. Johnson, '*The Merry Wives of Windsor*. Q1: Provincial Touring and Adapted Texts', pp. 154–55.

fourteen actors to cover the parts of the Quarto text on tour or elsewhere. Both Bracy and Johnson agreed on the theory of 'foul papers' and 'memorial reconstruction' after such concepts were beginning to be challenged, and Johnson continued this argument long after Warren and Urkowitz had posited other possibilities without acknowledging this alternative. In fact, Urkowitz had been even more forthcoming in 1988:

From the beginning of the twentieth century until today, a small group of influential critics set the paradigms now being followed by practically all editors of those Shakespearean plays which exist in significantly different early printed versions: W. W. Greg, especially in his work on *Merry Wives of Windsor* and *Two Elizabethan Stage Abridgements*, Peter Alexander on Shakespeare's early history plays, D. L. Patrick on *Richard III*, G. I. Duthie on *Hamlet* and Alfred Hart on the general problems of the 'bad' quartos. These critics argued that the first printed texts of *Merry Wives of Windsor*, *Romeo and Juliet*, *Hamlet*, *Henry V*, and *Henry VI, Parts 2 and 3* were illicitly published from actors' 'memorially reconstructed' and rough approximations of the scripts they had performed. Memorial reconstruction had also been used to explain the striking differences between the substantive texts of *Richard III* and *King Lear*, for example. Recently, however, an alternative paradigm has been recognized as a likely source for those variants: rather than quirks of a hypothetical pirate's memory, many textual differences may have been generated by Shakespeare himself in the process of revising his own scripts either before or after their initial theatrical productions.[41]

While Urkowitz and others had attempted to disprove the possibility of pirated or memorially reconstructed texts, he had not set forth why that theory had so convinced textual scholars like Pollard, Greg, McKerrow, or even Fredson Bowers. I think the reason why this unproven theory has been so influential is precisely the reason why the textual discrepancies between the Quarto and Folio *Merry Wives* are so important. They remind us of the economic conditions that produced them.

In a major essay published in 1990, Paul Werstine has shown how the false ideas of textual transmission were born and why they have remained so powerful: simply put, it is because they were both economical and apparently logical in their response to a deep yearning among textual editors to provide a narrative line for the birth and life of texts, a narrative biography. When, in 1918, Dover Wilson took on the First or 'bad' Quarto of *Hamlet* and then joined up with Pollard, in 1919, to extend their theory of the origin of 'bad' quartos to *Henry V*, *Romeo and Juliet*, and *The Merry Wives of Windsor*, they presented a most complicated genesis for all four texts — a theory of origin that incorporated a number of current narrative lines about Shakespeare's reworking of others' plays and about abridgement for provincial touring, as well as the newly popular idea of memorial reconstruction by an actor or actors. The 'bad' quartos, they speculated, were non-Shakespearean plays that had been both shortened for provincial playing — hence their comparative brevity — and partially revised by Shakespeare — hence the much larger measure of agreement between the 'bad' quartos and the 'good' Shakespeare texts in the early parts of these plays. Before being printed, the partially

---

[41] Steven Urkowitz, '"If I Mistake in Those Foundations Which I Build Upon": Peter Alexander's Textual Analysis of *Henry VI Parts 2 and 3*', *English Literary Renaissance*, 18 (1988), 230–31.

revised abridgements, they argued, had been worked over by a rogue actor or actors (who had played one or more parts in later fully revised Shakespearean versions of these plays) in a largely unsuccessful effort to bring the transcripts into line with the fully revised versions. Thus for Pollard and Wilson these 'bad' texts are partly Shakespearean.[42]

The simple beauty of this narrative was that whatever was thought bad was the work of a rogue, and whatever was thought good was written wholly by Shakespeare: the theory was self-fulfilling but, more attractively, it was both economical and loose enough to 'explain' and 'justify' any judgement or interpretation, and it was also capable of endless variation. In time W. W. Greg and F. P. Wilson, G. B. Harrison and Philip Edwards, and even Cambridge and Oxford editors subscribed to this master-narrative as well.

But, Werstine writes, it was the sense of narrative that convinced them.

Pollard's construction of holograph printer's copy for some 'good' texts of Shakespeare's plays rested on a general theory about the transmission of theatrical texts. Representing Shakespeare and his fellows as anxious about the possible theft of play manuscripts should they be multiplied through copying, Pollard argued (1) that Shakespeare would turn over to his company manuscripts of his plays in his own hand·— not scribal transcripts of them. [...] Then, according to Pollard, (2) the bookkeeper would annotate Shakespeare's holograph, which would serve as the 'Booke,' the theatrical document (often called anachronistically the 'promptbook') upon which performance would be based; Pollard sought to establish this practice by alluding to the use of holograph fair copies as 'prompt-copies' in the cases of Massinger's *Believe as you List*, Munday's transcription of *Sir Thomas More*, and Mountfort's *The Launching of the Mary*. Finally, (3) when the company decided to print the play, it would hand over the holograph — there was no other copy — to the printer, who was poor enough at his trade to introduce a quantity of errors in spite of having such fine copy before him. (p. 68)

The difficulty, according to Werstine, is that

no assertion in Pollard's narrative, except perhaps the last, can withstand much scrutiny. Since there is no evidence (that I know of) that a theatrical manuscript was ever stolen from Shakespeare's company, the fear of theft that Pollard projects upon the company seems groundless. Equally doubtful is Pollard's generalization from the Massinger, Munday, and Mountfort holographs to a universal practice of using authorial copy in the theatre. Each of the three cases cited can be represented as special: Massinger had recopied his play (after a fair copy of it, either authorial or scribal, had been submitted to the censor) to adapt it to the censor's commands; there is no evidence that *More* was ever performed; and the censor requested a more legible copy of the Mountfort piece. (pp. 68–69)

Indeed, Werstine claims never to have been able to locate an indisputable act of memorial reconstruction. Nevertheless, he shows that 'when W. W. Greg undertook an investigation of the "bad" Quarto of *Merry Wives of Windsor* in 1910', by dint of a good deal of improvising he made the master-narrative work:

[42] Paul Werstine, 'Narratives About Printed Shakespeare Texts: "Foul Papers" and "Bad Quartos"', *Shakespeare Quarterly*, 41 (1990), 65–86 (p. 66).

He sought to reduce to just one agent the three agents then thought to have produced 'bad' quartos: (1) the adapter, who may have abridged the play; (2) the reporter, who, Greg thought, attempted, by shorthand or by memory, to reconstruct a text; and (3) the reviser ('hack poet'), who may have rearranged the text provided him by the reporter or who may have embellished it. Because Greg believed that a dramatist as accomplished as Shakespeare could not have written anything so corrupt as the dialogue of Quarto *Wives*, Greg concluded that it must therefore have been the work of a reporter. Greg managed to eliminate the adapter through the strategy of arguing that the passages and scenes he had been credited with cutting were merely forgotten by the reporter in the process of memorial reconstruction. To explain omissions near the end of the play, Greg invoked mere fatigue by the reporter. Greg also saw no need to resort to the then conventional hack poet to explain the rearrangement of passages and scenes between Folio and Quarto or the Quarto's apparent additions or alternatives to Folio passages. According to Greg, such rearrangments as the Quarto offered had no intelligible purpose and so must represent distortions in the reporter's recollection rather than revision by a hack poet; apparent *additions* to the Quarto were, rather, accidental *omissions from* the Folio during its printing; and when Folio and Quarto provided alternative versions, as in the last act, Greg called upon the theory that *Wives* was revised (although not necessarily by Shakespeare) between Quarto and Folio. Even though Greg postulated such revision of the play, he offered as the thesis of his argument that a reporter *alone* could account for the variations of the 'bad' Quarto of *Wives* from the Folio version: 'I see no justification for conjecturing two agents where one will suffice.' (pp. 75–76)

But regarding the identity of the agent, of course, conjecture is just what he did: with no hard evidence whatsoever, he went on to speculate that the reporter was the Host of the Garter because his lines are more often carried over from Quarto to Folio, and so he set the narrative that Bracy and Johnson still advocate.

We know from Antony's closing words in *Julius Caesar* or from the last lines of an *Othello* or a *Hamlet* how strong the human pull toward narrative really is, even when that narrative has no documentation on which to stand. What I want to propose, however, but with the documentation given here from the Quarto and Folio *Merry Wives*, is a counternarrative which, given all the economic factors of the 1590s in England has much more to support it. The counternarrative would run something like this: that historic events and perceptions of them, social conditions, economic factors, and even climate are matters which cause plays to change in performance and scripts to change from one printing to the next. While I can agree with Urkowitz that there were two separate versions of *King Lear* over time, I think to establish authorial revision is to some degree dependent on establishing causes for change, and not at all certain. For we do not know just where Shakespeare's hand is in the variant texts, if with some texts it is there at all. Elsewhere Werstine has anticipated me in this: speaking of *Hamlet* he writes, "The only imaginable grounds for privileging Q2 and F with unassailable integrity would be evidence that each is independently linked to Shakespeare. While the historicity of the variants discussed [...] is evident from the printed documents themselves, just as the historicity of the playwright Shakespeare is well documented, there is no document to link the variants to the playwright.'[43]

If the new interest in history and in cultural studies has taught us anything, it has taught us that much of what profoundly affects literary texts comes initially from outside, rather than inside, those texts, just as dearth seems to have caused the Lord Chamberlain's Men (and probably later the King's Men) to relocate *The Merry Wives* until relative economic health returned to England and to Windsor, and a play about haves and have-nots, meant to be comic, would not run the risk also of scraping so painfully along the bone. The most significant counternarrative for *The Merry Wives* is, I think, primarily an economic narrative, as the very subject matter and language of the play, particularly in the Folio text, make so transparent. The counternarrative for *Henry V* is quite probably, as Patterson argues, political. Other counternarratives for other plays may take other forms and for other reasons. This is the primary lesson that the texts of *The Merry Wives* teach us. But *The Merry Wives* also issues a warning: we should not dismiss even the most wretched and fragmentary of texts until we ask, why was this put down in this way? What does it say or avoid saying? Does it represent a statement, a satire, an interrogation, or a conspiracy with silence? Even the roughest of writing has some motivation and purpose behind it.

[43] 'The Textual Mystery of *Hamlet*', *Shakespeare Quarterly*, 39 (1988), 1–26 (p. 24).

The Strange Tongues of *Henry V*

PAOLA PUGLIATTI

University of Florence

> KATHERINE A strange tongue makes my cause more strange, suspicious.
> (*Henry VIII*, III. 1.45)

1 *Both rabbit and duck*

The critical reception of *Henry V* seems to indicate that the play may be considered one of the definitely ambiguous or ambivalent works of world literature. There have, in fact, been critics who argue resolutely for a celebrative reading and critics who argue as resolutely for its contrary; and there have been, more and more frequently in the last decades, critics who dispute, and often brilliantly show, that the play 'points in two opposite directions'.[1] It is, indeed, impossible to write or speak about *Henry V* without taking sides in the king's trial and without accordingly pronouncing a final verdict, although all such trials end by rehearsing the usual catalogue of arguments: those in favour of Henry (many and self-evident) and those against (fewer and more indirect: his banishing and 'killing' Falstaff, his implicit acceptance of Canterbury's 'bribing', the violence of his speech before Harfleur, the killing of the French prisoners after Agincourt, his sending his old friend Bardolph to death, the charges of Court, Bates, and Williams, and a few more optional accusations which vary from essay to essay). Obviously, however, it is not only on Henry that a verdict is pronounced: part of the critical energies are, in fact, spent in connecting the judgement that the play seems to pass on the most celebrated and heroic of English kings to what we may guess about, so to speak, Shakespeare's political attitude.

Generally speaking, those critics who stand decidedly for an apologetic reading of Henry obviously suggest that the play is the [conformist] picture of a poet who [was on the side of power or who simply] admired Henry as a

---

[1] N. Rabkin, 'Either/Or: Responding to *Henry V*', in *Shakespeare and the Problem of Meaning* (Chicago: University of Chicago Press, 1981), p. 34. For a summary of the divergent opinions on *Henry V*, see G. Holderness, 'Prologue: the Histories and History', in G. Holderness, N. Potter and J. Turner, *Shakespeare: the Play of History* (Basingstoke: Macmillan, 1987), pp. 62–63. In the introduction to his edition of the play, Gary Taylor says that *Henry V* critics divide into 'partisans of Henry and partisans of pacifism' and adds that these last 'either dislike the play intensely, or believe that Shakespeare [...] himself intensely disliked Henry, and tried hard to communicate this moral distate to the more discerning members of his audience.' (*Henry V*, ed. by G. Taylor (Oxford: Oxford University Press, 1984), p. 1.) Taylor, clearly a partisan of pacifism, holds the sensible view that we cannot expect that Shakespeare might have wanted to communicate distaste for Henry, even though only to the more discerning. However, he evokes and discusses a series of elements which are evidently 'against', even arguing that 'the text unequivocally implies' that the killing of the French prisoners after Agincourt should be represented on the stage (p. 32).

patriotic hero and wanted to stage his reign in the tone of an epic celebration (the square parentheses contain the additions of a radical viewpoint). One might suppose that the opposite critical trend would be equally explicit in suggesting the presence of the opposite political attitude, namely, one of conscious disapproval or of disparagement. But things stand in a different way. Indeed, with few exceptions, the essays which strive to detect in the play arguments against Henry suggest more or less clearly that those arguments are not part of a conscious project.[2]

H. C. Goddard, for instance, produced one of the sharpest and most univocal responses to the play, piling up evidence to show that Henry, far from being depicted as the 'ideal king', appears to be the perfect ruthless Machiavellian. However, although Goddard believes that Shakespeare's Henry and the battle of Agincourt are strongly deglorified in the play, he contends, or at least implies, that deglorification was not a deliberate act: 'If Shakespeare had deliberately set out to deglorify the Battle of Agincourt in general and King Henry in particular it would seem as if he could hardly have done more.'[3]

The implication of this view may be either that Shakespeare's intention was to glorify Henry and Agincourt but that 'the text' eluded his decision and suggested a different picture (we have already heard it held that texts are stronger than authors) or that the conscious project (for obvious reasons of survival) was that of glorifying the king and the battle but a deeper deglorifying conviction ended by (unconsciously) emerging in spite of the poet's efforts to keep it in check.

In a different perspective, J. Dollimore and A. Sinfield engage in discussing the working of ideology in Shakespeare's representation of history, and they choose *Henry V* as a test-case. The authors, as is known, support a radical definition of ideology as inescapable 'material practice, woven into the fabric of everyday life'. They concede, however, that the institutional efforts, in the Elizabethan state, to achieve ideological unity were not always successful, 'for conflicts and contradictions remained visible at all levels'.[4] Thus, when they discuss the cracks in what should be the ideological surface of a play on Henry of Monmouth, they attribute them to a mechanism of contradiction which seems to be indicated as necessary and physiological:

---

[2] One of the exceptions is John D. Cox, *Shakespeare and the Dramaturgy of Power* (Princeton: Princeton University Press, 1989), Chapter 6, who elaborates a notion of 'opacity' as the main characteristic of Henry (*vs* the 'transparency' of, for example, Richard III), that he qualifies as a theatrical dissimulating capacity. Cox argues that 'Shakespeare's invention of the opaque self achieves its best expression in *Henry V*' (p. 111). This same dissembling capacity, that Puttenham indicated as an essential expression of power ('Qui nescit dissimulare nescit regnare') makes, Cox argues, the supreme ambiguity of Hal's (and King Henry's) figure, while it in turn reflects the theatrical opacity of public Elizabethan figures of power (the Queen, of course, but also Essex and Raleigh). In other words, in *Henry V* 'Shakespeare renders the ambiguities of theatrical opacity in contemporary politics' (p. 113).
[3] *The Meaning of Shakespeare* (Chicago: University of Chicago Press, 1951), I, 256.
[4] 'History and Ideology: the Instance of *Henry V*', in *Alternative Shakespeares*, ed. by J. Drakakis (London: Methuen, 1985), p. 211.

the idea is that ideology tends to incorporate the alternatives that it is engaged in neutralizing (p. 215).[5]

If we look at this argument bearing in mind our naïve idea of there being an author and our naïve curiosity about this author's political attitude in a particular text, here again we get the picture of somebody (consciously?) supporting the dominant ideology (epic celebration of Henry) who nevertheless unconsciously incorporates here and there in his celebration unfavourable elements which are necessarily introduced as the physiological antibodies of ideology. Again, in this case, no deliberate intention is conceded to the dramatist.[6] There is another position that I would like to discuss, which assigns to 'the author' a higher decisional capacity.

Norman Rabkin, in his essay entitled 'Either/Or', starts from the well-known description that Gombrich gives in *Art and Illusion* of the picture of an ambiguous zoomorph being (rabbit or duck?) and concludes that, like that drawing, *Henry V* is constructed in such a way as to look *either* one thing *or* the other. Rabkin's idea is, therefore, that having skilfully and deceptively included two opposite views in the same piece of writing, Shakespeare is daring us to choose one of the two figures he has woven into his carpet. In other words Rabkin believes that, as happens with the mutually excluding plots which torment the reader of *The Turn of the Screw*, only one of the pictures may be chosen as the true one.

Rabkin's essay proposes the interesting idea that 'Shakespeare's habitual recognition of the irreducible complexity of things has led him, as it should lead his audience, to a point of crisis' (p. 61). The critic, however, is too much tempted by what he has brilliantly described as the play's 'rival gestalts' ever to consider that the 'irreducible complexity of things' whose consciousness he is attributing to Shakespeare may suggest precisely that the play's two (or more) gestalts are by no means rival and that the point of crisis may well consist in the fact that Shakespeare is trying to present a polymorphous or polyphonic political picture, namely, '*both* a rabbit *and* a duck'. In other words, that the play is neither a riddle nor a trick; that, in spite of its contradictions, it is not an ambiguous political statement; on the contrary, it is a clear political assertion about how ambivalent political and historical issues can be. The complexity of the picture is precisely in the fact that no

---

[5] S. Greenblatt expresses a similar view: 'We may suggest that the subversive doubts the play continually awakens serve paradoxically to intensify the power of the king and his war even while they cast shadows upon this power.' ('Invisible Bullets: Renaissance Authority and its Subversion', in *Political Shakespeare: New Essays in Cultural Materialsim*, ed. by J. Dollimore and A. Sinfield (Manchester: Manchester University Press, 1985), p. 43).

[6] G. Holderness resumes the problem of authority and intentionality in connexion with history in these terms: 'It seems to us unwise [. . .] completely to surrender, in the course of reading history through the texts, the genuine possibility that some kind of authorial "mastery" shaped those texts, and shaped them deliberately to particular ends. The related critical problems of authorship and intentionality render impossible any straightforward definition of what "the author" meant: we can only speculate about the elusive, mysterious connections between William Shakespeare and the plays "he" "wrote". Such speculation may be inevitable, pleasurable, even illuminating; but we are still left, in the end, with a bookful of plays and a handful of dust.' (p. 16)

choice between the conflicting portraits of Henry and between the diverse possible readings of the events is to be made.[7]

II   *Drama and historical imagination*

I would suggest that Shakespeare's validating various gestalts in a history play, namely, his allowing contradictions to become visible in the telling of history should be considered as a historiographical (rather than humane or psychological) category. One, in particular, implies a *critical* perspective. I am considering the Greek root of the word *critical*, namely, the verb κρίνω (discern, distinguish, interpret, evaluate) and arguing that a *critical* presentation of a given reality is one that shows awareness of discrepancies and conflicts, that exposes diverse and diverging ways of viewing that reality and leaves the possibility of various interpretations open; in a sense, I am contrasting a *critical* presentation of a given reality with an *ideological* one (one, namely, that is engaged in hiding, or even suppressing alternative readings) or, in Bakhtin's terms, a polyphonic with a monologic attitude of texts. Shakespeare's dramatic execution of history is *critical* in that it raises historical and political issues, provides instruments for their interpretation and presents more than one aspect of a problem and more than one way to evaluate it.[8]

Although I am not going to use Bakhtin's terminology in any technical way, I am assuming his theory of dialogism as a conceptual background. In particular, the idea that language is a culturally and socially saturated tool and that, therefore, it is intrinsically dialogical and even conflictual; the idea

---

[7] Incidentally, the 'both-and' paradox is a recognized reasoning pattern in Renaissance thought. As a potentially dangerous procedure, it is discussed in that widespread treatise of rhetoric (or of political reasoning *sub specie rhetorica*) which is Puttenham's *Arte*. The word that Puttenham uses to characterize the 'both-and' effect is *Amphibologia*. Puttenham disapproves of the procedure and defines *amphibology* as 'vicious speech' which occurs 'when we speak or write doubtfully and that the sense may be taken two ways' (George Puttenham, *The Arte of English Poetry* (1589; rpr. London: Constable, 1895), p. 266). Puttenham's treatment of ambiguity in general and of the kind of ambiguity that he terms *amphibology* in particular is by no means merely rhetorical. On the contrary, he passes a clear judgement on the political dangerousness of this mode of expression, that he characterizes as a linguistic malady able to breed social and political diseases. Amphibology, Puttenham argues, ends by producing ambiguities which are uncontrollable: no mere courtly jokes or witty verbal skirmishes but, literally, a kind of discourse which may induce political subversion (Jack Straw's and Jack Cade's rebellions and Captain Kett's sedition were stirred, Puttenham holds, by 'certain propheticall rymes, which might be constred two or three wayes as well as to that one whereunto the rebelles applied it' (p. 267). The passage is commented on by Stephen Cohen, who distinguishes in this section of the *Arte* the illustration of two kinds of ambiguity: a first type in which we have a true meaning masked by a false one; and a second type (*amphibology*) in which 'truth and falsehood are unknowable and either option is equally likely' (*The Language of Power, the Power of Language* (Cambridge, MA: Harvard University Press, 1987), p. 16). S. Mullaney ('Lying Like Truth: Riddle, Representation, and Treason in Renaissance England', *ELH*, 47 (1980), 32–47, defines amphibology as a 'figure of treason and rebellion' (p. 41) and argues that for Puttenham 'the social and political threat posed by the figure of amphibology' is 'the figure of treason itself' (p. 36). Assuming Cohen's distinction, it would seem that a difference between what is ambiguous (of dubious meaning, equivocal, lacking clarity) and what is ambivalent or amphibologic (admitting two non-exclusive meanings) should be posed. The second is the kind of double meaning that concerns us here.

[8] That even a critical presentation of a given reality may be a way to appropriate ideology at a higher level, does not cancel the impression of variety and multi-perspectivism that certain texts determine.

that linguistic performances are never neutral and that they may, when directed to that end, become a weapon to express diversity, dissension, and conflicts of interests. From these views derives an image of the universe of discourse as a war-zone where the users of language engage in struggles for primacy and where eventually battles are won or lost. Certain texts — those that Bakhtin would define as *monologic* — tend to neutralize or 'etherize' the conflictual and controversial potential of language, while others exploit or even strive to enhance that potential. Shakespeare's *Henry V*, as I will try to show, is of the last type.[9]

To argue for polyphony and for a critical perspective in Shakespeare's plays may seem to reaffirm a set of 'humanistic' values, and therefore to hold a backward position, vaguely behind the times of what the interpretative community has been elaborating in recent years, especially as far as the issue of ideology is concerned. However, I am insisting on polyphony because I would suggest that the old-fashioned truism may be reconsidered and requalified as a historiographical category. Incidentally, although I am using the word *critical* in a rather intuitive way, I may mention the fact that this term was used by Hegel, Nietzsche, and Croce to illustrate one of the types of historiographical interpretation or approaches to historical exegesis. What I am arguing, therefore, is that in the staging of history (certainly of national history, but maybe also in a play like *Julius Caesar*) Shakespeare may have behaved as a historian (besides, of course, behaving as a dramatist); that his reading and rendering of historical sources may have been supported by principles and methods similar to those that we associate with historical investigation; that, in short, Shakespeare's dramatic presentation of history is to be appreciated also as an effort of historical criticism.

One of the few scholars who are ready to concede this is Graham Holderness, who argues that Shakespeare shared a new awareness of the pastness of the past and affirms that

Shakespeare's historical plays are not just *reflections* of a cultural debate: they are *interventions* in that debate, *contributions* to the historiographical effort to reconstruct the past and discover the methods and principles of that reconstruction. They are as much locations of historical controversy as the history books: they are, in themselves and not derivatively, historiography.

---

[9] The issue of polyphony and the related notions of dialogism and heteroglossia (or plurilinguism) are treated mainly in M. M. Bakhtin, 'Discourse in the Novel', in *The Dialogic Imagination*, ed. by M. Holquist (Austin: University of Texas, 1981) and in *Problems of Dostoevsky's Poetics* (Minneapolis: Minneapolis University Press, 1984). See also V. N. Vološinov, *Marxism and the Philosophy of Language* (Cambridge, MA: Harvard University Press, 1986), Part 3 in particular. Bakhtin's explicit denial that drama and poetry may share the polyphonic quality of the novel and his arguments about the 'intrinsic monologism' of drama have been by now effectively challenged. See, on this point, A. Serpieri, 'Polifonia shakespeariana', in *Retorica e immaginario* (Parma: Pratiche, 1986). Serpieri's essay is a close discussion of Bakhtin's qualification of drama as essentially monologic, followed by a reading of six Shakespearian plays. As regards Shakespeare and the Elizabethans, Serpieri argues for a culturally necessitated polyphony, determined by the dissolution of the comparatively monolithic medieval symbolic cosmos.

In short, Holderness concludes, 'the plays can be read as serious attempts to reconstruct and theorise the past — as major initiatives of Renaissance historical thought'.[10] Besides, Holderness touches upon the important issue of invention in the histories (an issue which deserves more attention than it has so far received). Discussing the *Henry IV* plays as 'less firmly attached to the solid *mimesis* of literary historiography' than *Richard II*, and as displaying 'an infinitely greater liberty of invented incident', he argues that 'the principal effect of this expanded form [. . .] is its enlarged capacity for the juxtaposition of contradictions'.[11] What Holderness remarks, in particular, as regards the mixture of genres and styles and the invented elements in the *Henry IV* plays is, I believe, true of all the histories, however closely they seem to reproduce the historical sources.[12]

The many forms of source corruption that Shakespeare perpetrates, apart from their obviously responding to dramatic exigencies, may be read, I consider, as marks of the historiographical quality of the texts. Not only the introduction of imaginary elements, but also temporal contractions, cuttings, displacements, expansions, foregroundings, the sequencing of events, the very demarcation of the plot boundaries, etc., denote a historian's interpretative activity and are to be seen as comments and glosses on the margins of the received historical tradition.

An example of the way in which scene sequencing is used as an equivalent of the conceptual category of historical commentary is Act II of *1 Henry IV*. The act is mainly devoted to the highway robbery and to the trick played on Falstaff by Hal and Poins. The hilarious Scene 2, where the prince and Poins rob Falstaff of his booty is abruptly interrupted by the appearance of Hotspur, alone, Hamlet-like, reading a letter. In the first moments of this scene, the strong discrepancy — linguistic, stylistic, and situational — prevents our appreciation of Hotspur's mood and our siding with the seriousness of his enterprise. However, the pressure of estrangement also works in the opposite direction. By the end of the Hotspur scene, in fact, emotion and sympathy have been raised mainly thanks to the dialogue which follows the appearance of Lady Percy; so that when, with equal abruptness, the Eastcheap scene is resumed, for a few moments laughter is blocked and we are compelled to absorb the irreconcilable diversity of the two worlds. Thus, by means of their simple juxtaposition, the two situations are made to react to, and comment on, each other. In this case, I am not sure

---

[10] *Shakespeare's History* (Dublin: Gill and Macmillan, 1985), p. 31.

[11] Holderness, Potter, and Turner, p. 42.

[12] S. Greenblatt argues that 'the closer Shakespeare seems to a source, the more faithfully he reproduces it on stage, the more devastating and decisive his transformation of it', 'Shakespeare and the Exorcists', in *Shakespeare and the Question of Theory*, ed. by P. Parker and G. Hartman (London: Methuen, 1985), p. 178. Discussing Canterbury's long speech on the Salic law in *Henry V*, 1.2, G. Taylor says that 'the play's greatest crux of interpretation involves, not a departure from or addition to or conflation of his sources, but an instance of almost slavish dependence upon one of them' (p. 34).

whose interests are served by the estrangement effect. Certainly, the audience's tendency to side with the prince is blurred, and we are compelled to
discern and discriminate, and mostly to consider that events are neither
neutral nor transparent.

Generally speaking, it is when the dramatist frees himself from the constraints of his historical sources, when he is free to invent non-historical events
and to evoke non-historical characters, that the texts tend to build up
alternative historical and political perspectives.[13] On these occasions, far
from providing moments of 'relief' from the burden of history, the dramatist
lays down an arena where a multiplicity of voices is allowed to take part in the
dialogue. These forms of polyphony are often employed to reveal symptoms of
social pathology or, more simply, the dissenting perspective or the uneasiness
of a category, a trade, or a group of people. Sometimes a person is allowed to
emerge from the anonymous crowd and to assume the consistency and
relevance of a character or a quasi-character: a soldier, a gardener, a citizen, a
bourgeois who may have a name or be nameless is from time to time called to
the historical proscenium and allowed to speak his mind with the wisdom of
his class or of his trade (or of what is conventionally understood as its
rhetorical equivalent), as he was never allowed to do in a history book.[14]

To these voices which come from the obscure side of history are sometimes
entrusted messages of great political relevance. The horror of civil war, for
instance, is never expressed with such dramatic evidence as when, in
3 Henry VI, II. 5, two anonymous characters (a son who has killed his father
and a father who has killed his son) are summoned to show the devastating
effects of war through their private grief. Thus, the mimesis of the greater,
visible (and in a sense immovable) history is rendered more varied and
complex by shedding light on the obscure zone of 'invisible' history: the zone
of what may have happened. Moreover, at those moments during which the
dramatist explores the blank margins of his book of chronicles, a sense of the
individuality, peculiarity, and uniqueness of the events represented arises,
so that the intuition of the particular is transmitted from the margins to the
core of greater history. In other words, the lighting of the obscure areas
makes possible the enactment of a number of individual, diverse, diverging,
and sometimes disturbing perspectives, the introduction of different voices
and different social discourses, all of which are presented as equally creditable and worthy of the audience's attention; and these, in turn, stress the
uniqueness of greater historical events.

The so-called 'political attitude' of these texts is probably to be looked for
precisely in those areas where the irreverence of historical imagination

[13] G. Taylor affirms that 'resemblances to the chronicles establish Shakespeare's use of them; but, as always, his departures from his sources most illuminate his intentions' (p. 31).
[14] There are also occasions in which the marginal voices are used to serve the interests of the people in power. A case in point might seem to be the commoners' perspective in Act I Scene I of *Julius Caesar*. Their appearance, however, allows the tribunes' dissenting perspective to be affirmed and the political conflict to be perceived from the very first lines of the play.

renders visible what are, properly speaking, the contradictions which are connected with the trivialities of everyday experience. However, I wish to make clear that when I speak of polyphony in a Shakespearian historical play, I am not in any sense implying the presence of an attitude of political resistance or disobedience. Rather, I am arguing for a structure which allows the presence of a variety of voices expressing diverse axiologies, some of which may imply adherence to the dominant ideology and some of which, on the contrary, may appear to challenge that perspective. Most probably, the consideration of the social heterocosm that Shakespeare was addressing (a problem which must have been more pressing when national historical and political issues were at stake) played an important role in suggesting a non-monolithic, non-monologic attitude in the staging of the nation's past. However, the mental habit which allowed the playwright to address with equal pertinence all the sectors of the playhouse was determined, in my opinion, much less by commercial considerations than by the perception of the compelling complexity of things historical.

Henry V stages this kind of complexity by means of a series of peculiar procedures which are, broadly speaking, linguistic. They include first of all the two main languages which are used (English and French), the way and the circumstances in which they are used, and the discrepancies which derive from their use; the regional linguistic variations (or better, the comic, mock-regional distortions of English), the use of various, socially connotated, discourse types; the mixture of different genres and styles, the distribution of verse and prose, etc. Finally, one particular instance of dialogue — or of reaction to one statement on other statements — concerns the Choruses. The way in which in *Henry V* these different, recalcitrant elements are woven together is the play's peculiar contribution to a reconstruction of the past or, at least, to an enactment of the complexity of that past.

My idea is that by deploying so explicit and endemic a plurilinguism, by crediting a number of social discourses and of political perspectives, the play foregrounds conflicts of interests and a variety of viewpoints. Languages, dialects, styles, and social discursive varieties mark the boundaries (and differentiate the spheres) of the various ethnic, national, and social components. And that the many disturbing and disuniting effects of many-voicedness are deployed in the play in which national unity is celebrated is, to say the least, noticeable.[15]

---

[15] Discussing the issue of 'brotherhood' in the play, A. Gurr remarks: 'No play of Shakespeare's makes so much use of differences in language, and has more language barriers. With one entire scene in French and another half in French, and the French nobles regularly starting their scenes by making use of French phrases, plus Llewellyn's, Macmorris's and Jamy's non-standard English and Pistol's theatrical and old-fashioned quasi-verse, let alone Mrs. Quickly's malapropisms, the play puts up a great show of non-communication. Yet the one thing you expect of brothers is that they speak the same language. The play is full of brothers (and sisters) who cannot communicate with each other.' ('A Performance Text for *Henry V*', paper read at the Conference on 'Shakespeare dal testo alla scena', Ferrara, 24–27 June 1991, p. 9).

III   *Henry's 'strange tongues' and the languages of the conquered*

In *2 Henry IV*, trying to soothe the anguish of the dying king at Hal's 'headstrong riot', the Earl of Warwick interprets with an apt linguistic metaphor the prince's attitude in turning things to his own advantage:

> The Prince but studies his companions
> Like a strange tongue, wherein, to gain the language,
> 'Tis needful that the most immodest word
> Be look'd upon and learnt; which once attain'd,
> Your Highness knows, comes to no further use
> But to be known and hated.
>
> (IV.4.68)[16]

It appears that between this moment and the beginning of *Henry V*, having 'gained', and hated, the strange tongue of his former riotous companions, Henry turned to learning, again to his own advantage, the many languages of power: those of divinity, commonwealth, affairs, war, and policy, as Canterbury says in praise of the king (I.1.38–59).

Henry's linguistic ordeal, however, is not yet concluded. The stage of his conquest is, in fact, a tangle of different languages and the conquest is largely a matter of linguistic integration. The king is going to meet more strange tongues and discourses on the way to national unity and to foreign conquest, although from now on it is not going to be a matter of learning, but of submitting, disfiguring, or turning those strange tongues into some form of 'English'.

Many of the conflicts that are enacted in *Henry V*, starting from the literal conflict of the war which follows the invasion of France, are in fact represented as linguistic conflicts. In the course of the play Henry will have to come to grips with his enemies' native tongue, with the 'dialects' of the components of his regionally variegated army (in a sense, Henry himself, whose Welsh origin is remarked, is a 'stranger'). He will be touched, although peripherally, by what remains of the 'strange tongue' of his former companions and by the shreds of the comic convention which becomes more and more extraneous to his person (until what remains of the comic plot is hanged on the gallows in the person of Bardolph); in a strange tongue, or better in a bastard tongue that looks more and more like English, he will conquer a woman for a wife whom he has already conquered as the daughter of his vanquished enemy; he will have to face the challenge of the conflicting discourses which raise doubts as to the holiness of his war and to his right and honourable cause, and which pose questions about the leader's responsibility as regards the death of his subjects in battle. He is going to meet the non-neutrality of alien discourses, the views and evaluations which belong to a perspective that challenges his own: words and forms, as Bakhtin says, 'populated by intentions'. In other words, while conquest and unity imply

---

[16] Here and elsewhere, quotations from Shakespeare are taken from the Arden editions of his plays.

the necessity of removing linguistic and cultural differences, these seem to resist the tendency to eliminate diversity and are, till the last scene of the play, presented as problematic.

IV   *National and regional heteroglossia*

Henry V is a play written by an English playwright for an English audience. It is not, however, a play written *in English*. There are scenes written in French (III. 4) which presumably were not understood by a large part of the contemporary audience and which may still create problems to both audience and actors, scenes in which both languages are spoken and which, therefore, require an interpreter for both the English character on the stage and the spectators (IV. 4 and part of v. 2), and scenes where the French king, the Dauphin, and the nobility signal from time to time their being French by introducing here and there expressions or exclamations in that language although, to the audience's benefit, they speak mainly in English.

That the play's 'traffic' is to present 'two mighty monarchies' inside whose national confines different languages are spoken is not enough, however, to explain the linguistic situation described above. In *1 Henry VI*, in fact (an even more Frenchified play) only a very small number of words in French are spoken. While, then, in *1 Henry VI* the convention that prescribes that characters, whatever their nationality, understand each other in the author's and audience's language obtains, this is only in part true in the case of *Henry V*. Moreover, in this play not only is French spoken in a number of circumstances but linguistic difference is also signalled as problematic: lack of knowledge of English is, in different degrees, pointed out as a source of trouble, from simple incomprehension to the possibility of losing a husband to that of losing one's head.

Why is heteroglossia presented as a problem in *Henry V* while it is not in *1 Henry VI*? Why is the encounter of the countess of Auvergne with Lord Talbot (*1 Henry VI*, II. 3) so entirely monolinguistic and therefore perfectly communicative? Why does the Pucelle speak to the English lords and the English lords to her with never the shadow of a linguistic impediment while Katherine is shown as having to learn the English tongue ('il faut que j'apprenne à parler')before she meets Henry? And why is the French soldier Monsieur Le Fer in danger of losing his life (*Henry V*, IV. 4) simply for not being able to grant Pistol a ransom in English? Is the scene only one more comic interlude or does it remind us, in a curious way indeed, that even Pistol, that image of cowardice, is now, linguistically too, the master of his better?

Obviously, losing one's language or at least learning the victor's is one of the prices that a conqueror imposes on the conquered. What makes the difference between the two plays, then, seems to be a matter of course: namely, the fact that in *Henry V* a conquest is staged while its sequel stages a loss. Nevertheless, even though we grant this truism, the persistent thematization of linguistic difference and of language learning is not completely explained, and the situation remains slightly paradoxical.

The learning of the conqueror's language is by no means given for granted and seems to encounter some resistance until the last scene of the play. Why does Henry describe the English tongue as 'rough' and his own capacity to teach it as weak? ('Our tongue is rough, coz, and my condition is not smooth' (v. 2. 304–05)). The adjective *rough* may illustrate an affirmative value of plainness and simplicity, in contrast with the elaborate elegance of French, but it may also indicate that English is not easily taught and learned; why is it suggested that Kate be 'not apt' (l. 303) to learn it? (Incidentally, in the expression 'my condition is not smooth', *condition* may mean, as both the editor of the Arden and of the Oxford editions suggest, 'disposition, temperament', but it may also mean 'position'). Finally, it is to be remarked that the only article of the treaty which is presented as problematic is the one that implies the naming of Henry, in formal documents, as heir to the throne of France in French and in Latin: 'in French, Notre très cher fils Henry, Roy d'Angleterre, Héritier de France; and thus in Latin, Præclarissimus filius noster Henricus, rex Angliæ, et Hæres Franciæ' (v. 2. 357–60). The French tongue, it would seem, will not stoop to England's will. The French king, in fact, has apparently suspended the signing of this article which represents the final seal on Henry's conquest by granting him succession, and will sign it only on Henry's explicit request. Until that article is signed (and it is understood, but never explicitly declared, that it will be signed only some thirty lines before the end of the play), therefore, Henry's *condition* cannot be considered *smooth*.[17]

If Henry's linguistic conquest of France is not as successfully performed as his military and political conquest, the linguistic integration of Wales, Ireland, and Scotland seems at first sight to be less problematic. Although Fluellen cannot 'speak English in the native garb' (v. 1. 79–80), there are no incomprehensions between him, the Welsh, the Scottish, and the English captain. Indeed, unlike what happens with the French, all these characters speak English, although in a remarkably corrupt form.[18] It may be agreed that, as Dollimore and Sinfield have remarked,

[17] Indeed, Henry's condition as foreign pretender and heir to the throne of France is as awkward as was the Scottish James Stewart's condition as foreign pretender to the throne of England. When Shakespeare wrote *Henry V*, the debate about Elizabeth's succession and the controversy between Stuart and Suffolk supporters was very hot. (On the succession debate, see M. Axton, *The Queen's Two Bodies* (London: Royal Historical Society, 1977).
[18] A different linguistic situation is presented in *1 Henry IV* (III. 1). The Welsh Owen Glendower speaks English and gives a reason for it (he has been 'train'd up in the English court' (l. 117)), while his daughter, Mortimer's wife, only speaks Welsh. However, although there is no linguistic communication between husband and wife, there seems to be a deeper form of correspondence (a 'feeling disputation' (l. 199)). Moreover, Welsh is here granted the full independence of a language because it is unsubjected and described, when spoken by the lady, as a music (ll. 201–04).

the jokes about the way Fluellen pronounces the English language are, apparently, for the Elizabethan audience and many since, an adequate way to handle the repression of the Welsh language and culture. (p. 224)

But it may also be that even there the situation is not as linear as that. In Fluellen's, Jamy's, and Macmorris's 'disfigured' English, a way of speaking where difference is made explicit, in fact, a form of resistance to cultural integration is objectively represented. If the process of unification tends to kill the native tongues, nevertheless the marginal cultures still express some form of centrifugal force, if nothing else, by corrupting the 'garb' of the prescribed unitary language.[19]

The process, which becomes comedy in Shakespeare, is explained as a recurrent cultural phenomenon by Bakhtin:

The victory of one reigning language (dialect) over the others, the supplanting of languages, their enslavement, the process of illuminating them with the True Word, the incorporation of barbarians and lower social strata into a unitary language of culture and truth, the canonization of ideological systems, [...] all this determined the content and power of the category of 'unitary language' in linguistic and stylistic thought [...].

But the centripetal forces of the life of language, embodied in a 'unitary language', operate in the midst of heteroglossia. At any given moment of its evolution, language is stratified not only into linguistic dialects in the strict sense of the word [...] but also [...] into languages of social groups, 'professional' and 'generic' languages, languages of generations and so forth.[20]

In *Henry V* neither the English tongue nor the True Word of ideologically saturated discourses succeed in eliminating differences by imposing a 'unitary language of culture and truth'. Indeed, we have ample evidence in the play of the persistence of heteroglossia also in the form of differently orientated kinds of discourse. Henry's most trying encounter with the resistance of a non-neutral language 'populated by intentions' and with a challenge to the unitary discourse of the holiness of his war is, of course, his dialogue with the soldiers Court, Bates, and Williams on the eve of Agincourt (IV. I), an obvious instance of the use of marginal voices which objectively undermine a celebrative reading of the events. It should be pointed out that the three soldiers' view of the imminent battle, their indifference to and incomprehension of the 'right cause' for which they are sent to die is given strength by its representing the view of a group, namely, by the three soldiers' standing for the whole army involved in the enterprise.

---

[19] A remark by S. Mullaney is appropriate here: 'National tongues were not without their role in exercising that power [the power of the throne]. "Language", as the Bishop of Avila remarked in 1492, "is the perfect instrument of empire". Yet if we find in the Renaissance an increasing awareness and deployment of the power of language — power in a real sense, as a weapon of conquest and control — we also find in it a charting of the boundaries of rule, beyond which authority can only watch and listen to the treason's amphibolic spectacle' (p. 38). The Bishop of Avila's text comes to Mullaney from S. Greenblatt's 'Learning to curse: Aspects of Linguistic Colonialism in the Sixteenth Century', in *First Images of America*, ed. by F. Chiapelli (Berkeley: University of California Press, 1976), p. 562.
[20] 'Discourse in the Novel', pp. 271–72.

Alexander Court, John Bates, and Michael Williams, in fact, whose position is made even more dramatically relevant and reliable by their being given names and surnames,[21] expresses the only serious opinion of the 'vulgar', namely, of those that followed Henry only because 'to disobey were against all proportion of subjection' (IV. I. 148–49). What we see of Henry's army apart from them is much less creditable, since it comes either from the company of thieves and cut-purses or from what is explicitly presented as an instance of military fanaticism (Fluellen's in particular). Nothing in the play endangers our sympathy with Henry's enterprise so much as this scene, which comes near to destroying everything the play has been presenting up until now as justification of the invasion of France. However we read this scene, the questions of why a celebration should be so perilously endangered, why the balance of arguments should be so delicate and uncertain and, most of all, why so profound an ideological *difference* should be shown if a celebrative mood were the only perspective of the play, remain.

v *Conflict and the comic plots*

Other forms of incomprehension arise, however, between the two spheres of the comic plot which, from a certain point on, seem to be utterly incompatible. Indeed, the Welsh (Fluellen's) is the rising one, while the English (Pistol's) is clearly doomed to disappear. Captain Gower's rebuke to Pistol in defence of Fluellen (v. 1) literally determines the death of Pistol's bravado and his final disappearance from Henry's universe, which clearly cannot contain this last, dispossessed residue of his past revels any longer:

GOWER   Go, go; you are a counterfeit cowardly knave. Will you mock at an ancient tradition, begun upon an honourable respect, and worn as a memorable trophy of predeceased valour, and dare not avouch in your deeds any of your words? I have seen you gleeking and galling at this gentleman twice or thrice. You thought, because he could not speak English in the native garb, he could not therefore handle an English cudgel: you find it otherwise; *and henceforth let a Welsh correction teach you a good English condition*. Fare ye well.
(v. 1. 72–83; my emphasis)

'Let a Welsh correction teach you a good English condition'.[22] Indeed, from the start, the division has been incurable. In the two comic spheres of the play not only are different languages spoken, but also these, in turn, betray different *conditions*. They do because they are differently positioned as regards the king, and their position largely depends on the way the comic conventions are treated. The 'old' comedy, that which derives from the *Henry IV* plays, maintains its non-conformist, subversive character, while the

---

[21] A. Gurr remarks that the fact that these three ordinary soldiers are given forename and surname is 'a feature which is unique in all Shakespeare' (p. 5).

[22] 'Teaching' and 'correction' are other pervasive topics of the play. Languages, manners, the respect of ancient traditions, the discipline of the wars, in a word, the unitary language of a 'good English condition' must be taught to the heteroglot, the ignorant, and the recalcitrant.

'new' comedy of Fluellen and his fellow captains is presented as observant and traditionalist ('Will you mock at an ancient tradition?').

Moreover, the collapse of the 'old' comic plot is carried out by means of a series of interferences which make it more and more alien to comedy (or which strengthen its non-conformist character as comedy). Indeed, from the start, the comic conventions themselves seem to be polluted by the discrepant language of pathos. The first and most contradictory of these discrepancies is, of course, Falstaff's sickness and death (the news of his illness literally interferes with the comic quarrel between Pistol and Nym regarding the hostess). The series of subsequent pathetic collapses that follows (the dramatic cruelty of the deaths of Bardolph and Nym and the even more incongruous and inexplicable, although indirect, news of the Boy's death),[23] culminate in Pistol's farewell speech, which immediately follows Gower's rebuke and his exit:

> PISTOL   Doth Fortune play the huswife with me now?
> News have I that my Doll is dead i'th' spital
> Of malady of France;
> And then my rendezvous is quite cut off.
> Old I do wax, and from my weary limbs
> Honour is cudgell'd. Well, bawd I'll turn,
> And something lean to cut-purse of quick hand.
> To England will I steal, and there I'll steal:
> And patches will I get unto these cudgell'd scars,
> And swear I got them in the Gallia wars.
>
> (v. 1.84)

Here, on the one hand we are made to think that with these lines the long scene of Pistol's, and of his companions', theatrical life is come to an end; on the other, the projection forward assures us that Pistol is going to survive (we may even hypothesize that by sparing Pistol Shakespeare is leaving open the possibility of his 'return' in a future play). Incidentally, 'my Doll' in l. 85 instead of 'my Nell' may be a material confusion between Nell Quickly and Doll Tearsheet, but it simultaneously evokes the two women of the company (it may be read as a con-fusion), now both dead in one person. Their death, and the death of the whole party of friends, has obviously been determined by Henry's desertion.

Until the last but one scene of *2 Henry IV*, the comic plot agreed with, and was supported by, the prince. In *Henry V*, again, we have agreement between comedy (the 'new' comedy, this time) and Henry. Here, however, the king's support has, so to speak, defaced comedy, drawing it into a conformist sphere of action. What remains of the old, subversive comedy does not even touch the king. We will never know whether Henry recognizes Pistol in their

---

[23] Unless we justify it as a means to give more strength and render more acceptable Henry's order to kill the French prisoners, although the text does not make it explicit that Henry knows of the French attack on the baggage train. We infer the Boy's death from Gower's words: ''Tis certain there's not a boy left alive' (IV. 7. 5). As regards Nym, we know of his death from a passing mention of the Boy (IV. 4. 71–75).

only encounter (IV. 1), although we more than suspect that he is conscious of sending his old friend Bardolph to death (in III.6.104–09 Fluellen names Bardolph as the man to be executed and describes him with extreme accuracy). Indeed, if languages and dialects are distorted, the nature of comedy and laughter is no less perverted: while 'genuine' comedy has been polluted by pathos and melancholy and eventually marginalized, what remains is a loyalist model of comedy, incongruous because fully 'authorized'.[24] Nothing, in any case, seems to grant the establishment of a unitary form of national comedy.

Dollimore's and Sinfield's comment on this point, especially as regards the contrast between the two comic plots, is worth discussing:

Increasingly, since 2 Henry IV, sympathy for these characters has been withdrawn; from this point on, there seems to be nothing positive about them. It is here that Fluellen enters, offering an alternative to Falstaff among the lesser gentry and an issue — the control of England over the British Isles — easier to cope with. Fluellen may be funny, old-fashioned and pedantic, but he is totally committed to the King and his purposes, as the King recognizes (IV.1.83–84). The low characters are condemned not only to death but to exclusion from national unity; it is as if they have had their chance and squandered it. (p. 223)

What has been withdrawn is, however, the king's sympathy, not ours. The audience has mixed feelings: while our sympathy for the pedantic Fluellen is by no means granted, we do resist, up to a certain point, the many attacks that are launched against the 'old' comedy. We are likely to side with Pistol (a more and more marginalized character who lacks the language of conformism which would integrate him into the bright future of national unity) when he is allowed to pronounce his farewell speech. Pistol's monologue quoted above is a mock-counterpart of the serious form of so many tragic farewell speeches; a mock-counterpart which, however, gives dramatic relevance to the character's disappearance. Whatever moral judgement the audience may pass on Pistol's plans of stealing and purse-cutting, the speech shows one last spark of the 'old' comedy's fire. Pistol may be going to disappear for ever, but he may survive and even come back. What his speech shows, in the last analysis, is in fact his capacity to oppose the attacks of both Fortune and the 'new' legalitarian comedy.

The most serious and insidious conformist attack the 'old' comedy has to face seems to be inspired directly from the king, although it comes from inside its own sphere. I am referring to the Boy's long monologue in Act III Scene 2 (incidentally, a speech which makes of what was until then only a functional element, an independent character, so that we may the better regret his death). What is noteworthy is in the first place the fact that the attack comes from one who is both younger and socially lower than even

---

[24] The discussion of the way in which dramatic conventions are contaminated in Henry V would imply in the first place a reckoning of the verse/prose distribution (see, for instance, the surprising decision to use prose in the courtship scene in V.2).

Bardolph, Nym, and Pistol; one, moreover, who speaks the language of wisdom and honesty that the king's former friends have never been able to speak; but mostly the fact that the Boy's critical attitude in this speech curiously remembers Hal's in his famous monologue in *1 Henry IV* (1.2.190–212). Only, when he pronounces his speech, Hal is ready to exercise his power in a different company, while the Boy is planning to offer his services to better men. So much the worse for the old company of friends, since this time the 'I know you all' criticism comes from below:

> BOY   As young as I am, I have observed these three swashers. I am boy to them all three, but all they three, though they would serve me, could not be man to me; for indeed three such antics do not amount to a man. [. . .] They would have me as familiar with men's pockets as their gloves or their handkerchers: which makes much against my manhood if I should take from another's pocket to put into mine; for it is plain pocketing up of wrongs. I must leave them and seek some better service: their villainy goes against my weak stomach, and therefore I must cast it up.
>
> (III.2.28–32, 49–57)

With whom does an audience side after so sensible a speech? Things, by this time, have become utterly confusing. A battle is ahead of us, and the audience's national feelings (and, indeed, the feelings of any audience) cannot but side with the hero. And the Boy's speech (an uncompromised speech, since it comes from 'one of us') contributes to the drifting and drowning of those who do not side explicitly with heroism and do not labour for a glorious victory. After all, a certain amount of conformism is maybe one of the few common denominators of all audiences.

VI   *The discrepant voice of the Choruses*

Prologues, Epilogues, and Choruses, apart from introducing, commenting on, and concluding the action, are, not metaphorically, cues in a dialogue. Being direct addresses to the audience, they aim at getting a specific, although silent, response and, as seems the case with *Henry V*, the acceptance of a certain reading of the text that they introduce. In other words, they may represent an external way to determine a certain viewpoint. External, in the first place because they are not part of the action, and in the second place because they contemplate the action from a temporally removed perspective, that of the contemporary audience.[25]

Henry V has six such appeals to the audience, which introduce the five acts and close up the play. Apart from expressing both the material and moral inadequacy of the stage, and of the company, to represent the exceptional events of Henry's reign, Prologue and Choruses illustrate the virtues of the

---

[25] The external and contemporary position of the Chorus is stressed in the overt allusion to Essex's expedition to Ireland (v. Chorus 29–35), which started in March 1599 and which, judging from the false forecast of a victory, was presumably not yet concluded when the Chorus was composed.

ideal king, anticipate the content of the following act, and fill up the gaps by telling the events that are not going to be represented. Their function, however, is not only metadramatic, since many evaluations are suggested, more or less directly, by them.

The voice responsible for these fragments obviously belongs to one of the company: an actor, a stage-manager or the author himself; one, in any case, who is professionally engaged in the staging of the play and who, therefore, knows the material inadequacies of the stage to evoke so huge an argument. What evaluations come to the audience from the Chorus, then, are felt as coming from a perspective that is nearer — temporally, but also socially — to the audience than most of the perspectives that are to be found in the play; nearer, and therefore, trustworthy (psychologically, if not historically). And what this voice tells us is all in favour of the glorious king. Indeed, if a reader were to read only these introductory and concluding speeches and disregard the body of the play, none of the doubts that have been so far discussed about the celebrative intention of the play would arise.

However, the voice of the Chorus runs the risk of losing its reliability and also its privileged contact with the audience since on many occasions it affirms things that the play's action belies. (Obviously, it cannot be the other way round, since what is acted on the stage is not simply affirmed, but it is also validated by the very fact of its happening then and there). These apparent discrepancies have been studied as so many textual cruces, and they probably are. Nevertheless, until their textual status is coherently and satisfactorily unravelled, we may suggest their interpretation in the light of what has been said until now regarding the play's conflicting views.[26]

Discrepancies of this kind include first of all contrasts between the way in which heroism is depicted by the Choruses and the kind of 'heroes' we are shown in the action. This contrast is particularly sharp in the case of Acts II and V, where the comic scenes with their anti-heroes immediately follow the exit of the Chorus.

A textual explanation of this and other discrepancies has been suggested as a consequence of the Choruses' possible 'later writing and insertion where they do not make a perfect fit'.[27] Later insertion may, indeed, explain some of the minor inconsistencies. For instance, a material slip may have determined the disagreement between Act III Chorus (no able bodied man has remained in England, and the country is 'guarded with grandsires, babies and old women' (III. Chorus 20)) and Westmoreland's wish that all the young men that have remained at home were in France (IV. 3. 16–18); it may explain the many denials, in the Boy's and soldiers' wish to be at home and their balancing honour and fame against safety, of what Act II Chorus says

---

[26] Although remarking different discrepancies, P. Rackin argues that 'the action Shakespeare dramatizes contradicts the story the Chorus tells' (*Stages of History* (London: Routledge, 1990), p. 82).
[27] A. Gurr, p. 2. The interpretative implications which may come from the hypothesis of a later writing and insertion of the Choruses are of great interest.

about all the youth of England being so impatient to follow Henry that they 'sell the pasture [. . .] to buy the horse' (II. Chorus 1–11); it may explain that the Chorus to Act II announces that the scene will be taken to Southampton while the act opens in Eastcheap; but it cannot explain the description that Act IV Chorus makes of Henry the night before Agincourt as comforting and heartening the troops, 'thawing cold fear' (IV. Chorus 45) and addressing the men 'with cheerful semblance and sweet majesty' (IV. Chorus 40). What we are shown is, in this case, in sharp contrast with what the Chorus has announced. Henry is hiding his 'sweet majesty' under a borrowed cloak, and his long conversation with Court, Bates, and Williams and the monologue that follows show a melancholy, vulnerable, and unsure young man, more trapped in his problems than able to solve them and utterly unable to dissipate the doubts and fears of his soldiers.

Moreover, the hypothesis of later insertion leaves the reading of the play even more open to further speculation about its inconsistency as epic celebration. Why should, in fact, the need to add these unequivocally celebrative passages have been felt if not to buttress the uncertain celebrative mood of the play?[28] But the most blatant discrepancy comes from the last Chorus, which overturns the optimistic mood with which the play closes and finally flouts the rules of the celebration game. The play's last speech, delivered by Henry, has sealed in a euphoric tone the king's conquest of France and of Katherine:

KING HENRY   Prepare we for our marriage: on which day,
My Lord of Burgundy, we'll take your oath,
And all the peers', for surety of our leagues.
Then shall I swear to Kate, and you to me;
And may our oaths well kept and prosp'rous be!

(v. 2. 388)

That neither conquest is shown on the stage as an accomplished fact is not, by the time Henry's and the play's last words are pronounced, noteworthy. A prospective ending, in fact, indicates, in terms of theatrical conventions, that what is purposed verbally is going to happen.[29] And even supposing that a part of the contradictions that have been enacted have left a mark in the consciousness of a few spectators, we may think that by now they have all been wiped out.

Moreover, the story of King Henry V closes with a promise of immortality which is unique in the stories of kings that Shakespeare had written until then: Henry does not die (years later, Henry VIII will be granted a like immortality). In the audience's eyes the fact that Henry's death falls outside

---

[28] The idea that later addition of the Choruses may have been determined by the necessity to shelter Henry from possible hostile readings has been formulated by A. Gurr. I am quoting from notes taken while attending a talk delivered by Gurr in May 1989 at the Shakespeare Institute in Stratford.

[29] There are other occasions in which this convention is flouted. We may remember Bolingbroke's never accomplished purpose of a voyage to the Holy Land at the end of *Richard II*.

of the temporal limits of the play suggests that he is going to live. The effect is that of a life eternal and, given the euphoric final tone, eternally happy.[30] Non-death of Henry is certainly what the spectators — whatever sector of the playhouse they are occupying — expect from the glorification of a national hero. They would be disappointed otherwise.

After the last speech, the royal train disappears, leaving behind a promise of life: peace and prosperity for the country and a happy marriage for the royal couple. Then, the final Chorus enters the empty stage. It speaks of what will follow: events that the audience knows ('which oft our stage hath shown'), but whose memory the play has succeeded in dispersing: Henry's death, the loss of what has been conquered and a bloody civil war. And while the Chorus speaks, we are struck by what now appears as the basic discrepancy of the play: its not being able to decide between an optimistic and a pessimistic model. We discover, or are reminded that, in spite of what the play's final words had promised, Henry is going to die, and that happiness and prosperity will last only a 'small time'. What we have been made to see and to believe was, we now perceive, as ephemeral as the play's two hours' traffic. The audience cannot but be disappointed.

Indeed, Henry dies untimely, even before we leave the playhouse, and in as short a time all his conquests are lost. What the final Chorus tells us, in plain words, is that *all* (the play's *all* as well as history's *all*) was for nothing.

---

[30] Juri M. Lotman discusses the different framings of literary works as representing different world models. In particular, a text which closes with the victory of the hero affirms a model where the hero can neither die nor be discomfited. Lotman's essay is in the Italian translation of his book *Struktura chudozestvennogo teksta* (Moscow: Iskusstvo, 1970): 'La composizione dell'opera letteraria', in *La Struttura del testo poetico* (Milano: Mursia, 1972).

The Myth Structure and Rituality of
Henry V

BROWNELL SALOMON

Bowling Green State University

I

As he planned his series of plays on the Lancastrian kings, Shakespeare surely realized at the outset that the climactic work, his dramatization of Henry V's 'exploits and mighty enterprises' (1.2.121), would call for quite a different approach.[1] The result was a bold experiment that succeeded, fully transcending the special constraints of the material. For certain attributes of the Henry V legend did in fact comprise a set of artistic givens which decided the playwright on a method of storytelling unique to *Henry V*: the use of a presenter–narrator, the Chorus, in so dominating a fashion as to alter its traditional function. The deeper implications of this metadramatic technique will be examined later in this essay. But I would first delve into those qualities of his subject matter that focused Shakespeare's perceptions and put him in effect under an unusual obligation, leading him to adopt the presentational strategy that he did.

One obvious factor was his noteworthy protagonist, the larger-than-life culture hero who epitomized the ideal king, one whom the dramatist could ringingly portray as 'the young Phoebus' (III. Chorus 6), 'a Jove' (II.4.100), a man 'full of grace and fair regard' (1.1.22), 'the mirror of all Christian Kings' (II.Chorus 6), and 'this star of England [. . .] in the very May-morn of his youth' (Epilogue 6; 1.2.120). Here indeed was right subject matter to challenge any would-be author to meet the exalted expectancies of heroical poetry which the admired Sir Philip Sidney had told his countrymen was

not only a kind, but the best and most accomplished kind of Poetry. For as the image of each action stirreth and instructeth the mind, so the lofty image of such worthies [Achilles, Cyrus, Aeneas, etc.] most inflameth the mind with desire to be worthy, and informs with counsel how to be worthy.[2]

But though Shakespeare exploits many of the best known epic devices in *Henry V* — the invocation to the Muse, epithets like 'the warlike Harry' (Prologue 6), and the like — such indebtedness to literary epopee are notable but hardly decisive, more an effort to attain the sublimity and mood

---

[1] Citations are to *The Riverside Shakespeare*, ed. by G. Blakemore Evans (Boston: Houghton Mifflin, 1974).
[2] Sir Philip Sidney, *An Apology for Poetry*, ed. by Geoffrey Shepherd (London: Nelson, 1965), p. 119.

of epic than to trade wholesale on formal resemblances. The Chorus, for example, though similar to an epic narrator, is in narrative terms actually a redundancy, providing us with no information absolutely necessary for our comprehension of the play.[3] My point is that Shakespeare's narrational-presentational mode in *Henry V* should not be pigeonholed as merely incidental epic borrowing, but can more plausibly be seen as an innovative adjustment to the *found* nature of his material. For unlike all historical persons and events used as sources in his earlier plays, King Henry's victory at Agincourt was incomparably a found story, niched firmly in the popular mind before Shakespeare took it up in 1599.

It had already been the subject of many popular ballads, of two dramatizations performed only a few years previous to Shakespeare's, and of 'The Agincourt Carol', described by an authority as a 'stirring song, perhaps the best-known carol in English not concerned with the nativity'.[4] To retell so familiar a story would oblige any playwright vigorously to offset any accustomedness on the part of his audience. And in this case the burden of responsibility was the greater because the story of Henry of Monmouth was almost too renowned, and there was also the fact of its uncommon prestige. It was, after all, *the* great national heroic narrative, in effect a culturally venerated emblem, a totem in verbal form that reminded the nation of that hallowed day *in illo tempore* long ago when England realized its highest aspirations for national solidarity. Some flavour of its momentousness for Elizabethans is conveyed in the description of Henry V's career by Samuel Daniel, lines which were among Shakespeare's sources: 'O what eternall matter here is found! | Whence new immortal *Iliads* might proceed.'[5] The events surrounding the victory at Agincourt were hardly the usual historical grist the playwright was free to alter at will for his own purposes. With its luminous celebrity, the story assumed an existence of its own, an identity ontologically prior to, independent of, and even superior to all its later redactions by Hall, Holinshed, and the others, or by Shakespeare himself. Not surprisingly, the exalted status of his subject inclined the dramatist to an unprecedented response. From the earliest moments of the play onward Shakespeare insists upon the prior autonomy of *the story*, elevating its

[3] A fact Samuel Johnson recognized in his 1765 edition of the play (Anthony S. Brennan, 'That Within Which Passes Show: The Function of the Chorus in *Henry V*,' *PQ*, 58 (1979), 40–52 (p. 43). Epic influences are reviewed by Edward I. Berry, '"True Things and Mock'ries": Epic and History in *Henry V*', *JEGP*, 78 (1979), 1–16.

[4] 'The Agincourt Carol' is so characterized in *The Early English Carols*, ed. by Richard Leighton Greene, 2nd ed. (Oxford: Clarendon Press, 1977), p. 474. For the ballads, see F. J. Child, *The English and Scottish Popular Ballads*, 5 vols (1882–1898; repr. New York: Dover, 1965), III, 320–26; and Thomas Percy, *Bishop Percy's Folio Manuscript*, ed. by J. W. Hales and F. J. Furnivall, 3 vols (London: N. Truber, 1867–1868), II, 158–73, 595–99. A complete verse of one ballad is sung in Thomas Heywood's contemporary play, *I Edward IV* (1592–1599; ed. by R. H. Shepherd, 6 vols (London: Pearson, 1874; repr. New York: Russell, 1964), II, 52): 'Agencourt, Agencourt! know ye not Agencourt?' For the previous plays, see *Henry V*, edited by J. H. Walter, Arden edition (Cambridge, MA: Harvard University Press, 1954), Introduction, pp. xxxvii–xxxviii.

[5] Samuel Daniel, *Civil Wars* (1595), IV. 6 (*Narrative and Dramatic Sources of Shakespeare*, ed. by Geoffrey Bullough, 8 vols (London: Routledge, 1962), IV, 421).

authority well above the present rendering. It is, indeed, 'so great an object', 'this great accompt', 'this history' (Prologue 11, 17, 32), and 'our history' that speaks now 'with full mouth' (1.2.230); it is an eternal example to posterity, for 'this story shall the good man teach his son' (IV.3.56). And 'to those that have not read the story', presumably few, the Chorus vouchsafes that he 'may prompt them' (v. Chorus 1–2). Finally, 'the story' is deferentially affirmed as one which 'our bending author hath pursu'd [. . .] with rough and all-unable pen' (Epilogue 1–2). Never before had Shakespeare made so pointed an issue of the primacy and obligating nature of his subject.[6]

II

Notwithstanding, perhaps all of the aforementioned characteristics of the Henry V narrative — its popular reputation, epic tone, and near-legendary protagonist — cannot wholly account for Shakespeare's presenting it in the unique fashion he did. Indeed, this essay will present modern narratological evidence to support the hypothesis that the author's obeisance to this story was likely fostered by an uncanny awareness that his source-narrative, even in its raw, diffuse state, possessed the integral qualities of a finished work. At the least, the proof is irrefutable that this 'great accompt' displayed a beauty of form that was strikingly literary even *before* Shakespeare began to exert imaginative control over it. Considered in its totality, there is a nicely balanced rondure, an organic symmetry of events which begin with the king's weighty resolve to invade France, reach a peak with the journey to and hard-won victory at Agincourt, and achieve satisfying closure with the Anglo-French reconciliation and Henry's betrothal to Princess Katherine. To be sure, all of the pivotal events of the play, including the conspiracy of Scroop and others, occur in the same chronological order as in Holinshed's *Chronicles*, the main historical source. But the way Shakespeare appears to have been led by the story, the way he admitted by-incidents to enhance but not alter the framework of salient actions in his prose source, argue that he intuited in 'our history' an already built-in determinacy.

No mere piecemeal aggregation of parts or episodes, here was the found integratedness of an artistic whole. Such congruency with intrinsic laws of

---

[6] Granted, expressions of authorial humility do have a basis in tradition: the so-called modesty topos, or formula, which harks back to classical oratory (Ernst Robert Curtius, *European Literature and the Latin Middle Ages*, trans. by Willard R. Trask (New York: Pantheon Books, 1953; repr. New York: Harper Torchbooks, 1963), pp. 83–85). And, in the Sonnets, Shakespeare uses such locutions as 'my pupil pen', 'my slight Muse', and 'these rude lines'. But the author's submissiveness in *Henry V* seems not so much the result of worry lest his retelling be flawed ('Mangling by starts the full course of their glory' (Epilogue 4)), as the result of objective doubts that his means themselves — the actors ('flat unraised spirits') and the stage ('this unworthy scaffold') — could uphold the extra-historical cachet of 'the story'.

configuration is what present-day Gestalt theorists refer to as wholeness-character or 'goodness in form'.[7] That ready unity which the playwright had merely to highlight in making it his own is today widely admired, one commentator remarking that '*Henry V* is an almost perfect realization of meaning in form. [. . .] In movement the play resembles a stately, cere-monial dance. [. . .] Indeed, it is less a drama than a celebration'.[8] Moody Prior, in his recent discussion of the work, assumes its status as a 'dramatic myth', an 'heroic fairy tale'.[9]

It would not ordinarily be possible to verify in concrete terms these enduring impressions that the narrative somehow reflects a timeless univer-sality ('eternall matter' to Samuel Daniel) or that its essentiality of form recalls folk history passed orally from generation to generation ('This story shall the good man teach his son' (IV. 3. 56)). Yet astonishingly, thanks to the findings of an influential research study of folk narrative by Vladimir Propp (1895–1970), which identifies in detail the controlling structural blueprint of many folktales and myths, we are now afforded proof positive that the suggestively ideal narrative design of Shakespeare's *Henry V* is so indeed because the play correlates in its entirety, point for point, with that selfsame ageless pattern of folktale and myth.

Propp's *Morphology of the Folktale*, published in Leningrad in 1928, had to wait thirty years for its first translation into English. Since 1958, the impact of this seminal work on folklorists, linguists, anthropologists, and literary critics has been enormous. The advent of a second edition in 1968 helped to further its reputation. Propp's achievement is his discovery, based on methodical inductive analysis, that all 177 Russian folktales of the well-known Afanasyev collection possessed a unitary compositional plan, a monotypical structure.[10] He noted, for example, that in one of the tales an eagle flies the hero away to another kingdom, in a second tale a horse carries the hero away to another kingdom, and in a third tale a little boat transports the hero away to another kingdom. Propp recognized in these examples that, while the incidental means of conveyance changed for the several heroes, their base actions remained a constant. Observing such

[7] See Floyd H. Allport, *Theories of Perception and the Concept of Structure* (New York: John Wiley, 1955), pp. 112–15.

[8] Rose A. Zimbardo, 'The Formalism of *Henry V*', in *Shakespeare Encomium, 1564–1964*, ed. by Anne Paolucci (New York: City College, 1964), 16–24 (p. 16). Compare Terry Hands, director of the RSC's honoured 1975 production starring Alan Howard: '*Henry V* is a remarkably structured play [. . .] a superbly balanced allegory' (in *The Royal Shakespeare Company's Production of 'Henry V' for the Centenary Season at The Royal Shakespeare Theatre*, ed. by Sally Beauman (Oxford: Pergamon Press, 1976), p. 26); and Herschel Baker: 'it is built of massive, block-like episodes, each with its own curve of action that contributes to the whole' (*The Riverside Shakespeare*, Introduction, p. 934).

[9] Moody Prior, *The Drama of Power: Studies in Shakespeare's History Plays* (Evanston, IL: Northwestern University Press, 1973), p. 339.

[10] Vladimir Propp, *Morphology of the Folktale*, 2nd edn, rev. and ed. by Louis A. Wagner with an introduction by Alan Dundes (Austin, Texas: University of Texas Press for the American Folklore Society, 1968); Vladimir Propp, 'Structure and History in the Study of Folktales (A Reply to Lévi-Strauss)', *Russian Literature*, 12 (1982), 11–32. The latter citation is the translation of an essay accompany-ing Propp's *Morfologia della Fiaba*, ed. by Gianluigi Bravo (Torino: Einavdi, 1966).

stable elements to constitute the fundamental components of the tale, he applied to them the term *function* (a character's action significant for the course of the narrative). Propp found, moreover, that the total number of functions derived from all of the tales was not infinite, but finite (only thirty-one), and that all functions universally occurred in strictly chronological, linear-sequential order. All thirty-one of them were not present in every tale of course, and one or more might perhaps be absent from a particular series (e.g., 4–5–7–8), but without exception there was no deviation in any tale from the irreversible, linear-sequential ordering. Unlike motifs, then, which occur randomly throughout a folkloristic text, functions are simultaneously units of structure and content which occur only in an invariate, syntagmatic — concatenated — order.

When Propp made this striking discovery, he believed modestly that he had revealed the morphological laws governing but one special class of Russian folktale — the 'magical folktale', or fairy tale, which today is subsumed under Aarne-Thompson tale types 300–749.[11] However, numerous investigators have since established convincingly the cross-cultural validity of Propp's model by implying it to a wide variety of narratives: namely, other bodies of folktale,[12] ancient Greek romances,[13] the Biblical adventure of Jacob,[14] and even the screenplay for Alfred Hitchcock's *North by Northwest*.[15] Alan Dundes intimates a relationship to epic structure, finding a distinct similarity between a nine-part sequence of Propp's functions and the last portion of the *Odyssey*.[16] Together, these studies show clearly that Propp's structural model pertains not exclusively to folktales but the gamut of folk narrative (and to some other types besides) from the slightest to the most serious, myth.

Propp himself has recently observed that certain classical myths — those of the Argonauts, of Perseus and Andromeda, of Theseus, and various others — are constructed according to the same morphological system as the folktale.[17] But this latter revelation only provides redundant confirmation for folklorists, who today universally agree that there are absolutely no

---

[11] 'Magical folktale' literally translates Propp's *volsebnaja skazka* and is the English form used by the 'Structure' essay in 1982; Lewis A. Wagner, reviser in 1968 of the first English translation of the *Morphology*, indicates his re-translation of the term as 'fairy tale' (Preface p. ix). Interestingly, Propp discloses that the Russian publisher of the *Morphology* in 1928 suppressed the delimiting word *magical* in the title, falsifying the author's intention in order to make the work appear to have wider interest ('Structure', p. 15).

[12] See Alan Dundes, *The Morphology of North American Indian Folktales* (Helsinki: Suomalainen Tiedeakatemia, 1964); Claude Brémond, 'Morphology of the French Folktale', *Semiotica*, 2 (1970), 247–76.

[13] Consuelo Ruiz-Montero, 'The Structural Pattern of the Ancient Greek Romances and the *Morphology of the Folktale* of V. Propp', *Fabula*, 22 (1981), 228–38.

[14] Roland Barthes, 'The Struggle with the Angel: Textual Analysis of Genesis 32.23–33', in *Structural Analysis and Biblical Exegesis: Interpretational Essays*, trans. by A. M. Johnson, Jr., Pittsburgh Theological Series, 3 (French edition 1971; Pittsburgh, PA: Pickwick Publications, 1974), pp. 21–33.

[15] Peter Wollen, '*North By Northwest*: A Morphological Analysis', in *Readings and Writings: Semiotic Counter-Strategies* (London: Verso Editions/New Left Books, 1982), p. 18–33.

[16] Dundes, 'Introduction to the Second Edition', *Morphology of the Folktale*, p. xiv.

[17] Propp, 'Structure', pp. 28–29.

structural or generic differences between myth and folktale.[18] Indeed, two leading students of the subject declare that myth is finally distinguishable from folktale and other traditional tales only by its serious purport.[19] Myth deals earnestly with 'origins and destinies', offering a society 'its pedagogic images of the nature and destiny of man'.[20] That the epic struggle involving national destinies confers upon *Henry V* the requisite seriousness of myth is unarguable; that the play conforms totally both to the content and formal paradigm of myth will be substantiated shortly. Furthermore, it is well to bear in mind about the ensuing analysis of *Henry V* as folk narrative, that this instance of Shakespeare's absorption in a story having folkloristic qualities is not unique. The plots of *The Taming of the Shrew*, *The Merchant of Venice*, *Macbeth*, *King Lear*, and *Cymbeline* have all been shown to have folktales either as analogues or sources.[21] This affinity with the very ground bass of the storyteller's art only corroborates what we doubtless knew all along, that Shakespeare is the quintessential universal dramatic poet.

As noted earlier, there are a total of thirty-one consecutive functions or points of narrative action in Propp's model. Of these, the following dozen, numbers eight to nineteen,[22] can be paired with reciprocal, similarly chronological events in *Henry V*:

'No. 8a. *ONE MEMBER OF A FAMILY LACKS SOMETHING OR DESIRES TO HAVE SOMETHING. [. . .] (2) Rationalized form: money, the means of existence, etc.*'
We learn at the outset that King Henry wishes to regain his lost birthright in France: 'his true titles to some certain dukedoms, | And generally to the crown and seat of France, | Deriv'd from Edward, his great-grandfather' (I.1.87–89).

'No. 9. *MISFORTUNE OR LACK IS MADE KNOWN; THE HERO IS APPROACHED WITH A REQUEST OR COMMAND; HE IS ALLOWED TO GO OR HE IS DISPATCHED. [. . .] (2) The hero is dispatched directly.*'

---

[18] See, regarding structural co-identity, Alan Dundes, *North American Indian Folktales*: 'morphologically speaking, myths and folktales are one and the same' (p. 110); Vladimir Propp, 'Structure', p. 28; E. Meletinsky and others, 'Problems of the Structural Analysis of Fairytales', in *Soviet Structural Folkloristics*, ed. by P. Maranda, Approaches to Semiotics Series, 42 (The Hague: Mouton: 1974—), I, 73–149 (pp. 74–75). With respect to generic co-identity, see Susan Reid, 'Myth as Metastructure of the Fairytale', in *Soviet Structural Folkloristics*, I, 151–72 (p. 168).

[19] G. S. Kirk, *Myth: Its Meaning and Functions in Ancient and Other Cultures* (Cambridge: Cambridge University Press, 1970), p. 40; William Righter, *Myth and Literature* (London: Routledge, 1975), p. 6.

[20] René Wellek and Austin Warren, *Theory of Literature*, 3rd edn (New York: Harcourt, Harvest book, 1956), p. 191.

[21] See Alan Dundes, ' "To Love My Father All": A Psychoanalytical Study of the Folktale Source of *King Lear*', in *Interpreting Folklore* (Bloomington, IN: Indiana University Press, 1980), pp. 211–22 (pp. 212–13); Anthony Landon, '*Macbeth* and the Folktale "The Fisher [sic] and His Wife" ', in *Proceedings From the Second Nordic Conference for English Studies*, ed. by H. Ringborn and M. Rissanen (Åbo, Finland: Åbo Akademi, 1984), pp. 423–35. Riddles, another folk form, figure importantly in *AWW*, *MV*, *Per.*, and *Cym.* (Phyllis Gorfain, 'Riddles and Reconciliation: Formal Unity in *All's Well That Ends Well*', *Journal of the Folklore Institute*, 13 (1976), 263–81 (p. 273).

[22] *Morphology*, pp. 35–55.

Gathering England's ranking churchmen and nobles in his presence chamber (1.2), Henry seeks moral allowance to attain his *lack*. To his inquiry: 'May I with right and conscience make this claim?', Canterbury directly urges the king to 'stand for your own, unwind your bloody flag' (ll. 96, 101). Ely, Exeter, and Westmoreland add their forceful assent (ll. 115–29).

'No. 10. *THE SEEKER AGREES TO OR DECIDES UPON COUNTERACTION.*'
Henry decides to counteract France:

> Now are we well resolv'd, and by God's help
> And yours, the noble sinews of our power,
> France being ours, we'll bend it to our awe,
> Or break it all to pieces.
>
> (1.2.222–25)

'No. 11. *THE HERO LEAVES HOME.*'
The king sets forth: 'I am coming on [. . .] to put forth | My rightful hand in well-hallow'd cause. [. . .] For we have now no thought in us but France' (1.2.291–93, 302); from London he proceeds directly to Southampton (11. Chorus 34–35).

'No. 12. *THE HERO IS TESTED, INTERROGATED, ATTACKED, ETC., WHICH PREPARES THE WAY FOR HIS RECEIVING EITHER A MAGICAL AGENT OR HELPER. [. . .] (8) A hostile creature attempts to destroy the hero.*'
Henry learns that France, future donor of the goal he seeks, has suborned the treachery of his countrymen, Cambridge, Scroop, and Grey (11.2.6–7). One of these would-be assailants, Lord Scroop, is even a bosom friend and court favourite (ll. 8–9).

'No. 13. *THE HERO REACTS TO THE ACTIONS OF THE FUTURE DONOR. [. . .] (4) He frees a captive. [. . .] (8) The hero saves himself from an attempt on his life by employing the same tactics used by his adversary.*'
In sly response to the French-leagued conspirators before him, Henry adopts their cunning to expose them. When he orders a prisoner freed ('Enlarge the man committed yesterday, | That rail'd against our person. [. . .] we pardon him' (11.2.40–41, 43)), the king's false friends argue for strict justice rather than enfranchisement. To their surprise, Henry accords them the capital punishment they had urged as the prisoner's due (ll. 177–78).

'No. 14. *THE HERO ACQUIRES THE USE OF A MAGICAL AGENT. [. . .] The forms by which [such agents] are transmitted are the following: [. . .] (2) The agent is pointed out. [. . .] (9) Various characters place themselves at the disposal of the hero.*'
Henry ascribes his protection to a supernatural agent: 'God so graciously hath brought to light | This dangerous treason. [. . .] We doubt not now | But every rub is smoothed on our way' (11.2.185–88). With a flourish of

trumpets, Henry's supporters join him on his expedition: 'Then forth, dear countrymen! [. . .] Cheerly to sea! The signs of war advance! | No king of England, if not king of France!' (II. 2. 189, 192–93).

'No. 15. *THE HERO IS TRANSFERRED, DELIVERED, OR LED TO THE WHEREABOUTS OF AN OBJECT OF SEARCH. [. . .] Generally the object of search is located in "another" or "different" kingdom. [. . .] (2) He travels on the ground or on water [. . .] on board a ship.'*
The Chorus asks us to 'suppose that you have seen | The well-appointed king at [Hampton] pier | Embark his royalty', and afterward to 'behold this fleet majestical, | Holding due course to Harflew' (III. Chorus 3–5, 14–17).

'No. 16. *THE HERO AND THE VILLAIN JOIN IN DIRECT COMBAT. [. . .] [There are two forms, distinguished by their results. If the hero gains the means for further searching from this unfriendly encounter, that is one.] If, on the other hand, the hero receives through victory the very object of his quest, we have [the following situations:] [. . .] (1) They fight in an open field.'*
Shakespeare uses both alternative forms of this narrative element in succession. The first combat at Harfleur ends successfully with the Governor's capitulation to King Henry's siege (III. 1–3). Winning Harfleur permits the hero's further striving toward his main goal, achieved through victorious battle in an *open field* near Agincourt (IV. 3–4).

'No. 17. *THE HERO IS BRANDED. [. . .] The hero receives a wound during the skirmish.'*
Though not actually wounded, the king is so affronted by the enemy's cowardly slaughter of the noncombatant luggage boys that the atrocity is tantamount to personal injury: 'I was not angry since I came to France | Until this instant. [. . .] They [Frenchmen at a distance] do offend our sight' (IV. 7. 55–56, 59). Also, moments before, Henry had been touched to the point of tears upon hearing that two brave countrymen were battle casualties (IV. 6. 33–34).

'No. 18. *THE VILLAIN IS DEFEATED. [. . .] (1) The villain is beaten in open combat.'*
The French Herald arrives to inform the king of the English victory: 'The day is yours' (IV. 7. 86).

'No. 19. *THE INITIAL MISFORTUNE OR LACK IS LIQUIDATED. [. . .] The narrative reaches its peak in this function. [. . .] (4) The object of a quest is obtained as the direct result of preceding actions. [. . .] [For example,] the princess is neither seized nor abducted, but she is nevertheless "obtained." She is obtained as the result of combat.'*
Henry obtains the hand of Princess Katharine as a direct result of the victorious battle. The French king bids him 'take her, fair son, [. . .] that the contending kingdoms | Of France and England [. . .] May cease their hatred' (V. 2. 348–52).

The foregoing demonstration goes far to account for potentialities latent in the Henry the Fifth story which urged Shakespeare to attempt a unique presentation dramaturgy for his play. There was of course the need to impress most forcefully upon his audience that this English heroic-epic story, whose prestige even 'The name of Agincourt' calls up (IV. Chorus 52), remains an undying example for the public good. But it is also very likely that the dramatist intuited in his source-narrative what has just been empirically confirmed: that the 'form-quality' of the story is identical with the structure of myth. Form-quality, say Gestalt psychologists, is what enables a listener to identify a melody even if it is transposed into different keys, or performed with different instrumental or vocal timbres or different harmonization, or even if the relative duration of its tones are lengthened or shortened.[23] We may infer that Shakespeare ideated the pattern because, in taking up the diffuse historical particulars in Holinshed, he concentrated and focused events to make the entire story reflect even more acutely the grammar of mythic narrative.

III

Catalyst for the playwright's metadramatic plan for *Henry V*, and thus a major constituent of the play's integral form, content, and meaning, is the Chorus. Differentiated by his non-character status from the other players and visually set apart from them, the Chorus assumes an unusual degree of prominence throughout the play, addressing the audience directly on a half-dozen strategic occasions which include the key framing moments of the Prologue and Epilogue. He is, moreover, separated from the others in time as well as space: allusions to Robert Devereaux the Queen's favourite and to stagings of the Henry VI plays (V. Chorus 29–34; Epilogue 13) pointedly establish him as a contemporary of the audience rather than of the medieval play-world. In modern productions, visual signs in costume such as a scarf, a turtleneck sweater, or a business suit convey this status. Not an author-figure who steps fictionally into the present, like the fourteenth-century poet John Gower in *Pericles*, this Chorus operates on the same plane of reality as the audience. He is our mediating agency to the story, its champion and interpreter. Not incidentally, the interplay with spectators breaks the dramatic illusion, accentuating the fact that we are watching a play. As with the Brechtian alienation effect, we are distanced from the theatrical action in order to be made more intellectually involved in it. One sure consequence is that the play's overall impact is remarkably enhanced.

---

[23] See Max Wertheimer, 'Gestalt Theory', in Willis D. Ellis, *A Source Book of Gestalt Psychology* (1938; repr. New York: Humanities Press, 1950), pp. 1–11 (pp. 4–5).

But another important effect is the instrumental, functional contribution the Chorus makes to the form of *Henry V* — a contribution uniquely serviceable for this play and unsuitable for any other by the playwright. Commentators have long noted the qualitative individuality of this play, wherein events are not merely depicted but in a real sense celebrated. Dover Wilson observes that the Chorus's reiterated appeal to the audience is 'comparable [. . .] to that of a priest leading his congregation into prayer or celebration'.[24] To Herbert Lindenberger, *Henry V* is 'a different kind of play' for Shakespeare because 'it depends on its ability to establish a communal experience with its audience'; it is 'ceremonial drama'.[25] In the following pages it will emerge that what these critics rightly identify as the distinguishing quality of *Henry V*, but use other words to describe, is rituality.

I use the terms rituality and ritualistic advisedly, for there is no intention to dub the work a thoroughgoing 'ritual play'; it is fully a drama, and a very popular and stageworthy one at that. Ritual, moreover, is known to be an elusive critical term, and students of the drama are justly mindful of the obligation to use it with due care. This is because of its history of being either too loosely applied to virtually any formal or ceremonial circumstance in the theatre, or misapplied, in the case of the so-called Cambridge school of criticism and its now discredited argument that myth originated in ritual. But rituality can have pertinence for literary criticism, provided we bear in mind its social functions. As Richard F. Hardin puts it: 'Rites cannot exist in an aesthetic or formalist vacuum; they require the context of community.'[26] Response to *Henry V* being so thoroughly conditioned by the communal, interactant experience of audience and Chorus, there results in performance a blurring of the line dividing secular rite from drama. To my mind, Shakespeare was pressed to meld rituality and mimesis in this play above all because the venerable folk status of the narrative — an important communal subject latently enframed in the stereotypic pattern of myth — begged for a special technique of defamiliarization: a Chorus, to throw the quotation marks of reality around the illusion of theatre, so to speak.

Ritual and theatre remain mutually exclusive categories of performance. And yet, as Richard Schechner has shown, despite their opposition both lie in dialectical relation to one another on a continuum: 'Whether one calls a specific performance ritual or theatre depends on the degree to which the performance tends toward efficacy or entertainment. No performance is pure efficacy or pure entertainment.'[27] To portray graphically the binary

[24] *King Henry V*, ed. by John Dover Wilson (Cambridge: Cambridge University Press, 1947), Introduction, p. xv.
[25] Herbert Lindenberger, *Historical Drama: The Relation of Literature and Reality* (Chicago: University of Chicago Press, 1975), p. 79.
[26] Richard F. Hardin, '"Ritual" in Recent Criticism: The Elusive Sense of Community', *PMLA*, 98 (1983), 846–62 (p. 847).
[27] Richard Schechner, 'From Ritual to Theatre and Back', in *Ritual, Play, and Performance*, ed. by Richard Schechner and Mady Schuman (New York: Seabury Press, 1976), pp. 196–222 (p. 207).

nature of ritual and theatre, Schechner lists their antithetical characteristics in facing columns. The table is presented here, as it affords an economical means of analysing their complementarity in *Henry V*:

EFFICACY ⟵⟶ ENTERTAINMENT	
(Ritual)	(Theatre)
results	fun
link to an absent Other	only for those here
abolishes time, symbolic time	emphasizes now
brings Other here	audience in the Other
audience participates	audience appreciates
criticism is forbidden	criticism is encouraged
collective creativity	individual creativity

(p. 207)[28]

It goes without saying that a performance of *Henry V* or any Shakespearean play is *fun*, a theatrical experience to be enjoyed for its own sake. None the less, for no other play does the dramatist push for ideological *results*, as when the Chorus inclines the audience to heed the example of 'this star of England' who, with compatriots of 'mighty men', achieved 'the world's best garden' (Epilogue 3–7). Ritual aspires to precisely this tradition-celebrating role: to revivify a group's sense of cultural unity and continuity by periodically recalling 'glorious souvenirs which are made to live again before their eyes'.[29]

Unlike ritual, theatre in its purest form exists *only for those here* in attendance; it involves the pretence that the performance is being enacted for the first time, without implications beyond the dramatic context. Ritual, however, intends a direct *link to an absent Other* — that Other being for generations of spectators of *Henry V* the emblematic memory of Agincourt, a true story of ancestors in 'the full course of their glory' (Epilogue 4) brought to a jubilant conclusion ordained by providence ('O God, thy arm was here' (IV. 8. 106)). The Chorus forges that link to the 'Other' in the play's opening moments, when he invokes a Muse that might transcend the pale illusion of theatre and recall to very flesh and blood the symbol of that time, 'warlike Harry, like himself' (Prologue 5).

Theatre *emphasizes now*; an audience at a dramatic entertainment suspends disbelief and pretends simultaneity with the fictional events enacted before it at any instant. But ritual *abolishes time*, the artificial construct it is in the

---

[28] Although the table is Schechner's, the definitional commentary is entirely my own. One pairing ('performer possessed, in trance' vs. 'performer knows what he's doing') is inappropriate to our analysis, and omitted.

[29] Emile Durkheim, *The Elementary Forms of the Religious Life*, trans. by J. W. Swain (1915; reprinted New York: Free Press, 1968), p. 420.

theatre, and substitutes a nontemporal perspective which contains the historical past but imbues it with relevancies of the present and future. This element of rituality is supplied in *Henry V* chiefly by the Chorus, whose every appearance breaks the dramatic illusion as he solicits our contemporary viewpoint. But a more incisive example of symbolic timelessness occurs on the day of the battle, when the king gathers his men about him to instill confidence at a moment of crisis. At one and the same instant, the actor impersonating Henry represents both the historical personage speaking the words in 1415 and the latest in an infinite succession of commemorators of this moment:

> This story shall the good man teach his son;
> And Crispin Crispian shall ne'er go by,
> From this day to the ending of the world,
> But we in it shall be remembered —
>
> (IV. 3. 56)

We in the audience are involved at this self-commentative juncture, a point where the theatrical illusion is very nearly broken, in our awareness that the king's prophecy fulfils itself now and forever in the timeless present. Seeing Henry's predicted future commemoration of Agincourt occur before our eyes fuses past and present, amplifying the national myth's communal significance. The aura of secular ritual intensifies further and the king foresees such memorializations becoming a calendrical rite each year on St Crispin's day (l. 45), when the present heightened sense of community ('we happy few, we band of brothers' (l. 60)) will be reaffirmed — as of course effectually it is with every performance of the play 'from this day to the ending of the world'. This moment, together with the Chorus's intrusions into depicted history in order to guide our perceptions in real time, are strategies that dissolve space and time to bring us into closer empathy and with the once and future meaning of 'this great accompt'.

Theatrical performance locates the *audience in the Other*. That is, insofar as the power of verisimilitude enables it, theatre urges the audience to identify vicariously with the onstage characters as if they were real persons in actual situations. Ritual, however, *brings the Other here*; the Chorus in *Henry V*, so far from easing the spectator's submission to mimetic illusion, instead calls attention to the theatre's imperfect attempts at make-believe which afford only pitiful 'mock'ries' of 'true things' (IV. Chorus 53). In this distinctly anti-illusionistic capacity, the Chorus functions as an agent in behalf of the 'Other' — the Agincourt story with its already subsistent form-quality and popular reputation — which, with our cooperation, he would redirect to us for purposes of demonstration ('force a play [. . .] eche out our performance with your mind' (II. Chorus 32; III. Chorus 35)). This strategy of effecting our virtual presence at the represented events coincides with Margaret Mead's definition of ritual itself as 'the repetition of those symbols which evoke the feeling of that primordial event which initially called the community into being with such power that it effects our presence in that event — in other words, represents the primordial event'.[30]

At theatrical entertainments the *audience watches* in rapt but passive attention the mimesis of life being simulated before it, as the performers meanwhile feign obliviousness to the presence of an audience. For ritual, however, at the invitation of an agent-officiator who addresses it directly, the *audience participates* in what is a celebratory event for the community. It is noteworthy, then, that the Chorus does not merely present *Henry V* to spectators but instead entreats them repeatedly to activate 'your imaginary forces' (I. Chorus 18) to help create the play and compensate for theatrical defects: 'Piece out our imperfections [. . .]. For 'tis your thoughts that now must deck our kings, | Carry them here and there' (ll. 23, 28–29). So prominent are these appeals that Dover Wilson was moved to set their frequency at 'no less than twenty-five times' (p. xv). The imperative mood is the recurrent technique for inducing the audience's symbolic participation, and nowhere is it as obvious as the seventeen instances used to effect our mental voyage with Harry of Monmouth across the Channel to Harfleur ('Suppose [. . .] behold [. . .] Hear [. . .] think [. . .] Follow, Follow!' etc. (III. Chorus)).

In the theatre, an *audience appreciates* emotionally and cognitively the various fictional conflicts represented onstage, without betraying its own true feelings or values. An audience constructively 'suspends its disbelief' for the duration of the performance. The nature of religious or secular ritual, however, is to have social efficacy; the *audience believes* its ideological content. That Shakespeare would transform his audience for *Henry V* from indifferent onlookers to partisan believers is consistent with the aims of heroic poetry generally, which Philip Sidney had argued 'doth not only teach and move to a truth, but teacheth and moveth to the most high and excellent truth' (p. 119). We might therefore expect the Chorus to warrant belief in the historicity of the Agincourt story ('this great accompt' of 'true things' (I. Chorus 17; IV. Chorus 53)) metadramatically, from 'without' the play. But another aspect of rituality is displayed in the way the audience is moved to link its own identity and allegiance with those of the protagonist. Ritual can effect cultural change by defining the participant's social identity: 'Ritual warrants our belief, and belief is usually concerned with questions of identity. [. . .] All real learning entails modification of behavior; all modification of behavior entails altered identity.'[31] Thus when the Chorus zealously bids the audience accompany Henry's expedition to France ('Follow, [. . .] And leave *your* England' (III. Chorus 17, 19; my emphasis)), subtly but

[30] Margaret Mead, *Twentieth Century Faith: Hope and Survival* (New York: Harper, 1972), p. 127, quoted by Richard F. Hardin, p. 851. Compare Walter Burkert: 'ritual is stereotyped action redirected for demonstration' (*Structure and History in Greek Mythology and Ritual* (Berkeley: University of California Press, 1979), p. 57).
[31] Langdon Elsbree, *The Rituals of Life: Patterns in Narratives* (Port Washington, NY: Kennikat Press, 1982), p. 9.

efficaciously he modulates the audience's identity from one of neutral observer to that of partisan of the English cause. Virtual identification of the audience with the onstage community is also achieved on the occasion, discussed earlier, of Henry's near-sacramental speech before the battle:

> We few, we happy few, we band of brothers;
> For he to-day that sheds his blood with me
> Shall be my brother.

(IV. 3. 60)

The type of communal bond the king now attains with his followers and with the audience as well, for the dramatic illusion nears the breaking point here, is what Victor Turner describes as the condition of *communitas*, an antistructural state produced by ritual whereby social barriers — differences of rank, social structure, or economic status — are removed and superseded by communal unity.[32]

In the theatre *criticism is encouraged*; an audience becomes involved in the performance's discursive flow of ideas and constantly brings its judgements to bear on the action. *Henry V*, being the theatrical work that it is, consists almost wholly of situations that invite critique. Two examples are Henry's amicable disagreement with Bates and Williams, and Pistol's self-serving capture of the French soldier for ransom (IV. 1. 4). But in the case of ritual, *criticism is forbidden*. 'Ritual discourages inquiry', declares a recent study, 'not only because it presents its material authoritatively, as axiomatic. It is itself a message stated in a form to render it unverifiable, separate from standards of truth and falsity. [. . .] Symbols used in ritual are presentational rather than discursive.'[33] It would seem, therefore, that Shakespeare's use of the Chorus as a presentational technique is only incidentally the equivalent of a bard or scop imparting the famous story of Henry V in the manner of oral epic. Rather more basic is how the Chorus inspires credence of the play, thus performing the authenticating, certifying functions of ritual: 'Ritual certifies that something is being done correctly, appropriately, efficaciously. Thus it also certifies the doer, the actor, the agent: he or she, self or other, has the particular power or status, is a believable model, can be recognized as an authority.'[34] Mediation of the Agincourt story through the Chorus forestalls criticism and promotes its social validation ('Admit me Chorus to this history'; 'sit and see, | Minding true things by what their mock'ries be' (I. Chorus 32; IV. Chorus 52–53).

---

[32] Victor Turner, *Dramas, Fields, and Metaphors: Symbolic Action in Human Society* (Ithaca, NY: Cornell University Press, 1974), pp. 45–47. For an analysis of *communitas* as one thematic key to the total pattern of scendes in *Henry V*, see my companion essay on structure, 'Thematic Contraries and the Dramaturgy of *Henry V*', *SQ*, 31 (1980), 343–56.

[33] Sally F. Moore and Barbara G. Myerhoff, 'Secular Ritual: Forms and Meanings', in *Secular Ritual*, ed. by Sally F. Moore and Barbara G. Myerhoff (Assen, The Netherlands: Van Gorcum, 1977), pp. 3–24 (p. 18).

[34] Elsbree, p. 9.

Our last contrast between rituality and theatricality is one that is easily discerned in the play. Theatre is the result of *individual creativity* on the part of the dramatist in collaboration with the actors. And normally, an author is pleased to accept responsibility and credit for the product of his invention. Ritual, we have noted, is an act of *collective creativity*, with the audience co-participating with an agent to achieve a socially purposeful result. *Henry V* is remarkable in the degree to which that authorial spokesman, the Chorus, inclines the play toward the ritual mode by stressing the audience's creative responsibility rather than the dramatist's. This strategy emerges at the inception, with the Prologue's belittlement of the author's chosen medium, the theatre ('this unworthy scaffold', 'this cockpit', 'this wooden O' (Prologue 10–13)). It is advanced thereafter by persistent calls for the spectator's imaginative participation to make the play work at all ('Play with your fancies', 'Grapple your minds', 'Work, work your thoughts [. . .] see' (III. Chorus 7, 18, 25)). Finally, in his Epilogue the playwright deprecates the role of his own creativity, while emphasizing deference to its source ('with rough and all-unable pen, | Our bending author has pursu'd the story' (Epilogue 1–2)). This gesture of self-effacement underscores the independence of the story as a folk object of lasting value to its inheritors. With each successive performance of the play, then, Chorus and audience interact in a collective ceremony that ritualizes, perpetuates, certifies Henry the Fifth as the cynosure of the nation's mythic past ('but in that small [time] most greatly lived | This star of England' (Epilogue 5–6)).

As stated earlier, all of the foregoing proofs of rituality taken together do not establish *Henry V* as an unqualified ritual play. And yet, while it remains a representational drama, the very obviousness and strategic placement in it of the agreed formal properties of ritual show unmistakably that it is the one Shakespearean work most fully under the aegis of rituality. We may surmise why the dramatist took what is ultimately a ritualistic approach to his play. The fact that the history of King Henry's 'exploits and mighty enterprise' was already fixed in the popular mind as the leading totemic document of British solidarity accounts somewhat for the need to innovate: to 'redirect' to the audience in a heightened fashion this vital yet almost too familiar subject. Another consideration was doubtless the story's clear affinities with the literary epic tradition. If the treatment of England's great hero were to compare in terms of artistic energy with depictions of Aeneas, Cyrus, Rinaldo, and the other champions of yore, then a 'Muse of fire' of sorts was required: some type of inventive stylization that would engage the audience more powerfully from a fresh, quasi-improvisational perspective.

Finally, as this essay sets forth, there is yet another probable basis for rituality in the play. It lies in the fact that the Agincourt story, long admired in its Shakespearean version for its organic perfection of form, is now known to replicate exactly the universal paradigm of folk myth. 'Our bending author' not only pursued the story but was manifestly attuned to its deep-structural harmonies in shaping his own narrative scheme. It was a found structure that ideally carried out the programmatic aims of myth as a cultural model or charter, for the determinate nature of its form mirrors what the play assumes to be the divinely intercessory, certain teleology of England in history ('Take it, God, | For it is none but thine!'; 'God fought for us. | [. . .] he did us great good' (IV.8.111–12; 120–21)). For reasons not likely fathomed by the playwright, the Agincourt narrative must have seemed in its totality a greater intensifying and universalizing vehicle than it did as the sum of its parts. Aware of its underlay of myth structure, we can appreciate why Shakespeare viewed this chronicle as virtually a self-dramatizing, autonomous thing-in-itself ('so great an object' (Prologue 11)), one whose treatment uniquely demanded the use of rituality.

'In Everything Illegitimate': Imagining the Bastard in Renaissance Drama[1]

MICHAEL NEILL

University of Auckland

In Conan Doyle's story 'The Adventure of the Priory School' Holdernesse Hall, the country seat of that stately patriarch the Duke of Holdernesse, is threatened by a peculiar revenant. Mr James Wilder is to all appearances a modern young man who occupies the mundane post of secretary to the Duke, but he is actually a sinister intruder from the past, whose family tree reaches back, through nineteenth-century melodrama and gothic fiction, to the bastard-figures of Jacobean tragedy.[2] An illegitimate son of the Duke, Wilder is a vindictive misfit, bent, like Edmund in *King Lear* or Spurio in *The Revenger's Tragedy*, on the displacement of the half-brother whose legitimacy he so bitterly resents. By comparison with his seventeenth-century kin he may appear somewhat colourless: unlike Spurio he does not actually seek to cuckold his father, but is content to sow a fatal discord in his marriage; his conspiracy against the legitimate sibling is limited to kidnapping and blackmail, and the story's only murder is an almost accidental consequence of his accomplice's attempt to avoid pursuit. Nevertheless, this bastard's identity as a dangerous social outsider, an incarnation of the disruptive anti-social energies associated with his begetting, is signified by his name, Wilder.[3] It marks him, evidently, as the symbolic denizen of that realm of unredeemed nature, the moor on which Holmes and Watson follow the tracks of his crime. Their task is made more difficult by the fact that Wilder has shod the horses of his kidnap vehicle with shoes 'shaped below with a cloven foot of iron' — supposed relics of the 'marauding Barons of Holdernesse in the middle ages'.[4] As well as equipping the villain with suitably gothic credentials and stamping him with the cloven-footed mark of the

[1] Originally written as a short paper for the Fifth International Shakespeare Congress in Tokyo (August 1991), this paper has also been presented in various forms to departmental seminars in the English and History departments at the University of Auckland, and the English Department at the University of Singapore. I am grateful to all of those who took part in those sessions, and in particular to Coppélia Kahn, Jonathan Lamb, Naomi Liebler, Carol Neely, Patricia Parker, and Kirpal Singh, for their invaluable comments and suggestions.

[2] Among his intermediate ancestors is the fratricidal (and apparently matricidal) 'monster', Robert Wringhim, the hero of James Hogg's *The Private Memoirs and Confessions of a Justified Sinner*, whose alleged bastardy is an important factor in his complex psychological motivation.

[3] For a suggestion that the identification of the 'natural child' with unredeemed nature derived from the practice of abandoning bastard children in the wilderness to survive, see Alison Finlay, 'The World so Swarms with Bastards Now: The Bastard in Elizabethan, Jacobean and Caroline Drama' (unpublished doctoral thesis, University of Birmingham, 1988).

[4] Arthur Conan Doyle, *The Complete Sherlock Holmes* (New York: Doubleday, n.d.), p. 558.

diabolic, these shoes, which are designed to 'counterfeit [...] the tracks of cows' reveal in him the passion for fraudulent substitution which sixteenth- and seventeenth-century dramatists identified as natural to his spurious kind. Their mysterious tracks, indeed, are nothing less than the spoor of Wilder's ancestry.

The reappearance of an identifiable theatrical type in so unexpected a context is a testimony to the imaginative power and persistence of the bastard figure as Renaissance dramatists created him.[5] Yet the genealogy of the literary bastard remains curiously obscure. More than ten years ago Peter Laslett lamented the lack of a proper cultural history of bastardy including its literary manifestations.[6] Despite a small flurry of recent interest in Elizabethan and Jacobean literary bastards, that history remains to be written — this paper is a preliminary essay towards such a history.[7]

'Why bastard? Wherefore base? [...] Why brand they us | With base? With baseness? bastardy? base, base?' What exactly did it mean to be branded a bastard in Edmund's world? A useful way to begin answering his questions might be with the outrage of a legitimate son. Returning from Paris, as Hamlet had returned from Wittenberg, on the news of his father's death, the enraged Laertes bursts into the court seeking revenge from Claudius; Gertrude, exactly as she has done with Hamlet in the first court scene, restrains him with an appeal for calm. Laertes's answering assertion of his natural right to grief is cast in language so hyperbolic that it would seem a mere extravagance if it did not exactly echo the terms of Hamlet's anguish:

> That drop of blood that's calm proclaims me bastard,
> Cries cuckold to my father, brands the harlot
> Even here between the chaste unsmirched brow
> Of my true mother.   (IV. 5. 118)

These words, with their striking paraphrase of the closet scene,[8] might be Hamlet's own. Indeed they serve as a reminder of the shocking possibility that lies, only half-articulated, beneath Hamlet's reaction to Claudius's magnanimous assumption of paternity: 'a little more than kin, and less than kind' (I. 2. 65). For if his aunt-mother is the whore that her precipitate

---

[5] The persistence of the type may even have something to do with the peculiar invective connotations of 'bastard' in modern English, where (in contrast to other European languages) the term is used to impugn the moral character of a man rather than to slight the honour of his family; more significantly, it can also be used to express a grudging admiration of exactly the sort invited by Elizabethan stage bastards.

[6] *Bastardy and its Comparative History*, ed. by Peter Laslett, Karla Oosterveen, and Richard M. Smith (Cambridge MA: Harvard University Press, 1980), pp. 4–5.

[7] The most comprehensive treatment of the topic is Alison Findlay's thesis (see note 2 above), which in turn acknowledges a debt to Leah Scragg, 'The Bastard in Elizabethan and Jacobean Drama', (unpublished master's thesis, University of Liverpool, 1964). In addition there are a number of papers, so far unpublished, which were contributed to the seminar on 'Shakespeare's Bastards' chaired by Mary Ann McGrail at the 1988 Shakespeare Association of America meeting in Vancouver.

[8] See III. 4. 40–44. 'Such an act | That [...] takes off the rose | From the fair forehead of an innocent love | And sets a blister there.' All citations from Shakespeare are to the Riverside edition, ed. G. Blakemore Evans (Boston: Houghton Mifflin, 1974).

marriage seems to make her, what guarantee remains of Hamlet's 'true' paternity?[9] It was, of course, the painful lot of that 'uncertain man' the bastard to be 'a little more than kin' — yet less than kind since he typically expressed the unnaturalness of his begetting by the monstrous unkindness of his nature. 'Wise men know well enough what monsters you make of them', Hamlet tells Ophelia (III. 1. 138–39); and the corollary of that horned monster, the cuckold, is that anomaly in nature, the mixed thing called a bastard.

Detached from legitimate sequence, and symbolically bastardized by an uncle-fathering whose illegitimate rule requires him to repudiate all the duties that 'nature' demands on behalf of his 'true' father, Hamlet (far more absolutely than Laertes) makes revenge a matter of legitimation — of proving himself Old Hamlet's 'true' and 'natural' son. Yet it is a proof that (as Freudian critics, approaching the matter from a slightly different angle, have observed), involves him in the profoundly unnatural act of killing the man who substitutes for (and might even be) his actual father. Hamlet's way of coping with this paradox is suitably paradoxical: like Prince Hal, another royal heir to regicide, coping with the perplexities of 'legitimate' inheritance in a usurper's court, he chooses, in effect, to play the part of 'a bastard son of the King's' (*2 Henry IV*, II. 4. 283), liberating himself from the constraints of legitimacy by embracing the indecorous licence proper to the child of sexual misrule.[10] Playing the bastard is what enables Hamlet to express the contradictions of his position: through it he at once mimes the illegitimacy of the heir-apparent role in which Claudius has cast him, and mocks the powerlessness that seems to compromise the 'truth' of his legitimate inheritance. It is a performance that, more than anything, is responsible for converting *The Tragedy of Hamlet Prince of Denmark* into one of those tragical-comical hybrids that so perplex Polonius's taxonomic skills; and it establishes him in unexpected kinship with Thersites, the bastard chorus of that masterpiece of dramatic illegitimacy which closely succeeded *Hamlet* — *Troilus and Cressida*.

The bastard, as I shall try to show, is habitually figured as a creature who reveals the 'unnaturalness' of his begetting by the monstrous unkindness of his nature. An 'out of joint' member of a hybrid genus, he is defined as neither one thing nor the other. To play the bastard, as Hamlet does, is to place oneself doubly outside the order of the 'natural', to become at once a counterfeit and a self-conscious anomaly: it is to break 'the mould of form', to become a creature of the uncertain margin — an 'antic' in both the theatrical and the grotesque senses of that slippery word, and a creature whose mixed

[9] Coincidentally, Ruth Nevo's paper, 'Mousetrap and Rat Man: an Uncanny Resemblance' (Shakespeare Congress, Tokyo, 1991), makes the same point about Hamlet's uncertainty — inevitable in the circumstances, one would have thought, though strangely ignored by earlier commentators.

[10] In a brilliantly suggestive article, '*Henry IV* and the Death of Old Double', *Essays in Criticism*, (40, 1990), 14–53, John Kerrigan explores the theatrical and verbal play on the 'bastard' and legitimate in the *Henry IV* plays, and notices their intimate association with ideas of counterfeiting (pp. 41–44).

nature is expressed in an idiom that systematically subverts the 'natural' decorums of kind. Energetic, witty, iconoclastic, and profoundly resentful of the legitimate order, the bastard, as John Danby put it, 'is the Elizabethan equivalent of 'outsider' [...]. He is outside Society, he is outside Nature, he is outside Reason',[11] so that he functions, in Kingsley Davis's words, as 'a living symbol of social irregularity.[12]

Thus when Spurio in *The Revenger's Tragedy* proclaims that 'adultery is my nature' he appeals to a whole set of cultural assumptions that made of the bastard a distinct sub-species amongst the swarm of attractive villains who populate late Elizabethan and Jacobean drama. Yet the reasons why the bastard should have acquired such archetypal presence as a transgressive bogeyman in the period are by no means obvious. In its origins 'bastard' had been a relatively neutral descriptive term. Apparently deriving from Old French *bast* ('pack-saddle'), it distinguished the placeless pack-saddle child from the established offspring of the marriage-bed. Social historians are generally agreed that, while the medieval period saw a gradual hardening of such distinctions, with the bastard being formally defined as *filius nullius* by the end of the twelfth century, the definition carried no particular stigma; rather it served, within the patriarchal system of primogeniture, simply to mark off the children who were entitled to inherit from those who were not. The *filius nullius* (as the rules of heraldic cadency imply) was not so much the son of nobody, as the *heir* of nobody.[13] Even in the later Middle Ages, when church attitudes were becoming more censorious, an allegation of bastardy was primarily a weapon in struggles over inheritance, rather than a slur on character and reputation. Historians generally argue that the condition of illegitimacy began to incur a significant degree of publicly articulated moral opprobrium only towards the end of the sixteenth century, when it attracted the attention of Puritan reformers on the one hand and of Poor Law administrators, keen to protect the parish from the charge of unwanted infants, on the other.[14] The zeal of reformers and officials alike was evidently exacerbated by what seems to have been a rapidly rising rate of illegitimate

---

[11] John F. Danby, *Shakespeare's Doctrine of Nature* (London: Faber, 1961), p. 44.

[12] Kingsley Davis, 'Illegitimacy and the Social Structure' in *Readings on the Family and Society*, ed. by William J. Goode (Englewood Cliffs, NJ: Prentice-Hall, 1964), pp. 21–23 (p. 21).

[13] See Chris Given-Wilson and Alice Curteis, *The Royal Bastards of Medieval England* (London: Routlege, 1984), pp. 43, 51–53; I. Pinchbeck, 'Social Attitudes to the Problem of Illegitimacy', *British Journal of Sociology*, 5 (1954), 309–23 (pp. 314–15); Alan Macfarlane, 'Illegitimacy and Illegitimates in English History' in Laslett, *Bastardy*, pp. 71–85 (pp. 75–65).

[14] Thus the section in the 1576 Poor Law 'Concerning bastards begotten and born out of lawful matrimony (an offence against God's and Man's laws) objects to their 'great burden of the [...] Parish, and [...] defrauding of the relief of the impotent and aged true poor of the same parish, [as well as to] the evil example and the encouragement of lewd life' constituted by their mere existence; the parents of such offspring are not only to provide for their maintenance, but to be treated as criminals and punished with whippings and imprisonment; see Pinchbeck, pp. 315–16; and see Given-Wilson and Curteis, p. 54; Martin Ingram, *Church, Courts, Sex and Marriage in England, 1570–1640* (Cambridge, 1987), pp. 151–58. For a suggestion that changing attitudes to bastardy reflect a more general shift towards a tighter regulation of sexual relations as part of the 'civilizing' process of the early modern period, see Norbert Elias, *The Civilising Process: The History of Manners*, trans. by Eduard Jephcott (Oxford: Blackwell, 1978), pp. 183–84.

births from the middle of the sixteenth century, reaching a peak in the years 1600 to 1620.[15]

However, whilst these social and demographic circumstances cast an interesting sidelight on such plays as *A Chaste Maid in Cheapside*, *The Witch of Edmonton*, and *Love's Sacrifice*, where unlicensed pregnancies and pack-saddle infants play an important part in the plotting, they can have only an oblique connexion with the emergence of the adult bastard as a type of subversive irregularity.[16] For theatrical bastards, after all, typically belong to the princely and aristocratic orders of society, amongst whom illegitimacy rates apparently underwent a sharp fall in the first half of the seventeenth century, and who, in any case, accorded bastardy a large degree of practical toleration.[17] Nor did the ambition of bastard princes, which was to become a seriously destabilizing factor in the later seventeenth century, significantly impinge on Elizabethan and Jacobean politics. Among contemporary royal bastards, Philip II's half-brother, the bastard Don John of Austria — a possible inspiration for the turbulent Don John in Shakespeare's *Much Ado About Nothing* — reputedly had designs on Mary Queen of Scots and the English throne, but the danger was not taken particularly seriously in England.[18] It is of course possible that heightened public concern over the moral and social aspects of bastardy, issuing in acts of Parliament in 1576 and 1610, may have exacerbated the embarrassments surrounding the uncertain legitimacy of Elizabeth, and even of her successor, James.[19] Still,

---

[15] Peter Laslett, 'Long-term trends in bastardy in England', in *Family Life and Illicit Love in Earlier Generations*, ed. by Peter Laslett (Cambridge: Cambridge University Press, 1977), pp. 113–15; Mac-farlane, 'Illegitimacy and Illegitimates', p. 82.

[16] By Alison Findlay's reckoning there are over one hundred plays from the period in which bastardy 'figures as a major subject', including fifty-seven featuring adult bastards (real or supposed), p. 2.

[17] See Ralph A. Houlbrooke, *The English Family 1450–1750*, (London: Longman, 1984), p. 117; Pinchbeck, 'Social Attitudes', p. 316; and Given-Wilson and Curteis, p. 54. Findlay includes some graphs designed to show (rather unconvincingly in my view) a correlation between peaks in numbers of plays featuring adult bastards and the early maturity of the crops of bastard children indicated in demographic peaks.

[18] On Don John's ambitions see J. H. Elliott, *Imperial Spain, 1469–1716* (London: Penguin, 1970), p. 265. As the hero of Lepanto, Don John also contributed to the paradoxical tradition of the Virtuous Bastard (see below, note 18), and it is thus that he appears in Webster's *The Devil's Law-Case* (IV. 2. 358–59, for example.

[19] The Tudor claim to the throne had been derived in the first instance from Henry VII's great-grandfather John Beaufort, a bastard son of John of Gaunt, and it was dubiously bolstered by his grandfather Owen Tudor's marriage to the widow of Henry V — a secret marriage of disparagement in which the clerk of the household's 'presumption in mixing his blood with that of the noble race of kings' caused much scandal. Elizabeth's personal claim was further clouded by Henry VIII's Second and Third Acts of Succession, in which he had successively bastardized and then legitmated Mary and Elizabeth, the daughters of his first two marriages; and Catholic propagandists, such as Cardinal Allen (*Admonition to the Nobility and People of England and Ireland*, 1588) were to use her alleged illegitimacy to argue the illegality of her succession. The princesses were bastardized to clear the way for the remarried King's expected male heirs; but when subsequent marriages produced only the sickly Edward, it seemed expedient to legitimize his daughters (see Given-Wilson and Curteis, pp. 47, 51–53). Later, Elizabeth herself was to decline marriage to Mary's widower, Philip of Spain partly on the grounds of an embarrassing parallel with Henry's marriage to his deceased brother's wife, Catherine of Aragon: 'If she approved the marriage of one man and two sisters, then she sanctioned the union of one woman to two brothers. And 'if that were a good Marriage, then she must be illegitimate"' (Jack Goody, *The Development of the Family and Marriage in Europe* (Cambridge: Cambridge University Press, 1983)). Possible connexions between Elizabeth's 'bastardy' and theatrical interest in bastard figures were pursued by contributors to the recent SAA seminar on 'Shakespeare's Bastards' (Vancouver, 1990). James's situation was less complicated, but the

while such awkwardnesses may have given particular piquancy to the dramatization of bastard ambition, they are hardly sufficient in themselves to account for the disruptive power of the bastard figure in the drama. To understand fully his transgressive potential, I think we need to look beyond the more or less rational realms of politics, moral judgement and social regulation into regions of more obscure anxiety.

I The Dirty Bastard

In the drama bastards are typically presented as a special class of transgressive male. Female bastard figures are exceptionally rare, the only significant example being Joan La Pucelle in *1 Henry VI*. While in practice at least fifty per cent of illegitimate children must have been female, this asymmetry is not necessarily surprising — legal bastardy being so much a category of disinheritance that, within a system of partiarchal primogeniture (where women could be, at best, only equivocally legitimate inheritors), it was almost automatically imagined as a male condition.[20] From this point of view La Pucelle's self-proclaimed bastardy is merely an extreme manifestation of her trans-sexual monstrosity: she usurps, as it were, the role of male usurper. At the same time bastard figures seem to have been typed as male because they embodied a certain kind of disruptive energy which was supposed to derive from the unfettered 'vehemence' of their begetting, a sexual drive imagined as essentially male ('some stirring dish | Was my first father' (*Revenger's Tragedy*, 1. 2. 180–81)). Bastardy, like cuckoldry, involved a transaction *between men*, in which the mother's role (as we may see from Lady Faulconbridge in *King John*) was confined to that of witness and mediator — a vehicle of pollution in the male line of descent.[21]

The factor of pollution is crucial however. In popular superstition the bastard was an oddly ambiguous figure; credited with exceptionally passionate energies, a 'composition and fierce quality' derived from the 'lusty stealth' of their begetting, bastards were also imagined as indelibly stained

---

Stuarts themselves traced their succession from a bastard line, and the circumstances of his own birth were muddied both by his mother's rumoured affair with David Rizzio and by her notorious involvement with the Earl of Bothwell, his father's assassin. Thus the king's own warnings in *Basilicon Doron* (Scolar Facsimile, pp. 96–97) against the propensities of bastards to 'unnatural' usurpation may be tinged with complex ambivalence. For further comment on anxieties surrounding Elizabeth's and James's birth and the question of inheritance, see Stephen Orgel's introduction to *The Tempest* (Oxford: Oxford University Press, 1987), pp. 37–40.

[20] There may indeed be a sense, as Janet Adelman suggests, in which daughters are always in some sense 'illegitimate', simply by virtue of their capacity to 'disrupt the patriarchal ideal, both insofar as they disrupt the transmission of property from father to son and insofar as they disrupt the paternal fantasy of perfect self-replication. Even more clearly than the mother's son, the daughter is but "the shadow of the male," carrying within her the disruptive sign of the mother's presence'. See Adelman, *Suffocating Mothers: Fantasies of Maternal Origin in Shakespeare's Plays, 'Hamlet' to 'The Tempest'* (New York and London: Routledge, 1992), p. 108.

[21] According to the 'logic of illegitimacy' which Adelman traces in *King Lear*, 'the female sexual place is necessarily the place of corruption, the "sulphurous pit" [...] that is Lear's equivalent to Edgar's "dark and vicious place"; present only as a site of illegitimacy, the mother [...] transmits her faults to her issue, the children whose corrupt sexuality records their origin' (*Suffocating Mothers*, p. 108).

by the viciousness of this origin (*King Lear*, 1.2.11–12).[22] Thus Donne's Problem IX, in explaining '*Why have Bastards best Fortune?*' invokes 'the old Natural reason [...] that these meetings in stolne love are most vehement, and so contribute more spirit then the easy and lawfull', together with 'the old Morall reason [...] that Bastards inherit wickednesse from theyr parents'.[23]

The belief that 'Bastards [...] have better wits and abilities'[24] no doubt contributed to a paradoxical tradition of Virtuous Bastardy, which cited Hercules, Romulus and Remus, Alexander the Great, King Arthur, and William the Conqueror among its heroes;[25] but the force of the paradox naturally depended on its running counter to the received view of the bastard's inherent viciousness.[26] According to Thomas Fuller's *Worthies*, popular etymology 'deduced bastard from the Dutch words *boes* and *art*, that is an abject nature';[27] while the jurist Sir John Fortescue justified the statutory disinheritance of illegitimate children by their inherently corrupt condition. Citing a passage in Judges 9 to show how there might be 'more wyckednesse in one bastarde chylde, then in lxxix lawfull sons', he asserted that 'if a bastard be good it commeth to him by chance [...] by speciall grace, but if he be evil that commeth to him by nature'. Drawing 'a certeyn corruption and stayne from the sinne of his parentes', a bastard was not merely 'the chylde of synners' but the 'chylde of synne' itself; and nature accordingly 'mark[ed] the naturall or bastard chyldren as it were with a certein prive mark in their soules'.[28] Thus the 'the steine of bastardy' described by one seventeenth century diarist was no mere heraldic metaphor, but a literal brand of infamy.[29]

There were in fact good scriptural grounds for such an idea, insofar as Old Testament law regarded the bastard as polluted by the very circumstances of his begetting, so that he was forbidden entry 'into the congregation of the

---

[22] For further evidence of the natural energy and vivacity attributed to bastards, see Findlay, pp. 36–37.

[23] John Donne, *Paradoxes and Problems*, ed. by Helen Peters (Oxford: Clarendon Press, 1980), p. 31.

[24] Donne, *Paradoxes*, p. 32.

[25] On Virtuous Bastards, see Findlay, Chapter 6, 'The Bastard as Hero', and Margaret Loftus Ranald, 'The British Bastard as England's Saviour', a so far unpublished paper from the Vancouver Shakespeare's Bastards seminar. I am indebted to the organizer, Mary Ann McGrail, for giving me access to several papers from this seminar.

[26] It is significant, in this context, that *The Misfortunes of Arthur* (1588), which presents Arthur as a type of virtuous bastardy is nevertheless at pains to emphasize that he is destroyed by Mordred, the bastard issue of his own incestuous adultery, whose usurping ambitions extend to the seduction of his stepmother, Gueneuora. Likewise, the otherwise heroic Spurio in Nabbes's *The Unfortunate Mother* (1639) is brought down by his incestuous passion for his own mother, meeting his end in a duel with the similarly ambiguous bastard, Notho, where each kills the other, as if in enactment of the self-cancelling energy of bastard appetite.

[27] Fuller wrote of Henry Fitzroy, natural son to Henry VIII, that he confuted this etymology 'and verified their deduction, deriving it from *besteard*, that is, the best disposition'; see Thomas Fuller, *The History of the Worthies of England*, ed. by P. A. Nuttall, 3 vols (London: Thomas Tegg, 1840), p. 499.

[28] John Fortescue, *A Learned Commendation of the Politique Lawes of England* (London, 1567; facsimile edn, Amsterdam and New York: Theatrum Orbis Terrarum, 1969) fols 95ᵛ–97ᵛ. Findlay cites a proverb 'Bastards by chance are good, by nature bad' (p. 33).

[29] *The Diary of William Lawrence*, (Beaminster: Stevens Cox, 1961), ed. by G. E. Aylmer p. 6; cited by Macfarlane, 'Illegitimacy', pp. 71–85 (p. 76).

Lord; even to his tenth generation' (Deuteronomy 23.20). Canon law followed this proscription by denying illegitimates ordination to the priesthood, as Fortescue observed;[30] and there are reasons for thinking that such superstitious fears of the bastard as a potential source of pollution may have been even more widely diffused. The social historian Alan Macfarlane, for example, finds in Thomas Becon's citation of this law (*Workes*, 1560) hints of 'a widespread view that bastards should not be christened'.[31] Why should mere illegitimacy have invited such symbolically charged ostracism? Part of the answer may be suggested by a sermon, preached by Dr Ralph Shaw at Paul's Cross on 22 June 1438, on the text 'Bastard slips shall not take root', which prepared the way for the bastardization of Edward IV's children and the accession of Richard III.[32] In the Geneva Bible the relevant passage (Wisdom 4. 3–6) reads:

the bastard plantes shal take no depe root, nor laye any fast fundacion [...]
For the unperfect branches shalbe broken, and their frute shalbe unprofitable and sower to eat, and mete for nothing.
For the children that are borne of the wicked bed, shalbe witnes of the wickednes against their parents when they be asked.

The implication here is that there is something inherently tainted about bastard stock — that their begetting constitutes an act of polluting mixture which renders the offspring in some sense unnatural or unclean.[33] So indeed it seems to Shakespeare's Lucrece as she justifies her suicide with a paraphrase of the same text: 'This bastard graff shall never come to growth. | He shall not boast who did thy stock pollute' (*Lucrece*. ll. 1062–63). The ultimate scriptural foundation for such views is to be found in the rules of separation laid out in Leviticus: 'Thou shalt not let thy cattle gender with a diverse kind: thou shalt not sow thy field with mingled seed' (Leviticus 19. 21). Commenting on this elaborate regime of differentiation in her chapter on 'The Abominations of Leviticus', Mary Douglas concludes that:

holiness is exemplified by completeness. Holiness requires that individuals shall conform to the class to which they belong. And holiness requires that different classes of things shall not be confused [...]. Holiness means keeping distinct the

---

[30] In support of the civil law's discrimination, Fortescue noted that the Church judged bastards 'unworthy to bee receaved into holye orders and rejecteth them from all prelacie' (fol. 95ᵛ). The same superstitious restrictions may help to account for the bastard's exclusion from membership of guilds and societies (see Findlay, p. 195). Practically speaking, bastards could, of course, be ordained on payment of a substantial fee of dispensation, as the presence of the Bishop of Winchester (a member of the illegitimate Beaufort clan) in *1 Henry VI* reminds us.
[31] Macfarlane, 'Illegitimacy', pp. 78–79. It was perhaps for this very reason that Sir George Buck thought it necessary to cite scripture when urging that it should be thought '[no] disparagement for a noble family to be descended from natural issue, considering that there [...] are infinite number of noble and princely families which are derived and propagated from bastards'. In addition to the Beauforts and the royal Stuarts, he cited 'this one example [...] above all, to wit, that Jesus Christ, the greatest and most noble king, was content to descend from Phares, a bastard', cited in Given-Wilson and Curteis, p. 53. Buck's other examples included the genealogies of Aeneas, Romulus, Theseus, Themistocles, Hercules, William the Conqueror.
[32] The text is also cited by Fortescue, fol. 95ᵛ
[33] On the 'unnatural' character of the bastard, see Findlay, Chapter 5, 'The Unnatural Child'.

Imagining the Bastard in Renaissance Drama

categories of creation. It therefore involves correct definition, discrimination and order. Under this head all the rules of sexual morality exemplify the holy.

Whilst not necessarily discounting the function of such sexual rules in the preservation of property rights and inheritance, Douglas insists that their primary function is to preserve the natural (divinely ordained) proprieties of separation:

Incest and adultery are against holiness, in the simple sense of right order. [...] Holiness is more a matter of separating that which should be separate than of protecting the rights of husbands and brothers.[34]

If bastards were forbidden the priesthood or banished from the congregation of the Lord, it was because they were unholy; and they were unholy because their adulterous procreation constituted an act of forbidden mixture which rendered them un-whole. Scriptural texts, significantly, do not always distinguish clearly between marital infidelity and simple fornication: either can be described as 'adultery', since each involves sexual mingling unlicensed by the fiction of nuptial union. Bastards are un-whole because they are the offspring not of 'one flesh' but of two bodies: there is an inherent and sinister doubleness about their begetting (one may think of Iago's 'beast with two backs') which renders them neither one thing nor the other, at once indeterminate and duplicitous. A bastard, as Spurio puts it in *The Revenger's Tragedy*, is 'an uncertain man', consigned by his very begetting to be a denizen of the unstable margin (*Revenger's Tragedy*, I. 2. 133). He is thus the human equivalent of dirt, as Mary Douglas defines it — matter in the wrong place, belonging to 'a residual category, rejected from our normal scheme of classifications',[35] a source of fundamental pollution.

This is the belief that underlies Talbot's speech in *1 Henry VI*, for example, when he scornfully offers to avenge his son's '*pure* blood' upon the '*contaminated*, base | And misgotten blood' of the Bastard of Orleans (*1 Henry VI*, IV. 6. 21–24; my emphasis); and it is expressed with peculiar intensity in Ford's *The Broken Heart*, where Penthea's conviction that her forced marriage to Bassanes is irremediably adulterous leaves her a prey to suicidal self-loathing, grounded in the belief that her blood is now tainted by 'mixtures of pollution' (IV. 2. 150).[36] Apart from its relation to Judaic rules of separation, this way of thinking about adultery is embedded in the etymology of the word itself. In Latin *adultero* meant not only 'to commit adultery' but also 'to pollute or defile', a pollution which once again seems to have been understood as the consequence of inadmissible mixture, since *adulterium* (adultery)

---

[34] Mary Douglas, *Purity and Danger: An Analysis of Concepts of Pollution and Taboo* (New York and Washington: Praeger, 1966)
[35] Douglas, p. 36.
[36] Joseph A. Candido, 'Blots, Stains, and Adulteries: the impurites in *King John*, in *King John: New Perspectives*, ed. by Deborah Curren-Aquino (Newark: University of Delaware Press, 1988), pp. 114–25, notices how the language used to describe John's death makes it seem an expression of his polluted blood (pp. 118–19). Findlay (p. 28) cites Alonzo's rebuke to the ambitious Gaspar in the anonymous *The Bastard* (1652): 'thy polluted blood | Thinks to pollute mine' (B²ᵛ).

also referred, for example, to the grafting together of different varieties of plant. This is the meaning which underlies the suppositious bastard Perdita's aversion to botanical hybrids as 'Nature's bastards' (*Winter's Tale*, IV. 4. 83).[37]

This way of thinking extended not only to plants and to the animal kingdom, but to the developing notions of racial difference and 'purity' which served to underpin the emergent ideology of empire. Thus in *1 Henry VI*, as Phyllis Rackin has shown, Talbot's pride of blood is inseparable from a strategy which impugns the legitimacy of the French cause by stigmatizing it with bastardy: if the French are led by a self-indicated bastard, Joan La Pucelle, under the patronage of another, the Bastard of Orleans, it is, by implication, because they are a 'bastard' nation. 'What ish my nation?' asks the *Henry V*'s furious Captain Macmorris in his bastard English. 'Ish a villain, and a basterd, and a knave, and a rascal' (III. 2. 123–24); he has no doubt been reading Spenser's *A View of the Present State of Ireland*, where the barbaric nature of the Irish is associated with their claim to Spanish antecedents: 'Of all nations under heaven [...] the Spaniard is the most mingled, most uncertain and most bastardly.'[38] It can hardly be accidental that the type of such adulterate mingling should be Caliban, the rebellious slave of Prospero's 'new world' empire in Shakespeare's profoundly ambivalent drama of colonization, *The Tempest*. The bastard nature of the island's only 'native'[39] is what symbolically disinherits him of a kingdom that he claims in the right of 'Sycorax, my mother' (I. 2. 331), and makes him naturally subject to Prospero's imperial authority.

Stigmatized by his master as a 'demi-devil [...] a bastard one' (V. 1. 272–73), Caliban is supposedly the offspring of his witch mother's unnatural commerce with 'the devil himself', as a result of which he is 'not honor'd with | A human shape' (I. 2. 283–84). his monstrous form is the sign of an inner deformity which renders him fundamentally recalcitrant to that 'print of goodness' which is the badge of submission to Prospero's civil order; and his adulterate origin is expressed in the desire to violate the honour of Miranda and to people the island with his own bastard kind. But that very

---

[37] Presumably we are to take this as a sign of the true-bred instinct of a child who has been cast out as the bastard offspring of her mother's adultery with Polixenes. The misogynist pamphlet *Hic Mulier: Or, The Man-Woman* (London: 1620), obsessed as it is by what the pamphleteer perceives as threats to the proper differentiation of gender which turn women to 'stranger things then ever *Noahs* Arke unladed, or *Nyle* ingendred', extends this notion of the bastard to the illegitimate mixtures in dress, the 'monstrousnesse of deformitie in apparell' which includes 'the false armoury of yellow Starch (for to weare yellow on white, or white upon yellow, is by the rules of Heraldry basenesse, bastardie, and indignitie)', Sig. A³ᵛ–A⁴.

[38] Edmund Spenser, *A View of the Present State of Ireland*, ed. by W. L. Renwick (Oxford: Clarendon Press, 1970), p. 44. Likewise, Sir John Davies's *A Discoverie of the True Causes why Ireland Was neuer entirely Subdued* (London, 1612), attributes Irish factiousness and want of civil government partly to the 'mischiefe' brewed by 'that Irish Custom of Gauel-kinde' which allowed all sons to inherit 'aswell Bastard as Legitimate' (p. 172).

[39] By this description I mean to exclude Ariel and the other spirit creatures (as Caliban himself does in remembering his lonely rule) — ultimately, of course, the island has no 'true' natives, only spirits and colonists, and no true inheritors either, since like any bastard, Caliban can claim only through the female line.

ambition serves as a reminder that Caliban's monstrousness is not simply to be understood as marking his status as sub-human Other, a creature of unregenerate nature awaiting the civilizing discipline of empire. For Caliban too is a colonist, cast away on the island with his mother in an uncanny prefiguration of Prospero's and Miranda's arrival. Of course his adulterate desire for Miranda anticipates the colonial fantasies of the black rapist with which so many commentators have associated it; but it is also, as Prospero's reluctant acceptance of his paternal foster-role ('this thing of darkness I | Acknowledge mine', (v. 1. 275–76)) implies, a kind of incest. If, from one perspective, the identification of Caliban-as-colonist anticipates the familiar colonialist mystification by which indigenous peoples are revealed as being no more than settlers themselves, from another he represents the enduring fear of 'degeneration' which might turn the colonizers into a 'bastard' people, such as the 'Old English' were supposed to have become in Ireland. According to Spenser's *View of the Present State of Ireland*, for example, these former settlers, as a result of the 'contagion [of] lycentious conversinge with the Irish, or marrying, or fostering with them', had become 'now much more lawlesse and lycencious then the very wilde Irish [. . .] growen to be as very Patchcockes as [them] [. . .] barbarous and bastard like', exhibiting their 'degenerate' condition by a 'devilish dislike of ther owne naturall country, as that they would [. . .] bite of the dugge from which they sucked lyfe'.[40] So it is that Caliban, notorious biter of the feeding hand, can be presented as the rival and degenerate double of Ferdinand, a figuration of all those adulterate desires (for both sexual conquest and political usurpation) that the young prince is required to suppress before he is licensed to inherit.[41]

II   *The Cheating Bastard*

The bastard, as the action of *The Tempest* with its pattern of usurpation, disinheritance, and illegitimate substitution suggests, is not merely the vehicle of polluting mixture, but an epitome of the counterfeit.[42] Perhaps

---

[40] Spenser, *View*, pp. 102–08.

[41] The quasi-allegorical scheme I outline will not of course encompass all of the play's notorious ambivalences: Caliban's lyrical response to the beauties of the island, together with Gonzalo's observation that the 'people of the island [. . .] though they are of monstrous shape [. . .] | Their manners are more gentle, kind, than of | Our human generation you shall find | Many, nay, almost any' (III. 3. 30–34), significantly complicate the meanings which attach to his seemingly 'monstrous' and 'unnatural' character and hence to the whole issue of inheritance in the play. In this context it is worth observing the existence a number of post-colonial texts in which bastards are figured as inheritors (or potential inheritors) of a recuperative hybridity — notably Brian Friel's plays *Translations* and *Making History*, and Salman Rushdie's novels *Midnight's Children* and *Shame*. Since *Midnight's Children* itself asks to be read as (among other things) a reply to Forster's *A Passage to India*, one might view its narrator, Saleem (a racial and cultural 'bastard' as well as a literal illegitimate), as embodying exactly the hybrid possibilities which Forster (who had made a bastard child the emblem of one kind of hybridizing 'connexion' in his novel of class, *Howard's End*) baulked at in his novel of empire.

[42] Thus for Coriolanus to adopt the hypocritically subservient role towards the plebeians that his mother requires of him will be to 'dissemble with [his] nature' and use 'words that are [. . .] but *bastards* and syllables | Of no allowance to your bosom's truth' (*Coriolanus*, III. 2. 62, 55–57, my emphasis).

because the unnaturalness of adulterous mingling must necessarily be reflected in false, impure issue, the Latin *adulter* came to mean not just an adulterer (or, in Vulgate Latin, the offspring of adultery: a bastard), but (usually in the form *adulter solidorum*) 'a counterfeiter or adulterator of coin'; while *adultero* similarly acquired the sense 'to falsify, adulterate, or counterfeit'. The same extended meaning is present in Medieval English *adulter* ('corrupt' or 'debase'), and is everywhere apparent in the expanded sixteenth- and seventeenth-century terminology of adultery.[43] Thus the Countess of Salisbury, in the anonymous *Edward III* (1592–95), wards off the king's advances by urging that the act of adultery would 'stamp his [God's] image in forbidden metal' (II.1.258).[44] Themselves counterfeit, since they are not the 'true' sons of their fathers, and carrying the taint of their 'double' origin, stage bastards are habitually stigmatized as counterfeits or associated with counterfeiting practice. In *The Troublesome Raigne of King John* (1588), for example, the illegitimate Faulconbridge is somewhat ambivalently identified as the 'lively counterfet | Of *Richard Cordelion*' (*1 Troublesome Raigne*, ll. 192–93); while in *Edmond Ironside* (1595) the 'degenerate bastard' Edricus boasts of the 'counterfeiting guile' and 'dissimulation' with which he advances his usurping ambitions (I.1.166, III.6.1238, IV.1.1426).[45] In *Troilus and Cressida* the bastard's counterfeiting becomes an agent of subversive mockery, as Thersites's imagination 'coins slanders like a mint, | To match [his legitimate superiors] in comparisons with dirt' (*Troilus and Cressida*, I.3.193–94). Thersites's satiric coining, like that of Patroclus, the rival whom he denounces as a 'gilt counterfeit' (II.3.25), itself frequently takes the form of degrading theatrical imitation — a form of counterfeiting that links him with that bastard-getting magnifico, Volpone. In Jonson's vicious comedy of unnatural fatherhood, the protagonist is an heirless patriarch who is nevertheless 'the true father of his family'; and Volpone's profligate coining of bastards is ironically matched by the fertile theatrical counterfeiting and getting of false heirs that enables him to 'coin [his

[43] Among the apparent coinages listed in *OED* are: adulterate, *v.* (1531); adulterate, *ppl.a.* (1590); adulterated *p.ppl.a.* (1607);adulterately, *adv.* (1619); adulterating, *vbl.sb.* (1610); adulteration, *sb.* (1606); adulterator, *sb.* (1625) adultered, *ppl.a.* (1624); adulterine, *a.* and *sb.* (1542); adultering, *ppl.a.* (1599); adulterously, *adv.* (1599). *Hic Mulier*'s tirade against the blurring of gender distinctions in dress similarly discovers in current fashions not merely bastard deformity but a species of adulterate counterfeiting, 'mimicke and apish incivilitie': its followers are 'but ragges of Gentry, torne from better pieces for their foule staines [...] adulterate branches of rich Stocks, that taking too much sap from the roote, are cut away, and imploy'd in base uses. [...] It is exorbitant from nature, and an *Antithesis* to kinde. [...] What can bee more barbarous, then with the glosse of mumming Art, to disguise the beauty of their creations? To mould their bodies to euery deformed fashion. [...] To haue their gestures as pyebald,and as motley-various as their disguises. [...] They turne Maskers, Mummers, nay Monsters in their disguises [...] [through] this *Misselanie* or Mixture of deformities', Sig. A³ᵛ, B¹–Bᶦᵛ, C², C³ᵛ.

[44] Cited from G. C. Moore Smith (ed.), *The Reign of King Edward III* (London, 1897).

[45] Cited from *Shakespeare's Lost Play, Edmund Ironside*, ed. by Eric Sams (New York: St Martin's Press, 1985). For further discussion of the bastard's propensity for dissimulation, see Findlay, pp. 176–81, who cites the bastard Fallacy's travesty of Edmund in Richard Zouche's *The Sophister* (1631): 'Sacred Deceit, to thee be consecrate | My temples, aid thou Godesse mine attempt' (A⁴), quoted p. 177.

victims] into profit' (I. 1. 86) — as he himself will ultimately be 'coined' by that spurious inheritor, Mosca (II. 2. 23).[46]

Nowhere, perhaps, is the notion of bastard counterfeiting more elaborately developed than in *The Revenger's Tragedy*, where the villainous Spurio, a bastard 'true-begot in evil' carries a name which means both 'bastard' and 'counterfeit'. For Spurio, the possession of his stepmother's body is an act of adulterous usurpation which prefigures his usurpation of the body politic, as the bawdy *double entendre* of 'a bastard scorns to be out' reminds us (v. 1. 168).[47] It is at once a confirmation of his adulterate nature and a revenge for it: by substituting himself in the old Duke's bed Spurio symbolically reverses the act of his own 'false' begetting, inscribing his father's wife with the mark of his own adulteration ('The pen of his bastard writes him cuckold', II. 2. 109), and thereby legitimates himself in the eyes of the Duchess ('His bastard son, but my love's true-begot', I. 2. 210). The satisfaction of this adulterine revenge is compounded in the bastard's scheme to displace his legitimate rival, Lussurioso, by surprising him in the adulterous act of fornication, thus wittily disinheriting him 'in as short a time | As I was when I was begot in haste' (II. 2. 125–26). In this way Spurio becomes a dramatized embodiment not only of the literal adultery which he claims as his birthright ('Adultery is my nature', I. 2. 177), but of the usurping desire for illegitimate substitution which drives the politics of this whole corrupt court. More than this, his counterfeit presence constitutes a kind of rebus for all those fraudulent politic stratagems of which the play's villain–hero, Vindice, is both the scourge and principal exponent. If the surreptitious vice of the court, in Vindice's hallucinating imagination, itself amounts to a species of counterfeiting ('Now cuckolds are a-coining', II. 2. 43), ironically it can be combated only with counterfeiting of his own, as he adopts the role of that 'base-coined pandar' described by Hippolito (I. 1. 80), and connives in the adulterous seduction of his mother and sister ('We must coin. | Women are apt you know to take false money', (I. 1. 102–03)).

If Vindice (whose own parentage will be placed under question by the discovery of his mother's viciousness (II. 1. 162–64)) has to coin new identities, to become so 'far [. . .] from [himself]' that it is 'as if another man had been sent whole into the world' (I. 3. 1–2), his need for histrionic counterfeiting merely mirrors the bastard's aboriginal condition as one who is, in

---

[46] An important detail in this complex system of ironic equivalences is Mosca's suggestion that coinage, in the form of gold, is the sovereign medicine which 'transforms | The most deformed, and restores them lovely' (v. 1. 117–18). It is also worth noting that the principal domestic function of Volpone's bastard brood is apparently theatrical counterfeiting, the 'pleasing imitation | Of greater men's actions, in ridiculous fashion' (III. 1. 13–14), and that their first performance concerns the systematic debasement of the soul of Pythagoras. This deformed counterfeiting supplies an ironic mirror for 'the too much licence' of contemporary dramatic practice by which, according to Jonson's Epistle Dedicatory, the poetasters of his day have 'much deformed their mistress [. . .] adulterated her form'.

[47] Compare the antipatriarchal stratagems of the aptly named bastard Antipater in Markham and Sampson's *Hero and Antipater* (1622), whose viciousness similarly stems from his sense of having been 'begot when sin was revelling' (II. 1. 157).

effect, born far from himself. This is the 'curse of the womb' that renders
Spurio 'the thief of nature' (I. 2. 159), as if self-robbed of his 'true' or 'natural'
self—which is to say his proper social identity — in the very act of coming to
be. Stamped with a name that signals only his inauthenticity,[48] Spurio
epitomizes the radical anonymity with which the bastard has to contend. In
King John the bastard Faulconbridge may 'come one way of the Plantagenets'
(v. 6. 11), but (as his rebaptism in Act I Scene I and the uncertain shifting of
his stage name in the Folio text both remind us) the *way* he comes does not
even endow him with a 'real' name.[49] In *King Lear* Edmund is equivocally
'acknowledged' by Gloucester, but only as a whore's son, fathered it seems
more by the 'good sport at his making' than by any deliberate act of
paternity. 'I cannot wish the sport undone', Kent laughs, 'the issue of it
being so proper' (I. I. 17–18); but his banter turns on a cruel pun, since to be
a 'proper' person in seventeenth-century England (as James Calderwood
has pointed out) is 'to be propertied [...] to possess',[50] while Edmund's
alienation from what Lear calls 'propinquity and property of blood'
(I. I. 114) renders him an 'unpossessing bastard' (II. 1. 67), fundamentally
improper. Coming 'saucily into the world' before his time, like his close kin
the 'rudely stamped' Richard of Gloucester (around whose monstrous birth
and physical deformity hang metaphoric suggestions of the very bastardy
with which he stigmatizes his own nephews),[51] the bastard too feels 'scarce
half made up' (*Richard III*, I. 1. 21). As a result he is compelled to shape
himself in the mirror of his own wit. Stripped of paternal authorization (like
Spurio, sardonically convinced that 'some stirring dish was my first father'
or that he was 'stolen' (counterfeited) by the obscene union of 'Damnation
[with] the sin of feasts, drunken Adultery'), he has no option but to become
his own maker.

   Spurio's sour jokes play on a post-Reformation distortion of the doctrine of
filius nullius, as a result of which the bastard 'became indeed the son of no-one,
isolated in law from all his natural relatives'.[52] The effect was to turn him
into a kind of living embodiment of that unnatural paradox 'the portrait of
nobody'. For the *filius nullius* became author of himself by desperate necessity, a kind of self-animated fiction — 'Caesar o nullo' as the celebrated

[48] In John Florio's dictionary, *Queen Anna's World of Words*, Spurio is glossed as 'a bastard, a baseborne.
Also adulterate or counterfeit'. Findlay, who also notices the virtual anonymity of the bastard, cites
William Clerke's *Triall of Bastardie* (1594, E1ᵛ), to the effect that *spurius* was the technical Latin term for
the son of a concubine and *nothus* for the son of an adulteress (pp. 26–28).
[49] Candido observes how counterfeiting extends even to the king himself, whose sense of 'being tainted
by a corrupt, debased, or illegitimate stock [...] manifests itself [...] in an almost compulsive strategy of
concealment and deception' ('Blots, Stains, and Adulteries', p. 117).
[50] James Calderwood, *The Properties of Othello* (Amherst: University of Massachusetts Press, 1989), p. 10.
[51] In *3 Henry VI*, v. 5. 115, he and his brothers are denounced by Queen Margaret as 'the bastard boys of
York' in a context where York's patronage of the usurper Cade (a counterfeit Plantagenet) and
appearance at the head of an Irish army associates the Yorkist faction with illegitimacy of all kinds.
[52] Pinchbeck, p. 315. The alternative description was *filius populus* as Fortescue, citing a popular rhyme,
points out: 'Your natural or bastard sonne is yᵉ sonne of yᵉ people. [...] To whom the people father is, to
him is father none and all. To whom the people father is, wel fatherles we may him call' (fol. 93ᵛ).

motto of Caesar Borgia in *The Divils Charter* (1607) has it.[53] The 'unpossessing bastard' of the drama, displaced from the narrative of history by the circumstances of his begetting, is cast loose to locate and possess himself by whatever invention he can contrive, discovering in his illegitimate condition something of the outlaw's paradoxical freedom.[54] He becomes a perfect figure for that spirit of ambivalent individualism, at once restlessly ambitious and full of the bitterness of displacement, which Thomas Hyde evokes in his study of the best known of all literary bastards, Giovanni Boccaccio. Hyde observes how the Italian writer turned his own illegitimacy 'into an image for the new age he helped to inaugurate. An illegitimate and upstart age, cast loose from historical succession [...] wishing for legitimacy but unwilling to accept its imaginative restraints, struggling greedily and guiltily to inherit'.[55]

From the defiance of the Bastard Falconbridge's 'mounting spirit' ('I am I, howe'er I was begot', *King John*, I. I. 175), to Don John's dyspeptic bile ('I cannot hide what I am. [...] Let me be that I am and seek not to alter me' *Much Ado*, I. 3. 13–37), and Edmund's sardonic wit ('Fut, I should have been that I am had the maidenl'est star in the firmament twinkled on my bastardizing' *Lear*, I. 2. 131–33), the stage bastard repeatedly insists on his own self-begotten sufficiency in overreaching language that insolently travesties the divine 'I am',[56] confounding his own essential formlessness and namelessness with the name of originary form itself. That such blasphemy is often echoed in the language of other Elizabethan overreachers merely serves to illustrate the representative character of the bastard:[57] if the bastard was, in Danby's formulation, 'the Elizabethan equivalent of [an] "outsider"', he was also a sinister insider — a surreptitious insertion into the body of the family. An alien graft who had struck root in the family tree, he could stand for all those obscure forces which threatened to corrupt and subvert society from within.

III   *The Monstrous Bastard*

Every bastard, then, in the scheme I have outlined, is like the 'filthy rogue' Thersites (*Troilus*, v. 4. 29) or the 'filth' Caliban (*Tempest*, I. 2. 346), a figure of

---

[53] Barnabe Barnes, *The Divils Charter*, IV. 2. 1980. Cited from the edition by R. B. McKerrow, Materialen zur Kunde des älteren Englischen Dramas, 60 (Louvain: A Uystpruyst, 1904). Compare Antipater's 'None or alone' in *Herod and Antipater* (quoted in Findlay, p. 142).

[54] The bastard-figure's propensity for 'willing of identity' is also noticed, from a rather different perspective, by Bruce Young in 'The Bastard as Self and Other: Levinas, Renaissance Attitudes and Shakespeare's Bastards', an unpublished paper from the Vancouver Shakespeare's Bastards Seminar.

[55] Thomas Hyde, 'Boccaccio: the Genealogies of Myth' *PMLA*, 100 (1985), p. 744; cited in Phyllis Rackin, *Stages of History: Shakespeare's English Chronicles* (Ithaca: Cornell University Press, 1990), p. 159. Gaspar, the hero of the anonymous *The Bastard* (1652), seems to make his bastard condition similarly representative: 'The world so swarmes with Bastards now, that I | Need no despair for want of Company; | I'm in among the Throng' (A⁴ᵛ), cited in Findlay, p. 223.

[56] Arguably even Caliban's invention of a history of usurpation in which he once figured as 'mine own king' fits this general pattern of egotistical self-sufficiency. For other examples of the blasphemous 'I am', see Findlay, pp. 143–44.

[57] Findlay, Chapter 2, 'The Bastard as Vice', traces some of the bastard's generalized viciousness to his descent from the Medieval Vice.

dirt (matter in the wrong place) and pollution (illegitimate mixture), whose very existence violates the natural order of things. But, at the same time, by his counterfeiting he also exemplifies a sinister sophistication or falsification of the 'true' or the 'natural'. When Spurio declares that 'Adultery is my nature' he is simultaneously quibbling on the idea of himself as a 'natural son' and elaborating a vicious paradox, according to which — by virtue of the 'nature' given him by his adulterate birth (*natura*) — he is naturally unnatural, essentially counterfeit, and purely adulterous: the proper fruit of a society where 'fruit fields are turned into bastards' (I. 3. 51), and the irregular epitome of a state whose officers of law have become 'authority's bastards' (III. 4. 73). In *King Lear* a similar series of quibbling associations underlies the counterfeiting Edmund's paean to the tutelary of bastards: 'Thou, Nature, art my goddess' (*Lear*, I. 2. 1). If Spurio expresses his adulterate nature by embracing the incestuous desires of his stepmother ('For indeed a bastard by nature should make cuckolds | Because he is the son of a cuckold maker' (*Revenger's Tragedy*, I. 2. 201–02)), Edmund equally displays his by contracting adulterous liaisons with Goneril and Regan. Together, these two characters reveal how, through one of those strange linguistic contradictions that expose cultural double-think, the bastard could be at once 'spurious' ('unnatural') and yet a 'natural child' — just as the term 'natural child' itself in sixteenth- and early seventeenth-century usage could be used to distinguish *either* legitimate or illegitimate offspring — an ambiguity nicely caught in Gloucester's embrace of Edmund as 'loyal and natural boy' (II. 1. 84). The naturally unnatural character of the bastard makes him into a living exemplar of those ironic mechanisms by which nature revenges itself on the perpetrators of vicious and unnatural acts. Adultery begets its own proper punishment — as Gloucester (like the dying Duke in *The Revenger's Tragedy*, his eyes forced open to witness himself made cuckold by his own bastard)[58] painfully discovers: 'the dark and vicious place where thee he got | Cost him his eyes' (*Lear*, V. 3. 173–74); so too, in *The Misfortunes of Arthur* (1588), King Arthur traces his downfall to the adultery and incest that shaped both his own and Mordred's bastard natures:

> Well: 'tis my plague for life so lewdly ledde,
> The price of guilt is still a heavier guilt.
> For were it light, that ev'n by birth my selfe
> Was bad, I made my sister bad: nay were
> That also light, I have begot as bad.
> Yea worse, an heire assignde to all our sinnes.   (III. 4. 18)[59]

The paradox of the bastard's unnatural kind is close to the heart of *King Lear* where notions of 'nature' and 'kind' are extensively problematized, and

---

[58] The ironic symmetries here are reinforced by the way in which the imagery of eating links Spurio's erotic banquet with the poison that gnaws the Duke's lips ('Those that did eat are eaten', I. 159) — it is as if Spurio *were* a devouring poison compounded of the Dukes's own blood/lust.
[59] Cited from *Early English Tragedies*, ed. by J. W. Cunliffe (Oxford: Clarendon Press, 1912).

where the oppositions between the 'true' and the 'bastard', the 'natural' and the 'unnatural', are alternately supported and confounded by the behaviour of Lear's and Gloucester's children. In a desperate endeavour to maintain the 'natural' boundaries between the legitimate and illegitimate, the two fathers rhetorically bastardize their legitimate children — making of Cordelia a *filia nullia*, denouncing Edgar as an 'unnatural. [...] monster' (I. 2. 76–94), and repudiating Goneril as 'degenerate bastard [...] more hideous [...] than the sea-monster' (I. 4. 254–61).[60] But for Lear the conviction that 'Gloucester's bastard son | Was kinder to his father than my daughters | Got 'tween the lawful sheets' (IV. 6. 114–17, begins to collapse all such distinctions into a misogynist vision of universal adultery, where all are bastardized and bemonstered by the very circumstances of their begetting between the Centaur thighs of their mothers.[61] In the context of such a vision, Edmund comes to seem less exceptional than representative — his bastardy, like Spurio's, an outward sign of the inner deformity afflicting a whole society where the 'unnatural' has become obscenely naturalized and 'humanity [...] prey[s] on itself, | Like monsters of the deep' (IV. 2. 49–50).

   This association of the bastard with the monstrous is by no means peculiar to *Lear*, of course. By the sixteenth century the word 'bastard' itself had acquired a range of meanings closely comparable to those of 'adultery' and its derivatives, referring not only to the 'spurious' or 'counterfeit', but also to the 'mongrel' or 'hybrid'[62] — in effect, the monstrous. The anomalous condition of the *filius nullius* was an expression 'the irregular intercourse of which he was the fruit',[63] defining him as monstrous because he represented the offspring of an unnatural union, one that adulterated what were proposed as among the most essential ('natural') of all boundaries.[64] So in Ford's *'Tis Pity She's a Whore*, for example, Hippolita's curse on her partner-in-adultery, Soranzo, for what she regards as his doubly adulterous marriage to Annabella, equates bastardy and monstrosity: 'mayst thou live | To father bastards, may her womb bring forth | Monsters' (IV. 1. 99–101); and her curse seems to have been granted a kind of ironic fulfilment when Soranzo discovers the existence of the 'gallimaufry' that is already 'stuffed in [Annabella's] corrupted bastard-bearing womb' (IV. 3. 13–14).

---

[60] In her unpublished paper, 'Filius Nullius: Bastards, Younger Sons, and Daughters in *King Lear*', delivered to the seminar on Shakespeare's Bastards in Vancouver, Kathy Howlett observes how accusations of bastardy abound in the play, embracing Regan, Edgar, and Oswald ('whoreson [...] son and heir of a mongrel bitch' (II. 2. 16–20)), as well as Edmund, Cordelia, and Goneril.
[61] The logic of this fantasy is beautifully traced in Janet Adelman's psychoanalytic account of the meaning of illegitimacy in *King Lear* (*Suffocating Mothers*. pp. 105–09). Adelman writes that 'maternal origin and illegitimacy are synonymous in the Gloucester plot — and throughout *Lear* because sexuality *per se* is illegitimate and illegitimizes its children; whether or not the son is biologically his father's, the mother's dark place inevitably contaminates him, compromising his father's presence in him' (p. 107).
[62] *OED* bastard, *sb.* and *a.*, B⁴, B², A³.
[63] Pinchbeck, p. 315; see also Findlay, p. 37.
[64] Kathy Howlett's *'Filius Nullius'* argues that in *Lear* Edmund's bastardy associated him with a whole range of characters whose nature 'cannot be bordered certain in itself' (IV. 2. 33) and who thus represent a threat to the categories and boundaries of 'an enclosed system'.

Being unholy, the bastard can never be 'whole': thus bastards are expressly linked with 'deformed persons, and eunuchs' in Francis Bacon's 'Of Envy' as creatures whose 'natural wants' may render them vicious;[65] and the same connexion is suggested by the deformity of the heteroclite brood — dwarf, eunuch, and hermaphrodite — which Volpone has supposedly begotten through adulterate commerce with 'Gypsies, Jews, and black-moors' (*Volpone*, I. 1. 506–07).[66] Thus when the Watch in *Much Ado About Nothing* uncover (with a telling Freudian malapropism) 'the most dangerous piece of *lechery* that ever was known in the commonwealth', and promise to expose the villains' accomplice, 'one *Deformed*' (III. 3. 161–67; my emphases), they speak wiser than the audience may suppose, since 'Deformed' is actually none other than that moral monster, Don John the Bastard. Nowhere, perhaps, is the deformed nature of the bastard more apparent than in that literal 'monster', the 'salvage and deformed slave', Caliban, who combines the physical malformation of Volpone's offspring with the misshapen psychology of a Don John, an Edmund, or a Spurio.[67]

This sense of the bastard's inherent deformity may attach itself even to those like Faulconbridge in *King John* whose character is in many respects attractive, even admirable. An invention of Shakespeare's principal source, *The Troublesome Raigne*, the bastard had already established himself as the effective hero of that play: but there his bastardy figured merely as a factor in the dramatized debate as to who should properly inherit the patriotic mantle (or lionskin) of Richard Coeur-de-lion. Shakespeare's adaptation, however, makes the issue of his illegitimacy symbolically central to a play in which (in Phyllis Rackin's words) 'every source of authority fails and legitimacy is reduced to a legal fiction';[68] and where, as a result, 'All form is formless, order orderless' (III. 1. 253). In *King John* the legitimacy of all claimants to the throne is under challenge: not only is bastardy polemically alleged against both Prince Arthur and his father in Act II, scene I (ll. 121–31), but the king himself is denounced in the opening exchange for the illegitimate usurpation

[65] Francis Bacon, *Essays* (London: Dent, 1906), p. 25. Significantly Deuteronomy 23. 1–2 similarly links eunuchs and bastards in its list of those forbidden to enter the congregation of the Lord (see also Leviticus 21. 18–20). Canon law accordingly excluded eunuchs as well as bastards from the priesthood — indicating that both groups were seen as polluted by their failure to conform fully to the category 'man'.
[66] By the same token Corbaccio's bastardizing of Bonario is mockingly announced by Mosca as a 'monstrous' wrong (III. 1. 91). The Bastard's monstrosity is compounded by the fact that through his very existence he proves his mother a whore, thus demonstrating her own monstrosity, since, as Nicholas Breton declared: 'A whore is no perfect woman; for every woman is either a maide, a wife, or a widow; and being neither of these, she must needs be a monster, and so an imperfect woman' (*Diverse Newes Out of Divers Countries* in *The Works in Verse and Prose*, ed. A. B. Gossart, 2 vols (Edinburgh: Chertsey Worthies Library, 1879, II, p. 8). Edmund is a 'whoreson [who] must be acknowledged', but ironically that very acknowledgement, as his lowering presence reminds us, publicly brands his mother as a whore.
[67] Findlay (pp. 53–55) notes that Caliban's deformity, like that of his kinsman Suckabus, bastard child of the witch Calib in *Seven Champions of Chistendom*, is also a reflection of his allegedly diabolic paternity. However she cites other examples of the association of the bastard with the monstrous and deformed, pp. 112–16.
[68] Phyllis Rackin, *Stages of History: Shakespeare's English Chronicles* (Ithaca: Cornell University Press, 1990), p. 184.

of his 'borrowed majesty' — a usurpation which the French king figures as
an act of violent adultery, by which John has

> Cut off the sequence of posterity,
> Outfaced infant state, and done a rape
> Upon the maiden virtue of the crown.   (II. 1. 96)

As 'the presiding spirit' of this play, 'the human embodiment of every kind of
illegitimacy',[69] the Bastard incarnates the deformity in the body politic
which is the consequence of John's adulterous usurpation of the crown, and
which Salisbury insists that Prince Henry is born to reform:

> for you are born
> To set a form upon that indigest
> Which he hath left so shapeless and so rude'   (V. 7. 25)

The expressive vehicles of this deformity are the 'rude' speech (I. 1. 64) and
'wild counsel' (II. 1. 395), with which he persistently subverts the shaping
authority of official language — as, for example, in the confrontation
between the rival kings at Angers, where his subversive asides disrupt the
very form and syntax of the verse itself —

KING JOHN	[. . .] I bring you witnesses,
	Twice fifteen thousand hearts of England's breed —
BASTARD	Bastards, and else.
KING JOHN	To verify our title with their lives.
KING PHILIP	As many and as well-born bloods as those —
BASTARD	Some bastards too.
KING PHILIP	Stand in his face to contradict his claim.

(II. 1. 274)

From the Bastard's perspective, however, the authorized language of
chivalric heroism is merely another version of the rhetoric of patriarchal
reproof that first pronounced his own illegitimacy:

> Here's a large mouth indeed [. . .]
> What cannoneer begot this lusty blood?
> He speaks plain cannon-fire [. . .]
> Zounds, I was never so bethumped with words
> Since I first call'd my brother's father dad.   (II. 1. 457–68)

It is this iconoclastic licence which, in a world tainted with illegitimacy,
makes Faulconbridge, as Joseph Candido observes, 'a sort of moral oxymoron [. . .] a true bastard to the time', endowing him with a paradoxical
quality of 'authenticity'.[70] Significantly Faulconbridge must surrender this
dialect of liberty before he can offer his 'true subjection' to the 'lineal state' of
King Henry, and become the choric spokesman of the legitimate and the

---

[69] Rackin, p. 186. For Joseph Candido, the Bastard's 'personal defilement' represents the impossibility
of untainted action in 'an adulterate world'. Candido discovers in the play 'a Hamletesque obsession with
sullied purity and [. . .] adultery' ('Blots, Stains', p. 114).
[70] Candido, 'Blots, Stains', p. 123. For some discussion of the bastard's association with chaos and
topsy-turveydom, see Findlay, pp. 133–36, 208.

'true' (v. 7. 101–05). For as long as it is sustained, however, it makes him the most energetic presence in the play;[71] and this disruptive idiom is one that he conspicuously shares not only with the likes of Spurio ('Old dad dead?)' (*Revenger's Tragedy*, v. 1. 111) and Edmund ('Fine word "legitimate"' *Lear*, 1. 2. 18), but above all with the most linguistically progenitive as well as the most degenerate, of all his bastard kin, Thersites.

Homer's Thersites was 'the ugliest man that had come to Ilium' and became proverbial for his deformity of body and mind.[72] But only in Shakespeare does he identify himself as a bastard; and in *Troilus and Cressida* his bastardy operates as a sign of the work's own generic illegitimacy. His function as the play's deformed chorus serves as a reminder that when the Renaissance thought of literary 'kind' it was not so much speaking meta-phorically as imagining the laws which governed a second order of nature. At every point, in its recurrent imagery of the monstrous, *Troilus and Cressida* seems aware of its affront to the 'natural' laws of composition. Spurning what Agamemnon would call the 'surmised shape' and 'promised largeness' of its epic design, it grows deliberately 'bias and thwart'. A piece of 'ridiculous and awkward action', a 'counterfeit' more shameless than any of Patroclus's or Thersites's strutting imitations, *Troilus* revels in its own illegitimacy. This play is bastard work *par excellence*, delighting in the humiliations it visits upon the head of Homer, the patriarchal begetter, whose frustrated yet defiant heir it seems to be.

With Thersites, more comprehensively than with any of his rivals, the deformity of the bastard infects his whole world, utterly subverting the generic integrity of a play whose monstrous design comes to mirror his own adulterate and irregular nature. *Troilus* is by common consent the most bafflingly mixed of Shakespeare's performances — a hybrid creation that from the very beginning has seemed to confound the taxonomy of kinds. First published as a 'History', in a quarto whose second state included a preface that identified it as a 'commedy' (and one that rivalled the best work of Terence and Plautus), it was nevertheless offered to readers of the Folio as *The Tragedie of Troilus and Cressida*; while twentieth-century rediscoverers of the play have variously labelled it a romantic tragedy, an abortive heroic tragedy, a comical satire, a mock-heroic burlesque, and a deliberate exercise in the grotesque. To Heinrich Heine, it was a play in which the tragic muse chose to 'act the clown' — 'it is as though we should see Melpomene dancing the *can-can* at a ball of *grisettes*, with shameless laughter on her pallid lips, and with death in her heart'; while Swinburne hailed the play as a marvellous artificial monster — 'this hybrid and hundred-faced and hydra-headed

---

[71] Although Faulconbridge's discovery of an unambiguously heroic-patriotic language at the end of the play signals a kind of legitimation, arguably 'The Four Voices of the Bastard' defined by Michael Manheim in Curren-Aquino, *King John* pp. 126–35, are themselves an illustration of his mixed nature.
[72] See Homer, *Iliad*, Book II; Erasmus, *Adages*, 'Thersitae Facies'.

prodigy'.[73] In the end *Troilus* is perhaps best described in the self-referential flourish that Swinburne unconsciously paraphrased — as a literary creature, which, like that 'blended knight', the 'mongrel' Ajax (II. 1. 13; IV. 5. 86), 'hath robb'd many beasts of their particular additions [...] [its] valour crushed into folly, [its] folly sauc'd with discretion [...] [having] the joints of every thing, but every thing so out of joint that [it] is a gouty Briareus, many hands and no use, or purblind Argus, all eyes and no sight' (I. 1. 19–30).[74] Less extravagantly, we might see it as a mocking exemplum of Sidney's 'mongrel tragicomedy';[75] or as a marvellous *reductio ad absurdum* of Guarini's paradoxical defence of the tragicomic hybrid — a genre in which the very mixtures that conventionally identify 'an unseemly and monstrous story' become the marks of 'a good and legitimate poem' because it imitates a world where contraries are naturally linked in all kinds of 'illegitimate' conjunction.[76]

It is entirely in accord with this indecorous decorum that a professing illegitimate should emerge as the moving spirit of a play which, like him, is 'bastard begot, bastard instructed, bastard in mind, bastard in valor, in everything illegitimate' (v. 7. 17–18). What more proper chorus than a bastard, after all, for a play that improperly corrupts the whole epic 'matter of Troy' into a battle for 'contaminated carrion' (IV. 1. 72), a fable of adultery in which 'all the argument is a whore and cuckold' (II. 3. 72–73)? The reductiveness of this parody of a Jonsonian *argumentum fabulae* is absolutely characteristic: for if Sidney objected to mongrel plays in which degree was violated by 'mingling kings and clowns', *Troilus* is a play which annihilates degree by rendering them systematically indistinguishable — so that Ajax, for example, takes the clownish Thersites for King Agamemnon himself (III. 3. 260–61). Helplessly nostalgic for an order of 'distinction' and 'authentic place' in which 'what hath mass or matter by itself | Lies rich in virtue and *unmingled*' (I. 3. 27–30, 108; my emphasis), and where the singleness of truth is expressed in sublime tautology ('as true as truth's simplicity', III. 2. 169) its denizens inhabit a world of degenerate and confused mixture where the very opposites of 'right and wrong', appear to 'lose their names' (I. 3. 116–18), and where truth becomes a false or bastard thing, since 'to say the truth' is to say 'true and not true' (I. 2. 98).

---

[73] Heinrich Heine, *Shakespeare's Girls and Women*, trans. C. G. Leland (1839; 1891); A. C. Swinburne, *A Study of Shakespeare* (1880); both in *Troilus and Cressida: A Casebook* ed. by Priscilla Martin (London: Macmillan, 1976), pp. 45, 55.

[74] Elsewhere Ajax appears as a kind of Plinian monster 'who wears his wit in his belly and his guts in his head' (II. i. 73–74); and if Ajax is a monster, so too is that horned beast Menelaus, for example, 'both ass and ox' in Thersites's estimate, and rhetorically tainted, too, with the qualities of 'a [dog], a moile, a cat, a fitchook, a toad, a lezard, an owl, a puttock, [...] a herring without a roe, [...] the louse of a lazar' (v. 1. 59–65).

[75] Sir Philip Sidney, *An Apology for Poetry*, in *English Critical Essays (Sixteenth, Seventeenth, and Eighteenth Centuries)*, ed. by Edmund D. Jones (London: Oxford University Press, 1947), p. 46.

[76] Giambattista Guarini, 'The Compendium of Tragicomic Poetry', in *Literary Criticism, Plato to Dryden*, ed. by Alan H. Gilbert (Detroit: Wayne State University Press, 1962), pp. 507, 513.

Symbolically speaking, Thersites is the polluted source of this plague of indistinction, the levelling satire which renders 'the mongril cur Ajax' indistinguishable from 'that dog of as bad a kind [...] the cur Achilles', or 'that same dog-fox Ulysses' (v. 4. 11–15), or ultimately from that '*whoreson indistinguishable* cur' Thersites himself (v. 1. 28–29; my emphasis).[77] It is the touch of Thersites's bastard nature that makes this whole world indistinguishably kin (but distinctly less than kind). Saluted by Achilles as 'crusty botch of nature' — at once a source of pustular infection, and a clumsily botched copy of humankind — Thersites is the monstrous 'core of envy' from which flows the stream of poisonous comparison that reduces Agamemnon himself to a 'botchy core' (v. 1. 4–5; II. 1. 6).

In Thersites' disintegrative vision of what Faulconbridge calls the 'undetermin'd differences of Kings' (*King John*, II. 1. 355), each particular warrior becomes merely a '*general*' symptom of the 'plague of Greece', 'The *common* curse of mankind, folly and ignorance' (II. 1. 12, II. 3. 27–28; my emphases). This is a play where kings and clowns are not merely thrust together by the head and shoulders, but where each becomes a simulacrum of the other, and both are mirrored in one supremely reductive image of debased mixture — Hector's last conquest of a warrior whose sumptuous armour is stripped to display a 'putrefied core' of filthy indistinction, the image of his own undistinguished death.[78]

Offering itself, in a characteristic oxymoron, as a pageant of 'monumental mock'ry',[79] *Troilus and Cressida*, far from defying the depredations of Time, monstrously collaborates in the oblivious work of that 'great-siz'd monster of ingratitudes' (III. 3. 147, 153), through its systematic debasement of heroic memory.[80] Its self-cancelling frenzy is perfectly expressed in its spurious chorus, whose final appearance brings him into confrontation with his fellow-bastard, Margarelon. Although Thersites may refuse this combat with a mirror-self as unnatural ('one bear will not bite another, and wherefore should one bastard?' v. 7. 18–20), the confrontation nicely epitomizes the self-devouring tendency of his satire. For Thersites is by his own confession 'lost in the labyrinth of [his] own fury' — at once minotaur and

---

[77] See René Girard, '*The Plague in Literature and Myth*': *To Double Business Bound*, (Baltimore: Johns Hopkins University Press, 1978); in *King John* too, adultery and bastardy are figured as symptoms of moral plague, in Constance's tirade against Elinor's alleged adultery and John's consequent illegitimacy: 'God hath made her sin and her the plague | On this removed issue, plagued for her, | And with her plague, her sin. [...] A plague upon her!' (II. 1. 185–90).

[78] At this point Shakespeare, like the author of *The Revenger's Tragedy* in the celebrated 'bony lady' scene, seems to produce a grotesquely literal version of Sidney's apocalyptic ideal of tragedy as 'show[ing] forth the ulcers that are covered with tissue' (*Apology*, p. 28). The figure must of course recall the Prologue, 'suited in like condition as our *argument*' who so pompously ushers in a play where 'all the *argument* is a whore and a cuckold'.

[79] For a brilliant exploration of this aspect of the play, see Rosalie L. Colie, *Shakespeare's Living Art* (Princeton NJ: Princeton University Press, 1974), Chapter 8, 'Forms and Their Meanings: Monumental Mockery'.

[80] Such self-cancelling paradoxes were particularly attractive to John Marston, with whose satiric writing *Troilus* is often compared: see for example his dedication of *The Scourge of Villainy*, 'To Everlasting Oblivion', repeated in the wry motto chosen for his own tomb, *Oblivioni Sacrum*.

victim, consumed in a satirical plague of his own generation. In this he is the true scion of a work whose bastardizing vision so levels distinction that language itself seems to fail, rendering it, for all its storms of rhetoric, once again like Ajax, 'a very land-fish, languageless, a monster' (III. 3. 263).

Nestor describes him as 'A slave whose gall coins slanders like a mint, | To match us in comparisons with dirt' (I. 3. 193–94); and his rhetoric perfectly embodies the undifferentiating tendency of dirt, as Mary Douglas describes it:

in [the] final stage of total disintegration, dirt is utterly undifferentiated. [...] Dirt was created by the differentiating activity of mind, it was a by-product of the creation of order. So it started from a state of non-differentiation; all through the process of differentiating its role was to threaten the distinctions made; finally it returns to its true indeterminable character [of] formlessness.[81]

The bastard, I have tried to suggest, is indeed the human equivalent of dirt — a category of being 'created by the differentiating activity of mind' as a by-product of the attempt to define and preserve a certain kind of social order; but his role, *by definition*, is also to challenge that order, 'to threaten the distinctions made'; and in *Troilus and Cressida* it is the bastard's adulterate vision that seems to reduce his world (and the whole fabulous 'matter of Troy') to the condition of pure dirt, of matter in 'its true indeterminable character of formlessness' imagined in Ulysses's nightmare of indistinction when 'the primogenity and due of birth' loses its 'authentic place' and 'each thing melts | In mere oppugnancy':

> the bounded waters
> Should lift their bosoms higher than the shores,
> And make a sop of all this solid globe;
> Strength should be lord of imbecility,
> And the rude son should strike his father dead;
> Force should be right — or rather, right and wrong
> (Between whose endless jar justice resides),
> Should lose their names, and so should justice too!
> Then everything include itself in power,
> Power into will, will into appetite,
> And appetite, an universal wolf
> (So doubly seconded with will and power),
> Must make perforce an universal prey,
> And last eat up himself.   (I. 3. 111)

[81] Douglas, p. 161.

Children and Suffering in Shakespeare's Plays

ANN BLAKE

La Trobe University

One way in which Shakespeare's England differed from ours was in the much larger proportion of children in the population. Despite the high infant and child mortality rates — about a quarter of all children failed to reach the age of ten — 'probably something in the region of 40 per cent of the population consisted of dependent children living at home with their parents'.[1] This meant, as Laslett wrote, that 'children were everywhere', a constant presence in all adult affairs, as in some of the paintings of the period where children are often seen playing in the background or crawling into the foreground.[2] The imaginary worlds of Shakespeare's plays do not, of course, reflect these proportions since they do not set out to be social documentaries; adults are more dramatically interesting than children, and the plays are concerned with them. Nevertheless a careful search reveals a surprisingly large number of parts for children, at least thirty. It is particularly interesting to discover that some of the more substantial roles are Shakespeare's invention. Young Lucius in *Titus Andronicus*, the Boy in *Henry V*, and Lucius, Brutus's page in *Julius Caesar*, have no counterparts in Shakespeare's sources, while the scenes of young Macduff and Mamillius grow from only the briefest hints. Children *were* everywhere in 1600, including in Shakespeare's company where they worked as apprentices to adult actors. But the quality of some of these parts makes us recognize that more is being done than giving the boy actors something to do until they graduate to the demanding task of playing women. In his histories and tragedies Shakespeare has created a number of child characters who come to a violent end. What follows is an attempt to define the dramatic significance in Shakespeare's tragic world of these scenes of children and their suffering.

The image of the child in Shakespeare's plays takes little account of the contemporary religious and educational sense of the imperfections of childhood. These children are tender-hearted and loyal, brave, and idealistic. Moreover, they are free from adult vices, and emphatically innocent. Milton expresses orthodox Christian doctrine on the child's position within fallen mankind when he writes: 'Assuredly we bring not innocence into the world,

---

[1] Keith Wrightson, *English Society 1580–1680*, Hutchinson Social History of England (London: Hutchinson, 1982), pp. 105–06.

[2] Peter Laslett, *The World We Have Lost further explored*, 3rd edn (London: Methuen, 1983), p. 119.

we bring impurity much rather.' Contemporary writing on the education of
the young begins with a sense of the innate imperfection of children as beings
who must be closely watched and severely disciplined for their own good, in
the hope that soon rational faculties will be sufficiently developed to restrain
natural evil impulses. That view of the young is perhaps reflected in
'schoolmaster' Prospero's efforts to 'nurture' the dark nature of the 'hag-
seed' Caliban, and his own noble daughter, but not in the characterization of
those who actually appear as young children. Though the language of the
plays reasonably enough attaches the adjective 'childish' to the recognized
disabilities of childhood: 'error', 'weakness', 'treble', 'fear', and so on, the
figures of the children themselves are felt to be not so much inferior as
innocent and defenceless.

When Polixenes in *The Winter's Tale* talks to Hermione of himself and
Leontes as boys, he describes such childhood innocence:

> We were, fair Queen,
> Two lads that thought there was no more behind
> But such a day to-morrow as to-day,
> And to be boy eternal [. . .]
> We were as twinn'd lambs that did frisk i' th' sun
> And bleat the one at th' other. What we chang'd
> Was innocence for innocence; we knew not
> The doctrine of ill-doing, nor dream'd
> That any did. Had we pursu'd that life,
> And our weak spirits ne'er been higher rear'd
> With stronger blood, we should have answer'd heaven
> Boldly 'Not guilty', the imposition clear'd
> Hereditary ours.
>
> (i. 2. 62–75)[3]

The dramatic context immediately comments on Polixenes's words with the
outbreak of Leontes's sexual rage. Polixenes's sense of innocence here, with
its proper acknowledgement of original sin, 'the imposition [. . .] hereditary
ours', is to be found, of course, in many contemporary poems addressed to
children, such as Milton's 'On the death of a fair infant dying of a cough'
which eloquently and comprehensively praises the 'heaven loved innocence'
of those who die young, and it informs Earle's rightly famous 'character' of
'The Child', with its images of 'nature's fresh picture newly drawne in Oyle
which time and much handling dimmes and defaces. This soul is yet a white
paper unscribled with observations from the world, wherewith at length it
becomes a blurr'd Notebook'. And in the world of Shakespeare's plays the
innocence of living children is consistently felt. They may tease and become
tiresome but they never practise that thoughtless cruelty which appears in
the imagery of the plays, most memorably in Gloucester's simile for the cruel
gods: 'As flies to wanton boys are we to th' gods. They kill us for their sport'

[3] All references to the texts of Shakespeare's plays follow William Shakespeare, *The Complete Works*, ed.
by P. Alexander (London and Glasgow: Collins, 1951).

(IV.1.37). No such boys occur in the plays; on the contrary the children themselves are seen primarily as victims, and in need of protection from adult wickedness. With one exception, William Page, who has the good luck to live in a comic world in *The Merry Wives of Windsor*, all Shakespeare's named children are fated to suffer. Their youth, weakness, and innocence ask for protection but they meet instead with cruelty and violence. Their sufferings and deaths constitute an image of human evil at its most ruthless: what Tyrrel, speaking of the murder of the little princes in *Richard III*, calls 'the most arch deed of piteous massacre', the horror of violence inflicted on those incapable of defending themselves, or even of understanding why they are to be hurt.

The most impressive of these scenes, and the one which has the most far-reaching dramatic significance, is the 'piteous massacre' of young Macduff. The boy becomes a target when Macbeth, warned by the Witches' apparition to 'beware Macduff', hears that Macduff has fled to England. In rage and frustration at this escape he declares he will have all Macduff's family killed. This massacre is, like Herod's Massacre of the Innocents, futile savagery. As soon as Macbeth announces his terrible intentions at the end of Act IV Scene 1, the audience begins to wait in dread for the murder:

> The castle of Macduff I will surprise,
> Seize upon Fife, give to the edge o' th' sword
> His wife, his babes, and all unfortunate souls
> That trace him in his line.
>
> (IV.1.150)

When Lady Macduff and her child come on stage at the beginning of Act IV Scene 2, the murderers are approaching; Ross warns of danger, Lady Macduff is fearful, but the audience is certain, and that gives a terrible edge to her words as she speaks to Ross of her husband's flight: it is a betrayal, and leaves them all exposed and vulnerable. Ross, though overcome with sorrow at their plight, can offer no comfort or reassurance, and he leaves. As Lady Macduff speaks with her son the suspense grows, rising further with the arrival of the Messenger, who urges Lady Macduff to fly 'fell cruelty' with her 'little ones'; but the warning is too late. She has time to make one speech of protest and then the murderers burst in. Only young Macduff is killed on stage, the slaughter of Lady Macduff and her other children, 'all my pretty chickens', is, like the murder of Duncan, left to the appalled imagination. Young Macduff dies with the courage and nobility characteristic of Shakespeare's children, defending his father's honour and trying to save his mother's life with a pathetically child-like phrase: 'Run away, I pray you' (IV.2.85). The suspense, and the horror of the butchery of the boy by the 'shag-ear'd' villains is appalling; no wonder the scene was omitted for eighteenth- and nineteenth-century audiences. It may not match in ghastly detail the threatened blinding of Arthur by red hot irons, but in *King John* the worst does not happen; Hubert spares the boy. The slaughter of young Macduff offers no escape: these assassins seem to enjoy what they are doing.

At the heart of the scene is the conversation between Lady Macduff and her son, Shakespeare's additions to his chronicle source,[4] where the pathos and fearfulness of their situation is heightened by Shakespeare's contrasting the innocent child's view with the experienced adult's. Left alone with her son, Lady Macduff gives release to her distress at her husband's betrayal of his family and her fear for their lives. She does this obliquely, playing a bitterly humorous game, telling her son that his father is dead. How will he live now? He is confident that he'll be able to get what he needs, as birds do. She recognizes this as the confidence of a child, founded, like that of the innocent creatures of the natural world, on ignorance of difficulty and danger: 'Poor bird! thou'dst never fear the net nor lime, | The pitfall nor the gin' (IV. 2. 34–35). With precocious wit he insists that he will survive since *he* is not a 'poor bird'. In her grief and anxiety Lady Macduff repeats that his father is dead (or as good as), and she throws back her question: 'How wilt thou do for a father?' But young Macduff's confidence is proof against her and manifests itself in pert sophistication: 'If he were dead, you'd weep for him; if you would not, it were a good sign that I should quickly have a new father' (IV. 2. 60–62). His reliance on his reading of his mother's mood is not justified, and with his pretence to worldly wisdom he skates over the terrible depths of her cares. But he is puzzled and questions his mother persistently: 'Was my father a traitor, mother?' and next 'What is a traitor?', a very child-like order of questions. His mother explains that a traitor is one that swears and lies, but her son, probably more familiar with the idea of the wickedness of swearing than with the act of swearing allegiance, brightly suggests that his father is in no danger: traitors, swearers, and liars will never be hanged since they out-number the honest men. Lady Macduff comments: 'Poor prattler, how thou talk'st' (IV. 2. 63); her capacity to indulge her precocious son is running out. That the pathos in this conversation comes across without any sentimentality is due in part to the sharp sense, in their dark situation, of the discrepancy between an adult's and a child's understanding of evil. Lady Macduff has the bitter knowledge that there may be no reason why she is in danger except that she is in 'this earthly world'. But young Macduff, for all his knowing talk, is innocent.

That youthful innocence, dramatized throughout the scene, is underlined by the words of the murderers as the child is killed: 'What, you *egg*?/ *Young fry* of treachery!' (IV. 2. 83). It is this scene between a child and a parent which brings together in a way unique in the play, and among such scenes in Shakespeare, images of tender care and nurture by parents of young children and by creatures of their young. Lady Macduff contrasts her husband's abandoning of his family with the wren who fights to defend her young in the

---

[4] Holinshed's *Chronicle* provides a striking visual parallel in the woodcut of Makdowald who, anticipating an attack on his castle by Macbeth, slaughters his wife and children and then commits suicide. See *The Historie of Scotland*, 1577, p. 240, reproduced in *Narrative and Dramatic Sources of Shakespeare*, ed. by G. Bullough, 7 vols (London: Routledge and Kegan Paul, 1964–75), VII, 491.

nest against the owl: Macduff 'wants the natural touch' (IV. 2. 9). As their conversation draws on these images, the scene centres on the tender relationship between parents and children, which here, most strikingly, incorporates pathetic humour in a situation of great danger. The vulnerability of the young and their need of protection is dramatically obvious. The whole scene gives new life to the play's clusters of images of babies, milk, and nurturing, of birds, eggs, and nests, which define a particular sense of natural bonding which Macbeth violates, and thereby loses. His assassins destroy the child, and the entire family, and we see this as the most simply hateful image of that warfare on humanity, including his own, which he wages all through the play, with such grim success.

The effect is similar to that in *Richard III*, where it is the murder of the little princes which most clearly invites the audience to respond to Richard's actions as cruel for the first time in the play. Before that, Richard has established a close, even confidential, relationship with the audience. Shakespeare chooses not to present the murder of the princes on stage, perhaps to avoid repetition after the murder of Clarence.[5] It has great impact nevertheless. Tyrrel's announcement is made straight to the audience, in soliloquy, and with passionate indignation. Responsibility for the slaughter is carried back to Richard, and the dramatic effect of the arch horror of the atrocity brings about a change in the allegiance of the audience who now turn against Richard, and thus are prepared to accept his defeat and death.

In *Macbeth* the effect of the murder of young Macduff is more complex. We can see why Bradley questioned whether the scene was needed to heighten our abhorrence of Macbeth's cruelty when Shakespare has already made us feel, with Macbeth himself, such abhorrence at the murders of Duncan and Banquo. His sense of the function of the scene stressed the appeal of its pathos: 'to touch the heart with a sense of beauty and pathos, to open the springs of love and tears'.[6] This it undoubtedly does, because Shakespeare engages our feelings so powerfully for this defenceless mother and child, and then for the bereaved father, Macduff. Emrys Jones sees this scene, together with the scene in England (IV. 3), as a single unit which is vital to the structure of feeling in the play. When Macduff hears the news of the slaughter of his family this is, Jones says, 'the first time in the play that what we see on stage has the effect of simply moving us'.[7] It may well be, as Bradley implied in his phrase 'to open the springs of love and tears' and as Jones explicitly argues, that the audience's pity extends even to promptings of 'deep tragic sympathy' for the king and queen. Shakespeare's remarkable achievement in *Macbeth* is to make us care for their fate in the last act, and

[5] See Bullough, III, 239. Bullough believes that Shakespeare chose not to show the murder of the princes because he was consciously avoiding materials recently dramatized in *The True Tragedy of Richard III*, perhaps because he had been recently accused of plagiarism by Robert Greene, and because he wished to prove his independence.

[6] A. C. Bradley, *Shakespearean Tragedy* (London: Macmillan, 1904), p. 391.

[7] Emrys Jones, *Scenic Form in Shakespeare* (Oxford: Clarendon Press, 1971), p. 221.

sympathy aroused in the first place by Macbeth's own victims contributes to this end.

In his first tragedy, *Titus Andronicus*, Shakespeare had introduced a child: young Lucius, the grandson of Titus, who, from this point of view, is an early and less successful version of young Macduff. As Kermode noted, his role is to contribute to the restoration of sympathy towards Titus.[8] And, again like young Macduff, though without himself becoming a victim, he heightens the sense of horror: through his innocent, partial comprehension he offers a distinctly pathetic perspective on the situation around him. His first appearance, in the Folio text, is at the family banquet (iii. 2), attended by the mad Titus and the mutilated Lavinia, where his distress for his grandfather is pitiful, especially because of his limited sense of adult griefs and wrongs. His idea of making Lavinia 'merry with some pleasing tale' fits his experience of life, but not theirs. The boy's tender impulse has a pathetic humour which anticipates the pathos and humour in the scene in *Macbeth*. However, at the end of the play the juxtaposing of pathos and horror goes awry. Young Lucius's father, now proclaimed emperor of Rome, grieves over Titus's body and calls on his son to join him:

> Come hither, boy; come, come and learn of us
> To melt in showers. Thy grandsire lov'd thee well;
> Many a time he danc'd thee on his knee,
> Sung thee asleep, his loving breast thy pillow;
> Many a story hath he told to thee,
> And bid thee bear his pretty tales in mind
> And talk of them when he was dead and gone.
>
> (v. 3. 160)

His reference to story-telling is too obvious an appeal: Mamillius in *The Winter's Tale* does his own story-telling, and thus creates a less predictably sweet picture. Moreover, the image of the loving grandsire is awkwardly juxtaposed to the Titus who has just served a Thyestean banquet, and stabbed his daughter and the Empress before being killed himself. Young Lucius's reply is just as disjunctive as his father's speech:

> O grandsire, grandsire! ev'n with all my heart
> Would I were dead, so you did live again!
> O Lord, I cannot speak to him for weeping;
> My tears will choke me, if I ope my mouth.
>
> (v. 3. 172)

This image of Titus evoked by the weeping grandchild seems, in the light of what precedes it, a mawkish indulgence, too obvious and unnecessary an appeal for sympathy for Titus. Keats, who had some interest in the sentimental, refused to accept as Shakespeare's these last moments of the play.

---

[8] Frank Kermode, Introduction to *Titus Andronicus* in *The Riverside Shakespeare*, ed. by G. Blakemore Evans (Boston: Houghton Mifflin, 1974), p. 1022.

The tragedies of Shakespeare's contemporaries and immediate followers include remarkably few child figures, and those that do exist draw attention, by their weaknesses, to the achievement of *Macbeth*, and to two difficulties apparent in *Titus Andronicus*: how to arouse simple pathos without falling into sentimentality, and how to bring together pathos and horror without also arousing incredulous laughter. Marston aims for the mixed effect of pathos and horror with the child Julio in *Antonio's Revenge*, but goes too far. Julio is killed on stage by Antonio and the scene of his death is an implausibly heightened version of the horror and sweetness juxtaposed in Arthur's scene with Hubert in *King John*. Little Julio loves Antonio dearly, and asks for a kiss: "Truth, I love you better than my father, 'deed.'[9] He pleads for his life but finally, with incredible gentle passivity, surrenders: 'So you will love me, do even what you will' (III.3.42). Antonio protests that he loves the boy and kisses him, but, being a more furious avenger than even Shakespeare's young Clifford, he will not hesitate to kill the child of his enemy, and he stabs Julio saying: 'Whilst thy wounds bleed, my brows shall gush out tears' (III.3.41). Marston contrives a final excess of revenge horror when Antonio lifts up the little dead body and drips the blood on his father's hearse.

The boy Hengo in Fletcher's *Bonduca*, after a prominent and pathetic role, also meets a spectacular death on stage: he is shot while suspended from a 'rock'. His loving uncle then hauls up the wounded child to die in his arms. Their protracted leave-taking is typical of Webster and Fletcher in its spun-out pathos. That Webster can present pathos successfully is witnessed — at least for some — by the Duchess of Malfi's lines, at the point of death:

> I pray thee look thou giv'st my little boy
> Some syrup for his cold, and let the girl
> Say her prayers, ere she sleep.[10]

Keeping the reins on pathetic dialogue between a child and an adult proves harder for both dramatists. (The Duchess's own children are, perhaps mercifully, silent.) Giovanni in *The White Devil* is, like Hengo, a 'lapwing' of a prince, boasting at length of the deeds he will perform to delighted relatives. Both catechize tender-hearted adults about death. Giovanni's weariness from grief: 'Lord, Lord, that I were dead, | I have not slept these six nights' (III.2.324–25), saves his speech from sentimentality; Hengo's speeches are beyond saving and go on for some forty lines. Shakespeare's scenes avoid this danger, first of all, by being brief. With the exception of the final slow-moving passage from *Titus*, the scenes allow no lengthy savouring of the feelings evoked. Further, Shakespeare presents sharply observed, *varied* childhood behaviour. His contemporaries sound single, unmixed notes: the valiant treble or the quiet child mourning lost parents, an episode whose

---

[9] John Marston, *Antonio's Revenge*, ed. by W. Reavley Gair, The Revels Plays (Manchester: University Press; Baltimore: John Hopkins University Press, 1978), III.3.5.
[10] *The Duchess of Malfi*, IV.ii.203–05, in John Webster, *Three Plays*, ed. by D. C. Gunby (Harmondsworth: Penguin, 1972). Quotations from Webster follow this edition.

appeal is easily predictable. Shakespeare, distinctively, brings together pathos, horror, and humour in scenes which contribute to the significance of the whole play, while Webster and Fletcher merely display children in pathetic cameos.

Each of the roles for children in Shakespeare's tragedies, *Titus Andronicus, Macbeth,* and *Coriolanus,* and in what might be called the tragic half of *The Winter's Tale,* bears a distinct stamp, and emphasizes different aspects of a child's nature or experience, to fulfil a particular dramatic function. For instance, Coriolanus's son, young Martius, makes only one appearance, in Act v. Scene 3, and speaks one speech, defying his father:

> 'A shall not tread on me!
> I'll run away till I am bigger, but then I'll fight.
>
> (v. 3. 127)

His brave words in a barely understood situation raise a smile and break the tension of the scene with an easily recognized moment when parents are amused by their child, and indulge him. Out of this pathetic humour emerges Martius's symbolic role. As Coriolanus struggles to remain unmoved by ties of country and family the presence of the child makes it less and less possible for him to maintain an unnatural distance from his mother and her demands. He wills himself to reject natural feeling:

> I'll never
> Be such a gosling to obey instinct but stand
> As if a man were author of himself
> And knew no other kin.
>
> (v. 3. 34)

But knowing kin is inevitable as his wife presents their son: 'This is a poor epitome of yours' (v. 3. 68). The boy's presence traps Coriolanus into admitting his natural human ties: 'That's my brave boy' he says as Martius kneels to him. While still speaking slightingly of the ties of kin — 'woman's tenderness' — he acts positively in response to them, and it is the child who has enabled these feelings to be presented simply and directly.

Mamillius in *The Winter's Tale* has different symbolic functions. His role in the first part of the play is to embody that state of sexual innocence which Leontes and Polixenes so insist on in their conversation about their youth, when they were 'pretty lordings'. All through Act I Scene 2 Mamillius, the innocent child, is on stage, and Leontes explicitly identifies his own childhood self with the boy, a 'kernel, | This squash'. Later in the scene Mamillius is the audience to Leontes's tirades of sexual jealousy, and in that pathetic situation, seen in earlier plays, of trying to cheer and please a distressed adult, the cause of whose distress he does not understand. The contrast between the innocent child's world and the world of adult sexuality (here leading to torment and misery) could hardly be more sharply realized than by these two, father and son, standing side by side. Mamillius's death occurs half-way through the play, but the idea of children as an 'unspeakable comfort' to their parents continues to be important. Children as a cure for melancholy and even a palliative to thoughts of death is a view of progeny that goes beyond the Sonnets' argument that children, like fame, offer a kind of immortality. The feeling for children here is more affectionate, their personalities are more important. Mamillius's strong dramatic presence makes his premature death an irreparable loss, poignantly recalled at the end of the play in Leontes's comparison of Mamillius with Florizel. Perdita is found, returning like her mother as if from the dead, bringing the cheering promise of young life, but not Mamillius.

For what emerges as a variety of purposes, Shakespeare chose to include children in the tragic world of extreme suffering, expanding their role from his sources or even inventing them altogether. The brief episodes in which they appear, made immediately distinctive for the audience by the fresh appeal of light voices, introduce a new perspective on the main action, a moment when the audience's emotional attention is disengaged from the protagonist. The children's deaths then directly invite the audience's pity. Of course, children are not the only innocent victims in the tragedies: Ophelia, Desdemona, and Cordelia certainly may all be seen as innocent. But as R. S. White rightly points out, comparison between them and the children, that is, between children and young adults, immediately creates an awareness that perfect innocence is only possible in children.[11] Some critical commentators may even try to persuade readers to see these young women as in some way contributing to their fate, through weakness, stubbornness, or pride. Those less willing to lay blame on these victims must acknowledge that even the most virtuous, acting with full adult scope and responsibility, meet with tension and conflict.

It is not necessary for innocence to be destroyed to have a powerful effect in the play. One of Shakespeare's inventions is Lucius, Brutus's page in *Julius Caesar*, who, though in many ways not typical of children in the tragedies, has a role which defines the essential place of children in Shakespeare's poetic perception of the tragic world. Lucius's immediate dramatic function is to modify our sense of Brutus by allowing him to be seen in a role which is unequivocally appealing: Brutus endears himself to us by his tender concern for this dutiful boy. In the last part of Act IV Scene 3 after the quarrel with Cassius, Lucius plays and sings for his master, finally singing himself to sleep. The appearance of the ghost of Caesar soon dispels this peaceful mood, and the troubled Brutus rouses Lucius and questions the drowsy child. This incident, the third time in the play that Lucius has been awakened by his master, repeats the contrast between the sleeping boy and the restless state of mind of Brutus in the garden night scene. Then Brutus has to call repeatedly to wake him, and he envies him: 'I would it were my

[11] R. S. White, *Innocent Victims: Poetic Injustice in Shakespearean Tragedy* (London: Athlone Press, 1986), p. 46.

fault to sleep so soundly' (II. 1.4). When the conspirators leave Lucius has again gone to sleep, and Brutus talks of the difference between Lucius and himself:

> Boy! Lucius! Fast asleep? It is no matter,
> Enjoy the honey-heavy dew of slumber.
> Thou hast no figures nor no fantasies.
> Which busy care draws in the brains of men;
> Therefore thou sleep'st so sound.

(II. 1.229)

Unlike Lucius, Brutus cannot sleep: 'Since Cassius first did whet me against Caesar | I have not slept' (II.1.61–62). He experiences that troubled state of mind when life becomes 'like a phantasma or a hideous dream'. Macbeth too, of course, knows that shaken state of man: his speeches poignantly evoke that peace of mind and ability to sleep which he no longer enjoys. Lucius in *Julius Caesar* enacts that blessed state. He stands clearly in the play as a credible figure who yet effortlessly assumes a symbolic significance which derives from a blended sense of his youth and carefree mind, his music, and his sleeping. Tragedy entails physical suffering and death, but pre-eminently suffering in the mind, mental anguish. An antithesis to that metaphorical storm and tempest in the mind is, as Wilson Knight made us see, music.[12]

From the early history plays Shakespeare gives dramatic prominence to scenes of the suffering and death of children, with the fate of young princes anticipating the fuller tragic perception of childhood innocence and its destruction. In these brief scenes the children ask unequivocally for pity. Their deaths simply condemn adult cruelty. This is true even of the very short episode in *3 Henry VI* where the child Rutland is killed on stage to satisfy Clifford's blood-thirsty craving for revenge. The grieving father York declares that in slaughtering a sweet, innocent child Clifford has overcome all restraints:

> That face of his the hungry cannibals
> Would not have touch'd, would not have stain'd with blood;
> But you are more inhuman, more inexorable —
> O, ten times more — than tigers of Hyrcania.

(I.4.152)

York's clamorous description of Clifford's inhumanity would perhaps not appear in a later play: the extremity of the deed would be allowed to make its point dramatically, as in Macduff's reception of the news of Macbeth's 'fell swoop' on his family: 'He hath no children'. But if dramatically redundant, what York says is just: the murder of young Rutland marks an absolute peak

---

[12] G. Wilson Knight, *The Shakespearean Tempest*, 3rd edn (London: Methuen, 1953), passim for the tempests of mortality; on *2 Henry IV*, see p. 46; on *Julius Caesar*, see p. 187. For the sleeplessness of Brutus and Macbeth, see *The Wheel of Fire* (London: Methuen, 1930), pp. 126–27.

of horror in the *Henry VI* plays, when their savage political rivalry and bloody carnage is simply felt as 'inhuman'. Equally, in *Richard III*, the murder of the little princes, which, as noted, turns the tide of audience sympathy against Richard, constitutes an extreme: the 'most arch deed of piteous massacre'. It is worth insisting that the princes' deaths affect the audience so strongly because Shakespeare has made the princes so engagingly child-like in their 'pretty prate'. Like early versions of young Macduff and Mamillius they speak with child-like directness, ask questions persistently, and mingle naïve idealism with precocious wit in life-like episodes of conversation between adults and children.

It is in *King John* that the role of the suffering child, Arthur, assumes central importance. Shakespeare has made him younger and less politically ambitious than his counterparts in the historical sources. Though he can speak nobly of his rights he appears in the first three acts as a pawn in a political game. It is his tender loving nature, revealed in the execution scene with Hubert, that is important (IV. 1). Arthur wants nothing so much as to live as Hubert's son, and to look after him, boasting 'I warrant I love you more that you do me' (IV. 1. 31). This is a scene of almost unbearable pathos, submitting the sweet, loving nature of the child to the fear of hideous pain, though the tyrant's cruelty is averted when Hubert's heart is softened and he refuses to carry out John's orders. Nevertheless, John's intention is accomplished as Arthur, flying from his enmity, dies in his jump from the castle walls, and Hubert, who spared his life, must now pick up his dead body as Faulconbridge comments:

> How easy dost thou take all England up!
> From forth this morsel of dead royalty
> The life, the right, and truth of all this realm
> Is fled to heaven; and England now is left
> To tug and scamble, and to part by th' teeth
> The unowed interest of proud-swelling state.
>
> (IV. 3. 142)

For him Arthur's significance is political. He is the legitimate but lost ruler of England; in contrast, those who are now struggling for power are no better than dogs fighting over a bone. But the audience responds to the destruction of the personal qualities of Arthur, Shakespeare's most prominent child character. His gentle, loving nature and perhaps his mother's grief at his death, provide the antithesis to the play's violent world of betrayal, conflict, and self-assertion. But like the reluctant monarch Henry VI, the 'unworldly' Arthur is doomed. The human values he represents are shown to exist in the execution scene when Hubert relents, but they cannot prevail in this political world.

In that later history, *Henry V*, Shakespeare incorporated a young victim who is not a dynastic enemy, but, like Brutus's Lucius, a young page: the boy who, after Falstaff's death, follows Pistol, Nym, and Bardolph to the wars in France.[13] He is young, as he admits, and small: the Frenchman calls him 'Petit Monsieur' (IV.4.49); he is a witty page like Moth and Falstaff's page in *2 Henry IV*, all neat jugglers with words and exposers of folly. But for all his poised wit, his too is an essentially innocent view of the world: adult folly and corruption sicken him. His vulnerable situation makes him even more pitiful and never more so than when he says, speaking for all in battle: 'Would I were in an ale house in London, I would give all my fame for a pot of ale and safety' (III.2.11–13). Shakespeare's inclusion of this figure gives the Chronicles' episode of the killing of the boys a personal focus and therefore a greater poignancy which serves to enforce a sense of the horror of war. *Henry V* repeatedly confronts the audience with cross-reflecting images of war, including the suffering of non-combatants, but none is as unequivocally appalling as the reported slaughter of this good page.

These powerful stage images in Shakespeare's histories and tragedies of adults plotting against children, and killing them, must have reminded the audience of the archetypal instance in Christian history of such cruelty in St Matthew's account of King Herod's massacre of the innocents. The story, read annually as the gospel for Innocents' Day, and recollected in medieval tales of Jewish cruelty against Christian children, such as that told by Chaucer's Prioress, formed one of the most dramatically powerful episodes in the cycles of miracle plays. As a scenic representation of pathos, horror, and suspense it was challenged only by the pageant of Abraham and Isaac. For some of Shakespeare's audience, no doubt, the Shakespearean scenes of the brutal killing of children or the threatened blinding of Arthur would have awakened memories of theatrical performances during the last years of the miracle plays: the last performances at Coventry, for instance, were in 1579. The fifteen-year-old Shakespeare may have seen them. It is possible, as Emrys Jones has argued, to speak of Shakespeare's indebtedness to these plays;[14] and it may be that he, and other dramatists (the author of *The Yorkshire Tragedy*, for instance) learned from them something of the theatrical possibilities, and management, of stage violence.[15] For audience and dramatists these horrific spectacles of violence against children, actual or threatened, constituted a potent part of their theatrical heritage.

---

[13] J. W. Draper, 'Falstaff's Robin and other Pages', *SP*, 36 (1939), pp. 476–90, sees the Boy, Falstaff's page in *2 Henry IV* and Robin in *The Merry Wives* as all the same person. W. Robertson Davies, *Shakespeare's Boy Actors* (London: Dent, 1939), also thinks that all three parts are 'probably' the same boy, and notes that the part which began as a mere stage property to set off Falstaff's size achieves real significance in *Henry V*; see p. 163.

[14] Emrys Jones, *The Origins of Shakespeare* (Oxford: Clarendon Press, 1977), Chapter 2.

[15] See *The Yorkshire Tragedy*, ed. by A. C. Cawley and Barry Gaines (Manchester: Manchester University Press, 1986), p. 80. A note on Scene v where the husband murders his two sons suggests 'the Jacobean dramatist may well have drawn on his memories of plays on the Massacre of the Innocents'.

Reviews

Traditional Oral Epic: The 'Odyssey', 'Beowulf', and the Serbo-Croatian Return Song. By
    JOHN MILES FOLEY. Berkeley, Los Angeles, and Oxford: University of
    California Press. 1990. xi + 424 pp. $60.

Outside a select band of true believers, the oral-formulaic theory has had a
somewhat dubious reputation. It has been criticized for its casual cross-cultural
comparisons of widely disparate genres, its efforts to establish on stylistic grounds
alone how a poem was composed, and its disregard for provenance and the whole
question of how and why an oral poem should ever have been written down in the
first place. In *Traditional Oral Epic* John Miles Foley goes to great lengths to avoid
these failings, substituting the more cautious concept of tradition-dependence for
that of pure orality and paying close attention to the differences as well as the
similarities between varying traditions. His revised version of the oral-formulaic
theory deserves consideration by anyone interested in oral culture.

Foley rejects as overly rigid previous efforts to reduce formulaic language to a
substitution system, a 'patchwork of ready-made phrases'. Instead he argues that
oral or oral-derived poetry consists of a spectrum of traditional phraseology
governed by certain fundamental rules. This poetic tradition incorporates both
formulaic and non-formulaic language. It is flexible and allows individual poets a
wide range of choice but is charged with internal associations to a far greater degree
than any written poetry. While its complexity and variety often defy conventional
formulaic analysis, traditional poetry remains rooted in oral composition. It 'carries
with it both compositional utility and aesthetic referentiality' (p. 276).

Foley demands that we recognize the fluidity of oral tradition. Rather than
accepting any single version of a poem as definitive, we must consider its various
stages. This strong diachronic emphasis, a further deviation from most previous
oral-formulaic studies, leads him into a detailed account of Indo-European prosody,
which is the source of the most fundamental rules of the tradition, and of the
provenance of the *Odyssey* and *Beowulf*. In his discussion of the early recensions of
Homer, for example, he cites the so-called 'wild' papyri as evidence of the fluidity of
the Homeric tradition.

A danger, which Foley himself alludes to in his conclusion, is that in avoiding the
grandiose claims of earlier scholars we will end up with a concept of the poetic
tradition so tentative and so hedged with caveats as to be virtually devoid of
meaning. It is worth noting, therefore, that although Foley severely undermines the
possibility of using formulaic analysis as a simple litmus test for orality, his
categories of 'traditional' and 'oral-derived' retain a strong link to oral composition.
It is on the basis of *Beowulf*'s 'demonstrably oral traditional character', for example,
that Foley rejects Kevin Kiernan's argument for a *Beowulf* coeval with the manuscript, since such a late date would 'in effect cut the poem off from its oral traditional
provenance' (p. 35).

Several of Foley's claims should prove controversial outside the field of oral-
formulaic studies. Despite its emphasis on the fluidity of the oral tradition and its use
of such mixed categories as 'tradition dependent', *Traditional Oral Epic* ultimately
tends to maintain a dichotomy between orality and writing, claiming that written
poetry 'no matter how dense with allusions and inherited figures' can never
command the 'open connotative field' of oral tradition (p. 2). This runs against the

direction of much recent work in both literary theory and cultural history. One
might compare *Traditional Oral Epic* to Jonathan Goldberg's *Writing Matter*
(Stanford, 1990), for example, which criticizes the oral/written dichotomy as a form
of logocentricism.

   Traditional Oral Epic is an impressive work. It is punctilious in its method and
shows a fine grasp of the philological complexities of three languages. Its treatment
of work inside oral-formulaic circles is comprehensive and painstaking, although it
shows little awareness of much of the work without. It is not, unfortunately, an easy
book to read. The very precision that distinguishes Foley from more exuberant
predecessors makes for intimidating and occasionally dreary analysis, some of
which would have benefited from more rigorous editing. I question, for example,
whether we really need five pages of detailed examination of the less than two per
cent of the lines in the return songs that are hypermetrical in order to establish that
'syllabicity is a constant and rigorous rule' (p. 94). Foley's deference to the work of
others in the field at times conceals the full force of his argument and his efforts to
establish a method that would be beyond reproach burden the book with repetitive
qualifications.

   Foley offers *Traditional Oral Epic* as a first step toward a unified poetics for oral or
oral-derived poetry. But the book significantly heightens our sense of the variety
within this poetry and the sheer complexity of traditional phraseology. If I remain
sceptical of the possibility of a unified oral poetics it is in part a tribute to the
sophistication and care of Foley's analysis.

TRENT UNIVERSITY, PETERBOROUGH, ONTARIO   ANDREW TAYLOR

The Battle of Maldon AD 991. Ed. by DONALD SCRAGG. Oxford: Blackwell in
     Association with The Manchester Centre for Anglo-Saxon Studies. 1991.
     xiv + 306 pp. £45.

The title intends us to be in no doubt that the book (marking the millennial
anniversary) is about the battle rather than the poem, although the poem inevitably
haunts its every part, often in quite unexpected ways. The dust jacket gives us in
monochrome realism a strong image of that rocky causeway across the Blackwater
mud, and hovers over the very spot where, a thousand years ago, Wulfstan son of
Ceola held the bridge — but we have been led to this present-day spot only by
believing in the historicity of an account some would rather see as a work of pure
imagination. The poem takes the leading place in the first of the book's four parts,
which consists of facsimiles, transcriptions, and translations of all the documentary
evidence for the battle, and, as the most detailed account, is appropriately given a
later section of discussion to itself. Another section studies the historical context,
military, political, economic, and topographical, while the last is devoted to
Byrhtnoth and the great man's relics at Ely. This plan, with its very deliberate
emphasis on history and its sources, while it denies any real platform to the
doubters, gives us something better: not only a commemorative history book, but a
much needed companion to the poem, at once balanced and stimulating; on the one
hand seemingly reserved on exclusively literary matters, but on the other full of
information and critical judgement on the nature and interpretation of *all* the
documents.

   An important part in the plan is played by the book's visual impact. The
facsimiles of the principal manuscripts in Part I, the often evocative photographs of
runic stones (notably the snow-swept monument of Harold Bluetooth at Jelling, and
the stone of Esbern who 'did not flee at Uppsala'), coins and other artefacts of metal,
wood, stone, and textile, the eighteenth- and nineteenth-century engravings, all

make us strongly aware both of the look and feel of the evidence (its often fortuitous and paradoxical character, to which Donald Scragg draws attention in his introduction), and of the 'real' events, places, and people to which it refers. We are encouraged to think that, despite modern embarrassment or scepticism, we still know where we might find Byrhtnoth's remains — although he himself, it seems, was no giant after all, but still appropriately taller than the Anglo-Saxon average at a little over six feet.

The scope of Simon Keynes's essay on the historical context of the battle gives it a central role, drawing much of the rest together. The reconstructed story of Æthelred's dealings with the vikings is necessarily qualified by many 'perhapses'. Pointing out that the A manuscript of the *Chronicle* is after all an independent witness, Keynes maintains that Olaf Tryggvason did command the viking force at Maldon, cheerfully accepting that to do so is 'to give oneself the benefit of the doubt, but such leaps of faith are the stuff of Anglo-Saxon history'. A convincing picture emerges, more complex than the *Chronicle* suggests, for the period immediately following the battle, of a wealthy country, far from devastated, led by a king with his advisers doing at least 'as much as could have been expected under the circumstances'. The battle epitomizes those circumstances, and Keynes's forceful representation of the nation's dilemma has a familiar ring. On the one hand 'governments should not, after all, give in to terrorists' demands'. But on the other, for all the 'little touch of Byrhtnoth' that may have been in each of Æthelred's advisers, 'what for him was a matter of principle had been turned by his death into a far more difficult choice'.

Keynes's account also offers a valuable perspective on the poem, his historian's reading providing a corrective to a too simple emphasis on heroic convention. If we assume, as he suggests, an audience capable of seeing both sides of a current 'fight or pay' debate ('The poet, through the messenger, presents a reasoned case for the payment of tribute'), it is certainly easier to reconcile ourselves to the poet's account of what then went wrong, stirring, but with its puzzlingly distributed emphases and disconcerting directness: Byrhtnoth did right not to pay, but made a mistake because of a pride so obvious as to require no further explanation. The poem's mixture of art and actuality has often led readers to simple either/or solutions (there is an analogy in modern responses to later medieval 'autobiographical' poetry) which this book thoroughly and consistently discourages. Scragg's assessment of the poem as history, carefully balancing the constraints of art with the historical event known to the audience, is only the first of many; and sometimes the contributors effectively balance each other. Where Scragg has warned us not to think of Byrhtnoth literally going into battle with a Germanic comitatus, Richard Abels argues that 'the poet's vision of the English army as the ealdorman's war band may contain more than a kernel of truth'. John Dodgson eloquently balances heroic ideal with an 'actual place' (still Northey Island, despite the claim of Osea) 'as well as an actual time and an actual person', and offers a tempting reason why Byrhtnoth might have chosen one Wulfstan to defend a bridge that lay no more than a mile from the man's own estate.

A striking case for the poem's historicity, and a modestly urged dating, is proposed in Nicholas Brooks's argument that its unheroic emphasis on spears rather than swords, together with the absence of helmets, and of byrnies (except on vikings), represents the actual poor state of English military equipment before reforms introduced in the first decade of the eleventh century. In the same section Margaret Locherbie-Cameron sets out the evidence for the existence of all men named in the poem, although the creation of fictional names for such essential figures as the hostage and the *ceorl* is surely at least possible. The importance of the eighteenth century for the transmission of the *Battle of Maldon*, and an interesting episode in the growth of Anglo-Saxon studies, is represented in Kathryn Sutherland's convincing account of why Thomas Hearne appended the poem to his edition of the *Glastonbury Chronicle*.

There are inevitably a few small errors in the text, including one of transcription in the F version of the *Chronicle*, where *primum* is given as *primo*, but these are not such as to mar a handsome volume that will, as its editor hopes, mark the millennium of the battle in a lasting way by providing a starting point and provocation for future work.

University of Reading   David J. Williams

Norm und Spiel in 'The Owl and the Nightingale'. By Rainer Holtei. (Studia Humaniora) Düsseldorf: Droste. 1990. 239 pp.

This book springs from the differing interpretations of the Middle English poem *The Owl and the Nightingale*, which vary from serious allegory to burlesque satire. Rainer Holtei finds these interpretations unsatisfactory partly because the poem needs to be interpreted within a concrete historical communicative situation and partly because many English-speaking critics have ignored work done on the poem, and on Middle English literature generally, which has appeared in German. In order to understand the poem one needs to remember that it is a game and a game has rules, but at the same time the conventions which govern the norms of the time may be adapted to provide suggestive meaning. There are important questions about the poem to be faced: what is the debate between the owl and the nightingale about; how is the desired judgement to be reached; why are the disputants represented as birds; why did the poet use English rather than Latin or Anglo-Norman; who comprised the intended audience? It is these questions which he tries to answer.

Important figures are the judge, Nicholas of Guildford, who provides the norms for the debate, and the narrator, who acts in many ways as a surrogate audience. Through him the audience learns to ask the questions which Nicholas would have to resolve. The poem is not unidimensional, but multidimensional, and in this the concept of norms plays a significant part. There are three types of norm. The first consists of binding norms. These include the fact that the poem is a game which has rules. The birds take part in a debate, a *plait*, which is based on the forensic method of plea and counter-plea. The debate must be carried out in accordance with fair play. The birds accept the norm that their usefulness to mankind is the definitive feature of the debate, and that *riht luve* is the only basis for the social, moral, and judicial contest about love and marriage. The second type of norm comprises the open norms of debate in the tradition of debate literature. The choice of protagonists and the topics of debate are free. The debate is a *plait* in which the birds focus on each other's *custe* through their song. The third type of norm is the use of stereotyped characteristics in the pleading of the birds. Each makes emotional appeals to the audience through the narrator; each generates different literary echoes, but neither is linked with a single concept and neither is traditionally linked with the other. In his choice of birds the author is able to play with the norms in anticipating that his readers will follow what he keeps from the traditional norms and what he has adapted. The audience must be understood as sophisticated, for they would recognize the various literary echoes and the norms emanating from debate and animal literature, from *lais* and fables, and from the conventions of education found in the *trivium*. The choice of English may be motivated by the greater freedom this gave the poet to play suggestively with the norms his audience would be familiar with in Latin texts. Many of the assumptions they might make from the educated background of Latin could be called into question by the use of English so that the poet both exploits and questions the norms. In this way the poem fits into the questioning style of the late twelfth century. Although the poem is to be understood literally, it is not about an owl and a nightingale. It is about the need for conventions and norms: the limits which they provide, the directions they give us for thinking intellectually to some purpose, and the way in which they need always to be questioned. The poem is about how to form a judgement rather than about a specific judgement.

This is an important book which contains far more suggestive criticism than I can comment on here. It is to be hoped that the fact that it is in German will not hinder it from being widely read; it deserves to be.

UNIVERSITY OF SHEFFIELD   N. F. BLAKE

The Legends of King Arthur in Art. By MURIEL WHITAKER. (Arthurian Studies, XXII)
    Cambridge: Brewer. 1990. x + 363 pp. £49.50.

In *The Legends of King Arthur in Art* Muriel Whitaker deals with all aspects of illustration of the legends in all media from the earliest illuminated manuscripts of the twelfth century to a feminist interpretation by an artist of the 1980s. Her research has been extremely thorough. The result is a book both difficult to read and to review fairly: its chief value lies in its wide range and painstaking accumulation of material, yet this can also be counted its chief failing. It is exhaustively descriptive, but leaves the reader with no sense of an overview of the subject. Although it is suggested on the dust-jacket that the writer's 'emphasis on content, rather than form, offers an original perspective, different from that of the art historian', too often this lack of art historical background seems to result not in fresh perceptions, but in a tendency to describe works of art rather than to analyse them. On a related point of presentation, it is inconvenient that no plate numbers are given in the text. It would also have been helpful if art historical convention had been followed in giving the size of works of art in the list of illustrations.

Again according to the dust-jacket the book's purpose is 'to explain the social, political, religious, and aesthetic conditions which influenced the form and content of representations of Arthurian legends in various historical periods'. This is a daunting task but a very worthwhile one: a more readable and a more satisfactory work of scholarship would have resulted if the author had kept this aim firmly in mind and ruthlessly excluded material not immediately relevant. As it is, there seems to have been little selection. This is a pity because some excellent ideas remain undeveloped, and are almost lost in an accumulation of detail. The services of a ruthless editor to excise and to encourage the author towards a tighter organisation of her material would have been invaluable.

This proliferation of detail may partially result from a failure to decide whom this work is meant to address: other academics and students in the field or a more general readership? At first, it seems that Whitaker assumes little, if any, knowledge on the part of the reader. In the first chapter the development of Arthurian romance is dealt with in detail which is unnecessary if a specialist readership is assumed, yet terms such as *topos* (p. 5) *locus amoenus* (p. 6), likely to be unfamiliar to the general reader, go unexplained. This criticism is valid throughout the book: the work of T. S. Eliot, for example, is described in terms which are condescending even to the general reader, who surely does not need to be told that image of the waste-land symbolizes 'modern man's physical, intellectual, moral, spiritual and aesthetic impoverishment' (p. 315).

Where Whitaker attempts an interpretation of the social and political conditions which influenced representation of the legends, her judgements are too often superficial. The neglect of the legends both as literature and as the subject of illustration during the seventeenth and eighteenth centuries is not accounted for; the subsequent revival of interest in the ninteenth century and the problems which the Victorians had in accommodating the legends is inadequately explained. For example, Whitaker seems largely unaware of the precise nature of the difficulties faced by William Dyce when in 1847 he was commissioned to paint frescoes illustrating Malory's *Le Morte D'Arthur* in the new Palace of Westminster. She refers simply to 'the difficulties of adapting a literary subject to a fixed architectural theme and at the same time satisfying the commissioners and their royal chairman' (p. 179). It was adapting this particular literary subject for this particular setting which was more specifically a serious problem: Dyce had to adapt for the decoration of Queen Victoria's Robing Room a story in which an adulterous queen plays a central role. Similarly Whitaker fails to make any reference to the background of intense religious controversy over the Oxford Movement at the time when Dyce, himself a High Churchman, had to decide how to treat the Grail Quest. She shows little awareness of what is one of the most fascinating aspects of her subject: the tremendous gulf between medieval and nineteenth century responses to, and perceptions of, the legends as reflected in the visual arts.

HOMERTON COLLEGE, CAMBRIDGE   CHRISTINE POULSON

Ritterliche Ideale in Chrétiens 'Yvain' und im mittelenglischen Gedicht 'Ywain and Gawain': Von 'amour courtois' zu 'trew luf', vom 'frans chevaliers deboneire' zum 'man of mekyl myght'. By ULRIKE DIRSCHERL. (Sprache und Literatur. Regensburger Arbeiten zur Anglistik und Amerikanistik, 33) Frankfurt a.M., Bern, and New York: Lang. 1991. 432 pp. £36.

The Middle English verse novel *Ywain and Gawain* has often been compared with its source, Chrétien's *Yvain*, and most critics (including the present reviewer) have concluded that the English poet, for all his narrative skill and competent versifying, has not really understood (or cared for) the French poet's real concerns and was much more interested in the dramatic story-line than in the subtleties of *amour courtois* and chivalric codes of behaviour. Too little attention has, no doubt, been paid to the possible reasons for the English adaptor's changes, his omissions and, even more importantly his additions to the story. Ulrike Dirscherl is quite right to direct our attention to these aspects of the 'translation', though she seems to overrate the novelty of her approach and she has a tendency to belabour her subject almost to the point of exhaustion. This is apparent already in her first chapter on previous research and even more when she discusses the well-worn problems of 'courtly love' and its transformation in the hands of the English poet. She sensibly points out that his idea of 'luf' was evidently very different from Chrétien's elaborate concept of *amour courtois* and that the chief difference lies in the supreme value he puts on the ideal of 'trewth' in its full variety of senses. In her view, this is not, as has been claimed, the reduction of a complex idea but a deliberate re-interpretation for an audience very different from Chrétien's.

The same applies to the concept of chivalry, another traditionally problematic term. Dirscherl gives a useful if lengthy account of controversial definitions, in particular the relationship between literary ideals of chivalry and actual practice: she cautiously agrees with those scholars who have found close correspondences between actual ideals and literary idealization and have claimed that these influenced each other in many ways. There are two long chapters on forms of battle and on the knight's place within the social structures reflected in the two poems. Dirscherl gives numerous examples of how the English poet adapted descriptions of fighting and battle in order to focus on the hero's 'prowess' rather than the ritual of knightly combat and warfare. For the English poet, as for Chrétien, fighting is only one aspect of the code of 'curtaysye', but the word clearly has an entirely different meaning in English, being more closely related to 'charity', 'mercy', and 'trowthe' than the French equivalent. Ywain's prowess, more physical than Yvain's, is usually employed in the service of others, especially those in need of his help. At the same time, the class to which he belongs appears less rigidly defined and there is some indication that the decline of chivalry as well as the rise of other professions and their entry into the ranks of knighthood has left its mark on the poem. Few would quarrel with Dirscherl's conclusion: 'Beide Dichter konnten sich nicht den jeweiligen gesellschaftlichen und politischen Verhältnisen völlig entziehen' (p. 254), and there is much to be said for her claim that *Ywain and Gawain* is not just an inferior imitation. It is more than plausible that the English adaptor had a clear idea of the kind of audience he was addressing, that he was familiar with English traditions, particularly in the portrayal of Gawain and of King Arthur, and that he consistently shaped his material in accordance with his own ideas of love and knightly ethos.

Dirscherl's study gives a useful overview of previous research on all aspects of the poem and its background; it is full of sensible observations and helpful references. Yet the persuasive but on the whole unsurprising conclusions do not always justify the relentless thoroughness of her presentation. The book is regrettably, another instance of a doctoral dissertation forced unabridged on to the overcrowded market under the German Universities' law of *Druckzwang*, instead of having been pruned into a slim book or, even better, a concise article (in English) which would have made its worthwhile point much more effectively and served the scholarly community much better.

UNIVERSITY OF BONN   DIETER MEHL

The Romance of Merlin: An Anthology. Ed. by PETER GOODRICH. (Arthurian Studies from Garland) New York and London: Garland. 1990. xix + 418 pp. $50 (paperbound $18.95).

This book is meant as a teaching text for undergraduates, and unless one objects in principle to translations or to anthologies of extracts, the idea behind it is a good one. For a thousand years, authors have cast Merlin in roles that provide contrasting insights into the mentalities of those who heard or read about him. Some of their stories embody profound thought about power or the human imagination: others are no less revealing for being driven by crude sensationalism.

The texts are well chosen to illustrate these themes: part or all of the Lailoken fragments, the early Myrddin poems, Geoffrey of Monmouth's *Historia* and *Vita Merlini*, the French prose *Merlin*, its Vulgate and Post-Vulgate continuations, the Didot *Perceval*, *Of Arthour and Merlin*, the English prose *Merlin*, Malory's *Morte Darthur*, Spenser's *Faerie Queene*, Heywood's *Life of Merlin*, Tennyson's *Merlin and Vivien*, Twain's *Connecticut Yankee*, Edwin Arlington Robinson's *Merlin*, T. H. White's *Sword in the Stone* and *Once and Future King*, and C. S. Lewis's *That Hideous Strength*. Welsh, Latin, and French is translated, and the older English glossed on the page. There are no notes, but each text has a short historical and interpretative introduction and a select bibliography, and there is a general introduction with a chronology, embracing nine languages, of Merlin's major literary appearances.

The plan is sound, but the implementation is uneven. Of the translations, which Peter Goodrich delegated to others, the Welsh are excellent, the French lively but rather free, and the Latin adequate —but the late John Jay Parry should have known better than to translate the office of *custos Angliae* as 'custodian of the realm'.

With the English texts, however, editing and glossing are so hit-and-miss as to suggest that Goodrich does not know such things can affect meaning. Sometimes they don't: when Grisandol meets the Emperor *upon the greces*, it is unimportant that she is coming not 'over the grass' but 'up the steps'; but that Merlin's writing *in grewe* over the palace doorway is not 'engraved' but 'in Greek', that the *Sarasyns* who invade Britain are not 'Saxons' but 'Saracens', and that Merlin's oath *on my parel* is not a knightly 'on my honour' but (from a devil's son) a Christian 'on my salvation' all affect the themes that Goodrich's readers will be trying to discern.

The background material is also uneven. It includes much useful information and (on recent texts particularly) some thought-provoking criticism, but also too many errors of fact and presentation, and too much sloppy prose. Most of its shortcomings, from the misleading conflation of courtly love and Christianity in the account of the *Faerie Queene* (perhaps an attempt to assimilate both to late twentieth-century ideological pluralism) to the furry print and chemical paper, are those of the daily press, without the excuse of the daily deadline. Although this book will (as house-agents say) serve its purpose, its intended readers should use it as a tool, not as a model.

UNIVERSITY OF WALES, BANGOR   P. J. C. FIELD

Arthurian Literature X. Ed. by RICHARD BARBER. Cambridge: Brewer. 1990. vi + 160 pp. £29.50.

This latest volume offers an interesting collection of material. A. H. W. Smith explores the significance of the claim of Ludovicus Ponticus Virunius that, when he compiled his *Historia Britannica* of 1508, he drew not only upon Geoffrey of Monmouth's *Historia Regum Britanniae*, but also upon a manuscript of poetry written by a certain Gildas. Virunius would seem to have used perhaps the oldest document describing the legend of the Britons and, since the manuscript is lost, he would now offer the most direct access to it. But Geoffrey of Monmouth also frequently refers to a certain Gildas when presenting material not found in the *De Excidio*, the extant work of the writer of that name. If would certainly seem possible that Geoffrey and Virunius had employed the same source material (albeit indirectly in Geoffrey's case). A. H. W. Smith also offers 'A Supplementary Bibliography of Twentieth-Century Arthurian Literature', an update of material which appeared in *Arthurian Literature II*. Here, 'Arthurian' is taken in its very broadest sense, as, indeed, is literature, for the check-list includes films, operas, comics, and pop-up books. Nearly every entry is accompanied by a descriptive note and by an indication of the category to which it belongs (even though most of the abbreviations describing these categories are self-explanatory, it would not have come amiss to explain them again at the head of the list). One can only admire the enthusiasm of Smith and his fellow-compilers. Readers will now have a better idea of what they should seek out amongst modern Arthuriana and what they should avoid. Another useful list is provided by Christine Poulson, a subject index on Arthurian legend in fine and applied art in the nineteenth and early twentieth centuries, complementing the index arranged according to artist which appeared in *Arthurian Literature IX*. This is more messy than her first index: there is an overlap between subjects and she has to include a category embracing subjects not covered elsewhere.

A large part of this volume is devoted to an article by Armel Diverres, 'The Grail and the Third Crusade: Thoughts on *Le Conte del Graal* by Chrétien de Troyes'. The argument put forward is a bold and fascinating one. Drawing partly on proposals made by Helen Adolf, Diverres suggests that there is a crusading dimension to Chrétien's romance: the poet was commissioned to write a work which would reflect the links of the family of Philip of Flanders with the ruling house of the kingdom of Jerusalem. Episodes in the work reflect incidents in the life of his patron: in short, Perceval represents Philip of Flanders, the Fisher King the leper-king, Baldwin IV of Jerusalem. But when news of the death of Philip reached Chrétien in the summer of 1191, he was forced to change tack. He developed another set of adventures centred on Gauvain, in which an informed public would recognize the presentation of the qualities required by a crusader. There are many good things about this article. Diverres restates the case in favour of the unity of the romance, he rightly points out that in the grail procession it is the host which sanctifies the *graal* and not the reverse, and he comes to the commonsense conclusion that there is an association between Chrétien's prologue and the main body of the romance. However, it proves difficult to endorse the whole of Diverres's hypothesis, tempting though this may be. At one point, when considering a detail, he admits that 'it is impossible to say whether Chrétien had this in mind or not', and the same would seem true for the whole. There are a number of incidental features with which one can quibble. When Chrétien describes a tower as being unique in the area from here to Beirut, it is surely the absence of such a tower which is being emphasized and not the existence of a tower *beyond* Beirut. Moreover, it does seem difficult to equate Perceval's diffidence at the Grail Castle with Philip of Flanders's meddlesome behaviour on his first visit to the kingdom of Jerusalem in 1177–78. Nevertheless, this monograph is an important contribution to Chrétien studies and, like the other articles in the volume, will become a valuable source of reference.

University of Durham   G. N. Bromiley

Chaucer's 'Troilus and Criseyde'. By C. David Benson. (Unwin Critical Library) London, Boston, and Sydney: Unwin Hyman. 1990. viii + 226 pp. £25.

C. David Benson's is the second Chaucerian offering in the series in which it appears, following Derek Pearsall's account of the *Canterbury Tales*, and emulating its successful dialogue with previous criticism in a style which is declaratory and clear. But a second and more distant echo is apparent in words commencing the chapter on 'Love', which begins: 'Everyone knows that *Troilus and Criseyde* is a poem about love.' The allusion is to C. S. Lewis's *Allegory of Love*, but it is Lewis's paper on Chaucer's modifications to *Il Filostrato* which in fact provides the book's strategy. Chapters on a series of topics — *Il Filostrato*, reader response, the representation of Troy, characterization, love, fortune, and Christianity — are all referred back to Boccaccio's work: a comparative method which stimulates insights into the chosen topics, but excludes mention of textual history or the role of plot structure, and perhaps contributes to a narrowing of scope in respect of contemporary English contexts.

Although employing C. S. Lewis's phrasing to open Chapter 6, Benson's use of it is not comparably coercive: indeed, his attitude to interpretation is thoroughly liberal. He adroitly exploits discrepancies between critical readings to argue that Chaucer's modifications to his major source took no consistent direction, but contributed to a richness and complexity which validates a spectrum of differing interpretations. A similar position was argued for the Clerk's Tale and for *Troilus and Criseyde* by Elizabeth Salter, implying that Chaucer's creativity was rarely subject to an overarching strategy, but responded locally to various stimuli in his source material.

A book which orchestrates bibliography so skilfully, offering critical alternatives as the vehicle of individual judgement, does not invite disagreement, but one or two reservations may be mentioned.

Although acknowledging in principle the variety of modes in characterization employed, Benson does not exploit this principle as fully as might be; for, in allegorical mode, Criseyde's love is clearly (?pre)figured in the dream of the exchange of hearts (II.925–31), and so it is probably too agnostic to see the first evidence of Criseyde's having fallen in love only when she admits it to Troilus in Book III (ll. 1210–11). On the other hand, although admitting that the same character may at once be a literary type and an individual, acknowledgement of a more complex realism seems admissible in Book II, where realistically conceived characters play out scenes in which they are shown to adopt literary roles. This is no binary choice between convention and realism: rather the latter is made more complex by its ability to adopt the patterns of the former in order to achieve purely practical ends.

This example is perhaps symptomatic of the feature which many readers of Chaucer will find least satisfactory in an otherwise attractive book: its lack of resolution; its willingness to support diversity rather than impose synthesis. Is it indeed the case that Chaucer considered his work to be so open? The poetics of his time was heavily intentionalist, seeing the poet as transmitting his meaning to an audience through his art; and Chaucer is crucially concerned with his meaning. He prays that even if the poetry is destroyed by copyists, his meaning will survive and be understood; and he implicitly accepts responsibility for it in his Retractions.

Chaucer's concern with morality in a pagan context, found also in the Knight's Tale, *Legend of Good Women*, and *Parliament of Fowls*, is underestimated (because external to the book's strategy), and the poem's morality is cast in terms of a 'Robertsonians' versus 'others' dichotomy. It is unfortunate that the reader is left with this sense of diversity: with alternatives rather than both. The moral perspectives of the poem are clearly critical of Criseyde, but also, although less obviously, of Troilus himself. But the remarkable feature of the poem is that neither is much diminished in our estimation by knowing this. Culpability does not preclude amiability. Perhaps the adversarial spirit of C. S. Lewis, with his opposition between secular and religious love, has been allowed to influence too much the view of the poem presented, concealing essential syntheses to be found within diversity.

But these are minor objections outweighed by the virtues of a book which will be readily accessible and genuinely useful to Chaucerian readers of all kinds.

UNIVERSITY OF SHEFFIELD

J. D. BURNLEY

Chaucer's Sexual Poetics. By CAROLYN DINSHAW. Madison: University of Wisconsin Press. 1990. x + 310 pp. $37.50 (paperbound $15).

Central to this study is the analogy of text and the female body. This insistence that 'literary activity has a gendered structure' is historically anchored here in medieval allegorical traditions about reading and interpretation which speak of text as flesh and of flesh as woman. Arising from such ways of talking about writing is a masculine erotics of the text which occludes female desire: the pleasurable seduction by post-lapsarian language, particularly but not only in the form of pagan sources, must eventually give way to the chastening proper to what Jerome calls 'a matron of the true Israel'. Jerome compares the Christian appropriation of classical style to the abduction of the woman in Deuteronomy 21.10–13: 'If thou [...] seest in the number of the captives a beautiful woman, and lovest her and wilt have her to wife, Thou shalt bring her into thy house: and she shall shave her head, and pare her nails.' Carolyn Dinshaw's fascinating introduction traces the implications and variations in this figure of text as woman, clothed and naked, in the Latin exegetical

tradition, elucidating its essentially patriarchal meaning by reference to anthropological and psychoanalytic theory, particularly Lacan and Levi-Strauss.

According to Dinshaw, in Chaucer, too, literary activity is invariably gendered;
her Chaucer is generally less of a breaker of the moulds than Jill Mann's. Much of
this book underlines what it sees as the masculine aspects of Chaucer's work,
particularly of *Troilus*, *The Legend of Good Women*, and *The Man of Law's Tale*. Chaucer
is commended not for constructing a new order but for bringing into the clear light of
day the structure of the old. His method reveals a pointedly masculine narrator, a
Troilus, and a Pandarus who all ultimately 'read like men', glancing away from
disorder and contradiction and opting instead for the chimera of wholeness; his
Criseyde, his Cassandra, and, up to a point, aspects of his Pandarus indicate that,
whatever one's native gender, it would be possible to read otherwise, were it not for
the constraints of the world as it is, a world in which Hector's 'we usen here no
wommen for to selle' is 'a cover for the real workings of patriarchy' (p. 61). The
'slydynge' of Criseyde's 'corage', potentially a liberatingly disruptive aspect of her
as reader, turns out to be convenient for the social organization in which she is *read*,
'a thing passed between men' (p. 58).

Dinshaw reads *The Legend of Good Women* as the masculine narrator's 'defensive'
use of the saint's life genre to control the feminine, whose capacity for endangering
masculine desire had thus become visible in *Troilus*. Here she associates control of
the femine text with the anti-individualizing narrative methods of hagiography, in
which the swapping about of bits of biographies was justified by the theory that, as
Gregory of Tours put it, 'it is better to talk about the *life* of the fathers than the *lives*
[. . .] the life of one body nourished them all'. This part of Dinshaw's book is perhaps
most interesting for the questions it raises, but does not answer: one might want to
debate this yoking of literary stylization and lack of individuality with that which is
restrictive, controlling, and particularly masculine. Caroline Walker Bynum's
Holy Feast and Holy Fast (Berkeley and London: University of California Press, 1987)
provides a convincing alternative to the narrowly negative reading of feminine
passivity; her findings and approach would have enriched this discussion.

Drawing on Irigaray, Dinshaw describes the Wife of Bath in terms of playful
mimesis; she 'mimics patriarchal discourse [. . .] not in order to "thwart" it
altogether, to subvert it entirely, but to *reform* it, to keep it in place while making it
accommodate female desire' (p. 116). Unlike Hector, she cheerfully admits that 'al
is for to selle', suggesting ways in which women can get in on the 'economy of
possession'. Far from justifying the misogynistic tradition, she 'appropriat[es] the
Other created by ideology' for her own purposes. Chaucer poses rape, always
potential in a system which disregards female desire, as the actuality which sparks
off her tale: ultimately, however, the story is closed by a male fantasy fictively
represented as a woman's.

Other chapters discuss at length *The Man of Law's Tale* and *The Clerk's Tale*, but
by far the most stimulating and original is that devoted to the Pardoner and his
radically unsettling implications for all that has gone before — in particular, for
the gendered hermeneutic of the veiled feminine body as text and meaning. Seen
by the narrator as of uncertain gender and sexual orientation, the Pardoner is,
perhaps, a 'gelding'; he is exhibitionistically involved with his clothes and his
relics, fragments of bodies apparently but fraudulently of great significance. His
words and his things are at once signs of lack and substitutes for wholeness. He is
finally silenced by the very masculine Host's obscene threat that he would like to
produce the ultimate relic from the Pardoner's questionable sexual parts, a threat
which perhaps reveals the Host's sense that his own manhood and wholeness are
in danger. Reading the Pardoner as a study in fetishism, and noting a medieval
nostalgia for wholeness and unslipperiness in language, Dinshaw argues that the

Pardoner suggests an alternative hermeneutic: one not based on gender 'but perhaps on something unmediated'. Perhaps there *is* no body beneath the veils.

BIRKBECK COLLEGE, LONDON   CATHERINE LA FARGE

Reformist Apocalypticism and 'Piers Plowman'. By KATHRYN KERBY-FULTON. (Cambridge Studies in Medieval Literature, 7) Cambridge, New York, and Melbourne: Cambridge University Press. 1990. xii + 256 pp. £30; $49.50.

This study on the 'new apocalypticism' of the later Middle Ages compares interestingly with the other Cambridge Study in Medieval Literature to focus on *Piers Plowman* that by Wendy Scase, on the 'new anticlericalism'. Both immerse the reader in the pool of some learned tradition from which there are only occasional landings to review the poem, for which no overall 'reading' is offered. Wendy Scase's material is less well known, and her findings are more original, but this book sometimes offers equally convincing contexts for the same passages. It is a pity that they did not compare notes behind the scenes at Cambridge University Press.

Kathryn Kerby-Fulton's interest is in two traditions of Apocalyptic writing: the 'visionary' symbolism of *The Shepherd of Hermas*, Hildegard of Bingen, and Bridget of Sweden; and the 'exegetical' Apocalypticism written from the thirteenth century by William of St Amour, Joachim of Fiore, and John of Rupescissa (this is the 'new Apocalypticism'). Like Morton Bloomfield she sees Langland's apocalypticism as an expression of his faith that the world can be perfected now, before its end, and some of the authors she considers (particularly Joachim of Fiore and his followers) share this optimistic hope for the future. But so do some of Langland's near-contemporaries, writing 'political prophecy' in English, and it is difficult to see why she has not also included them in her commentary on, for example, Consciene's Utopia of B.III. 284–330. Such texts as 'When Rome is removed' (R. H. Robbins, *Historical Poems of the XIVth and XVth Centuries*, No. 45) share not only a symbolic alliterative style with *Piers Plowman*, but also his political context, which for all her insistence on the contemporary concerns of Langland's eschatology, she does not discuss. Nor, in spite of her interest in 'vision', does she mention the flowering of Apocalyptic art and sculpture in Langland's England. By neglecting such popular or vernacular sources, and by choosing Latin texts (which she does not translate) from such a wide span of time, she does not give me a convincing context for Langland's Apocalypticism. Nor does she tell the whole story of how it invades the poem, leaving out, for example, the possibility of relating Meed to the Whore of Babylon, and Holy Church to the Woman Clothed with the Sun. What we are given is more a survey of how clerical authors placed the present times in an overall pattern of history, with some insights on how Langland shares this tradition.

Of the texts she does cover, I found the *Shepherd of Hermas* and the *De Periculis* of William of St Amour the most relevant to Langland. These comparisons are not new, but her analysis is subtle and raises interesting questions. She compares, for example, not only the figure of The Shepherd with Langland's Piers, but also the concatenation of images which haunt both this text and the *Apocalypse of Esdras*, with Langland's loose image structures. William of St Amour was a thirteenth-century secular priest who wanted to abolish the friars altogether, and she carefully distinguishes his and his imitators' 'nihilistic' use of certain Biblical texts, from Langland's similar but 'reformist' use of the same texts. In fact the friars become a central focus for this study, because Langland seems to have made use not only of anti-fraternal Apocalypticism, but also the pro-fraternal exegesis of the Franciscan Joachim of Fiore and his followers (in for example Reason's 'prophecy of repristinisation' in Passus v). Kerby-Fulton has highlighted an important inconsistency here in Langland's attitude to mendicancy, and one that surfaces again in his simultaneous condemnation of begging, and his apparent faith that Will (or Piers, or Hawkyn) should trust to God to provide for him. Her suggestion that Piers's promised return to earth recalls the Joachite visions of an Angelic Pope and of the Last World Emperor rolled into one, raises another possible contradiction. If she is right, why does Langland crown Conscience King at the end of the poem, and leave him, the embodiment of any struggling Christian, to solve the 'crisis of leadership' on his own?

But this author, rather like Langland, prefers to spiral around problems, returning to them at different places and in different contexts, than to give answers. Too many of her arguments, either about Langland's meaning or about his possible sources, break off before the point of commitment. Even on the question of Joachite influence she leaves us to decide whether it is really there, concluding only that 'we know at least that the problem is more complicated than the traditional eschatology allows for' (p. 199), Nor, in the many passages in the book where she deals not with Langland but with the Latin source material in which she has made herself so expert, does she venture beyond the claims made by the accepted guides to such territories: Reeves, McGinn, Knowles, Szittya, for example. I would prefer a clearer and more courageous line of argument. She may feel that her book, like Langland's again, should convey a journey, not an arrival, but this approach is apt to be a little disappointing for those who are travelling the road with her.

NEWNHAM COLLEGE, CAMBRIDGE   ANNA BALDWIN

John Gower's Poetic: The Search for a New Arion. By R. F. YEAGER. (Publications of the John Gower Society, II) Cambridge: Brewer. 1990. vii + 289 pp. £35.

Those who have worked hardest to promote Gower's reputation in this century have tended to value him more as a moralist than as a poet. R. F. Yeager is intent on taking him seriously as a poet, though none the less of a moralist as well: he portrays Gower as an active reformer both of his society and of his language, who strove to create a poetic language that was adequate to his high moral themes. Only the first chapter of Yeager's book deals directly with Gower's style, and it focuses all but exclusively on the *Confessio Amantis*; in it, Yeager accounts for the irreproachable regularity of both Gower's meter and his rhyme as his conscious attempts to set new standards for the language in response to the metrical discord of his English predecessors. The more important part of his argument concerns Gower's appropriation of the language of the previous works from which he drew. Yeager has discovered an important precedent for the manner in which Gower composed his *Vox Clamantis* — by weaving together extracts and quotations from classical and medieval poetry — in the late classical *cento*, especially as practised by the Christian poet Anicia Faltonia Proba. He sees here a model for Gower's adaptation of old verse for new contexts in his other poems as well. In his French verse, the *Mirour de l'Omme*, which Yeager describes as 'an anatomy of good and wicked desires' (p. 84), and his lyrics, where the context is the promotion of chaste marriage, this borrowing amounts to an 'adversarial rewriting' of the amoral and indelicate treatment of love by his French predecessors, particularly the *Roman de la Rose*. This same procedure provides the basis for Yeager's account of the structure of the *Confessio Amantis*. In this poem, he asserts, Gower offers himself as a 'new Arion', the poet whose 'lusti melodie' brought peace and harmony into the world, whom he invokes at the end of his Prologue. The long, fictive love-confession, modelled on traditional love-allegory, is his 'lusti melodie'. It is also the story of the narrator's growth in wisdom, offering both a redefinition of love and a discussion of the roots of political harmony, and culminating in the narrator's prayer for peace in the epilogue. In each respect in which Gower has broadened the discussion of love, he has redirected traditional love-poetry to a new end, and has surpassed its ethical limits even while imitating its form. The *Confessio* is thus 'a love poem designed to outgrow itself' (p. 265) and another conscious attempt to reform the language of the poetic tradition from which it springs.

An argument of this sort on a six-hundred-year-old poem must necessarily be more provocative than persuasive, especially to the extent that the case for Gower's artfulness depends on establishing his attitudes and intentions rather than merely describing effects. Even if the notion of 'adversarial rewriting' is not merely anachronistic, it is quite difficult to know Gower's feelings about the *Roman de la Rose*, or about the relation of his own work to its sources. The specific examples of recognizable borrowing in the *Mirour* and the lyrics are too slight and too few to sustain the argument that Yeager builds on them; similarly, the lines he quotes from the opening of the *Confessio* may reflect, but do not prove, a belief in the poet's high calling that matches Virgil's and Dante's. Yeager's speculations on Gower's use of his predecessors also depend on assumptions about both the breadth and depth of his reading that are contradicted by some of his own comments on the nature of Gower's sources. In giving so much weight to the didactic purpose of the *Confessio*, moreover, many will feel that he has overlooked the major importance of this poem as a 'lusti melodie', an objection that is frequently made to those critics (once exclusively American, but increasingly international) who exalt Gower as poet of social reform rather than of love.

Yeager is at his best, however, in discussing precisely the most overtly didactic portions of the poem, and in that respect his book has much to offer. His chapter on the 'hard cases', the long apparent digressions in the *Confessio*, is particularly instructive on the thematic interconnexions within the work; he makes good use, for instance, of St Paul's condemnation of avarice as a form of idolatry to explain Gower's discussion of pagan religions within the course of his treatment of Avarice in Book 5. Elsewhere, his comments on the thematic structures of the *Mirour de l'Omme* and of Gower's two sequences of lyrics are more useful and revealing than anything else that comes to mind. Yeager has thought long and hard about Gower's works; and in taking Gower so seriously as a poet, he has succeeded most of all in explaining some of the ways in which Gower's morality gives structure to his verse.

University of Hawaii at Manoa   Peter Nicholson

The Myths of Love: Classical Lovers in Medieval Literature. By Katherine Heinrichs. University Park and London: Pennsylvania State University Press. 1990. vii + 270 pp. £27.

The myths of love in Katherine Heinrichs's title are the relatively small group of stories, mostly from Ovid's *Heroides* and *Metamorphoses*, which are commonly alluded to by the European courtly love poets of the late fourteenth century, principally Boccaccio, Machaut, Froissart, and Chaucer. Heinrichs's contention is that these allusions (she rejects the term 'digressions', as applied by C. S. Lewis and others) have fixed values, and that they can therefore be used as indices of the attitude of the writers who employ them. Mostly those values are negative; these secular lovers tend to exemplify concupiscent love *par amours*, inadequate in the Christian order, so the protagonist of the Christian era (such as the black knight in *The Book of the Duchess*) suffers from a calculated guilt by association. This 'mining of Pagan gold' — extracting moral value from pagan texts and euhemerizing it — offers limited ethical substance but has considerable use as what E. D. Hirsch calls 'narrowing data': information which helps to resolve the status of the morally indeterminate. It helps to resolve, for example, the vexed issue of whether to interpret naïve narrators as devices of disingenuous irony, implying the opposite of what they say, or as honest enquirers whose ingenuity allows the truth to emerge.

These issues are very enlighteningly treated in Heinrichs's first chapter. She then turns to a consideration of the so-called mythographers in the book's most crucial chapter, headed 'Classical Lovers and Christian Morality'. What she says here is not particularly new but it is admirably clarifying. The typical situation is that 'passionate sexual love is first praised, classical *exempla* are adduced, and finally love is regarded *sub specie aeternitatis* and found wanting'. The third chapter considers what is termed 'spiritual pilgrimage', negatively defined through the declarations about love of foolish authorities such as the Friend and the old woman (the Wife of Bath's prototype) in the *Roman de la Rose*. The folly of these false authorities is again to be inferred from their classical illustrations, as it is in the lesser works of Boccaccio considered here. The fourth chapter deals with love debates where the moral is again deduced from the foolish lover. Throughout the book Heinrichs has made an impressively strong case for her texts which are the least repected corner of medieval literature (especially among Anglophone critics); her enthusiasm gets out of hand when she claims that Machaut's *Jugement dou Roy de Navarre* 'is one of the cleverest productions in all literature, in which practically every line has several sorts of comic or ironic resonance', even if her excellent analysis of the poem does show that the poem works in a sophisticated way to a judgement opposed to the ostensible one. The final chapter approaches Chaucer's dream poems with the notion of irony that has been implicit throughout the book (the notion of it used by D. W. Robertson, Robert Hollander, and by I. A. Gordon on *Troilus and Criseyde*).

Even though the dream poems are the works of Chaucer most closely related to the writings examined here, it is a pity that the book does not turn to more weighty English works: *Troilus*, or *The Canterbury Tales* more generally, or *Confessio Amantis*. I say this less in criticism than in tribute to a considerable contribution to the interpretation of medieval literature, which develops criteria that offer some certainty of judgement. There are some flaws: texts in Latin and French are sometimes translated, sometimes not; occasionally a kind of critical shorthand glosses over complex matters (for example Dante's *Epistola* x is cavalierly introduced by 'to Can Grande he writes'); the authoritative anthology of the mythographic tradition by A. J. Minnis and A. B. Scott (*Medieval Literary Theory and Criticism c. 1100–c. 1375: The Commentary Tradition* (Oxford: Clarendon Press, 1988)) should have been mentioned, as should Rosamund Tuve's *Allegorical Imagery* which raised problems about 'narrowing data' that Heinrichs goes some way towards resolving. A short bibliography would have helped define the field.

But these are minor matters in an important and elegantly written book. Its greatest value for the English medievalist is that it gives pause to the generally accepted 'Ricardian poetry' view that the touches of naturalism and *voltes face* of late fourteenth-century English writers are an English phenomenon. They are well attested in Froissart. This book has unlikely virtues: it is a triumph for moderately applied Robertsonian historical criticsm, and it sends the reader back to Machaut and Froissart with revived appetite.

Magdalen College, Oxford   Bernard O'Donoghue

Latin Poetry and the Classical Tradition: Essays in Medieval and Renaissance Literature. Ed. by Peter Godman and Oswyn Murray. Oxford: Clarendon Press. 1990. xi + 243 pp. £30.

This book containing eleven essays by some of the leading scholars in medieval and renaissance Latin is the result of a conference held at the Warburg Institute in

London at the end of 1988. That the participants should have been allowed a free rein for their papers is normal, but when these are presented in book form the need for a summing up by the editors, including perhaps elements of any discussions, is sorely felt. A postlude should be *de rigueur* in these situations. Particularly regrettable is the lack of any overall theoretical base for what constitutes the classical tradition. Only Peter Godman's 'Literary Classicism and the Latin Erotic Poetry of the Twelfth Century and the Renaissance' tries to tackle the problem, albeit by reference to discussions of classicism in music. But is musical theory totally transferable to poetry, or to prose? Some essays, such as Peter Dronke's 'The Archpoet and the Classics', demonstrate a sure and sensitive intuitive feel for the topic while others, such as Giovanni Orlandi's 'Classical Latin Satire and Medieval Elegiac Comedy', seem to be flailing about, at times unable to recognize the tradition, at others wilfully jettisoning it. Two of the later period papers, Jozef Ijsewijn's 'Poetry in a Roman Garden', pointing out the likelihood of unconscious echoing of previous authors because of the technical constraints of vocabulary and metre, and G. W. Pigman III's 'Neo-Latin Imitation of the Latin Classics', recalling the rôle of memory and rote-learning, would have helped Orlandi to begin to sort out his ideas (and ours, too). It is interesting to note the implicit reminder from the Renaissance specialists to the medievalists that the search for manuscripts to bolster one's arguments may be unnecessary. Learning by rote could be passed on by generations of teachers without any of them actually setting eyes on the actual text, though, of course, Dronke is absolutely right when suggesting that Orleans was the place where knowledge of Tibullus and Propertius would have been available in manuscript form.

As might be expected from such a topic, all three 'renaissances' (Carolingian, twelfth-century, and 'The Renaissance') are covered, but it is a pity not to find a paper on an author working on his own, without the stimulus of a group of like-minded contemporaries. The Carolingian period is quite oddly represented by Murray's 'The Idea of the Shepherd King from Cyrus to Charlemagne', who finds that discontinuity, 'because it is a new creation [...] belongs to the continuing history of the classical tradition'. The adaptation of the classical to the Biblical described by Murray is more firmly grounded in Jan Ziolkowski's 'Classical Influences on Medieval Latin Views of Poetic Inspiration', ending with the Archpoet, and in Paul Gerhard Schmidt's 'The Quotation in Goliardic Poetry', where even classical metres have to fit into structures that are alien to them. Michele Feo's 'The Pagan Beyond of Albertino Mussato' gives an implicit revenge of classicism over the Bible when Dante's *Inferno* is replaced by a Virgilian Hades. According to Feo the reasons are to be sought in politics. A. C. Dionisotti's 'Walter of Châtillon and the Greeks' also brings in political motives and anti-Roman feelings, but there are other factors involved. There is the problem of what epic poetry should be, with the schools of Reims having different opinions from those of the Chartrians. I hesitate to suggest that a glance at the introduction of my edition of the first three books of Joseph of Exeter's *Trojan War*, another Reims text referred to by Dionisotti, might have given some help in this direction. Godman's study of Peter of Blois's version of classicism is beautifully done, though the admiration one feels for Peter's cleverness and poetic dexterity cannot totally redeem the content. However subtly or allusively worded, the poem 'Grates ago Veneri' is nevertheless a first person account of the narrator's rape of a young girl, and reading it leaves one with a feeling of unease, only slightly alleviated by the girl's supposed gratitude for having been raped. Ovid's flippant 'all girls like being raped' (in his sophisticated Rome everyone was playing a game) is here replaced by a more uneven contest, similar to that of the Pastourelle, and the narrator's confidence in his masculinity that taught the girl a pleasure previously unknown does not find much approbation with this reader. The

second half of Godman's article, on the 'Basia' of Johannes Secundus, is far more
speculative, opening up a few approaches that seem viable in the present parlous
state of our knowledge of the man. The link between Peter of Blois and Johannes is
an attitude, that of the poet against the critic (though in the twelfth century it could
also be expressed in terms of *antiqui* and *moderni*). Godman's remarks on Johannes
should be read in conjunction with Walter Ludwig's chronological study of 'The
Catullan Style in Neo-Latin Poetry', and this in turn takes us back to Pigman, albeit
somewhat tangentially, for it is one of Catullus's first imitators, Pontano, who exerts
more influence on the Catullan-style writers than Catullus himself did. Pigman also
raises the intriguing extra difficulty of evaluation involved when poets like Vida
consciously echo poets who are echoing poets who may well be echoing poets . . . . All
in all this is a generally fascinating collection of essays with few 'longueurs'.

UNIVERSITY OF READING   KEITH BATE

Studies in 'The Vernon Manuscript'. Ed. by DEREK PEARSALL. Cambridge: Brewer.
   1990. xi + 238 pp. £35.
This collection of essays is intended, as Derek Pearsall remarks (pp. ix–x), to act as a
complement to the publication of the facsimile of the Vernon manuscript (Cambridge: Brewer, 1987, with an introduction by A. I. Doyle). Like the texts in the
Vernon manuscript itself, the essays fall into well-defined groups.
   The first group consists of 'General Essays' that deal with primarily codicological
aspects of the manuscript. Fittingly, the opening essay is an updated revision of
A. I. Doyle's 'The Shaping of the Vernon and Simeon Manuscripts', arguably the
most influential piece of work ever done on these sister manuscripts.
P. R. Robinson's contribution is a nice blend of lexicographical and manuscript
information that examines the terms 'coucher book' and 'ledger book', concluding
that, although medieval usage is rather vague, it is appropriate to apply the former
term to the Vernon manuscript. Thorlac Turville-Petre relates the Vernon manuscript to the Clopton manuscript both through their Worcestershire dialect and
through their texts of the *Euangelie*, which may have been copied from the same
exemplar. The picture that emerges is of an energetic and thriving scribal industry
in the south-west midlands, producing religious (and other) texts for a primarily
armigerous, orthodox gentry. N. F. Blake's essay views the contents and organisation of the manuscript as the work of a monastic compiler-editor who had access to a
wide variety of texts, often in more than one version, whose intention was to provide
a comprehensive, orthodox anthology, possibly for a community of women religious.
By concentrating on the choice of predominantly prose texts in Part 4 of Vernon and
on their internal wording, S. S. Hussey argues that the book was intended for a
devout lay audience. Given the complexity of the manuscript, however, such
divergence of possibilities is quite in order.
   The second set of essays deals with individual texts or groups of texts and is
subdivided into smaller groups that treat religious texts, the so-called 'romances',
and the lyrics. Thomas J. Heffernan first sets the copying of the Vernon manuscript
in the troubled social and religious contexts of the late fourteenth century and then
identifies, by close textual comparison, the manuscript's (and Simeon's) version of
the *Northern Homily Cycle* as a representative of a tradition distinct from that of the
original recension. Avril Henry's examination of the 'Pater Noster in a table
ypeynted' (of which a colour plate is provided) is a sensitive iconographic and
textual interpretation that relates the English and Latin text to scholastic schemati-
zations of doctrine. The essay continues with a succinct account of selected doctrines
and their sources in other Vernon works and of how these are partly communicated

322 *Reviews*

through structure and style. Drawing on a wide range of texts, Carol M. Meale places the Marian miracles solidly within their tradition, although the specific sources may remain elusive. Her tentative suggestion that the combination of text and illustrations might have been modelled on continental books raises, as she notes, intriguing implications for how Vernon was generated. C. W. Marx carefully delineates the relationship between the Middle English *Lamentation of Mary to Saint Bernard* and its immediate source, the Anglo-Norman verse *Plainte de la Vierge*, and the ultimate source, the Latin *Quis dabit*, an interesting 'transformation of a text from one medieval genre to another' (p. 157).

There follow two essays on the Vernon 'Romances' (so marked and questioned in the table of contents). As others have done, A. S. G. Edwards questions traditional definitions of the romance, preferring to view *Robert of Sicily*, *The King of Tars*, and *Joseph of Arimathea* as what Dieter Mehl calls 'homiletic romances'. As such, these works fit well into the didactic context of the Vernon manuscript, as they do in the other manuscripts in which they appear. Edwards makes the plausible hypothesis that *Joseph of Arimathea* was a local, Worcestershire composition, possibly written specially for Vernon, by implication at Bordesley Abbey. Karl Reichl's contribution is an analysis of the language of *The King of Tars* that neatly utilizes both traditional, phonological dialect features with information from *The Linguistic Atlas of Late Mediaeval English*. He then uses dialectal and textual comparison between the texts of the Auchinleck and Vernon manuscripts to show that 'the romance reached the Vernon MS essentially through a chain of written transmission' (p. 186), though some variations are best explained by memorization of the text by the scribe.

The collection is rounded off by two essays on the Vernon lyrics. John Burrow examines, with some elegant speculation, 'the number, order and identity of [the] constituent stanzas' in the twenty-three lyrics with refrains, comparing them, where possible, with other copies of the poems. Finally, John J. Thompson uses the complete set of twenty-seven lyrics to provide information about the assembly of material for the Vernon and Simeon manuscripts, before using such, and other, codicological evidence to show how great the search must have been for material for these manuscripts.

This is a fine collection of essays, distinguished particularly by the emphasis given by its authors to viewing the Vernon manuscript within a wide context of other manuscripts and texts. Doyle's update of his important essay of 1974 is highly useful, though it is unfortunate that references to it elsewhere in the volume are to its original appearance. There are some inconsistencies in the style of footnote citations, but what few inconsistencies of substance there are in the individual essays are acceptable as reflecting alternative interpretations of the evidence. In light of the importance, at least in date, of the manuscript's copy of *Piers Plowman*, an essay on the Vernon text of the poem (perhaps by the editor?) would have been welcome. This is, however, a grand complement to the Brewer facsimile of the Vernon manuscript and, indeed, serves partly as a tribute to Ian Doyle's scholarship on the manuscript.

MICHIGAN STATE UNIVERSITY   LISTER M. MATHESON

Shakespeare's Festive World: Elizabethan Seasonal Entertainment and the Professional Stage. By FRANÇOIS LAROQUE. Trans. by JANET LLOYD. (European Studies in English Literature) Cambridge, New York, and Melbourne: Cambridge University Press. 1991. xvi + 423 pp. $45; $64.50.

It is a pleasure to welcome European scholarship into the subject of the English Renaissance, but it would appear, sadly, that this work has suffered from François

Laroque's distance from the subject. The first half is a study of festivity itself and, in this, Laroque's section on Shrove Tuesday is extremely good; the material quoted, and there is much of it, all from contemporary sources, provides a reliable picture of the indulgences and excesses of London's youth. It comes as a shock, therefore, to find elsewhere historical errors, as for example, nineteenth-century Mummers' play texts used as evidence for Renaissance and even of medieval mummings: 'Saint George [...] up until the mid-sixteenth century [...] had been celebrated with jollifications and parades in the towns and by performances of stereotyped popular dramas similar to the Mummers' play' (p. 110); 'St George and the dragon made [sixteenth-century Inn-signs] their last home, ending a career that speaks volumes about the continuous decline undergone by the great popular festivals ever since the Middle Ages [when St George and the dragon] were the subjects of the Mummers' folk plays' (p. 111). Following too closely in the footsteps of E. K. Chambers here leads to a quagmire, yet Chambers's 1903 work does not make the same crude equation between early and late material. It must be that Laroque has here misunderstood his source, since his conclusion about the decline of St George plays ignores the fact that they were written about four centuries later than he says, therefore they cannot have experienced quite such a drastic end in 1600.

The second half is a sympathetic, conservative (see pp. 244–45, 253), and even contradictory view of the function of festivity in Shakespeare's work; as when the first half of his book, on the ubiquity of Shrovetide, Mayday, and Whitsun customs in about 1600, is negated with a line from Levi-Strauss, 'the débris of what was once a social discourse' (p. 191). The most successful parts, such as on *The Winter's Tale* and *Othello* are those where his understanding of festive time and charivaris is put to sustained use. But the slips are such that in a small space one must speak of them. For this work lacks objectivity and one constantly feels that a momentary hobby-horse has blinded Laroque to overall realities.

In the Jack Cade scenes in *2 Henry IV*, he makes an interesting reference to the work of Le Roy Ladurie, who wrote that the 'sword dance was to put "an end to the activities of an evil landlord who would terrorize peasants or rape their daughters"'. The social and economic emancipation connected with class struggle is inseparable from the defence of sexual integrity, as Jack Cade reminds his followers' (p. 251). Laroque here overlooks his previous page where he had approved Cade's own 'loudly proclaimed sexual demands. He was for instance, to claim for himself the rights of *jus primae noctis* and licence to take his pleasure with other men's wives whenever he wished'. Surely some comment should have been made here on Cade's own hypocrisy, of which the audience would have been aware. Just how positive *is* the portrayal of this leader? Had Laroque remembered his own interesting obser-vations on the 'pendulum' (p. 204) and 'hour-glass' (p. 220) qualities of festive time: vigorous/positive at one moment, feeble/negative at the next, the contradiction could have contributed to his argument instead of demolishing it. There are many more such moments, and in a work for which so much is claimed, the lack of consistency overshadows his very real feeling for the value of the seasonal calendar. As a result, the riches of his source material require judicious sifting from the reader.

UNIVERSITY OF GLASGOW   SANDRA BILLINGTON

Shakespeare's Tragic Cosmos. By T. McALINDON. Cambridge, New York, and Melbourne: Cambridge University Press. 1991. xvii + 306 pp. £30.

For many readers the most significant feature of this book will be its unequivocal repudiation of the central arguments of cultural materialism (though T. McAlindon prefers the label Marxism). He states in his introduction that it is a 'textually demonstrable fact that Shakespeare consciously and systematically referred the contradictions that troubled him most to a transhistorical model of human and universal nature', and in his conclusion that 'Shakespeare's tragic art is radically informed by essentialist notions of a transhistorical human nature and of unchanging laws encoded in universal nature'. McAlindon is an unpolemical writer, but this, along with his earlier *English Renaissance Tragedy*, represents the most direct challenge to the school of criticism promoted by Jonathan Dollimore which has yet been published.

It is, however, far from being a restatement of the Tillyardian world picture. McAlindon does not dismiss Tillyard, but argues that his version of a hierarchical order of nature has to be supplemented by the more important horizontal model which derives from Empedocles. The Empedoclean cosmos is one of universal contrariety in which nature is governed by the opposing forces of Love and Strife in a system of *concordia discors*, and this conception of nature is ultimately held to be responsible for Shakespeare's characteristic mixing of comedy and tragedy. The continuous dialectic of Love and Strife produces harmony from division and division from harmony, hence comedy from tragedy and tragedy from comedy. But McAlindon also takes issue with such critics as Norman Rabkin, and more recently Graham Bradshaw, who in emphasizing the dialectical quality of Shakespearean drama argue for its open-endedness and for the impossibility of reconciling the conflicts of valuation which the texts pose. His own thesis is that such contradictions 'are at root conflicts of natural forces and feelings rather than ideas' and are therefore 'by definition capable of some kind of reconciliation'. To put it another way, Shakespearean tragedy dramatizes the conflicts of the human heart which are in turn reflected in the 'harmonious contrarietie' of universal nature. Its essence can be seen in terms of a pun on the word 'kind' as meaning both 'natural' and 'loving' , and it is this that forms the basis of a reading of the tragedies which stresses their movement towards resolution.

The corollary of this — that there is an underlying discord in Shakespearean comedy — is acknowledged in the second chapter where McAlindon discusses the importance of Chaucer's Knight's Tale for English Renaissance literature and for *A Midsummer Night's Dream* in particular. These two works are undoubtedly well suited to illustrate the principle of *concordia discors* (or *discordia concors*). The remaining chapters of the book are devoted to individual tragedies from *Romeo and Juliet* to *Antony and Cleopatra*, with the exception of *Timon* and *Coriolanus*. Those last two plays are certainly very ill suited to support McAlindon's general thesis, and it is also true that McAlindon has difficulty with some of the tragedies which he does discuss. The most obvious example seems to me to be *Hamlet*. It is reasonable to wish to rescue the play from philosophical over-interpretation, but it is unclear whether the play is concerned with conflicts of natural feeling *rather* than ideas, or whether we think of Hamlet principally as 'a man of warm and loving nature'. Furthermore, statements such as that the play is a 'site of endless semiotic disorder', that 'bafflement is an integral part of the play's meaning', and that 'all this excess, dislocation, and confusion in language is likened to the state of primal chaos: the word and the world are one' would seem to contradict the author's own premises and align him with those critics he wishes to challenge.

But if McAlindon is occasionally inconsistent this may be due to the enormous weight of prior critical commentary which he has taken on board. There is a slightly weird moment in the notes to the *Hamlet* chapter where he cites Peter Alexander's *Hamlet, Father and Son* only to prefer Nigel Alexander's book on the same play; one has the feeling of being suddenly transposed into a critical metadrama. The enormous amount of reference to earlier critics is, however, a measure of McAlindon's scrupulousness as a scholar, and this is undoubtedly a work of genuine scholarship. Some of the best moments in the book are such insights as the significance of 'hands' in Romeo and Juliet's wooing sonnet, the suggestion that Sinon at Troy is a model for Iago, and the fascinating discussion of the importance of the *Metamorphoses* and Plutarch's 'Isis and Osiris' for *Antony and Cleopatra*.

To complain of weak links in the argument is not to suggest that McAlindon's thesis is fundamentally unconvincing. The chapter on *King Lear*, for example, is extremely successful in demonstrating that 'the drama of the human heart is the drama of the natural world'. This is a humane study and one of real intellectual integrity. It also offers a radical revision of Tillyard which the tediously repetitive mockery of his 'world picture' by cultural materialists does not.

UNIVERSITY OF ST ANDREWS   NEIL RHODES

The Merchant of Venice. By JAMES C. BULMAN. (Shakespeare in Performance) Manchester and New York: Manchester University Press. 1991. viii + 164 pp. £25 (paperbound £8.95).

Henry IV. Part One. By SCOTT McMILLIN. (Shakespeare in Performance) Manchester and New York: Manchester University Press. 1991. viii + 132 pp. £25 (paperbound £8.95).

These two valuable studies join the growing number of contributions in recent years devoted to adding recognition of the problems of performance to the practice of drama criticism.

It is difficult to do justice to James C. Bulman's outstanding book in a short, shared review. I suspect that readers will learn more about *The Merchant of Venice* from this than from any other criticism. Bulman's opening chapter raises various problems in order to lead into the richly documented account in the second chapter of Sir Henry Irving's patriarchal, tragically ennobled Shylock, which dominated the later nineteenth century both in England and America. Complementing the opening, a closing chapter confronts, perhaps inevitably, 'Shylock and the Pressures of History'. Astute, acutely observant, and balanced, Bulman surveys the various uses and abuses of the play in the century of the Holocaust.

At conservative Stratford, Theodore Komisarjevsky's 1932 production, steeped in modernist Europe, evolved an eclectic anti-naturalist style to dispel the spectre of his sombre British predecessor. Cubist, Fauvist, and Expressionist elements went into the set, while the acting was festively ludic and theatrically fantastic, restoring *commedia* to Venice, with its comic Jew, and to Belmont, with its romance. The *regisseur* ruled here, not the actor-manager.

In the 1970 production at the National, Jonathan Miller reverted to Irving's concept but 'updated' the play to the Victorian period. Some severe cuts were made (including 'I hate him for he is a Christian') to present Laurence Olivier's Shylock in terms of 'more intricate and codified [...] social tensions'. From the body of Shakespeare's text so many directors really have had their pound of flesh, blood and all. However, ten years later, as executive producer for the BBC Shakespeare, in his influence on the director Jack Gold, Miller reversed his approach. The sixteenth-century caricature returned in the guise of Warren Mitchell, or at least that was the intention. To some, Mitchell merely echoed the Yiddisher comic butt of the twentieth-century music-hall.

Bill Alexander's psychologically provocative direction for the Royal Shakespeare Company (1987) refused to opt for polarized resolutions, actually intensifying the problems of the text. Anthony Sher portrayed Shylock as archetypal blood-lust Jew, the Venetians were closet homosexuals — 'Shylock has become their monster [...]

offering them a grotesque image of their own Christianity' — all bent on overt brutality and vilification in a corrupt materialist society.

The first production of *1 Henry IV* considered by Scott McMillin was that of 1945 with Olivier and Richardson doing a patriotic Carry on Shakespeare at the Old Vic, perpetuating the star system with the conventional theatrical prominence of Hotspur and Falstaff (McMillin shrewdly notes the influence of Richardson's renowned Peer Gynt on the latter). Crucial for a conceptual shift to Hal's *bildungsroman* was the still remembered Prince of Richard Burton at the Shakespeare Memorial Theatre in 1951. Burton's Danish angst in the role gives him the claim to be the first of the Angry Young Men of the fifties. More importantly this was the first of the post-war 'cycle' productions considered here (Peter Hall and the Stratford RSC 1964; Terry Hands and the RSC 1975; Michael Bogdanov with the English Stage Company, 1986).

One of the fascinating strengths of this book is McMillin's recognition of the inextricable cultural factors — critical, financial, political, and institutional — which instigated the largely misleading idea of a cycle, whether that of one or two tetralogies, or the completely barmy 'Falstaff cycle'. Generic disjunction and difference mark Shakespeare's provisional development, not the dramatic juggernaut of some Wagnerian *weltanschauung*.

A final word for Orson Welles's film *Chimes at Midnight* (1966). McMillin generously praises the cinematic quality. However, this entirely Quixotic venture recycles Cervantes in terms of Shakespeare. No wonder it was made in Spain.

UNIVERSITY OF READING RONALD KNOWLES

These Valiant Dead: Renewing the Past in Shakespeare's Histories. By ROBERT C. JONES. Iowa City: University of Iowa Press. 1991. xvii + 172 pp. $24.

Taking his title from the exhortation of the Bishop of Ely in *Henry V* to 'Awake remembrance of these valiant dead, | And with your puissant arms renew their feats' (1.2.115–16), Robert C. Jones sets out to investigate the manner in which Shakespeare's History Plays invoke the past as a means of validating the present. The story he tells, from the plays for the First Tetralogy, through *King John*, to the Second Tetralogy, is one of gradual loss, coupled with the increasing need to reproduce history as fiction, culminating in the final play of the Second Tetralogy in a revitalization and a restatement of the substantial veracity of a 'real' history.

Jones announces his aim 'to trace the possibilities as they are suggested through the histories, for crediting a vital relationship between past and present in which the valiant dead can be renewed to benefit their successors' (p. xiii). Despite occasional reference to the neo-Foucauldian historiography of Hayden White, Jones does little more than domesticate what White has called 'the peculiar dialectic of historical discourse' (*Tropics of Discourse: Essays in Cultural Criticism* (Baltimore, MD: Johns Hopkins University Press, 1978), p. 129).

The view which emerges of the two tetralogies is a broadly teleological one, not too dissimilar from that of Tillyard, despite avowals to the contrary, which brushes aside irony and contradiction. The theme of loss in the *Henry VI* plays is familiar, and it is not surprising that Jones should find discontinuity emerging as the realm sinks into confusion. He identifies Talbot as a figure who hangs on to a real sense of historical continuity, using 'historical precedents positively as models for heroic action', as opposed to 'the factionalists [who] use their history and their memories wilfully and destructively, and hence wrongly' (p. 12). What passes Jones by is the ideological investment in different versions of historical narrative, and the manner of justification that is frequently used. In his discussion of *2* and *3 Henry VI* he suggests rather glibly that 'revenge tends to stifle whatever recourse to history might otherwise make its claim on these contentious lords' allegiance' (p. 24), strongly implying a right and a wrong reading of 'history' itself, as opposed to an authoritative or a legitimizing one. Later we are told that 'memory floods the world of *Richard III*' (p. 31) but that the play 'virtually inverts the ideal of "remembrance" embodied in Talbot' (p. 32). Well, yes, but so what? In passing he takes a swipe at feminist interest in Shakespeare's female characters — 'consciousness on the rise' (p. 158 n. 2) — and concludes with the view that 'if Richard would undo the past, however, Richmond does little to revive it and nothing to "awaken remembrance" of the "valiant dead" in his own person' (p. 42). Of *King John* he notes that the play problematizes 'truths' and 'fictions of history' (p. 68), but he has nothing to say about the challenge which this play poses to traditional hierarchies of power beyond the view that the bastard Falconbridge is 'a fictive character acting a non-historic role' (p. 65).

Jones's treatment of the Second Tetralogy builds towards a theme which, as he states it, is not particularly profound or interesting. These plays are littered with references to the past and they intersperse a range of historical narratives. The idea of Hal producing a historical narrative of his rise to power, his appropriation of Hotspur's 'honour' (p. 109), and the emergence of Falstaff as 'a characteristically unique permutation of the lost leader figure — a dead anti-hero whom the living hero must *forget* in order to fulfil his own role as leader, but whose remembrance colours our view of that hero and reminds us of what he has lost in his triumph' (p. 144) jumbles insight with commonplace, and exposes the severe limitations of Jones's perspective on these plays. He gestures towards an ironic reading of *Henry V* without considering the question of the problematical nature of theatrical representation which the play foregrounds through the figure of the Chorus, and concludes with a peculiar distinction between historical 'truth' on the one hand and fictional representation on the other. His conclusion is that 'there *was* an Agincourt and a Henry V who won it' but that 'the play asks us to celebrate that heroic feat as true, to share in its spirit by awakening its remembrance' (p. 154). Such a heroic reading of the play, perfectly in keeping with both Tillyard, and the Laurence Olivier film, edits out ruthlessly many of the issues which recent criticism of the Histories has attempted to investigate. In his footnoting Jones shows that he is aware of some of these issues, but his analysis demonstrates that they have done nothing to budge a rather stodgy orthodoxy.

University of Stirling   John Drakakis

Shakespeare, Plautus and the Humanist Tradition. By Wolfgang Riehle. Cambridge: Brewer. 1990. x + 309 pp. £39.50.

If it is probable that Shakespeare studied Plautus at school, possible that he acted in his plays, and nearly sure that like Jonson he would have preferred his *vis comica* to the blander charms of Terence, the teachers' pet, then a likelihood exists that Plautus was the first major dramatist to have had a formative influence on his art. Wolfgang Riehle's thesis that this was so has the strength of inherent plausibility. Although not a new idea, it can scarcely be said to have won widespread acceptance. It deserved to be re-examined.

One hint of a fresh approach is Riehle's disclosure that he formed his conviction not in the study but while directing rehearsals of *Menaechmi* and *The Comedy of Errors* over several months. The germ of that experience was not quite killed by the rigorous deskwork that followed, and it informs the best part of his book, a dramaturgical comparison of those two plays together with the tragicomic

328   *Reviews*

Amphitruo, which he thinks impressed Shakespeare profoundly. First, however, he must clear away modern misconceptions. Building on the rehabilitation of Plautus in classical circles by older scholars such as Fraenkel and Duckworth, and on studies such as Segal's *Roman Laughter* (Cambridge, MA: Harvard University Press, 1968) and Slater's *Plautus in Performance* (Princeton, NJ: Princeton University Press, 1985) which themselves reflect the influence of Shakespeare criticism, he is able to argue that the Roman writer had much more to offer the sixteenth century than empty stock characters and farcical plots. As well as being funny he could be serious, moral, and even 'romantic' in his sympathetic treatment of frustrated love. He must have appealed to boys trained in spoken Latin as a sophisticated wordsmith, master punster, and metrical wizard. More significantly still, he claimed attention as a man of the theatre with an evident interest in stagecraft and a bent for the metatheatrical, expressed through his characters' enjoyment of audience-address and their consciousness of role-playing and crises of identity. Riehle argues that in all those respects Plautus's example surpassed those of models available to Shakespeare from the native tradition. But while challenging those who take an opposite view, his contention is rather that the gulf between native and classical comic traditions would not have seemed to yawn as wide to Shakespeare as it did to Sidney and does to most modern historians. (He concludes, indeed, by asserting a continuous awareness of New Comedy throughout the middle ages and subscribes to the view that its staging was recalled in that of the mystery-cycles and the Elizabethan public theatre).

Not being much concerned with source-study, Riehle's case for Plautus's influence is barely susceptible to proof: persuasiveness is all. At times he forgets this, resorting to the logic of Lewis Carroll's Bellman, but in general he puts his case well so long as he keeps his eye fixed on the workings of his chosen texts. He makes clear where he stands on each issue, sensibly writing of differences and transformations as much as of affinities or debts, and where his research leads to negative results (as in the chapter on metre) he willingly says so. Sad, then, that some of his book's authority is weakened in its last hundred pages. An understandable quest for wider horizons leads the author to look beyond Plautus to relate, not only *Errors*, but most of Shakespeare's comedies and romances to what is called his 'humanist interests'. A patchy chapter on onomastics in *Errors* comes to rest on Luciana, who motivates a chapter on renaissance Lucianism, which is then gathered up with New Comedy and much else to be diversely applied, in a very long chapter, to some seventeen plays. Like any lively jumble-stall this contains much intriguing material but is so diffuse and indiscriminate as to risk leading readers to review their assent to the more disciplined argument of the central thesis.

That defect apart, this is a solid book on a subject that should still matter to students of Shakespeare and renaissance comedy. Well mannered, well documented, and well produced, it is worthily dedicated to the memory of Wolfgang Clemen.

McMaster University, Hamilton, Ontario   Douglas Duncan

Massinger: The Critical Heritage. Ed. by Martin Garrett. (The Critical Heritage Series) London and New York: Routledge. 1991. xiv + 249 pp. £60.

To appreciate the unfairness of Massinger's critical reputation one need only look at the famous theatrical painting reproduced on the jacket of this volume: Edmund Kean as Sir Giles Overreach in the mad scene that ends *A New Way to Pay Old Debts*, which he first played in 1816. It was during this scene that Byron felt what he later described as convulsions; according to Hazlitt ladies were frightened into hysterics;

The Times reviewer noticed that even one of the actresses was shaken. Yet Massinger himself was to be blamed, virtually from that time to this, for his inability to touch the heart. Until recently, there has been no opportunity to test this judgement, since, after a few other revivals and adaptations, his plays largely dropped out of the repertory from the mid-nineteenth century onward. As Martin Garrett points out in the introduction to this collection, the first indication of a possible Massinger comeback was the publication of the fine edition of his works by Philip Edwards and Colin Gibson. Then came major productions of a few of his plays and (in 1985) a collection of new critical essays edited by Douglas Howard. And now, apparently, it has become worth studying the history of his critical reception.

It is obvious that such a collection as Garrett's will be mainly a history of decline, and, from the point of view of most readers, a history of bad criticism. This is fair enough when it exposes critics' dependence on each others' opinions and phrases, less fair when it shows them, like Coleridge, enthusing over Massinger's writing in scenes which are now ascribed to Fletcher, or when it reprints judgements which they would not have made if they had known, for instance, the satiric verse letter to Davenant, discovered only in 1980, which effectively demolishes the Victorian image of gentle, melancholy Massinger.

Predictably, the qualities which the eighteenth century admired in the playwright worked against him in the next century, when he was often compared, to his disadvantage, with the more obviously exciting Webster. But it is surprising that so many writers in both centuries reserve their highest praise for his metrical skill — not a quality much valued nowadays. Perhaps inevitably, Garrett's introduction is most sympathetic towards those whose approach is political. The latter has become so much the orthodoxy of the late twentieth century that the Royal Shakespeare Company's revival of *A New Way to Pay Old Debts* began and ended with images foreshadowing the Civil War, while the programme of a London fringe production of *The Roman Actor* declared as a matter beyond question that the play represented Massinger's reaction to Charles I's absolutist tendencies. It is a pity that Garrett does not reprint the historian S. R. Gardiner on 'The Political Element in Massinger's Plays' (1876); presumably, this doesn't count as criticism, but then, by these criteria, neither do half the essays in Howard's collection. The selection does, however, offer an interesting review from the *Westminster Magazine* for 1779, which claims that Richard Cumberland's adaptation of *The Bondman* owed its success to its political allusions, and Samuel Rogers's recollection of the excitement that the plays inspired in the young Charles James Fox. The apparent paradox of Massinger's reputation — cold and correct on the page, exciting in the theatre — can perhaps be resolved by a recognition that political excitement is as real as poetic excitement.

UNIVERSITY OF DELAWARE   LOIS POTTER

A Register of English Theatrical Documents: 1660–1737. Compiled and ed. by JUDITH MILHOUS and ROBERT D. HUME. Volume 1: *1660–1714*; Volume 2: *1714–1737*. Carbondale and Edwardsville: Southern Illinois University Press. 1991. xxxix + 521 pp.; 522–1079 pp. $90 two volumes.

Theatre historians have grown accustomed to being in the debt of Judith Milhous and Robert Hume. Anyone interested in late seventeenth-century theatre comes to realize that the string of articles and books issuing from the Milhous and Hume industry has transformed and immeasurably deepened our knowledge of the organization and practice of professional theatre in the period. Shedding 'new light' — a favourite phrase in the titles of their articles — has become a habit for them but one born of complete knowledge of the work of other scholars, prolonged searches of archives, county record offices, and, above all, the PRO, combined with their ability confidently and imaginatively to reinterpret the evidence as it has steadily accumulated. The end-product of this effort will, I presume, be the long-promised revision of the early volumes of *The London Stage*, building on the pioneering work of van Lennep and Avery to produce a far more detailed picture of the daily operations of the theatres than could have been drawn twenty-five years ago.

In the meantime, their latest work, *A Register of English Theatrical Documents: 1660–1737*, marks another vital stage in their mapping of the period's theatre history. The two volumes record, in as accurate a chronological order as possible, the complete extent of the documentary evidence so far known for the management and regulation of the theatre. Year by year, they list each and every document they know of, giving it a title, identifying its location, summarizing its contents and indicating published sources. A complicated system of brackets indicates where dates are to varying degrees hypothetical. The two volumes are adequately indexed with a helpful appendix listing documents misdated by earlier scholars; it is a tribute to their careful scholarship that there are so many entries in this appendix. Their principles for inclusion and exclusion are clearly set out; I would have wished for the inclusion of printed material directly connected with performance, e.g. libretti distributed at theatre — a category they have opted to exclude — but there is in fact little to carp about.

As the authors readily acknowledge, *A Register* is no more than a provisional listing, dependent on the work of other scholars, as well as their own future labours, to add and correct. They suggest a revision in fifteen years; I hope they may be persuaded to issue occasional pamphlet supplements in the meantime to make it easier for the rest of us to keep up-to-date. Spot-checking of numerous entries showed extremely high levels of accuracy. Of course, the interests of comprehensiveness have meant the inclusion of much mundane material but any year reveals fascinating snippets, sending one back to the materials afresh. Sandwiched between the search for and arrest of Martin Powell in January 1692, for example, comes a summary of Shadwell's letter on the costuming of Brady's *The Innocent Imposter*: in full he wrote, 'I would have had it acted in Roman habits and then with a Mantle to have covered her hips Mrs Barry would have acted the part'.

Most importantly, perhaps, the volumes will act as a spur to others to attempt to fill the gaps. As Milhous and Hume readily admit, the volumes have little to record of theatre outside London. As the great labours of the *Records of Early English Drama* project continues to unveil pre-Restoration provincial theatrical activity, it only shows how much needs to be done to map the full extent of non-metropolitan theatre after 1660. It is unlikely that a comparable project for the later period will ever be undertaken but the records are waiting to be listed. *A Register* may encourage someone to make a start. As it is, the accumulated scholarly debt to Milhous and Hume continues to grow alarmingly fast.

TRINITY HALL, CAMBRIDGE   PETER HOLLAND

Shakespeare Verbatim: The Reproduction of Authenticity and the 1790 Apparatus. By MARGRETA DE GRAZIA. Oxford: Clarendon Press. 1991. xii + 244 pp. £30.

Shakespeare Verbatim is evidence that radical cultural history is not necessarily cavalier with its sources, and that bibliographical scholarship does not have to be boring. This is an important book. It is also substantial, thorough, and detailed.

The thesis of *Shakespeare Verbatim* is that many of the materials we take for granted as essential to the study of Shakespeare became so at a specific historical moment, and in response to a particular cultural situation. It was the Enlightenment which produced for the first time a controlled, ordered, disciplined Shakespeare, located in a historical period, and complete with a life, an image, and an interiority, which together made it possible to unify the diverse and discontinuous texts, and fill the gaps in meaning that appeared within and between them. Edmond Malone's *The Plays and Poems of William Shakspeare* (spelt that way because that was how Shakespeare himself wrote it), was published in ten volumes in 1790. It was reissued in an expanded and revised edition by James Boswell in 1821. Margreta de Grazia's argument is that Malone's monumental work was not the culmination of previous editions of Shakespeare. It did not evolve from the work of Rowe, Pope, Theobald, Johnson, and others. On the contrary, it constituted a quite new departure in response to emerging cultural imperatives. In consequence, the model of editorial work it represents, which is still familiar to us in the twentieth century, is neither universal nor inevitable. It owes nothing to nature and a great deal to its specific epoch.

The Enlightenment characteristically presented its constructions as truth. Malone's extensive research among the documents produced an 'authentic' Shakespeare, whose portrait resembled the man himself as he appeared in 1607, whose biography was properly pruned of apocryphal details, and whose works were duly listed in chronological order. The result was a less wayward, more respectable author. Shakespeare emerges as a serious, responsible, and deservedly prosperous citizen, the proprietor of his own writings, which are to be seen as a repository of moral values. Any lapses of taste in the texts could be attributed to the habits and preferences of the newly identified Elizabethan period: they were thus not the dramatist's personal responsibility.

What Malone excluded in the course of disciplining Shakespeare was extravagance, irregularity, indeterminacy. He dismissed as unauthenticated the transgressive Shakespeare of earlier accounts, who poached deer in his youth and began his literary career by writing a scurrilous ballad. Shakespeare was now a knowing, rational, autonomous individual, whose unified consciousness was the source of the identifiable, unitary meanings of his works. And while the texts themselves provided direct and unmediated access to the author's mind and experience, doubtful readings could be resolved in terms of what Shakespeare was likely to have thought, to have had, precisely, in mind.

Malone's edition miraculously produced presence out of absence. There were in existence no guaranteed likenesses, no original manuscripts direct from the pen of the dramatist, no sure accounts of a life. But Malone's documents, records, and annotations stood in for the missing 'originals'. By these means Malone constructed an Author, who was able to take their place, who constituted the free-standing origin of the meanings of the texts and the guarantee of the correct reading of his work. Victory, as Roland Barthes might have said, to the editor. And victory, too, in due course to the literary institution, which would valorize editorial expertise and locate it in a neutral, objective realm, prior to interpretation.

The Malone Shakespeare, much refined and emended, is recognizable now. But another more shadowy figure is beginning to appear in recent criticism, at the same time as Enlightenment values begin to elicit a certain scepticism. This postmodern Shakespeare, more plural, more differentiated, though less worthy, perhaps, is also constructed, it becomes possible to see, this time out of slightly different materials, and in response to other, more recent cultural imperatives.

Shakespeare Verbatim is not an instance of New Historicism in the Greenblatt mould: there are no anecdotes, no unexpected readings of Renaissance texts. But it is in an independent and important sense historicist. It locates in history not only Shakespeare himself, but also editorial practice, raising by implication profound questions for those who are currently working to produce editions of Shakespeare's texts. Like all good historicist analysis, it thus relativizes our own present, locating it as one moment in a continuing cultural history. And at the same time, since it is a fluent and scholarly discussion of Malone's work, *Shakespeare Verbatim* is also in an important sense new. It offers a model of sophisticated, theorized work on the processes by which Shakespeare has been produced for his modern admirers.

UNIVERSITY OF WALES COLLEGE OF CARDIFF   CATHERINE BELSEY

Mock Kings in Medieval Society and Renaissance Drama. By SANDRA BILLINGTON.
    Oxford: Clarendon Press. 1991. xiii + 287 pp. £35.

In the first three chapters of Part 1 of this study Sandra Billington assembles the various materials of medieval mock-kingship into appropriate categories of outlaws and rebels, kings of winter festive groups, summer kings and queens, and kings of fortune. Mock kings, or lords of misrule, are surveyed, from aristocratic outlaws and seasonal peasant festivities, to university entertainments, and the Inns of Court. This multifarious and engaging historical material constitutes about a third of the book. Thereafter, in Part 2, this 'evidence' is applied to a variety of Renaissance plays in both general and specific chapters. *The Troublesome Reign of King John* and *The Misfortunes of Arthur* are paired together as examples of 'the strongest evidence' for the 'variety of mock king interpretations and analogies' to 'provide another kind of understanding' of Renaissance texts. An apt quotation from Part 1 of *The Troublesome Reign*, identifying John as a temporary summer king, seems to provide direct evidence, but thereafter a major problem in the whole book arises as it becomes evident that argument rests on the rather shaky 'evidence' of increasingly tenuous analogy. Many kings in Renaissance drama are not quite up to the job, make a mockery of it, or are mocked by others, thus they may be seen as 'mock kings'. Relying on a slide from inept kings to mock kings, this reasoning is very weak. In fact it is hardly reasoning at all and becomes mere labelling — as in 'summer king behaviour'.

However, a chapter is devoted to Shakespeare's Plantagenet plays and a figure such as Jack Cade would certainly seem to fit very well into the lord of misrule pattern. Clearly Billington could extensively and fruitfully have applied her researches to illuminate arguably the most challenging personage of the *Henry VI* plays. Regrettably, barely more than a page is taken up with Cade. Here, where Billington's evidence, argument, and example are at their strongest the critical opportunity is passed up because she wishes to claim more than her approach warrants. Again, Falstaff is an obvious candidate, but the author cannot resist pushing the thesis too far. Not only Falstaff, but Henry and Hotspur are 'competing misrule lords'.

At one point Billington notes that 'criticism is always a selective exercise', but the method employed here is of occlusion and superimposition, not selection. For example, it is claimed that Richard III is 'a misrule lord *par excellence*, combining evil and festive characteristics'. Not a word is said about the generally accepted morality vice background. Again, in *Timon of Athens* is is not sufficient to accept the poet's account of his play for Timon in his own words: 'I have upon a high and pleasant hill | Feign'd Fortune to be thron'd'; for Billington his story 'establishes Timon as a summer king, in hilltop terms'. Following the chapter on *Tamberlaine* and *Timon* are chapters devoted to comedy; Festive Tragedy (*Troilus and Cressida, King Lear,* and *Antony and Cleopatra*); Political Dissent and Drama; Moral Political Criticism through Saturnalia in Jacobean Drama.

In discussing comedy once more a logical slide takes place. The coordinates of folly-disorder-misrule are loose enough to slip around in and can even seem convincing in some places, as with the crudity of *An Humorous Day's Mirth* but when applied to Sir Epicure in *The Alchemist* we are pulled up short by 'Mammon's [fantasy] to become lord of the philosopher's stone'. Gradually the mock king notion is expanded to incorporate saturnalia and *mundus inversus* topoi thereby deploying the shotgun school of criticism: let fly at the object and something is bound to get hit. For example, sighting *Troilus and Cressida* by way of the conjectural Inns of Court venue, firstly Pandarus in the epilogue is seen as 'the lord of misrule who had presided over the now ended Christmas entertainment', and then the Greeks, imitating Achilles, are blasted as 'a series of arrogant and useless imitation, or mock, lords'. This is tendentiousness run riot. Of Lear's arraignment of Goneril we read that 'he can do no more than lead parodic debate on political misrule in the manner of a seasonal, Temple lord'. Shakespeare's contemporaries would have recognized the fallacy of accident here: that which belongs to an accident or adjunct is attributed to a substance. This is the case with much of Billington's criticism; consider this distorting and wholly reductive remark on *Antony and Cleopatra*: 'Antony's form of misrule follows the precepts of the Gray's Inn Prince d'Amour'.

Other matters give cause for concern. The following works, all gleaned from a brief random sampling, are not found in the index, even though the last two also appear in the text with full page illustrations: *Jack Straw; Robin and Marian; An Humorous Day's Mirth; Mankind; Misogonus; The Romance of Arthur; Eikon Basilike.* Presumably anyone who could write the following, towards the close of the book, 'Pericles's words at the end of his travels "my twelve months are expir'd", specifically recall the annual cycle of mock king election [. . .] Fortune imposed such Christmas prince status on him', has lost all judgement?

UNIVERSITY OF READING   RONALD KNOWLES

The Dragon and the Dove: The Plays of Thomas Dekker. By JULIA GASPER. (Oxford English Monographs) Oxford: Clarendon Press. 1990. x + 241 pp. £27.50.

Julia Gasper cuts a swathe through much previous discussion of Dekker by pursuing the convincing thesis that he subscribed to a 'militant Protestant' outlook and that his dramatic works are organized to express it. Since a confessional foreign policy was never on James I's agenda and any conformity of decisions of state (actually guided by pragmatic judgements on national and personal security) with a putative apocalyptic role was coincidental, Dekker and like-minded London citizens experienced incremental frustration.

The Whore of Babylon reassembles events of Elizabeth's reign into an education, directed in the aftermath of the Gunpowder Plot at the pacific faintheart James, in the unremitting enmity of the Roman Whore and the bellicose fearlessness with which the (internationally conceived) True Church must meet it. It is difficult to judge how literally Dekker's mind framed history as an apocalyptic scenario, but apocalyptic discourse (even if reticently deployed) could effect a decentring of royal authority: its moral absolutes could both elevate and reproach historical actors. Gasper persuasively identifies Essex as the figure whose death warrant Titania (Elizabeth) signs, which is ostensibly inconvenient to her argument since Essex was the champion of belligerent Protestantism; but on this occasion Elizabeth (generally representing the True Church) flips over, by echoing the murderous Nero's expressed wish not to have learned to write, into the role of Antichrist. The allusion is necessarily oblique but Gasper gives good reason to think that Seneca's *De Clementia* is being invoked (along with its retroactive irony that Seneca himself fell victim to Nero's tyranny); and she later provides confirmation from *If This Be Not A Good Play* where King Alphonso, paralleling James's early pardon to Essex's accomplices, quotes the same phrase in order to forestall such crocodile tears. This typifies the flexible astuteness with which, once she has assumed the dualistic apocalyptic spectacles, Gasper reads clues.

Whether discussing *The Magnificent Entertainment* (where she makes short work of Jonathan Goldberg's simple notion of the pageant as an imperial triumph) or *The Virgin Martyr* (where the easy assumption of Catholic baroque influence is displaced by evidence of Protestant martyrology emotively deployed to rally support for the beleaguered Frederick and Elizabeth), Gasper reveals in Dekker's work a combination of topical lobbying and propagandizing which attests a politically alert city culture. *Match Me In London* is Dekker's riskiest satiric venture, his title alone seeming to direct the audience to parallels with James: the play is about a Spanish king, a timorous tyrant with James's foibles, one of which is his appointment of a 'Vice-Admirall' as vicious and incompetent as the Lord Admiral of England, Buckingham. This play was relicensed for performance by the Princess Elizabeth's Company in August 1623 while Charles and Buckingham were pursuing the Prince's amorous mission to Spain. By comparison, Gasper suggests, *A Game At Chess*, put on a year later, went with the flow of official sentiment after the pair's humiliation. Though Gasper hints at answers — Sir George Buck's dotage (when the original licence was granted), possible tacit sympathies with the Protestant cause, the king's summer absence — it remains a mystery how Dekker got away with this one.

Since so much of the book is engaged with topical detail one might have liked a concluding assessment of Dekker's militant Protestantism, especially since Gasper thinks our attitude to his principles will govern our estimation of the plays. She surely does not mean that to value them one must be committed to advancing the international Protestant cause by violent means? What is the relationship of the beliefs that constitute Dekker's stance? Gasper suggests, for example, that, while a Calvinist, he was not much interested in predestination. Yet her explanation of the sorry treatment of Hammon in *The Shoemaker's Holiday* (to Calvinism hypocrites could not escape that identity however hard they tried) relies on the idea of predestination; so too does *The Virgin Martyr*'s spectacular visitation of irresistible grace (Theophilus, rabid persecutor of Christians, did not know or control the spiritual identity secreted in his name), which she convincingly sees as triumphantly clinching the story's appropriation by Protestant martyrology. Were such beliefs merely used in an adventitiously tribal way, guided chiefly by the predicted reflexes of a known audience? Which beliefs mattered, and why? Answers are somewhat dispersed; yet Gasper's trenchant and well-informed study makes sense of a great deal in Dekker and in the political culture he was addressing. It is the most illuminating book on him.

UNIVERSITY OF MANCHESTER   JOHN STACHNIEWSKI

Ben Jonson. By RICHARD ALLEN CAVE. (English Dramatists) Basingstoke and London: Macmillan. 1991. ix + 184 pp. £30 (paperbound £8.99).

This is a Theatre Studies Jonson, an examination of his plays as works for the stage, focused primarily on the way he 'exploits all the devices that constitute the art of performance until performance comes to have the flexibility of reference (philosophical, emotional, and social) of a metaphysical conceit' (p. 5). At its best this offers extremely lucid and revealing readings of the plays, demonstrating time and again how a knowledge of the theatrical conventions which Jonson was manipulating can inform our understanding of the issues at the heart of the drama and the subtle discriminations he makes in respect of them. So, in *Sejanus*, it is 'the sordid reality of power politics as advocated by Machiavelli that is Jonson's subject, not, as the theatrical convention would have it, the seductive glamour' (p. 35). In the chapter on *Bartholomew Fair*, the best and most invigorating in the book, Richard Allen Cave shows how the 'puppet-play is in fact the best and most intricate of a carefully graduated sequence of strategies, which simultaneously entertain while inviting us to explore our laughter and so probe deeply into the psychology of performance and audience response' and argues most convincingly that 'Jonson may introduce the citizens to us as stereotypes, but he endows them steadily with unexpected complexity' (pp. 98–99, 108).

But there are limits to the usefulness of this approach, and Cave is not always as engaged as he is in these examples, so that the quality of the book as a whole is uneven. In respect of *Volpone*, for example, he breathes new life into the truism of the Fox as the consummate actor, and rings interesting changes on it by suggesting that Celia is the exact antithesis, a non-actor, 'a dutiful, god-fearing, eminently bourgeois *wife*' (p. 45). But why then does she throw down her handkerchief to 'Scoto of Mantua'? The equation is surely not quite as clear-cut as he suggests. The attention to recent productions of the plays (and some not so recent, such as Dickens's *Every Man In His Humour*) is welcome and helpful, though not as sustained as it might be, and sometimes seems to serve as a vehicle for narrow prescriptions about the 'right' way to stage the plays. We are told that Bill Alexander's 1983 *Volpone* showed 'the proper approach to Jonson' (p. 61), while Trevor Nunn's casting of Ian McKellen as Face in *The Alchemist* (1977) 'was to touch the pulse of Jonson's comedy' (p. 92).

If Cave seems over-rigid at such moments he is oddly cavalier about what he chooses to cover in the book. He purports to be dealing with the comedies, but gives one of his best chapters to *Sejanus* (while never so much as mentioning *Catiline*), is rarely more than dutiful about 'The Caroline Jonson' (though he pays lip-service to the post-Anne Barton 'rediscovery' of the late plays), yet finds time for a very half-hearted chapter on masques. This purports to fill the gap of Jonson's retirement from the stage, 1616–1625, but says nothing about the most shrewd and daring product of that period, *The Gypsies Metamorphosed*; it might also give an unwary reader the impression that Jonson and Inigo Jones between them invented court masques, and that all of their collaborations involved the use of a proscenium arch, which is by no means the case. His haziness on such matters is symptomatic of a rather cursory attention to the historical conditions under which Jonson wrote. He chews over the impossibility of reconstituting the precise effects of using boy actors for female roles (and so the difficulty today of effecting the ending of *Epicoene*) but shows little curiosity about how the use of an entire cast of boy actors might centrally have shaped that play, *Cynthia's Revels*, and *Poetaster*. He castigates Danny Boyle's 1989 production of *Epicoene* at the Swan because the Collegiates were 'too obviously played as Jacobean progenitors of the pantomime dame yet absurdly by very young actresses for whom it was a genial romp' (p. 74). But may that not be a fair 'translation' of the original conception? In the same ahistorical vein he credits Jonson with a 1616 volume of Collected Plays (p. 6), rather than of *Works*, a distinction which meant a great deal to contemporaries who mocked him for it.

Within his own terms, Cave is a perceptive analyst of what in Jonson has worked or, such as *Sejanus*, he argues, might well work in the modern theatre. But the criteria by which he judges this are inherently conservative, encouraging (with a few local adjustments) the long-held conviction that Jonson wrote a handful of timeless masterpieces but that most of what he wrote is beyond resurrection. More attention to the question of how ambivalently and contentiously Jonson related to his original audiences might make us realize that a good deal more of what he wrote is still

336 *Reviews*

capable of speaking urgently to us (even possibly on the stage, if we are inventive enough); though we still might not exactly enjoy what he has to say to us.

LANCASTER UNIVERSITY

RICHARD DUTTON

The Poetics of Primitive Accumulation: English Renaissance Culture and the Genealogy of Capital. By RICHARD HALPERN. Ithaca, NY, and London: Cornell University Press. 1991. vii + 321 pp. $47.50 (paperbound $15.95)

For me, reading this book was like listening to Beethoven play the piano after he lost his hearing: the performance was brilliant, but I was embarrassed for the performer because he couldn't hear when he was making mistakes. Richard Halpern is spiritually tone deaf — a consequential misfortune when he is writing about literature with a richly varied spiritual palette. I was embarrassed for him, for example, when I read his analysis of Lear's reunion with Cordelia. Halpern argues that their relationship is essentially feudal, hence 'charged with the counter-challenge that inheres in sacrifice' (p.250). Their reunion therefore consists of a triumph for Cordelia: 'Cordelia's motives [...] should not be allowed to conceal the actual result of her actions: she wins a total victory over her father, who by the end of the play is reduced to grovelling and self-abasement. "No, Sir," she can say at the delicious moment of emotional triumph, "you must not kneel"' (IV. 7. 58). Such tone deafness is related to two principal problems I noticed with this book: its ignorance about the Reformation and about ethics. An unrelated problem is Halpern's failure to engage other Marxist critics.

But first, the brilliance. 'Primitive accumulation' is Marx's phrase, denoting the acquisitiveness of a pre-capitalist economy. Halpern argues that the modes of production accompanying primitive accumulation also accompany particular cultural characteristics that he finds inscribed in texts by Skelton, More, Spenser, and Shakespeare. The scope of the book invites comparison with *Renaissance Self-Fashioning*, but Halpern incisively distinguishes Greenblatt's concern with explicit 'juridical' power from his own concern with a pervasive socio-economic power that affects politics but is implicit and unrecognized. Halpern puts his argument forward lightly, fairly, and eruditely. He corrects Marx on Adam Smith, and he is as familiar with the texts and complexities of Tudor humanism as with those of modern Marxist theory.

Halpern acknowledges the Reformation when it has a direct bearing on the text he is interpreting — as in *The Shepherds' Calendar* — but the dissolution of the monasteries becomes 'the primitive accumulation of church lands' (p. 75), as if Henry were swept up by socio-economic forces beyond his own control and knowledge, an unlikely characterization of his tyranny and greed. Halpern's summary of James's constitutional debate with Parliament is well informed and informative (pp. 219–25), but he fails to note that arguments over the precedence of royal or parliamentary power had a venerable heritage in arguments about the precedence of papal and imperial power that were extremely important for the Tudor Reformation, as pointed out by Frances Yates and others.

'Ethical' for Halpern describes 'a mode of thought which takes a free and volitional subject as its basis and starting point' (p. 87). This will do for Kant, who has no bearing on Halpern's authors, but not for Christian ethics, which begin with the premise of volitional bondage. Properly speaking, what Halpern sees as Marx's rejection of 'an ethical prolematic' in Adam Smith (p. 65) is Marx's reassertion of the social justice that was preached by Christian pastors in the Middle Ages and sporadically during the Tudor regime. Greenblatt is more insightful about the ethical motives of the early Marx (*Renaissance Self-Fashioning*, p. 37).

Where other Marxist critics of Renaissance literature are concerned, Halpern acknowledges Walter Cohen (three times) and Jonathan Dollimore (once) for readings of specific texts, but he fails to engage them as fellow theorists. This is particularly unfortunate in the case of Dollimore, who begins *Radical Tragedy* by distinguishing his position from Louis Althusser's — a theorist to whom Halpern is explicitly indebted. Halpern nowhere mentions Frank Whigham's *Ambition and Privilege*, though Whigham anticipates Halpern's argument in some quite specific ways.

HOPE COLLEGE, HOLLAND, MICHIGAN   JOHN D. COX

Marcus Tullius Ciceroes thre bokes of duties, to Marcus his sonne, turned oute of latine into english, by Nicolas Grimalde. Ed. by GERALD O'GORMAN. (The Renaissance English Text Society) Washington: Folger Books; London and Toronto: Associated University Presses. 1990. 265 pp. £25.

Cicero wrote his treatise on moral duties, *De Officiis*, during his enforced retirement from politics. Before long, in 43 BC, he was to be murdered by his enemies. The ruin of the Republic in whose service Cicero had once earned the title of 'father of his country' casts fingers of shadow over his work. *De Officiis* is nevertheless concerned above all with the exercise of virtue in public life. The highest and best form of action (it tells us) is that which, informed by wisdom, works for the benefit of society. Cicero had sent his son to Athens to study philosophy, but he believed that he himself had much to teach him about how moral philosophy might further public good through political activity, especially by means of oratory. In fact the best constructed parts of his treatise are the two books on moral goodness and expediency in which he took the second-century Stoic Panaetius of Rhodes as his principal guide. The third, which deals with possible conflicts between the two, a subject which Panaetius had not reached, is more discursive, repetitious, and anecdotal.

Cicero was never forgotten during the Middle Ages, but his posthumous reputation as a stylist and moral philosopher probably reached its zenith during the Renaissance. His treatise on duties then enjoyed enormous influence. A fervent admirer, Sir Thomas Elyot, communicated his excitement in a vibrant passage of his *Boke named the Governour* (1531). The *De Officiis* (here coupled in the same sentence with the works of Plato) contained, Elyot wrote, 'incomparable swetnesse of wordes and mater [...] wherin is joyned gravitie with dilectation, excellent wysedome with divine eloquence, absolute vertue with pleasure incredible'. Cicero and Demosthenes were held to be the two greatest masters of oratory, and only gradually, from the later sixteenth century onwards, did admiration for Ciceronian style decline in England. Cicero's advice about the individual's involvement in public affairs appeared to complement Christian teaching, which was not directly concerned with this subject. Much of his writing was permeated with a Stoical spirit which seemed to anticipate Christianity in such things as its contempt for sensual pleasures, its insistence that only what was right could be expedient, and its emphasis on the voluntary subordination of individual interests to the general good. Perhaps Cicero spoke especially eloquently to the better educated gentlemen of mid-Tudor England, many of whom were, like him, lawyer administrators. His message of public service, so useful in the development of a flattering self image, was accompanied by a thoroughly acceptable social conservatism and a welcome contempt for menial occupations (among which Cicero did not, however, count large-scale trade, especially if 'satisfied with gaine [...] it chaunge from the haven into landes': a fact no doubt reassuring for gentlemen preparing younger sons for commerce, or merchants aspiring to gentility). His advocacy of a discreet and moderate charity chimed in with (and had perhaps helped to inspire) currently fashionable ideas about poor relief. Less obviously palatable was Cicero's steadfast republicanism, though through his countless readers this may have had a significant influence on English political culture in the century before the civil war.

The first English translation of *De Officiis* to be published, Robert Whittinton's, appeared in 1534. But Nicolas Grimald's 1556 version was far more successful. By about 1600 it had gone through eight editions, and at least six thousand copies of it had been printed. Grimald's translation is here reprinted for the first time since the death of Elizabeth I. In his short introduction Gerald O'Gorman first gives some examples of influential Tudor educationalists who had a high opinion of *De officiis* and then gives a brief account of Nicholas Grimald. He shows that the Latin text he used was probably the one published by Carolus Stephanus in 1554–55, even though it was not the version which was to be printed in parallel with Grimald's translation from 1558 onwards. He reconstructs, as far as possible, the printing of the first edition and provides careful bibliographical descriptions of all editions down to the eighth, of *c.* 1600. The marginal notes in the first edition are set out separately at the end, followed by press-variants, some editorial notes, a glossary, and a select bibliography. A more extensive appraisal of the translation and a somewhat fuller glossary might have been useful. But O'Gorman and the Renaissance English Text Society have performed a valuable service in making Grimald's translation available in this attractively presented edition.

UNIVERSITY OF READING

R. A. HOULBROOKE

Andrew Marvell and Edmund Waller: Seventeenth-Century Praise and Restoration Satire. By A. B. CHAMBERS. University Park and London: Pennsylvania State University Press. 1991. viii + 208 pp. $27.50.

Who is this book written for and what is its purpose? Its subtitle, when taken with the main title, suggests a study of satire and panegyric in Marvell and Waller, while remarks made early in the book hint at a desire to encourage readers to reassess Waller and Marvell as satirist. So, in his Preface A. B. Chambers rightly claims that Marvell's 'Last Instructions' has 'received considerably less recognition than [...] such astonishing vigor and virtuosity merits [*sic*]', while on p. 12 it is intimated that Chambers wants to support Earl Miner's high valuation of Waller's 'On St. James's Park': and a modest case both can and should be made for Waller, whose elegance and poise should not obliterate one's sense of a considerable intelligence. But if Chambers is seeking to make this case and to encourage revaluing of Marvell as satirist he has shot himself in the foot.

This is nowhere more evident than in the book's second chapter, on the hew/glew/dew controversy in 'On His Coy Mistress', where the ransacking of, in particular, the Bible and biblical commentary reaches almost parodic heights:

As Lapide (942B), quoting Gregory the Great, points out, it is the 'impetus carnis', the driving force of the flesh, which impels the 'reprobus' toward a gluttonous palate 'ad gulam' and such things as 'rixas' or — as Marvell has it 'strife'. (pp. 38–39)

Anyone who writes so densely has either to accept that his words will be heard only by fellow pedants or to demonstrate the need for such arcane commentary. It is unfortunate for Chambers that this problem is so acute so early in his book, because later chapters are relatively straightforward and include some sensible thoughts. Even so, both style and judgement remain suspect. Early infelicities include '"Lycidas" sets a standard that few poems of any age, including Milton's other funeral verse, can scarcely measure up to' (p. 5), and 'Bellarmine points out that the ointment could scarcely flow from the head nor from the beard' (p. 28). So far as judgement goes, Chambers seems to invent a problem (p. 110) about the linking of satire with eulogy; he refers to Conrad (p. 104) where Donne's epigram 'A Burnt Ship' would be more appropriate; and he seems to know little about the traditions of panegyric and advice to princes.

On p. 53 we read that 'the probability seems strong that Marvell was working from within a tradition, using concepts and words with connotative values and associations at one time recognized though now largely unfamiliar'. This alerts us to the fact that Chambers is struggling with familiar problems. When (p. 18) he tells us that he proposes to look 'at Marvell's words as carefully as I can' we might suspect a planned revival of the New Criticism, but the concern with 'context' would indicate some kind of historicism. A few pages of, say, David, Poole, Bellarmine, Ainsworth, Lapide, Galen, Theophrastus, Aquinas, and Cajetan (all p. 41) suggest a concern with intellectual history rather than the New Historicism. But Chambers never grapples with the theoretical issues involved with his approach, taking refuge instead in quips and edgy qualifications (see pp. 16, 31). If it is true that Marvell uses 'concept and words [...]' at one time recognized though now largely unfamiliar', we need to ask 'recognized by whom?' if we are to define a Marvell audience, and to consider what to do about our unfamiliarity with the concepts and words in question. If the only way to read Marvell is by constructing the field of learning Chambers uses, we shall have to accept that this great poet will only be read by a tiny minority. If the long-unfashionable Edmund Waller is to be revived it will have to be without the leaden learning and leaden prose of this book.

NOTTINGHAM   GEORGE PARFITT

Marvell & Alchemy. By LYNDY ABRAHAM. Aldershot and Brookfield, VT: Scolar Press. 1990. xii + 364 pp. £35.

Long relegated to quaintness and obscurity, alchemy has had something of a revival over the past few decades — not, of course, as a recipe for turning base metals into gold, but as a tradition of esoteric teachings which deserves serious historical study. This revival has been due partly to the Jungian interpretation of alchemy in psycho-therapeutic terms, and partly to the historical interest in Renaissance magic awakened by Frances Yates and others. These have suggested new meanings and contexts for alchemy, and have led in particular to a re-evaluation of its influence, in Europe and England, during the sixteenth and seventeenth centuries.

One area of alchemy's influence was its literature, with its marvellous lexicon of code-names — the 'green lion', the 'virgin's milk', the 'secret fire' — and its fondness for highly-charged and often surreal parables to describe various phases of the alchemical *opus*. This peculiar linguistic richness, widely available in print by the end of the sixteenth century, was a fertile source for the metaphor-hungry poets of the period, and so this revival of interest in alchemy has fed into literary studies. The poems of Donne, the comedies of Jonson, and the later plays of Shakespeare have all proved rich in alchemical imagery, and to these names may now be added that of Andrew Marvell.

In *Marvell & Alchemy*, Lyndy Abraham presents a sharply focused and compellingly argued account of alchemical motifs in some of Marvell's best-known poems. She provides a concise introduction to the literature on the subject that was available to Marvell: not just the classic texts, but also a new flowering of English alchemical writing — Elias Ashmole's great collection, *Theatrum Chemicum Britannicum* (1652); and the texts of Robert Fludd, Thomas Vaughan, and the mysterious Eirenaeus Philalethes.

Abraham deals in detail with 'Upon Appleton House', Marvell's elusive meditation on the home of his patron, Lord Fairfax. She shows that one of the poem's

guiding conceits is an ingenious comparison between the actual history of the house
— the 'dissolution' of the original nunnery during the reign of Henry VIII, and its
refurbishment in finer form by Fairfax's great-grandfather — and the chemical
processes of dissolution and reconstitution which are fundamental to the *opus*. She
sums up the political message that Marvell conveys: 'Out of the corrupt nunnery has
been born a new house, a new line, and a new order.'

In 'To His Coy Mistress', Abraham finds a similar appropriation of alchemical
imagery, associated with the climactic phase of the *opus* known as the *coniunctio* or
'chymicall wedding'. In this there is a clear continuity from Donne's love-poetry,
particularly the emblematic coitus of 'The Ecstasy'.

A book like this has to negotiate a narrow path. There is no doubt that there are
alchemical notations in these poems, but there is also the danger of over-
interpretation, of dragooning the poet's vocabulary into a single, narrow provenance. It is part of the nature of alchemical writing that it presses this sort of
reading *à clef* into one's mind. The alchemists liked to claim that the whole of Greek
mythology was a concealed 'riddle' about the Philosophers' Stone. It is necessary to
resist this tendency. Some of Abraham's parallels seem over-zealous in this way, but
she has written an important and lucid book, which adds to our awareness of
alchemy as a covert but powerful presence in the mainstream of seventeenth-century
literature.

HEREFORD

CHARLES NICHOLL

Literature and the Visual Arts in Tudor England. By DAVID EVETT. Athens and London:
   University of Georgia Press. 1990. xiv + 366 pp. $35.

David Evett joins a line of audacious scholars, beginning with Wylie Sypher, who
have attempted to define the style or styles of the artistic and literary production of
Tudor England. Although stimulating theories and even new insights into individual works often emerge from such inter-arts stylistic studies, previous writers have
tended to force literature into rigid art historical classifications with little of use to
show for it. Evett, in contrast, designs his own terms for the two major sixteenth-
century English styles, which he calls Traditional and renascence, and reserves the
label Renaissance for the later Stuart art produced in conscious imitation of the
Italian Renaissance. So far, so good; but even he ends up wallowing about in the
muddy waters of Mannerism in Chapter 9 of a book that has already voiced bitter
complaints against such dubious comparisons between English literature and
Italian art.

Far more interesting are the author's two major stylistic divisions and their
definitions. The first is the Traditional style growing out of medievalism, which is
both self-advertising and decorative, an art of surfaces resulting in what he calls a
'plane style'. It is ceremonial in intent, as were civic pageants or funeral processions,
and thus is organized on the principle of 'aggregative repetition' and characterized
by seriation and the commitment to *copia*. Above all, it is rhetorically 'paratactic'
like a picture gallery. Evett provides convincing examples from art, architecture,
and literature to illustrate this style, which he says continues until the end of the
sixteenth century.

Simultaneously, upperclass education influenced the introduction of the later
renascence style based on classical models. Its characteristics include the establishment of an artistic point of view through the use of linear perspective, self
consciousness, irony, and Platonic idealism. It is rhetorically 'hypotactic' since the
parts are logically subordinated to a controlling central idea. After considering the
definitions of these two styles, however, I wonder if we are not simply being given

new terminology for the older stylistic divisions of 'medieval' and 'Renaissance' in a book already overburdened with technical jargon.

Evett also discusses three distinct modes in English art: the 'Demotic' or practical (as he defines it), the Grotesque or fantastic used for borders or transitions, and the Idealistic or emblematic. Perhaps the most successful section of this book is the author's analysis of Spenser's literary use of stylistic grotesqueries in *The Faerie Queene*. On the other hand, in the artistic decoration of homes and furnishings the elaborate grotesqueries were not usually the product of local imagination and thus 'subversive' of renascence idealistic art, as the author claims, but were actually copied from continental pattern books of the period. For example, Theodore de Bry adds a number of such pattern pages to his *Emblemata Nobilitatis* of 1593, and borders as well as *picturae* from other emblem books were commonly traced by English artisans and embroiderers of the Tudor period.

The *de rigueur* Marxist or post-modernist considerations of patronage and the economic status of artists seem out of place in this study, since the author does not demonstrate any particular connexions between style and economy. A stylistic analysis of the elaborate English gardens of the period and their spatial relationship to the architectural styles of country houses would have been considerably more appropriate here. Although Evett has much of importance to say about new perceptions of landscape in renascence poetry and painting, he makes no mention of Bruce R. Smith's brilliant essay 'Landscape with Figures' in *Renaissance Drama*, n.s. 8 (1977), 57–111, which might have been helpful.

Unhappily, the reader stumbles across some rather shocking errors of fact in this study, provocative though it may be as a whole. Evett ascribes to Amy Lowell the famous Marianne Moore poetic formula for 'imaginary gardens with real toads in them' (p. 155); he misspells Erwin Panofsky's first name as 'Irwin' (p. 158 and repeatedly thereafter), and later he wrongly assigns Plato's discussion of the *Sileni Alcibiadis* in *The Symposium* to the same author's *Apology* (p. 323, n. 30).

Such quibbles aside, the major value of *Literature and the Visual Arts in Tudor England* seems to lie in its demonstration that a traditional rhetorical analysis applied to poetry, architecture, and painting does indeed work rather well in a discussion of stylistic similarities among the sister arts.

BETHESDA, MARYLAND   PEGGY MUÑOZ SIMONDS

Melodious Tears: The English Funeral Elegy from Spenser to Milton. By DENNIS KAY. (Oxford English Monographs) Oxford: Clarendon Press. 1990. 296 pp. £30.

'Let streaming teares be poured out in store': thus Spenser's Colin Clout in 'November', one of the first pastoral elegies in English, and one of the most influential tributaries of the widening waters that make up the history of the elegy, pastoral and otherwise. Dennis Kay's *Melodious Tears: The English Funeral Elegy from Spenser to Milton* usefully follows a stretch of the genre's headwaters in the Renaissance, the value of his study being the detailed mapping by which he situates such principals as Spenser, Jonson, Donne, and Milton among hosts of accompanying elegists, thereby broadening the object of study while also sharpening our sense of what the more successful elegies do and do not share with their lesser companions. Companionship in this period is often close, unlike the relative isolation of later elegies, and much of Kay's book focuses on a succession of funeral anthologies, such as those for Sidney, Queen Elizabeth, and Henry, Prince of Wales. Indeed, the very notion of a community of mourners is crucial to the genre, and the story of the increasingly vexed, competitive, and fragmenting nature of that community — along with the intensifyingly self-conscious particularity of individual authors — is one of the most interesting elements of this book. *Melodious Tears* opens with a retrospect of the generally impersonal, sententious, and often metronomic funeral verses of the so-called 'drab' Tudor writers, among whose works Kay nevertheless notices the nascent individualism with which Grimald and Churchyard moved from old humanist and heroic formulae toward a more personal expressiveness and a more fluent vernacular style. Against this background Surrey's precocious poems for Wyatt take on renewed interest and invite further analysis; but it is with Spenser and Sidney that Kay's account begins to measure the powerful blend of innovation and deepened, continental-classical traditionalism that marks one of the strongest currents of the genre. With a newly deliberate virtuosity and an elevated awareness both of poetic vocation and of the resources of fiction and poetic form, Spenser and Sidney rediscovered in pastoral a renewable mythology as well as a repertoire of ways in which to stage their canny, although at times pessimistic, negotiations between the private and public reaches of art. So too, Spenser's impresario-like management of 'Astrophel' and its accompanying procession of poems by other elegists — this is the first vernacular funeral anthology — is an especially influential moment not only in the 'invention' of Spenserian poetry, but also in the diversifying and co-ordinating of personal and collective responses to death. As Kay writes, 'Spenser's performance [...] as the shaping intelligence whose own contribution frames, informs and reinterprets the efforts of his fellow mourners, established a significant precedent' (p. 66), a precedent whose managerial design and generic variety will influence subsequent collections and (yet more interestingly) even such later, single-author works as *The Anniversaries* and 'Lycidas' ('more an anthology than the volume it concludes'). One of the values of Kay's study is in fact its underscoring of the plural, anthologist elements in the origin of Donne's and Milton's elegies, and its defence of these unprecedentedly inclusive poems against narrow notions of generic unity.

With the elegies for Queen Elizabeth and then again for Prince Henry, Kay pursues the genre's increasingly overt sensitivity to political, cultural, and vocational issues. Here the analysis could be methodologically more penetrating, particularly given the recent work of Greenblatt, Patterson, Goldberg, Montrose, Crewe, Berger, and others; but the survey of assemblages and poems by such as Chettle, Newton, and Petowe for Elizabeth, and of the large number of works for Prince Henry two decades later, provides an indispensable catalogue. These two occasions are of course separated by Donne's *Anniversaries*, and it is fascinating to see how in varying proportions the later works (from Gorges, Peacham, Niccols, Davies, and Drummond, to Sylvester, Cornwallis, Chapman, Webster, and many others) show the first confluences of Spenser's and Donne's achievements. For it was Donne whose worldly, direct, and versatile argumentative manner broke through the more mediate fictions of Spenser or Sidney to achieve a non-pastoral mode that could accommodate the new extra-literary complexities of the time.

By this point in his study, Kay has interestingly suggested the relation between the emerging elegy and the sonnet (itself used, often in sequences, for explicitly funerary purposes). Questions of sincerity, loss, inexpressibility, formal constraint, self-presentation mark both kinds of poem; additionally, it would be worth speculating further on the complex entanglements of eros and grief in the poems under discussion. From its Greek origins, to such attempted extrications as those of Donne's friend George Garrard, or Milton's 'tangles of Neaera's hair', through to the elegies of Tennyson and Hardy, this admixture deserves closer study; and just as Kay's generally straightforward readings could be deepened and complicated by a more trenchant cultural and political poetics, so they could become more intriguing in the light of a fuller approach to erotic and sexual-political elements of the genre.

Introducing his final chapter (on elegies from Jonson to Milton), Kay writes: 'The increasingly self-conscious politicization of literary discourse during the reigns of James I and Charles I had as an incidental consequence the effect of turning the elegy into a highly political genre, one where the poet's choice of mode was an expression of political view, and where, under the veil of literary commentary, political and religious points might be made more or less obliquely' (p. 205). While this competitive aspect of the elegy has been there since its Greek eclogic origins, Kay's watchful account gives us a good view of the kind of literary scrapping and rivalry that marked the ideological divergences of the Jacobean and early Stuart periods. With a brief look at Ben Jonson's neo-classical restraint, the more impressive when viewed against the rising self-obsessiveness of his contemporary elegists, the discussion moves by way of Daniel, Chapman, and Drayton, to the triumphant renovation achieved by Milton. Here again, Kay's patient charting of the territory gives us a fuller sense of Milton's recapitulations and his originality, his way of carrying the combined traditions of Spenser, Sidney, and Donne to new levels of diversity and power. With *Melodious Tears*, the reader now has a fair-minded and scrupulous survey of the many and various examples of the genre, individual and anthologized, that precede Milton's 'Yet once more'.

THE JOHNS HOPKINS UNIVERSITY   PETER SACKS

Fleeting Things: English Poets and Poems, 1616–1660. By GERALD HAMMOND. Cambridge, MA: Harvard University Press. 1990. viii + 394 pp. $41.95.

Our Halcyon Dayes: English Prerevolutionary Texts and Postmodern Culture. By LAWRENCE VENUTI. Madison and London: University of Wisconsin Press. 1989. 320 pp. $37.50 (paperbound $18.75).

One could hardly ask for more striking evidence of a crisis in the humanities than the simultaneous appearance of these two books, covering more or less the same ground, with nothing whatsoever in common. Lawrence Venuti's *Our Halcyon Dayes* bristles with hard words like 'interpellation', 'symptomatic reading', 'determinate contradictions', 'discontinuous textual work', 'schizzes of desire', never for an instant relaxing its vigilance against such individualist deviations from the true faith as liberal humanism, organic form, and subjectivity. His opening words are '*Our Halcyon Dayes* is a Marxist intervention into Renaissance studies' (his decentring of the subject extends to treating his own 'intervention' as a passive product of 'the Marxist discourse which processes this writing'), whereas Gerald Hammond begins 'I learned to enjoy poetry'. It is hard to imagine a conversation between these two scholars, in a chance encounter in a railway carriage, lasting more than thirty seconds.

Venuti's approach can be called deferential Marxism: tributes to Althusser, Jameson, and Eagleton litter the opening pages, and though, following poststructuralist fashion, he looks for 'interrogative', 'indeterminate' texts, they all seem to ask the same questions, to which Venuti gives the same answers. The argument is relentlessly circular, as Jacobean city comedy, the plays of Massinger, the court masque, and Cavalier love poetry are all passed through the sausage grinder to reappear as reflections of class conflict in seventeenth-century society. Scenes in Massinger's *The Maid of Honour* (c. 1621) involving a peace-loving, vacillating king, a corrupt, powerful catamite favourite, and a discontented 'patriotic' court faction headed by the king's warrior brother might be thought to bear some relationship to the England of James I during Buckingham's ascendancy, and in particular to the contentious issue of the Palatinate. Indeed, the title of the play might suggest that different attitudes toward honour in a number of characters, male and female, are being juxtaposed dramatically. But for Venuti the figures in the play are all 'determinate subjects in process, characters whose essence dissolves into inconsistent actions determined by the contradictions of the class struggle in which they are locked' (p. 78). Half a dozen pages of Margot Heinemann's *Puritanism and Theatre* are far more illuminating on the historical context of Massinger's plays than Venuti's whole chapter: here as elsewhere in the book, the terms governing the analysis are too crude and inflexible to be of much use, and patient historical investigation is not Venuti's forte.

Venuti, consistent here as elsewhere, sees his own critical practice in *Our Halcyon Dayes* as no less determined by the iron laws of historical necessity than his shackled authors, presenting his method of 'symptomatic reading' as the product of the 'social conjuncture' of 'a late phase of capitalism' which he identifies as postmodernist. Gerald Hammond's *Fleeting Things*, in contrast, seems to come from a leisured, more gracious time, protective of idiosyncracy and welcoming eclecticism, where books are products of inquiring minds set free to roam in well-stocked libraries. Occasionally, the air of gentlemanly nonchalance seems excessive, though the authorial strategy of foregrounding poetic texts, juxtaposing the unfamiliar and familiar, and ignoring the disputes of twentieth-century critics makes the book far more entertaining to read than the lumbering solemnities of *Our Halcyon Dayes*. Nevertheless, the virtual absence, even in footnotes, of any reference to the vast body of criticism dealing with seventeenth-century literature in the last thirty years does add to the sense of a time-warp, with the author an erudite and witty Rip van Winkle.

One thing the two books have in common is an emphasis on 'discontinuities', seen as revelatory of the strains and tensions inherent in the court society with which both authors are concerned. In *Our Halcyon Dayes* it's all relatively simple and predictable, once a reader has mastered the author's recondite vocabulary: contradictions in the class struggle lead in dramatic works to inconsistency in characterization and in lyric poems to 'ideological subversiveness' independent of the author's intent. Hammond, more alert to nuance, to the 'coded conventions' of genre, and to the problematical in interpretation, is far more illuminating in his detailed, sensitive commentaries on poems written during the 1630s which 'threaten to be torn apart from within' as they seek to 'contain the country's dissensions within the ideal vision of kingship'. Like a number of recent critics concerned with revaluing the poetry and drama of the middle years of the seventeenth century — Lois Potter, Martin Butler, Leah Marcus, Kevin Sharpe, and others — Hammond in his opening chapters emphasizes 'the need to write in praise of powerful people' as a spur to composition. But in his scrupulous attention to the historical context of the works he discusses, Hammond, unlike Venuti, at no point treats literature as a mere epiphenomenon of material forces, and though the relationship between literature and public events is one of his principal concerns, it is only one of a number of interrelated topics in this wide-ranging, fascinating book.

One of the great strengths of *Fleeting Things* is the unexpectedness of the connexions it finds as, with a studied appearance of randomness, a *sprezzatura* appropriate to the Cavaliers, it unearths poems on lopped-off fingers, blushing, vertigo, ships, dreams, building up by accretion the picture of a vanished age preserved in poems which make ephemera seem significant and emblematic. One recurrent concern in Hammond's book is 'mergings of life and death'; another, in its treatment of stylized erotic encounters and of custom and ceremony, is a sense of 'how thin a shell of civilization covers turbulent passions'. In two excellent chapters, Jonson, in Yeatsian terms, is presented, once again balancing opposites, as a poet who 'fuses an immense respect for tradition to a language studded with expressions of resistance and revolt', both in poems with an explicitly ethical and political dimension and in poems, written late in his life, on the confinement of old age.

Hammond's style is aphoristic, his method inductive, as he roams freely among the poems of the period, making the familiar strange and the obscure familiar. This kind of close critical commentary, witty, relaxed, and intelligent, may be out of fashion, but *Fleeting Things*, like the poets it celebrates, is concerned with the 'civilized transactions' which, by one means or another, can endure vicissitudes.

QUEEN MARY & WESTFIELD COLLEGE, LONDON   WARREN CHERNAIK

A Fine Tuning: Studies of the Religious Poetry of Herbert and Milton. Ed. by MARY A. MALESKI. (Medieval & Renaissance Texts & Studies, 64) Binghamton, NY: Medieval & Renaissance Texts & Studies. 1989. xii + 317 pp. $40.

This is a *festschrift* for Joseph H. Summers, which includes, after the editor's introduction, a generous tribute to him from a colleague, Russell A. Peck, followed by a bibliography of his scholarly writings. The essays derive from papers given at the Sixth Annual Le Moyne Forum on Religion and Literature, where the two keynote speakers were Louis Martz and Barbara Lewalski. Martz's paper leads six articles in the Herbert section, Lewalski's seven in the Milton.

In the Herbert section, where several contributors gracefully relate to *George Herbert: His Mind and Art*, the essays have varying weight and scope. The first two stand together to suggest a broad churchmanship allowed by *The Temple*, in reaction to scholarship of the late 70s and early 80s, which stressed the more strictly 'Protestant' figurations in Herbert's language. Martz argues for a 'generous ambiguity', pointing to the rather uncalvinistic use of the eucharist in many of the poems, and perceives changes between the Williams manuscript and the edition of 1633, drawing support from the analysis by Nicholas Tyacke of changes within the early seventeenth-century English church. The Laudian Herbert seems to have become more liberal in managing tone in his poems. In the next essay Sidney Gottlieb compares the closing sequences of Williams and 1633. Circumspectly, he claims that the later ending has a 'less imperious, more gentle and familiar God', and that the deep sense of unworthiness is now modified by greater playfulness and confident humour. Both essays implicitly involve matters of art as well as of doctrine.

After this harmonious opening come three studies of individual poems and one more general essay, by Diane McColley, on musical dimensions in *The Temple*. She proffers helpful, even over-detailed readings of poems such as the two *Antiphons* and *Easter*, reconstructing awareness of musical theory and practice in Herbert's texts. Of the three smaller studies, Michael Schoenfeldt performs new-historically on 'Dedication', reading much in little, interrogating cultural pressures and strategies of self-representation. If, in a world of patronage, tensions are always displayed in dedications between self-assertion and submission, how much more so when the 'onelie begetter' is God himself. Thomas Hester offers a perhaps overwrought analysis of 'The Altar', wanting the poem to display a dynamic altering of the speaking self, not just fixity within emblematic form. The least rounded piece of the three, from Chauncey Wood, is an Augustinian reading of 'The Pulley, using a promising quotation from near the beginning of *Confessions*. The play on the word 'rest', however, works better in English than Latin, and Herbert's poem is too widely allusive to fit such a single key.

There is wider variation in method on Milton. The material of Barbara Lewalski's substantial opening, 'Generic Multiplicity and Milton's Literary God', will be familiar to readers from *Paradise Lost and the Rhetoric of Literary Forms* (Princeton, NJ: Princeton University Press, 1985), Chapter 5. This is the only genre study. Two essays overlap in having sexuality for subject. Noam Flinker tries cross-cultural intertextuality with the Song of Songs, Ranter writings, and the unfallen Adam's

346

Reviews

attitude to sex. (Adam is 'refined Ranter'.) Despite lively quotations about spirituality and group sex, sharp new definition of *Paradise Lost* is not very obvious. Also
involving much comparative quotation, Fannie Peczenik's essay clarifies Adam's
account of Eve's creation from his rib by showing how differently rabbinical and
Christian exegesis had treated the story. To claim that Milton's account amounts to
a critique of others' is too much, but she highlights special characteristics in Milton's
narrative partly by showing what he chose *not* to say. In this reading misogyny
belongs only to the discourse of the fallen, or falling, Adam.

Another two essays pair in subject-matter, whilst showing further variations in
technique. William Schullenberger and Marshall Grossman read Milton's individual Christology, as evidenced in the much later *De Doctrina Christiana*, back into 'The
Passion'. Both are interested in Milton's supposed incapacity to write on that
subject; neither is light-handed. In an unballasted journey of speculation into a
windy sea of metaphoric land, Shullenberger sees doctrine so inscribed into the
figures of Milton's language, that the death of the god-man obliterated language
itself: 'Christ's passion is a death-blow to the passion which is poetry.' A death to
think. In his doctrinal/linguistic/psychoanalytic conjectures — a series of 'would
be's, what it *might* have meant to write of the passion if one already had that
Christology — Grossman is also concerned with impossibility: the passion would
represent 'a transforming moment which exists in time but cannot be represented in
language'.

More traditionally involved in ambiguity and difficulty, Christopher Grose
examines the peculiar nature of the tempter in *Paradise Regained*, considering him a
'white devil' who takes over some of the narratorial functions. Finally, in explicatory
mode, Alinda Sumers claims a new solution for the 'two-handed engine' in
'Lycidas', quoting Puritan rhetoric of the kind Milton would have known, but she
does not actually prove that the pilot is Christ or that the engine is simply
conscience. She does, however, without saying so, furnish a teasing possibility for
the fiend who stands behind Guyon in Spenser's Cave of Mammon.

This collection has had a difficult birth. The conference was in October 1983; the
volume was in press about 1987. It is difficult to hide the delays which occurred
before and after going to press. This is not a *fresh* tribute to the honoured scholar, and
some penalties of delay are substantial. Lewalski's 'keynote' contribution is a
shorter, earlier version of her chapter of 1985. Questions about the point of
publishing the 1983 version subsequently come to mind. Grose's essay is likewise an
earlier version of material in *Milton and the Sense of Tradition* (New Haven and
London: Yale University Press, 1988), Chapter 7. Then again, one or two essays in
the volume might be thought a bit thin or marginal in quality. Some of these essays
contribute in their fields, and a decorum is to be noted in having the *festschrift*
published by MRTS — that house re-issued Summer's classic books on Herbert and
Milton — but one could also identify some things in this tardy offering which suggest
that the distinguished have been kidnapped as much as the chief guest honoured.

University of Reading

Cedric C. Brown

Milton and the Drama of History: Historical Vision, Iconoclasm, and the Literary Imagination.
By David Loewenstein. Cambridge, New York, and Melbourne: Cambridge
University Press. 1990. x + 197 pp. £25; $34.50.

David Loewenstein's slim volume bears an imposing title. Far from sinking beneath
the burden, however, his study of Milton's 'imaginative responses to the processes of
history', and of how these inform both the verse and prose, proves strikingly
successful. The main inspiration is Hayden White's *Metahistory* (Baltimore, MD:

Johns Hopkins University Press, 1973), a formalist account of the nineteenth-century historical imagination. White's insights into the poetics of history, especially his proposition that every history is also a particular kind of story (determined by its 'emplotment' as epic, romance, tragedy, comedy, or satire, as the case may be), are here transposed to the seventeenth century. This opens up an embarrassment of interpretative riches, allowing Loewenstein to bring out (in Chapter 1) the unexpectedly tragic dimension of Milton's anti-prelatical tracts, and (in Chapter 3) to offer the spectacle of Milton simultaneously deconstructing *Eikon Basilike* and recasting the king's erstwhile tragic image in comic and satiric forms. Chapter 5, devoted to teasing out the competing comic and tragic visions of history in the last two books of *Paradise Lost*, does much to reinvigorate material which had become the subject of some sterile controversy. The startling picture of God as 'proto-iconoclast' developed there leads finally into an account (once again largely untrammelled by critical orthodoxies) of Milton's fullest 'expression of radical iconoclasm', *Samson Agonistes*.

Ironically, the work which ought to be most amenable to this kind of treatment, *The History of Britain*, proves the most resistant. Loewenstein (in Chapter 4) sees it as 'aborted', with intimations of epic outweighed by 'signs of strain and weariness' as Milton confronted 'the problem of presenting history unworthy of record'. While the *History* is a notoriously difficult text (and always has been: Whigs were as baffled as Tories were hostile), it is surprising that he does not canvass the possibility that its 'emplotment' is satirical or even — delving further into Hayden White's tool-box — that its master trope is Irony.

The focus throughout is on the rhetorical features of the texts themselves with little on their sources or social context, a policy which means that there is, for example, no place for Shakespeare in the examination of the 'theatrical tropes in *Eikonoklastes*' (or anywhere else for that matter). This may be just as well because his forays outside the canon tend to misfire. Thus an attempt to bracket Milton's reminder to Parliament in *Areopagitica* that it was free to repeal any of its predecessors' acts with Richard Overton's view that, as 'men of the present age', we should 'be absolutely free from all kindes of [...] *Arbitrary Power*' comes to grief on the fact that the arbitrariness Overton was exclaiming against *was* Parliament's tendency to behave as if Magna Carta and the Petition of Right did not exist.

Loewenstein's own highly idiosyncratic prose style is further cause for concern . Bludgeoned by, *inter alia*, 'dynamic' (used twenty-five times in the fifteen pages of Chapter 2), 'mythopoetic(ally)' (eighteen times in the eighteen pages of Chapter 4) and 'troubled', 'troubling', 'turbulent' and 'turbulence' (more than seventy times in all), the reader comes to feel that repetition is being substituted for argument.

But these blemishes and irritations should not be allowed to obscure the merits of a book which generates so many apposite conjunctions and insights. On page 1, the author announces that it is his aim to show 'how deeply [Milton's] controversial prose affected and shaped his major poetic achievements': it is no small triumph if, a hundred and fifty pages later, we can say that he has done much to accomplish exactly that.

Royal Holloway and Bedford New College,   Martin Dzelzainis
London

John Bunyan and his England: 1628–88. Ed. by Anne Laurence, W. R. Owens, and Stuart Sim. London and Ronceverte: The Hambledon Press. 1990. xxiv + 181 pp. £25.

'The book has its origins', the editors' introduction tells us, 'in a conference held at the Open University, Milton Keynes, in September 1988 to mark the tercentenary of Bunyan's death, a conference deliberately designed to celebrate and to explore Bunyan's many-faceted personality and career in a wide historical and cultural perspective'. Part 1 is 'primarily historical in focus', with chapters by Christopher Hill and others on topics such as Bunyan's contemporary reputation, the Parliamentary Army, seventeenth-century Radicalism, Persecution, Millenarianism. Part 2 'deals chiefly with Bunyan's autobiographical and fictional writings', and has chapters by the late Roger Sharrock and others on *Grace Abounding*, on Salvation and Damnation, on Bunyan in the light of modern concepts of gender. In addition there are eleven verses called *Pilgrims Crossing*, by Patricia Beer.

It is a feature of the volume that it avoids using the word 'Puritan' to describe Bunyan, and seeks rather to see him in relation to terms like 'Dissent', 'Radicalism', and 'Counter-Culture'. This wisely closes the door on some futile attempts at making distinctions about the past, and welcomes Bunyan into late twentieth-century debate on ethics and politics. 'Puritan' (a French word anyway) is defined by the Oxford English Dictionary as 'a member of that party of English Protestants who regarded the reformation of the church under Elizabeth as incomplete': a definition clouded in its very origin by the fact that so many of those who were permitted to engineer that 'reformation' regarded their own work as shamefully incomplete. 'Puritan' is perhaps a political label, and like other such labels also a weather-cock. The joint decision made in this volume not to apply it to Bunyan is, unavoidably, a political decision. It is part of Bunyan's challenge, in any age, that he cannot be dismissed under any label.

This is a welcome volume, to be read and thought about. If it is of mixed quality, and more convincing in some places than others, so is Bunyan himself. The historical Part 1 seems (to this reader at least) to have more to say to the present age than the more ambitiously 'relevant' Part 2. One exception is Roger Sharrock's 'Spiritual Autobiography: Bunyan's *Grace Abounding*'. Set at the head of Part 2, it makes a bridge between our own age and Bunyan's. Roger Pooley's '*Grace Abounding* and the New Sense of Self' is a worthy companion to it. Both exemplify a quiet, patient, scholarly approach to Bunyan which is not lavish of words or splashy with ideas. Pooley, for instance, reminds us of something embarrassing in our world: that Bunyan reposed in 'the power of God'. It is not easy to hijack such a sensibility in the name of twentieth-century concerns: yet Bunyan concerns us. He is so pertinent to our history that he returns to trouble our present.

One of those troubled is N. H. Keeble, whose 'The Feminine in the Thought and Work of John Bunyan' moves towards the conclusion that, as far as Bunyan is concerned, 'the liberty wherewith Christ hath made women free (Galatians 5.1) does not, after all, offer any emancipation from, or revolutionary redemption of, traditional gender rôles'. Class, and literary deviousness, may have something to do with this. It is much harder, for example, for any attentive reader to reduce Milton to a male chauvinist than may be the case with Bunyan. Yet N. H. Keeble's starting-place distresses me. As an example of Bunyan's 'casual, off-hand' view of women these words from *Grace Abounding* are quoted: 'I came where there was three or four poor women sitting at a door in the Sun, and talking about the things of God.' Ever since I read those words (more years ago than I care to remember) I have regarded them as the most sublime evocation of sanctity (always excepting the Authorized Version of the Bible) in the English language. Milton cannot compete. Shakespeare is not in the running. Perhaps there is an irony of conscious challenge in choosing this passage as a spring-board for an account of Bunyan's devaluing of women.

University of Warwick   Malcolm Hardman

Reason, Grace, and Sentiment: A Study of the Language of Religion and Ethics in England, 1660–1780. Volume I. Whichcote to Wesley. By ISABEL RIVERS. (Cambridge Studies in Eighteenth-Century English Literature and Thought, 8) Cambridge, New York, and Melbourne: Cambridge University Press. 1991. xiii + 277 pp. £35; $49.50.

This is the first of a two-volume study, and so any verdict must be provisional; none the less, it gathers conviction as it proceeds, and is liable to displace the work of G. R. Cragg in late seventeenth-century history of ideas. It is not a radically modernizing account, though. There is no armoury of theory to be put on with a flourish before doing battle with the texts, no attempt to dismiss previous accounts. Isabel Rivers acknowledges her precursors Mark Pattison and Leslie Stephen, not to mention the Cambridge English Moralists paper. The method is that of a history of ideas, written with the conviction that attention to the language — which often just means the vocabulary — will be as revealing as an abstracted treatment of ideas. (This is different from the Restoration Anglicans she discusses, who dismissed dissent as mere carping over terms.) Nor is there any appropriation of old religious controversies for contemporary, secular use, foregrounding politics, and gender over religion. One might say that Rivers's self-effacing approach to these issues is startlingly traditional. She just wants to let these old voices speak, without taking sides. Fair enough, and a difficult task, even if there are no reservations about the implied liberalism of such an approach. Unfortunately, the effect is sometimes to under-dramatize. Take the opening chapter, 'The Conflict of Languages in the Mid-Seventeenth Century': the Whichcote-Tuckney letters provide a useful summary of opposing views on the priority of faith, reason, and works; then there is a convincing, but somewhat flat account of the way Hammond, Jeremy Taylor, and the author of *The Whole Duty of Man* set about undermining Puritan popular piety. She avoids the spurious thrills of taking sides and reconstituting old passions; but the student reader, at least, might be left wondering why it was all so important.

Her scope remains wide — the 'Latitude-men' of the late seventeenth century, Dissent from Baxter to Doddridge, and a culminating chapter on Wesley. The analysis comes down to major figures most of the time, though; while she, rightly, treats the Latitudinarians as a composite (with Whichcote and Wilkins more prominent than usual), the tradition of Dissent is shrunk to Baxter and Bunyan, Watts and Doddridge, for much of the time. That means that the Quakers get pushed to the margins rather too quickly, but it has compensations. It gives her the space to put Anglican and dissenting ideas alongside each other, which is in itself illuminating; and the sustained comparison of Baxter and Bunyan in Chapter 3 is the most rewarding part of the book. Concluding this volume with John Wesley brings both Anglican and dissenting traditions together. Rivers demonstrates well the extent to which Wesley was attempting a synthesis of Reformation doctrines (minus Calvin) with subsequent developments in the religion of the heart. Her grand narrative of the period becomes clearer in this chapter, but the reader is still often left to infer it.

A study of this kind also depends for its success on an accumulation of revising detail and re-centred texts, and here Rivers scores strongly. To take a number of examples from my list, there are the anti-Catholic writings of the Latitude-men as redefining the relation of faith and reason, the rescue of Edward Fowler from Bunyan's caricature, Watts's wary use of polite language to engage in enquiry with the unconvinced, and Wesley's revisions/distortions of diverse writers (Bunyan particularly) to fit them into his ecumenical *Christian Library*.

So, let us hope the next volume has a big conclusion. For example, why does she think that dissent was more influential, or at least more interesting than Anglicanism, in its development of a language for the affections? Will she break her silence on gender issues? Whatever happens, we will learn something new.

UNIVERSITY OF KEELE   ROGER POOLEY

The Courtship Novel, 1740–1820: A Feminized Genre. By KATHERINE SOBBA GREEN. Lexington: University Press of Kentucky. 1991. viii + 184 pp. $23.

By alternating 'broader discussion of narrative techniques and themes with chapters devoted to selected authors' (p. 7), Katherine Sobba Green has fashioned a mountain of material into an elegantly structured examination of enlightenment advocacy for companionate marriage, and its implications for women's attitudes to their suitors, parents, and themselves. Most of the novels discussed are by women. Trying to free themselves from a 'gender-specific association between textual and sexual availability' (p. 11), they 'feminized their genre, avoiding or ameliorating the deleterious associations between their bodies and their works' (p. 13). Through the predicaments of sometimes literally aphasic heroines, they 'demonstrate what is now a commonplace, that language has too frequently been appropriated by the male hegemony or that women often find themselves, in one way or another, at a loss for words' (pp. 6–7). Courtship novels nevertheless achieved an impressive amount of discreet disruption; concentrating 'on the brief and limited opportunity for autonomy that women enjoyed before they married', they aimed 'to disturb established ideas about how dutiful daughters and prudent young women should comport themselves during their courtships' (p. 161), especially if these ideas entailed the restriction of female education to trivial superficialities, the commodification of girls in the marriage market, or mercenary matches that made no concession to affective individualism.

Green avoids dangerous pitfalls. She brings a wide range of modern critical and political interpretation to bear on her texts, but always reads them on their own terms; whatever we might think of domestic bliss as a goal for women today, she leaves us in no doubt that, two hundred years ago, women's right to 'self-determination in marriage' was a 'feminist cause' (p. 138). While using Lawrence Stone's historical theories and terminology, she refuses to engage in the contentious task of establishing their relationship with extratextual phenomena: 'Whether or not the British population actually changed its nuptial practices, historians have demonstrated that, at least within the realm of ideas — that is, within period texts — companionate marriage made a substantial impact on eighteenth-century England' (p. 14). Faced with the awkward fact that 'about half of the two dozen women courtship novelists who did marry eventually separated from their husbands', she observes that authors discouraged naïve optimism by providing 'several exposés of failed marriage' for every 'love match' (p. 53).

There are occasional minor slips. When Green says Terry Eagleton sees eighteenth-century feminism as a 'byblow' (p. 45) of the bourgeoisie's stuggle with the aristocracy, she appears unaware that the word means 'bastard'. The heroine of Jane Austen's *Sense and Sensibility* (1811) is, of course, Elinor, not 'Louisa' (p. 116). Less venial, because more substantive, is her assumption that Charlotte Lennox's Lady Arabella is a 'middle-class ingenue' (p. 50).

The richness of Green's material allows no opportunity for discussing the links of courtship novels with other literary forms, apart from conduct books and periodicals. Yet contemporary poets and playwrights of both sexes frequently engaged with similar issues, while her quotation from Igor Webb, that 'the children are "possessed of a knowledge the adults do not have"' (p. 137), applies to many literary lovers, from Daphnis and Chloe to Romeo and Juliet. Furthermore, the contexts of enlightenment feminism still require examination. When Henrietta Courteney leaves home rather than abandon the Protestant faith, her 'resistance to the partriarchal order' (p. 59) expresses itself as conformity with the larger partiarchy of British established religion. Green notes the absence of 'the subject positions of daughters' (p. 138) from *Considerations of the Cause of the Present Stagnation of Matrimony* (1772), although it attacks the commodification of women: is the author less concerned with vindicating female autonomy than increasing the upper and middle class population? *The Courtship Novel* opens interesting areas for future research.

READING UNIVERSITY   CAROLYN D. WILLIAMS

Blake and His Bibles. Ed. by DAVID V. ERDMAN with an introduction by MARK TREVOR SMITH. (Locust Hill Literary Studies, 1) West Cornwall, Connecticut: Locust Hill Press. 1990. xvii + 237 pp. $30.

At first glance, *Blake and His Bibles*, a collection of six articles on widely diverse aspects of William Blake's understanding of the Bible and on his attempts to reshape it in his texts and pictures, may well exacerbate a widely shared, frustrated puzzlement: why are there so few sustained, book-length treatments of this vastly important subject? (Leslie Tannenbaum's *Biblical Tradition in Blake's Early Prophecies* (Princeton, NJ: Princeton University Press, 1982), bites off a significant chunk of Blake's work but still only a fraction thereof. Michael Tolley's *William Blake's Use of the Bible* (unpublished doctoral thesis, University of London, 1974) remains very possibly the most highly esteemed and oft cited unpublished dissertation in living memory. Having read the six articles at hand, however, one begins to realize, or realize anew, just why such book-length studies should prove daunting. Not only is it true that the Bible spreads to the farthest reaches and penetrates to virtually every recess of Blake's thought and work in both media, but his expressed attitudes toward the Bible, along with the revisionist versions of it that he created, are almost certainly the fruits of a complicated series of spiritual conversions, of which we have few reliable indices outside of his problematic verbal and pictorial works themselves. The danger of circular thinking and interpretation is obvious. Moreover, it has become increasingly clear (from the work of Robert N. Essick, for example) that some of Blake's seemingly most bizarre notions and locutions refer very concretely to contemporary issues — especially about linguistics and theology — unintelligible without an exceedingly thorough mastery of cultural history in the seventeenth and eighteenth centuries, analogous to David V. Erdman's expertise in the politics of Blake's era.

The importance of cultural history emerges most vividly in an engagingly modest but enormously learned, informative, and engrossing essay by Sheila A. Spector on Blake as a Hebraist, wherein the author shows that Blake's seemingly crude attempts at Hebrew are probably in fact rather sophisticated. The 'errors' in his Hebrew, one learns, are conditioned by virulent contemporary controversies over the Scriptures and the Hebrew language, waged among linguists, theologians (Jewish and Christian, orthodox and radical), mythologists, deists, and plain anti-Semites. Scholarly investigation and thinking do not come any better than in this marvellous piece. Similarly revealing about Blake's contemporary milieu is Florence Sandler's essay on Blake's annotations to Bishop Watson's attack on Tom Paine; the bishop emerges as a religious liberal, not a mossback, and Blake, for all his vehemence, emerges as a man torn by some interesting self-contradictions. The paradoxical turn of Blake's mind is also illuminated by Mark Trevor Smith; taking off from Los's often-quoted declaration in *Jerusalem* about the need to create a system, Smith argues lucidly that the creation and demolition of systems are ultimately, for Blake, identical liberating enterprises.

The other three contributors, amplifying valuable work they have done else-where, are also ultimately concerned with Blake's ideas but approach him through his pictures: J. M. Q. Davies addresses the *Nativity Ode* illustrations, while John E. Grant and Mary Lynn Johnson address, respectively, the *Night Thoughts* illustrations and those Blake did for the Psalms. Although these three essays tend to focus on a familiar question about Blake, namely the extent to which his illustrations reflect the original authorial intent or creatively transform that intent, they all make thought-ful, substantial new contributions, showing how much can and still needs to be done by way of a methodology no longer, in itself, novel. The breadth of knowledge of the Bible directly and indirectly evinced in the Johnson essay, and in her other writings about Blake, suggests that she is one of the few people well qualified to treat the biblical illustrations *in toto*.

UNIVERSITY OF ARKANSAS, FAYETTEVILLE   BRIAN WILKIE

In the Pride of the Moment: Encounters in Jane Austen's World. By JOHN A. DUSSINGER. Columbus: Ohio State University Press. 1990. xiii + 213 pp. $39.50.

John Dussinger selects *Emma* as the central text in his study of Jane Austen's narrative strategy. He argues that Austen's 'artistic strength lies not so much in the larger design of the story as in its minute encounters' (p. 16), and that 'her refusal in *Emma* to tidy up everything that has aroused our curiosity' is only a 'stumbling block for readers insistent on eternal verities and smooth surfaces' (p. 11). Dussinger concentrates on the characters' 'states of being, their encounters in everyday situations, which may be discrete experiences and do not always contribute to the resolution of the plot' (p. 13). In the course of his argument he revives the 'little bits of ivory' metaphor for Austen's art: the 'minute encounters' in her novels are 'ivory miniatures revelatory of the characters' inner life' (p. 16). By focusing on these exclusively he risks making Austen once again appear slighter than she really is.

Dussinger is at his more persuasive when he describes those almost wordless encounters in Austen's novels where two characters are caught up in a dance, a game, or other social event, 'in which their individual selves merge for the moment of the experience' (p. 21), 'all their feelings concentrated' (p. 28). The traditional patterns in such rituals 'summon a less fragmented culture' than Austen's 'present one'. Whether or not he is right in assuming that her culture was more fragmented than its predecessors, he well describes how such moments do appear to take place outside the 'everyday world' of her novels. He does not draw the reader's attention to many of these moments, however, or describe precisely how each of them works. Dussinger also includes an interesting discussion of Austen's characteristic use of the narrative voice. 'Austen's narrative renders the character as perceiving subject caught in the exigencies of the moment' (p. 13). The narrator, 'unlike Fielding's or Sterne's [...] usually fades into the central character's point of view, becoming identical with it through free indirect discourse' (p. 93). The latter is a form of reported speech in which a character's external dialogue and private thought merge into one another, sometimes becoming indistinguishable. 'As scholars have pointed out', (Norman Page, Roy Pascal, Graham Hough) 'Austen is the first English novelist to have grasped the full range of effects produced by this technique' (p. 87). But here again he does not enlarge on an interesting subject in much detail.

Essentially Dussinger's study is a series of notes on *Emma*, with cross references to Austen's other novels. He uses Freud and Sartre, and a variety of philosophical and linguistic approaches to describe the encounters in *Emma*. The chapter headings are 'Play', 'Desire', 'Character', 'Speech', and 'Text'. Occasionally his approaches conflict with each other. At one point characters are discussed in terms of their past experiences, at another they are said to have 'a short memory or almost none at all' (p. 37). When subjected to one kind of critical approach, they are treated as 'psychologicl entities', and when subjected to another they are treated as 'linguistic artefacts'. In one place an event is said to be of 'momentous importance' for those who took part in it; in another it is said to be 'a kinetic arrangement of intentions lasting only for the moment' (p. 39). Such inconsistencies are sometimes ascribed to Jane Austen rather than to Dussinger himself: 'Besides [Miss Bates's] function in reflecting the insincerity of polite discourse and the inherent fragmentariness of any communication [. . .] elsewhere in the text her words bear comparison with the most authoritative voice heard, including the hero's. Perhaps uneasy about presenting this character so inconsistently, Austen has little use for her once the secret engagement becomes known' (p. 139).

Dussinger's fragmentary approach yields its most satisfying results when he examines the inner lives of some of the more important secondary characters in Austen. His fullest chapter is 'Speech', which is about Austen's compulsive talkers, whose garrulity sometimes conceals disturbing depths. He illustrates how, 'among Miss Bates' various functions, perhaps the most intriguing is the expression of an existential loneliness that no other characters can voice in their polite conversation' (p. 113), and how 'Mr Woodhouse's prodigious "inner life" [is] encoded in his text' (p. 168). On the other hand Dussinger cannot encompass figures like Emma Woodhouse or Elizabeth Bennet, who remain present throughout their respective novels. This reveals a major flaw in his theory that Austen's 'artistic strength lies not so much in the larger design of the story as in its minute encounters' (p. 16).

UNIVERSITY OF CALIFORNIA, SANTA BARBARA   LOGAN SPEIRS

Women and Romance: The Consolations of Gender in the English Novel. By LAURIE LANGBAUER. (Reading Women Writing) Ithaca, NY, and London: Cornell University Press. 1990. xii + 271 pp. $35 (paperbound $10.95).

Laurie Langbauer points out in this stimulating book that the categories 'women' and 'romance' have been linked together so frequently that their connexion has come to seem natural. In her study of the relation between them, she is concerned not to offer another definition of these terms, but to study the how and the why of their yoking together, the mechanism of connexion. Similarly, in analysing what is conventionally held to be the opposition between the novel and romance, she is concerned less with the content than with the how and the why of this opposition. Drawing on poststructuralist theory, she offers an understanding of it in terms of the Derridean logic of the supplement, whereby no term can escape the contamination of its opposite, and also invokes the Foucauldian notion that contradiction is always implicated in any power system it appears to contest. From this perspective, she argues that the supposed opposition between the novel and romance is a false one, for each term is deeply implicated in its opposite. However, it has been in the interests of a dominant male tradition to cast romance repeatedly as the 'other' of the novel, all that it does not want to be. (Female) romance, she suggests, has thus been repeatedly 'scapegoated' by the dominant (male) novel form, made to represent 'the chaotic negative space' whose exclusion defines the novel. Women and romance thus reflect a 'consoling illusion of privilege' for men and novels.

Langbauer takes issue with traditional accounts of the 'rise of the novel' whereby romance is seen as an inferior form which is superseded as the novel form develops, and suggests instead that such an evolutionary view of literary history may itself be a kind of romance, or illusion. In a discussion of the novels of Meredith she demonstrates that romance, supposedly 'left behind' by the time of the late nineteenth century, resurfaces repeatedly even in texts such as *Diana of the Crossways* which explicitly disavow it. She also traces the way in which the romance of history operates for Meredith, who constructs history in order to put an end to it via a wishful identification with the pre-Oedipal (and pre-historical) mother. Langbauer suggests that similarly dubious impulses may lie behind the 'recourse to history' of some contemporary feminist criticism: feminists must be wary of the pitfalls built into 'the concept of history as it is frequently used'.

It could be argued that 'history' is the repressed other of Langbauer's own text, repeatedly 'scapegoated' by her in order to justify what remains an essentially formal analysis of the relations between women, romance, and the novel. Through-out her book Langbauer maintains a double focus, moving between the nineteenth-century novel/romance and issues of contemporary feminist scholarship. Such movement is predicated, of course, on a belief that similar structures are implicated in the inscription of 'woman' in these different periods. So in her discussion of Dickens Langbauer employs the metaphors of 'the streetwalker' and 'the home-body' to denote Dickens's 'two types of women': she goes on to link the wayward 'streetwalker' with wayward deconstructive theory, the homebody with Foucaul-dian analysis of constraints, and then suggests that both deconstructive and Foucauldian analysis use the figures of the streetwalker (or hysteric) and the homebody (or mother) to support their theoretical propositions. As the recourse to bracketed terms might suggest, this is an analysis which can seem to strain its terms of comparison: it is more ingenious than substantive, perhaps.

Langbauer is at her best where she registers more sharply the historical determi-nants behind the inscription of women in different periods, for example in a fine concluding chapter in which she traces the connexion between George Eliot's 'pessimism' and the position of feminists today. She argues that Eliot's novels, with their emphasis on the intractability of our social relations and the powerlessness of the human will, lead to the same crux that confronts contemporary feminism, which is 'how to think our way out of the very constraints determining our thought'. Langbauer is aware, in other words, of the potential conflict between her acceptance of poststructuralist theory and a feminist commitment. On the one hand such theory contains its own consolations, offering an implicit reassurance because it seems to have 'blocked off' all possible objections to itself. On the other hand, a system which seems to have incorporated all possible contradictions can seem to pre-empt criticism and thwart any movement towards change. In this it is very like the philosophical determinism which troubled Eliot. Despite this, Eliot's fiction, like feminism itself, constantly urges, in Langbauer's words, 'the necessity for continu-ing to resist what we cannot imagine how to overcome'. This (strictly) illogical conclusion is the nearest the author comes to indulging in the consolations of her gender in this intricate and closely argued study.

UNIVERSITY OF LEICESTER   CLARE HANSON

Bicycles, Bangs, and Bloomers: The New Woman in the Popular Press. By PATRICIA MARKS. Lexington: University Press of Kentucky. 1990. x + 222 pp. $22.

So generous is Patricia Marks with her quotations that there is a temptation to browse through her book much as one might through one of the periodicals she describes. Observing the curious along with the significant, sifting gossip from information, one would still have to admit that she has disinterred more material on the 'New Woman' than anyone before her, and that overall it provides further evidence of a growing and complicated relation between radical impulses and what we would call 'media publicity'. And among her *faits divers* Marks offers, in addition, some genuinely new information about womens's clubs, women's education, and women's fashion.

It is not to deny the activities of independent women in the period, nor an emergent feminist sensibility, to conclude that, as far as the periodicals were concerned, the 'New Woman' was in large part a male invention. In her looks and attitudes the cartoon 'New Woman' is closer to a male fantasy than any female reality. This often has the odd effect of making the satire seem more inventive as well more pointless and offensive. Noting the tendency among cartoonists to turn 'New Women' into hard-drinking, cigar-smoking, be-tweeded club-men Marks rightly observes that 'What seems to be happening is that the male illustrators read their own somewhat doubtful activities into their counterpart's lives and then accuse women of being "manly".' That, in a way, is to credit the enemy with a degree of complexity.

Energy and wit are never the prerogative of the objectively clear-sighted. The Victorian passion for parody and caricature required from journalists a knowledge of prosody and of verse forms, and a graphic dexterity capable of challenging the reader's expertise. Shakespeare and Tennyson were continually reworked, visual styles endlessly adapted, as Marks reveals.

Where she sometimes lets us and herself down is in her failure to pursue the ways in which periodicals solicited their readers' responses. Nor does she always stand sufficiently apart from her source-material to understand its full reference. An instance occurs in a late chapter where Marks reports a correspondence between a woman physician and a Mrs L. Ormiston Chant about women and physical exercise as if their respective positions were self-evident. It would help to be told more about Mrs Chant here because she was a formidable woman whose campaigning zeal has often been reviled. In fact she presents precisely the kind of contradictory figure whose endeavours to protect women from exploitation sometimes led to the kind of prudery and surveillance we find so uncongenial today. Like other strong women of her day she was an easier person to satirize than to understand in her full social situation.

There are other areas where a larger context would have helped: the careers of individual jounalists such as Robert Buchanan for instance, or the editorial control behind journals such as *Truth*. In fact there is a certain imprecision about Marks's methods overall: the continual movement between England and America elides cultural difference, while a wider sampling of journals to include the dailies (especially the newer prints of the nineties) would have raised questions about the 'popular press' that, although suggested in the sub-title, are never confronted. To take full account of the 'New Journalism' would be to raise further questions about the 'New Woman' in the light of an assumed or desired readership — questions of class, of market, and, of course, of gender.

UNIVERSITY OF WARWICK   JOHN STOKES

The Comic Art of Barbara Pym. By MASON COOLEY. (AMS Studies in Modern Literature, 18) New York: AMS Press. 1990. 292 pp. $42.50.

Mason Cooley's subject is new and necessary: earlier critics have been content to glance briefly at Pym's comedy and praise her as a comic artist before getting on to the serious stuff about lonely spinsters, something to love, transience, and mortality. Such gestures in the direction of her comedy are inevitably inadequate or merely provocative. An example of the former is Robert Liddell's loosely drawn chapter on Pym's comedy in his *A Mind at Ease* (London: Owen, 1989); of the latter, Lord David Cecil's bull's-eye comment that Pym wrote 'the finest examples of high comedy to have appeared in seventy-five years'. Cooley undertakes a methodical study of Pym as humorist. His thesis, given in his first chapter is as right as rain; the comic spirit is central to Pym's fiction, everything radiates from that: 'It is the decisive element, the shaping spirit. That is true from the beginning of her career to the end, from the hilarity of her first novel to the elegiac mood of her last' (p. 3). He is quite right to point out that the sadness always present in Pym's fiction is distanced and transmuted by her comic sensibility.

Cooley notes well that Pym's fictions are all in one way or another autobiographical and that she knew that detachment from her experience (she often used the Wordworthian phrase 'emotion recollected in tranquility') was necessary to allow her transformation into comedy of what was for her terribly sad. He makes an important point in noting Pym's propensity to form her fictional situations within 'conventional literary modes of framing experience' (p. 8). By this he means, I think, that Pym's heroines are always transforming experience through the lense of literature — one good example being that one-time Oxford tutor, Jane, of *Jane and Prudence*.

Although he is generally accurate in describing his author's literary practice, he repeats an irritating and misleading truism at times: 'These heroines retain the traditional old-maidish qualities; they are love-starved, timid, moralistic, and intensely curious about other people's affairs' (p. 9). And they are gallant and kind, intelligent and observant, many-sided, and so on. All of them? One failure of Pym criticism overall is to ignore the diversity of her characters (and of her novels more generally), especially her leading female characters. The above description ('love-starved', 'timid,' 'moralistic') certainly does not fit Leonora Eyre, whose kind and gallant feelings towards the elderly are expressed in her firm judgement: 'One has to be tough with old people [...] otherwise they *encroach*.' 'Her spinster heroines tend to be the only characters who are clear-headed and generous-minded,' says Cooley (p. 9). Some, maybe — many of them are just the opposite in one way or other. Is Belinda clear-headed? Prudence Bates or Jessie Morrow generous? Perhaps there has been too much critical emphasis on the uniformity of the Pym World: 'It's very Barbara Pym.'

Cooley's determination to treat all the novels in sequence becomes a little tedious; inevitably there must be repetition. Thus there are at times languors in a book that quite often makes good sense and points the way to further study and awareness.

UNIVERSITY OF ILLINOIS, URBANA-CHAMPAIGN   ANTHONY KAUFMAN

Critical Essays on Harold Pinter. By STEVEN H. GALE. (Critical Essays on British Literature) Boston, MA: Hall. 1990. x + 356 pp. $40.
Critical Essays on Tom Stoppard. By ANTHONY JENKINS. (Critical Essays on British Literature) Boston, MA: Hall. 1990. x + 230 pp. $35.

None of the Pinter materials collected here by Steven H. Gale has been reprinted before. He thus avoids the re-cycling often found with such volumes and achieves a minor editorial coup by beginning with Harold Hobson's prescient review of the first production of *The Room*. The following section on 'Interviews' includes the lengthy 1971 New York exhange with Mel Gussow with much of great interest including Pinter's relationship with Beckett and a fascinating aside on sentimentalism. The interviews with John Barber and Miriam Gross bring out strongly the mature Pinter's preference for Proust over Joyce. From British readers the availability of these materials can save a time-consuming trip to Colindale. The rest of the articles and essays are divided in 'The Dramas', 'The Films', 'The Element of the Theatre' and 'Overviews', 'within each category the arrangement of the articles reflects the chronology of the works being examined'.

The first section begins very strongly with Elin Diamond on the parodic element in *The Dumb Waiter*. Though there are aspects of *Pinter's Comic Play*, from which this is taken, with which one would beg to differ, this is excellent (but why isn't the obvious source of Hemingway's short story *The Killers* mentioned, and the early film version which coincided with Pinter's cinema-going youth?). It seems a pity that Katherine Burkman has never been responsive to the parodic element in Pinter and thus intially failed to see it with the Golden Bough allusions in *A Slight Ache*. As a consequence Burkman has created a whole structure of fertility myth ritual which reappears here in a ludicrously strained fashion applied to *Betrayal*. In an essay especially written for the collection Linda Ben-Zvi argues persuasively for the place of *Monologue* in Pinter's work, while Alrene Sykes, though concerned with one of Pinter's most discussed plays, *The Caretaker*, is nevertheless both shrewd and sensitive in her close reading. Those who, like Gale and Gay Gibson Cima, turn to the fascination of *Old Times*, might find a more controlling focus with the recognition that in the first production, as Anna swept down from the darkened window backstage, she was wearing a post-war Dior A-line dress in contrast to Deeley and Kate's contemporary (late sixties) style.

Other articles have rewarding details: Francis Gillen's suggestion of the Jonsonian quality of *The Hothouse*; V. M. Jiji's observation, in the midst of Freudian wanderings, on the Italian campaign remarks of Lenny and Ruth in *The Homecoming*; Thomas P. Adler's comparison of *No Man's Land* with Pirandello. There is arguably a whole study in this last topic. The end of *No Man's Land* echoes the conclusion of Pirandello's *Enrico Quarto*.

Many rather wayward things have been said about *The Basement* which C. C. Hudgins carefully addresses here in his able insistence on the work as film rather than text, a point anticipating the section on film. All the essays here — on *The Servant* (Elayne P. Feldstein), *The Go-Between* (Foster Hirsch), 'The Losey-Pinter Collaboration' (Beverle Houston and Marsha Kinder) 'Cinematic Proust ...' (Stephanie Tucker) — make apparent the homogeneity of all of Pinter's work, how criticism of one area enriches that of another, and conversely how to neglect one aspect would be to impoverish criticism elsewhere.

For Pinter's early acting background in repertory theatre of the fifties, the work of David T. Thompson and Leslie Smith is essential reading and both are justly represented here.

Drama is realized by way of the semiological manifold of theatre, not just dialogue, and this was the fundamental weakness of Austen Quigley's *The Pinter Problem* which propounded a Wittgensteinian rejection of the reference theory of meaning and a concomitant rejection of 'subtext'. However, Quigley provided the most theoretically disciplined and exacting of Pinter studies and the lengthy section reproduced deserves its place. Ironically, Quigley's old adversary, Martin Esslin, in spite of the weakness of his arguments, here seems to get closer to the experience of a Pinter play.

Though is is not clear why several critics have been neglected by Susan Hollis Merritt, her bibliography will be very useful for students of Pinter's work.

Proliferation and doubleness seem to pervade Stoppard (his English not his original Czech name) as the opening interview of Anthony Jenkins's collection makes plain, even in the repeated adjustments and varying editions of plays. Clive James, anticipating some concerns of *Hapgood*, draws the Newton-Einstein analogy with physics; a fixed world, but variable viewpoints. Jenkins cleverly takes this as the principle of structure in this volume. Even in the Quixotic surrealism of *Lord Malquist and Mr Moon*, *Fons et origo* of so much later theatre as Michael Billington shows, the eponymous heroes are like wave and particle. For Normand Berlin 'Stoppard does not root the intellectual in felt experience' whereas Jenkins on the same topic of 'Death in *Rosencrantz and Guildenstern*' finds 'a debate whose very theatricality persuades us emotionally as well as intellectually'.

Again, Roy W. Perrett argues for the richness of philosophical material in *Jumpers* against Jonathan Bennett's essay. Tim Brasswell, effectively supporting Perrett, provides basic background material on Logical Positivism and the 'Vienna Circle' of the twenties with its English disciple A. J. Ayer challenged by C. E. M. Joad. Mention of the latter reminds us of the somewhat Stoppardian realities of life itself — Joad, a distinguished professor of philosophy who had become a household name through his participation in the B.B.C's *The Brains Trust*, was disgraced when found fiddling his fares on public transport.

The title *Travesties* itself invites a bi-focal respose and finds defenders in R. A. Cave's and Michael Billington's essays. 'Logics of the Absurd' by T. R. Whitaker engages with the Agatha Christie detective context of *The Red Inspector Hound* and the surrealism of *After Magritte*. The plays since 1977 are discussed in essays by C. W. E. Bigsby and Neil Sammells. For Bigsby *Every Good Boy Deserves Favour*, *Professional Foul*, and *Night and Day* dramatize 'the liberal resistance to a modern spirit of bogus nationalism and private and public pragmatism'. But Sammells, at the conclusion of his examination of *Night and Day*, *The Real Thing*, and *Squaring the Circle*, challenges Stoppard for the emerging conservatism of his work. The acerbic sharpness of Sammells' indictment here is one of the most provocative things in the book.

A pun is an instrument of doubleness and the essays by Hersh Zeifman and Jim Hunter examine this and other aspects of linguistic inventiveness in Stoppard's work. Hunter mentions rhetoric; knowledge of the difference between paronomasia, antanaclasis, and syllepsis, would have sharpened both essays. *Hapgood* as a name seems to intimate two contrasting aspects of one person, 'hap' (accident, misfortune) and 'good'. Jenkins explores *Hapgood's* world of espionage and the internal analogue of quantum physics while Doreen Thompson surveys women in Stoppard's work in a specially written essay entirely free of theory and feminism: quite a feat these days. But is Hapgood not a moral androgyne in a metatheoretical play which uses the cover of espionage and physics to stymie feminists?

UNIVERSITY OF READING   RONALD KNOWLES

Pinter in Play: Critical Strategies and the Plays of Harold Pinter. By SUSAN HOLLIS
    MERRITT. Durham, NC, and London: Duke University Press. 1990.
    xxiii + 343 pp. £37.95; $48.95.

In her introduction, Susan Hollis Merritt urges her academic readers to pause before contributing further to the 'vast industry' of literary criticism and scholarship, and 'to become more vigilant regarding their reasons for doing so, and to contribute more carefully and more responsibly'. In publishing such a huge study Merritt is either extremely confident or somewhat lacking in a sense of irony. As bibliographical editor for *The Pinter Review* the author probably knows more about Pinter criticism than anyone else. This and her knowledge of contemporary critical theory qualifies her for a metacritical study which undertakes a rather complex task — to analyse Pinter criticism and critics in terms of their 'class, gender, sexual-role orientation and other social, and psychological traits'.

The difficulty here is that at least three books seem to be being written at once: a survey and analysis of Pinter criticism; a socio-psychological study of the academic institutionalization of criticism; an evangelical feminist critique of dominant maleness in criticism and theory. It could have been done. As a bibliographer, Merritt has to be meticulously disciplined and her *Pinter Review* articles provide an essential reference, but let loose on a book the result is, I regret to say, questionable. Two fundamental problems bring this about, organization and selection. Not until Chapter 3, page 51, do we get to actual Pinter critics, namely Almansi and Henderson. Before that Merritt admits that Chapter 2 is largely a review of *What is Criticism?* edited by Paul Hernadi. This at least formalizes the centrifugal fling in Chapter 1. Merritt cannot control or resist the constant accretion of asides, name after name, theorist after theorist. The two-page discussion of Almansi and Henderson's postmodernist approach is excellent, but again it is sandwiched between what seem random theoretical notes. In this respect, the whole book, page after page, needs severe pruning.

Chapters 4 to 7 examine various critics and approaches: the debate in *Modern Drama* concerning *The Dumb Waiter*: Steven Gale's thematic approach; Katherine Burkman's anthropological interpretation; the 'psychoanalytic manoeuvres' of Gordon, Esslin, and Gabbard; the Wittgensteinian analysis of Quigley; Dierdre Burton's use of discourse analysis; Sakellaridou's feminist study. What is of value here is to have not only Merritt's analysis but the occasional inclusion of varying reviewer's comments. If this had been stuck to throughout this study it would have become an indispensable work of reference for all students of Pinter's work. What is inexplicable is Merritt's principle of selection. Given the scope allowed by the publishers why was the opportunity not taken of simply working through the body of Pinter criticism?

Hayman and Hinchcliffe's early books, though undistinguished, could have received some consideration in the establishment of Pinter's early reputation, as could Arthur Ganz's early 'Twentieth Century Views' collection. Martin Esslin's *Theatre of the Absurd*, for better or for worse, arguably the most influential categorization of Pinter in all criticism, is ignored. Hollis's early study was more than a mere survey. A slur on Baker and Tabachnik by a reviewer on Esslin is the only mention they receive, yet Baker's chapter on the East End remains very useful for non-Londoners. Kerr's questionable 'existential' view is mentioned but never discussed, while Dobrez's consideration of the context of European dramatic existentialism is ignored. One could continue — what of Lahr's 'casebook' on *The Homecoming*? Dukore's *Where Laughter Stops*? Trussler? Sykes? All these are omitted; yet the whole book is characterized by redundance. The following example is not atypical.

Yet any reviewer who is 'friends' with a playwright must be somewhat conscious of the potential effects of subsequent reviews on their friendship. Though it is possible that judgments may not be altered by the circumstances of a friendship in any crucial way, such a relationship does differentiate reviewers' judgments regarding evaluations of a friend's work from their other decisions. The actual personal and social relationship between a reviewer and the author whose book is being reviewed (or otherwise commented on) may inhibit what the reviewer says about it. (p. 222)

As Merritt says towards the close of her study, 'we are accountable for our acts of scholarship and criticism'.

UNIVERSITY OF READING   RONALD KNOWLES

Edith Wharton's Letters from the Underworld: Fictions of Women and Writing. By CANDACE
WAID. Chapel Hill and London: University of North Carolina Press. 1991.
x + 237 pp. $32.95 (paperbound $12.05).

Edith Wharton and the Unsatisfactory Man. By DAVID HOLBROOK. (Critical Studies
Series) London: Vision Press; New York: St. Martin's Press. 1991. 208 pp.
£21.95.

In her study of Edith Wharton Candace Waid focuses on the novels, stories, and
poetry which she denotes as centrally concerned with textual relations: relations
between Wharton and her predecessors in both European and American literature
and between Wharton's protagonists and their ability to 'author' their own stories.
Waid discusses *Artemis to Actaeon*, two of the major novels: *The House of Mirth* and *The
Custom of the Country*, three novellas: *The Touchstone, Ethan Frome*, and *Summer*, the
short stories with which Wharton launched her career: *The Greater Inclination*, and
those with which she closed it: *Ghosts*. Whilst all Waid's readings of these texts are
cogent, meticulous, and insightful, it is her work on *The Custom of the Country* which is
the most startling and revelatory. She describes the novel as 'the marriage of
capitalism and sentimentalism that embodies Wharton's most apocalyptic vision of
America', worrying the text from a number of perspectives and positions to obtain
the definitive reading of Undine Spragg as the 'devouring muse'.

This study is predicated on Waid's reading of her subject's concern with 'realism
and the real' as 'gender-related and often sexually charged terms'. She locates
Wharton's interest in architecture, in structure and design as 'the formal
requirements of the real' in opposition to the 'feminine aesthetic that focuses on
surfaces'. The early stories and *The House of Mirth* are discussed in terms of letters: as
alphabet, epistles, literature, or as statements of metaphoric intent — Wharton's
delineation of Carrie Fisher as 'embodying a spicy paragraph' or Alice Weatherall
as 'an animated visiting list'. Waid's interpretation of the novel relies in part on
establishing an intimate relationship between the nature of the fall of Lily Bart and
Wharton's lifelong preoccupation — both within and without her fictions — with
the *Oresteia*, as well as the myth of Persephone, the latter acting as the informing
spirit behind the whole study. What Wharton herself described as the 'building
material' of her work she also identified as the masculine sensibility and the failed
authors in her writing are determined by Waid to be women who, like Lily Bart,
cannot come to terms with the world of 'surfaces' and go down in a confusion of the
written word: wills, envelopes, cheques, appointments, and letters, none of which
adequately represent their condition. In reading *Ethan Frome*, however, Waid's
emphasis switches to the struggle with silence and those who are mute, with the
absence of not only the written but the spoken word. This is inextricably linked to a
reading of the text as centrally concerned with 'female barrenness and relentless
infertility', with the young woman replacing the old in a ritual of death and decay
rather than renewal and regeneration.

Waid engages with Wharton's repeated attempts to refute those of her critics who
dismissed the New England novellas as written by an expatriate who knew knothing
of the real conditions of existence of the native population of Massachusetts. Indeed,
the impetus behind Waid's reading of *Summer* is what she describes as Wharton's
'argument' with the local colorists, and in particular with Mary Wilkins Freeman.
Freeman's story, 'Old Woman Magoun' is examined in great detail and *Summer*, 'a
narrative about survival rather than death and resurrection' is presented as being in
dialogue with this narrowly precursive text. This approach, though new and not
without interest does rather leave *Summer* untouched; the difficulties of the text, the
elisions, the looseness of the prose, are not engaged with. Also, perhaps, the
belatedness of Wharton's introduction of any idea of dialogue between her and her

predecessors in the New England subject is not given sufficient credit. The close scrutiny to which Waid subjects the language of *The Custom of the Country* is missing from her treatment of *Summer*, her notion of the former being about 'unfinished books' might have illuminated the darker corners of the New England novella. In the placing of Ralph Marvell at the centre of authorial concern in *The Custom of the Country* Waid points to Wharton's personal identification with her creation, the failed writer 'who is seduced by the siren song of a false muse'. She goes on to equate, in a powerful and persuasive argument, 'the struggle between art and artifice' with that between 'culture and what Wharton calls a "phantom 'society'"'. Waid also conducts an extensive examination of the relationship between the poetry of Andrew Marvell and Wharton's writing in *The Custom of the Country*; she compares Wharton's portrait of Undine with the visual representations of parallel narratives by Turner and Boucher. A further insight might perhaps have been gained by a consideration of Francis Picabia's painting, 'udnie (jeune fille americaine; danse)' which arose from his visit to New York in 1913; the water nymph here being a point of reference for the portrait of the quintessential American girl.

Waid's study of Wharton is impressive for a number of reasons: the range of allusion, the marshalling of evidence in pursuit of an argument, the felicitous expression of her most radical insights into the texts. Any reading of Wharton's fiction is partial; the range and denseness of her literary achievement and ambition make this unavoidable. In essence, I believe that the critical issues tackled by Waid are those placed firmly in the foreground by Wharton herself.

Nothing could provide more of a contrast to Waid's detailed and meticulous probing of Wharton's ficition than David Holbrook's *Edith Wharton and the Unsatisfactory Man*. Whilst I strongly recommend Waid as provocative and inventive and likely to be inspirational to students and teachers alike, Holbrook's study compounds misprint with error with misreading with inaccuracy. The book does not seem to have been proof-read. Even those names at the centre of interest in a novel are confused and jumbled. Quotations bear little resemblance to Wharton's words: for instance Lily Bart's demonstration of her ability to live cheaply: 'but I can trim my own hats!' becomes 'but I contain my own hates', a dramatically different kind of utterance. In discussion of *The Reef* we are given Sophy Viner, supposedly in Wharton's words: 'She has a child after all', instead of: 'She was a child after all' — a serious difference for an unmarried young lady in 1912. Newland Archer's very specifically *yellow* roses for Ellen Olenska in *The Age of Innocence* become — carelessly — red. The clichés are in Holbrook's prose and ideas, not Wharton's.

Holbrook's theory is that Edith Wharton could only place sexual confidence in her own father and his reading of Wharton's novels is based on the search for father figures to substantiate this notion. The novels are read biographically, with the odd psychological gloss on plot and character. His reading of *The Custom of the Country*, and particularly the role of Undine Spragg, bears no relation to the novel that I can discover: 'She suffers so much, over her second husband's death, for instance, that the reader even finds relief in the last episode, in which she takes refuge in the arms of Elmer Moffat — with whom she encounters the good, solid old American values.' Presumably the values Holbrook means are those typically manifested by Moffat: cheating your competitors, lying to procure the de Chelles Tapestries, giving false testimony in court, visiting prostitutes, inciting Undine to elope with him (both as married and unmarried woman), etc. etc.

Throughout his study Holbrook uses the term 'Jamesian' liberally. As it is never made clear whether this term is used for denigration or praise one is only able to conjecture that it is a positive term when he starts to use 'Scott Fitzgeraldese' as a term of abuse. *Edith Wharton and the Unsatisfactory Man* is a hasty, half-formed study of a writer judged constantly by someone else's standards; *Edith Wharton's Letters*

From the Underworld is a detailed, serious study of a writer in dialogue with her own art.

ROEHAMPTON INSTITUTE   JANET GOODWYN

Painterly Abstraction in Modernist American Poetry: The Contemporaneity of Modernism. By
    CHARLES ALTIERI. (Cambridge Studies in American Literature and Culture)
    Cambridge, New York, and Melbourne: Cambridge University Press. 1990.
    viii + 529 pp. £40; $49.50.

Charles Altieri's previous book, *Self and Sensibility in Contemporary American Poetry*
(Cambridge: Cambridge University Press, 1984), sought to salvage, defend, and
maintain what Pound called in 1913 the seriousness of art. He attended to the
self-consciousness of contemporary lyric poetry as a means of confronting the
cultural pressures which persisted from the Modernism of the century's earlier
years. Altieri's defence of poetry was directed against those interpretive languages
holding authority over our social life: those discursive practices which 'map' human
motives and capacities into 'the discreet, manageable structures proposed by the
social sciences', and one of poetry's primary social functions was thus to resist such
structures which were viewed as encouraging a 'dangerously reductive image of
human agency'.

    The present exercise probes this crisis of contemporaneity by returning to its
manifestations in Modernism itself and restructuring its basic terms into a struggle
between poetry as 'infinite incantations of ourselves' and the impositions of 'empiri-
cal description'. The crisis is productively re-read through poetry's affinities with
the experimentations in the visual arts: 'Modernist art demonstrated the capacity of
formal energies to reject mimetic structures and still retain extraordinary semantic
force by relying directly on the production of exemplary attitudes that an audience
might project into extraartistic contexts.' Consequently, we receive challenging new
readings of Eliot, Williams, Moore, Stein, and, particularly, Pound and Stevens, as
well as illuminating analyses of Impressionism, Cubism, and Vorticism; of
Cezanne, Braque, Picasso, Malevich, and Mondrian. Stevens's cry for abstraction,
worked by Altieri into a rich series of complex figurations, becomes the vehicle for
sustaining incantatory agency on behalf of 'individual resistance to hegemonic
cultural values'.

    So abstraction becomes clothed within a liberal and humane value system which,
paradoxically, implicitly applauds the ahistoricism of the postmodernist self —
proposing the 'eloquence of song' where selves are both elicited and defined by
'teasing out expressive needs' in order to create 'an imaginative state that various
selves can enter because the expression ceases to belong to any one producer'.
Altieri's interest in the 'release from bondage to the representational principles
fostering empiricist values', the shared ground of Modernist poetry and painting,
thus becomes, in his own phrase, 'aesthetic idealism'. Here, he proclaims his
resistance to both history and what he calls the 'prevailing "advanced" critical
positions' in seeking to examine the 'ideal structures' proposed by Modernist poetry
'on their own terms' so as to 'provoke us to more accurate and more intricate
versions of our own contemporaneity'.

    The great strength of Altieri's account lies in its proclamation of poetry's
constructivist office: 'The artist's efforts to replace representational values with
principles capable of unmaking and remaking very powerfully entrenched aesthetic
and moral expectations about art.' This is an important recognition, but Altieri
turns it to worrying and misleading ends. Constructivist energy, he argues,

possesses its expressive power largely because it has no possible social sanction or use. That
cold refusal to accommodate itself to practical judgement exacted a substantial social price: it

drew the art, and the artists, into alliance with political systems that shared their impatience with human imperfection. This very danger, however, ultimately deepened the artists' need to make the art unrecouperable by any social vision.

To say the least, this does not square easily with, say, Pound or Williams, both of whom were wholly committed to a 'social vision'. And its manipulation of that most urgent of democratic positions — the world as subject to the manufacture of human agency — is, at best, perverse: or, more accurately, a result of Altieri's creed of abstraction. Altieri is a gifted reader, but this book falls prey to unrecognized distortions of his own admission: 'Getting straight about abstraction takes an embarrassing amount of abstraction.'

UNIVERSITY OF KEELE IAN F. A. BELL

Irony and the Discourse of Modernity. By ERNST BEHLER. Seattle and London: University of Washington Press. 1990. xiii + 154 pp. $20.

According to Ernst Behler, 'being modern means essentially a departure from exemplary models of the past, a decentering of habitual ways of viewing the world, and the necessity for producing normative standards out of oneself' (p. 3). For Behler, these constitute the key elements of a sense of modernity which has determined 'our own' condition, since, that is, the late seventeenth century. It follows that writing about 'one's own modernity' is done with an awareness of paradox: that of automatically relegating modernity to the past while still aiming to explore its present-ness. Far from being problematic, however, this paradoxical quality is but an aspect of (any) modernity's self-reflexive gesture. Having stated such an awareness, Behler proceeds to give an account of 'Modernism and Post-modernism in Contemporary Thought' and takes us briefly through the work of contemporary theorists/exponents of what should be read as conflicting positions. Thus, Jürgen Habermas and Jean-François Lyotard are seen as advocates of modernism and postmodernism respectively, while the views of Richard Rorty and Jacques Derrida are ushered into the debate as points of reference, but also legitimation, of the postmodernist side.
    The problem here is not so much the schematic exposition of the above theorists' arguments, as the author's own hesitant assumptions about the *post* in 'post-modernism': is it 'a radicalized, intensified version of modernism', or is it 'that situation in which all the ideals of modernity have come to their exhaustion' (p. 5)? Can it really be both? Behler does not avoid the question, but comes up with an answer which accommodates both positions, that is, with a typically postmodern — playful, twisted, and confused — evasion: 'Postmodernity therefore reveals itself as an ironic notion communicating indirectly, by way of circumlocution, configuration, and bafflement, the necessity and impossibility of discussing the status of modernity in a straightforward and meaningful manner' (pp. 4–5).
    Leaving the notions of modernity/modernism and postmodernity/postmodernism thus intertwined, Behler continues with a survey of modernist concepts of the aesthetic in the Romantic age and then focuses on irony as the critical term which 'is a decisive mark of literary modernity' (p. 73). From Socrates to Schlegel and Nietzsche to Derrida, Behler traces irony as a revealing and fruitful mode for the discussion of the theoretical physiognomy of modernity, only to conclude in his final chapter that postmodernism, in its self-referentiality, is a valid continuation of that same mode. Here, Habermas is finally attacked and Derrida applauded, the former for his 'desperate' effort to resuscitate the discourse of rationality and progress and the latter for being the supreme ironist. Furthermore, and with no apparent justification, Rorty's views on the matter are once more offered as authoritative

statements on the present state of philosophy and the modernism/postmodernism debate. Behler implicitly endorses Rorty's claim that '[philosophy] has become more important for the pursuit of private perfection rather than of any social task' (p. 145), and that, consequently, Habermas is missing the point. Thus, Rorty's 'matter-of-fact pragmatism of small solutions and relative decisions' is to be preferred to Habermas's 'totalitarian foundationalism', the one 'new and interesting', the other 'traditionalist and conservative'.

This is not the first instance of an attack on Habermas as the killjoy-reminder of the incompleteness of the project of modernity and the author is certainly entitled to choose sides. Ernst Behler's case for the postmodern as ironic *par excellence* is put forward in a lucid and informative way and his study is a useful intervention in the modernity/postmodernity debate. One only wishes that the polemical thesis in the book were argued in a more dialogic manner: if it is the discourse of modernity which encompasses that of postmodernity, even in the corrective form of the ironic trope, then Habermas's suspicion about the ongoing claims of its demise and transgression should not be so hastily dismissed.

University of Strathclyde   Vassiliki Kolocotroni

New Readings of the American Novel: Narrative Theory and its Application. By Peter Messent. Basingstoke and London: Macmillan. 1990. viii + 328 pp. £35 (paperbound £9.99).

This narratological account of eight major American novels sets itself a two-way project: to introduce the primary characteristics of narrative theory, as practised by such structuralist thinkers as Gérard Genette, Mikhail Bahktin, Wolfgang Iser, Paul Ricoeur, and Roland Barthes (this list is not exhaustive), and to provide exemplary readings which demonstrate the analytical uses to which the theory may be put. The resulting negotiations between text and theory are seen in relation to *The Great Gatsby, The Sound and the Fury, The Sun Also Rises, A Lost Lady, The Portrait of a Lady, The House of Mirth, Huckleberry Finn*, and *Their Eyes Were Watching God*. There is here an implicit chronological limitation at work which produces a largely unvoiced appeal to the idea of modernism: an idea which would seem to set in play a whole range of assumptions that work with the theoretical assumptions explored. Yet one of the achievements of this book is the impression of diversity which it produces, both among the texts with which it deals and within the structuralist orthodoxy which provides the controlling principles.

New Readings of the American Novel is, as its subtitle makes clear, motivated by a pedagogical rationale. The discussion is directed at students of critical theory and their teachers, both of whom will find very useful these model applications of theory to familiar texts. This worthwhile project is qualified, though, by the admission, made early on, that a certain selectivity is in operation here. Only aspects of each theory are explored according to their relevance to the text under discussion. It must be assumed, then, that the text somehow determines the appropriateness of the analytical tools applied to it. There is a circularity to this logic which seems to arise from a profound unwillingness to surrender the primacy of the text, a resistance which is at odds with the book's ostensibly structuralist reasoning.

This ambivalence, this less than complete commitment to structuralist theory, is most clearly perceptible in the book's attempt to redefine narrative theory in such a way as to challenge the concept of the American canon. In response to the common complaint that structuralism is a formalism that ignores, at its peril, the historical, cultural, and political dimensions of the text, Peter Messent sets himself the task of using structuralist methods to produce an image of the text as a reflection of

American heterogeneity. Placed at the end of a lengthy study of the major novels of the modern American canon, this attempt is certainly presented as ambitious. But is it really? Messent takes as his marginalized or non-canonical narrative Zora Neale Hurston's *Their Eyes Were Watching God*, a classic text of the Harlem Renaissance and a staple of academic courses on twentieth-century Afro-American writing. Here again, the pedagogical conception of the book betrays its analytical force. For without the necessity to appeal to practical classroom situations, Messent could have provided us with a really searching critique of canonicity. Undoubtedly he possesses the learning, the intelligence, and the argumentative skill required to theorize in this way. As it is, the immense potential of this book is compromised by the need to adapt theory to the constraints imposed by pedagogy. *New Readings of the American Novel* will prove valuable in the classroom for its highly readable and informative presentation of narratological theory and practice which is also, and importantly, affordable (at least in the paperback edition).

UNIVERSITY OF LEICESTER   DEBORAH L. MADSEN

American Photography and the American Dream. By JAMES GUIMOND. (Cultural Studies of the United States). Chapel Hill and London: University of North Carolina Press. 1991. xi + 341 pp. $39.95 (paperbound $17.95).

James Guimond's book is a history of the secularization of the 'American Dream' in this century, in which he writes about the work of those photographers who used the camera as an instrument of social and sociological observation. These are the documentarists, whose subjects were the 'unimportant, unglamorous, unnoticed', to cite Robert Frank, the ordinary people whose labours in the farms, offices, and factories of the United States provide a different spectacle of the human chronicle than that encoded in the national myth of scientific and industrial progress so confidently asserted in the last years of the nineteenth century, and which is reiterated in a variety of idioms throughout the twentieth century. This is an intriguing and irritating book, so saturated with sociological data that the photographic images which illuminate it often receive less attentive analysis than they seem to deserve. Occasionally, Guimond refers to a popular and striking image, but does not give an illustration of it, and in one late chapter, on William Klein, Robert Frank, and Diane Arbus, his enterprise is seriously qualified because he was unable to get permission to reproduce work by either Frank or Arbus. I think there are several excellent short books contained in this rather expansive study, whose reach is too long, moving as it does from Francis Johnston's *Hampton Album* of 1900 to Susan Meiselas's *Nicaragua* (1981) and Dale Maharidge and Michael Williamson's *Journey to Nowhere* (1985).

The problem is that this history is too complex for any one book, whatever the primary focus, and the binding unity of 'documentary' photography seems to me inadequate to bear the weight of the general social and political history Guimond is committed to. In addition, Guimond seems unduly hesitant in his definition of what constitutes the documentary image, and how it differs from photojournalism, the objectivism of informational photography, or the manipulative intent of propagandist photography, and settles somewhat unconvincingly on the likeness of documentary photography to modernist 'art' photography. To call on Eugene Atget, along with Paul Strand and Walker Evans, as photographers who work in both idioms, is at least disturbing. Atget's 'documentary' treatment — if it is that — of Parisian streets, buildings, parks, and architectural monuments, is striking for its persistent erasure of the human, and it was for this, in part, that the Surrelists took him up in the twenties. The drama of the specifically human is rarely present in Atget, and it is this drama that the documentary photographers were concerned to record. But the desire to narrate the story of the common people is surely in conflict with the aesthetic primacy of the image in art photography, and the simple opposition between 'story' and 'form', between document and art, remains an obdurate fact.

This difficulty is demonstated in Guimond's otherwise entirely persuasive chapter on Lewis Hine. Citing a journalistic response to the sociological work of Hine as compared to the art photography of Stieglitz in relation to images of the railroads, where Stieglitz's famous image 'The Hand of Man' is called on in illustration, Guimond argues that Hine understood the human cost of the locomotive industry, whereas for Stieglitz 'the locomotive was essentially an icon of power signifying human dominance over nature' (p. 87). But this depends absolutely on how you read 'The Hand of Man', as a celebratory image, or as irony? This will look a minor cavil in response to this large and impassioned study, but it demonstates something of what is lost in detail precisely because Guimond's scope is so extensive.

The cultural history Guimond unfolds begins with the advent of a populist dream of material riches and social fulfilment associated with Theodore Roosevelt and Woodrow Wilson during the Progressive Era. His account of Frances Johnston's *Hampton Album*, meant to illustrate the effectiveness of the vocational education programme for black and native Americans, initiated by General Samuel Chapman Armstrong at the Hampton Institute, Virginia, in the aftermath of the Civil War, is at once responsive to Johnston's idealist sympathies, whilst recording her unchallenging representation of a programme acceptable to conservatives as well as reformers because the second rate education it provided was deemed appropriate to its students. There is an excellent chapter on Lewis Hine's subversive practices in recording the extent and conditions of child labour in the early years of the century, and the human cost of industrial expansion through the twenties, and an informative description of the work of Walker Evans, Arthur Rothstein, Dorothea Lange, and Carl Mydans for the Farm Securities Administration in the thirties, a history which surely deserves a lengthier study than Guimond can provide here. Finally, though there is a good bibliography, and copious notes, there is no list of illustrations, nor an index to them, an odd omission from a study of this kind.

LIONEL KELLY   UNIVERSITY OF READING